CEDU쎄듀는 A **C**omprehensive **E**nglish e**DU**cation(종합적 영어교육)의 약자입니다.

펴낸이	김기훈 ㅣ 김진희
펴낸곳	(주)쎄듀 ㅣ 서울특별시 강남구 논현로 305 (역삼동)
발행일	2022년 4월 30일 제1개정판 1쇄
내용문의	www.cedubook.com
구입문의	콘텐츠 마케팅 사업본부
	Tel. 02-6241-2007
	Fax. 02-2058-0209
등록번호	제 22-2472호
ISBN	978-89-6806-253-7

첫단추

듣기실전편

BUTTON

듣기 모의고사

20회

저자

김기훈   現 ㈜ 쎄듀 대표이사

現 메가스터디 영어영역 대표강사

前 서울특별시 교육청 외국어 교육정책자문위원회 위원

저서 천일문 / 천일문 Training Book / 천일문 GRAMMAR

첫단추 BASIC / 쎄듀 본영어 / 어휘끝 / 어법끝 / 문법의 골든룰 101

절대평가 PLAN A / 리딩 플랫폼 / ALL씀 서술형

Reading Relay / The 리딩플레이어 / 빈칸백서 / 오답백서 / 독해비

첫단추 / 파워업 / 절대유형 / 수능실감 등

쎄듀 영어교육연구센터

쎄듀 영어교육센터는 영어 콘텐츠에 대한 전문지식과 경험을 바탕으로
최고의 교육 콘텐츠를 만들고자 최선의 노력을 다하는 전문가 집단입니다.

이혜경 전임연구원

마케팅	콘텐츠 마케팅 사업본부
제작	정승호
영업	문병구
인디자인 편집	올댓에디팅
디자인	쎄듀 디자인팀
영문교열	Eric Scheusner

이 책을 내며

듣기는 여러 언어 기능 중에서 가장 많이 사용되는 기능으로서, 우리는 평균 말하는 양의 두 배를, 읽는 양의 네 배를, 그리고 쓰는 양의 다섯 배를 듣는다고 합니다. 또한, 듣기와 읽기 기능은 서로 매우 밀접하게 연관되어 듣기를 잘하는 사람이 독해도 잘 할 수 있습니다.

수능 영어에서는 이와 같은 듣기의 중요성을 반영하여 영어 듣기 능력을 시험하기 위한 평가도 함께 치러집니다. 영어 듣기를 잘하는 방법은 많이, 꾸준히, 그리고 무엇보다도 정확하게 듣는 것입니다. 충분한 양의 질 좋은 문제로 꾸준한 학습을 하는 것에 더하여 대화나 담화의 내용을 **정확하게 듣고 이해하는 능력**이 요구됩니다.

정확하게 듣고 이해하기 위한 효과적인 학습 방법 중 하나가 바로 영어를 들으며 글로 받아 적는 Dictation(받아쓰기)입니다. 딕테이션을 할 때에는 단순 청취를 할 때보다 더 높은 집중력이 요구됩니다. 대화나 담화를 들으며 대략적인 글의 흐름을 이해하는 것에서 그치지 않고, 단어 하나하나를 모두 듣고 받아 적어야 하므로 정확하고 꼼꼼한 듣기 능력이 길러집니다. 또한, 받아 적지 못한 부분을 눈으로 직접 확인함으로써 자신이 부족한 점이 무엇인지를 알고 보완해 나갈 수 있습니다.

본 〈쎄듀 첫단추 듣기실전편 듣기 모의고사 20회〉는 양질의 문제와 딕테이션을 통해 정확하고 꼼꼼한 듣기 능력 향상을 목표로 기획되었습니다. 이 책은 수능 출제기관인 교육과정평가원과 각 시도 교육청에서 출제한 대표 기출 문제들을 바탕으로 이와 가장 유사하게 만들어진 질 높은 문제만을 엄선했습니다. 또한, 각 회 문제 뒤에 이어지는 페이지에서 전 문항에 대한 딕테이션 코너를 마련하였습니다. 딕테이션 효과가 특히 뛰어난 곳을 받아쓰기 할 수 있도록 하였고, 쉽고 짧은 구에서부터 보다 길고 복잡한 문장까지 단계적으로 발전시킬 수 있도록 구성하였습니다.

듣기 학습은 듣는 것에서 끝나는 것이 아닙니다. 이제, 듣기에 딕테이션을 더해 정확하고 꼼꼼한 실전 대비의 첫단추를 끼울 차례입니다. 부디 이 교재를 통해 영어 듣기 능력을 키우기 원하는 모든 학습자가 자신의 실력 향상을 직접 확인하고 그에 따른 강한 자신감을 갖게 되기를 바랍니다.

저자

딕테이션에 관한 모든 것 Q&A

Q
'딕테이션(Dictation)'이란 무엇인가요?

A '딕테이션(Dictation)'이란 우리말로 '받아쓰기'입니다. 즉, 누군가가 말하는 것을 그대로 글로 받아 적는 것을 의미합니다. 우리가 처음 한글을 배울 때 낱말과 문장을 소리 나는 대로 받아썼듯이, 스크립트를 보지 않고 영어를 들으며 그것을 그대로 받아 적는 학습법이 바로 '딕테이션'입니다.

Q
딕테이션이 영어 학습에 어떻게 도움이 되나요?

A 딕테이션은 청취, 이해, 쓰기, 읽기가 모두 내포된 과정입니다. 따라서 딕테이션을 통해 영어 듣기 능력을 기른다면, 청취력 향상은 물론, 말하기, 읽기, 쓰기에 이르는 전반적인 영어 실력이 향상되는 긍정적인 효과를 얻게 될 것입니다. 딕테이션이 각 부분에 어떻게 구체적으로 도움이 되는지는 다음과 같습니다.

1 자연히 청취력이 향상됩니다.
딕테이션을 할 때는 단순히 문제를 풀기 위해 청취를 할 때보다 집중력이 높아집니다. 또한 학습자가 잘 들리지 않는 부분을 여러 번에 걸쳐 집중적으로 반복해서 들어야 하므로 본인에게 부족한 부분을 듣는 능력이 효과적으로 향상될 수 있습니다.

2 익숙하지 않은 영어 발음에 익숙해집니다.
학습자는 본인이 생각한 것과는 다르게 발음되는 단어의 발음을 익히게 됩니다. 여기서 발음에는 강세, 연음 등도 포함됩니다. 예를 들어 '묻다, 매장하다'의 뜻을 가진 영단어 bury는 [búri]가 아닌 [béri]로 발음됩니다. 또한 '감소(하다)'의 의미인 decrease는 품사에 따라 강세가 달라집니다(동사: [dikríːs], 명사: [díːkriːs]). 꾸준한 딕테이션을 통해 학습자는 단어의 발음을 이해하고 이에 익숙해질 수 있습니다.

3 저절로 문법·어법을 익히게 됩니다.
주어가 단수일 때 현재동사에 '-(e)s'가 붙는다거나, 간접의문문의 경우 '의문사+S+V'의 어순으로 쓰인다는 것, 능동관계와 수동관계, 가정법 구조 등 단순 청취만으로는 지나치기 쉬웠던 부분을 짚어 가며 자연스러운 문어법 학습이 가능합니다.

4 추론 능력이 향상됩니다.
학습자는 빈칸 앞뒤의 상황을 통해 빈칸에 들어갈 내용을 유추합니다. 모르는 단어나 표현이 들리더라도 대화나 담화의 흐름으로 대부분 추론이 가능합니다. 이를 반복적으로 학습하면서 듣기뿐 아니라 독해에서도 문맥에 따른 어구의 의미를 추론하는 능력을 키울 수 있습니다.

Q

그렇다면 어떤 순서로 딕테이션을 해야 하나요?

A 중간에 멈추지 않고 녹음을 들으며 한 회분의 문제를 풉니다. → 채점을 합니다. → 다시 녹음을 들으며 딕테이션의 빈칸을 채워 봅니다. → 들리지 않는 부분이 있다면 두세 번 연속해서 듣습니다. → 스크립트를 확인하며 틀린 이유를 확인합니다. → 모르는 어휘나 표현은 암기하고, 잘 들리지 않았던 발음을 학습합니다. → 다시 녹음을 들으며 내용을 확인합니다.

Q

딕테이션을 할 때 주의할 사항이 있나요?

A 1 중요한 것은 철자(spelling)가 아닙니다.

물론 딕테이션을 하며 모든 철자를 올바르게 쓸 수 있다면 좋겠지만, 단어나 구, 문장이 소리 나는 발음과 쓰임, 의미를 이해한다면 철자가 틀린 것에 크게 집착할 필요는 없습니다. 이는 이후 스크립트를 보며 정확한 철자를 확인하고 익히는 것으로 충분합니다.

2 무작정 반복해서 듣는다고 좋은 것은 아닙니다.

여러 번 반복해서 들어도 전혀 감이 오지 않는 발음은 처음 본 단어 혹은 알지만 정확한 발음을 들어본 적이 없는 단어일 경우가 많습니다. 그러한 경우 과감히 넘어가고, 스크립트를 확인하며 새로운 단어와 발음을 익히는 것이 현명한 학습법입니다.

3 처음부터 스크립트를 먼저 확인하지 않습니다.

어떤 단어나 표현이 나오는지 미리 알고 있다면 그건 순전한 본인 실력이 아닙니다. 딕테이션의 목적은 본인의 부족한 점을 한눈에 파악하여 보완해나가는 데 있으므로 스크립트를 미리 확인한다면 학습 효과는 자연스레 낮아집니다.

Q

이 책의 '딕테이션'은 어떻게 구성되어 있나요?

A 일반적인 딕테이션의 방법은 들리는 모든 문장을 완벽하게 받아 적는 것입니다. 하지만 이제 막 첫단추를 낀 학생들에게 스크립트의 모든 내용을 받아쓰는 것은 결코 쉽지 않습니다. 따라서 쉬운 단어, 짧은 구부터 시작하여 보다 더 긴 구, 복잡한 문장에 이르기까지 딕테이션 학습법을 단계별로 적용하는 과정이 필요합니다.

이 책은 1회부터 10회까지는 1~5단어의 짧은 단어, 구, 간단한 문장을, 11회부터 20회에서는 보다 더 길고 복잡한 문장을 받아 쓸 수 있는 공간이 마련되어 **실력 향상을 위한 단계별 학습이 가능합니다.**

또한, 정답의 근거가 되는 핵심 내용, 수능 영어 듣기에서 자주 쓰이는 표현, 문어법 상 중요한 부분, 잘 들리지 않는 발음(연음, 생략되는 음, 불완전한 음)을 정확히 분석하여 이를 위주로 빈칸을 구성했으므로 본 교재만으로도 최적의 학습 효과를 누릴 수 있습니다.

이 책의 구성과 특징

01회 ★ 첫단추 듣기실전편

ANSWER p.2

01 다음을 듣고, 여자가 하는 말의 목적으로 가장 적절한 것을 고르시오.
① 학교 오케스트라의 역사를 안내하려고
② 학교 오케스트라 단원 모집을 공지하려고
③ 연주회 중 발생한 정전에 대해 사과하려고
④ 연주 중간에 자리를 뜨지 말 것을 당부하려고
⑤ 연주회 중 휴대전화 전원을 끌 것을 요청하려고

02 대화를 듣고, 여자의 의견으로 가장 적절한 것을 고르시오.
① 선물은 감사를 표현할 수 있는 방법이다.
② 향수는 화학물질이 있어 건강에 좋지 않다.
③ 선물을 할 때는 상대의 취향을 고려해야 한다.
④ 물건을 살 때 판매 직원의 추천을 받는 게 좋다.
⑤ 유행보다 자신에게 어울리는 향수를 찾아야 한다.

03 대화를 듣고, 두 사람의 관계를 가장 잘 나타낸 것을 고르시오.
① 의사 – 환자 보호자   ② 약사 – 손님
③ 상사 – 부하 직원   ④ 교사 – 학부모
⑤ 파티 주최자 – 초대 손님

04 대화를 듣고, 그림에서 대화의 내용과 일치하지 않는 것을 고르시오.

05 대화를 듣고, 남자가 할 일로 가장 적절한 것을 고르시오.
① 택시 부르기   ② 여행 가방 싸기
③ 전등 소등 확인하기   ④ 여권 분실 신고하기
⑤ 우편배달 중지 신청하기

06 대화를 듣고, 두 사람이 지불할 금액을 고르시오.
① $22   ② $27   ③ $34
④ $39   ⑤ $44

07 대화를 듣고, 여자가 자전거를 타러 갈 수 없는 이유를 고르시오.
① 시험공부를 해야 해서
② 자전거를 잘 타지 못해서
③ 할머니 댁을 방문해야 해서
④ 헬멧을 아직 구비하지 못해서
⑤ 좋아하는 밴드 콘서트에 가야 해서

08 대화를 듣고, 두 사람이 [ ] 않은 것을 고르시오.
① 뮤지컬 제목
③ 상연 일시
⑤ 극장 위치

09 Knoxville Art Contest[ ] 않은 것을 고르시오.
① 주제는 '물 없는 하[ ]
② 작품은 4월 3일과 [ ]
③ 한 사람이 하나의 그[ ]
④ 색연필로 그린 그림[ ]
⑤ 저작권이 있는 캐릭[ ]

★ 실전과 꼭 같은 듣기 모의고사!

실전과 꼭 같은 유형 배치와 엄선된 문제로
실전에 완벽히 대비할 수 있습니다.

---

01 DICTATION

녹음된 내용을 들으면서 빈칸을 알맞게 채워 보세요.

ANSWER p.2

01
W: Welcome, everyone. Thank you for coming to the Carlton High School Orchestra Concert this evening. The Carlton High School Orchestra, _____ 1979, has a long history. Tonight the orchestra will perform a variety of music from Mozart to jazz, which we're sure you're going to enjoy. At this time, we would like to make an announcement. All your cell phones must _____. We hope you will not just turn off the ringer, but turn it off completely. Checking text messages or reading news on a smartphone during the concert makes no sound, but the bright light will be _____ _____ in a darkened hall. Thank you again, and we hope you have a great time.

02
W: Ethan, you look upset. What's wrong?
M: It was Nora's birthday yesterday. I gave her a birthday gift, but she didn't _____.
W: What did you get her?
M: I bought a perfume the sales clerk recommended. It smelled sweet and nice.
W: Oh, that wasn't _____. Nora doesn't really like perfume. Couldn't you tell she never wears it?
M: No, I didn't know that.
W: You should have thought about _____ _____.
M: The sales clerk said that perfume is very popular among young women.
W: There's nothing that everyone likes in the world. You need to find _____.
M: You're right. She probably was disappointed in me.
W: It's okay. She'll understand.

03
M: Hello. Peter Cromwell speaking.
W: Good morning, Mr. Cromwell. This is Charlotte Mills. I'm calling for my daughter, Emily. She's not feeling well today.
M: I'm sorry to hear that. I hope it's not too bad.
W: It's not serious. She has a fever and feels dizzy, so I think _____ today.
M: I hope she feels well soon.
W: Thank you. Anyway, I'm concerned about her math class. Can I get _____ for today?
M: OK. Is it all right for me to send the homework _____?
W: That would be great. Do you have my e-mail address?
M: Hold on, please. Hmm... I have eliza79@gmail.com. Is that correct?
W: Yes, that's correct. Thank you for your help, Mr. Cromwell.
M: My pleasure. Tell Emily I said, "_____."

04
W: Take a look at this. Lilian and I made this two-story dollhouse.
M: Wow! You guys did such a great job! It's nice to be able to see inside the house.
W: Can you see the staircase on the left side?
M: Yes. You put _____ on the stairs. They're so cute!
W: Lilian made them with colorful clay. She also made the flower vase on the coffee table.
M: You mean the table in front of the sofa? Excellent! I like _____ of the sofa.
W: That was my choice. Take a look at the bed _____. Isn't it pretty?
M: Yeah! That must be the bed that Lilian chose.
W: She also added a big window behind the bed.
M: Why didn't you _____ on the window? I think the bedroom would look more beautiful with curtains.
W: That's a good idea. I'll talk to Lilian about that.

★ 받아쓰기를 통해 기초를 탄탄히!

정답 근거, 주요 표현, 연음을 위주로
받아쓰기 연습을 할 수 있는 Dictation을
전 회 단계별로 수록했습니다.

CONTENTS

[책 속의 책] 정답 및 해설

※ **유형별 접근 Tip을 수록한 정답 및 해설!**

유형별 접근 Tip을 포함한 꼼꼼하고 친절한
해설로 혼자서도 충분한 학습이 가능합니다.

Zach   Barri   Leo

Jane   Tracey   Mikaela

※ **다양한 성우와 살아있는 표현!**

다양한 원어민들의 목소리와 억양에 익숙해질 수 있도록
총 6명의 남/여 성우가 녹음했습니다.

01회 * 첫단추 듣기실전편

01 다음을 듣고, 여자가 하는 말의 목적으로 가장 적절한 것을 고르시오.

① 학교 오케스트라의 역사를 안내하려고
② 학교 오케스트라 단원 모집을 공지하려고
③ 연주회 중 발생한 정전에 대해 사과하려고
④ 연주 중간에 자리를 뜨지 말 것을 당부하려고
⑤ 연주회 중 휴대전화 전원을 끌 것을 요청하려고

02 대화를 듣고, 여자의 의견으로 가장 적절한 것을 고르시오.

① 선물은 감사를 표현할 수 있는 방법이다.
② 향수는 화학물질이 있어 건강에 좋지 않다.
③ 선물을 할 때는 상대의 취향을 고려해야 한다.
④ 물건을 살 때 판매 직원의 추천을 받는 게 좋다.
⑤ 유행보다 자신에게 어울리는 향수를 찾아야 한다.

03 대화를 듣고, 두 사람의 관계를 가장 잘 나타낸 것을 고르시오.

① 의사 – 환자 보호자
② 약사 – 손님
③ 상사 – 부하 직원
④ 교사 – 학부모
⑤ 파티 주최자 – 초대 손님

04 대화를 듣고, 그림에서 대화의 내용과 일치하지 않는 것을 고르시오.

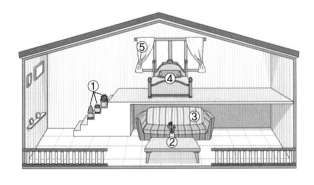

05 대화를 듣고, 남자가 할 일로 가장 적절한 것을 고르시오.

① 택시 부르기
② 여행 가방 싸기
③ 전등 소등 확인하기
④ 여권 분실 신고하기
⑤ 우편배달 중지 신청하기

06 대화를 듣고, 두 사람이 지불할 금액을 고르시오.

① $22   ② $27   ③ $34
④ $39   ⑤ $44

07 대화를 듣고, 여자가 자전거를 타러 갈 수 없는 이유를 고르시오.

① 시험공부를 해야 해서
② 자전거를 잘 타지 못해서
③ 할머니 댁을 방문해야 해서
④ 헬멧을 아직 구비하지 못해서
⑤ 좋아하는 밴드 콘서트에 가야 해서

08 대화를 듣고, 두 사람이 보려는 뮤지컬에 관해 언급되지 않은 것을 고르시오.

① 뮤지컬 제목
② 티켓 가격
③ 상연 일시
④ 주연 배우
⑤ 극장 위치

09 Knoxville Art Contest에 관한 다음 내용을 듣고, 일치하지 않는 것을 고르시오.

① 주제는 '물 없는 하루를 상상해보기'이다.
② 작품은 4월 3일과 7일 사이에 제출해야 한다.
③ 한 사람이 하나의 그림만 출품할 수 있다.
④ 색연필로 그린 그림도 출품 가능하다.
⑤ 저작권이 있는 캐릭터를 그리면 안 된다.

10 다음 표를 보면서 대화를 듣고, 두 사람이 예매할 영화를 고르시오.

Movies Now Playing at Palace Cinema				
Title	Genre	Age Rating	Time	Review Scores
① The Dark Town	horror	R-rated (Restricted)	2:00 p.m.	7
② Home Again	comedy	G-rated (General audiences)	12:30 p.m.	8.5
③ Chapter 2	drama	R-rated (Restricted)	1:30 p.m.	7.5
④ Justice League	action	G-rated (General audiences)	2:00 p.m.	6.5
⑤ Finding Mory	adventure	G-rated (General audiences)	2:30 p.m.	8

11 대화를 듣고, 여자의 마지막 말에 대한 남자의 응답으로 가장 적절한 것을 고르시오.

① Wow. It smells so good.
② Sure. I promise I'll do that.
③ Thanks. First, draw a heart.
④ Yes. She likes chocolate cake.
⑤ It looks great. I'm proud of you.

12 대화를 듣고, 남자의 마지막 말에 대한 여자의 응답으로 가장 적절한 것을 고르시오.

① I have to go. Talk to you later.
② Sorry. I promise not to be late again.
③ Great! I'll come by sometime tomorrow.
④ Maybe some other time. Thanks anyway.
⑤ Okay. I'll pick you up in front of the library.

13 대화를 듣고, 남자의 마지막 말에 대한 여자의 응답으로 가장 적절한 것을 고르시오. [3점]

▶ Woman :

① Sure, let's go find what we need.
② All right, if that's what you want.
③ I'm glad you're so understanding.
④ The game will start at 2 p.m. sharp.
⑤ Yes, I wish I could get away like that.

14 대화를 듣고, 여자의 마지막 말에 대한 남자의 응답으로 가장 적절한 것을 고르시오. [3점]

▶ Man :

① Wonderful! Spain is a big country.
② Okay. Next time I'll try another topic.
③ Of course! Together, we can do better.
④ Thank you. Your script was great, too.
⑤ I'm sorry I forgot to invite you to the play.

15 다음 상황 설명을 듣고, Brayden 선생님이 Grace에게 할 말로 가장 적절한 것을 고르시오. [3점]

▶ Mr. Brayden :

① You're not ready, but I'm still proud of you.
② I'm sorry. It was the best I could do for you.
③ Thank you. I'm glad to know you care about me.
④ It's all right. You can learn from your mistakes.
⑤ Don't worry. I won't tell anybody about your failure.

[16~17] 다음을 듣고, 물음에 답하시오.

16 남자가 하는 말의 주제로 가장 적절한 것은?

① how to make exercise fun
② benefits of group activities
③ ways of organizing group games
④ the necessity of exercise to keep fit
⑤ what to do when friends get together

17 언급된 활동이 아닌 것은?

① basketball　　② baseball
③ swimming　　④ biking
⑤ dancing

01

W: Welcome, everyone. Thank you for coming to the Carlton High School Orchestra Concert this evening. The Carlton High School Orchestra, _____ 1979, has a long history. Tonight the orchestra will perform a variety of music from Mozart to jazz, which we're sure you're going to enjoy. At this time, we would like to make an announcement. All your cell phones must _____. We hope you will not just turn off the ringer, but turn it off completely. Checking text messages or reading news on a smartphone during the concert makes no sound, but the bright light will be _____ _____ in a darkened hall. Thank you again, and we hope you have a great time.

02

W: Ethan, you look upset. What's wrong?

M: It was Nora's birthday yesterday. I gave her a birthday gift, but she didn't _____.

W: What did you get her?

M: I bought a perfume the sales clerk recommended. It smelled sweet and nice.

W: Oh, that wasn't _____. Nora doesn't really like perfume. Couldn't you tell she never wears it?

M: No, I didn't know that.

W: You should have thought about _____ _____.

M: The sales clerk said that perfume is very popular among young women.

W: There's nothing that everyone likes in the world. You need to find _____.

M: You're right. She probably was disappointed in me.

W: It's okay. She'll understand.

03

M: Hello. Peter Cromwell speaking.

W: Good morning, Mr. Cromwell. This is Charlotte Mills. I'm calling for my daughter, Emily. She's not feeling well today.

M: I'm sorry to hear that. I hope it's not too bad.

W: It's not serious. She has a fever and feels dizzy, so I think _____ today.

M: I hope she feels well soon.

W: Thank you. Anyway, I'm concerned about her math class. Can I get _____ for today?

M: OK. Is it all right for me to send the homework _____?

W: That would be great. Do you have my e-mail address?

M: Hold on, please. Hmm... I have eliza79@gmail.com. Is that correct?

W: Yes, that's correct. Thank you for your help, Mr. Cromwell.

M: My pleasure. Tell Emily I said, "_____."

04

W: Take a look at this. Lilian and I made this two-story dollhouse.

M: Wow! You guys did such a great job! It's nice to be able to see inside the house.

W: Can you see the staircase on the left side?

M: Yes. You put _____ on the stairs. They're so cute!

W: Lilian made them with colorful clay. She also made the flower vase on the coffee table.

M: You mean the table in front of the sofa? Excellent! I like _____ of the sofa.

W: That was my choice. Take a look at the bed _____. Isn't it pretty?

M: Yeah! That must be the bed that Lilian chose.

W: She also added a big window behind the bed.

M: Why didn't you _____ on the window? I think the bedroom would look more beautiful with curtains.

W: That's a good idea. I'll talk to Lilian about that.

05

W: Honey, have you finished packing? We have to leave in 10 minutes.

M: Don't worry. I have.

W: Make sure to carry your passport.

M: Oh, dear! Have you seen my passport? I can't remember _____.

W: Oh, no! What are you talking about? When did you _____?

M: Well... I put it on the desk. Then maybe I put it in my backpack. Right. Here it is.

W: Oh, _____! You really scared me.

M: I think we're ready. Did you ask the mailman to stop mail delivery?

W: Yes, I already did it. Can you please check _____ _____ before we leave?

M: Okay. I'll take care of it.

W: Thanks. Now I'll _____.

06

W: Dylan, look at these key rings. Aren't they cute?

M: Fantastic! They are so beautiful and unique.

W: Why don't we get some for our friends? I think they'll be _____.

M: Good idea. I think seven key rings are enough. Which ones do you like?

W: I like flag key rings. They're $6 each.

M: Why don't we get some tower key rings, too? They're $5 each.

W: Then let's get _____ key rings and _____ key rings, okay?

M: Sure. That comes to... $39.

W: No, that's not correct. Look at the sign that says you _____ if you spend more than $30.

M: You're right. That will save some money.

W: Let's go to the cashier.

07

W: Hi, Jacob. _____?

M: Hi, Olivia. What happened? Did you finally get your favorite band's concert ticket?

W: No, sadly I didn't get it. Instead, I got a new bicycle.

M: Cool. Is it your birthday gift?

W: Yes, my grandma sent it to me. It's very strong and lightweight.

M: _____. Now you and I both have bicycles. How about going biking with me in the park now?

W: I'd love to, but I can't go biking now.

M: Do you need to study for the exam? Come on. We only need just _____.

W: No, I _____. It's dangerous to go biking without a helmet.

M: That's right. Then maybe next time after you buy one.

W: Okay. See you later.

08

M: Isabella! I just got two tickets to the musical you wanted to see. Look at these!

W: Oh, dear! Is it "Mamma Mia!"? _____ _____, but weren't those tickets expensive?

M: I got a 20% discount on them with my membership card. It _____ for two.

W: Thank you! When is the performance? Oh, it's Thursday the 17th.

M: Seven o'clock is all right with you, right? We don't have to rush after work.

W: Yes. Who will perform _____ on that night?

M: Matilda Fletcher. She is one of the best musical singers.

W: Exactly. I'm a big fan of her. By the way, _____ _____ the theater?

M: We can take a subway and transfer to a bus at City Hall Station.

W: Sounds good. I can't wait!

09

W: Could you go a day without water? What if we didn't have water to drink or shower with, or for firefighters to put out fires? Let your imagination run free, and put your ideas into a painting for the Knoxville Art Contest. The theme is "Imagine _____." This contest is open to all the students of Knoxville from grade 1 through grade 8. _____ _____ their artwork between April 3rd and April 7th. Paintings must be the work of one individual student, but _____ from the same student will be accepted. Any medium, such as paint, colored pencils, or markers, can be used. However, paintings with _____ or images will not be accepted. For a full list of rules and information, please visit our website, www.knoxville.org/artcontest.

10

M: Honey, let's go to see a movie with our kids tomorrow.

W: Good idea. Then we need to book tickets now. What should we watch?

M: Hmm, I don't think horror movies are good for our kids.

W: I agree. And we also should choose _____ _____ since our kids are 8 and 12 years old.

M: You're right. Kids cannot see R-rated movies. So we can choose from among these three.

W: Why don't we go to see a movie _____ _____ at a restaurant?

M: All right. There is a nice Italian restaurant near the cinema. Then we can see one that _____ _____.

W: Yeah. Now we have these two options. Which one do you prefer?

M: Let's choose the one with _____ _____.

W: Okay. I'll book four tickets.

11

W: Sean, don't touch that! It's your sister's birthday cake.

M: It looks lovely. Mom, _____ the cake myself? Please! I'd really love to do it.

W: Hmm, it's a good idea. But you have to _____ _____, okay?

12

M: Hello, Haynes Auto Repair. _____ _____?

W: This is Emma Clarks. I took my car in for repair yesterday. Is it ready?

M: Sure, Ms. Clarks. You can _____ anytime between 9 a.m. and 6 p.m.

13

W: Michael, look out the window. It's really cloudy outside.

M: Uh-oh! I don't think we can go on our canoe trip at the lake today.

W: That's too bad. I was really _____ _____ our trip.

M: It'll be too difficult to take the canoe with all the fog.

W: You're right. What should we do then?

M: Should _____ instead?

W: It looks like it'll rain. I don't feel like _____ _____ from the rain. How about going shopping?

M: You know how much I hate that. Oh, I have an idea. _____ a talk show on TV.

W: We do that all the time.

M: I heard Edward Robinson will appear on today's show. He is a terrific football player.

14

M: Natalie, I'm happy you and I are a team for the Spanish class project.

W: So am I. I'll do my best.

M: We should make a five-minute play in Spanish by next Friday. Let's choose a topic first.

W: How about _____ that happens on an airplane?

M: Sounds interesting. Let's make a funny situation between a rude tourist and a smart flight attendant.

W: Um, Dylan, I'd rather _____ on my own if you don't mind.

M: What do you mean?

W: I'm a terrible Spanish speaker, so I want to play _____ part.

M: That makes no sense! We're making a play, not a presentation.

W: I'm just worried I might make mistakes and ruin your grade.

M: Come on, Natalie. If I help you with speaking and you help me with writing, we can _____ _____.

W: Do you really think so?

15

M: Grace is a high school student and a violinist in the community orchestra. The conductor of the orchestra is Mr. Brayden. The orchestra is having _____ next month, so they have to practice every day. Grace practices the violin for hours in the practice room every day. Because the violin has an important role in the piece they're playing, Grace wants to do _____. But during practice today, Grace made _____ _____ while playing. After the practice, she goes to Mr. Brayden and apologizes to him for her mistakes. Mr. Brayden thinks _____ _____ because they're still practicing. He wants to make her feel better. In this situation, what would Mr. Brayden most likely say to Grace?

16~17

M: For many people, it is more fun to watch television than to run 5 miles. Yet, if you don't exercise, your body _____. You start to move, and maybe even think, more slowly. But why do something that isn't fun? Well, there are many ways to _____ _____. Many group activities can provide you with exercise and fun. Think of the times when you are just _____ with your friends. You go outside and jump rope, play basketball or baseball, run races, and so on. Soon, you are all laughing and having a good time. But there are times when you are by yourself. Then what? You can _____ just by walking, biking, or even dancing. For example, you can take an enjoyable morning walk with your dog in a park. You can ride your bike while listening to your favorite songs or practice the newest dance by yourself. Before long, you will be the fittest dancer of all your friends!

01 다음을 듣고, 남자가 하는 말의 목적으로 가장 적절한 것을 고르시오.

① 자동차 안전 운전을 당부하려고
② 대중교통 수단 확대를 요청하려고
③ 자동차 정비의 중요성을 강조하려고
④ 주 1일 승용차 안 타기를 제안하려고
⑤ 대기 오염 측정 장비 설치를 촉구하려고

02 대화를 듣고, 여자의 의견으로 가장 적절한 것을 고르시오.

① 감자는 대량으로 구입하지 말아야 한다.
② 싹이 난 감자는 싹만 제거하고 먹을 수 있다.
③ 싹이 난 감자는 독소가 있으므로 버려야 한다.
④ 감자는 냉장 보관하면 영양소가 파괴될 수 있다.
⑤ 감자를 보관할 때 사과를 넣어주면 오래 보관된다.

03 대화를 듣고, 두 사람의 관계를 가장 잘 나타낸 것을 고르시오.

① 토크쇼 진행자 – 농구 선수
② 비행기 승무원 – 조종사
③ 잡지 기자 – 영화배우
④ 영화감독 – 소설가
⑤ 만화 독자 – 만화가

04 대화를 듣고, 그림에서 대화의 내용과 일치하지 <u>않는</u> 것을 고르시오.

05 대화를 듣고, 여자가 할 일로 가장 적절한 것을 고르시오.

① 친구 병문안 가기　② 저녁 설거지하기
③ 차고 정리하기　④ 미용실 예약하기
⑤ 자동차 전시회 방문하기

06 대화를 듣고, 여자가 지불할 금액을 고르시오. [3점]

① $2,650　② $2,700　③ $2,750
④ $2,800　⑤ $2,900

07 대화를 듣고, 여자가 동백꽃(camellia)을 살 수 <u>없는</u> 이유를 고르시오.

① 가격이 너무 비싸서
② 꽃이 피는 철이 아니라서
③ 꽃 수입에 문제가 생겨서
④ 병충해로 재배가 되지 않아서
⑤ 꽃말이 약혼식에 적절치 않아서

08 대화를 듣고, Junior Tennis Tournament에 관해 언급되지 <u>않은</u> 것을 고르시오.

① 대회 일자　② 참가비
③ 등록 마감일　④ 대회 장소
⑤ 주최 기관

09 Timber Library Bazaar에 관한 다음 내용을 듣고, 일치하지 <u>않는</u> 것을 고르시오.

① 모든 구매는 쿠폰으로 해야 한다.
② 음식 판매는 아직 시작하지 않았다.
③ 중고 의류와 새 의류를 구분해 판매한다.
④ 책과 장난감은 도서관 앞에서 판매한다.
⑤ 수익금은 아프리카 관련 도서 구입에 쓴다.

10 다음 표를 보면서 대화를 듣고, 두 사람이 예약할 리조트를 고르시오.

Resorts in the Ecrins Area

Resort	Distance (driving hours)	Accommodations	Kids Program	Price
① A	5 hours	hotel	no	$170
② B	2 hours	hotel	no	$110
③ C	2 hours	hotel / camping	yes	$150
④ D	3 hours	hotel / camping	no	$140
⑤ E	3 hours	hotel / camping	yes	$120

11 대화를 듣고, 여자의 마지막 말에 대한 남자의 응답으로 가장 적절한 것을 고르시오.

① How nice! You're an awesome wife.
② Not at all. That really helps me out.
③ No, that's easy. Let's have it tonight.
④ Never mind. I'm sorry to trouble you.
⑤ Glad you like it. Help yourself to more.

12 대화를 듣고, 남자의 마지막 말에 대한 여자의 응답으로 가장 적절한 것을 고르시오.

① Not really. Do you have any special plans then?
② You're right. What is the best thing to help them?
③ I have no idea. How much can you afford to give?
④ You can. Why don't you come along with me now?
⑤ I admire you. How have you done it all these years?

13 대화를 듣고, 남자의 마지막 말에 대한 여자의 응답으로 가장 적절한 것을 고르시오. [3점]

▶ Woman :

① Okay. Tell your son I'll cheer for him.
② I know. You always make me feel better.
③ That's for sure. I hope he starts feeling better.
④ That's true. It's not easy to get into that school.
⑤ Yeah. You must enjoy watching basketball games.

14 대화를 듣고, 여자의 마지막 말에 대한 남자의 응답으로 가장 적절한 것을 고르시오. [3점]

▶ Man :

① Okay, I'll call someone else. Thanks anyway.
② That's okay. Don't forget to bring what you said.
③ Sure. I'll tell him to call you back this evening.
④ Great. I'm looking forward to visiting the museum.
⑤ Thank you for your time. I'll be in touch with you.

15 다음 상황 설명을 듣고, Justin이 청중에게 할 말로 가장 적절한 것을 고르시오.

▶ Justin :

① We apologize for our carelessness.
② Fortunately, she wasn't seriously injured.
③ I promise you I will pay you back for this.
④ She won several awards for her artistic talent.
⑤ We're sure you won't be disappointed with her acting.

[16~17] 다음을 듣고, 물음에 답하시오.

16 여자가 하는 말의 주제로 가장 적절한 것은?

① the necessity of taking breaks
② effects of lack of sleep on efficiency
③ relationships between sleep and health
④ some problems caused by lack of sleep
⑤ causes of and solutions to lack of sleep

17 언급된 질병이 아닌 것은?

① high blood pressure
② diabetes
③ irregular heartbeat
④ blood cancer
⑤ heart attack

01

M: Cars are one of the great mixed bags of our time. They are wonders of engineering and a serious threat to life on Earth at the same time. They create convenience and also _____ _____. In the U.S., about 28% of all greenhouse gas emissions come from cars. If you are truly trying to lighten your environmental impact, the easiest thing to do is _____ your car once a week. If you leave your car at home one day a week, you prevent 55 pounds of pollution each year from _____ into our air. Would you be willing to make a public commitment to leave your car at home and take a bus _____ for work? You'll not only save energy and your money but also get a chance to relax and exercise.

02

M: I bought three pounds of potatoes for a dollar at the grocery store.

W: That's _____. I don't know how that store makes money.

M: They were cheap, but some of the potatoes _____ _____.

W: Really? Potato sprouts are toxic and can give you a headache and other digestive symptoms.

M: Oh, then I should _____.

W: No need to throw them out. If you simply _____ _____ any sprouts, the potatoes will be quite safe to eat.

M: Are you sure? I don't want to get sick after eating them.

W: Absolutely. _____ the sprouts and any soft spots, and your potato should be fine to use.

M: Thanks for telling me. I'll make potato soup tonight.

W: Sounds delicious. Have a nice dinner.

03

W: Next question, do you like your job?

M: Absolutely. I enjoy my job very much.

W: What do you like about your job?

M: I can be anybody. I can be a pilot, a police officer, or even a superhero. I feel like I'm living so _____.

W: That must be exciting. Which character do you like playing the best?

M: I especially like _____ because that was my dream when I was young.

W: I understand. What do you do in your spare time?

M: Oh, I do many things.

W: Would you share them with the readers of our magazine?

M: I travel, read, and play basketball, and recently I've started to _____ for a children's hospital.

W: Sounds like you're really enjoying your life. Working hard, playing hard, and helping other people.

M: Well, I just try to _____ this life.

04

W: Look over there. What are those people doing? They're all dressed in white with their hands and faces painted in white.

M: They're performing artists on the street. They look like living statues.

W: Oh, yes. That person who is sitting on a chair with his right hand _____ looks like he's imitating Rodin's famous sculpture.

M: Right! *The Thinker*, I guess. I like the woman with wings next to *The Thinker*. She has _____ _____.

W: She is a praying angel. The man next to her has the most difficult job out of them all.

M: Yes, he is _____ in his right hand. He's trying to throw it.

W: Isn't he also imitating a famous sculpture?

M: I think so, and I think the man on the right _____ an old warrior.

W: He is holding a long sword with both hands, and there is _____ beside his feet. By the way, what is that white jar in front of them for?

M: It's a tip jar. People _____ in the jar. Why don't we tip them?

W: Okay, it's a good performance. I will.

05

M: Mila, I'm going to San Francisco tomorrow and coming back on Sunday.

W: What are you talking about? We have to do a major house cleaning this Saturday.

M: Actually, Joel _____ to the San Francisco Auto Show, but he got into an accident this morning.

W: You mean your co-worker Joel? Is he okay?

M: Yeah, but now I have to go there _____ _____.

W: I understand. I was hoping you could clean the garage this Saturday.

M: I'll _____ tonight instead.

W: All right. Since you'll be out, I'll go to the beauty salon to get a perm this Saturday.

M: Sounds like a good idea. Why don't you _____ _____ right now?

W: Thanks for reminding me. Otherwise, Saturday will be completely booked.

06

W: Excuse me. How much does this leather sofa cost? It looks great.

M: It's $2,500, _____. It's a premium Italian leather sofa.

W: You mean the price doesn't include delivery charge?

M: No, it doesn't.

W: Oh, that seems kind of expensive.

M: It's _____ than average — that's true. But this sofa will last longer, and you'll save money in the long run.

W: I see. Then how much is the delivery charge? I live in an apartment.

M: Does your building have elevators?

W: I'm afraid not. The only access is through a staircase. My apartment is on the 3rd floor.

M: The standard delivery charge is $_____, but it's only for the first floor. There'll be an additional charge of $50 per floor.

W: Okay, so I'll have to pay _____. How soon would you be able to deliver it?

M: Let's see... We could deliver it _____.

W: All right. Here is my credit card.

07

M: When will you have your engagement party?

W: In two weeks. I have no idea _____ _____ for the occasion.

M: I'll do whatever I can for you. For engagement parties, I usually suggest classic flowers like roses and lilies for decorating.

W: Okay, and I love camellias. I'd like to add camellias to the selection.

M: Well, camellias _____ at this time.

W: But these days so many flowers are imported into our country from all over the world. _____ _____ pay high prices.

M: You're right, but even these days, not every flower is available in all seasons.

W: Oh, that's so disappointing. I want them because they're _____ love and beauty.

M: I know what you mean. But the season for camellias is late winter to early spring. I'm afraid they aren't available in summer.

W: Oh, okay.

M: Let me show you other flowers that will _____ _____.

08

W: Hello, you've reached Caroline's house.

M: Hello, Mrs. Caroline. This is Henry O'Brien, Bret's tennis coach.

W: Oh, hello. How is Bret doing with his lessons?

M: He's doing very well. _____ I'm calling you. I asked him to participate in the Junior Tennis Tournament.

W: I heard that. _____ October 28th _____ December 2nd.

M: Yes, there will be games for singles and doubles, and Bret will play in the doubles.

W: So, _____ to register for the tournament?

M: It's $40 per player. He has to sign up _____ _____ September 23rd. I'll give Bret the form tomorrow.

W: Okay. Oh, one more question. _____ _____?

M: It's the Mesa Tennis Center, near Lawrence University.

W: All right. Thank you for calling.

09

W: This announcement is for all those attending the Timber Library Bazaar. If you would like to buy something, you must first _____. To prevent a lack of change, we ask that you buy all goods with these coupons. Any unused coupons _____ at the cashier. The food tables are still being set up. We will start selling food at 11:30 a.m. We will be selling used clothing on the right side of the library hall. New clothing will be sold on the left of the hall at greatly _____. We are selling books and toys in front of the library. DVDs will be available there, too. _____ _____ to send books to poor regions of Africa. We thank you for coming to this bazaar and _____ _____ to libraries in Africa. We hope you have a good time today.

10

M: Let's get away this weekend with the kids.

W: Good idea. How about staying at a resort? There is _____ in this flyer.

M: Okay. But I don't want to spend _____ _____ each day.

W: Me, neither. Let's choose a resort that's no more than a 4-hour drive away.

M: How about staying in a tent for a night?

W: I'd love to. I think it'll be a great experience for the kids.

M: All right. Then we'll choose a place that has _____.

W: Good. We should also look for something that has a program for kids.

M: Well, it looks like there are two options. Let's go to the one that's closer. We don't want to _____ _____ a long drive.

W: Wait a second. We should think about the price. I want _____.

M: That's a good point. I'll make reservations right now.

11

W: Honey, would you _____ tonight? It's my turn, but I'm very busy preparing for a presentation.

M: Sure. What would you like to have for dinner?

W: I really like your spaghetti with oil and garlic. Is it _____ for you?

12

M: I heard you're going to _____ for the people who were injured by the hurricane.

W: Yes, I am. South Texas Blood Center is asking for _____.

M: Sounds great. I'd also like to make a donation.

13

M: Hello, Miss Lynn. It's a beautiful day, isn't it?

W: Oh, hello, Mr. Robinson. The weather is gorgeous. Are you on your way out?

M: I'm _____ see a basketball game. I'm just waiting for my wife to come out.

W: I see. Well, I hope you have a wonderful time.

M: Thank you. I'm going to see the high school basketball finals. My son _____.

W: Oh, I had no idea your son was _____ _____!

M: He's one of the top shooting guards on his team.

W: Wow, very impressive. Is he planning to _____ _____ once he graduates?

M: Well, he was asked to join the NBA, but he plans to go to university first.

W: He sounds _____ his age. You must be proud of him. I'm sure he will be a wonderful person.

M: Thanks for saying so. Oh, there comes my wife. I should leave now.

14

W: Hello?

M: Hello. Can I talk to David? This is Julian, his friend.

W: David isn't home. _____ his cell phone?

M: I did, but he didn't answer. His phone was off.

W: Maybe his phone's battery died. Do you want to _____?

M: Yes, please. I'm calling to ask him about our field trip tomorrow. Did you hear about the trip?

W: Ah, yes. I remember him talking about that.

M: We're going to the Museum of Science tomorrow. Do you happen to know _____ _____ to the museum?

W: I'm sorry, but I don't know. David won't be home until late, so why don't you _____ _____?

15

W: Justin Kidwell is a producer of a local theater company. His theater company decided to _____ the musical *Don Quixote*, and has been preparing for it. Finally, they will perform the musical at the community theater today. But unfortunately, Helen Myles, who plays _____, fell down some stairs. It's not serious, but she is _____ _____ to perform tonight. So, Julia Smith will replace her. Since she has been practicing this role along with Helen, she will do fine. Now Justin goes onto the stage and informs the audience about the change. He says he is sure that Julia's performance will be just as good. He wants to _____ in tonight's performance. In this situation, what would Justin most likely say to the audience?

16~17

W: How many hours did you sleep last night? These days, it seems most people aren't _____ _____. This can be a real problem. Although it may not seem serious at first, lack of sleep can have side effects. Sleeping less can lead to _____, including high blood pressure, stroke, and diabetes. In addition, frequent sleep loss can _____ for irregular heartbeat, or even a heart attack. Getting too little sleep can also affect how well we learn. Studies have shown that sleepy people _____ memory and concentration. Tired people also make mistakes on the job, which can cause injury. Perhaps even more importantly, _____ affects your mood. Tired people are more nervous, less adaptable, and less flexible. What can you do to stay rested and cheerful? Go to bed at the same time every night. And remember, going to work _____ is like starting your day with one foot in a hole.

03 회 ✳ 첫단추 듣기실전편

01 다음을 듣고, 여자가 하는 말의 목적으로 가장 적절한 것을 고르시오.

① CCTV 규제법 확립을 촉구하려고
② CCTV 설치 청원 참여를 부탁하려고
③ CCTV 찬반 토론회 개최를 공지하려고
④ CCTV와 범죄율 감소의 관계를 설명하려고
⑤ 육아시설의 CCTV 설치 의무화를 주장하려고

02 대화를 듣고, 남자의 의견으로 가장 적절한 것을 고르시오.

① 애완동물을 기르는 것이 자녀의 정서 교육에 좋다.
② 집안의 해충을 없애려면 전문가의 도움이 필요하다.
③ 너무 깨끗한 환경이 건강에 오히려 안 좋을 수 있다.
④ 대청소보다는 매일 하는 청소가 위생에 도움이 된다.
⑤ 실내를 깨끗이 유지해야 알레르기 발생을 줄일 수 있다.

03 대화를 듣고, 두 사람의 관계를 가장 잘 나타낸 것을 고르시오.

① 가구점 직원 – 손님
② 호스텔 직원 – 투숙객
③ 부동산 중개인 – 의뢰인
④ 홈스테이 보호자 – 유학생
⑤ 학교 행정직원 – 외국인 학생

04 대화를 듣고, 그림에서 대화의 내용과 일치하지 않는 것을 고르시오.

05 대화를 듣고, 여자가 할 일로 가장 적절한 것을 고르시오.

① 미용실 위치 알려주기
② 할인 쿠폰 가져다주기
③ 남자의 동생 연습 돕기
④ 남자의 동생 연주회 가기
⑤ 인터넷으로 미용실 검색하기

06 대화를 듣고, 두 사람이 지불할 금액을 고르시오.

① $1,080   ② $1,200   ③ $2,160
④ $2,400   ⑤ $2,640

07 대화를 듣고, 두 사람이 Molly's Bakery에서 쿠키를 주문하지 못한 이유를 고르시오.

① 주문이 너무 많이 밀려서
② 준비한 재료를 다 소진해서
③ 아들이 원하는 쿠키가 품절되어서
④ 점포 이전하느라 임시 휴업을 해서
⑤ 영업 부진으로 폐업을 하게 되어서

08 대화를 듣고, Spearfish에 관해 언급되지 않은 것을 고르시오.

① 인구수   ② 세워진 연도
③ 주변 경관   ④ 이름의 유래
⑤ 관광 시설

09 Victorville 초등학교 여름 축제에 관한 다음 내용을 듣고, 일치하지 않는 것을 고르시오.

① 한 달 후에 개최될 예정이다.
② 올해는 바다를 주제로 한 장식과 활동이 있다.
③ 학생식당 건물 뒤 야외에서 열린다.
④ 우천 시에는 행사가 취소된다.
⑤ 점심 식사로는 해산물이 제공된다.

10 다음 표를 보면서 대화를 듣고, 남자가 구매할 장난감 블록을 고르시오.

Toy Blocks of Toy Land					
Toy Blocks	Age Limit	Material	Pieces	Price	Features
① Mega Blocks	1-3 years	plastic	80	$20	oversized
② Alphabet Blocks	2-3 years	wood	40	$26	alphabet blocks
③ Fantasy Blocks	1-3 years	wood	40	$38	organic color finish
④ Green Blocks	0-3 years	recycled milk containers	20	$24	eco-friendly
⑤ Lincoln Logs Set	3-6 years	wood	100	$48	tin box for storage

11 대화를 듣고, 여자의 마지막 말에 대한 남자의 응답으로 가장 적절한 것을 고르시오.

① I'm afraid I don't like this table.
② I'll be your waiter. Here's your menu.
③ Yes, a table for three. Come this way.
④ I'm sorry. I couldn't make a reservation.
⑤ Wait a second. I'll check with the kitchen.

12 대화를 듣고, 남자의 마지막 말에 대한 여자의 응답으로 가장 적절한 것을 고르시오.

① Hold on. Sorry, she's on another line.
② Maybe in an hour. I'll tell her you called.
③ That's right. Maybe the phone is out of order.
④ Thank you. But I want to speak to her directly.
⑤ We have a bad connection. I'll hang up and call again.

13 대화를 듣고, 남자의 마지막 말에 대한 여자의 응답으로 가장 적절한 것을 고르시오. [3점]

▶ Woman :

① Everyone's tastes differ, but I will try.
② Please turn down the music. It's too loud.
③ Right. Classical music is worth listening to.
④ I try to be better. I wish you could understand me.
⑤ I'm disappointed in you. I thought I could trust you.

14 대화를 듣고, 여자의 마지막 말에 대한 남자의 응답으로 가장 적절한 것을 고르시오. [3점]

▶ Man :

① Anyway, let's hurry down. It's good to be safe.
② Oh, no. I think you've read too many fairy tales.
③ You're right. It's dangerous to be here after dark.
④ Wonderful! The sun has set beyond the mountain.
⑤ Yes. I'm sure there are plenty of bears around here.

15 다음 상황 설명을 듣고, Oliver가 Lucy에게 할 말로 가장 적절한 것을 고르시오. [3점]

▶ Oliver :

① I didn't know that. But I don't care.
② You're lucky. Now you have enough time.
③ What a relief! Thanks for letting me know.
④ I'm begging you. Please show me your paper.
⑤ Don't be late. Make sure to turn in the paper by six.

[16~17] 다음을 듣고, 물음에 답하시오.

16 여자가 하는 말의 주제로 가장 적절한 것은?

① the causes of test takers' stress
② how to improve study habits and skills
③ effective ways of managing test anxiety
④ treatment methods for anxious individuals
⑤ tips for answering test questions correctly

17 언급된 장소가 아닌 것은?

① a bedroom　　② a garden
③ a park　　④ a backyard
⑤ a beach

01

W: Hello, community residents. Recently, there have been _____ in our neighborhood, which has alarmed many residents. Our community has been known to be a very safe area, where children can walk alone during the day. But it seems that we are no longer safe. In order to prevent any further crimes, we have decided to ask the city to install _____ _____ throughout our neighborhood. We strongly believe this will stop further criminal behavior and protect our streets. A letter asking the city to install CCTV cameras will be passed around the neighborhood, and we ask that you give us your full support _____ your name. We need your help to _____ _____.

02

W: I need to clean the floor.

M: Amelia, you already did it this morning.

W: Think about our kids. _____ I keep my home, _____ they will be.

M: I just read an article about that. It said environments that are too clean cause allergies.

W: Really? I can't believe that. You mean we should not clean our home?

M: They're not suggesting bringing harmful bacteria into the home, but data does suggest that being too clean _____.

W: Then I have been doing it wrong.

M: Maybe. They do say early exposure to bacteria or pet hair may be linked to _____ later in life.

W: Oh, I've spent a great deal of time in cleaning.

M: I know. Of course we should clean our home, but don't be _____ about cleaning.

W: I'm confused. Let me read that article.

03

W: Come here. This is your room, Minho.

M: Thank you. It's large and bright. I really like it.

W: Glad you like it. _____ all of the closet and dresser space for your clothes.

M: I really appreciate it. May I ask _____ _____?

W: It's just down the hall. Oh, I'm afraid it's not the same as in Korea. There aren't any drains in the floor here.

M: I see. I'll try not to get any water on the floor.

W: Okay. What else? _____ around seven, so we eat breakfast about 7:30 a.m. It'll give you plenty of time to catch the school bus.

M: When and where can I catch my school bus?

W: It's 8:30 a.m. at the corner across from our house, and your class starts at 9:30 a.m.

M: I see. I'm excited to see my new school.

W: Oh, if you want to _____ in Korea, you can use the phone downstairs.

M: Thanks, but I can use my smartphone app to call them for free.

04

W: What are you looking at? I want to see.

M: I took some photos from the barbecue party that my family had last weekend. Here, take a look.

W: Is that your grandfather who _____ on the barbecue?

M: Yes, it is. And the girl who is holding the dishes next to him is my sister, Layla.

W: The girl with _____ in her hair? She's so cute. How old is she?

M: She's 8 years old. She wanted to grill the meat, but she's too young to use the grill.

W: Who is the woman with a baby _____, to the right of your sister? She has a big smile.

M: That's my aunt, Angelina. Can you see the man who is holding a bucket near the table? He is her husband, my uncle Jerome.

W: Then who is the man with sunglasses on the right?

M: He is my father. _____ and trying to open the parasol since it was very hot.

W: It looks like you had a wonderful time.

05

M: Hi, Grace. Oh, you _____, didn't you? Your hair looks absolutely gorgeous!

W: Thanks. I found a really good hair stylist.

M: Great! Actually, my sister was looking for a good hair stylist. She needs to _____ since she'll be playing the violin in a school concert.

W: Your younger sister? Wow! That's great! I'll tell you where my beauty salon is.

M: How much does a perm cost there?

W: I think it's more than 100 dollars.

M: It's so expensive! I guess it's _____ _____.

W: Hold on. I'll give you the coupon I received. You _____ the price with that coupon.

M: That's great. My sister will be very pleased.

W: Just wait here, and _____ right now. It's in my backpack in the library.

M: Thank you, Grace.

06

W: William, I think I found a great new refrigerator for us to use.

M: You know we don't have a lot of money right now.

W: They have very good payment plans where we can pay for it _____. We can choose between 12-month and 24-month plans.

M: I think the interest must be very high.

W: No, they have an interest-free payment plan available on this refrigerator.

M: No interest? That's good. What's the payment each month?

W: We can either pay _____ for one year or pay $100 each month and finish in 2 years.

M: Well, if we pay all at once, is there any discount?

W: Yes, they offer _____ for a one-off payment. It's quite a lot.

M: If we sell the old one at a used market, I think we can afford that. Let's pay all at once.

W: Okay! We really need a new refrigerator.

07

M: Christie, _____ cookies from Molly's Bakery for Daniel's birthday party?

W: Good idea. Their cookies are fantastic! They use the best ingredients.

M: We can order their cookies online. Let's see.

W: I think we need a box of chocolate cookies and peanut butter cookies.

M: I see. Oh, no. They aren't taking _____ now.

W: Why? Do they have too many orders? Are they _____?

M: No, it's not that.

W: The bakery didn't close, did it?

M: No, it says they'll _____ a new store on Anselmo Street, so the store is _____ _____ until this coming Sunday.

W: Oh, that's too bad. Our party is this Saturday.

M: Yeah, but I think we can order cookies from another bakery. I will search.

08

M: I heard you just moved here to our city. Where are you from?

W: I'm from Spearfish in South Dakota. It's a small town, so it's much different from this city.

M: Oh, really? _____ from your hometown?

W: This city is so big and full of people. If you can believe it, Spearfish only had about 11,000 people living in it!

M: Wow, _____. How old is your town?

W: It was founded in 1876. The town is surrounded _____, and there are streams and canyons.

M: Sounds great. It must be very beautiful.

W: Yes. Actually, it got its name from the fact that it is on a stream where Indians _____ _____.

M: Interesting. I'm sure the town attracts a lot of outdoor lovers.

W: That's right. Spearfish is ranked one of the best small towns.

09

M: Parents, I'm here to announce that Victorville Elementary School will be having its annual summer festival _____. Our theme this year is "Under the Sea," _____ _____ and activities. The festival will take place outside, right behind the cafeteria building. If it rains on that day, all the decorations and festival activities will be moved _____. You may take your children to any part of the festival you choose. But please stay with them at all times. Don't let them run off on their own! Our lunch will be served at 12:30 p.m. Our kitchen chefs have planned a fantastic meal of _____ _____. I'm sure it's going to be a great day!

10

M: I'm looking for a gift for my nephew's birthday. I want to get him something special. Can you recommend something for me?

W: Sure. I think he'd like toy blocks. Toy blocks _____ and develop important skills. Look here.

M: Good. Can you help me pick one?

W: How old is he? It's important to buy _____ _____ for kids.

M: He is two years old.

W: Then you can choose one among these four. Which material would you like?

M: Anything will be fine _____. And I think the block set should have more than 30 pieces.

W: You have these two options. Which would you like?

M: I'll take this one. It's more expensive, but it uses _____. It may be safer.

W: You're right. Kids often put toys in their mouth.

11

W: Excuse me. I have a reservation in the name of "Jones." We're _____.

M: Let me see... I'm sorry but the name is not on the list.

W: Are you sure? Oh, right! My friend made the reservation! Please check again with "Mason."

12

M: Hello! This is Ryan Wilson. Can I speak to Jennifer Hume, please?

W: Hi, Ryan. Sorry, but _____. Why don't you call her cell phone?

M: I tried, but she didn't answer. When is she expected back?

13

M: What are you listening to, Abigail?

W: Oh, hi, Carter. I'm listening to Nirvana songs.

M: Nirvana? Is it a band?

W: Yes, Nirvana is a famous rock band. Do you want to listen together?

M: No, thanks. It was music for _____ _____, wasn't it?

W: No, they're in many top-ten lists of the best rock bands of all time.

M: They were, but I think rock music is _____ _____ now. Why don't you listen to the latest music?

W: _____ do you listen to?

M: I listen to only the latest hip hop music. Try it.

W: It's the latest, but I don't think it's the greatest. I have my own _____.

M: Well... I'm sure you'll like it if you give it a chance. I really recommend it.

14

M: Wow! This hiking is really difficult.

W: It's been a while since you've been hiking — that's why. You'll be all right.

M: I don't think I can go any further.

W: Okay. Let's _____. Hmm, it's already six.

M: Really? Then it will _____. How are you planning to get down in the dark?

W: We'll be all right. We can get down in about an hour.

M: I don't think so. We're going to have to run down.

W: Listen, Luke. There's no way we're going to _____.

M: But it's getting really late. What if we _____ _____ in the dark?

W: Hey, it's June. The sun won't go down for another couple of hours.

15

M: Oliver is a college student. He is taking a religion and culture course this semester. In the class, he has to _____, and it's due today by six p.m. Unfortunately, his laptop is broken, so he has to go to the computer room to finish his paper. Oliver rushes to the computer room because he _____ _____. Then he runs into Lucy, his classmate. She asks him _____. When Oliver says why, Lucy tells him the due date for the paper has been postponed a week. The professor had e-mailed the announcement to all his students, but Oliver hadn't got it. He _____. In this situation, what would Oliver most likely say to Lucy?

16~17

W: If you feel nervous before an exam, you're not alone. This is test anxiety. In some ways, _____ is a good thing. It helps to focus the mind and get the adrenaline going. Too much, though, is not so good. Fortunately, there are a couple of simple things you can do to control your test anxiety. First, eat regular, nutritious meals, and _____ wherever possible. This will keep your energy levels up. Exercise regularly, and _____ _____ so you can concentrate. Be positive. Instead of thinking that you are going to fail, imagine that you're not. Replace anxious, negative thoughts with positive ones. _____ _____ or place that you remember as peaceful, restful, beautiful, and happy. It can be your bedroom or your garden. You can _____ _____ in the park or walking on the beach. Remember that not every method is the perfect choice for every individual. Try several different techniques before you decide which ones are best for you.

01 다음을 듣고, 남자가 하는 말의 목적으로 가장 적절한 것을 고르시오.

① 자전거 자물쇠 사용을 촉구하려고
② 자전거의 보관대 주차를 당부하려고
③ 자전거 절도 방지 캠페인을 홍보하려고
④ 자전거의 보행자 도로 주행을 경고하려고
⑤ 자전거 주행 시 보행자 보호를 주의하려고

02 대화를 듣고, 여자의 의견으로 가장 적절한 것을 고르시오.

① 화성의 주거지 개발은 민간이 주도해야 한다.
② 화성 개발에 투입되는 정부 예산을 줄여야 한다.
③ 우주 개발에서 직접적 경제 이익을 얻기 어렵다.
④ 우주 개발보다는 인류를 돕는 데 돈을 써야 한다.
⑤ 우주 개발은 과학 기술을 획기적으로 발전시켰다.

03 대화를 듣고, 두 사람의 관계를 가장 잘 나타낸 것을 고르시오.

① 백화점 점원 – 쇼핑객
② 항공사 발권 직원 – 여행객
③ 공항 보안검색 요원 – 탑승객
④ 전자제품 수리 직원 – 의뢰인
⑤ 여행사 직원 – 관광객

04 대화를 듣고, 그림에서 대화의 내용과 일치하지 않는 것을 고르시오.

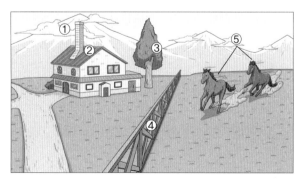

05 대화를 듣고, 남자가 할 일로 가장 적절한 것을 고르시오.

① 회의 연기하기　　　② 회의에 참석하기
③ 식사 예약 취소하기　④ 회의 문서 복사하기
⑤ Johnson 씨에게 전화하기

06 대화를 듣고, 남자가 여행 경비로 지불할 총액을 고르시오.

① $2,400　　② $2,600　　③ $2,700
④ $3,500　　⑤ $3,600

07 대화를 듣고, 남자가 학교 야구부원을 그만두려는 이유를 고르시오.

① 아버지가 반대하셔서
② 코치가 너무 엄격해서
③ 너무 많은 시간을 빼앗겨서
④ 프로 선수로 선발이 되어서
⑤ 팀 동료들과 사이가 안 좋아서

08 대화를 듣고, Easter Island에 관해 언급되지 않은 것을 고르시오.

① 섬의 위치　　　　② 소속 국가
③ 최초 발견 탐험가　④ 섬 이름의 유래
⑤ 섬에 석상을 세운 목적

09 Skanes Zoo에 관한 다음 내용을 듣고, 일치하지 않는 것을 고르시오.

① 개장한 지 30년이 조금 안 되었다.
② 미니 기차는 정거장마다 승하차가 가능하다.
③ 건물 안에서는 사진을 찍을 수 없다.
④ 동물원 내 극장에서 두 시간마다 영화를 상영한다.
⑤ 안내 데스크에서 동물원 지도를 구입할 수 있다.

10 다음 표를 보면서 대화를 듣고, 여자가 임대하려는 집을 고르시오.

House	No. of Bedrooms (& Bathrooms)	Monthly Rent	No. of Stories	Available Date
① A	3 (2)	$2,200	1	September
② B	2 (1)	$2,000	1	October
③ C	4 (2)	$2,500	2	September
④ D	3 (2)	$2,300	1	October
⑤ E	4 (2)	$2,800	2	September

Houses Available on Westridge Drive

11 대화를 듣고, 여자의 마지막 말에 대한 남자의 응답으로 가장 적절한 것을 고르시오.

① So, you want to switch shifts with me.
② I'm sorry, but I didn't do it on purpose.
③ You have to stand in line over there, then.
④ Hey, don't cut in line. Go to the back of the line.
⑤ Please save my place while I go to the restroom.

12 대화를 듣고, 남자의 마지막 말에 대한 여자의 응답으로 가장 적절한 것을 고르시오.

① Yes, I'll do that. Thanks for the help.
② Sorry for the time change. See you there.
③ Send me an e-mail. I'd be glad to help out.
④ Don't worry. It'll be discussed at the meeting.
⑤ Oh, okay. I should reschedule the appointment.

13 대화를 듣고, 여자의 마지막 말에 대한 남자의 응답으로 가장 적절한 것을 고르시오. [3점]

▶ Man :

① Don't do that. We need to save energy.
② I feel the same way. Let's do it right now.
③ Take it easy. You don't have to decide now.
④ If that's the case, you should change the plan.
⑤ Don't worry. Let's call and ask tomorrow morning.

14 대화를 듣고, 남자의 마지막 말에 대한 여자의 응답으로 가장 적절한 것을 고르시오. [3점]

▶ Woman :

① Please! Don't interrupt me until I'm done talking.
② I agree. A circus is a great attraction for children.
③ Good idea. It's so important to keep good company.
④ Then that works out perfectly. Thanks for inviting her!
⑤ How nice! You should be happy to have such a lovely kid.

15 다음 상황 설명을 듣고, Charlotte가 Gabriel에게 할 말로 가장 적절한 것을 고르시오. [3점]

▶ Charlotte :

① Don't worry about it! I'll be there on time.
② You can rely on me. I can keep your secret.
③ I'll call you back. Thanks for understanding me.
④ If you don't show up on time, we'll miss the train.
⑤ I'm sorry I'm late. I should have gone to sleep earlier.

[16~17] 다음을 듣고, 물음에 답하시오.

16 남자가 하는 말의 주제로 가장 적절한 것은?

① how to select and care for indoor plants
② types of popular potted plants in a classroom
③ the influence of nature on increasing attention
④ positive effects of plants on classroom performance
⑤ how to improve children's ability to learn new things

17 언급된 식물이 아닌 것은?

① lavender ② lily
③ rosemary ④ spider plants
⑤ snake plants

01

M: Hello, students. As you know, bicycles are _____ of transportation around campus. You probably have also heard the news that there have been some bike robberies on campus. If you want to keep your bike safe, _____ to a bike rack. Bike racks are located near almost every building. In addition, _____ block walkways and present serious danger for people who use wheelchairs or walking sticks. So, it's important to use the bicycle racks. Please don't park your bike _____ of travel to stairs, ramps, doorways, or door buttons. Furthermore, bikes locked to trees can cause _____ to or even kill the trees. Please help keep the campus beautiful and keep your bikes safe by locking your bike to a bike rack.

02

M: Chelsea, I read about the coolest thing in the newspaper yesterday.

W: What was that?

M: It said humans could soon live inside Mars in underground caves. This project is really amazing, isn't it?

W: Well, that's cool, but I think it's better to use the money for humans _____.

M: So you think it's a waste of money.

W: Yeah, I heard the budget to bring just 4 people to Mars was over $6 billion. Why should we spend so much money on that?

M: Well, it's important for our country to work with the newest technology.

W: Yeah, it _____ give us good things. But why should we spend all this money exploring space and finding out _____ on Mars?

M: You know, we do get useful scientific knowledge from space exploration.

W: Maybe, but I think the needs of common people should always _____. While there are people on Earth who need help, we should help them first.

M: I see what you're saying.

W: Common people on Earth are _____ priority. Keeping the human race alive is a necessity.

03

M: Next!

W: Here's my ticket.

M: Please _____ and put them into a plastic bin. And step through the scanner.

W: Okay. What's wrong? I took off my watch and belt.

M: Please step to the side.

W: Certainly.

M: Do you have any coins or keys _____?

W: No, but I just put my necklace into my pocket.

M: Ah, that might be _____. Put your necklace in this basket and walk through the scanner again.

W: Okay.

M: Good. _____ empty your pockets before you go through here next time. And _____ bring your boarding pass.

W: I'll keep your advice in mind. Thank you.

04

W: Kevin, how was your vacation to Bulgaria?

M: It was so amazing. I'll never forget it. Oh, I have a picture here.

W: Wow, it's a beautiful landscape. There are mountains in the background.

M: Yeah. You wouldn't believe _____! They're so tall, and some of them were covered by clouds!

W: Oh, there is a cute house on the left of the landscape.

M: Yes, it has a tall chimney!

W: I also like the tall tree next to the house. Do you know _____?

M: I never got to meet them. Oh, do you see the long

fence in the center?

W: Yeah, there are two horses _____ on the right side of the fence. They're lovely!

M: I think the owners of the house might have had a horse ranch.

W: I see. Did you see the horses run?

M: No, I didn't. They were _____ eating grass. Anyway, it was really a great experience!

05

W: Hey, Steven! Are you busy now?

M: Hi, Julia. I'm just finishing up some work. Can I help you with anything?

W: Actually, yes. I'm going into a meeting, but I don't have enough time _____. Can you help me?

M: Absolutely. What can I do for you?

W: I need _____ of this document — one for each person who will be in the meeting.

M: All right. I'll do it right away. Anything else?

W: Please call Mr. Johnson and tell him that I won't be able to make it to our dinner appointment tonight.

M: I'll call him as soon as I finish the other job _____.

W: Oh, hold on. I forgot I had a question for him, so don't call Mr. Johnson. I'll just call him myself after my meeting.

M: Okay! I'll get going with that _____ _____!

W: Thank you, Steven.

06

W: Hello, can I help you?

M: Oh, yes, I took this brochure yesterday, and now I'd like to take one of your holiday packages.

W: Okay. Which one _____?

M: This one here, on page 36. I'd like to travel to Europe. How much is this fifteen-day tour?

W: It costs 2,000 dollars per person, and it's a five-

nation trip.

M: Oh, that's a bit expensive. How about this nine-day tour which visits 3 countries?

W: That one's a special offer. It was originally _____, but you can get a 10 percent discount. Is it what you want?

M: Yes, that's the one. I would like to book this tour for 2 people.

W: Good. Could you _____ this booking form? We need your full address and _____ _____ 100 dollars. You can pay by credit card.

M: Oh, I see. _____ the rest of the money?

W: We need to receive the money at least ten days before the tour begins.

07

W: Conner, I heard you are a member of the school baseball team.

M: Yes, _____ last month, and the coach said I was talented.

W: You're good at baseball! Your father must be proud of you.

M: Yes, he is, but I'm thinking of quitting the team.

W: Really? Is the coach too strict? Or don't you _____ with your teammates?

M: No, he is nice and my teammates are also okay.

W: Then why? You are _____, and the coach is nice. Now _____ is help them win as much as possible!

M: But I have to attend training at 7 a.m. every weekday morning before classes start.

W: That's not bad, I think.

M: Not only that. I have to train for _____ _____ every day! And Sundays are spent playing other teams!

W: Oh, that sounds like hard work.

M: I just want to enjoy baseball. I'm not going to be a professional player.

W: I see, now I understand you.

08

W: Have you ever heard of Easter Island? It's an amazing island.

M: I've heard its name, but I don't know _____. Where is it located?

W: It's a Polynesian island in the Pacific Ocean about 3,600 km off the coast of Chile.

M: Oh, I remember. It's part of Chile. Wasn't the island _____ a Spanish navigator?

W: No, a Dutch sea captain, Jacob Roggeveen, was the first navigator to visit the Island in 1722 on Easter Day.

M: That's why it was named Easter Island. Anyway, _____?

W: One of the reasons is that it has 887 huge stone statues, called *moai*. Look at this picture.

M: Oh, yeah, I've seen them. _____ these stone statues?

W: We just know that the people who first inhabited the island were from Polynesia. But the mystery is yet _____.

M: I'd love to visit there sometime.

09

M: Welcome to the Skanes Zoo. The Skanes Zoo has been open for _____. We have about 20,000 animals here. I will tell you about the zoo and the animals _____ on this small train. This train goes around the zoo. There are several stops where you can _____ the train. Please use your cameras to take pictures if you want to, but you must not take pictures inside the buildings. To your left, you can see a movie theater which shows _____ _____ every two hours. To your right, there is the Visitors' Center. It has an information desk where you can get _____ of the zoo. It shows where all the animals are in the zoo. Today, you can all discover a wonderful world of animals. We hope you enjoy your visit.

10

M: So, are you looking for a house on Westridge Drive?

W: Yes, it's near my office, and I hear there's a good school nearby.

M: That's right. We have 5 houses _____ _____ on Westridge Drive. How many bedrooms do you need?

W: We have two kids, so we want a house with at least 3 bedrooms and 2 bathrooms.

M: Okay. And _____ are you interested in?

W: Somewhere between $2,000-$2,500 a month including utilities.

M: Then you have these three options.

W: _____ of stairs, because it's too easy for a child to slip and fall down the stairs.

M: So, you want a _____ home. You can choose one of these two. When would you like to move in?

W: Next month, around _____. Hmm, I think this one is exactly what I want. Can I go and see it now?

M: Sure.

11

W: Excuse me. Is this the line to buy tickets?

M: No. This is the line to get into Adele's concert. I'm afraid the tickets for her concert are _____.

W: Oh, no. I want to buy tickets for the museum, not the concert. Do you happen to know _____ _____?

12

M: Stephanie, you also need to attend the meeting tomorrow morning.

W: Really? Well, I have to go to the dentist tomorrow morning. _____ from the meeting?

M: I'm sorry, but that's difficult. We really _____ _____ at the meeting.

13

M: Kaylee, you look really busy.

W: Yes, I am. Please _____ me right now.

M: Hmm... What's wrong with you? You look upset.

W: Oh, I'm sorry, but I'm really annoyed. Why is this _____?

M: What are you trying to do?

W: Well, I'm just trying to use my new photo printer. There isn't any button! I can't _____!

M: Why don't you look at the manual? I'm sure it'll help.

W: I've already studied the manual and followed the directions. But it still doesn't work.

M: Let me take a look. Oh! There is a phone number for _____ right here.

W: But it's already 11 p.m. _____ _____.

14

M: Hailey, did you hear that the circus is coming to our town?

W: I did, and my daughter is so excited about it. She really wants to go, but my husband is _____ _____!

M: Oh, do you have any plans to take her?

W: I really want to, but I just learned that I have to work the night shift. I'm going to be working all the nights that the circus is here.

M: Oh, really? _____.

W: I know. I wish I knew _____.

M: Well, here's an idea. I mean, I have a daughter, and I know she really wants to go.

W: Do you have time to take her?

M: Yes, I do. And I certainly _____ taking one extra kid.

W: Oh, that would be great! But I really don't want to bother you.

M: _____! Plus, I'm sure my kid would love to meet your daughter.

15

W: Gabriel and Charlotte are friends. They plan to go hiking tomorrow. They are taking a trip to Copper Mountain, _____. They decide to take the train to Copper Mountain. It will take about _____ to get there. The train runs only _____, one in the morning and the other in the evening. If they miss the 7 o'clock morning train, their hiking plan will have to be canceled. Charlotte is very concerned because Gabriel is never on time. She warns Gabriel that their plans _____ _____ if he's late and misses the train. She wants to remind him again that he has to _____. In this situation, what would Charlotte most likely say to Gabriel?

16~17

M: You may have heard that having plants around the home and office greatly improves people's moods and reduces depression. But do you know plants can do _____ than increase levels of positive energy? Recent research shows that children who spend time around plants _____ _____. For example, children with attention deficit disorder who learn in a natural environment engage more with classwork. In another experiment, keeping plants in children's learning environments enhanced learning capabilities by _____. For these benefits, some plants work better than others. Potted plants, such as lavender, rosemary, or aloe, in the classroom reduce children's tendency towards distraction and help them to better focus on schoolwork. Specifically for children with problems paying attention, spider plants or snake plants can have a dramatic positive effect on learning. In addition, _____ of natural beauty help to minimize the anxiety that would otherwise occupy their minds. So if you want to help your children learn better, _____ their learning environment.

05회

01 다음을 듣고, 여자가 하는 말의 목적으로 가장 적절한 것을 고르시오.

① 강 살리기 캠페인 참여를 촉구하려고
② 강 주변 생태 환경 조사를 제안하려고
③ 지방 단체장 선거 출마 선언을 공표하려고
④ 생태학과 신입생 모집 설명회를 홍보하려고
⑤ 환경 프로젝트에 대한 재정 지원을 요청하려고

02 대화를 듣고, 남자의 의견으로 가장 적절한 것을 고르시오.

① 사진 촬영을 부탁할 때는 예의를 갖춰야 한다.
② 각자 의견이 다르니 남에게 강요하지 말아야 한다.
③ 멋진 여행 사진을 남기려면 사진 기술을 배워야 한다.
④ 여행을 할 때 사진으로 남겨야 여행이 오래 기억된다.
⑤ 여행에서 사진 촬영보다는 직접 보는 순간을 즐겨야 한다.

03 대화를 듣고, 두 사람의 관계를 가장 잘 나타낸 것을 고르시오.

① 분장사 – 단역 배우　　② 배우 – 의상 디자이너
③ 감독 – 무대 디자이너　　④ 모델 – 행사 진행자
⑤ 마술사 – 특수효과 담당자

04 대화를 듣고, 그림에서 대화의 내용과 일치하지 않는 것을 고르시오.

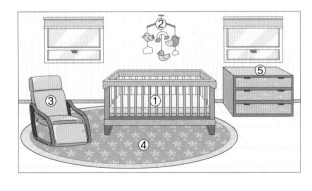

05 대화를 듣고, 여자가 할 일로 가장 적절한 것을 고르시오.

① 세탁물 수거하기
② 아침 식사 제공하기
③ 회의 시간 조정하기
④ 택시 회사에 전화하기
⑤ 지하철 노선도 알려주기

06 대화를 듣고, 여자가 지불할 금액을 고르시오.

① $60　　② $81　　③ $90
④ $162　　⑤ $180

07 대화를 듣고, 여자가 Stephanie의 남편에게 전화를 걸려는 이유를 고르시오.

① 파티에 못 가게 되어서
② 약속 장소가 변경되어서
③ 주차 장소를 알아보기 위해서
④ 교통 체증으로 약속에 늦어서
⑤ 생일 선물을 미리 보내야 해서

08 대화를 듣고, Stephen King에 관해 언급되지 않은 것을 고르시오.

① 출생연도　　② 책 판매 부수
③ 최초 출간 소설　　④ 출간 작품 수
⑤ 이전 직업

09 Halloween 무서운 이야기 대회에 관한 다음 내용을 듣고, 일치하지 않는 것을 고르시오.

① 이야기의 길이는 500단어 이하여야 한다.
② 이야기는 타자로 치거나 손으로 써야 한다.
③ 1등 상금은 1000달러짜리 상품권이다.
④ 입상자 발표는 10월 30일에 한다.
⑤ 입상작만 Jackson County Times에 게재된다.

10 다음 표를 보면서 대화를 듣고, 여자가 구매할 로봇 청소기를 고르시오.

Robot Vacuum Cleaners for Sale				
Model	Scheduled Cleaning	HEPA Filter	Price	Remote Control
① Roomba	◯	◯	$690	◯
② Neat Bot	×	×	$220	×
③ Robopower	◯	×	$350	◯
④ Robot Vac	◯	◯	$450	×
⑤ Bot King	◯	◯	$520	◯

11 대화를 듣고, 여자의 마지막 말에 대한 남자의 응답으로 가장 적절한 것을 고르시오.

① I'm glad you like it. Please come again.
② That sounds good. I'd like some of that.
③ Here's your salad. Your fish is on its way.
④ Sorry. We don't have any strawberries today.
⑤ Okay. I recommend the grilled fish with lemon.

12 대화를 듣고, 남자의 마지막 말에 대한 여자의 응답으로 가장 적절한 것을 고르시오.

① Here you go. May I see your passport, please?
② That's right. It was delayed due to bad weather.
③ I'm sorry. All the seats are taken at the moment.
④ All right. Could you line up in the order of arrival?
⑤ I'm not sure. Why don't you ask at the information center?

13 대화를 듣고, 남자의 마지막 말에 대한 여자의 응답으로 가장 적절한 것을 고르시오. [3점]

▶ Woman :

① Good for you! But I'm going to miss you.
② That's a good idea. We can start it right now.
③ Give me a call. We can have dinner some-time.
④ I'm sorry. You must have called the wrong number.
⑤ That's very kind of you. But I'm afraid I can't come.

14 대화를 듣고, 여자의 마지막 말에 대한 남자의 응답으로 가장 적절한 것을 고르시오. [3점]

▶ Man :

① Hurry up. Our flight leaves in an hour.
② Don't worry. We have time to go shopping.
③ Sorry. But all the available seats are taken.
④ You're right. We've done everything we can.
⑤ I think he will do fine. He knows where to park.

15 다음 상황 설명을 듣고, Jessica가 남자에게 할 말로 가장 적절한 것을 고르시오. [3점]

▶ Jessica :

① Where is the cashier? I'd like to buy this.
② When is it finished? I have to pick up my kids.
③ Sorry, but could I go first please? I'm in a hurry.
④ How long did you wait here? It takes a long time.
⑤ Where can I find a cart like that? It looks convenient.

[16~17] 다음을 듣고, 물음에 답하시오.

16 여자가 하는 말의 주제로 가장 적절한 것은?

① business gift-giving etiquette tips
② the dos and don'ts of exchanging gifts
③ the art of giving gifts for all occasions
④ taboos of gift giving in different countries
⑤ how to choose a proper gift in other cultures

17 언급된 선물이 <u>아닌</u> 것은?

① clocks   ② meat   ③ wine
④ roses   ⑤ dolls

01

W: Hello, I'm Leah Andrews, an ecology professor at Stevenson University. I studied the condition of the environment for many years, but I was never an activist. I thought if I _____ protecting the environment, I would see things less objectively during my research. However, as I was studying the Gray River, I found it was in a _____. That's why I decided to _____ the local residents to save Gray River. We all want to protect and _____ so that we can safely use the water and swim in the river. We are planning to hold a meeting on July 12th at Stevenson Hall to start our campaign _____ _____. There will be a lot of scientists there to tell you what's going on in the river. We hope to see all residents there.

02

M: Oh, look at the Alhambra Palace in the sunset! It's breathtaking!

W: Wow! I should take some pictures. These are beautiful!

M: Amelia, there's _____ to the sunset that is right in front of you.

W: Of course. But I want to capture the moment. I take photos for the memories.

M: Don't you think you're missing the _____ while taking all those pictures?

W: I just want to preserve the beauty forever.

M: You always take so many pictures wherever we visit. I think your desire to capture the moment actually _____.

W: What do you mean by that?

M: I mean we should see the sunset _____ _____. Just enjoy the scenery and this moment.

W: I understand, but don't push me too much. You like seeing scenery, and I like _____.

03

M: Excuse me, are you Leah Jones?

W: That's me! What can I help you with?

M: I'm David Clark. Mr. Miller, the director, told me I could meet you here.

W: Nice to meet you, David. You'll be _____ _____ in the play, right?

M: Exactly. This is _____, so I'm very nervous.

W: I'm sure you'll do a great job. Now, the magician should be an attractive character, so I'll make a fancy costume.

M: The makeup designer said something similar. Did you already read the script?

W: Of course. We need to understand the roles to make the costumes. Now I'll _____ _____.

M: Okay. I'm looking forward to seeing _____ _____.

W: I'll do my best.

04

M: Honey, I'm home! What are you doing?

W: William, look! I just decorated our baby's room.

M: Oh, how lovely! You put the baby bed near the wall between the windows.

W: Yes, and I _____ the bird mobile _____.

M: It's nice! I heard mobiles help the baby's brain to develop.

W: That's right. And I put an armchair beside the bed near the window.

M: Wow! It's a good place for you to play with the baby. I also like _____ on the floor.

W: I put it on the floor for safety. I also bought the chest of four drawers on the right.

M: Perfect! You can keep all the baby supplies in it.

W: I was planning to buy a chest of three drawers, but I _____ because I guessed four drawers would hold more things.

M: That was a good purchase. Three drawers _____.

05

W: Good morning, sir. How can I help you?

M: Hi. Where is the restaurant for breakfast?

W: It's right over there, sir.

M: Thanks. I also have some laundry that needs _____. When will the clothes be returned if I send them this evening?

W: Well, it usually takes a day. What is your room number? I'll send someone to _____ this evening.

M: Thank you. It's 809. And I have to be at a business conference at 10 o'clock at Plaza Hotel. Can I take the subway to get there?

W: Well, yes, but you need to transfer twice. I think it's better _____.

M: Isn't it far away from here?

W: No. It's only a 20-minute drive from this hotel.

M: That's good. Could you _____ for me at 9:20 a.m.?

W: Sure, sir. _____ right away.

06

M: Good afternoon! Do you want to sign up for a class?

W: Yes. _____ would you recommend?

M: What is the goal of your workout? If you want to build muscle, I suggest taking the body building class. It's 60 dollars a month.

W: No, I don't want to exercise too hard. I want something to _____, and that's all.

M: Well... Do you like running? We have a special class on Mondays and Fridays for runners.

W: Sounds good. How much is the fee?

M: It costs _____. This class usually runs outdoors but runs indoors on rainy days.

W: I think that sounds good. I'd like to sign up now.

M: If you pay for _____, you can receive _____.

W: Sounds great. Then I'll pay for 3 months in advance. Here's my credit card.

M: Okay. Hold on, please.

07

W: Jack, what time is it? We are going to be late for the party!

M: No. It's around six. _____.

W: But I think we have to be at Stephanie's house by 6:30 for her surprise birthday party.

M: Don't worry. We're not going to be late.

W: I don't think we can make it because there is a lot of _____ at this time of day.

M: I'm sure _____. We're not far away now.

W: Are you sure? We'll probably spend more than 10 minutes to find a parking place.

M: You're right. Then why don't you call Stephanie's husband and ask him _____ our car?

W: Okay. I'll call him now.

M: Don't worry. Anyway, the party starts at 7.

08

M: Hi, Sophia. What are you reading?

W: Hi, Brandon. I'm reading this book I just bought. Have you ever heard of the author Stephen King?

M: Yeah, he is a very famous author of horror fiction. He is quite old, I guess.

W: Right. He _____ 1947. And did you know 350 million copies of his books have been sold?

M: That's amazing. Why the sudden interest in Stephen King?

W: Well, I read his _____ novel, *Carrie*, and I found it very interesting. So I kept on reading his books.

M: He has written numerous novels. Did you read all of them?

W: No, I've only _____. I also saw some movies made from his work.

M: Wow! You are a big fan of him! By the way, it's almost 1:30. We have English class now!

W: Okay. Oh, that reminds me, Stephen King was once _____ in a high school.

M: Really? Anyway, let's hurry. We don't want to be late for class.

09

M: Welcome to the Halloween Scary Story Contest. It's our biggest contest. You already know the basic rules. Your story must be _____ _____, and be an original. Stories should be typed or _____. Stories have to be in before our deadline. The deadline is September 30th. First place wins a $1,000 gift card, second place wins a $500 gift card, and third place wins a $250 gift card. We will announce and post the winners on _____! And, if we like your story, _____ winning or not, you have a chance of being published in our Halloween print issue of *Jackson County Times*. We are looking for _____ _____ this time. Please scare us!

10

W: I'm so busy these days, so I'm thinking of getting a robotic vacuum cleaner.

M: Good idea. Robot vacuum cleaners are a convenient way to _____.

W: I want a cleaner that can clean my house while I'm out.

M: Then you should get one that has a _____ _____ function.

W: Great. My child has allergies, so is there a vacuum cleaner that has a special filter?

M: Of course. You should get something that has a HEPA filter. It _____ all micro dust.

W: I definitely like that. His allergies have been getting worse.

M: I see. How much are you willing to spend?

W: I don't want to spend more than $600.

M: Then you can choose between these two.

W: I'll take the one that has _____. That will be more convenient.

11

W: And would you like a dessert?

M: Yes, please. _____ anything?

W: Well, today we have strawberry cheesecake. It's _____ our best desserts.

12

M: Excuse me. This is terminal C, right?

W: Yes, that's right.

M: Do you know _____ United Airlines flight 235 _____?

13

W: Hello, there! You're Julian! Wow! It's great to see you here again.

M: Sarah! Hello! _____! I haven't seen you in ages.

W: Yeah, what are you doing here in Louisville? Are you just visiting?

M: I just got a new job here in accounting, so I'm shopping for some new clothes.

W: That's great! Where do you live now?

M: I'm renting an apartment on Kent Street. Well, this is a small world.

W: Really! Oh, I have to go back to work. We must _____.

M: Okay, but I don't have your phone number now. _____ my cell phone number?

W: No, I lost my phone. Here is my new number.

M: Okay. I'll save your number.

14

M: It's 5:20. We should board the plane now.

W: But Tim _____. Why don't you call him again?

M: I just did, but he didn't answer. He is impossible. He promised me not to be late, but he is late again.

W: He probably had a hard time finding a parking space.

M: No, he said he would take an airport limousine. He has _____.

W: Oh, really?

M: Yes. I _____ even if he missed the plane.

W: We've been waiting for him for almost an hour.

M: Oh, there is the last announcement for our flight. I think we should go.

W: I think so. The gate will be closing soon. We _____ now.

15

M: Jessica has two children who are both elementary school students. She always has to pick up her children from school at 3:30. Today, she _____ a supermarket to do some grocery shopping. She picks up a few things she needs and goes to the counter to _____. Unfortunately, the line at the counter is very long. It's almost 3 o'clock and there is still one person in front of her. Jessica _____ to pick her children up. The man before her in line has a lot of stuff in his cart. It will surely take a long time. Jessica wants to ask the man if she can pay _____. In this situation, what would Jessica most likely say to the man?

16~17

W: Giving gifts is a popular way to show affection all around the world. However, certain gifts are viewed by people in other cultures as _____. For example, clocks are not good gifts to give to your Chinese friends, because the word in Chinese for "clock" is very similar to the word for "death." The Japanese are a little picky about _____; giving nine of anything is considered bad luck, and therefore it's recommended that you always give _____. Meat and leather goods are not good in India, where people never eat cows. Also remember that many Muslims don't drink alcohol, so purchasing a bottle of wine for them is probably not the best idea. Flowers are welcomed in many cultures around the world, but they have some different meanings _____. For instance, red roses, a traditional lovers' gift, would appear _____ at a business meeting. Yellow roses commonly suggest mistrust in France, and death in Mexico.

06 회 * 첫단추 **듣기실전편**

01 다음을 듣고, 여자가 하는 말의 목적으로 가장 적절한 것을 고르시오.

① 놀이기구 사용법을 안내하려고
② 어린이 실외 운동을 장려하려고
③ 입장 시 질서 유지를 요청하려고
④ 놀이터 안전수칙 준수를 당부하려고
⑤ 어린이에게 좋은 운동을 소개하려고

02 대화를 듣고, 남자의 의견으로 가장 적절한 것을 고르시오.

① 어린이의 TV 시청 시간은 연령에 따라 조절해야 한다.
② 어린이의 TV 시청은 잘 관리하면 긍정적 효과가 있다.
③ 어린이의 TV 시청 시간과 독서하는 시간은 반비례한다.
④ 부모의 TV 시청 습관이 자녀의 TV 시청에 영향을 준다.
⑤ 장시간의 TV 시청은 어린이 두뇌발달에 안 좋은 영향을 준다.

03 대화를 듣고, 두 사람의 관계를 가장 잘 나타낸 것을 고르시오.

① 교사 – 양호교사
② 환자 보호자 – 구급 대원
③ 의사 – 간호사
④ 상사 – 비서
⑤ 접수원 – 물리치료사

04 대화를 듣고, 그림에서 대화의 내용과 일치하지 않는 것을 고르시오.

05 대화를 듣고, 여자가 할 일로 가장 적절한 것을 고르시오.

① 아이 숙제 도와주기
② 복숭아 사러 가기
③ 파이 만들기
④ 학교 바자회 참석하기
⑤ 인터넷에서 조리법 검색하기

06 대화를 듣고, 남자가 받게 될 총 보상 금액을 고르시오.

① $1,700   ② $2,200   ③ $2,700
④ $3,200   ⑤ $3,700

07 대화를 듣고, 여자가 나비 장식 머리띠를 구입하지 않은 이유를 고르시오.

① 재질이 딱딱해서
② 디자인이 복잡해서
③ 보석 장식을 싫어해서
④ 할인을 해주지 않아서
⑤ 착용 시 귀 뒤쪽이 아파서

08 대화를 듣고, Marina Hotel에 관해 언급되지 않은 것을 고르시오.

① 수영장 시설   ② 어린이 놀이 시설
③ 공항 셔틀버스 제공   ④ 하루 숙박비용
⑤ 인터넷 사용 가능 여부

09 Book Talk에 관한 다음 내용을 듣고, 일치하지 않는 것을 고르시오.

① Columbus County의 성인을 대상으로 한다.
② 매달 마지막 수요일 저녁에 모임을 갖는다.
③ 다음번에는 역사 소설을 읽고 토론을 한다.
④ 토론에 참여하려면 미리 등록을 해야 한다.
⑤ 토론 모임 후 가벼운 다과가 제공된다.

10 다음 표를 보면서 대화를 듣고, 여자가 선택한 농산물 배달 상자를 고르시오.

		Door-to-door Produce Delivery Service		
Box Type	Type of Produce	Frequency	Box Size	Organic
① A	Vegetables	Twice a week	small	all
② B	Fruit & Vegetables	Once a week	small	vegetables only
③ C	Fruit & Vegetables	Twice a week	medium	all
④ D	Fruit & Vegetables	Once a week	large	vegetables only
⑤ E	Fruit & Vegetables	Once a week	large	all

11 대화를 듣고, 여자의 마지막 말에 대한 남자의 응답으로 가장 적절한 것을 고르시오.

① Yes, I take the subway to work.
② Well, it's half an hour's journey.
③ Right. It's a little too far to walk.
④ No, I've got another 20 miles to go.
⑤ Actually, there is a traffic jam ahead.

12 대화를 듣고, 남자의 마지막 말에 대한 여자의 응답으로 가장 적절한 것을 고르시오.

① Of course. Try on another pair.
② I don't think so. I'll fix the hole.
③ Right. Your pants are a bit tight.
④ No way. Those are too much work.
⑤ I agree. That's what pockets are for.

13 대화를 듣고, 남자의 마지막 말에 대한 여자의 응답으로 가장 적절한 것을 고르시오. [3점]

▶ Woman :

① I really hate myself. I am good for nothing.
② Don't be hard on yourself. Just forget about it.
③ Anybody can make a mistake. So I forgive him.
④ Sorry. I didn't charge your cell phone last night.
⑤ I know you did your best. I'll buy you another one.

14 대화를 듣고, 여자의 마지막 말에 대한 남자의 응답으로 가장 적절한 것을 고르시오. [3점]

▶ Man :

① All right! Calm down and tell me slowly.
② Cheer up! You can visit there next time.
③ Wow! No wonder you're going to be busy.
④ You look exhausted. Take care of yourself!
⑤ Right! Autumn always seems to be a busy time.

15 다음 상황 설명을 듣고, Nora가 Michael에게 할 말로 가장 적절한 것을 고르시오. [3점]

▶ Nora :

① That's amazing! Good luck to you.
② Hang in there! Don't be disappointed.
③ Try it! You're young enough to start.
④ Good! Plan well and achieve your dream.
⑤ Thanks! I'm preparing for audition programs.

[16~17] 다음을 듣고, 물음에 답하시오.

16 남자가 하는 말의 주제로 가장 적절한 것은?

① effective techniques for reading books
② how to improve imagination and creativity
③ reading as a tool of improving imagination
④ benefits of reading different types of books
⑤ differences between TV watching and reading

17 언급된 책의 종류가 아닌 것은?

① mystery   ② spy novel
③ history book   ④ horror novel
⑤ biography

01

W: Hello, guys! It's nice weather, so I hope you have a good time here on the playground. You can run, slide, climb, and jump! But if you don't _____ _____, this can be a very dangerous place. First, you need to _____ before using the equipment. People should slide down the slide one person at a time. You must use the stairs _____ the slide. Also, your feet must come first when riding down the slide. Do not slide down standing up or on your stomach. When using the swing, you must tightly hold onto the handles. In addition, _____ _____ or jump on the seesaw. If you follow all of these basic rules, you can really enjoy yourself here. Now have fun!

02

W: Honey! Can you _____ Lily tonight? I have a dinner appointment with Carrie.

M: Well, actually, I need to send e-mails to my clients, but it'll be okay. I'll let Lily watch TV while I work.

W: Hmm, I don't think it's a good idea.

M: Don't worry. I'll put on a children's program.

W: I heard watching TV can be bad for kids' brain development.

M: I don't think so. TV is not all that bad for kids. Children's programs can even be _____ _____.

W: But if kids watch TV, they won't want to read books or exercise.

M: I read an article about it in the newspaper. If you monitor their viewing, you will find TV has a _____ children.

W: All right. It's up to you tonight.

M: Don't worry. I've got it under control.

03

M: You look so tired.

W: Yes, _____. It's been a very busy day.

M: The emergency room is always busy, but today seemed busier than ever.

W: I know... Anyway, you must be hungry, right? I have some sandwiches. Would you like some?

M: No, thanks. I don't feel like eating now. By the way, do I have more patients to check on?

W: No, but Mr. Johnson, who came in _____ _____, is still complaining about the pain.

M: How about his temperature? Did you give him his medicine and a shot?

W: Yes, I did. His temperature has gone down to normal, 37°C. But he appears very anxious.

M: Have we received his scan results?

W: No, _____ them yet.

M: Well, I'll see him shortly.

04

M: Olivia, look at this paper. This article is about my son's basketball team winning the championship.

W: Oh, it's Miller Grove High School's basketball team. Is your son holding up the championship trophy?

M: The boy in the far left? No. Try to guess _____ _____. People say that my son resembles me.

W: It's _____ from this picture. Well, is he the boy who is holding a basketball?

M: No, you're wrong again. My son is holding a banner in the center.

W: Oh, he's so good-looking. It says "2018 Boys Basketball Champions" on the banner. You must be proud of him!

M: Yes. And the man with a striped shirt and a tie is their head coach. I've met him several times. He's very good with the students.

W: That's great. By the way, why is the coach holding up 7 fingers?

M: Because it's their 7th championship win.

W: That's amazing! That's why the boy _____ _____ is raising _____ in the air.

M: Maybe. They do look happy with their victory.

05

M: Mom, I am home. What are you cooking? It smells so good.

W: I am cooking dinner. This is your favorite, baked salmon.

M: It looks really yummy. And I see some pie over there, too. Is it our dessert?

W: No, your sister has to take it to the school bazaar tomorrow. I found _____ on Today's Cooking's website.

M: Oh, what is it? Did you try the new recipe?

W: Yes, it's a recipe for peach pie. Since this is _____, I thought it would be a good choice.

M: I want to try some. Can you bake one for me? I'll go to the supermarket and buy some peaches now.

W: You don't have to. There are some peaches left. I'll _____ now.

M: That's great. Do you need any help, Mom?

W: No, you can go do your homework and leave it to me.

M: Thanks, Mom. Call me whenever it's ready.

06

W: Good afternoon, Mr. Brown. Have a seat.

M: Good afternoon, Ms. Thomas. I've brought all the documents you asked.

W: Okay. Would you like _____?

M: No, thanks. As I told you over the phone, I broke my arm and had an operation.

W: Yes, so you want to _____ on your insurance.

M: My medical bill came to $2,200, and my medicine bill was $500. Will you pay for everything?

W: Yes, your insurance plan _____. And you can get an extra $500.

M: Really? That's great news.

W: Yes, because you hurt yourself in a car accident, you can get extra money from our special coverage.

M: Good. I'm glad I have insurance.

W: This is why our customers are _____ _____ Pacific Insurance. We'll pay you in ten days.

07

W: I'd like to get a hair band. Are these all on sale?

M: No, there are a few that _____. Which one would you like?

W: Hmm, I'd like something simple with a small decoration.

M: Let me see... Then what about this band with a butterfly decoration? This butterfly is decorated with pearls and crystals.

W: Wow, it looks pretty. That's _____ _____. How much is it?

M: It was originally $35, but now it's on sale for $22.

W: Sounds great. Can I see it?

M: Sure. Here it is. It's very flexible and soft. Simple but fancy. Would you like to _____?

W: Okay. Hmm... Oh, I don't think I can wear it for a long time. _____ just behind my ears.

M: Then why don't you try another one?

W: No, thanks. I have to go now. I'll come back another time.

08

M: Hello. This is Marina Hotel. How can I help you?

W: Yes, I'm thinking of _____ to your hotel for our summer holiday. But first, can you tell me about your facilities?

M: Certainly, ma'am. We have two swimming pools and saunas.

W: I have two children. Is there any _____ _____? I'm worried they'll get bored.

M: Sure. Lots of kids seem to have a great time at our go-cart track. We also have a games room.

W: That's wonderful. We'll be coming by airplane. Do you run a bus from the airport to the hotel?

M: Yes, we run a shuttle bus every half hour.

W: Okay. And I need to check my e-mail. Is there _____ there?

M: Certainly, ma'am. We offer Wi-Fi all around the hotel. And there is also the Business Center.

W: Do you know what it costs to use _____ _____?

M: I'm not quite sure, but it costs less than $30 a day.

W: Okay. Thanks.

09

M: Welcome to Columbus County Library. The Columbus County Library offers a book discussion group called Book Talk. Book Talk is a book discussion group that _____ _____. Book Talk is open to adults from Columbus County. The group generally meets at 7 p.m. on the last Wednesday of every month in the library's conference room. Sarah Wise, the librarian, selects books for discussion. The title for the discussion on Wednesday, December 27 is a historical fiction, *Salt to the Sea* by Ruta Sepetys. There is no need _____ to join Book Talk. Just read the book and come to the group ready to talk about it. After the meeting, _____ are provided. For more information about Book Talk, contact Sarah Wise at 940-782-5280.

10

M: How can I help you?

W: I'd like to _____ your produce delivery service.

M: Thanks. You have several options to choose from. Would you like fruit and vegetables, or just vegetables?

W: I would like fruit and vegetables, please. _____ get the delivery box?

M: We can send it to you once a week or twice a week.

W: I prefer once-a-week delivery. Can I have them delivered on Mondays?

M: Sure. And we have small, medium, and large boxes, so you can _____. Which one do you want?

W: Since I have a large family, I definitely need the large boxes.

M: Would you like your fruit and vegetables both to be organic or just the vegetables?

W: I definitely want _____ to be organic.

M: Okay. Can you fill out this form?

11

W: So, Mr. Philips, how do you _____?

M: I take the ferry to Manhattan. It's a beautiful ride, and it's free! After that, I take the subway and get off at 72nd Street Station.

W: Sounds great. _____ is your ride on the subway?

12

M: Mom, the pocket in my pants has _____ in it.

W: You just bought those pants a month ago. I said you shouldn't carry your keys and pens in your pocket.

M: I see. You're right. Anyway, I think I need to _____ this weekend.

13

W: You look upset. Is something wrong?

M: I think I _____.

W: Are you sure? You just bought it a month ago. Did you call your phone?

M: Yes. I keep calling my phone, but no one is answering.

W: Where do you think you lost it?

M: Maybe... I think I lost it _____ a roller coaster over there. I couldn't find my phone after riding it.

W: Really? You mean that crazy roller coaster?

M: Yes, I put the phone in my sweatshirt pocket, but the pocket is really small.

W: Too bad. If that's the case, there's _____ it, and even if you did, the phone is probably ruined.

M: I don't understand why I put it in this pocket. I'm such an idiot.

14

W: Oh, no! I can't believe summer's over, can you?

M: _____. I had a really good time this summer vacation, but now we have to go back to school.

W: I know, but I'm excited now because I _____ for this semester.

M: I'm going to join the golf team. Do you want to join with me?

W: I'd _____, but I'm already on the swim team, so I don't think I would have time.

M: You can do both if you change your swimming schedule.

W: I don't think so. I need to do a lot of volunteer work, too.

M: _____ volunteer work are you involved in?

W: I'm a member of the local "Habitat for Humanity," so I'll spend all of my weekends to help build houses. And I'll also visit the local senior center.

15

W: Michael is a coworker of Nora. They work in a small trading company. Today their company has a picnic to help strengthen teamwork and have fun. There is a song competition in the program. Michael participates in the song competition and wins first prize. He sings so well, just _____ _____. Nora is amazed and tells him that if she could sing like him, she would be a singer. Michael says he once thought about becoming a singer. But he thinks he's a little _____ a singer now even though it has always been his dream. Nora doesn't think so. There are some audition programs on TV, and she thinks it's not too late _____ _____. She wants to encourage him to share his talent. In this situation, what would Nora most likely say to Michael?

16~17

M: How often do you watch television? Do you know that you're using your imagination while watching TV? Yes, you are! Watching television does use your imagination, but it's only _____ _____. When reading, however, you use active imagination. Why? When you read, your mind tends to _____. Suppose you are reading a mystery or a spy novel. Your mind will imagine a mysterious setting that matches what you have _____ _____. A good science fiction writer creates a picture with the characters, scenes, and settings in his or her story. But that is all a writer can give you. The rest is _____. The more you read, the more your imagination improves. If you read different types of books, such as history books, biographies, and romance novels, you will start to _____ more creative ideas. To get the most out of your imagination, don't forget to check out the bestselling books online or at a bookstore.

01 다음을 듣고, 여자가 하는 말의 목적으로 가장 적절한 것을 고르시오.

① 화재 발생 시 대피 요령을 안내하려고
② 건물의 화재 경보 오작동을 사과하려고
③ 건물 안전 진단의 중요성을 설명하려고
④ 정기적인 화재 대피 훈련을 권유하려고
⑤ 화재 경보 시스템 시험 작동을 공지하려고

02 대화를 듣고, 남자의 의견으로 가장 적절한 것을 고르시오.

① 건강을 위해 일정 시간 햇빛을 쬘 필요가 있다.
② 햇빛에 노출되면 피부암 발병의 확률이 커진다.
③ 흐린 날에도 자외선 차단제를 꼭 사용해야 한다.
④ 자외선 차단제의 화학물질이 피부에 해로울 수 있다.
⑤ 자외선 차단제를 선택할 때 꼭 성분을 확인해야 한다.

03 대화를 듣고, 두 사람의 관계를 가장 잘 나타낸 것을 고르시오.

① 경찰관 – 신고자
② 은행원 – 은행 고객
③ 세관 직원 – 수입업체 직원
④ 웹사이트 관리자 – 사용자
⑤ 세무서 직원 – 세금 문의자

04 대화를 듣고, 그림에서 대화의 내용과 일치하지 않는 것을 고르시오.

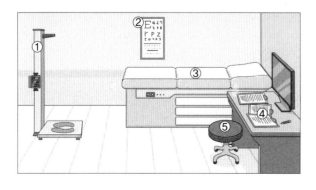

05 대화를 듣고, 여자가 할 일로 가장 적절한 것을 고르시오.

① 보고서 작성 끝내기
② 아이 병원에 데려가기
③ 봉제 동물 인형 구입하기
④ 아이에게 동화책 읽어주기
⑤ 아이에게 따뜻한 음료 가져다주기

06 대화를 듣고, 남자가 지불할 금액을 고르시오. [3점]

① $400   ② $600   ③ $700
④ $800   ⑤ $900

07 대화를 듣고, 남자가 네팔 여행을 가지 못하게 된 이유를 고르시오.

① 부모님의 허락을 받지 못해서
② 여름 학기를 수강하게 되어서
③ 비행기 표가 모두 매진되어서
④ 휴가 일정이 갑자기 바뀌어서
⑤ 여행 경비를 다 모으지 못해서

08 대화를 듣고, Douglas County 산불에 관해 언급되지 않은 것을 고르시오.

① 시작된 날   ② 피해 면적
③ 피해 가옥 수   ④ 발화 원인
⑤ 동원된 소방대원 수

09 Big Rock 청소년 등반 대회에 관한 다음 내용을 듣고, 일치하지 않는 것을 고르시오.

① 11월 17일 금요일에 대회가 열린다.
② 8세에서 18세까지 누구나 참가할 수 있다.
③ 참가자는 무료로 등산화를 빌릴 수 있다.
④ 대회 등록은 온라인으로 해야 한다.
⑤ 일찍 등록하면 참가비가 더 저렴하다.

10 다음 표를 보면서 대화를 듣고, 남자가 구매할 자동차를 고르시오.

Tony's Used Cars					
Car	Type	Engine Size	Number of Doors	Price	Seating
① A	car	2.4 liter	4	$5,500	5
② B	car	2.0 liter	4	$4,900	5
③ C	car	1.8 liter	2	$4,800	4
④ D	SUV	2.0 liter	5	$5,200	7
⑤ E	truck	2.5 liter	2	$4,600	2

11 대화를 듣고, 여자의 마지막 말에 대한 남자의 응답으로 가장 적절한 것을 고르시오.

① Certainly. You can pick it up at 6 p.m.
② Sure. You can find one behind that building.
③ Yes. It's a little cheaper than the parking lot.
④ Here's your ticket. Call us when you need your car.
⑤ No. They're reserved parking spaces for the residents.

12 대화를 듣고, 남자의 마지막 말에 대한 여자의 응답으로 가장 적절한 것을 고르시오.

① He is a terrific actor. I'm a big fan of him.
② Let's turn off the TV now. It's time to study.
③ The game will be over in 10 minutes. Please wait.
④ Let's play the game again. I'll beat you this time.
⑤ Please do not feel too bad. It's no fault of yours.

13 대화를 듣고, 남자의 마지막 말에 대한 여자의 응답으로 가장 적절한 것을 고르시오. [3점]

▶ Woman :

① Right. Don't forget to exercise regularly.
② You look great. I also want to get in shape.
③ I don't think I can do that. I'm not an early bird.
④ Okay. Just come in comfortable workout clothes.
⑤ It sounds like having my own trainer. I'll try that.

14 대화를 듣고, 여자의 마지막 말에 대한 남자의 응답으로 가장 적절한 것을 고르시오.

▶ Man :

① What a great plan! You're so sweet!
② You're a skilled carpenter. I admire you!
③ I think so. I'll build a smaller object first.
④ Yes. This book teaches you how to make it.
⑤ Right. It's really hard to find a good tool kit.

15 다음 상황 설명을 듣고, Owen의 어머니가 Owen에게 할 말로 가장 적절한 것을 고르시오. [3점]

▶ Owen's mother :

① Great. I feel that I've been rewarded for all my effort.
② Congratulations. I'm happy to tell you that you won it.
③ I know how hard you've worked for this. I'm proud of you.
④ Okay. Like any plan, you need to set a goal and run for it.
⑤ That's true. The most important thing is enjoying your job.

[16~17] 다음을 듣고, 물음에 답하시오.

16 남자가 하는 말의 주제로 가장 적절한 것은?

① how to use a microwave effectively
② why the microwave is so popular everywhere
③ the health effects of using a microwave oven
④ reasons why people prefer not to use a microwave
⑤ differences between a microwave and a regular oven

17 언급된 장소가 <u>아닌</u> 것은?

① restaurants   ② trains
③ cafeterias   ④ supermarkets
⑤ bakeries

01

W: This is an announcement from your maintenance office. I'm sorry to interrupt your working day by shouting over the building's sound system like this. But I wanted to _____ that we will be conducting a test of the building's _____ shortly. These frequent tests are essential to your well-being in the event of an emergency. We urge you _____ during this test so that we can ensure your safety in the future. This is only a test of the system, _____, so there will be no need to leave the building at this time. However, if you need or want to leave the building, you are _____. Thank you again for your patience.

02

M: Jennifer, why don't we go out for a walk?

W: Good idea, but hold on. I have to _____ _____ before I leave the house.

M: It's cloudy, so don't worry about it too much.

W: You must wear sunscreen any time you'll be out. _____ the UV rays even on cloudy days. We just can't see them.

M: Isn't that what cosmetic companies want you to believe?

W: But it's true that getting a sunburn can increase your risk for skin cancer.

M: Well, I think that _____ on your face is worse for you. It's _____ of chemicals.

W: UV rays can make your skin older and even give you skin cancer!

M: Actually, sunscreen itself _____ because it contains harmful chemicals. You should think about that.

W: Oh, I hadn't heard that. I can't believe sunscreen itself is harmful.

M: I'll send you an article about that. Then you'll be convinced.

03

M: Good afternoon. How can I help you?

W: I got a call and was told that I had a problem with my personal _____.

M: Your income tax?

W: Yes, and they asked my account number and PIN number over the phone.

M: You didn't give them the numbers, did you?

W: Well, I gave the first number but stopped. It didn't feel right.

M: Good for you! It sounds like voice phishing.

W: Yes, I wasn't sure if _____ to the tax office or to the police. So I decided to come here first to check _____.

M: Good. Can I have your ID card and account number, please?

W: Here's my ID and account number.

M: Hmm… _____. Well, no one withdrew any money from your account today. If you get another phone call like that, please _____.

W: I see. I'm so relieved. That really scared me. I don't know how these people knew my name and phone number.

04

M: Hi, Ms. Moore. Mr. Wilson asked me to help you with the student physical checkups.

W: Hi, James. Thanks. You _____ the kids through their checkups.

M: All right. Should I line the kids up in front of this room?

W: Yes. And bring kids _____ to the scale on the left side of the room.

M: I see. You'll measure their heights and weights with it.

W: Right. And they'll have their eye exams.

M: Oh, there is an eye chart on the wall above the bed. By the way, what will you use the bed for?

W: We won't use it this time. Oh, when you bring kids, you _____ their names on the charts which are placed on the desk.

M: Do you mean the desk on the right?

W: Yeah. And while I examine a kid, have two kids wait _____ next to the desk.

M: Okay. I can do that.

05

W: Honey, I'm worried about Chloe. She doesn't want to go to bed tonight.

M: It's almost 11 p.m. Doesn't she feel well?

W: No, she is healthy. Recently she gets so worried before going to sleep at night.

M: Really? Do you know the reason why _____ _____?

W: Hmm... I don't know exactly, but I think she's just _____.

M: It's quite common at her age. How about buying some stuffed animal toys for her?

W: She already has _____, such as teddy bears and cuddly rabbits.

M: Oh! _____ read her a storybook before she goes to sleep?

W: That's great. Will you do it now?

M: I'm afraid I can't do it now. I've got to finish this report. What about you?

W: Okay. I'll _____ while you finish your work.

M: That's good. I think it will make her feel much more safe and relaxed.

06

W: Do you need any help?

M: Yes. How much is this wonderful coat?

W: It's $1,500. It's made of all cashmere wool.

M: Wow! It's way above _____.

W: There are some nice coats which are being sold at a 20% discount. How about this one? It was originally $500, but it's now 20% off.

M: That's a good price, but I don't like _____ _____.

W: Then you'll like this coat. It was originally $1,000, but you can also get a 20% discount on it. Why don't you try it on?

M: Looks good, but it's also _____ _____.

W: May I ask what price range you have in mind?

M: I'm hoping to spend no more than $700.

W: Well, it is really warm and lightweight. I think you _____ a little extra _____.

M: Hmm... Okay. I'll take it.

07

W: Hi, Jeremy. I heard you're going to Nepal this summer. When are you leaving?

M: Unfortunately, my trip's been canceled.

W: Oh, sorry to hear that. Your parents didn't want you to travel, right?

M: No, they said I could go, and I've worked at a restaurant every weekend.

W: You must have saved _____ then.

M: Yes, but it is useless now. I can't make the trip this summer after all.

W: Why? Do you have to take summer school?

M: No, I don't. When I tried to _____ _____, I found all the tickets to Nepal were completely _____.

W: That's too bad. Why don't you put your name on the waiting list?

M: I already did, but there are _____ on the list ahead of me. So I gave up.

W: How about going somewhere else? There are a lot of beautiful countries you can go to.

M: No, going to Nepal has been my dream. I just decided I would go there next time.

08

M: There was a huge wildfire in Douglas County.

W: Yes, I saw it on the news.

M: _____ on Friday, October 5th

and quickly spread across the county.

W: I heard it _____ across 1,400 acres. I think that's because it's very dry in October.

M: Right. One of my friends lives there, and he said he's never seen anything like that.

W: Oh, really? I think lots of people were harmed. Is he safe?

M: Yeah, he and his house are safe, but about 40 houses _____.

W: I feel so sorry for those people.

M: They are not sure _____ in the first place, but we always should be careful in the forest.

W: They must have needed a lot of firefighters to put out the fires.

M: I heard there were about _____ on scene, but more firefighters should have been there.

09

M: The Big Rock Youth Climbing Competition is back! The Big Rock Youth Climbing Competition is an opportunity for you to test your climbing ability and have fun in a friendly atmosphere. It'll _____, November 17th in the Big Rock Climbing Center. Since it was started in 2010, this is the 9th competition this year. It's _____ from age 8 to 18. No experience is necessary, and you can _____ for $3. There will be 12 routes to choose from. Registration is needed to participate. You must register online by November 10th. The entry fee is $15, but it will be reduced to $10 if you _____ by October 30th. For more information, please contact Joe Mason at 405-992-3746.

10

W: Can I help you find something?

M: Yes, I'm looking for a used car. We need a family

car.

W: May I ask what kind of car you're looking for?

M: We don't need a truck, since _____ _____.

W: Okay. What size engine do you want?

M: I don't want anything _____ 2 liters.

W: I understand. The bigger ones drink far more fuel.

M: Certainly. And I don't like 2-door cars because _____ to ride in the back seat.

W: Then you can choose between these two. How much is your budget?

M: Well, I'd like to stay under $5,000. Oh, I like this one.

W: Oh, well, this one is just a little bit over $5,000, so it doesn't really _____.

M: But I think such a small amount over is okay. And _____, so my family will really like this one. I'll take it.

11

W: Excuse me. Can I _____ on this side of the street?

M: No, you can't. It's a No-Parking Zone until 6 p.m.

W: Well, then where can I park until 6? Are there _____ around here?

12

M: Sue, can I _____ another channel? I'd like to watch my favorite TV show.

W: No. I'm watching a basketball game now. _____ your show online? It's a rerun, isn't it?

M: My laptop monitor is too small. I'd like to watch it on TV.

13

M: You look serious. What's wrong?

W: I'm trying to lose weight, but I _____ _____.

M: You look good. But if you want to be in better shape and you're too busy, find other ways to include activity _____.

W: Like what?

M: You can walk quickly to the office or climb up and down the stairs instead of taking the elevator.

W: That sounds like a good idea. But I don't think I'd be encouraged to keep going.

M: I use a fitness app on my smartphone. It'll encourage you to walk more.

W: What's that? And how does it help me _____ _____?

M: It can track your activities, like steps, distance walked, and calories burned, using your phone.

W: That's cool! What's the name of the app? Do I have to pay for it?

M: No, it's a free app called the Daily Fitness App. It _____ your daily activities.

14

W: Honey, is there anything you've been wanting to buy lately?

M: Hmm... I don't know. Why do you ask?

W: Christmas is coming up, and I want to know the things I could _____.

M: That's so sweet of you, honey! But you've already given me far too much.

W: Just tell me, please. Can you think of anything you'd want?

M: Hmm... Well, you know I'm _____ _____.

W: Certainly. You said you wanted _____ _____ when you were young.

M: I found a nice tool kit for woodworking at K Mart the other day. If I had it, I'd like to make _____ _____ for our backyard.

W: That sounds like a great idea for Christmas! Maybe I can help you _____ during the holiday!

15

W: Owen is a high school student, and he wants to major in photography at an art school. In the hopes of _____, he decides to enter an international photography competition which is open for students. Owen always takes a camera with him and takes _____ he can. He gets up early in the morning at 5 a.m. to take pictures of the sunrise. He tries to put emotion and feelings in his photographs. Finally, he sends his photos to the competition organizers. And today he _____ _____ he will receive third prize. When his mother hears the news, she is very pleased and wants to _____ rather than the outcome. In this situation, what would Owen's mother most likely say to Owen?

16~17

M: What do you think is the most commonly used device in homes today? As you may have guessed, it is the microwave. Because using a microwave can cut _____, they are used by many families. But microwaves aren't just used in the home. They're everywhere — in restaurants, trains, cafeterias, college dormitories, and break rooms in workplaces. It's not surprising that microwaves are popular. Workers and students can _____ from last night's dinner in the microwave, heat them for a few minutes, and eat a delicious lunch. Supermarkets also _____ of microwaves because they sell different types of "microwaveable" meals. Some people say that using a microwave _____ from the pleasure of cooking. But, for many modern people who do not believe cooking is fun, microwaves are a wonderful device to make their lives _____ _____.

08회

✳ 첫단추 듣기실전편

01 다음을 듣고, 여자가 하는 말의 목적으로 가장 적절한 것을 고르시오.

① 교내 운동장 개방을 알리려고
② 학부모에게 학생 훈육을 부탁하려고
③ 학교 운동장 방범 순찰을 요청하려고
④ 방과 후 운동장 사용 금지를 공지하려고
⑤ 학생 지킴이 자원봉사 신청을 독려하려고

02 대화를 듣고, 남자의 의견으로 가장 적절한 것을 고르시오.

① 주택의 담장 설치를 의무화해야 한다.
② 사슴에게 먹이를 제공해 공존해야 한다.
③ 사냥으로 사슴의 개체 수를 조절해야 한다.
④ 전기 철조망 설치를 정부가 보조해야 한다.
⑤ 숲을 파괴하는 개발 계획을 수정해야 한다.

03 대화를 듣고, 두 사람의 관계를 가장 잘 나타낸 것을 고르시오.

① 비서 – 상사
② 식당 직원 – 손님
③ 호텔 직원 – 투숙객
④ 전자제품 판매원 – 고객
⑤ 통신회사 직원 – 이용자

04 대화를 듣고, 그림에서 대화의 내용과 일치하지 않는 것을 고르시오.

05 대화를 듣고, 여자가 할 일로 가장 적절한 것을 고르시오.

① 노트북 컴퓨터 고쳐주기
② 태블릿 PC 구입 도와주기
③ 방에서 스마트폰 가져오기
④ 무료 컴퓨터 강좌 알려주기
⑤ 이메일로 사진 보내는 법 알려주기

06 대화를 듣고, 두 사람이 북카페로 재개장하기 위한 총 예상 금액을 고르시오. [3점]

① $3,400
② $3,800
③ $5,400
④ $6,200
⑤ $7,200

07 대화를 듣고, 두 사람이 집을 구매하지 않는 이유를 고르시오.

① 해변에서 너무 가까워서
② 동네가 안전하지 않아서
③ 집값이 예산을 초과해서
④ 뒷마당 관리가 어려워서
⑤ 자동차 소음으로 시끄러워서

08 대화를 듣고, 여자가 면접 본 직장에 관해 언급되지 않은 것을 고르시오.

① 근무 장소
② 근무 시간
③ 건강 보험 혜택
④ 유급 휴가 일수
⑤ 연봉 액수

09 Championship Chess Camp에 관한 다음 내용을 듣고, 일치하지 않는 것을 고르시오.

① 6월 21일부터 5일 동안 열린다.
② 1학년부터 6학년 학생을 대상으로 한다.
③ 초보자도 숙련자도 모두 참여할 수 있다.
④ 캠프 비용에 간식은 포함되어 있지 않다.
⑤ 등록 신청은 온라인과 전화로 할 수 있다.

10 다음 표를 보면서 대화를 듣고, 두 사람이 택한 버스 관광 상품을 고르시오.

One Day Bus Tours

Bus Tour	Time	Tourist Course	Price (per person)	Lunch Included
① A	9 a.m. – 4 p.m.	Valley	100 euros	×
② B	11 a.m. – 7 p.m.	Cathedral / Palace	70 euros	○
③ C	8 a.m. – 2 p.m.	Palace / Museum	60 euros	○
④ D	10 a.m. – 4 p.m.	Beach	80 euros	×
⑤ E	9 a.m. – 5 p.m.	Farm & Lake	80 euros	○

11 대화를 듣고, 여자의 마지막 말에 대한 남자의 응답으로 가장 적절한 것을 고르시오.

① Sorry, I didn't mean it.
② No, it's totally up to you.
③ Well, I guess I have no choice.
④ Right. That's exactly what I thought.
⑤ Good. Anytime after 1 p.m. is fine today.

12 대화를 듣고, 남자의 마지막 말에 대한 여자의 응답으로 가장 적절한 것을 고르시오.

① Please don't rush me. I need time to think.
② I promise to be on time. You don't need to worry.
③ I didn't know that. Thanks for the information.
④ You can get there by train. Here's the train schedule.
⑤ I'm sorry. I missed the ferry due to a delayed train.

13 대화를 듣고, 남자의 마지막 말에 대한 여자의 응답으로 가장 적절한 것을 고르시오.

▶ Woman :

① Good idea. It'll be sunny tomorrow.
② Fantastic! It feels like Christmas already.
③ All right. Let's get out of the cold for a bit.
④ Yes. I love hiking, but it's great to be home.
⑤ Okay. I'll bring my chair over to the fireplace.

14 대화를 듣고, 여자의 마지막 말에 대한 남자의 응답으로 가장 적절한 것을 고르시오. [3점]

▶ Man :

① You need to take care of yourself more.
② I'm not sure, but I guess it's worth a try.
③ I do it because it gives me an opportunity.
④ It's very kind of you to listen to my problems.
⑤ If you want to be healthy, you should eat better.

15 다음 상황 설명을 듣고, Dominic이 Green 부인에게 할 말로 가장 적절한 것을 고르시오. [3점]

▶ Dominic :

① Would you mind if I put this box here?
② Could I give you a hand with that box?
③ Are you sure you can do it by yourself?
④ If you don't mind, could you give me a ride?
⑤ Why don't you ask somebody to help you with it?

[16~17] 다음을 듣고, 물음에 답하시오.

16 남자가 하는 말의 주제로 가장 적절한 것은?

① the negative effects of songs
② various types of modern songs
③ the use of songs to boost moods
④ songs as a means of communication
⑤ the importance of songs in everyday life

17 언급된 음악의 장르가 아닌 것은?

① folk songs   ② jazz
③ ballads   ④ rock
⑤ hip hop

01

W: Hello. Recently, it has come to my attention that there have been several students staying and playing in the schoolyard after school. The schoolyard is not safe after school because there are no teachers or school staff _____ _____. Besides, as there is no fence around the yard, anyone can enter the yard. And school property might be damaged, or worse, children could even be seriously injured. So our school has decided that _____ _____ on the schoolyard after school. This is now _____. Once school finishes, the yard must _____ students until the next day. If we find anyone after school, they'll be punished and their parents will be notified.

02

M: Did you hear that a deer destroyed a vegetable garden in our neighborhood?

W: Yes, I heard that. There are so many deer around here.

M: There has been _____ caused by them on farms and in gardens.

W: They're harmful animals to us now. I think the government should do something to control their population.

M: You're right. I think hunting is _____ _____ to solve this problem.

W: But isn't it too cruel? I believe it's better to build electric fences around neighborhoods. They're effective for keeping out deer.

M: It costs way too much. We can control the deer population _____. This also prevents deer from _____ food.

W: Well, I think electric fences are safer. Maybe the government can help pay for electric fences.

M: Hmm... Maybe... But I think the cheaper and easier solution is best.

W: It still seems kind of cruel to me, but I see your point.

03

W: Good evening. How can I help you?

M: I've got some network problems. I can't connect to your Wi-Fi. The login screen doesn't appear.

W: Oh, I see. We'll send someone _____ _____.

M: Can you send him immediately? I have to send an e-mail now.

W: If it's urgent, why don't you _____ _____? There is free Wi-Fi in the lounge.

M: No, I'll wait for the technician in my room. How long _____?

W: It will be about 20 minutes.

M: That'll be okay. And I'd like to have some breakfast and coffee delivered to my room tomorrow morning at 7 o'clock.

W: _____ would you like, the English or continental breakfast?

M: Continental, please. I'll pay my bill when I check out.

W: All right, sir. I'm arranging everything right now.

04

W: This is the initial draft of the poster for our Thanksgiving dinner. What do you think?

M: Well, it looks great. I like _____ _____ the words, "HAPPY THANKSGIVING" on the banner at the top!

W: Thanks, and I drew two owls on the branch.

M: They're really cute! The owl on the left is wearing a black hat with a buckle on the front.

W: Yes, _____ a pilgrim's hat. And the owl on the right is wearing an Indian feather hat.

M: Great. They're both symbols of Thanksgiving. But it looks like we need to _____ here at the bottom.

W: What do you want to change?

M: You drew some leaves at the end of the branch. Why don't you draw a pumpkin and some corn _____?

W: Good idea. I'll change them. How about the time and location of the dinner at the far right?

M: I like it. I think it's the most important information on the poster. Thank you. It's really great.

05

M: Becky! Can you give me a hand?

W: Sure, Grandpa. What do you need?

M: I've just started to take a free computer course at the senior center.

W: Wow! Good for you! But is your laptop _____ _____? It's been more than ten years, I guess.

M: Don't worry. I bought a used tablet PC. By the way, you're a computer expert, aren't you?

W: Well, no, I wouldn't call myself a computer expert, but I think _____.

M: Okay. My computer teacher asked me to _____ _____ to his e-mail, but I forgot how to do it. Can you explain it for me?

W: Sure. It's very easy once you know how. Is your picture you want to send to him on your tablet PC?

M: No, it's on my smartphone. I feel embarrassed about forgetting.

W: Grandpa, I'm proud of you. Most people at your age hardly try to learn about technology, so don't feel discouraged.

M: Thank you. Anyway, I'm going to _____ _____ in my room.

06

M: Carla, I've got an idea for getting more customers to come to our coffee shop.

W: What's that?

M: There are many coffee shops including ours around here, right? But there aren't any book cafes here.

W: So are you suggesting _____ _____ of our own?

M: Definitely. I'm sure there are people who want to read books with coffee and tea.

W: That's a good idea, but I'm not sure _____ _____ for that right now.

M: I have a business plan. We need $3,000 for the remodeling costs.

W: We also need to buy books and other stuff.

M: That will be _____. I think we can afford it.

W: Don't forget we'll need money for marketing and advertising. How much do you think it costs? Around $1,000?

M: I already thought about that. _____ _____ for that.

W: Not bad. I agree with you. We can do this.

07

W: Robert, look at this house for sale. I really like this house.

M: Yes, it's a beautiful house.

W: It's in a great neighborhood, and the beach is _____.

M: But the house is on the corner. That means it gets twice as much traffic and noise.

W: Don't worry. There is _____ in this area. Best of all, it's got a big backyard.

M: I'm sure our kids would love to play basketball in the backyard.

W: Let me see its price. Uh, oh. _____ this house.

M: Are you sure? I think we can afford it.

W: If we buy this house, we'll be house rich, but cash poor. Think about the monthly payment.

M: Hmm... You're right. We have to find a _____ _____.

08

W: By the way sir, can you tell me a little about the position?

M: Sure. What do you want to know?

W: If I get this job, will I be working at the office or at the stores?

M: You'll be spending most of your time _____ _____.

W: I see. And when are the office hours? Is it from nine to five?

M: No, it'll be _____. If you have more questions, please ask me freely.

W: Thanks. I'd like to know more about _____ _____.

M: The company pays for 90% of your health insurance for you and your family. But you have to pay your medical bills until the total reaches $1,500.

W: Okay. I heard that I'll get 10 days of vacation a year. Is it paid vacation?

M: Yes, you get a 10-day _____ each year. And you already know about the annual salary for this job, right?

W: Yes, I'm satisfied with the salary. Thank you.

M: We'll be contacting you soon. It was nice meeting you, Ms. Johnson.

09

W: Trinity School will have its Championship Chess Camp, starting from June 21st to the 25th, for 5 days from 8 a.m. to noon. This annual tradition is open for _____, and it has always proved fun and a great learning experience for them. All students, from _____ _____ to the experienced competitor, are welcome to join. There will be _____ for beginners, guided play, and game play. A mini-tournament will make a fun and exciting conclusion to this camp. The cost for the camp is $210 and includes _____. You can register for it either online, www.trinityatl.org, or by contacting Anna Lewis at 910-287-4468. Don't miss out on this great opportunity to have fun, learn, and play more chess.

10

M: What should we do tomorrow?

W: I walked more than 6 hours today, so I'm tired of walking. Let's take a bus tour tomorrow. I got this brochure in the hotel lobby.

M: Good idea. We can choose _____ _____. What would you like to choose?

W: We reserved a flamingo show at 7 p.m. tomorrow. We have to choose one which finishes _____ _____.

M: That's right. Which course are you interested in?

W: We already saw so many historic sites such as cathedrals and palaces. I'd like to do _____ _____ tomorrow.

M: Then it looks like we have these three options. Let's choose one of the cheaper ones.

W: I'd like a tour _____ if they're the same price.

M: You have a point. We won't need to spend time to search for restaurants. Let's take this one.

W: Okay. I'll call and reserve it.

11

W: Your cavity has gotten so bad. It looks pretty serious. You _____ earlier.

M: I've been so busy with work.

W: I won't be able to treat it in one visit. I'll have to _____ for several weeks. Is that okay with you?

12

M: How can I help you?

W: I'd like an 8:30 a.m. train ticket to Green Harbor. I have to take the morning ferry, _____ at 10 a.m. there.

M: Then I recommend the 8:00 a.m. train because you need to arrive at the harbor at least _____ _____ the ferry.

13

M: Are you all right, Ella?

W: Actually, no. It's really cold outside! The weatherman was wrong again.

M: Yes, they said the cold weather _____ _____ yesterday.

W: They never get the weather right. If they said it would be cold like this, we wouldn't have gone hiking today.

M: You're right, and this strong wind is making it feel so much colder.

W: I feel like my toes are freezing.

M: We're nearly to the town. _____.

W: Look! There is a coffee shop over there. Do you mind _____? We can have some warm coffee.

M: Sounds great. It seems that there is a fireplace inside.

14

M: Hi, Hannah. How's it going?

W: Hi, Carter. Not so good.

M: You look really tired. Are you sick?

W: No, I'm not getting much sleep these days.

M: Is something _____?

W: Not really. I don't really have a serious problem. I just can't get a good night's rest.

M: Hmm... Getting plenty of sleep is so important to our health.

W: I know. So _____, but it makes me even more tired.

M: Well, I suggest you avoid caffeine in the afternoon and evening. Instead, drink some warm milk before you go to bed.

W: Do you think _____?

15

M: Dominic is a high school student. Today, he is on his way home from school. Since he knows almost _____ on his block, he greets everyone he meets as he's walking along. As he comes near his house, he sees Mrs. Green, _____ to him, walking out of her front door. She is carrying a big box from the house to her car in the driveway. Mrs. Green is an elderly woman at the age of 65, and she is having difficulty carrying the box. Dominic would like to help her to carry the box. But he knows Mrs. Green is a very independent woman, so he wants to _____. In this situation, what would Dominic most likely say to Mrs. Green?

16~17

M: What do you usually do when you feel down? Some people might eat delicious food, and others might go on a trip. But many people would agree that the easiest way to cheer up is _____ _____. The genre of music doesn't really matter. There are lots of great pop and folk songs that can touch you with beautiful stories. Jazz, ballads, and hip hop songs can also _____ with sweet rhymes and smooth rhythms. CD players, smartphones, and YouTube enable you to _____ _____ the particular kind of song that you like most. Make a list of the songs that you love most. _____ at a specific time, such as on your way to work or just when you want to be motivated. As you listen, imagine yourself succeeding in what is most important to you right now. You will find that songs automatically give you _____ and well-being.

01 다음을 듣고, 남자가 하는 말의 목적으로 가장 적절한 것을 고르시오.

① 아파트 건설 공사 일정을 설명하려고
② 수도관 교체로 인한 단수를 공지하려고
③ 노후 아파트 재건축 추진을 요청하려고
④ 수돗물 개선을 위한 반상회를 안내하려고
⑤ 공사로 인한 수도관 파열 사고를 사과하려고

02 대화를 듣고, 남자의 의견으로 가장 적절한 것을 고르시오.

① 페이스북의 친구 수락은 신중해야 한다.
② 페이스북 사용 제한 연령을 낮춰야 한다.
③ 아이에게 페이스북 사용이 해로울 수 있다.
④ 아이에게 페이스북 사용 시간을 정해줘야 한다.
⑤ 페이스북은 교우관계를 유지하는 데 도움이 된다.

03 대화를 듣고, 두 사람의 관계를 가장 잘 나타낸 것을 고르시오.

① 취업 면접관 – 지원자
② 학교 선생님 – 학부모
③ 경품 행사 담당자 – 참여자
④ 퀴즈쇼 진행자 – 출전자
⑤ 레크리에이션 지도자 – 수강생

04 대화를 듣고, 그림에서 대화의 내용과 일치하지 않는 것을 고르시오.

05 대화를 듣고, 남자가 여자에게 부탁한 일로 가장 적절한 것을 고르시오.

① 숙제 도와주기
② 서점에서 책 찾아오기
③ 친구에게 대신 연락하기
④ 도서관에서 책 대출하기
⑤ 서비스 센터에 데려다주기

06 대화를 듣고, 남자가 항공권과 숙박비로 쓴 금액을 고르시오. [3점]

① $850   ② $900   ③ $950
④ $1,000   ⑤ $1,100

07 대화를 듣고, 남자가 여름방학에 집에 돌아가지 않는 이유를 고르시오.

① 부모님이 해외여행을 가셔서
② 축구팀의 여름 훈련이 있어서
③ 방학 중 배낭여행을 가기로 해서
④ 성적이 나빠 여름학기를 신청해서
⑤ 대학 박물관에서 일을 하게 되어서

08 대화를 듣고, Junior Cooking Competition에 관해 언급되지 않은 것을 고르시오.

① 대회 개최 일자   ② 참가 가능 연령
③ 대회 참가비   ④ 참가 신청 방법
⑤ 가족 참관 가능 여부

09 Culture Night에 관한 다음 내용을 듣고, 일치하지 않는 것을 고르시오.

① 매년 하는 행사로 이번이 아홉 번째로 열린다.
② 4월 21일에 오후 5시부터 9시까지 열린다.
③ 일반인과 UMC 학생 모두 무료로 입장할 수 있다.
④ 7시부터 세계 전통 의상 패션쇼가 진행된다.
⑤ 페이스북으로 행사 자원봉사를 신청할 수 있다.

10 다음 표를 보면서 대화를 듣고, 두 사람이 구매할 책상을 고르시오.

CHILDREN'S DESKS

Desk	Drawers	Frame	Price	Color
① A	○	metal frame	$90	light pink
② B	○	wooden frame	$93	dark grey
③ C	○	wooden frame	$105	dark green
④ D	○	wooden frame	$95	light yellow
⑤ E	×	metal frame	$85	light blue

11 대화를 듣고, 여자의 마지막 말에 대한 남자의 응답으로 가장 적절한 것을 고르시오.

① Wow. The baby just began to walk.
② Certainly. It depends on how hard I work.
③ Thanks. I just had to share the good news.
④ Don't flatter me so much. It makes me blush.
⑤ That's right. She's sensitive to others' feelings.

12 대화를 듣고, 남자의 마지막 말에 대한 여자의 응답으로 가장 적절한 것을 고르시오.

① I'm wondering if you can change seats with me.
② I would like to apologize for kicking your seat.
③ Please come this way, and I'll show you around.
④ You can move to a vacant seat after the movie begins.
⑤ You aren't allowed to bring any drinks inside the theater.

13 대화를 듣고, 남자의 마지막 말에 대한 여자의 응답으로 가장 적절한 것을 고르시오. [3점]

▶ Woman :

① I'm sorry. I don't have time to do it right now.
② I know that now. I should have asked you first.
③ What a relief! He gave me a few days' extension.
④ You're right! I'll ask him if I can submit it early.
⑤ Hurry up! Or you won't finish the paper on time.

14 대화를 듣고, 여자의 마지막 말에 대한 남자의 응답으로 가장 적절한 것을 고르시오. [3점]

▶ Man :

① We will put your donation to good use.
② I'm worried we will make it difficult for them.
③ I'm glad to know that I can help in some way.
④ You need to take this form and fill out the blanks.
⑤ You can save these children because of your interest.

15 다음 상황 설명을 듣고, Daniel이 Olivia에게 할 말로 가장 적절한 것을 고르시오.

▶ Daniel :

① Never mind. You can always try it again.
② I'm sorry. I can't do anything else about it.
③ I don't know for sure. But that's your fault.
④ Good for you. You can learn from mistakes.
⑤ I know how you feel. Don't let it get you down.

[16~17] 다음을 듣고, 물음에 답하시오.

16 남자가 하는 말의 주제로 가장 적절한 것은?

① how to meditate for beginners
② the healing power of meditation
③ meditation as a powerful motivator
④ a comparison of exercise and meditation
⑤ ways to balance physical and mental health

17 언급된 병명이 <u>아닌</u> 것은?

① sleeplessness ② depression
③ lung cancer ④ the common cold
⑤ heart disease

ANSWER p.42

01

M: The Westville Apartment Management Office would like to make an announcement to all Westville residents. We have good news for those of you who have complained about the yellow water that flows through our old water pipes. As you know, the pipes are nearly 40 years old. In order to provide you with cleaner water, we will _____ with new ones. The construction will start from Apartment B. The water _____ _____ on Apartment B most of the day on March 19th starting at 8 a.m. We apologize for the inconvenience but ask for your cooperation, as we will provide you with cleaner water. We suggest that you _____ you need before the construction. Please call 751-907-9589 for further questions.

02

W: Alex, Joshua really _____ a Facebook account.

M: Really? I heard there is a Facebook age limit.

W: It's 13, and Joshua will be 13 years old next month. He said many of his friends have already opened Facebook accounts.

M: Well, that's not really a good reason to do something.

W: But at his age, doing something together is very important to make friends.

M: Maybe. But I'm worried about the effect Facebook will have. He will probably spend a lot of _____.

W: You're right. He needs to play outdoors instead of spending time posting on his Facebook.

M: I think Facebook itself is okay, but it's hard for us to monitor him all the time. It could be _____ _____.

W: I understand. Why don't you talk to Joshua about it?

M: Yes, I will.

03

M: Great, Rebecca! You've just entered our bonus round. How do you feel?

W: Thank you. I'm so nervous.

M: Who did you come here with?

W: My husband and my two children. They're over there.

M: Let's say hello to Rebecca's family! Now you're _____ the $10,000 cash prize. If you win, what will you do with all that money?

W: I really don't know at this moment.

M: All right. When the buzzer goes off, you must _____ within 5 seconds. Are you ready?

W: Yes, I'm ready.

M: Gandhi was often called "Mahatma" by the Indian people. What does _____?

W: That means "Great Soul."

M: You are correct!

04

M: Do you want to see pictures of me in a costume? Here, look at this picture.

W: Oh, you took it at Comic Con. There is a big monitor _____ behind you guys.

M: Yes, it showed an animated UFO. We took this picture in front of an animation booth.

W: Yeah, there is a signboard standing on the left. I like this comic character, one of the Ghostbusters.

M: I like him, too. Can you guess who I am?

W: Hmm, are you the one who is wearing a black mask and has a long sword in his hand?

M: No, that's not me. I'm the one _____ _____ with a big star in the center.

W: Wow, you're Captain America! But it's a bit strange. Why did you print the letter B on your mask? Shouldn't it be the letter A?

M: _____ because my name is Brandon, which begins with B. And the man on the right is my friend, Sean.

W: He is holding _____. He must be

Thor! You guys had a lot of fun!

M: Absolutely! It was a great experience.

05

M: Hello, is Carrie there?

W: Yes, this is she speaking. _____, please?

M: It's me, Carlos. Do you have plans to go downtown today by any chance?

W: Actually, I'm already in the downtown area to meet some friends. Do you want to join us?

M: Thanks, but I can't. I just dropped my smartphone in some water so _____ to the service center now.

W: Sorry to hear that. That's why you didn't call with your phone.

M: Yes. The problem is that I have to pick up a book I ordered for my history class at the Stanley Bookstore. But I don't have enough time.

W: Oh, the one near Union Plaza?

M: Yes, so I was wondering _____ pick it up for me. I really need that book for tomorrow's class.

W: Okay. _____ and stop by your place on the way home.

M: Thanks a million.

06

W: Julian, I heard you recently traveled to New York.

M: Yes, it was just great. _____ there?

W: No, but I'm planning to visit there next month. How much did you pay for your flights and hotel?

M: Well, I spent $450 for _____.

W: Oh, it's quite cheap. Where did you stay?

M: I stayed at the Chelsea Hostel _____, and that was _____. It's clean and located in one of the safest neighborhoods in New York.

W: Sounds great. Did you have your own room?

M: No, it was a dormitory room. If you want a single room, you have to pay $65 a night.

W: I don't mind dormitories. If I save some money on hotels, I can watch a Broadway musical.

M: Good idea. But there is no elevator in the hostel, so you should ask for a room _____ _____.

W: That's good to know. Thanks for the information.

07

W: Chris! Why haven't you gone home yet?

M: I'm not going home this summer. What about you?

W: I've got _____ at the University Museum until next week. So, I'll leave next Saturday. But what's going on with you?

M: Well, something happened.

W: What is it? Is it because of summer training for the school's football team?

M: No. I quit the team two months ago. It's nothing _____.

W: Hmm... Are your parents going on an overseas trip?

M: No. Well, it's _____. I got two D's in math and physics.

W: I can't believe it! You always get good grades. What happened?

M: I've been lazy about studying these days. So I decided to _____ to focus on my studying.

W: I understand. But your parents are going to miss you.

M: I miss them, too. But I have no choice.

08

W: Hello, this is the Junior Chef Academy. How can I help you?

M: _____ your Junior Cooking Competition held on November 11. I'd like to ask a few questions about it.

W: Sure. What do you want to know?

M: Is there an age limit _____ the competition?

W: Yes, the age limit will range from 8 to 17.

M: Okay. And I'd like to know the entry fee.

W: It's $50. You can pay it online.

M: I see. Can my friends and family _____ _____ the competition?

W: Yes, of course! There are 500 _____ _____, and their admission is free.

M: Sounds good. Thank you.

W: My pleasure. You can find further information on our website.

09

W: Attention, students! You are all invited to our _____. Culture Night is the biggest event on campus. Last year we hosted more than 1,400 students and community members. It'll be _____, April 21st from 5 p.m. to 9 p.m. This event is also open to the public. Admission tickets are $5, but _____ UMC students. You can taste a variety of free foreign food and learn about cultures and traditions at multiple student exhibits. From 7 o'clock, there will be cultural performances and _____ of traditional costumes from around the world. We also need volunteers to help with setting up, decorating, and serving and organizing food. To volunteer, please register online through our Facebook.

10

W: David, Ashley is starting elementary school this year, so we need to get a desk for her.

M: Yes, I know. Let's order it online since they offer the best prices.

W: Okay. Let's do it now.

M: Do you think she needs _____?

W: Absolutely. She needs drawers to store and organize her stuff.

M: Okay. What sort of frame will be good for her? I think metal frames are strong.

W: I don't think Ashley would like it. She is a young girl. A desk with a metal frame looks like office furniture.

M: You're right. Then we'll choose _____ _____. Now we have these three options. I don't want to _____ $100.

W: I agree with you. And dark colors won't match with her room's atmosphere. _____ _____.

M: Got it. Then let's get this one.

11

W: You look happy, Andrew. What's new?

M: Maria is going to have a baby! I can't believe we're going to _____!

W: Oh my, that's great news! Congratulations. I'm really happy for you two.

12

M: Excuse me, I'd like to _____ in the back since it's better to see a movie from farther away.

W: What's your seat number?

M: It's 11E. Is that _____?

13

M: Stephanie, how's it going?

W: Oh, I'm okay. How about you?

M: Very good. It's Friday! But you look worried.

W: Yes, I'm worried about my paper for Professor O'Hara's sociology class.

M: What's the problem? We have plenty of time left before the deadline.

W: Yes, the paper is _____, but I'm leaving next Wednesday to go to Santa

Barbara and coming back on Saturday. My cousin is getting married there.

M: Did you tell Professor O'Hara about it?

W: Yes, but he said I should _____ on Friday.

M: Then why don't you turn in your paper _____ _____? I think it'll be fine.

14

W: Hi, Jacob.

M: Oh, Vivien. What are you doing here? A campaign _____?

W: Yes, more than 200 million children between 5 and 17 are employed.

M: Really? That's a lot! That doesn't include house chores or part time jobs, does it?

W: No. Listen, you might have an after-school job, or maybe you help out with chores around the house. That's not child labor.

M: Oh, I see. Then it's much more serious.

W: Yes. They can't go to school, and many are _____. Every year a lot of children die from accidents related to their work.

M: That's awful. I didn't know that.

W: This pamphlet will tell you more about child labor.

M: Can I offer _____ of some kind?

W: Sure. Please fill out this form to make a donation. I'd really appreciate it.

15

W: Olivia and Daniel are co-workers. Today, Olivia is late to work, and their boss is angry with her because there is an important meeting in the morning. Olivia looks sad, so Daniel gives her a cup of coffee with warm words. Olivia tells him that she is having _____ today. She says that her car stopped in the middle of the street. And then she had to have it taken to a repair shop. _____,

when she tried to call the office, she dropped her cell phone and broke the screen. And her boss never listened to why she was late and got angry with her. She is very depressed. Daniel wants to _____. In this situation, what would Daniel most likely say to Olivia?

16~17

M: Good morning, everyone. I'm Chris from the Johnsville Meditation Center. Are you looking for something better in life? Then meditation can help. Just as you can train your body through exercise, you can train your mind through meditation. Meditation _____ the mental and emotional muscle you need to live a happier, more positive life. When you meditate, the mind becomes calm and relaxed. Several studies have shown that just 30 minutes of meditation daily _____ of anxiety, sleeplessness, or depression. On top of that, we now know that the mind has a direct impact on the body. You might have noticed that the health of some people gets worse when they are stressed out for a long time. Meditation helps in improving _____. In fact, the practice of meditation for a period of time can even help cure the common cold, a severe headache, or heart disease. Now that you have meditation as _____ to all your big and small problems, why worry? Just meditate!

10회

✻ 첫단추 **듣기실전편**

01 다음을 듣고, 남자가 하는 말의 목적으로 가장 적절한 것을 고르시오.

① 강연회 연사를 소개하려고
② 동창회 개최 환영사를 하려고
③ 시 대회 시상식 시작을 알리려고
④ 교우 관계의 중요성을 강조하려고
⑤ 졸업 파티 지연에 대해 사과하려고

02 대화를 듣고, 여자의 의견으로 가장 적절한 것을 고르시오.

① 고래 사냥을 모두 금지해야 한다.
② 고래 고기 판매법을 제정해야 한다.
③ 각국의 식문화 차이를 인정해야 한다.
④ 멸종 위기 동물은 특별히 관리해야 한다.
⑤ 고래 사냥을 고통 없는 방법으로 바꿔야 한다.

03 대화를 듣고, 두 사람의 관계를 가장 잘 나타낸 것을 고르시오.

① 상점 주인 – 고객
② 경찰관 – 민원인
③ 자동차 정비사 – 운전기사
④ 아파트 관리인 – 주민
⑤ 주차장 경비원 – 주차인

04 대화를 듣고, 그림에서 대화의 내용과 일치하지 않는 것을 고르시오.

05 대화를 듣고, 남자가 할 일로 가장 적절한 것을 고르시오.

① 머리 염색하기
② 두피 관리하기
③ 잡지 가져다주기
④ 음료수 가져다주기
⑤ 헤어스타일 검색하기

06 대화를 듣고, 남자가 지불할 금액을 고르시오. [3점]

① $30
② $50
③ $70
④ $90
⑤ $110

07 대화를 듣고, 여자가 영화를 보러 갈 수 없는 이유를 고르시오.

① 쇼핑 계획이 있어서
② 바이올린 연주회에 가야 해서
③ 외국으로 자원봉사를 하러 가서
④ 자선모금을 위한 음악회를 열어서
⑤ 자선 바자회에서 판매를 담당해서

08 대화를 듣고, Anytime Fitness에 관해 언급되지 않은 것을 고르시오.

① 주차 공간
② 사물함 제공
③ 등록 방법
④ 운동 시설
⑤ 월 회비

09 Foodtown 특별주간에 관한 다음 내용을 듣고, 일치하지 않는 것을 고르시오.

① 과일과 채소는 최소 10프로 할인한다.
② 소고기와 양고기의 특별 판매가 있다.
③ 냉동 해산물은 폭풍우로 공급이 어렵다.
④ 베이커리에서 커피를 무료로 제공한다.
⑤ 지역 특산 식품을 시식할 수 있다.

10 다음 표를 보면서 대화를 듣고, 여자가 구매할 토스터를 고르시오.

Toasters for Sale

Model	Size	Color	Price	Cover
① A	4-slice	black	$99.99	○
② B	2-slice	silver	$43.99	×
③ C	2-slice	pink	$44.99	×
④ D	2-slice	red	$53.99	○
⑤ E	2-slice	olive green	$49.99	○

11 대화를 듣고, 여자의 마지막 말에 대한 남자의 응답으로 가장 적절한 것을 고르시오.

① I agree. It'll be a good way to save money.
② Great. Please send them my congratulations.
③ I'm sorry. I can't come to their anniversary.
④ It's costly, but it's worth it for our future goal.
⑤ Then we can afford that. Let's order it for them.

12 대화를 듣고, 남자의 마지막 말에 대한 여자의 응답으로 가장 적절한 것을 고르시오.

① Exactly. That's why I'm doing it.
② Right. Nobody cares what you do.
③ You did a good job. I'm proud of you.
④ Don't worry. I understand how you feel.
⑤ Good luck. I hope you achieve your goal.

13 대화를 듣고, 남자의 마지막 말에 대한 여자의 응답으로 가장 적절한 것을 고르시오.

▶ Woman :

① No way. I don't think I can afford it.
② Thanks. I really need an expert's help.
③ It might not work well. But I'll try again.
④ That'll be great. I'll invest all of my money.
⑤ He's not ready yet. He'll call you tomorrow.

14 대화를 듣고, 여자의 마지막 말에 대한 남자의 응답으로 가장 적절한 것을 고르시오. [3점]

▶ Man :

① We need to find a way to protect wild animals.
② I'll adopt a cat at the local animal shelter tomorrow.
③ We should at least try to find someone who can keep it.
④ Raising a pet is a great learning experience for children.
⑤ I think people who abandon their pets should be fined.

15 다음 상황 설명을 듣고, 상담 선생님이 Katie에게 할 말로 가장 적절한 것을 고르시오. [3점]

▶ The counselor :

① It's entirely up to you. I don't mind it at all.
② Life will teach you a lesson. You'll remember it.
③ You won't always have what you're looking for.
④ You seem to be doing all right so far. Don't spoil it.
⑤ You'd better quit working. Do the important thing first.

[16~17] 다음을 듣고, 물음에 답하시오.

16 남자가 하는 말의 주제로 가장 적절한 것은?

① jobs that will disappear in the future
② the most promising jobs of the future
③ how to prepare for the jobs of the future
④ the demand and supply of skilled workers
⑤ the growth and popularity of the robot industry

17 언급된 직업이 <u>아닌</u> 것은?

① nurse   ② pharmacist
③ dentist   ④ food engineer
⑤ robot operator

01

M: Good evening, ladies and gentlemen! I'm Timothy Whittier. Sorry for the delay. We are all so excited to meet each other, and we've been absorbed _____. I'm so glad to see all of you here. It already has been 10 years. This must be a very special and _____ for all of us. And there are many more _____ today but wanted to. Among us who are here, we have classmates like Edward, who flew back all the way from Singapore. My classmate Jonathan gave me a card some 10 or 11 years ago with a little children's poem on it that goes: "There are big ships; There are small ships; But there is_____." Welcome to the AAHS Class of '08, 10 year reunion! Let's celebrate!

02

W: Christian, have you ever seen that documentary about whales?

M: No, I haven't. Did you see it?

W: Yes, I saw it yesterday. It's a good documentary, but so sad.

M: I heard whales are _____.

W: Yeah, every year Japan, Norway, and Iceland kill around 1,500 whales.

M: Well, I saw an interview with a Japanese whale hunter. He said it's a cultural thing.

W: It's different. We _____ whale meat to live, as we have farm animals such as pigs and cows that provide plenty of food.

M: Oh, I agree. We certainly don't need to eat whale meat these days.

W: Actually, in Japan, whales are even _____. About three million whales were killed in the 20th century alone.

M: That many? That's a lot more than I'd guessed.

W: Plus, whale hunting is really cruel. There is no kind way to kill a whale at sea. Many die a slow, painful death. _____.

M: I should watch the documentary.

03

M: Good afternoon. Can I help you?

W: Good afternoon. I'd like to speak to you about _____ I noticed last night.

M: What was the problem that you experienced?

W: I was parking my car in the parking lot in the back of the building.

M: Did somebody park their car in your designated parking space?

W: No, I had no trouble parking in my space. But it was very dark out there.

M: Oh, maybe some of the bulbs _____.

W: Right. They need to be fixed because a dark parking lot can be a dangerous place.

M: I agree. I'll go out there after dark and _____.

W: Thanks. And would you mind talking to the person in apartment 2C and asking him to _____ after 10 at night? I can't sleep at night.

M: Oh, okay. I'll talk to him about that.

04

M: You look tired, Madison. What's wrong?

W: My daughter planned a slumber party in our house this evening, so I was very _____ for it yesterday.

M: What is a slumber party?

W: It's a party where young girls spend the night together at one of their houses. Look at this photo in my cell phone. My daughter and I decorated her room.

M: Fantastic! There are two tents on each side of the room. You _____ with flowers on top.

W: Can you see a teddy bear in the tent on the left side? It's my daughter's favorite.

M: How cute! You _____ a big picture with a moon and stars _____. It's lovely. Is the table under the picture for snacks?

W: Yes, there's _____ now, but I'll put some cookies and cupcakes on it this evening.

M: Oh, I like the cushion in the tent on the right side. I like _____ on it. How many friends did your daughter invite?

W: She invited five friends.

M: I hope they'll have a great party. You're the best mom.

05

M: Good afternoon, Mrs. Stuart. Have a seat.

W: Good afternoon. Mr. Glenn.

M: Would you like some coffee or orange juice?

W: No, thanks. I already drank some coffee.

M: Okay. _____ your hair done? Would you like it a bit shorter today?

W: Yes, my hairstyle is _____. I'm ready for a new image, but I don't want too much cut off.

M: Okay, then I could just cut a little. Do you _____ a particular style _____?

W: Well, actually I'm not sure. Can you recommend one?

M: How about putting some color in your hair?

W: I think it'll damage my hair.

M: Don't worry. These days coloring doesn't damage your hair as much. Do you want to _____ _____ that feature the latest hairstyles? I'll go get them.

W: Yes, please. I'll also _____ _____ with my smartphone.

M: Okay. Wait a second.

06

M: Excuse me. Does that bus go to Greenville?

W: Yes, you need to buy a bus pass here.

M: Okay. How much does it cost for a bus pass?

W: It depends on _____. There are passes for a day, a week, and a month.

M: How much are the day pass and the weekly pass?

W: The day pass is $5, and the weekly pass is $_____.

M: I'd like some weekly passes, then.

W: Sure. _____?

M: I have three children. Is there _____ on them?

W: Yes, the weekly pass for _____ is $20.

M: Then I'd like to buy three child passes and one adult pass.

W: Here you go. Thank you for your purchase.

07

M: Chloe, _____ if we could go to see a movie this Saturday.

W: That sounds like fun, but I can't.

M: Are you busy with your homework?

W: No, actually, I'm planning to help people _____.

M: Sounds great! Do you plan to go to one of those countries?

W: No, my friends and I are planning to _____ _____ this weekend.

M: Oh, how will you raise money? Are you going to sell something?

W: No. You know my major is violin. We'll _____ _____ in front of the Evergreen Shopping Mall this Saturday.

M: I admire you. There are always plenty of people passing by.

W: Yes, _____ this Saturday.

M: Oh, okay. I'll go there to see you then.

W: I really appreciate it.

08

M: Hello, Anytime Fitness.

W: Hello, I'd like to ask a few questions about your fitness club.

M: Sure. What can I do for you?

W: I'd like to _____ there. Where can I park my car while I'm exercising?

M: We have a large, _____ in front of the building.

W: Good. Do you provide changing rooms and lockers?

M: Of course. We offer _____ _____ and lockers for men and women, free of charge. We recommend that you bring your own lock.

W: That's great. How do I sign up for the classes?

M: You need to come here and _____ an application form. Then you can choose the class you want.

W: Okay. Can you tell me how much _____ _____ is?

M: It's 40 dollars a month.

W: Thanks! I can't wait to get started.

M: No problem. I'll see you soon!

09

M: Good evening, ladies and gentlemen! This week is a special week at Foodtown because we are celebrating our first anniversary. All fruits and vegetables are _____, and meat products are at least 20 percent off. We have special buys on beef steaks for grilling and imported legs of lamb. We regret that our fresh seafood is _____, due to continuing storms off the coast. But frozen seafood _____ at bargain prices. While you shop at Foodtown, please enjoy _____ _____ coffee in the bakery department. You are also _____ our many delicious local and imported speciality foods. Thank you for shopping at Foodtown.

10

W: Hi, I'm looking for a toaster.

M: We have a great selection here. Which type of toaster are you looking for?

W: Well, I'm not quite sure. What could you recommend?

M: How big is your family? If you have a big family, I'd recommend this 4-slice model.

W: No, I have _____ of three. I don't need a 4-slice toaster. How about the extra features?

M: Actually, all of these have basic functions; timer, a cancel function, and bagel settings.

W: If so, I'd like one of _____. I don't like silver or black colors.

M: Okay, and _____ do you have in mind?

W: I'd like to stay under $50.

M: Then you can choose between these two.

W: Hmm... Then I'll take the one with a cover. _____ while it's not in use.

M: Good choice. It also prevents children's hands _____.

11

W: Dylan, our parents' 20th wedding anniversary is next month. What do you think of _____ _____ for them?

M: That sounds great, but it must be very expensive.

W: Not really. Actually, _____ a hundred dollars.

12

M: My doctor advised that I _____ for my health. I'll run for an hour every day.

W: Good for you! You'll feel much better if you do.

M: I'm going to _____ and eat more vegetables. I'll do my best to lose weight.

13

W: I'm thinking of _____ .
M: Good idea. Where do you want to live?
W: I want a house near Orchard Street and Oxford Street.
M: I know where that is. It's _____ to live.
W: Absolutely. And that area is really good for children, since there are many good schools in the neighborhood.
M: Did you find a house that you really like?
W: Not yet. I'll visit a real estate agent next week. Do you happen to know any _____ around there?
M: One of my friends is a real estate agent.
W: That's great. Can you _____ ?
M: Sure. If you want, I'll call him right now.

14

M: Emily, look! There's a kitten in this box!
W: It's very cute. But why is it here?
M: Someone _____ it here! Who would do such a thing?
W: That might not be the case. It could just be lost.
M: I don't think so, since it's in a box. Oh, poor thing. _____ . It could die in this cold weather.
W: Let's call the _____ first. They might be able to find its owner.
M: Well, I'd like to keep it at home while we search for its owner.
W: Charles, we don't have anything that _____ _____ in our home.
M: We can go buy a few things. If it doesn't have an owner, let's raise it. Otherwise, it might _____ _____ .
W: I know, but it's all very sudden.

15

M: Katie is a high school student. She took a math exam last week but didn't get a good score. Today, Katie visits the school counselor's office _____ _____ about university. Since her math grade was really bad, the counselor asks her why. Katie says she couldn't study much because she's been _____ a clothing store every weekend. The counselor asks her what she wants to do after high school. She wants to major in computer science and become a computer technician. The counselor says she needs _____ _____ in math to get into the computer science department. The counselor wants to tell her _____ for studying. In this situation, what would the counselor most likely say to Katie?

16~17

M: Every year, the United States government issues a report on what _____ will be in the future. Based on information provided by the biggest industries, this report predicts how quickly these industries will need new employees. Recently, the reports have said that some of the "hottest" jobs are in the _____ . Jobs in the service industry include jobs in health care, medical technology, and food services, for example. There are many reasons why certain industries will have more jobs available in the future. One reason is that people are _____ _____ nowadays. This means more people are needed to take care of the old. Therefore, nurses, dentists, and food engineers _____ be some of the "hottest" jobs in the near future. In addition, with robots slowly _____ manual labor jobs, robot operators will be needed in specific industries. Will you be ready for one of the "hottest" jobs in the future?

01 다음을 듣고, 여자가 하는 말의 목적으로 가장 적절한 것을 고르시오.

① 청년 실업의 심각성을 지적하려고
② 취업 면접 시 주의 사항을 설명하려고
③ 취업에 성공한 체험 수기를 공모하려고
④ 취업 면접을 계속 시도할 것을 조언하려고
⑤ 재학생을 위한 취업 강의 수강을 권유하려고

02 대화를 듣고, 여자의 의견으로 가장 적절한 것을 고르시오.

① 양복 정장이 가장 예의 있는 옷차림이다.
② 상황에 따른 적절한 옷차림을 해야 한다.
③ 시간 약속을 철저히 지키는 것이 예의이다.
④ 주최자가 요구하는 드레스코드를 따라야 한다.
⑤ 모든 연주회에는 격식 있는 옷차림이 필요하다.

03 대화를 듣고, 두 사람의 관계를 가장 잘 나타낸 것을 고르시오.

① 사진작가 – 기자
② 부동산 중개업자 – 구매자
③ 조명 업체 직원 – 고객
④ 인테리어 디자이너 – 의뢰인
⑤ 무대 디자이너 – 감독

04 대화를 듣고, 그림에서 대화의 내용과 일치하지 않는 것을 고르시오.

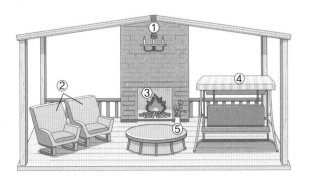

05 대화를 듣고, 남자가 할 일로 가장 적절한 것을 고르시오.

① 여분의 타이어 빌려주기
② 자동차 타이어 교체하기
③ 자동차 정비소에 전화하기
④ 자동차 정비 공구 빌려주기
⑤ 자동차 뒤에 주의 표지판 두기

06 대화를 듣고, 여자가 지불할 금액을 고르시오. [3점]

① $1,400   ② $1,600   ③ $1,700
④ $1,800   ⑤ $2,000

07 대화를 듣고, 남자가 자전거를 사지 않은 이유를 고르시오.

① 부모님이 위험하다고 반대해서
② 일하다가 자전거 사고를 당해서
③ 형이 타던 것을 물려받기로 해서
④ 미술 대회 상품으로 받게 되어서
⑤ 마이애미 여행으로 돈을 다 써서

08 대화를 듣고, Breakfast Club에 관해 언급되지 않은 것을 고르시오.

① 참여 대상   ② 운영 시간   ③ 제공 메뉴
④ 등록비   ⑤ 등록 방법

09 Paradise 원자력 발전소 관광에 관한 다음 내용을 듣고, 일치하지 않는 것을 고르시오.

① 제한 구역에서는 노란 선 안에 있어야 한다.
② 12세 이하의 어린이는 부모와 동반해야 한다.
③ 사진 촬영은 모든 구역에서 금지된다.
④ 음식과 음료는 반입이 허용되지 않는다.
⑤ 가이드가 방문객을 15명씩 인솔한다.

10 다음 표를 보면서 대화를 듣고, 여자가 구매할 전자책 리더기를 고르시오.

		Top 5 Best E-book Readers of 2018			
Brand	**Price**	**Screen Size (inches)**	**Weight (grams)**	**Battery Life (hours)**	
① Glowlight	$130	6	300	14	
② Jetbook	$149	8	220	21	
③ Paper	$119	6	150	21	
④ Aura	$149	6	150	28	
⑤ Boox	$199	8	300	21	

11 대화를 듣고, 여자의 마지막 말에 대한 남자의 응답으로 가장 적절한 것을 고르시오.

① That was a great badminton game.
② We can't win this game without you.
③ It's very nice of you to show the way.
④ I was impressed with your performance.
⑤ I hope I can live up to your expectations.

12 대화를 듣고, 남자의 마지막 말에 대한 여자의 응답으로 가장 적절한 것을 고르시오.

① Of course. Your total comes to 45 dollars.
② It hasn't started yet. You are in time for the movie.
③ Here are your tickets. You need to go to screen 7.
④ That's right. This film has been showing for two months.
⑤ Please let me check. We have 5 seats available at 6:15.

13 대화를 듣고, 남자의 마지막 말에 대한 여자의 응답으로 가장 적절한 것을 고르시오. [3점]

▶ Woman :

① I'm sorry, but the doctor is not taking new patients.
② Dr. Harris is away. Instead, you can see Dr. Jones now.
③ We'll see you then. Please pay at the cashier over there.
④ No problem. We have a 3 o'clock opening next Thursday.
⑤ Thanks for waiting. You can see Dr. Harris in ten minutes.

14 대화를 듣고, 여자의 마지막 말에 대한 남자의 응답으로 가장 적절한 것을 고르시오. [3점]

▶ Man :

① I have a job interview tomorrow. Wish me luck.
② Don't worry. I'm sure you'll do better next time.
③ I think so. This will be a great opportunity for you.
④ Thank you for your help. I've been looking for this.
⑤ You can do it as well. Don't give up and keep trying.

15 다음 상황 설명을 듣고, Kevin이 Michael에게 할 말로 가장 적절한 것을 고르시오.

▶ Kevin :

① That's okay. You can learn from your mistakes.
② I'll help you find your watch. Let's go to the library.
③ You're in big trouble. You've gone too far this time.
④ Everyone makes mistakes. I understand why you did.
⑤ Tell her the truth. It will be worse if she finds out later.

[16~17] 다음을 듣고, 물음에 답하시오.

16 남자가 하는 말의 주제로 가장 적절한 것은?

① different types of art
② ways of decorating the home
③ the functions and value of art
④ art as a tool of communication
⑤ art that is alive in our daily life

17 언급된 활동이 아닌 것은?

① basket making ② flower arrangement
③ car decoration ④ cake decorating
⑤ paper folding

01

W: We all know that the economy these days isn't good. It's very hard to find a job. However, many young people use this as an excuse to stay home and not go out and look for a job. It's important _____, even if you fail a few times before you succeed. Even if it takes you a long time to find a job, you'll meet a lot of great people along the way. It will also give you useful experience. As you do _____ _____ job interviews, you'll learn what interviewers are looking for in people. You'll get _____ those interviews! Plus, although it might take a few tries to find that perfect job, you'll feel that much more proud when you finally get a job you love.

02

M: Mom! Hurry up! We're going to be late for the concert.

W: Don't worry. I'm almost done. Oh, Leon! Look at you! Please _____.

M: Why? I like this sweatshirt and jeans.

W: If you plan to go to a baseball game, a sweatshirt and jeans are perfect. But it's a symphony orchestra concert!

M: What do you want me to wear?

W: Well, I want you to dress more formally. It's important _____ _____.

M: You mean I should wear a tuxedo?

W: No, you don't need to dress as if you _____ _____ at the White House. But you need to dress more formally than now.

M: But I want to listen to music in comfort.

W: A symphony concert _____ a concert of popular music. Here are your jacket and shirt. Please hurry up!

M: Okay. Okay.

03

M: Mrs. Wilson. I'd like to talk about the living room now.

W: All right. I have some time to talk.

M: _____ for the wallpaper?

W: I'd like my living room to be warm and inviting _____.

M: How about putting in maple floors and cream colored wallpaper?

W: Maple? What color is that?

M: It's a light brown color. I have some pictures of some samples here.

W: Let me see. I like it. And as for the lighting, I'd prefer LED lighting.

M: Got it. _____ _____, LED lighting is more practical than others. How about this pendant lighting?

W: That's very nice. It's very unique. Oh, I'm afraid I have to leave now. I have a meeting with a real estate agent.

M: Okay. We'll talk about the details for the children's rooms later.

W: Thanks.

04

W: I visited Victoria's house yesterday. It has a really nice terrace.

M: Was it her housewarming party? A house with a terrace is my dream house.

W: Yes, I took a picture of her terrace with my phone. Do you want to see it?

M: Sure. Oh, it has a roof and looks fancy. I like this lamp _____.

W: It looks like there are three candlesticks on it. Can you see these two armchairs on the left?

M: Yes, they look comfortable. Wow! There is a fireplace in the center! Fantastic!

W: Yeah, she made a fireplace in the stone wall. That's the best part of it.

M: Yeah, I agree. She also _____.

W: Yes. She said her kids really wanted to put a swinging bench there, but she decided to put a sofa because _____ on the terrace.

M: A swinging bench might be dangerous for kids anyway. There is a round table in front of the fireplace.

W: Victoria put a flower vase on it. She really has _____.

M: She really does!

05

M: Excuse me! Ma'am! _____ _____ here. You could get a parking ticket if you leave your car here.

W: I know that, but I have a flat tire so I'm stuck.

M: Oh, really? Why don't you call a repair shop or your insurance company?

W: I'd like to call a repair shop, but I don't know their phone number. _____ the number of one?

M: No, I don't. Well, do you have a spare tire in your car's trunk?

W: Yes, but I'm not sure of how to change it. Besides, I don't have the proper tools.

M: I have some tools on hand, so I can change the tire for you.

W: Oh, are you sure? It's very kind of you. I really hope I'm not bothering you too much.

M: It's no problem at all. Could you place this "caution" sign behind your car _____ _____?

W: Yes, I will. Thanks a million.

06

M: Hello, Green Publishing Company.

W: Hi, I'm Mila Hamilton from Westville University Bookstore.

M: Okay. How can I help you?

W: _____ for one of your books, *A-Level Biology*. How much is it?

M: Its original price is twenty dollars.

W: Can you offer me a discount? I'd like to get one hundred copies.

M: Let me see. Yes, we can offer you a discount. _____ the original price.

W: Just 10%? Can I get a 20% discount? We're a regular customer and plan to place a big order next semester.

M: Hmm... Okay. _____. But this is an exception.

W: Thank you very much. I'll send you an e-mail with the delivery address.

M: All right.

07

W: You look really excited. What's going on?

M: Yeah! I'm going to Miami next week.

W: Sounds great! But I think the trip will cost a lot. How did you get the money? Did your parents give you some?

M: No, I've been saving my money _____ _____.

W: But you've saved that for a bike, haven't you?

M: Yes! But _____ anymore.

W: Do you mean that you gave up the bike to go to Miami?

M: No. Do you remember the drawing contest the Cube Bike Shop was holding last month?

W: Yes, I heard about that. The prize was a bicycle. Oh, my goodness! Did you win?

M: Yes. _____ from that drawing contest! So I can go to Miami, also.

W: I didn't know you could draw so well. This is amazing!

08

W: Honey, I finally got a job. But I have to go to work at 8 in the morning.

M: Congratulations! Then both of us _____ _____. Then we should think about Melissa. Her school starts at 9 a.m.

W: Don't worry. There is Breakfast Club in her school. It's a service that provides a breakfast for children in the morning. It's open _____ _____.

M: That's a good service. Does it run every weekday?

W: Yes. It's open from 7:15 to 8:45 a.m. each day.

M: Sounds great. _____ _____?

W: They provide a variety of cereals, hot foods, toast, fruit, and milk. After breakfast, there is time to play with friends.

M: That's perfect!

W: I'd like Melissa to attend Breakfast Club. Do you agree with me?

M: Absolutely. Should we _____ _____?

W: Yes, we can book through the online booking system on the school's website.

M: Let's do it right now.

09

M: Welcome to a tour of the Paradise Nuclear Generating Station. During the tour, we will pass through a restricted area. While you are in that area, we ask that you remain _____ _____ painted on the walkway. Children 12 years and under must stay with their parents at all times. You _____ in all areas. We do ask, however, that you turn off your flash; you won't need it because there is plenty of light. _____ at all points on the tour. Experienced guides lead each group of 15 visitors and teach you about nuclear generating facilities. Visitors are advised that anyone not obeying these rules will be escorted to a waiting area. Shall we begin?

10

W: Hi, Chris. I'd like to buy an e-book reader. I heard the screens look like paper, so _____ _____.

M: Exactly. I have used one for several months. It weighs about one tenth of paper books but can store thousands of full books.

W: Great. Can you help me choose the best one? I can pay _____.

M: Okay. Look at this site. They compare the top 5 best e-book readers.

W: Great. I can make a decision after comparing.

M: There are _____: 6-inch and 8-inch. Which one would you like?

W: I want a 6-inch screen because _____ _____.

M: Then you also want the lighter one. I think one which weighs less than 200 grams would be all right. Now you have these two options.

W: I'll take this one _____ even if it's a bit expensive.

M: Good choice.

W: Thanks for helping me.

11

W: I'm proud of you! You're the winner of the BWF World Championships.

M: Thank you very much.

W: Keep up the good work. I believe _____ _____ in the next Olympic Games.

12

M: I'd like to buy five tickets for *Kingsman* at 5:20, please.

W: Sorry, we don't have any seats available for that show. They're sold out.

M: Oh, that's too bad. What about other times? _____ _____?

13

M: Excuse me. Dr. Harris said to me that I need to make the next appointment here.

W: Yes, you need to see him in January. What day would be good for you?

M: Well, Tuesdays or Fridays are good.

W: Why don't you come on Tuesday, January 9th at 10 in the morning?

M: I'm afraid I'm working at 10. _____ _____ after 3 p.m.?

W: Dr. Harris doesn't take any appointments on Tuesday and Friday afternoons.

M: Then on what days does he take afternoon appointments?

W: Mondays and Thursdays. _____ _____ on Monday, January 15th?

M: I'd prefer Thursday, if that's all right. _____ _____ ?

W: That's fine. How does 3 p.m. sound?

M: That would be great. Thanks for your help.

14

M: Jasmine, why do you look so down?

W: Oh, nothing is working out these days. I'm so depressed.

M: What's wrong?

W: _____ at Louisville Company in Langford.

M: Oh, I guess you didn't pass the company exam. I heard their exam is quite difficult.

W: Actually, I passed the examination with a high score. I studied really hard.

M: Then what was the problem?

W: The problem was the interview. It was my first interview, and I was _____ . I could barely breathe. So, I didn't get the job.

M: That's really too bad. I'm sorry to hear that.

W: I was _____ . I really wanted to get the job.

15

M: Michael has a nice watch. He got it as a birthday gift from his mother. Since he often loses things, his mother has warned him _____ _____. Today, _____ somewhere in the library. He looks everywhere in the library for it, but he can't find it. He goes to the lost-and-found, but it hasn't been turned in. Then he runs into his friend, Kevin. He tells Kevin that _____ to tell his mother that he lost her gift. Actually, his mother didn't want to buy him that fancy watch because he is careless, but he asked her to buy it. Kevin thinks that Michael should tell his mother what happened _____ .

In this situation, what would Kevin most likely say to Michael?

16~17

M: Many people think that art is created by really talented people _____ and produce it. But most of us have always played with and created art. Art is in every part of our lives; what we wear, the design of our homes we live in, and even what our cars look like. We ourselves produce those kinds of art in everyday activities. For example, _____ _____ are ways of expressing our feelings in an artistic way. A taxi driver hangs a decoration like a dancing toy on the cab dashboard to give pleasure to passengers during the hours of work. A chef may carefully arrange _____ on a dish and pile different colored vegetables around the edges. When we throw a housewarming party, we may decorate our rooms by choosing a wallpaper color and arranging furniture and other home decorations. We also make cake decorations for our children's birthday parties. Like this, we often _____ _____ . It even happens each morning when we choose our clothes and matching accessories for the day.

12 회

✱ 첫단추 듣기실전편

01 다음을 듣고, 남자가 하는 말의 목적으로 가장 적절한 것을 고르시오.

① 학교 행사를 홍보하려고
② 운동회 개회를 선언하려고
③ 초대한 운동선수를 환영하려고
④ 스포츠맨십의 의미를 설명하려고
⑤ 학교 체육의 필요성을 주장하려고

02 대화를 듣고, 여자의 의견으로 가장 적절한 것을 고르시오.

① 원자력이 화석 연료보다 더 친환경적이다.
② 다양한 전기 공급원을 연구해 개발해야 한다.
③ 여름철엔 가급적 에어컨 사용을 줄여야 한다.
④ 안전을 위해 원자력 발전소 사용을 멈춰야 한다.
⑤ 안정된 전기 수급을 위해 원자력 발전소는 필요하다.

03 대화를 듣고, 두 사람의 관계를 가장 잘 나타낸 것을 고르시오.

① 연구소장 – 연구원　　② 교장 – 동문회장
③ 물리학 교사 – 졸업생　④ 대학교수 – 강연 의뢰인
⑤ 신문 기자 – 우주 과학자

04 대화를 듣고, 그림에서 대화의 내용과 일치하지 않는 것을 고르시오.

05 대화를 듣고, 남자가 할 일로 가장 적절한 것을 고르시오.

① 노트북 컴퓨터 꺼내기
② 무료 전자책 파일 보내주기
③ 공공도서관까지 차를 태워주기
④ 온라인에서 보고서 자료 찾아주기
⑤ 무료 전자책 제공 사이트 알려주기

06 대화를 듣고, 여자가 지불하게 될 총금액을 고르시오.

① $720　　　② $768　　　③ $960
④ $970　　　⑤ $1,200

07 대화를 듣고, 남자가 오늘 저녁 식사를 함께하지 못하는 이유를 고르시오.

① 초과 근무를 해야 해서
② 퇴근하다 다리를 다쳐서
③ 직장에서 회식을 하게 되어서
④ 다친 동료를 데려다줘야 해서
⑤ 어머니와 저녁 식사를 하게 되어서

08 대화를 듣고, Sequoia 관광 투어에 관해 언급되지 않은 것을 고르시오.

① 소요 시간　　　　② 옷차림
③ 준비물　　　　　④ 점심 제공 여부
⑤ 예약 방법

09 Fall Costume 대회에 관한 다음 내용을 듣고, 일치하지 않는 것을 고르시오.

① 10월 15일에 마을의 광장에서 열린다.
② 가상 인물의 의상을 입는 것도 가능하다.
③ 심사는 시장과 마을 기업가들이 한다.
④ 4개의 수상 부문에서 각각 상을 수여한다.
⑤ 작년 수상자들의 의상은 공개되지 않는다.

10 다음 표를 보면서 대화를 듣고, 남자가 구매할 식물을 고르시오.

Verde Plant Shop

Plants	Air Cleaning	Need for Water	Size	Price
① A	×	once a month	tall	$120
② B	○	every day	short	$70
③ C	○	once a week	tall	$80
④ D	○	once a week	short	$60
⑤ E	○	once a month	short	$90

11 대화를 듣고, 여자의 마지막 말에 대한 남자의 응답으로 가장 적절한 것을 고르시오.

① Sure. I'll stop by the pharmacy.
② Okay. Take this pill after every meal.
③ All right! Let me get some water, too.
④ That's right. It will soon work on you.
⑤ Yes. The doctor gave me the prescription.

12 대화를 듣고, 남자의 마지막 말에 대한 여자의 응답으로 가장 적절한 것을 고르시오.

① Thanks for coming. You're welcome anytime.
② Just bring yourself. We have everything we need.
③ Wonderful. It would be great if you bring drinks.
④ It sure is. You can expect us there on Saturday.
⑤ That sounds like fun. Just drop me an invitation.

13 대화를 듣고, 남자의 마지막 말에 대한 여자의 응답으로 가장 적절한 것을 고르시오. [3점]

▶ Woman :

① Don't worry about it. You did very well.
② You can do as you want. I won't force you.
③ You can count on me. I'll be there on time.
④ You have a point. I'll register us both in the class.
⑤ No, thanks. I'd rather do something more exciting.

14 대화를 듣고, 여자의 마지막 말에 대한 남자의 응답으로 가장 적절한 것을 고르시오. [3점]

▶ Man :

① Stop putting yourself down and let it go.
② I know it takes some time to finish the job.
③ You did a good job and must feel very proud.
④ Don't be stupid and give it up before it's too late.
⑤ I told you to calm down and not to be so excited.

15 다음 상황 설명을 듣고, Natalie가 Maria에게 할 말로 가장 적절한 것을 고르시오. [3점]

▶ Natalie :

① I don't know how to thank you. You're a lifesaver.
② I'm afraid I have to cancel my trip. I have no choice.
③ It's my pleasure. I love dogs, and I'm glad to help you out.
④ Sorry about that. I'll make sure it never happens again.
⑤ That's right. If you help me, I promise to return the favor.

[16~17] 다음을 듣고, 물음에 답하시오.

16 남자가 하는 말의 주제로 가장 적절한 것은?

① respecting your body when exercising
② advantages and risks of doing exercise
③ how to burn calories without exercising
④ benefits of staying healthy through exercise
⑤ the necessity of regular exercise and good diet

17 언급된 운동이 <u>아닌</u> 것은?

① walking   ② bicycling
③ hiking   ④ hockey
⑤ baseball

01

M: Ladies and Gentlemen. Boys and Girls. It gives me great pleasure to be here. This is truly a wonderful opportunity. And I want to _____ _____ to all the participants and physical education teachers. This event shows just how much we all respect and admire our athletes. I am sure that we will witness some amazing performances of athletic skill over the course of this championship. Do your best and compete _____ sportsmanship and fair play. And take the opportunity to _____ _____. Indeed, the Annual Sports Meet is incredibly important to our school's image and our students' reputation. In closing, I wish you every success and good health. I am so happy to _____.

02

W: Lucas, please set the air conditioner on low. In summer, people use a lot of electricity, and this can cause power failures.

M: I see. I think we _____ nuclear power plants.

W: What are you talking about?

M: I heard that power plants using fossil fuels cause global warming. Nuclear energy is relatively _____.

W: That's not true. Think about the 2011 disaster in Japan. It's clearly unsafe.

M: But that kind of accident doesn't happen often. And I think it's getting safer.

W: What about _____? They are highly dangerous, too.

M: We can find a good way to deal with the waste.

W: It sounds almost impossible. Moreover, nuclear power plants can be a target for terrorism. _____ _____.

M: Well, nuclear power may not be good, but it's a realistic choice.

03

W: Come on in, Mason. It's been a long time. You look great!

M: Thanks, Ms. Baker. You haven't changed a bit in the last 20 years.

W: Really? What have you been doing?

M: I became _____ of NASA. How about you?

W: Very good. Congratulations! I'm very proud of you.

M: Thanks. You taught me _____ _____ and encouraged me to be a scientist. I really appreciate it.

W: I was very happy to teach you. You were indeed one of the brightest students I had. By the way, _____?

M: Some of my high school classmates planned a get-together, so I was wondering _____ _____.

W: Really? Are you sure you want me there?

M: Yes, we'd like to invite you. When we were high school students, _____ _____, including how to live and how to dream.

W: I'd be happy to. Let me check my schedule.

04

W: Hey, Oliver! What's that picture on your desk?

M: It was taken when I went Boy Scout camping last month.

W: It looks like a great time. There are _____ _____. Did you set up those tents?

M: Yes, after setting up the tents, we prepared lunch.

W: I see you here near the campfire. You're _____ _____ in your hand, right?

M: Right. I tried to make a fire for cooking.

W: I see the big pot near the campfire. What is this boy sitting at the picnic table doing?

M: He is Matthew, the leader of the Boy Scouts. _____ _____.

W: He looks focused! Oh, there are _____ _____ behind the table.

M: Yes, actually we took three flags there. But somebody _____ the car.

W: I see. Anyway, it must have been great fun.

05

M: Elizabeth, did you finally borrow the book for your history class?

W: No, not yet. The school library didn't have it.

M: You said you need it _____.

W: Yeah, so I was thinking of going down to the public library this afternoon. Can you _____ _____ there?

M: Sorry, I have a dentist appointment this afternoon. By the way, you can use free books on the Internet.

W: Really? I didn't know that. How can I use them?

M: There are some websites _____ _____. They have tons of free books for you _____ or download to your computer.

W: Wow! That sounds great.

M: Yeah, _____ some of them.

W: Thank you! Let me take out my laptop.

06

M: Hello. How can I help you?

W: I'd like to get a new smartphone, the Sky Phone advertised on TV.

M: Good choice. It has a super HD touch screen and 64 gigabytes of internal memory.

W: I see. Are you offering _____?

M: Well, yes, but it depends on _____ _____ this phone.

W: What's the best plan?

M: There are two pricing options: a 30-month plan and a 24-month plan.

W: How much should I pay each month?

M: You need to pay $30 per month for _____ or $40 per month for _____.

W: Hmm... I'll sign up for a 24-month plan.

M: Okay. _____?

W: I need a phone case and a protective film for the screen.

M: The phone case is free, but you need to pay for _____. It is $10.

W: Okay. I'll buy it.

07

W: Hello?

M: Hello, Jennifer. It's Gabriel speaking.

W: Gabriel! Are you still in the office? I'm waiting for you.

M: Jennifer, that's why I'm calling. We were supposed to eat out tonight, but I _____ _____.

W: Oh, why? I've been looking forward to this dinner.

M: I'm really sorry I have to miss it.

W: Do you _____?

M: No, do you know my co-worker, Benjamin? He _____ when he left the office, and I had to take him to the hospital.

W: Oh, dear! Is he okay?

M: Yes, he is okay now. I'm waiting for him to be treated. He lives alone, so _____ _____.

W: If that's the case, that's okay. By the way, my mother called me and said she'll visit me next month. Would you like to meet her?

M: Certainly. I'd love to see her. Let's talk about it later.

08

M: Hello, Sequoia Sightseeing Tours. How can I help you?

W: Hello. I'd like to ask something about the tour. How long is the tour?

M: Our full-day tour is generally _____, and the half-day tour is 3 and half hours long.

W: _____ during the tour in this season of the year?

M: Well, it's very difficult to predict. But as you know, it's usually very hot in the summer.

W: Okay. Can you tell me what I should bring?

M: _____ your camera, water, snacks to eat, and sunscreen.

W: Oh, thanks. Does the tour include lunch?

M: Yes, _____ at Wuksachi Lodge.

W: I see. How do I book a tour?

M: _____ through our website or call us at this number.

W: Thank you. Let me think about it and call back to you.

09

W: If you've ever dreamed about dressing up as your favorite movie or TV character, this is your chance! Our town will hold a Fall Costume Contest in the town square next Saturday, _____. Any costume is welcome, whether you're dressing as a real or _____ _____. The costumes _____ _____ our mayor, Sarah Turner, and business owners in town. Prizes will be given for the top costume of _____.
The categories are the most creative costume, funniest costume, most beautiful costume, and scariest costume. You can find last year's winners on the City's website. But it's not permitted to imitate past winners' costumes. The costume you dress up in _____. Give it a try and come to see everyone's costumes!

10

W: How can I help you?

M: I'd like to get a nice plant for my mother for Mother's Day. Do you deliver?

W: Of course. Is there a particular plant you're interested in?

M: Honestly, I don't know much about plants, but I'd like to get her _____.

W: We have houseplants that clean the air. Anything else?

M: I think a plant that _____ _____ would be good for her.

W: All right. We have plants that only need to be watered once a week or even once a month.

M: Both are good. And my mother _____ _____ because they can cover the windows and block the light.

W: That narrows down your choices to these two. How much _____ to spend?

M: No more than $80.

W: Well, I think this is what you want.

M: Great. Please deliver it to this address.

11

W: Aiden, can you get me my medicine? It is _____ _____.

M: Sure. Is it an oval or round shaped tablet?

W: The pill I need is a round one. _____ _____?

12

M: Hi, Eliana. _____ to invite you and your husband to our place this Saturday night.

W: It's so kind of you to stop by. We would love to come and join you.

M: The dinner starts at about 6 o'clock. _____ _____?

13

W: Thomas, I want to learn a new sport!

M: Sounds great. What do you want to learn?

W: I'm going to take a Brazilian Jiujitsu class. _____ with me?

M: Brazilian Jiujitsu? Isn't it a martial art?

W: Yes, it is. I really want to _____.

M: Then why don't you try swimming or tennis?

W: Brazilian Jiujitsu will help me get in shape. Plus, the way you earn different levels of belts is exciting!

M: It sounds fun, but _____ _____ others.

W: You don't have to worry about that. In the beginning, you don't fight at all!

M: Well, _____ I'd be very good. It seems too difficult.

14

M: Madison, cheer up. Want some tea?

W: No, thanks.

M: A cup of tea will give you relief. Why don't you try some?

W: No, _____. I can't believe I dropped the ball.

M: It's just one of those things.

W: I _____ the ball, but I dropped it. If I hadn't, we would have won the game.

M: You did your best. That's enough.

W: No, _____. I'm sure the coach must be very angry with me.

M: No, he isn't. _____.

W: I hate myself. I feel so stupid.

15

W: Maria lives with two dogs. She is planning to travel Eastern Europe with her friends for a month this summer. But _____ on her trip. She also can't put her dogs in a shelter for dogs because her dogs don't like to stay in shelters. And her other friends can't help her because they live in a "no pets" apartment. So _____ in the newspaper in hopes to find someone who will look after her dogs. Unfortunately, _____ _____ the advertisement. She is really worried about it. Today, she _____ _____ her neighbor, Natalie, and tells her about it.

Natalie _____ her dogs for a month. Maria deeply thanks Natalie. But Natalie thinks it's no big deal because she likes pets. In this situation, what would Natalie most likely say to Maria?

16~17

M: Hello, everyone. I'm Daniel, a fitness trainer. You may think that the harder you exercise, the stronger you become. But you should know exercising can _____ if you are not careful. When you _____ _____ to get fast results, your body can easily get injured. So, start slowly and build up gradually. _____ _____ to warm up with easy walking or gentle stretching. Then speed up to a pace you can maintain for five to ten minutes. As your stamina improves, gradually increase the amount of time you exercise. Work your way up to 30 to 60 minutes of exercise most days of the week. Your workout routine can include various light activities, such as walking, or bicycling. You can go hiking or play baseball with your family on weekends. But _____. If you feel pain, shortness of breath, or dizziness from exercising too much, take a break. _____ _____. If you're not feeling good, give yourself a day or two off.

01 다음을 듣고, 남자가 하는 말의 목적으로 가장 적절한 것을 고르시오.

① 기후변화의 심각성을 경고하려고
② 방송 프로그램의 변경을 통보하려고
③ 물건 사재기를 자제할 것을 당부하려고
④ 강풍과 폭설에 대비할 것을 안내하려고
⑤ 재난 대피 훈련에 참여할 것을 촉구하려고

02 대화를 듣고, 여자의 의견으로 가장 적절한 것을 고르시오.

① 지나친 조기 교육은 아이의 성장을 방해한다.
② 취학 전 어린이는 부모와 애착 관계가 중요하다.
③ 어린이 조기 교육은 사회성 발달에 도움이 된다.
④ 어린이 조기 교육은 미래의 성공을 위해 필요하다.
⑤ 활동적인 아이의 집중력 향상에는 악기 교육이 좋다.

03 대화를 듣고, 두 사람의 관계를 가장 잘 나타낸 것을 고르시오.

① 건물 관리인 – 택배 기사
② 보안 담당자 – 교수
③ 실험실 경비원 – 연구 조교
④ 수리 기사 – 사무실 직원
⑤ 연구원 – 연구 의뢰인

04 대화를 듣고, 그림에서 대화의 내용과 일치하지 않는 것을 고르시오.

05 대화를 듣고, 여자가 할 일로 가장 적절한 것을 고르시오.

① 정리함 사러 가기
② 필기구 사다 주기
③ 머그잔 가져다주기
④ 책상 서랍 정리해주기
⑤ 연필 깎는 칼 빌려주기

06 대화를 듣고, 두 사람이 지불할 금액을 고르시오. [3점]

① $270
② $280
③ $300
④ $370
⑤ $470

07 대화를 듣고, 여자가 수영 수업을 택할 수 없는 이유를 고르시오.

① 수영을 전혀 할 줄 몰라서
② 다른 수업과 시간이 겹쳐서
③ 수영장 수심이 너무 깊어서
④ 수영장 사용료가 너무 비싸서
⑤ 수영장 물에 알레르기가 있어서

08 대화를 듣고, 영화 시사회(the movie preview)에 관해 언급되지 않은 것을 고르시오.

① 영화감독
② 시작 시간
③ 주연 배우
④ 사진 촬영 장소
⑤ 영화의 장르

09 Diamond 광산 투어에 관한 다음 내용을 듣고, 일치하지 않는 것을 고르시오.

① 안전모와 안전화를 착용해야 한다.
② 12세 미만의 아이는 입장할 수 없다.
③ 카메라는 가지고 들어갈 수 없다.
④ 터널 탐방 시간은 약 15분이다.
⑤ 큰 가방은 사물함에 보관할 수 있다.

10 다음 표를 보면서 대화를 듣고, 두 사람이 선택한 카펫 회사를 고르시오.

Carpet Companies				
Carpet Company	Price	Cleaning Service	Years in Business	Customer Review
① Abbey Carpet	$850	◯	25	●●●●●
② North West Carpet	$490	✕	10	●●●
③ Arrowhead Carpet	$550	✕	12	●●●●
④ Carpetright	$690	◯	3	●●●
⑤ Mill Creek Carpet	$750	◯	21	●●●●●

11 대화를 듣고, 여자의 마지막 말에 대한 남자의 응답으로 가장 적절한 것을 고르시오.

① No. I'm not afraid of making mistakes.
② It's okay. Just relax and trust in yourself.
③ I know. You did very well your first time.
④ No problem. Thank you for encouraging me.
⑤ Of course. Remember that this is not the end.

12 대화를 듣고, 남자의 마지막 말에 대한 여자의 응답으로 가장 적절한 것을 고르시오.

① I'm afraid I have another appointment then.
② I'd like to bring my friend with me tomorrow.
③ I just want to do my best to get good grades.
④ I don't have any exams scheduled for Friday.
⑤ I'm always so stressed with school and studying.

13 대화를 듣고, 남자의 마지막 말에 대한 여자의 응답으로 가장 적절한 것을 고르시오. [3점]

▶ Woman :

① I'm glad you like it. I made it for you.
② Thank you. I'm going to throw a party.
③ I'll take that muffler. I like its green color.
④ It's beautiful. That color looks better on me.
⑤ I'd like to learn how to make a muffler like that.

14 대화를 듣고, 여자의 마지막 말에 대한 남자의 응답으로 가장 적절한 것을 고르시오.

▶ Man :

① You're welcome. Thanks for your time.
② That's what I think. You should be careful.
③ We need to put the fish back into the water.
④ I agree. I've never seen such a beautiful sight.
⑤ Yes. It's important to take good care of the sea.

15 다음 상황 설명을 듣고, Dylan이 아버지에게 할 말로 가장 적절한 것을 고르시오. [3점]

▶ Dylan :

① Do you think I should quit this job?
② How should I prepare for the interviews?
③ Could you set up a meeting for me now?
④ Which offer do you think I should accept?
⑤ Are there any job openings at your company?

[16~17] 다음을 듣고, 물음에 답하시오.

16 여자가 하는 말의 주제로 가장 적절한 것은?

① advantages and disadvantages of reading fiction
② fiction reading as a way to improve reading skills
③ understanding human nature through hero stories
④ the value of fiction as a tool for learning social skills
⑤ secrets for developing children's ability to read and write

17 언급된 문학 장르가 <u>아닌</u> 것은?

① fairly tales   ② hero stories
③ fantasy stories   ④ legends
⑤ myths

01

M: We interrupt regular programming for this breaking news. We have been informed by the National Weather Office that a big storm is moving in. It is bringing _____ _____. City officials have been advised to close down all public buildings, including schools. We must ensure that everyone is prepared for heavy snow. The storm _____ _____ and will bring at least two meters of snow. So do not expect to follow _____ _____ for a minimum of six days or more. Everyone should have on hand plenty of food and fuel. _____ for further instructions. We now return to our regular programming.

02

W: I want to give Camilla violin lessons. Music School at Ohio University has just opened a violin class for kids.

M: Violin? Camilla is already taking soccer class and drawing class.

W: Playing the violin improves children's concentration and memory.

M: Since she's still young, _____ _____ is enough, don't you think?

W: _____ is so important. During that time, the human brain develops rapidly.

M: I know, but that doesn't mean we have to force it.

W: What you need to succeed in life is established before _____. Research has shown that.

M: Well, Camilla is very active. For a girl like her, all these classes can be very stressful.

W: I don't think so. The violin class will be just once a week.

M: It'll put too much pressure on her. I know she'd rather do something physical.

W: Actually, I think she would probably _____ _____. Besides, I'm sure they'll be good for her.

M: Hmm... Okay. I'll consider your suggestion.

03

M: Is there a problem?

W: This ID scanner can't read my ID card. The door isn't opening.

M: Hold on. _____. Do you work here?

W: Yes, I am a graduate student and _____ _____ of Dr. Herold here. I didn't have a problem yesterday.

M: Your personal information isn't coming up on my monitor. You have to go to the office over there and ask about it.

W: I already went there, but no one is in the office right now.

M: I'm afraid there's nothing I can do at the moment. I have to be able to check _____ _____.

W: Here's my ID card with photo. Can't you _____ _____ this one time?

M: Sorry, I can't do that. It's a laboratory safety policy. Why don't you call a researcher in your lab and ask for help?

W: Okay. I'll call.

04

W: Justin, I made the poster for opening our library. Would you like to take a look?

M: Let me see. You drew a big tree in the center. It creates _____.

W: Yeah, and it symbolizes growth and development. I also drew two birds in the tree.

M: Good. But there's one thing I'd like to change.

W: Don't you like the three books under the tree?

M: I like them. The image of the books _____ _____. But you drew a headset near the books. I think this headset looks strange.

W: Really? Why?

M: Well, I think putting a pair of _____ _____ than a headset because the poster is for a library.

W: Okay. _____ right away.

M: But I like the way you wrote the title "READ" in the bottom center.

W: I think too many words are not effective, so I just wrote "The Parkville Library Opens" and "Monday, August 27" under the title.

M: That looks impressive.

05

W: Austin! Can I borrow a pencil knife?

M: Sure. It's somewhere on my desk.

W: On your desk? Oh, Austin! _____ _____. I can't find it.

M: Then I'm going to find it for you. I need to organize my desk. Oh, here it is.

W: You need to clean up your desk soon.

M: No problem. It's easy. First, I'll move all my books here to the bookshelf.

W: There are so many pencils and pens all over your desk.

M: I'm thinking of putting them into one of the desk drawers.

W: Hmm, no. Why don't you _____? That way you can find them easily, but they won't make a mess.

M: I don't have an extra mug. I should _____ _____.

W: You don't have to. I have one. _____ right now.

M: Thanks.

06

W: Honey, I can't believe we're having a baby in just three months.

M: I can't believe it at all. We've got to prepare baby furniture. I've found a nice online store. Look

here!

W: Great. _____. What do you think of this grey one?

M: It costs $200. But this brown one looks better.

W: Its price is $300. It's a little more expensive than the grey one.

M: But they're having _____ this brown baby bed. I think we can afford it.

W: All right. Let's order the brown baby bed. And we need a dresser.

M: How about this 5-drawer dresser? It's $200.

W: It's too high. I want to use it as _____ _____.

M: You mean you'll change our baby's diapers on it?

W: Right. So I think _____ should be enough. It's just $100.

M: I see. Let's order them now.

07

M: What's up, Laura? I didn't know you're a member of this fitness club.

W: Hi, Eric! I just joined here today. It's a very good place to exercise.

M: It's nice to see you here. Aren't these facilities really nice?

W: Yeah, but _____ is so high.

M: It's worth it. By the way, what class are you taking?

W: I'm taking aerobics and yoga. How about you?

M: I'm taking tennis and swimming. There are very nice tennis courts here.

W: I know, but _____ tennis.

M: Oh, how about swimming? There is an Olympic size swimming pool.

W: Sorry, but I can't. I enjoyed swimming when I was young, but now _____ in swimming pools.

M: That's too bad. I'd hoped _____ the same class.

W: That would be fun. Anyway, I'm glad we bumped into each other.

08

W: Hi, I'm Alyssa. I'm the photographer for *Film News*.

M: Hello, Alyssa. It's nice to meet you. So, you're here for the movie preview?

W: Yes, I am. My boss wants me to take pictures of all the famous actors and actresses who come down the red carpet for the preview.

M: As you know, there will be a lot of actors and actresses _____ Christopher Martin. He is a genius.

W: I think so. Do you know _____ _____?

M: The show starts at 7 p.m. They usually start to arrive about 30 minutes before the show.

W: Okay, I'll be ready for it. Where is the photo spot?

M: Over there, by the door. All of the actors and actresses will _____, so you can get some great photos from there.

W: Thank you. I'll move there.

M: Since it's an action movie, I think a lot of people will _____.

W: I see. Thanks for your advice. You've been a great help.

09

M: May I have your attention, please? Welcome to the Diamond Mine Tour! We _____ our first tunnel. Safety helmets and safety shoes are required beyond this point. If you go through the entrance on the right, you will be provided with helmets and shoes. I see some children in the group. I am sorry, but for safety reasons, _____ _____ on the mine tour. They can wait in the waiting area. _____, so please leave your cameras in a locker. We will be entering the underground facility _____ _____, which will allow you time to put on all the equipment. You can also put any inconvenient large-size bags in a locker before entering the tunnel. Thank you.

10

W: Carlos, I've contacted five different carpet companies since we have to replace our carpet.

M: Did you find a company that _____ _____?

W: I wanted to discuss it with you first. Let's take a look at this list.

M: Wow, excellent! I think the price is the most important factor for us. I don't want to pay more than $800.

W: I agree.

M: Why don't we go with the company that offers us the cheapest price?

W: I want the carpet cleaning service, but the company that offers the cheapest price doesn't offer this service.

M: Then choose the one that gives us the best offer and provides _____, too.

W: Well, this company has only been in business for 3 years. I can't trust them.

M: _____ some customer reviews?

W: They don't have good reviews. I'd like to choose this company that has more experience and better reviews.

M: Okay. Let's choose that. _____ _____.

11

W: Oh, there are so many people in the audience. It's _____ onto the stage, right?

M: Yes, but don't worry. You had plenty of practice. Are you ready, Sophia?

W: I'm not sure. _____, and my legs are shaking.

12

M: Do you think you'll be able to make it to my party this weekend?

W: Sorry, I can't. I have to _____. I have an important final exam coming up!

M: Really? You still _____ before final exams! Why are you studying so early?

13

M: Mrs. Campbell. How are you feeling today?

W: Oh, Daniel. You've come again. I'm doing well, thank you.

M: You mentioned that your legs _____ _____ last week. Is everything all right?

W: They feel much better now. It's so wonderful of you to see me every Friday like this.

M: It's my pleasure, and _____.

W: But it's not easy cleaning and looking after a disabled elderly woman.

M: Mrs. Campbell, I come here because I really enjoy the visits.

W: You're so kind! Daniel, I want to give you this muffler. Please take it.

M: Oh, my! Thank you so much. I don't know what to say. It's lovely!

W: You don't have to say anything. I just wanted to show my appreciation.

M: It feels warm, and it's my favorite color. _____ _____ tonight.

14

W: This aquarium is amazing! Look over there, Pablo!

M: Where? Wow! It's like being under the sea.

W: Yes, and doesn't _____?

M: What? Weren't you pointing to that colorful fish?

W: I was talking about the female diver next to the fish. She looks like a mermaid.

M: What is a mermaid?

W: It's a legendary creature _____ and upper body of a female human and the tail of a fish.

M: Ah, I knew that. But that diver doesn't have a fish tail. Anyway, she looks like the queen of the underwater world.

W: She is swimming with sharks and _____ _____.

M: Wow! It's like a rainbow with all these colorful fish.

W: It's amazing. They all look like they're dancing. I'm glad we came here to this aquarium.

15

W: Dylan has been looking for a job for the past several months. He's been to several job interviews. And today _____ by two companies. Dylan is very happy because he had been out of work for such a long time. But now he has to choose _____ _____. However, it's very difficult to choose because both are excellent companies which offer great benefits and salary. Dylan _____ _____ which to accept. He finally calls his father. Dylan explains to his father why he can't make up his mind. He's _____ _____ from his father. In this situation, what would Dylan most likely say to his father?

16~17

W: Do you remember the very first book you read? Probably it was a short story with a fictional character. Some people claim that reading fiction such as fairy tales or hero stories is a waste of time. They say, "Those stories usually begin with a perfect world. The ending is always happy for the one who has overcome failure. It's false and unreal!" But reading fiction can do more than provide relaxation and entertainment. Reading fiction allows us _____ _____ and, as a result, helps us behave properly. One study showed that children ages 4-6 who read a lot of children's storybooks had a significantly stronger ability to read _____ _____ of other people. Similarly, psychologists have found that traditional tales, from legends to myths, perform the essential work of _____ and act as a kind of social glue. Thus, reading fiction can be a great way of learning to _____ _____.

14회

✳ 첫단추 **듣기실전편**

01 다음을 듣고, 여자가 하는 말의 목적으로 가장 적절한 것을 고르시오.

① 댄스 안무 창작을 요청하려고
② 댄스 공연 후 노고를 칭찬하려고
③ 마지막 총연습 참석을 당부하려고
④ 댄스 대회 출전 전 최종 당부를 하려고
⑤ 댄스 초보자에게 기본자세를 설명하려고

02 대화를 듣고, 남자의 의견으로 가장 적절한 것을 고르시오.

① 눈을 보며 이야기하는 것이 예의이다.
② 옷차림으로 사람을 판단해서는 안 된다.
③ 여행자는 그 나라 문화를 존중해야 한다.
④ 남성도 여성 인권을 위해 노력해야 한다.
⑤ 여행에서 안전을 최우선으로 생각해야 한다.

03 대화를 듣고, 두 사람의 관계를 가장 잘 나타낸 것을 고르시오.

① 학생 – 양호교사
② 가수 – 매니저
③ 연주자 – 무대감독
④ 배우 – 분장사
⑤ 토크쇼 사회자 – 방송국 PD

04 대화를 듣고, 그림에서 대화의 내용과 일치하지 <u>않는</u> 것을 고르시오.

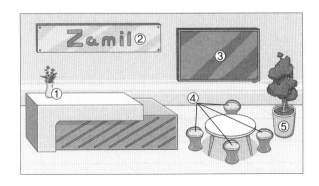

05 대화를 듣고, 남자가 지금 할 일로 가장 적절한 것을 고르시오.

① 설거지하기
② 쓰레기 버리기
③ 야구 하러 가기
④ 친구 책 돌려주기
⑤ 저녁 식사 준비 돕기

06 대화를 듣고, 여자가 사무실 파티를 준비하는 데 드는 금액을 고르시오.

① $150
② $180
③ $230
④ $280
⑤ $430

07 대화를 듣고, 남자가 이전 직장을 그만둔 이유를 고르시오.

① 봉급이 낮아서
② 일이 너무 많아서
③ 건강이 안 좋아져서
④ 상사와 불화가 있어서
⑤ 마라톤 선수가 되기로 해서

08 대화를 듣고, Evans 중고 서점에 관해 언급되지 <u>않은</u> 것을 고르시오.

① 영업시간
② 휴무일
③ 위치
④ 주차 공간
⑤ 웹사이트 주소

09 Bruce Canyon 공원에 관한 다음 내용을 듣고, 일치하지 <u>않는</u> 것을 고르시오.

① 유럽에서 드문 다양한 동식물이 있다.
② 여름에는 낚시와 수영을 할 수 있다.
③ 크리스마스 날을 제외하고 1년 내내 개방한다.
④ 낮 시간의 이용은 입장료가 무료이다.
⑤ 야영객에게 장작이 무료로 제공된다.

10 다음 표를 보면서 대화를 듣고, 두 사람이 구매할 병따개를 고르시오.

	Model	Material	Shape	Attachment	Price
	Bottle Openers for Promotional Gifts				
①	A	metal	rectangular	Magnet	$1.20
②	B	plastic	owl	Key Ring	$1.00
③	C	metal	square	Key Ring	$1.50
④	D	metal	bear	Key Ring	$2.50
⑤	E	metal	round	Magnet	$1.90

11 대화를 듣고, 여자의 마지막 말에 대한 남자의 응답으로 가장 적절한 것을 고르시오.

① Well, I don't want it. That's it.
② Oh, I forgot it! How stupid of me!
③ How terrible! I lost my sunglasses.
④ Yes. I'll be careful when swimming.
⑤ Don't worry. I'll wash it after swimming.

12 대화를 듣고, 남자의 마지막 말에 대한 여자의 응답으로 가장 적절한 것을 고르시오.

① Cheer up! You'll do better next time.
② I'm sorry. I don't think you can make it.
③ Welcome. I hope you enjoy your work here.
④ You deserve it. I'm sure you'll do a great job.
⑤ Don't worry about it. It's none of your business.

13 대화를 듣고, 남자의 마지막 말에 대한 여자의 응답으로 가장 적절한 것을 고르시오. [3점]

▶ Woman :

① That's right. You need to study harder.
② You're a lifesaver. I feel relieved already.
③ I know what I should do. But it's not easy.
④ That's okay. I don't think I need them anymore.
⑤ You look pale. You should go home and take a rest.

14 대화를 듣고, 여자의 마지막 말에 대한 남자의 응답으로 가장 적절한 것을 고르시오. [3점]

▶ Man :

① You're right. He is an old friend of mine.
② Sounds great. I'll bet he enjoyed this party.
③ I promise to ask you next time. Thank you.
④ Let's be practical. You can't have everything.
⑤ Calm down. Your anger will not solve the problem.

15 다음 상황 설명을 듣고, Robert가 투숙객에게 할 말로 가장 적절한 것을 고르시오. [3점]

▶ Robert :

① I apologize. Your room is on the tenth floor.
② Yes. Room service is available until 9 o'clock.
③ I'm sorry for the mistake. I'll remove the charge.
④ Of course. But you must get your bag by 3 o'clock.
⑤ Excuse me. There is another customer ahead of you.

[16~17] 다음을 듣고, 물음에 답하시오.

16 남자가 하는 말의 주제로 가장 적절한 것은?

① an effective and simple diet plan
② effective ways of going on a diet
③ some problems caused by obesity
④ the causes and treatment of obesity
⑤ the harmful effect of obesity on health

17 언급된 음식이 <u>아닌</u> 것은?

① milk   ② soft drinks
③ chocolate   ④ pie
⑤ potato chips

01

W: We're finally finished with rehearsals. We've practiced for six months, and our dance performance will be evaluated sometime later. Don't be too nervous. Think of this performance as just another one of our rehearsals. When you _____, don't think of this as your first performance. Most importantly, you must make sure that _____ _____. Just as we've done before, you must not only concentrate on your movement but the entire group's. Emma, don't forget to take a step forward when you're doing your solo. Also, always listen to the music and try to get into the rhythm of it. We are not here to win a contest but to have a good time. All right, _____ _____. Is everyone in line?

02

W: Asad, I'll travel to your country next month.

M: That's great. I'm sure you'll like its beautiful scenery and kind people.

W: Yeah, I'm very excited. _____ _____ for me?

M: Well, one of the most important things is _____ _____ with local men.

W: Really? In my culture, it's basic etiquette to make eye contact when I'm speaking to someone.

M: In my culture, there are strict gender rules. Women should not make too much eye contact with men.

W: Oh, then I should wear dark sunglasses.

M: That's a good idea. And don't wear short pants or a tight top. Those clothes will send the wrong message to local men.

W: That's not fair! Think about the temperature in the desert in your country!

M: Well, I understand. But fair or not, it's our culture. _____ to be a welcome guest.

W: I see. I'll keep that in mind. Thanks for your advice.

03

W: Donald, can I have some water?

M: Here it is. How do you feel? Don't you think you should see a doctor?

W: No, I'm not that sick. I feel better after getting some rest.

M: _____ this evening. Will you be all right?

W: Sure. Don't worry about that.

M: Here's tonight's performance program. This is the final performance. You can take a rest tomorrow.

W: Okay. Anyway, what are all those flowers for? There are so many.

M: _____. They also sent you some chocolate. Do you want some?

W: No, thanks. But I'm grateful. Let's have a rehearsal. I'll get makeup after the rehearsal.

M: Okay. If it's too hard, why don't you _____ _____?

W: I don't want to do that. It's so unprofessional. Is the band here?

M: Of course. They're all waiting for you.

04

M: This is the design for our company booth for the State Fair.

W: You placed the information counter on the left side. Good.

M: How about the flower vase on the counter? It'll _____.

W: Good idea. And I like the name of our company, "Zamil," on the banner on the left side of the wall.

M: It's for balance because there is a large monitor _____.

W: Okay. We can also play our company's promotional video clip throughout the day.

M: Yes. And I put a round table under the monitor.

W: Perfect. It's for our booth visitors, right? _____ _____. Hmm...

M: Do you think we need more chairs?

W: Yes, I think four chairs will be better than three.

M: Okay! I'll change the design. How about _____ _____ near the table?

W: I like it. You did a good job.

05

W: Alex, what are you doing? _____ _____?

M: I'm sorry, Mom. I have to hurry up and finish my homework. After that I'm going over to Blake's house.

W: Are you going over there to play baseball?

M: No. I borrowed his book yesterday, and _____ _____ this evening.

W: I guess that means you can't help me for five minutes.

M: Five minutes? Then I can help you. I thought you wanted me to wash the dishes.

W: No. I just finished cleaning the kitchen, and there's a lot of trash.

M: Do you want me _____?

W: Can you? It's quite heavy, so I don't think I can carry it.

M: All right. _____ right away.

W: Good. I'll prepare dinner.

06

W: Jonathan, I need your help. I'm _____ _____, but I don't even know where to begin.

M: I planned last year's office party; maybe I can help you out. First, what do you have in mind for the location?

W: Well, there's a room at the community center that we could rent, but it's going to cost $200 for the night.

M: I can save you that money pretty easily. Why don't we have the party here at the office? _____ _____.

W: Then what about decorations? We need balloons and banners.

M: Don't worry. If you go to the decorations store, you can find "Party in a Box." It's $50 _____ _____!

W: I think I'll do that! Then, the last thing is refreshments.

M: Snacks usually run $100 for a party package, and drinks usually run $80 on K-mart's website. They also offer free delivery.

W: Okay, _____. Thanks for helping me.

M: My pleasure. Just tell me if you need any help.

07

W: Hi, Sam! Good to see you here. Are you jogging?

M: Yes, actually I'm preparing for the Phoenix Half Marathon.

W: Wow! That sounds great! But aren't you busy? You said you've been terribly busy since you became a manager.

M: Actually, _____ last October.

W: Really? Did you have some problem with your boss or some health problems?

M: Not at all. My decision to quit _____ _____ those things. By the way, I got a new job.

W: Good. You changed jobs because the new job pays you more money, right?

M: No, actually not. I got paid better in the previous job.

W: Oh, I see. _____ at your previous job?

M: Yeah, _____ every day. I felt like I was a machine.

W: I understand why you quit. You look happy now.

M: Yes, I'm happy. I work eight to four, and I can enjoy running.

08

M: Good afternoon, Evans Used Bookstore. How can I help you?

W: Hello, I'd like to sell some of my used books. Can I ask you _____?

M: The price is decided based on the type of book and _____.

W: Then I should bring the books there. I'd like to visit your store this evening. When do you close?

M: We are open from 10 a.m. to 7 p.m.

W: Oh, I don't think I can make it this evening. Do you open on Saturday?

M: Yes, we're open until 3 p.m. on Saturdays, but _____.

W: _____, exactly?

M: It's 198 Luis Street, near Union Square.

W: Thanks. Is there any place I can park my car around your bookstore?

M: We don't have a parking lot, but you can use street parking.

W: Okay. Thank you.

09

M: Hello, I'm Robert Moore, manager of Bruce Canyon Park. The park has a wide variety of wild plants and animals _____. It also has clear mountain streams, and you can enjoy fishing and swimming on a hot summer day. The park is open all year _____. The park is open from 9 a.m. to 6 p.m. for day visitors. There is _____, but there are fees for overnight camping. Each campsite is limited to 2 tents and begins at a base rate of $15.00 per night. Fires are permitted in grills, but _____ at the camp office. Please come out and enjoy nature in Bruce Canyon Park.

10

W: Let's give away bottle openers as promotional gifts for the grand opening of our store.

M: Good idea. How about this plastic bottle opener? It is owl-shaped. Isn't it cute?

W: It's cute, but it doesn't fit the image of our store. _____.

M: Okay. Do you like any of the animal-shaped openers, like the bear?

W: No, I'd like to go with a simple design.

M: Then let's choose among these three. There is a key-ring type opener. _____ would be good advertising.

W: I don't think people would like it. I've never seen key rings hanging on the wall.

M: Then _____ on the back of it.

W: Yes, I think it's better and more useful. People can attach it on the refrigerator.

M: Okay. Now which one do you prefer? Would you like the cheaper one?

W: Absolutely. Let's go with the cheaper one.

11

W: Sam, _____? Check if you forgot anything.

M: Don't worry, Mom. I've got an extra pair of underwear, sunglasses, and a long sleeve shirt, _____.

W: Okay, have fun at the beach. Oh, one more thing, Sam. You did _____, didn't you?

12

M: I'm really excited about my new project at work. It's something I'd hoped _____.

W: Good for you. It sounds like a great opportunity for you.

M: That's right. I don't know _____, but this is something I've wanted for a while.

13

M: Hello, Ashley. _____?
Were you on a trip? I haven't seen you around.

W: No, I've been sick.

M: I'm sorry to hear that. What was wrong?

W: I've been seeing my doctor _____
_____ because of bad headaches.

M: That's terrible.

W: I'm okay now. But I have a lot of stress these days.

M: Why is that? I guess _____.

W: Yes, I haven't been able to attend any of my classes for a week. My final exams are coming up, and I don't know what to do.

M: Oh, don't worry about it. I can help you if you want.

W: I don't want to bother you. Are you sure?

M: Yeah. What are friends for? I'll _____
_____ all my notes.

14

M: Honey, what's your schedule like next weekend?

W: I'll have to check my planner. Well, I'm planning to go shopping.

M: Uh, well, you can go shopping sometime later, can't you?

W: Yeah. Why are you asking?

M: Well, it's just that I've invited some people over from work.

W: What? To our house? _____?

M: Thomas is leaving the company next week. So I'm throwing him a farewell party.

W: You decided to do this without asking me?

M: I'm very sorry. He looked so depressed, so _____
_____.
I think about seven people are coming.

W: Charles! _____.

M: I'm really sorry. We'll have a barbecue. So, I'd really appreciate it if you made some salad for us.

W: Hmm... All right. But if you don't ask me in advance next time, I'm _____.

15

W: Robert works at a small hotel. He takes reservations at the front desk as well as handles check-ins for hotel guests. As usual, he's at the front desk today. He's very busy with a large tour group _____. At this time, a female guest wishes to check out. She also asks if the front desk can hold her bag until 3 o'clock after check-out. Robert says it's possible and _____. The guest stayed in a standard room for three nights. Robert sees that she's also used room service. As soon as she looks at her charges, she tells him that she's never used room service. After double checking, Robert realizes that he's _____ with another guest's and that she is right. In this situation, what would Robert most likely say to the guest?

16~17

M: Are you thinking about dieting to lose weight? Before you start, it's important to learn _____
_____, since there can be many factors. For example, you may have bad food habits. Foods that are high in fat, sugar, and salt provide more energy than the body needs. Do you have easy access to food? Many stay-at-home moms _____ since they have more access to food at home. Another reason to overeat is an inactive lifestyle. Many people are not physically active enough for good health and spend too much time sitting. So, _____?

To begin, eat the right amount of the right stuff. Try to drink milk instead of soft drinks. Don't have chocolate, potato chips, or cookie jars around you. Don't stay up late playing computer games or watching TV. Eating out on a regular basis is also something you should avoid. I hope you keep all these points in mind and _____
_____.

01 다음을 듣고, 남자가 하는 말의 목적으로 가장 적절한 것을 고르시오.

① 강연회 연사를 소개하기 위해
② 결혼한 부부를 축하하기 위해
③ 복권 당첨자를 발표하기 위해
④ 시상식 후보자를 공표하기 위해
⑤ 동창회 초대 손님을 환영하기 위해

02 대화를 듣고, 여자의 의견으로 가장 적절한 것을 고르시오.

① 시간별로 계획을 세워 공부를 해야 한다.
② 공부는 늦은 시간에 하지 않는 것이 좋다.
③ 공부를 잘하기 위해서는 체력이 중요하다.
④ 수학 실력은 장기간에 걸쳐 쌓이는 것이다.
⑤ 공부 중 휴식 시간을 가지는 것이 바람직하다.

03 대화를 듣고, 두 사람의 관계를 가장 잘 나타낸 것을 고르시오.

① 서점 직원 – 구매자
② 도서관 사서 – 학생
③ 식당 종업원 – 손님
④ 복사 가게 직원 – 손님
⑤ 인터넷 카페 직원 – 이용자

04 대화를 듣고, 남자가 구매한 선물 바구니 그림에서 대화의 내용과 일치하지 <u>않는</u> 것을 고르시오.

05 대화를 듣고, 남자가 할 일로 가장 적절한 것을 고르시오.

① 은행에서 환전하기
② 면세점에서 쇼핑하기
③ 비행기 탑승수속하기
④ 서점에서 잡지 구매하기
⑤ 커피숍에서 커피 마시기

06 대화를 듣고, 남자가 지불할 금액을 고르시오. [3점]

① $95 　　② $98 　　③ $105
④ $118 　　⑤ $175

07 대화를 듣고, 남자가 Jack에게 화가 난 이유를 고르시오.

① 보고서를 빌려 가 베껴서
② 빌려 간 돈을 갚지 않아서
③ 의견이 달라 심하게 다퉈서
④ 책을 망가뜨리고 피해 다녀서
⑤ 시간 약속을 자주 지키지 않아서

08 대화를 듣고, 컴퓨터 사용 시 주의점에 관해 언급되지 <u>않은</u> 것을 고르시오.

① 올바른 자세
② 손목 받침대
③ 마우스 모양
④ 모니터의 각도
⑤ 모니터와의 거리

09 Wichita Symphony Concert에 관한 다음 내용을 듣고, 일치하지 <u>않는</u> 것을 고르시오.

① 순서에 청중과 함께 노래 부르기가 있다.
② 12월 14일 금요일 저녁에 열린다.
③ 티켓은 예약할 수 없고 당일에만 판매한다.
④ 12세 미만 아동의 티켓 가격은 10달러이다.
⑤ 연주회 시작 두 시간 전부터 입장할 수 있다.

10 다음 표를 보면서 대화를 듣고, 여자가 택할 강좌를 고르시오.

Rochester Fitness Center

Class	Purpose	Time	Fee	Instructor
① Swimming	Weight Loss	Tue., Thu. 3 p.m.	$45	Jane (Female)
② Squash	Weight Loss	Mon., Fri. 7 p.m.	$65	Mark (Male)
③ Weight Training	Strength	Mon., Wed. 2 p.m.	$50	Tom (Male)
④ Kick Boxing	Weight Loss	Tue., Thu. 8 p.m.	$45	Scott (Male)
⑤ Aerobics B	Weight Loss	Mon., Wed. 7 p.m.	$40	Kara (Female)

11 대화를 듣고, 여자의 마지막 말에 대한 남자의 응답으로 가장 적절한 것을 고르시오.

① You never know until you try.
② I'm going to be a good president.
③ I need some help with the election.
④ We will support any other candidate.
⑤ You can reduce your campaign budget.

12 대화를 듣고, 남자의 마지막 말에 대한 여자의 응답으로 가장 적절한 것을 고르시오.

① You're right. First things first.
② This is on me. I'll pay for you.
③ Sounds great. But I'm afraid I can't.
④ Good job. That's quite an improvement.
⑤ Thanks for your help. See you tomorrow.

13 대화를 듣고, 남자의 마지막 말에 대한 여자의 응답으로 가장 적절한 것을 고르시오.

▶ Woman :

① Nice job! I'm so glad you could make it!
② It seems like a dream! I finally got a job!
③ It's very difficult. But I'm sure it'll be worth it.
④ I need help. I don't know what's wrong with me.
⑤ Don't worry. You have plenty of other options.

14 대화를 듣고, 여자의 마지막 말에 대한 남자의 응답으로 가장 적절한 것을 고르시오. [3점]

▶ Man :

① The ferry isn't as popular since most people drive.
② The ferry is not in service during the weekends.
③ They can save time since many offices are along the river.
④ They can enjoy the beautiful night view from the bridge.
⑤ That's because it's considered to be a landmark of the city.

15 다음 상황 설명을 듣고, 교수님이 Jerry에게 할 말로 가장 적절한 것을 고르시오. [3점]

▶ Professor :

① Don't worry. I'll postpone the test just for you.
② I'm sorry, but I don't think I will take your late paper.
③ In this case, I'll accept the paper without any penalty.
④ I'm sorry to hear that. I hope she will recover soon.
⑤ If so, I suggest that you visit your grandmother.

[16~17] 다음을 듣고, 물음에 답하시오.

16 남자가 하는 말의 주제로 가장 적절한 것은?

① educational effects of pets on children
② how to keep household pets safe and healthy
③ advantages and disadvantages of raising pets
④ a pet's influence on a child's physical growth
⑤ tips for adopting a household pet for children

17 언급된 동물이 <u>아닌</u> 것은?

① dogs   ② turtles   ③ snakes
④ fish   ⑤ hamsters

01

M: Good afternoon, ladies and gentlemen. Thank you for sharing this very special day with Rosie and Chris. For those of you who don't know me, I'm Brandon. I've known Chris since middle school. Chris is really the best friend I've ever had. I'm very proud to stand by his side today. Rosie, I think we can all agree that you're beautiful this afternoon and that Chris _____. Rosie and Chris, this afternoon _____ _____. We all wish you a lifetime of happiness, love, health, success, and laughter. I hope you can always find humor in the bad and appreciation for the good. And I hope your love continues to grow throughout all the years to come. _____ _____. Cheers!

02

W: Nick, are you okay? You look so down.

M: I received my report card today. I really studied math hard, but I got a terrible grade anyway.

W: Have you thought about _____ _____?

M: I don't know. I stopped playing computer games and playing baseball for two weeks. I really did my best this time.

W: I know that you tried hard this time. But studying hard just for _____ won't improve your math grades.

M: What do I need to do?

W: Studying for math is like a marathon. _____ _____ instead of cramming right before an exam.

M: Are you saying that I should study at a steady pace?

W: Exactly. Don't expect quick results but set a strong foundation and build _____.

M: I see. It sounds difficult, but I'll try.

03

W: Excuse me. You're _____ _____ your drink here.

M: Oh, really? But the woman over there also brought her drink.

W: She's got a tumbler with a cap. Covered drinks are allowed.

M: Oh, I see. I'm a foreign student and this is my first time here, so I didn't know that. Umm, could you tell me _____?

W: Tell me which book you want, or you can use the computers over there.

M: Can I use those computers for free?

W: Sure. Just type keywords from the title or the author's name into the search box.

M: Thanks. _____ at a time?

W: If you're a student here, you can check out 10 books for 2 weeks.

M: I see. One more question: Are there copy machines inside?

W: Of course. You need to buy a copy card to photocopy materials.

M: Thank you. I'll go out to drink this and come back again.

04

M: I'd like to get some chocolate and candy for my little sister. She just graduated from kindergarten.

W: If you want something special, why don't you make your own gift basket?

M: Good idea. I'd like that. Can you help me to make it?

W: Sure. First, you need to choose a basket. I recommend this basket _____ _____.

M: Great. And a teddy bear is the first thing to put in the basket. My sister really likes teddy bears.

W: Okay. I'll put a teddy bear in the middle of the basket. And which chocolate box do you want?

M: Does this square box have chocolates and candy?

W: No, it only has chocolates. This heart-shaped box has _____ of chocolates and candy.

M: Then I'd like _____. Put it on the left side of the teddy bear.

W: Sure. How about putting these three roses in the basket?

M: Good idea. She loves roses. And could you decorate _____ with a big ribbon?

W: Certainly. Here you go. How do you like it?

M: It looks great. Thank you.

05

M: Okay. Now we've finished our flight check-in.

W: Honey, you got our boarding passes, right?

M: Yeah, here's yours and here's mine. Our flight leaves in two hours.

W: We don't need to wait at the boarding gate, do we?

M: Of course not. It's okay to be there an hour before the departure time.

W: Since we still have some time, _____
_____?

M: To tell you the truth, I hate shopping. It's so boring!

W: Then what do you want to do? Would you like to get some coffee at the coffee shop?

M: That sounds good. But before we do that, _____
_____? I'd like to get a magazine.

W: Okay. Oh, hold on. _____
_____. I need to go to the bank first.

M: Then let's do what we each want and meet at the information desk later.

W: Good idea. Let's meet there later.

06

M: Good morning. I have to send this package to Brazil.

W: OK, could you put it on the scale? Let's see _____.

M: Sure. I want to send it by airmail. How long does it take to get there?

W: It'll take about 7 days.

M: How much is it?

W: It weighs 5 kilograms, so _____. You also have the option of using "International Signed For."

M: What is that? I've never heard of it.

W: Your item will be fully tracked. And the person in Brazil has to _____ when the postman delivers it to them.

M: It sounds much safer. How much does that cost?

W: An extra $20. You will receive up to $70 _____
_____ during shipping.

M: That's good. I'd like International Signed For service.

W: Do you need anything else?

M: No, thanks.

07

W: Oh, there's Jack. Hi, Jack!

M: Jack? You mean Jack Tylor? Where is he?

W: Oh, he just walked away. Maybe he didn't see us.

M: I'm sure _____.

W: Why? What has he got against you? Did you guys have a fight or something?

M: No, we didn't fight. I just got angry with him. He borrowed my book and _____ _____ all over it.

W: Oh, my goodness!

M: I had to read the book for a report, but I couldn't read _____.

W: That's too bad. Did he apologize and buy you a new book?

M: He just said, "I'm sorry!" and _____ _____. I should buy the book again.

W: Oh. I think he should make a sincere apology to you.

08

M: Megan, aren't you tired?

W: Yes, I'm tired. I've been on the computer for a long time.

M: I noticed your posture _____ _____. You look so uncomfortable.

W: I was so focused on writing a paper that I didn't realize what I was doing.

M: You need to sit up straight. Push your hips _____ _____ in the chair.

W: I'll be careful about that. And my wrists really hurt, too.

M: How about using a wrist pad when you're using the mouse? It'll support your wrist, and you'll feel less pain.

W: Thanks for pointing that out.

M: And you can change your mouse to a vertical mouse. _____, you can move your hand without a problem.

W: I've heard about that. I'll think about it.

M: And make sure to _____ _____. You should keep yourself at least 40cm from the monitor.

W: I got it. Thanks for your good advice.

09

M: If you're dreaming of a musical Christmas, don't miss the Wichita Symphony's Annual Holiday Concert! The concert will open up with a choir, directed by Jay Decker. And _____, the concert will include our popular audience sing-along. The concert will be held on Friday, December 14, 7:30 p.m., at Wichita University Auditorium. _____ _____, and they can only be purchased individually on the night of the concert. Tickets will be $25 for adults and $10 for children under 12. Wichita University students _____ with student ID. Doors open at 6:30 p.m. So, _____ _____ before the start of the concert. For more ticket information, please visit the Wichita Symphony's website.

10

W: Excuse me. I want to sign up for one of your classes.

M: Some classes are already full, but several classes are still open. Here's the list of all the classes you can register for.

W: _____.

M: Then I recommend this swimming class.

W: Oh, but it's on Tuesday and Thursday afternoon. I can't take it since I work 9 to 6. I'm only free weekday evenings.

M: Then you can choose one of the evening classes.

W: Okay. Why is this class so expensive _____ _____?

M: It's because it offers private lessons. I'm sure this will be very effective.

W: But _____. As for the fee, I'd like to stay under 50 dollars a month.

M: Then it looks like you have two options. Which one do you prefer?

W: I'd like to _____.

M: All right. Then this is what you want.

11

W: I've been really busy these days. _____ _____ of my club.

M: That's great. I hope you get elected.

W: I don't think I can win. My rival has _____ _____ with this kind of thing.

12

M: Sarah, are you free tomorrow?

W: No. Actually, I have _____ due next Friday.

M: _____. Let's go to the Hip Hop concert tomorrow evening. I have tickets.

13

M: Miranda, what are you doing? _____ _____?

W: I applied at Soft Tech Company, and they're announcing the people who are hired today.

M: _____? Do you see your name?

W: I can't find my name. I really thought I was going to get this job. Soft Tech is hiring a lot of new employees, and I was hoping to be one of them.

M: Let me see. The names are all _____ _____.

W: Oh, my! I'm not on the list.

M: Wait a minute! The last names are in alphabetical order, not first names.

W: You're right. Let's see. T... Townshend.

M: Look! I see Townshend! There you are, Townshend, Miranda!

W: Really! Are you sure? Oh, Tim! Thanks a million.

M: _____. It's your doing. Congratulations!

14

W: This river _____ is really awesome.

M: Isn't it? I don't think this city would be here without this river.

W: The trees on the riverside are beautiful.

M: Yes, it's even more beautiful at night when the bridge and _____.

W: I should come here at night one day. There are a lot of tourists this morning.

M: Those people aren't tourists. They're people who are going to work across the river.

W: Really? I thought this ferry was for tourists.

M: Yeah, you would think so. But many people save time going to work by taking the ferry in the morning. If they didn't, _____ _____.

W: That's a good idea. Is the fare cheap?

M: Not really. It's much more expensive than the bus.

W: Really? Then _____?

15

W: Jerry is a college student. He's taking Professor Walker's biology class this semester. He had to _____ for his biology class last week. But his grandmother in Boston had a heart attack and was taken to the hospital. Jerry had to stay with his grandmother for a week. Fortunately, _____, but Jerry's paper for the biology class is now a week late. Today, Jerry wants to give the paper to the professor, so he explains to the professor _____ _____. Normally, the professor doesn't accept late papers, but she thinks _____ _____ because of what happened to him. In this situation, what would the professor most likely say to Jerry?

16~17

M: Did you care for a pet in childhood? The excitement of raising another being creates lifelong memories. While it's clear that _____ _____, did you know it can also teach your child in a positive and meaningful way? Having a pet in the family home brings great joy but also creates additional household chores. These chores are where children can learn important values and virtues _____ _____. For example, dogs can teach children to be responsible. Children who have to feed a dog, give a dog water, and walk a dog _____ _____ the life of another being. Cats also teach children responsibility, and also, children who own a cat learn about independence. Snakes, fish, and hamsters are also good _____ _____ about cleanliness and proper bathing habits. Thus, adopting a pet is a huge responsibility and shouldn't be taken lightly, but it might be _____ for your kids' childhood.

01 다음을 듣고, 여자가 하는 말의 목적으로 가장 적절한 것을 고르시오.

① 미술관 견학 순서를 공지하려고
② 손 씻기의 중요성을 강조하려고
③ 예술 작품 감상법을 안내하려고
④ 미술관 관람 주의사항을 알리려고
⑤ 미술관 단체 견학 신청을 권유하려고

02 대화를 듣고, 여자의 의견으로 가장 적절한 것을 고르시오.

① 지구 온난화에 대비해야 한다.
② 의류용 보온재를 개발해야 한다.
③ 멸종 위기 동물을 보호해야 한다.
④ 의류에 모피 사용을 중지해야 한다.
⑤ 동물 보호 기금 모금에 동참해야 한다.

03 대화를 듣고, 두 사람의 관계를 가장 잘 나타낸 것을 고르시오.

① 의사 – 환자   ② 경찰관 – 신고자
③ 보건교사 – 학부모   ④ 구급차 운전자 – 간호사
⑤ 구급 대원 – 환자 보호자

04 대화를 듣고, 그림에서 대화의 내용과 일치하지 않는 것을 고르시오.

05 대화를 듣고, 남자가 할 일로 가장 적절한 것을 고르시오.

① 케이크 주문 도와주기
② 함께 볼 영화 예매하기
③ 식당 안내 앱 다운받기
④ 이탈리아 식당 예약하기
⑤ 앱에서 식당 리뷰 조사하기

06 대화를 듣고, 두 사람이 지불할 금액을 고르시오. [3점]

① $146   ② $160   ③ $166
④ $180   ⑤ $186

07 대화를 듣고, 남자가 제시간에 출근할 수 없는 이유를 고르시오.

① 교통 체증으로 길이 막혀서
② 자동차가 갑자기 고장 나서
③ 타고 온 비행기가 연착해서
④ 공항으로 어머니 마중을 가서
⑤ 회의 발표 준비를 끝내지 못해서

08 대화를 듣고, 음식의 역사 수업에 관해 언급되지 않은 것을 고르시오.

① 수강 대상   ② 담당 교수   ③ 수업 방식
④ 수업 교재명   ⑤ 평가 방법

09 Blue Lake 하이킹에 관한 다음 내용을 듣고, 일치하지 않는 것을 고르시오.

① 2일 동안 진행되는 여행이다.
② 하이킹 초보자도 참가할 수 있다.
③ 첫날은 약 5시간 정도 하이킹을 한다.
④ 호수 주변에서 야영을 한다.
⑤ 트레킹 장비를 모두 제공한다.

10 다음 표를 보면서 대화를 듣고, 남자가 예약할 홀을 고르시오.

Concert Halls in Richmond City				
Hall	Available on June 22nd	Seats	Fee	Location
① A	×	180 seats	$450	downtown
② B	○	180 seats	$320	downtown
③ C	○	300 seats	$550	near school
④ D	○	170 seats	$600	downtown
⑤ E	○	200 seats	$400	near school

11 대화를 듣고, 여자의 마지막 말에 대한 남자의 응답으로 가장 적절한 것을 고르시오.

① It depends on where we want to go.
② I'd like a return ticket for my journey.
③ I've taken the airport limousine before.
④ It'll take about the same time for both.
⑤ The subway station is not far from here.

12 대화를 듣고, 남자의 마지막 말에 대한 여자의 응답으로 가장 적절한 것을 고르시오.

① Make sure you finish all your assignments.
② If I were you, I would talk to the professor.
③ If you didn't do it, then don't let it bother you.
④ Don't rely on chances, but do the best you can.
⑤ If you want a good grade, you have to be diligent.

13 대화를 듣고, 남자의 마지막 말에 대한 여자의 응답으로 가장 적절한 것을 고르시오. [3점]

▶ Woman :

① It's not fair. You can't say that.
② Okay. I'll have to read it here, then.
③ Thanks for telling me. Now I understand.
④ I see. I'd like to check out these two books.
⑤ Sorry. There is nothing you can borrow now.

14 대화를 듣고, 여자의 마지막 말에 대한 남자의 응답으로 가장 적절한 것을 고르시오.

▶ Man :

① Yes, there is. It's big enough for us.
② Don't worry. We will go look at it now.
③ It sounds excellent. Let's sign the contract.
④ Then I think this is exactly what you want.
⑤ Sure. You don't have to decide right away.

15 다음 상황 설명을 듣고, Tiffany가 Paul에게 할 말로 가장 적절한 것을 고르시오. [3점]

▶ Tiffany :

① I'll polish your shoes. Then they'll look better.
② Call customer service. I'm sure they can help you.
③ Go straight. You can find the shoe store on the right.
④ Call the shoe store. They can find larger sized shoes.
⑤ They look really good on you. The black color suits you well.

[16~17] 다음을 듣고, 물음에 답하시오.

16 여자가 하는 말의 주제로 가장 적절한 것은?

① ways of improving bone density
② the necessity for regular exercise in the teen years
③ the role of calcium in maintaining strong bones
④ developing habits that support good bone health
⑤ the importance of building strong bones in the teen years

17 언급된 활동이 <u>아닌</u> 것은?

① dancing   ② hiking
③ jogging   ④ yoga
⑤ walking

01

W: Hey, guys! Welcome to ZQ Art Gallery. Before we enter the gallery, I'm going to tell you some things that you should _____. First, respect the place we are going to visit. It's not a playground, so don't shout or run around. And make sure to only look at works of art _____ _____, not with your hands. Everyone has oils on their hands that can damage the art. So please don't touch. Just look and appreciate the works of art. _____ _____, about one meter away. You can take photos, but _____. You can feel hungry while exploring art, but you should enjoy your drinks and snacks only in the lobby and third-floor cafe. Now, are you ready to find a work of art that tells a story? OK! Let's go!

02

M: Mom, I'd like to get that jacket with a fur-lined hood. It looks very warm and comfortable.

W: Is the fur real or fake?

M: The clerk said it's real fox fur. Doesn't it look fancy?

W: Josh, I don't want you to wear anything with real fur.

M: I know _____, but it's just a small amount of decoration. And fur has been worn for centuries.

W: Yes, people have traditionally worn fur to survive cold winters, but they had no choice. But today we have _____.

M: Oh, yeah. I understand.

W: And modern technology provides us with good heating systems. Even worse is that _____ _____ to keep their fur at the best quality.

M: Really? That's terrible.

W: _____. Killing animals for fashion is wrong.

M: I see. I'll choose another jacket.

03

M: Where is your daughter?

W: She's in the living room. Please follow me.

M: Is she still _____?

W: She's getting better but still having trouble. Here she is.

M: What's her name?

W: Amber.

M: OK, Amber. I'm going to _____ _____. It'll help you breathe. Just relax. How long has she been this way?

W: It started around 8 o'clock, after dinner. She didn't have anything unusual for dinner. Will she be okay?

M: The oxygen mask is helping.

W: Oh, I know I shouldn't panic, but it really scared me. _____.

M: Don't worry. She's breathing normally now. But we really should _____ for some tests.

W: Okay. I'll prepare to leave right now.

04

W: Dad, I've just finished my drawing for the art contest.

M: Oh, let me see. Wow, it's a lovely drawing! This drawing seems to tell a story.

W: Yes, it's a story about a princess and a dragon.

M: Oh, it's a dragon! Right. It has _____ _____. It's sitting on a chair.

W: Yes, the dragon wants to have a cup of tea with the princess.

M: So there's a tea pot and _____. I like this table cloth with a flowery pattern. What is _____?

W: It's a mouse. This mouse wants to rescue the princess from the dragon.

M: What a great story! That's why the princess doesn't look so happy. Oh, _____ to drink some tea.

W: Yes. Can you see the tall tower on the right? She has been locked up there.

M: Oh, I see _____.
Does that have some meaning?

W: No, I just drew it. Should I remove it?

M: No, no. You really did a good job. I love this drawing.

05

M: Sarah, I'm going to see a movie this Saturday with Bruce and Scarlet. Do you want to join us?

W: I can't. It's my mother's birthday this Saturday. _____ and order a birthday cake.

M: You're a nice daughter. Oh, I've been to Yang's Kitchen downtown. They serve nice Chinese food.

W: Sounds great, but my mother doesn't like Chinese food. She likes Italian food.

M: I see. Why don't you look at _____?

W: Oh, that's a good idea. _____. I hope it's not too confusing.

M: Just choose one that has good reviews. I'm sure the reviews will help you decide. If you're busy, _____ for you.

W: How nice of you! That would be great.

M: Okay. I'll call you soon.

06

M: Kaitlyn, how about going to the musical, *Chicago*? Our local theater is performing it next month.

W: Sounds fantastic! I've always wanted to see it.

M: I'll get the tickets then.

W: How much are the tickets for that?

M: The most expensive seats are $150, and the cheapest ones are $50.

W: Wow, _____.

M: Let's get _____. They're rear orchestra seats, so they should be nice.

W: The total for both is $200. That's too expensive!

M: Don't worry. I got _____ coupon.

W: Really? That's great. But there should be a reservation fee, I guess.

M: That's right. But it's only a _____ _____. I'll reserve the tickets now.

W: Thank you so much. I'll treat you to dinner then.

07

W: Hello. You've reached Watson Company. Jennifer Rubin speaking.

M: Hello, Jennifer. It's Simon Kien. I'm afraid I'm going to be late today.

W: _____, or is your car having trouble?

M: No, it's not that. My mother _____ _____ at the airport last night, but she arrived this morning.

W: I guess _____.

M: Yes. Due to weather conditions, the flight couldn't take off on time.

W: All right. Oh, your mother lives in Vietnam, doesn't she?

M: Yes, she flew out to visit me. So I had to be there _____.

W: I see. You must be excited. And you have a meeting at 10 a.m. Will you be able to attend the meeting?

M: Sure. I just arrived home now. So _____ _____ 9:30 a.m.

W: Okay. If you can't make it, just call me.

M: Thanks, Jennifer.

08

W: Marcus, did you take the class, History of Food?

M: Yes, I took that class last semester. It's a freshmen class, isn't it?

W: No, _____.
The professor is James Mayers, right?

M: Yes, that's right. His class was interesting, and I liked the way he taught. And the class was _____.

W: How are discussions held?

M: He gave students the reading list for the class. We had to read the books before the class so that _____ in class.

W: That sounds a bit tough. What about the exams and grading?

M: There will be two tests, a mid-term and final, and a final essay. The professor evaluates your grade _____ and the essay.

W: Okay. Thanks for the information. I'll think about taking this class. See you.

M: I recommend it. It was a very worthwhile experience.

W: I'll keep that in mind.

09

M: Do you want to go hiking in green forests and visit a clear blue lake? Join us on this 2-day hike to Blue Lake, at the base of Mount Lapa. This is a tour _____.
On the first day, we will begin to hike at Santiago Village at nine. After hiking _____, we will reach Blue Lake (4,350m) at the base of Mt. Lapa. Later, we will camp _____. After breakfast, on Day 2, we will guide you to a small lookout to enjoy some special views. Later, we will go back down to Santiago Village. We will provide tents and tables. But you need to _____, such as sleeping bags and lanterns. Don't miss this amazing experience!

10

M: Hey, Jane. We have to find a hall to rent for our band's 3rd concert. Could you help me out?

W: Sure. First, when are you planning to hold the concert?

M: I'm planning to hold it _____.

W: Okay. How many people are you expecting?

M: I'd like a place that holds more than 150 people.

W: If you're looking at more than 150, how about getting a bigger place?

M: Well, if _____, it'll be too big. There'll be too many empty seats.

W: All right. What about your budget? How much can you spend?

M: We'd like to _____. We're trying to save money.

W: Then you have these two options. Look here. Which one do you like?

M: I like this one. Since _____, it'll be more convenient.

W: Sounds great. Then let's make a reservation.

11

W: Now _____ the downtown Grand Hotel from here?

M: We have two options. _____ the airport limousine _____ the subway.

W: Which one will get us there faster?

12

M: I got a D in History 201. I don't understand _____ _____.

W: Really? There must be something wrong. You had good attendance, and you did well on your exams.

M: That's exactly my point. _____.

13

W: Excuse me, _____?
Where can I find books about Old English?

M: Go to Section L over there. Can you see the sign?

W: Yes, I see. Thanks.

M: Excuse me. You _____.
It can be dangerous.

W: I'm sorry, but I couldn't find a ladder around here.

M: Do you want to get a book from _____
_____?

W: Yes, the book I want is on the top shelf, but I can't reach it.

M: I'll get it for you. Which one do you want?

W: The thick green book, titled "A Dictionary of the Old English Language."

M: Wait a second. Here you go.

W: _____ this book?

M: I'm sorry, but you can't. It's a reference book, so _____.

14

M: Come in, please. As I said, this is the biggest house on Maple Street.

W: Oh, _____! The living room is bright and spacious.

M: Right. It's got three bedrooms and two bathrooms.

W: First I'd like to see the kitchen.

M: It's right here. It's quite modern and _____
_____ — dishwasher, oven, microwave, and refrigerator.

W: That's very good. Is there a washing machine?

M: Yes, there's a washing machine and a dryer in the basement.

W: The house is perfect, but it's a little _____
_____.

M: You'll never find a house like this anywhere around here.

W: I know. Can you give me _____
_____?

15

W: Paul bought a pair of shoes cheap at a shoe store last week. He goes to school wearing those shoes this morning. When he takes off his shoes in the evening, he finds his feet are _____
from the color in the shoes. He calls the store _____ an exchange.
But the salesclerk _____.
The salesclerk says there is no refund or _____
_____. Paul is upset and asks his friend, Tiffany, for some advice. Tiffany feels that the store should change Paul's shoes with another pair. She had a similar situation before and dealt with the same problem. Tiffany wants to tell Paul _____. In this situation, what would Tiffany most likely say to Paul?

16~17

W: You may not think much about your bones, but you can't make a move without them. Strong bones help you look good, stay active, and feel your best. During the teen years, we make most of the bone that must _____.
Bone building is so important for teens because the teen years are _____
when new bone growth occurs faster than bone loss. If you don't gain sufficient bone strength as a teen, your bones are more likely to _____
_____ later in life. Moreover, those with weak bones are unlikely to recover quickly from injury. _____
_____ as a teenager, you can take part in a variety of fun activities, such as dancing or hiking with your friends. Or you can even go jogging or walking by yourself. Getting enough calcium is also critical. The important thing is that you should build bones that are _____
_____ during this time.

17회

01 다음을 듣고, 여자가 하는 말의 목적으로 가장 적절한 것을 고르시오.

① 청소 전문가의 강연을 소개하려고
② 간편한 청소 요령을 설명하려고
③ 청소 도구 판매를 광고하려고
④ 청소대행업체 이용을 권유하려고
⑤ 전자 제품점 할인 행사를 안내하려고

02 대화를 듣고, 남자의 의견으로 가장 적절한 것을 고르시오.

① 작은 일에 연연하면 큰일을 망칠 수 있다.
② 자녀가 스스로 자기 일을 하게 해야 한다.
③ 실수를 두려워하지 말고 일을 추진해야 한다.
④ 자녀의 실수를 질책하지 말고 격려해야 한다.
⑤ 여행 가방 싸는 것은 부모의 도움이 필요하다.

03 대화를 듣고, 두 사람의 관계를 가장 잘 나타낸 것을 고르시오.

① 작가 – 사진기자
② 광고 감독 – 광고주
③ 무대 감독 – 영화배우
④ 잡지 기자 – 편집장
⑤ 상점 직원 – 상점 주인

04 대화를 듣고, 그림에서 대화의 내용과 일치하지 <u>않는</u> 것을 고르시오.

05 대화를 듣고, 여자가 할 일로 가장 적절한 것을 고르시오.

① 수학 시험공부 도와주기
② 병원까지 차로 데려다주기
③ 교수님에게 사정 이야기해주기
④ 교수님에게 시험 연기 부탁하기
⑤ 교수님 전화번호 찾아 보내주기

06 대화를 듣고, 두 사람이 지불할 금액을 고르시오.

① $75
② $100
③ $120
④ $140
⑤ $160

07 대화를 듣고, 남자가 축구 동아리를 그만둔 이유를 고르시오.

① 식당을 개업하게 되어서
② 수영에 더 흥미가 생겨서
③ 축구 경기 중 부상을 당해서
④ 의사가 그만두라고 조언해서
⑤ 먼 곳으로 이사를 하게 되어서

08 대화를 듣고, Westside 통나무집에 관해 언급되지 <u>않은</u> 것을 고르시오.

① 숙박 요금
② 애완동물 허용 여부
③ 근처 상점과의 거리
④ 수도 시설
⑤ 인터넷 가능 여부

09 Trivia Track 게임 쇼에 관한 다음 내용을 듣고, 일치하지 <u>않는</u> 것을 고르시오.

① 현재 4명이 게임쇼에 출전하고 있다.
② 1등은 5만 달러의 상금과 여행 상품을 받는다.
③ 먼저 버저를 눌러야 답을 말할 수 있다.
④ 질문에 대한 답이 틀리면 5점을 잃는다.
⑤ 30점을 먼저 얻어야 1라운드에서 승리한다.

10 다음 표를 보면서 대화를 듣고, 여자가 선택한 자원봉사 그룹을 고르시오.

Volunteer Programs

Groups	Major	Type of Work	Required Language	Period
① A	science	helping research	English	6 months
② B	any	volunteer with elephants	English	one year
③ C	science	healthcare program	Spanish	3 months
④ D	architecture	temple repair	English	one year
⑤ E	any	child care program	Spanish	6 months

11 대화를 듣고, 여자의 마지막 말에 대한 남자의 응답으로 가장 적절한 것을 고르시오.

① Why? You have more than three days.
② I am very sorry for my late homework.
③ Let's work hard not to let it happen again.
④ Let me know if you need another extension.
⑤ I'm afraid I don't accept any late homework.

12 대화를 듣고, 남자의 마지막 말에 대한 여자의 응답으로 가장 적절한 것을 고르시오.

① Don't worry. Now try it and see if it works.
② Yes. It won't turn on if they're not connected.
③ That's a shame. I'm going to order a new one.
④ It's not dark enough. I think the ink has run out.
⑤ Really? I'd never even thought to check that!

13 대화를 듣고, 남자의 마지막 말에 대한 여자의 응답으로 가장 적절한 것을 고르시오. [3점]

▶ Woman :

① If you give me another 10% off, I'll buy them.
② I'll buy them then. I can't afford them right now.
③ That's how you can get the item at a cheaper price.
④ That'll be okay. But you'll have to wait a long time.
⑤ We might not have them by then. You should buy now.

14 대화를 듣고, 여자의 마지막 말에 대한 남자의 응답으로 가장 적절한 것을 고르시오. [3점]

▶ Man :

① It was so noisy that I couldn't sleep well.
② I agree with you. That was really irritating.
③ You can rely on me. I won't disappoint you again.
④ Same here. I should have asked for it to be warmer.
⑤ It was amazing. It created wonderful, dynamic sound.

15 다음 상황 설명을 듣고, Alex가 Caroline에게 할 말로 가장 적절한 것을 고르시오. [3점]

▶ Alex :

① I didn't mean to be late. There's heavy traffic.
② Please don't be mad at me. I want to be honest.
③ I'm sorry. I should have listened to what you said.
④ You were so stubborn. You made us late for dinner.
⑤ I'm sorry to hear that. You must have been frustrated.

[16~17] 다음을 듣고, 물음에 답하시오.

16 여자가 하는 말의 주제로 가장 적절한 것은?

① exercises for protecting our eyesight
② ways of helping prevent near-sightedness
③ effects of eating habits on our eyes' health
④ reasons for the increase of near-sightedness
⑤ the importance of proper lighting when reading

17 언급된 음식이 <u>아닌</u> 것은?

① carrots ② spinach ③ broccoli
④ almonds ⑤ strawberries

01

W: Yes! The famous blogger Masha Wells strongly recommended Wipe All. Its stainless steel handle and frame makes your cleaning easier and faster. It includes 2 wet mop pads and 1 dust mop pad _____ and effectively than cotton mops. When you clean your house, _____ the mop pads here and gently wipe. Take a look. Isn't the floor completely clean? Wipe All _____ _____ the floor perfectly clean. This is the time you've all been waiting for. We're giving you this great product _____ _____ of $36, 30% off the original price! Call us at 080-244-2290. Please hurry and order Wipe All now.

02

M: Honey, what are you doing?

W: _____ for Blake. He is going on a trip to New York.

M: Sophia, our son is old enough to pack his stuff for a trip.

W: But he's careless and always forgets something.

M: I understand it's hard to sit back and watch him make mistakes. But he'll _____ _____.

W: But if I don't pack his stuff, he'll be in trouble in New York.

M: I don't think so. By the way, where is he now?

W: He is reading a comic book in his room.

M: If he can't do his own packing, what can he do _____?

W: Okay. I'll _____ his suitcase now.

M: Yeah. We're just a guide. In life, there are no mistakes, only lessons.

03

W: Mr. Martin, I heard you wanted to see me.

M: Ah, Nicole. Have a seat here, please.

W: Sure.

M: It's about your article. I _____ your article with other members of the editing department.

W: You mean _____ with Conner McCarthy?

M: Yes, Conner McCarthy, the famous actor.

W: Is there anything wrong with it?

M: No, it's well-written, but _____ _____ in the magazine. The actor's face should be clearer and more natural.

W: I got it. I have several other photos. I'll send them to you as soon as possible.

M: All right. Then we can choose the proper photos among them. And you know _____ _____ is the 20th. Please send them soon.

W: Don't worry. I'll send them tomorrow morning.

04

M: Congratulations on opening your restaurant!

W: Thanks. I can't believe it. I just got the sample design of the exterior now.

M: Is this the sample? I like _____ _____ the main entrance.

W: I love how it goes so well with our door.

M: The sign board _____ is excellent.

W: The designer drew a fork, a spoon, and a knife on it. I really like them.

M: The chalkboard sign near the door is a great idea. You can _____ the day's specials and prices.

W: What about _____ the restaurant's front window?

M: It's a great idea for customers who are waiting. But I think a long bench would be better.

W: That's a good idea. They can wait on it together. Oh, what about the parasol on the right?

M: Nice idea. _____ from strong sunlight.

W: I'm glad you like it.

05

W: Tristan, you look worried. What's wrong?

M: I just got a phone call from my neighbor, and she said my mom _____ and got hurt.

W: How awful! Then you need to go home and take her to the hospital, don't you?

M: She called 911 for an ambulance, but I have to go to the hospital.

W: Oh, you should. I hope it's not serious.

M: Well, but _____ this afternoon. It's an important test.

W: Don't worry. If that's the case, I'm sure the professor will understand and you can take it another time. Who is your professor?

M: Dr. Heywood. Philip Heywood.

W: I know him. I think he can understand. If you want, I'll _____.

M: Well, no, I think I should tell him myself. Diana, could you find his phone number and _____ _____? I have to go to the hospital now.

W: Okay. I will. Go ahead.

06

W: Michael, look at that mug. It looks like a ceramic mug, but it's a stainless steel mug.

M: Wow, great. It's been made specifically to keep coffee warm.

W: And it's lighter than ceramic mugs.

M: That's true. Should we give this mug as a gift for all our employees? They're only 15 dollars each.

W: It's been a year since our store's opening, and I think it's a good idea.

M: Oh, there are _____. Each set includes one mug and ten tea bags. _____ _____.

W: They're more expensive, but I think our staff would like them better. Let's get some tea sets then.

M: We have _____,

right?

W: No, we can't forget the part-time employees.

M: That's right. We have _____ _____, right?

W: Yes. Let's get them.

07

W: Oh, hi, Stephen. I didn't expect to see you here.

M: Hi, Jasmine. We seem to be running into each other everywhere.

W: I know. What brings you here? It's Friday, and your soccer club practices every Friday, doesn't it?

M: Yeah, but _____.

W: Why? Was it too tough?

M: Actually, I have heart problems. _____ _____ that I should swim _____ _____.

W: Oh, is it serious?

M: No, but my doctor said the best thing is to _____. How about you?

W: I just love the water because I was raised by the beachside. After moving to the city, I've tried to come to the swimming pool as often as I can.

M: Anyway, how about having lunch with me?

W: Sounds good. There's a restaurant that has great pasta around here.

08

M: I'm here to find out some information for my summer vacation.

W: Please have a seat. Where are you planning to go?

M: I'm _____ a log cabin in Colorado for a week from June 12th.

W: Then we have a good place. Look at this photo. This Westside Log Cabin is located near Pikes Park. It's priced _____.

M: It looks great. Oh, I have a dog. Can I take my dog?

W: Sure. _____ in this log cabin. It has two bedrooms and a kitchen.

M: Good. Are there grocery stores in the area for me to pick up food?

W: Of course. It's just _____ the grocery store.

M: Does it have Wi-Fi service or Internet access?

W: No, the log cabin has electricity _____ _____ Internet service.

M: No problem. I'll just leave my laptop at home then. It's not a big deal. Can you make the arrangements for me?

09

M: Hello and welcome to our game show, Trivia Track! Now _____ our grand prize. As you know, _____ _____ $50,000 in cash and a six-day vacation to Bali! The rules are very simple. The first round is basic question and answer. I'll ask a question, and whoever knows the answer _____ _____ in front of them. The person who answers the question correctly gets five points. If the answer is wrong, you lose two points. If you don't know an answer, say "pass." _____ wins the first round. Have you got it? Now, for the first question. Listen carefully and push the buzzer as soon as you know the answer. Which European river flows through six different countries?

10

W: I saw your advertisement in the newspaper for various volunteer programs, and I'd like to sign up for something.

M: Thanks for coming. What type of work would you like to do?

W: I'm not quite sure. _____.

M: Then you can choose these four groups.

W: All right, but I don't think I can do healthcare work. I'm _____ another healthcare program.

M: Oh, okay. Can you speak Spanish by any chance?

W: No, I'm afraid not.

M: Okay. Then you can't choose this one because they want volunteers _____. How long could you volunteer?

W: I'd like to volunteer _____. I'm going to join a camp this winter, so I can't work any longer than that.

M: Okay. I guess this is your only option, then.

W: Thanks. I'd like to sign up now.

11

W: Excuse me, professor. I have to talk to you about my biology homework. I wasn't able to finish it.

M: _____, isn't it?

W: Yes, it is. But I was sick. Could you _____ _____ my paper until Thursday?

12

M: Natalie, what's wrong with the computer? Let me take a look at it.

W: The printer isn't working. _____ the repair center?

M: No, there's nothing wrong with the printer. _____ _____.

13

M: Hello. How can I help you?

W: I'd like to get a pair of sandals.

M: How about these white sandals? I guess you're a size 7 or 8. Would you like to try them on?

W: Yes, my size is 8. _____.

M: They look great on you.

W: Oh, dear! Is the price $189 like it says here on the price tag? Are you offering any discounts by any chance?

M: _____ right now.

W: Oh, I see. That would definitely be _____ _____. When do you plan to have a sale?

M: The department store will have _____ _____ on the 11th of this month.

14

M: How did you like the movie?

W: Actually, it was a little disappointing.

M: I agree. _____ my expectations.

W: I think I expected too much from the movie because of the reviews. This movie got such good reviews, didn't it?

M: Yeah, right. But _____ _____.

W: The storyline was bad. I didn't understand why the main character refused to explain anything to his friends.

M: Exactly! That _____ _____.

W: Also, the heating system in the theater was awful. _____ a bunch of bees buzzing and was far too hot.

15

M: Caroline and Alex are a couple, and they've been invited to one of their friends' houses. The dinner is at 6 o'clock, and they leave their home early. Unfortunately, their GPS isn't working. They try to call their friend, but his phone is turned off. Caroline _____ at a gas station and _____, but Alex refuses to ask for help. He says he can _____ since he's been in this area before. But they get lost. Finally, Caroline finds someone who gives clear directions. Still, they are late for the dinner appointment in the end. When they arrive at the friend's house, Alex _____ Caroline for what he did. In this situation, what would Alex most likely say to Caroline?

16~17

W: Hello, class. Do you wear glasses? More and more teenagers wear glasses because they can't see far objects easily. What can you do to prevent this condition? First and foremost, doctors strongly suggest you get _____ for possible signs of near-sightedness. Early detection is crucial. Also, _____ _____ of moisture within your eyes is one of the most important things you can do to keep your eyes healthy. Make sure _____ _____ when reading a book. You can also help your eyes by getting plenty of vitamins A and C. Some foods containing vitamin A are sweet potatoes, carrots, and spinach. Broccoli, strawberries, and oranges have a lot of vitamin C. Since your eyes are put under constant strain and stress while watching TV and staring at computer screens and smartphones, you must _____ from time to time. You should treat your eyes like you do your body by exercising them and giving them rest. I hope you keep these points in mind to maintain good eye health.

18회

✻ 첫단추 듣기실전편

01 다음을 듣고, 남자가 하는 말의 목적으로 가장 적절한 것을 고르시오.

① 강변 안전시설 확충을 요청하려고
② 농구 우승 축하 행사를 공지하려고
③ 장학 기금 모금 참여를 당부하려고
④ 선행 학생에게 장학금을 수여하려고
⑤ 의사자 추모 장학금 제정을 기념하려고

02 대화를 듣고, 여자의 의견으로 가장 적절한 것을 고르시오.

① 영화 제작에서 표현의 자유를 제한해서는 안 된다.
② 지나치게 폭력적인 영화는 사회에 해로운 영향을 준다.
③ 영화의 청소년 관람가 등급을 엄격하게 적용해야 한다.
④ 불법 영화 복제를 근절해야 영화 산업이 발전할 수 있다.
⑤ 많은 사람이 관람했다고 해서 반드시 좋은 영화는 아니다.

03 대화를 듣고, 두 사람의 관계를 가장 잘 나타낸 것을 고르시오.

① 선생님 – 학부모
② 마라톤 코치 – 선수
③ 취업 면접관 – 지원자
④ 스포츠 기자 – 아나운서
⑤ 선거 운동원 – 선거 후보

04 대화를 듣고, 그림에서 대화의 내용과 일치하지 않는 것을 고르시오.

05 대화를 듣고, 남자가 할 일로 가장 적절한 것을 고르시오.

① 부동산 방문하기
② 사업계획 제출하기
③ 사촌에게 전화하기
④ 제빵 기구 구입하기
⑤ 창업 자금 신청하기

06 대화를 듣고, 남자가 지불할 금액을 고르시오. [3점]

① $30
② $50
③ $80
④ $100
⑤ $120

07 대화를 듣고, 남자가 책을 할인해 준 이유를 고르시오.

① 중고 도서라서
② 단골 고객이라서
③ 표지가 손상되어서
④ 적립금을 사용해서
⑤ 학생 할인을 해줘서

08 대화를 듣고, Guinea Pigs에 관해 언급되지 않은 것을 고르시오.

① 크기
② 먹이
③ 평균 수명
④ 보충 영양제
⑤ 성향

09 Green Sports Center에 관한 다음 내용을 듣고, 일치하지 않는 것을 고르시오.

① 개장한 지 5년이 되었다.
② 대학 재학생의 연회비는 37달러이다.
③ 등록은 월요일부터 목요일에 가능하다.
④ 등록 시 학생증과 사진이 필요하다.
⑤ 시설 이용 시 학생증을 지참해야 한다.

10 다음 표를 보면서 대화를 듣고, 두 사람이 구매할 냉장고를 고르시오.

	Refrigerators — Good House Keeping				
	Model	Door Type	Price	Customer Review	Warranty (years)
①	A	4-door	$2,200	★★★★☆	3
②	B	3-door	$1,800	★★★★☆	3
③	C	2-door	$1,900	★★★★⯪	5
④	D	3-door	$2,400	★★★⯪☆	5
⑤	E	2-door	$1,700	★★⯪☆☆	2

11 대화를 듣고, 여자의 마지막 말에 대한 남자의 응답으로 가장 적절한 것을 고르시오.

① Don't worry about it. I'll take care of it.
② I think so. It's time to try something new.
③ Exactly. I also scored pretty well on tests.
④ You always say that. That's just an excuse.
⑤ I was upset. I made a big mistake on my test.

12 대화를 듣고, 남자의 마지막 말에 대한 여자의 응답으로 가장 적절한 것을 고르시오.

① Sorry. But I've never taken the class before.
② I can show you. I have a class around there.
③ All right. I'll sign up for the class on Monday.
④ No problem. Just tell me which building it's in.
⑤ Very good. There are two classes that are still open.

13 대화를 듣고, 남자의 마지막 말에 대한 여자의 응답으로 가장 적절한 것을 고르시오. [3점]

▶ Woman :

① Thank you so much. I'll never forget this day.
② My pleasure. It was really nice to meet you, too.
③ That's right. The "cheese" sound makes you smile.
④ You need to calm down a bit. You're so excited.
⑤ I really envy you. I want to meet him in person, too!

14 대화를 듣고, 여자의 마지막 말에 대한 남자의 응답으로 가장 적절한 것을 고르시오. [3점]

▶ Man :

① That's right. They are due back in a month.
② I'm sorry. I'll return them as soon as possible.
③ There is nothing that I can do if it doesn't work.
④ It's because there are late fees for unreturned books.
⑤ Don't worry. I'm sending the book list by e-mail.

15 다음 상황 설명을 듣고, Laura가 Nelson 선생님에게 할 말로 가장 적절한 것을 고르시오.

▶ Laura :

① I'll see if I can figure out the problem.
② I think you should encourage your children.
③ I feel relieved to hear she behaves well in school.
④ I think I should advise her to be polite in your class.
⑤ I've always been proud of you ever since you were a kid.

[16~17] 다음을 듣고, 물음에 답하시오.

16 여자가 하는 말의 주제로 가장 적절한 것은?

① health benefits of home cooking
② negative effects of eating instant foods
③ how to grow vegetables in an organic way
④ the importance of eating a widely varied diet
⑤ the value of eating plain and simple food for health

17 언급된 음식이 <u>아닌</u> 것은?

① corn ② salmon ③ melon
④ onions ⑤ tomatoes

01

M: We are gathered here today to remember a special person. Jonathan Adams was an Asher High School student. He was a basketball player, and he was _____ whenever he could. A year ago on this day, Jonathan was running along a riverbank. When he saw two boys fall into the river, he jumped into the water immediately and saved them. But after rescuing them, he was swept away by the river. Today, Asher High School has set up _____ _____ Jonathan Adams. This scholarship will help students who are not financially able to go to college. This is _____ _____ and remember him the best way we can.

02

W: What did you think of the movie?

M: I liked it. I like these kinds of movies.

W: Really? I didn't like it. I don't know _____ _____.

M: They probably want to show how cruel humans can be.

W: Then, they should do it in a more artistic way, not this way of just showing blood.

M: Well, just enjoy it. You're too serious sometimes.

W: But it is serious. Violent movies can affect people.

M: Do you really think so?

W: Yes! Some movie producers make these kinds of movies for money, but they really _____ _____.

M: I don't think so. People like violent movies because violence is part of human nature.

W: These movies _____ _____. They're very dangerous.

03

M: Are you ready, Erin?

W: I'm not sure.

M: _____. You've had plenty of practice for the past few months.

W: I just hope I can do what I did during my practice sessions.

M: I'm sure you'll do even better. Just remember _____ in the beginning. Twenty-six miles is a long run.

W: I know. I'll keep that in mind.

M: You already know the course. When you're running, try to hold the same pace.

W: Got it. Do you think I can break my own record?

M: I trust you. _____, so all you have to do is do your best.

W: I'll take your word for it. I guess that's all I can do.

M: Now, let's do some warming up.

04

M: What is this picture? It looks like a wax museum.

W: Yes, a wax museum in Seoul. It's the room of "Great Men of Korea."

M: Who is this woman on the left? She is sitting _____ _____.

W: She was a famous artist. And the man next to her was a great general.

M: Oh, he is wearing a hat with feathers and holding a stick.

W: Can you see me near him?

M: Yes, you're standing next to him and _____ _____.

W: Actually, I wanted to raise both my hands, but I couldn't because of the bag in my left hand.

M: You look good. Is the man on the right a king? He is sitting on a large chair.

W: Yes, he is King Sejong the Great. He created the Korean alphabet, Hangeul. _____ _____.

M: Oh, there's a big book behind him, too!

05

W: Greg, you'll never believe this. I just got the most amazing news!

M: What? What happened?

W: I just got the money I needed to open my own bakery!

M: Really? That's great news. Congratulations!

W: I _____ pies and cupcakes since those are my favorite things to bake!

M: That sounds like a wonderful idea. And now _____!

W: It has! Now I need to find the location for my bakery. It's the most difficult thing for me.

M: Do you need professional help? My cousin is _____. If you want, _____.

W: Can you do that? I really need some advice.

M: Sure. _____. I'm sure he can be very helpful to you.

W: That sounds good.

06

W: Hello. I'm calling from "Angel Covers" foundation.

M: I don't want to buy that. I'm busy.

W: No, I'm not a telemarketer. We're _____ _____.

M: Oh, you're doing fine work.

W: I'm calling you to ask if you would like to _____ _____. They're $10 per box.

M: Well, can I ask what you do exactly?

W: We work to provide food, health care, and education to people in need.

M: Oh, I see. How many cards are in the box?

W: Each box includes 12 different cards. And these are designed just for Angel Covers.

M: Oh, then I'd like _____.

W: Thanks. Most of the purchase price goes to people in need.

M: That sounds great. _____ _____.

W: Thanks a lot.

07

M: Can I help you? Are you looking for something?

W: Yes, _____ the foreign language section.

M: Oh, it's right above you. That is the foreign language section up there.

W: I'm looking for Garcia Marquez's novel. Oh, it's on the top shelf. Can you get the red book _____ _____ for me?

M: This one? Here it is.

W: Thanks. It's 26 dollars. Oh, _____ _____. Do you have another copy?

M: No, that's the last one.

W: What should I do? It looks like a used book.

M: It's not a used book, but _____ a 50% discount because its cover is damaged.

W: Really? That would be great. I'll take it.

M: Okay. Please follow me.

08

W: Patrick, do you have a pet?

M: Yes, I have two guinea pigs. I have a picture of them in my cell phone. Look!

W: Oh, how cute they are! _____?

M: They are about 10 inches long and weigh 2 to 3 pounds.

W: Their cage is pretty big.

M: Yes, they need a lot of room to run, so I made a large homemade cage for them.

W: That's very good. How long do guinea pigs live?

M: On average, they live about 5 to 7 years. Do you know they need to _____ _____ like humans?

W: Really? That's interesting! So do you give them vitamin C tablets?

M: Yes. Also, they are very _____ and _____.

09

W: Thank you. Welcome to the Green Sports Center. I'm happy that so many of you have been coming here to use _____ since we opened 5 years ago. All students at the college can be members of this sports center for an annual fee of $37. To register, you need to _____ _____ in the lobby, between 2 and 6 p.m., Monday to Thursday. Now, there are two things that you must remember _____ _____ when you come to register. These are your student card and a recent photograph of yourself. After registering, you will receive a sports card, and _____ _____ with you whenever you use the Sports Center facilities.

10

W: Honey, what about buying a new refrigerator? Ours is so old.

M: Yeah, we really need a new refrigerator. _____ _____ online. How about this one?

W: I don't like the 4-door type. They don't have much room inside.

M: Then let's choose a 3-door or 2-door type.

W: Okay, and I think we can pay up to 2,000 dollars. But _____.

M: I agree. But the cheapest one got bad customer reviews. It received 2.5 out of 5 stars.

W: I don't want to buy it. Let's choose one which got 4 or 4.5 stars _____.

M: Then there are two options we can choose from.

W: I think a warranty is very important. Let's choose the one _____.

M: I agree. Let's order this one right now.

11

W: You're late again, Steve. I think you need to do some studying and prepare for the final exam.

M: Mom, I can't study all the time. I need a break once in a while.

W: If you want to get a good grade, you need to _____.

12

M: Excuse me. I can't find my class. Could you _____ _____?

W: Of course, what room number is it?

M: It's room 612 in the Pearson building.

13

W: Excuse me, but are you Mr. Downey?

M: Yes, that's right. Are you a tourist?

W: Yes, I'm here in Bali on vacation. I can't believe _____ here.

M: Well, it's really me.

W: I'm a huge fan of yours. I've been a fan since your first movie.

M: Really? Then _____.

W: Yeah, I've sent you many fan letters in the past. Meeting you here is like a dream come true.

M: It's a pleasure to meet you, too.

W: Oh, can I _____ here? My name is Anne Palmer.

M: I'd be honored to, Anne.

W: Would you mind _____ _____?

M: Of course not. Say "cheese!"

14

M: Hello? This is Dr. Russell.

W: Dr. Russell, this is Jessica Blower in the Central Library.

M: Oh, hi. I was trying to call you. _____ _____?

W: Let's see. Uh... They will arrive in two weeks. Is that okay with you?

M: Yeah, it will be all right.

W: By the way, Dr. Russell, did you receive the list of books that _____?

M: List? No, I don't think so.

W: We e-mailed an individual list to each professor. We hope that you will return _____ _____ by July 10th.

M: Just a moment. I'll open my e-mail. Yes, I got the mail.

W: There are many books that have not been returned. So we ask all professors _____ _____ by July 10th.

15

W: Laura is the mother of 11-year-old Christine. Today is Parent-Teacher Conferences at Christine's school. She goes to her daughter's school and sees her teacher, Mr. Nelson. Laura asks him _____ in school. Actually, she is worried about Christine because she is quiet and shy but sometimes _____ _____. But to her surprise, Mr. Nelson says Christine is a very good student. When Laura tells him she is worried about her daughter, Mr. Nelson says Christine _____ _____ and learning. He says she tries to actively participate in the class activities. Laura is very surprised but feels good. In this situation, what would Laura most likely say to Mr. Nelson?

16~17

W: Are you a person who enjoys eating out? If so, I'd like to give you some advice. Much of today's cooking, particularly in restaurants, is designed to excite the senses more than to provide _____ _____. This comes with the risk of forgetting the pleasures of simple foods. Can you still _____ an ear of sweet corn, just picked, lightly cooked, and eaten plain without butter or salt? Or a slice of really fresh salmon only with lemon? Or a section of perfectly ripe melon? If you cannot imagine salad and tomatoes without creamy dressing, then _____ plain foods. I am not urging you to live on oatmeal and water. Once we become accustomed to eating spicy foods, we want even stronger flavors. My concern is that if strong flavors are the main appeal of food, _____. The ingredients that create these strong flavors can cause a variety of health problems as well as stomach pain. So, why not try to relearn _____ _____ for your health?

01 다음을 듣고, 남자가 하는 말의 목적으로 가장 적절한 것을 고르시오.

① 구취 방지 요령을 소개하려고
② 치아 미백 제품을 광고하려고
③ 치아 교정의 부작용을 설명하려고
④ 치아 건강의 중요성을 강조하려고
⑤ 인체에 무해한 치약 개발을 촉구하려고

02 대화를 듣고, 여자의 의견으로 가장 적절한 것을 고르시오.

① 쓰레기 분리수거를 의무화해야 한다.
② 바다의 중금속 오염 방지 대책이 필요하다.
③ 환경을 위해 충전용 건전지를 사용해야 한다.
④ 오염을 막기 위해 폐건전지는 재활용해야 한다.
⑤ 지하수 오염을 막기 위한 법규 개정이 필요하다.

03 대화를 듣고, 두 사람의 관계를 가장 잘 나타낸 것을 고르시오.

① 식당 종업원 – 손님   ② 관광 가이드 – 여행객
③ 박물관 직원 – 관람객   ④ 서점 직원 – 지도 구매자
⑤ 관광안내소 직원 – 관광객

04 대화를 듣고, 그림에서 대화의 내용과 일치하지 <u>않는</u> 것을 고르시오.

05 대화를 듣고, 여자가 할 일로 가장 적절한 것을 고르시오.

① 파티 일자 변경 알리기
② 친지에게 안부 전화하기
③ 생신 케이크 주문 취소하기
④ 식당 예약인원 변경 알리기
⑤ 생신 파티 초대 명단 만들기

06 대화를 듣고, 남자가 지불할 금액을 고르시오. [3점]

① $60   ② $70   ③ $80
④ $90   ⑤ $110

07 대화를 듣고, 여자가 룸메이트를 바꾸고 싶은 이유를 고르시오.

① 친구를 많이 초대해서
② 컴퓨터로 밤새 영화를 봐서
③ 방을 너무 더럽게 사용해서
④ 시끄러워 공부할 수 없어서
⑤ 자기 물건을 허락 없이 써서

08 대화를 듣고, 독서 클럽에 관해 언급되지 <u>않은</u> 것을 고르시오.

① 모임 인원   ② 모임 장소
③ 모임 횟수   ④ 책의 종류
⑤ 책 선정 방법

09 Four Corners Community Band에 관한 다음 내용을 듣고, 일치하지 <u>않는</u> 것을 고르시오.

① 매주 월요일 밤에 모임을 갖는다.
② 18세가 넘는 성인이면 참가할 수 있다.
③ 오디션은 1월과 7월에 실시한다.
④ 회비는 연습실 대여료로 사용된다.
⑤ 신청자는 이메일로 접수하면 된다.

10 다음 표를 보면서 대화를 듣고, 두 사람이 구매할 텀블러를 고르시오.

Tumblers for Sale

Model	Volume(ml)	Material	Handle	Price
① A	350	plastic	✕	$19
② B	450	stainless	✕	$27
③ C	500	stainless	✕	$35
④ D	500	stainless	○	$38
⑤ E	700	plastic	○	$30

11 대화를 듣고, 여자의 마지막 말에 대한 남자의 응답으로 가장 적절한 것을 고르시오.

① Of course. I have read it several times.
② Why not? I'll let you know when I'm done.
③ Thanks for understanding. I'll return it tomorrow.
④ Okay. I was wondering if you can lend me the book.
⑤ That's what I think. You'll get better grades next time.

12 대화를 듣고, 남자의 마지막 말에 대한 여자의 응답으로 가장 적절한 것을 고르시오.

① You're still not prepared to meet him now.
② If so, we need to leave this area immediately.
③ I have no choice but to cancel the meeting then.
④ The weather information isn't available at this time.
⑤ Call him and find out the reason for the cancellation.

13 대화를 듣고, 남자의 마지막 말에 대한 여자의 응답으로 가장 적절한 것을 고르시오.

▶ Woman :

① Sorry. I'll pay attention for such a call.
② Yes. Please give me Mr. Carter's number.
③ I understand. We could talk about it later.
④ Okay. I'll try not to let anyone disturb you.
⑤ Don't worry. I'll order a sandwich for lunch.

14 대화를 듣고, 여자의 마지막 말에 대한 남자의 응답으로 가장 적절한 것을 고르시오. [3점]

▶ Man :

① I see. Thanks for your advice.
② Great. I'm sure it'll refresh you.
③ My pleasure. It's no trouble at all.
④ Yes. I'm concerned about your grade.
⑤ That's okay. I don't want to bother you.

15 다음 상황 설명을 듣고, Deborah의 상사가 Deborah에게 할 말로 가장 적절한 것을 고르시오. [3점]

▶ Deborah's boss :

① Sure. The hospital is across the street.
② Don't worry. We need you to be healthy.
③ I can trust him this time. He's got one more day.
④ I understand. You'll have to do Ronald's work.
⑤ The project is due tomorrow. We need to hurry.

[16~17] 다음을 듣고, 물음에 답하시오.

16 여자가 하는 말의 주제로 가장 적절한 것은?

① nutrients for shaping children's bodies
② effective ways to strengthen children's bodies
③ how to help children have the ideal body shape
④ the necessity of preparing children for changes
⑤ the importance of building positive body images for children

17 언급된 증상이 아닌 것은?

① depression
② anxiety
③ excessive thirst
④ a lack of minerals
⑤ growth delay

01

M: Would you like to light up the room with your smile? It can be done. Most people aren't aware of _____ a bright smile. Our product can be used at home without visiting the dentist. Just apply the product to your teeth every night after your regular brushing. It's that simple. Maintain your usual cleaning habits, and after just a few days, your teeth _____ _____. Unlike similar products, ours is guaranteed not to hurt sensitive gums. Why wait? _____ at www.whiteteeth.com and _____. You'll see why our company has the highest sales of all dental product companies in the nation.

02

W: Bruce, can you help me clean the basement?

M: Sure, Mom. Oh, there are some old batteries in this box here.

W: They're used batteries. I've kept them there.

M: Can I throw away these old batteries with the other garbage?

W: No, you shouldn't do that. They contain harmful metals and chemicals _____ _____ and water supply.

M: Really?

W: Yes, if you do that, _____ _____. American people throw away about 180,000 tons of batteries per year.

M: Wow, that's a lot of batteries.

W: Yes, _____.

M: Oh, I see. Then what should we do?

W: I'll send them to a battery recycling center tomorrow.

M: Okay. Then I'll just leave this box here.

03

M: If you have any questions while we're going along, please _____.

W: I have a question actually.

M: Sure, what's that?

W: _____ once we get inside the museum?

M: Oh, I'm glad you asked that. I forgot to mention that taking photographs inside the art gallery and the museum is not allowed.

W: Okay. And what time do we have lunch?

M: After visiting the museum, _____ _____ at 12:15 exactly. Then we'll have lunch.

W: Okay. I have another question. I'd like to know if we're going to visit any castles today.

M: No, I'm afraid all of the castles are far from the city. We're going to visit them tomorrow.

W: Oh, thanks for the information.

M: My pleasure. I'll give you a map. It shows where _____.

04

W: Brian, our wedding planner just e-mailed us our wedding-invitation card design.

M: Let me see. Oh, it's pretty.

W: Yeah, they put a banner saying "WEDDING DAY" at the top left.

M: Right. There are _____ _____ under the banner.

W: I like this heart between them. And they placed our names, Brian and Emily, under the birds.

M: That's great. There's also the wedding date and time at the bottom left. June 16th, Saturday, 3 o'clock in the afternoon. Perfect!

W: What do you think of this bride-and-groom image on the right?

M: The bride looks great. She is wearing a wedding gown and a long veil.

W: I agree. But _____ _____. It looks funny.

M: I think so. Why don't you call them and _____
_____? That's the only thing
we want to change.

W: Okay. I'll do that.

05

W: Honey, did you order a cake for your mother's
birthday party?

M: No, I didn't yet. _____.
Oh, did you make a reservation for the birthday
dinner already?

W: Of course. Seven Hills is a fancy and popular
restaurant, so _____.

M: How many people did you reserve for?

W: I reserved a table for twelve people.

M: Then we need to _____
_____ to ten.

W: Why?

M: I just got a call from Aunt Sophia this afternoon.
Her husband, Uncle Jerry, hurt his back.

W: I'm sorry to hear that.

M: She said she has to take care of him, so those two
can't come to the party.

W: Okay. I'll call the restaurant and _____
_____ while you order the
cake.

M: Thanks, honey.

06

W: Good afternoon. How can I help you?

M: I'd like to buy some coffee beans.

W: We have various types of coffee beans. _____
_____?

M: I like coffee from Kenya. Can I know its roasting
date?

W: Its roasting date was a week ago. _____
_____ are from Ethiopia and Columbia.

M: How much are they?

W: The Ethiopian coffee and Kenyan coffee are
_____ a pack, and the Columbian coffee is
_____ a pack.

M: Hmm... I'll take one pack of Ethiopian coffee and
one pack of Columbian coffee. The fresh coffee
_____.

W: Right. Is there anything else?

M: I also want one pack of paper filters, the big size.
_____.

W: They are _____ a pack. Okay. One Ethiopian
coffee, one Columbian coffee, and a pack of coffee
filters.

M: Right.

07

M: Hi! What are you doing here at the library? Are
you studying?

W: No, I watched a movie in the media room. What
about you?

M: I'm _____. You look upset.
What's wrong?

W: It's because of my roommate. I don't want to go
into our room.

M: Oh, does she always have guests over?

W: No, she doesn't have many friends.

M: Then does she _____
_____?

W: No, she doesn't. But _____
_____. Her hair covers the floor, and she throws
away her trash on the floor.

M: Oh, that's terrible.

W: Yeah! I have cleaned the room, but it gets dirty
again two hours later.

M: Did you talk to her about it?

W: Yes, I did, but nothing's changed. I'll ask the
dormitory manager _____.

08

M: Oh, hi, Rachel. You're reading a book.

W: I've got my book club this evening, but I haven't had time to finish the book.

M: You're in a book club? What do you do? I mean what is the club?

W: Well, we're a group of friends. _____ _____. We meet in a local cafe and talk about the book we've read.

M: You like reading. So _____ _____?

W: It's usually a novel, but sometimes we read a biography or something like that.

M: And who chooses it?

W: We all do. We suggest books that _____ _____ and then decide together.

M: That's cool.

W: If you are interested, just tell me.

M: Okay. I'll think about it!

09

M: I'd like to invite anyone _____ _____ a high school band to join the Four Corners Community Band. We meet _____ _____ from 7 p.m. to 9 p.m in the Cortez Community Hall. The band plays all styles of music, including classical and jazz. The band is open to _____. Membership fees are $20 twice a year. Members must pay in January and again in July. Membership fees are used for the rental of our practice room. _____. If you want to join us, please e-mail us! We'd love for you to come join us!

10

W: We need to get tumblers for Christmas gifts for our staff.

M: Of course. Let's buy them online.

W: Okay. Let's check a price comparison website.

M: There's one here. It has _____ to choose from. First, which size of tumblers do you want?

W: Between 350 to 500 ml. Something bigger than 500 ml is _____.

M: Okay. I think plastic would be better since it's much lighter.

W: No, stainless steel is better because it's the safest material for hot drinks and easy to clean. _____ _____.

M: All right. I didn't know that. And how about _____? Sometimes the handles are inconvenient with a car's cup holders.

W: I agree. Then let's order this one because our maximum price is $30 per tumbler.

M: All right. I'll order 15 tumblers.

11

W: Hunter, _____ which Dr. Levi recommended to us?

M: Yes, I did. It's almost $60, quite expensive. I've almost finished the book.

W: Well, when you're finished with the book, _____ _____?

12

M: Camila! All flights to Florida have been canceled due to the hurricane.

W: Really? My flight is scheduled for 2:35 p.m. I have a meeting with a client there.

M: That's too bad! _____ _____.

13

M: Good afternoon, Sydney. Did anyone call me while I was out?

W: Yes, Mr. Carter called an hour ago. He'd like you _____ at this number as soon as possible.

M: I see.

W: Mr. Carter said _____.

M: Okay. I'll call him right away. By the way, _____ my appointment with the dentist?

W: Yes, it's next Tuesday afternoon at 3 p.m.

M: Good. I'm quite busy today. I have to finish up this report by 2.

W: I see. If you don't have time for lunch, I'll prepare some sandwiches.

M: Thanks, Sydney. I want to fully focus on my report. Whoever calls me, _____ _____.

14

M: Miranda, you look depressed. Is there anything wrong?

W: I made many mistakes in the mid-term exam.

M: Come on. _____. I'm sure you'll do better next time.

W: Lately I can't seem to remember what I've studied.

M: Maybe you should _____. That might help your memory.

W: Are you sure?

M: Yes! A lot of research has shown that after exercise, people _____ of memory and attention.

W: _____.

M: If your brain has to concentrate for hours at a time, it loses the ability to remember things.

W: Okay. I'll walk when I feel tired while studying.

15

M: Deborah recently took on a big project at her company and she is working very hard. Today she doesn't feel very well and has _____ _____. Seeing that Deborah is really sick, her co-worker, Ronald, tells her to go home and take a rest. Since Deborah is finding it difficult to work, she asks her boss if she can take the rest of the day off. Her boss says _____ because he clearly sees that she is ill. Deborah apologizes because she has so much left to do for the project. But her boss thinks that _____ _____ to perform well for the project. In this situation, what would Deborah's boss most likely say to Deborah?

16~17

W: We want our kids to feel great about themselves and their appearance. But most teens say they don't feel thin enough or attractive enough. Although 80% of youth have a normal body weight, over 60% are unhappy _____ _____ and want to change their weight. In a society where thinness is important, young people's weight and appearance naturally affect _____. This can quickly become a huge problem with symptoms of depression, stress, and anxiety. Body image worries can lead to unhealthy dieting and food obsessions. These behaviors can result in a lack of vitamins and minerals, and growth delays. We can help our children lay the foundation for _____ _____ early on. We can give our kids the sense that they are beautiful regardless of how they look. We can support them by _____ about the body. Remember, the body concept our sons and daughters develop in their early years _____ _____ into adulthood.

20회

01 다음을 듣고, 여자가 하는 말의 목적으로 가장 적절한 것을 고르시오.

① 신축 개장한 호텔을 광고하려고
② 호텔 개축 공사 지침을 제시하려고
③ 호텔 신입 사원들에게 호텔을 안내하려고
④ 관광객에게 호텔 편의 시설을 홍보하려고
⑤ 사원들에게 회사의 경영 방침을 설명하려고

02 대화를 듣고, 여자의 의견으로 가장 적절한 것을 고르시오.

① 음악 교육은 조기에 시작할수록 더 좋다.
② 음악을 크게 듣는 것은 청력에 좋지 않다.
③ 폭력적인 가사는 아이들에게 나쁜 영향을 준다.
④ 어린이를 위한 노래를 다양하게 만들어야 한다.
⑤ 최신 음악보다 취향에 맞는 음악을 들어야 한다.

03 대화를 듣고, 두 사람의 관계를 가장 잘 나타낸 것을 고르시오.

① 커피숍 종업원 – 손님
② 건축가 – 건축 의뢰인
③ 정원 설계 의뢰인 – 정원사
④ 집주인 – 부동산 중개인
⑤ 주택 구매자 – 은행 직원

04 대화를 듣고, 그림에서 대화의 내용과 일치하지 않는 것을 고르시오.

05 대화를 듣고, 여자가 할 일로 가장 적절한 것을 고르시오.

① 추가 금액 송금하기
② 회사 로고 프린트하기
③ 회사 상호와 로고 보내주기
④ 스포츠 물병 가격 조사하기
⑤ 상사에게 주문 물품 보고하기

06 대화를 듣고, 여자가 지불할 금액을 고르시오.

① $250   ② $320   ③ $355
④ $390   ⑤ $425

07 대화를 듣고, 여자가 보고서 성적을 나쁘게 받은 이유를 고르시오.

① 주제 선택을 잘못해서
② 보고서 분량이 너무 짧아서
③ 자료의 출처를 밝히지 않아서
④ 보고서에 이름 쓰는 걸 잊어서
⑤ 다른 학생의 보고서 내용을 베껴서

08 대화를 듣고, Paua 진주 양식장 투어에 관해 언급되지 않은 것을 고르시오.

① 운영 요일   ② 소요 시간
③ 이용 요금   ④ 점심 제공 여부
⑤ 특별 체험

09 자전거 주차 공간에 관한 다음 내용을 듣고, 일치하지 않는 것을 고르시오.

① 자전거 회사가 후원한다.
② 경기 두 시간 전에 개방된다.
③ 자전거 주차 요금은 무료이다.
④ 개인 자전거 자물쇠를 가져와야 한다.
⑤ 직원이 없으므로 귀중품을 남겨두면 안 된다.

10 다음 표를 보면서 대화를 듣고, 두 사람이 구매할 텐트를 고르시오.

King Camp Camping Tents				
Tent	Season	Sleeping Capacity (person)	Price	Weight (kilogram)
① A	3 season	2-3	$85	3.7
② B	4 season	4	$193	4.5
③ C	3 season	2-3	$105	2.6
④ D	3 season	4	$129	5.2
⑤ E	4 season	2	$165	3

11 대화를 듣고, 여자의 마지막 말에 대한 남자의 응답으로 가장 적절한 것을 고르시오.

① There's no way we can repair it in time.
② It'll be fixed for free under the warranty.
③ First, we need to order the parts we need.
④ We'll send someone out as soon as possible.
⑤ Please put it over there, and I'll take a look.

12 대화를 듣고, 남자의 마지막 말에 대한 여자의 응답으로 가장 적절한 것을 고르시오.

① Please don't do it. It's not that bad.
② Yes. There are some pencils in the box.
③ Wait. I'll clear out all the old junk there.
④ Okay. That way it will stay where I put it.
⑤ Right. It's much more expensive than yours.

13 대화를 듣고, 남자의 마지막 말에 대한 여자의 응답으로 가장 적절한 것을 고르시오. [3점]

▶ Woman :

① Tell the kids that I love them. I'll call again soon.
② I understand if you have to delay your arrival.
③ That's wonderful news! The kids will be so happy.
④ I hope your business will succeed thanks to this trip.
⑤ Chinese food doesn't agree with me sometimes.

14 대화를 듣고, 여자의 마지막 말에 대한 남자의 응답으로 가장 적절한 것을 고르시오. [3점]

▶ Man :

① No problem. Actually I don't like action movies.
② Sounds great. Let's go to a rock concert instead.
③ We have no choice. Let's see a movie on Sunday.
④ Hurry. The audience of the next showing is waiting.
⑤ Too bad. We'll have to watch the movie on DVD then.

15 다음 상황 설명을 듣고, Carol이 Jeff에게 할 말로 가장 적절한 것을 고르시오. [3점]

▶ Carol :

① What a relief. Where are your security cameras?
② How awful! When did your car have an accident?
③ Thanks! Can you come with me to check them out?
④ It looks great. How much did you pay for your car?
⑤ Why don't you park your car in front of the building?

[16~17] 다음을 듣고, 물음에 답하시오.

16 남자가 하는 말의 주제로 가장 적절한 것은?

① how to be a great dinner guest
② the usual ways to eat healthier
③ ways of planning a dinner party
④ tips for choosing a gift for a host
⑤ table manners from around the world

17 언급된 선물이 <u>아닌</u> 것은?

① flowers   ② wine
③ a candle   ④ a plate
⑤ a houseplant

01

W: Welcome to the Fairmont Hotel chain. As a hotel employee, many opportunities await you. You may be starting out as housekeepers, but any one of you _____ as you gain experience. Our goal at the Fairmont Hotels is to provide the highest level of service possible. Our customers pay high rates to stay at our hotels, and they expect _____ in return. In order to meet this expectation, a positive and professional attitude is required on the part of our employees. We expect the highest quality service from all of you. Now, we _____ _____ of the hotel before you begin work. We'll begin right next door in the dining room, and then move on to the kitchen. This way, please.

02

W: Brandon, what are you listening to?

M: Oh, Mom. I'm sorry if it's too loud. It's the most popular song nowadays.

W: Are you sure? I was very shocked by the words. _____.

M: Mom, it's a rap song. Please don't _____ _____. It's just for fun.

W: Brandon, you're only 11 years old, and I won't allow you to listen to any music like this.

M: It's not that bad.

W: This song is for adults not children.

M: But everybody listens to hip hop and rap music in our school.

W: Think about what it's saying. _____ _____, and the language is extremely unpleasant to me.

M: Oh, I see.

W: In addition, the violent lyrics could have _____ _____ you. It could change your behavior.

M: Okay. I won't listen to it.

03

W: Do you want some coffee? I have a fresh pot.

M: Yes, please. Thanks. You have a beautiful garden with flowers, trees, and a fountain.

W: Thanks. My husband is a gardener, so we've taken very good care of the garden.

M: Great. Actually, a well-maintained garden can _____. There are four bedrooms, right?

W: Yes. It also has a great view of the beach from upstairs.

M: Yes, it's a lovely house. The only problem is that _____.

W: I think I can get that much.

M: The prices have been falling in this area recently. I think you need to lower your price a bit.

W: Oh, I'll talk it over with my husband.

M: Okay. I need to take some pictures of your house to _____. Is it okay with you?

W: Sure. Go ahead.

04

W: Our department store is planning to hold a Santa Claus event. This is my design plan for the event.

M: Let me see. Wow, _____ on the left. Good idea!

W: I think a fireplace is the best place for Christmas gifts.

M: Exactly. So you put three big gift boxes in front of the fireplace.

W: I also put _____ in the center. It's for Santa Claus to sit on.

M: That's good. I like this arch behind the chair. You put up _____ saying "SANTA" _____ _____.

W: Yes. And I placed a Christmas tree on the right.

M: Well, _____ _____. How about putting a Santa hat there instead of a star?

W: Oh, it's a good idea. I'll change it.

M: Thanks. You did a good job.

05

M: This is Promotions Now. How can I help you?

W: This is Sarah Palmer from Silvertech Company. We're interested in your sports bottles on your website.

M: Great. We have several different sports bottles. _____?

W: I like your aluminum sports bottle. Its model number is 204PB.

M: That's the top seller. How many do you need?

W: Four hundred bottles. Can you offer a quantity discount?

M: Yes, we can give you a five-percent discount.

W: Thank you. Can you put _____ _____ the bottles?

M: Sure. Why don't you e-mail us your company's name and logo? We can print it on the bottles.

W: Great. _____ right away. By the way, do I have to pay an extra charge for the logo print?

M: No, it's free _____ more than 300 bottles.

06

M: Speedy Car Rental. How may I help you?

W: Uh, this is Angela Ford speaking. We've rented a car from you for two weeks from next Friday. But _____ to a week later.

M: Hold on, please. Yes, Ms. Ford. You wanted a compact car for two weeks.

W: Yes, that's right. Our total was $_____.

M: Sorry, but if you change the reservation, we'll have to give you a bigger car. Is that all right?

W: Is that more expensive?

M: Yes, you need to pay 35 dollars more per week.

W: Oh, dear. So _____ _____ for the two weeks?

M: I'm afraid so.

W: Okay. _____. I'll reserve that car. Thanks.

M: I'll send you the updated information. Goodbye.

07

W: Excuse me, Mr. Goldstein.

M: Come on in. What's up?

W: Uh, I didn't get my paper back yet.

M: I have a paper with no name on it. Is this yours?

W: That's it! Oh, I got a D minus. Is it because I didn't write my name on it?

M: No, that _____ the grade.

W: You said the paper should be two pages long, so I wrote two and a half pages.

M: Yes. And your ideas for the theme were creative. But you _____ into your paper.

W: No! I never copied anyone's paper.

M: Some of the ideas came from books. But you made it seem like they were yours.

W: Oh, I didn't know that would be such a big problem.

M: It's a huge problem. _____ _____ is dishonest and wrong.

08

W: Hello, this is Paua Pearl Farm.

M: Hello. We're planning to visit your pearl farm. I'd like to know _____.

W: Our farm is open from Monday to Saturday, and we offer guided tours for visitors on Friday and Saturday.

M: How long does the tour take?

W: It takes about one hour. You can discover how the pearls come to be and see _____ _____.

M: Good. Do all tours include lunches?

W: No, all tours include tea and snacks, but you need to _____.

M: Are there any special experiences offered?

W: Sure. You can make a unique souvenir from pearls by yourself.

M: Okay. Thanks for the information.

09

M: Do you want to ride your bike to the game at the main stadium? Madison City provides free bicycle parking. The bicycle parking space _____ _____ Saria Bike Company. The space will be available for bicycle parking from two hours before the game until one hour after the Madison City football game ends. There is _____ the bicycle parking space. Staff there will greet you and provide instructions for parking your bike. _____ _____ for your bike. The space will also _____, but don't leave any valuables with your bicycle.

10

M: Honey, we really need to buy a tent since we go camping every weekend. So I brought a brochure of tents.

W: That's a good idea.

M: Do you think we need a four-season tent?

W: I don't think so. We're not going camping in the winter. Let's _____.

M: Okay. Then think about the size. How about a tent for four people? It has more space inside.

W: I prefer a tent for _____. A bigger tent is heavy to carry. And it's difficult to find a big enough space to set up the tent.

M: Okay. We'll choose a 2 or 3 person tent. Now there are two options left.

W: Of course, _____, _____.

M: But the cheaper one is heavier. And there is only a 20-dollar difference in prices.

W: That's true. _____.

11

W: I need someone to fix my washing machine. It isn't working.

M: Okay. Can you tell me its model number and when you purchased it?

W: The number is MA17, and I bought it seven months ago. _____?

12

M: Do you know where a pencil sharpener is? We have two, but I can't find either.

W: _____. How about buying an electric pencil sharpener?

M: Good idea. _____ _____ on the bottom.

13

W: Hello?

M: Honey, it's me!

W: Oh, Anthony, I was hoping I'd hear from you soon! How is your business trip to China going?

M: It's going well. _____ over there?

W: Well, you know, same as usual. Life's good, except that I miss you so much!

M: I miss you too. How are the kids?

W: They miss you _____. They ask about you every day.

M: I think about you guys all the time, too.

W: Well, I've told them that you'll be coming back in a month, so they can't wait for that.

M: Well, honey, things are going so well over here that I think _____ _____ next week.

14

M: Lauren, how about seeing the movie, *Bumblebee*, this Saturday?

W: Great idea. I'd like to see it.

M: Let's have lunch at a nice restaurant and see the movie.

W: Oh, hold on. Aren't we going somewhere this Saturday?

M: Oh, right. I completely forgot. We _____ _____ my grandmother.

W: Well, how about watching the movie Friday evening?

M: I have a dinner appointment Friday evening. What about Thursday evening?

W: No, I have a dentist appointment on Thursday. I probably _____ a movie then.

M: Let's check when they stop running the movie. Oh, they _____ this Saturday.

W: I guess _____.

15

M: Jeff and Carol are friends. Today Jeff runs into Carol in the parking lot of his office building. Jeff notices Carol is very upset and asks her why. Carol says she's visited this building _____ _____. She parked her car there and she's just found a scratch on her parked car. Someone hit her car and ran away _____ _____. Her car is almost brand-new, so she is very upset. Jeff knows that there are some security cameras in the parking lot. So, he advises Carol to go to the parking lot office and check the cameras. Carol _____ _____ because he works in the building. In this situation, what would Carol most likely say to Jeff?

16~17

M: If a friend or family member invites you over _____, there are certain rules that _____. Remember, this person took the time to invite you, plan a meal, clean their house, pay for food, and get everything set up. So call the host and ask if there's anything you can do to help. You can bring dessert or _____ _____. If the host insists they don't need any help, bring over a small gift such as flowers, a bottle of wine, or a candle. A houseplant or a picture frame is terrific too. Always _____. During your meal, make sure you don't speak with your mouth full or _____ _____. This is considered rude and distasteful. Finally, it's common for people to send a thank-you card after the meal. A simple thank-you card with a few words will be enough. _____ _____ the next time you're invited to a dinner party.

ANSWER

01회

01 ⑤ 02 ③ 03 ④ 04 ⑤ 05 ③ 06 ③ 07 ④ 08 ⑤ 09 ③ 10 ⑤
11 ② 12 ③ 13 ② 14 ③ 15 ④ 16 ① 17 ③

02회

01 ④ 02 ② 03 ③ 04 ④ 05 ④ 06 ④ 07 ② 08 ⑤ 09 ⑤ 10 ⑤
11 ③ 12 ④ 13 ① 14 ① 15 ⑤ 16 ④ 17 ④

03회

01 ② 02 ③ 03 ④ 04 ⑤ 05 ② 06 ③ 07 ④ 08 ⑤ 09 ④ 10 ③
11 ③ 12 ② 13 ① 14 ① 15 ③ 16 ③ 17 ④

04회

01 ② 02 ④ 03 ④ 04 ⑤ 05 ④ 06 ③ 07 ③ 08 ⑤ 09 ⑤ 10 ①
11 ③ 12 ⑤ 13 ⑤ 14 ④ 15 ④ 16 ④ 17 ②

05회

01 ① 02 ⑤ 03 ② 04 ⑤ 05 ④ 06 ② 07 ③ 08 ④ 09 ⑤ 10 ⑤
11 ② 12 ⑤ 13 ③ 14 ④ 15 ③ 16 ④ 17 ⑤

06회

01 ④ 02 ② 03 ③ 04 ⑤ 05 ③ 06 ④ 07 ⑤ 08 ④ 09 ④ 10 ⑤
11 ② 12 ② 13 ② 14 ③ 15 ③ 16 ③ 17 ④

07회

01 ⑤ 02 ④ 03 ② 04 ⑤ 05 ④ 06 ④ 07 ③ 08 ④ 09 ③ 10 ④
11 ② 12 ③ 13 ⑤ 14 ① 15 ③ 16 ② 17 ⑤

08회

01 ④ 02 ③ 03 ③ 04 ④ 05 ⑤ 06 ④ 07 ③ 08 ⑤ 09 ④ 10 ⑤
11 ③ 12 ③ 13 ③ 14 ② 15 ② 16 ③ 17 ④

09회

01 ② 02 ③ 03 ④ 04 ④ 05 ② 06 ② 07 ④ 08 ④ 09 ③ 10 ④
11 ③ 12 ④ 13 ④ 14 ③ 15 ⑤ 16 ② 17 ⑤

10회

01 ② 02 ① 03 ④ 04 ④ 05 ③ 06 ④ 07 ④ 08 ④ 09 ③ 10 ⑤
11 ⑤ 12 ⑤ 13 ② 14 ③ 15 ⑤ 16 ② 17 ②

11회

01 ④ 02 ② 03 ④ 04 ④ 05 ② 06 ② 07 ④ 08 ④ 09 ③ 10 ④
11 ⑤ 12 ⑤ 13 ③ 14 ② 15 ⑤ 16 ⑤ 17 ⑤

12회

01 ② 02 ④ 03 ③ 04 ⑤ 05 ⑤ 06 ④ 07 ④ 08 ② 09 ⑤ 10 ④
11 ③ 12 ④ 13 ② 14 ① 15 ③ 16 ① 17 ④

13회

01 ④ 02 ④ 03 ③ 04 ④ 05 ③ 06 ④ 07 ⑤ 08 ③ 09 ④ 10 ⑤
11 ② 12 ⑤ 13 ① 14 ④ 15 ④ 16 ④ 17 ③

14회

01 ④ 02 ③ 03 ② 04 ④ 05 ② 06 ③ 07 ② 08 ⑤ 09 ⑤ 10 ①
11 ② 12 ④ 13 ④ 14 ③ 15 ③ 16 ④ 17 ④

15회

01 ② 02 ④ 03 ② 04 ③ 05 ④ 06 ③ 07 ④ 08 ④ 09 ⑤ 10 ⑤
11 ① 12 ③ 13 ② 14 ③ 15 ② 16 ① 17 ②

16회

01 ④ 02 ④ 03 ⑤ 04 ⑤ 05 ⑤ 06 ③ 07 ④ 08 ④ 09 ⑤ 10 ⑤
11 ④ 12 ② 13 ② 14 ⑤ 15 ② 16 ⑤ 17 ④

17회

01 ③ 02 ② 03 ④ 04 ④ 05 ⑤ 06 ⑤ 07 ④ 08 ④ 09 ④ 10 ①
11 ⑤ 12 ⑤ 13 ② 14 ② 15 ③ 16 ② 17 ④

18회

01 ⑤ 02 ② 03 ② 04 ③ 05 ③ 06 ③ 07 ③ 08 ② 09 ⑤ 10 ③
11 ① 12 ② 13 ① 14 ② 15 ⑤ 16 ⑤ 17 ④

19회

01 ② 02 ④ 03 ② 04 ⑤ 05 ④ 06 ③ 07 ③ 08 ③ 09 ③ 10 ②
11 ② 12 ③ 13 ④ 14 ② 15 ② 16 ② 17 ③

20회

01 ③ 02 ③ 03 ④ 04 ⑤ 05 ③ 06 ④ 07 ③ 08 ③ 09 ⑤ 10 ③
11 ② 12 ④ 13 ③ 14 ⑤ 15 ③ 16 ① 17 ④

고등 기초부터 ──○─── *New* ───○── 수능 준비까지

믿고푸는 **독해 4단계**

수능 독해의 유형잡고   모의고사로 적용하고

기본 다지는
첫단추

1 유형의 기본을 이해하는
**첫단추
독해유형편**

2 기본실력을 점검하는
**첫단추 독해실전편
모의고사 12회**

실력 올리는
파워업

3 유형별 전략을
탄탄히 하는
파워업 독해유형편

4 독해실력을 끌어올리는
**파워업 독해실전편
모의고사 15회**

* 위 교재들은 최신 개정판으로 21번 함의추론 신유형이 모두 반영되었습니다.

① 구문

판매 1위 '천일문' 콘텐츠를 활용하여 정확하고 다양한 구문 학습

끊어읽기   해석하기   문장 구조 분석   해설·해석 제공   단어 스크램블링   영작하기

② 문법·서술형

쎄듀의 모든 문법 문항을 활용하여 내신까지 해결하는 정교한 문법 유형 제공

객관식과 주관식의 결합   문법 포인트별 학습   보기를 활용한 집합 문항   내신대비 서술형   어법+서술형 문제

③ 어휘

초·중·고·공무원까지 방대한 어휘량을 제공하며 오프라인 TEST 인쇄도 가능

영단어 카드 학습   단어 ↔ 뜻 유형   예문 활용 유형   단어 매칭 게임

④ 선생님 보유 문항 이용

Online Test   OMR Test

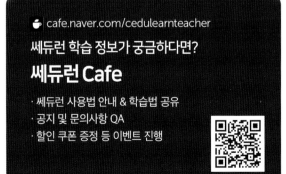

 cafe.naver.com/cedulearnteacher

쎄듀런 학습 정보가 궁금하다면?

쎄듀런 Cafe

· 쎄듀런 사용법 안내 & 학습법 공유
· 공지 및 문의사항 QA
· 할인 쿠폰 증정 등 이벤트 진행

첫단추

듣기실전편

BUTTON

듣기 모의고사 🎧

20회

정답 및 해설

쎄듀

첫단추

듣기실전편

듣기 모의고사 🎧

20회

BUTTON

정답 및 해설

01회

01 화자가 하는 말의 목적   ⑤

* 담화의 일부 내용이 아니라 중심 내용을 파악해야 한다. 본 담화는 연주회에 온 청중에게 감사함을 전하며 오케스트라가 창립된 해를 말하면서 역사가 길다는 이야기로 서두를 시작했지만, 전체 내용은 연주회를 위해 휴대전화 전원을 완전히 끌 것을 요청하고 있다. 그러므로 답은 ⑤이다.

W: Welcome, everyone. Thank you for coming to the Carlton High School Orchestra Concert this evening. The Carlton High School Orchestra, **founded in** 1979, has a long history. Tonight the orchestra will perform a variety of music from Mozart to jazz, which we're sure you're going to enjoy. At this time, we would like to make an announcement. All your cell phones must **be turned off**. We hope you will not just turn off the ringer, but turn it off completely. Checking text messages or reading news on a smartphone during the concert makes no sound, but the bright light will be **distracting to others** in a darkened hall. Thank you again, and we hope you have a great time.

여: 여러분, 환영합니다. 오늘 저녁 Carlton 고등학교 오케스트라 연주회에 와주셔서 감사합니다. 1979년에 창립된 Carlton 고등학교 오케스트라는 오랜 역사를 가지고 있습니다. 오늘 밤 오케스트라는 모차르트부터 재즈에 이르기까지 다양한 음악을 연주할 것인데, 여러분이 그것들을 즐기실 거라고 확신합니다. 지금 안내 말씀을 드리려고 합니다. 여러분 모두의 휴대전화는 반드시 꺼야 합니다. 저희는 여러분이 단지 벨소리만 끌 것만 아니라 휴대전화를 완전히 끄시길 바랍니다. 연주회 중간에 스마트폰으로 문자 메시지를 확인하거나 뉴스를 읽는 것은 소리를 내지 않지만, 그 밝은 빛이 어두운 홀에서 다른 사람들을 방해할 것입니다. 다시 한번 감사드리며 좋은 시간 보내시기를 바랍니다.

어휘 **found** 창립하다, 세우다; (~에) 기초[기반]를 두다   **perform** 연주[공연/연기]하다   **a variety of** 다양한   **announcement** 발표 (내용); 공고   **ringer** (전화기 등의) 벨소리를 내는 장치   **distract** 집중이 안 되게 하다   **darken** 어둡게 하다; 어두워지다

02 의견   ③

* 우선 지시문에서 명시한 화자의 성별을 보고 어느 화자의 말에 주목할지를 판단해야 한다. 특히 의견이나 주장을 표현하는 어구(I think ~, You should ~ 등)가 이끄는 내용을 잘 들어야 한다. 친구에게 준 선물로 속상해하는 남자에게 여자는 상대가 좋아하는 선물을 찾아보는 게 필요하다고 하고 있다. 그러므로 여자의 의견으로는 ③이 적절하다. 판매 직원이 추천한 향수를 선물했다가 실패한 상황이므로 ④는 답이 될 수 없고 Nora가 향수를 사용하지 않으므로 ⑤ 역시 답이 될 수 없다.

W: Ethan, you look upset. What's wrong?
M: It was Nora's birthday yesterday. I gave her a birthday gift, but she didn't **seem to like it.**
W: What did you get her?
M: I bought a perfume the sales clerk recommended. It smelled sweet and nice.
W: Oh, that wasn't **a good choice**. Nora doesn't really like perfume. Couldn't you tell she never wears it?
M: No, I didn't know that.
W: You should have thought about **her likes and dislikes.**
M: The sales clerk said that perfume is very popular among young women.
W: There's nothing that everyone likes in the world. You need to find **a gift that she likes.**
M: You're right. She probably was disappointed in me.
W: It's okay. She'll understand.

여: Ethan, 속상해 보이는데, 뭐가 잘못되었니?
남: 어제가 Nora의 생일이었어. 그 애에게 생일 선물을 주었지만 좋아하는 것 같지 않았어.

여: 뭘 주었는데?
남: 판매 직원이 추천한 향수를 샀어. 달콤하고 좋은 냄새가 났거든.
여: 아, 그건 좋은 선택이 아니었어. Nora는 향수를 정말 좋아하지 않아. 그 애가 향수를 전혀 쓰지 않는 걸 알지 못했니?
남: 응, 그걸 몰랐어.
여: 너는 그 애가 좋아하는 것과 싫어하는 것에 대해 생각해봐야 했어.
남: 판매 직원이 그 향수가 젊은 여성들 사이에서 아주 인기 있는 거라고 했어.
여: 세상에 모든 사람이 좋아하는 건 없어. 넌 그 애가 좋아하는 선물을 찾아보는 게 필요해.
남: 네 말이 맞아. 그 애는 아마 나한테 실망했을 거야.
여: 괜찮아. 이해할 거야.

어휘 **sales clerk** 판매 직원   **disappointed** 실망한, 낙담한

03 관계   ④

* 직업을 나타내거나 추론할 수 있는 힌트가 대화 전반에 걸쳐 드러나므로, 대화를 전체적으로 이해하는 것이 필요하다. 본 대화는 여자의 딸이 아파서 오늘 집에 있겠다고 전화한 상황이다. 여자가 남자에게 딸의 수학 숙제를 알 수 있겠냐고 묻고 남자가 여자의 이메일로 수학 숙제를 보내주겠다고 하는 것으로 보아 교사와 학부모의 관계임을 알 수 있다. 아프다는 언급이 있다고 해서 의사와 환자 보호자의 관계로 오해하지 않도록 유의한다.

[Cell phone rings.]
M: Hello. Peter Cromwell speaking.
W: Good morning, Mr. Cromwell. This is Charlotte Mills. I'm calling for my daughter, Emily. She's not feeling well today.
M: I'm sorry to hear that. I hope it's not too bad.
W: It's not serious. She has a fever and feels dizzy, so I think **she'd better stay home** today.
M: I hope she feels well soon.
W: Thank you. Anyway, I'm concerned about her math class. Can I get **her math homework** for today?
M: OK. Is it all right for me to send the homework **to your e-mail**?
W: That would be great. Do you have my e-mail address?
M: Hold on, please. Hmm... I have eliza79@gmail.com. Is that correct?
W: Yes, that's correct. Thank you for your help, Mr. Cromwell.
M: My pleasure. Tell Emily I said, "**Get well soon.**"

[휴대전화 벨이 울린다.]
남: 여보세요. Peter Cromwell입니다.
여: 안녕하세요, Cromwell 선생님. 저는 Charlotte Mills입니다. 제 딸 Emily 때문에 전화했어요. 오늘 그 애가 몸이 좋지 않아서요.
남: 그거 유감이군요. 너무 나쁜 게 아니길 바랍니다.
여: 심각한 건 아니에요. 열이 있고 어지러워해서 제 생각에는 애가 오늘 집에 있는 게 나을 것 같아요.
남: 몸이 빨리 좋아지기를 바랍니다.
여: 고맙습니다. 그런데, 그 애의 수학 수업이 염려되어서요. 오늘 딸아이의 수학 숙제를 알 수 있을까요?
남: 알겠습니다. 제가 어머님 이메일로 숙제를 보내도 괜찮으신지요?
여: 그렇게 해주시면 좋지요. 제 이메일 주소를 갖고 계세요?
남: 잠깐만요. 음… eliza79@gmail.com이 있습니다. 맞나요?
여: 네, 그게 맞습니다. 도와주셔서 감사합니다. Cromwell 선생님.
남: 천만에요. Emily에게 제가 "쾌유를 빈다."고 했다고 말해주세요.

어휘 **fever** 열, 발열; 열기   **dizzy** 어지러운

04 그림 불일치   ⑤

※ 대화가 나오기 전에 각 사물의 위치 관계와 외형(형태나 무늬, 개수 등)의 특징을 미리 확인하는 것이 좋다. 창문에 커튼을 달 것을 추천하는 남자의 말에 여자가 좋은 생각이라면서 이야기해보겠다고 했으므로 그림의 창문에는 커튼이 없어야 한다. 그러나 그림에서는 창문에 커튼이 있으므로 ⑤가 대화의 내용과 일치하지 않는다.

W: Take a look at this. Lilian and I made this two-story dollhouse.
M: Wow! You guys did such a great job! It's nice to be able to see inside the house.
W: Can you see the staircase on the left side?
M: Yes. You put **three little plant pots** on the stairs. They're so cute!
W: Lilian made them with colorful clay. She also made the flower vase on the coffee table.
M: You mean the table in front of the sofa? Excellent! I like **the striped pattern** of the sofa.
W: That was my choice. Take a look at the bed **on the second floor**. Isn't it pretty?
M: Yeah! That must be the bed that Lilian chose.
W: She also added a big window behind the bed.
M: Why didn't you **put up curtains** on the window? I think the bedroom would look more beautiful with curtains.
W: That's a good idea. I'll talk to Lilian about that.

여: 이걸 봐요. Lilian하고 내가 이 2층 인형의 집을 만들었어요.
남: 왜! 둘이 정말 멋진 일을 해냈군요! 집안을 볼 수 있게 하다니 멋진데요.
여: 왼쪽의 계단이 보여요?
남: 네. 계단에 3개의 작은 화분을 놓아두었군요. 너무 귀여워요!
여: Lilian이 컬러 찰흙으로 그것들을 만들었어요. 그 애가 또 커피 탁자 위에 있는 화병도 만들었답니다.
남: 소파 앞에 있는 탁자 말인가요? 훌륭해요! 난 소파의 줄무늬 패턴이 마음에 드는군요.
여: 그건 내 선택이었어요. 2층의 침대를 한 번 봐요. 예쁘지 않아요?
남: 네! 저건 Lilian이 선택한 침대임이 틀림없군요.
여: 그 애는 또 침대 뒤에 큰 창문을 추가했어요.
남: 창문에 왜 커튼을 달지 않았어요? 커튼이 있으면 침실이 더 아름다워 보일 것 같은데요.
여: 그거 좋은 생각이군요. 그것에 대해 Lilian하고 이야기해볼게요.

어휘 story (건물의) 층   staircase 계단(= stairs)   plant pot 화분   clay 찰흙, 점토   flower vase 화병   striped pattern 줄무늬 패턴   floor 층; 바닥

05 추후 행동   ③

※ 대개 대화는 어떤 일을 하게 되는 상황이 먼저 제시된 뒤에 남자와 여자가 각각 할 일들과 이에 대한 수락/거절의 응답이 나열되는 식으로 전개된다. 본 대화는 부부가 함께 여행을 떠나는 상황이다. 짐 싸는 것은 이미 했고 여권도 찾았으며 우편배달 중지 신청도 했다. 여자가 남자에게 전등을 껐는지 확인을 부탁하고 남자가 처리하겠다고 했으므로 남자가 할 일은 ③이다. 택시 부르는 여자가 할 일임에 유의한다.

W: Honey, have you finished packing? We have to leave in 10 minutes.
M: Don't worry. I have.
W: Make sure to carry your passport.
M: Oh, dear! Have you seen my passport? I can't remember **where I put mine**.
W: Oh, no! What are you talking about? When did you **last have it**?
M: Well... I put it on the desk. Then maybe I put it in my backpack. Right. Here it is.
W: Oh, **what a relief**! You really scared me.
M: I think we're ready. Did you ask the mailman to stop mail delivery?
W: Yes, I already did it. Can you please check **all the lights are off** before we leave?
M: Okay. I'll take care of it.
W: Thanks. Now I'll **call a taxi**.

여: 여보, 짐 싸는 것 끝냈어요? 우리는 10분 후에 떠나야 해요.

남: 걱정하지 말아요. 했어요.
여: 여권은 꼭 가져가요.
남: 아, 이런! 내 여권 봤어요? 내 걸 어디 두었는지 기억이 안 나요.
여: 설마! 무슨 말을 하는 거예요? 언제 마지막으로 갖고 있었어요?
남: 음… 책상에 그걸 두었어요. 그러고는 아마 내 배낭에 넣었을 거예요. 맞아요. 여기 있군요.
여: 아, 정말 다행이에요! 당신 때문에 정말 깜짝 놀랐잖아요.
남: 준비가 된 것 같아요. 집배원에게 우편배달을 하지 말라고 요청했어요?
여: 네, 벌써 했어요. 우리가 떠나기 전에 모든 전등이 꺼져 있는지 확인해줄 수 있어요?
남: 알겠어요. 내가 그걸 처리할게요.
여: 고마워요. 이제 난 택시를 부를게요.

어휘 pack (짐을) 꾸리다; 포장하다; 포장 꾸러미   relief 안심; (고통·불안 등의) 경감[완화]   delivery 배달(물); 연설; 분만, 출산

06 금액   ③

※ 여러 개의 수치 정보가 등장하므로 필요한 정보를 메모하면서 듣는 것이 좋다. 6달러짜리 깃발 열쇠고리 4개와 5달러짜리 탑 열쇠고리 3개를 사서 39달러를 지불해야 하는데, 상점에서 30달러 넘게 구매 시 5달러를 할인해준다고 했다. 그러므로 두 사람이 지불할 금액은 34달러로 답은 ③이다.

W: Dylan, look at these key rings. Aren't they cute?
M: Fantastic! They are so beautiful and unique.
W: Why don't we get some for our friends? I think they'll be **great souvenirs**.
M: Good idea. I think seven key rings are enough. Which ones do you like?
W: I like flag key rings. They're $6 each.
M: Why don't we get some tower key rings, too? They're $5 each.
W: Then let's get **four flag** key rings and **three tower** key rings, okay?
M: Sure. That comes to... $39.
W: No, that's not correct. Look at the sign that says you **get 5 dollars off** if you spend more than $30.
M: You're right. That will save some money.
W: Let's go to the cashier.

여: Dylan, 이 열쇠고리들을 봐요. 귀엽지 않나요?
남: 환상적이네요! 정말 아름답고 독특해요.
여: 우리 친구들을 위해 몇 개 사는 건 어때요? 그것들이 멋진 기념품이 될 거라고 생각해요.
남: 좋은 생각이에요. 열쇠고리 일곱 개면 충분할 것 같군요. 어떤 게 마음에 들어요?
여: 난 깃발 열쇠고리가 좋아요. 하나에 6달러군요.
남: 탑 열쇠고리도 좀 사는 게 어때요? 그건 한 개에 5달러예요.
여: 그러면 깃발 열쇠고리 네 개하고 탑 열쇠고리 세 개를 사죠. 괜찮아요?
남: 그럼요. 그러면… 39달러군요.
여: 아뇨, 그건 정확하지 않아요. 30달러 넘게 사면 5달러를 할인해준다고 쓰여 있는 표지판을 봐요.
남: 당신 말이 맞네요. 그게 돈을 좀 절약해주겠군요.
여: 계산원에게 갑시다.

어휘 key ring 열쇠고리   unique 독특한; 고유의   souvenir 기념(품)

07 이유   ④

※ 지시문을 통해 여자가 자전거를 타러 갈 수 없는 상황이며 여자의 말에 단서가 있을 가능성이 큼을 미리 파악한다. 여자는 시험공부 때문이 아니라 헬멧이 아직 없어서 자전거 타러 갈 수 없다고 했으므로 답은 ④이다. 좋아하는 밴드의 콘서트 티켓은 구하지 못했고 할머니는 자전거를 선물로 보내주셨다고만 언급했음에 유의한다.

[Cell phone rings.]
W: Hi, Jacob. **Guess what**?
M: Hi, Olivia. What happened? Did you finally get your favorite band's concert ticket?
W: No, sadly I didn't get it. Instead, I got a new bicycle.
M: Cool. Is it your birthday gift?

W: Yes, my grandma sent it to me. It's very strong and lightweight.
M: **How nice of her**. Now you and I both have bicycles. How about going biking with me in the park now?
W: I'd love to, but I can't go biking now.
M: Do you need to study for the exam? Come on. We only need just **a couple of hours**.
W: No, I **don't have a helmet**. It's dangerous to go biking without a helmet.
M: That's right. Then maybe next time after you buy one.
W: Okay. See you later.

[휴대전화 벨이 울린다.]
여: 안녕, Jacob. 무슨 일이게?
남: 안녕, Olivia. 무슨 일이 있었니? 네가 좋아하는 밴드의 콘서트 티켓을 마침내 구했니?
여: 아니야. 슬프게도 사지 못했어. 대신에 새 자전거가 생겼어.
남: 멋지다. 네 생일 선물인 거야?
여: 응. 할머니께서 내게 그걸 보내주셨어. 아주 튼튼하고 가벼워.
남: 정말 좋으신 분이다. 이제 너하고 나 둘 다 자전거가 있네. 지금 공원으로 나랑 자전거 타러 가는 건 어때?
여: 가고 싶지만, 지금은 자전거 타러 갈 수 없어.
남: 시험공부를 해야 하는 거야? 이봐. 우리는 단지 두 시간만 필요한 거라고.
여: 아니야, 난 헬멧이 없어. 헬멧 없이 자전거 타는 건 위험해.
남: 그건 맞아. 그러면 네가 그걸 사고 나서 다음에 같이 가자.
여: 좋아. 나중에 봐.

어휘 lightweight 가벼운, 경량의

08 언급하지 않은 것 ⑤

❋ 대화의 진행은 대개 선택지와 같은 순서이므로, 선택지를 보면서 언급된 내용을 소거하는 식으로 푸는 것이 좋다. 극장 가는 방법에 대해서는 이야기했지만 극장 위치는 언급하지 않았으므로 답은 ⑤이다.

M: Isabella! I just got two tickets to the musical you wanted to see. Look at these!
W: Oh, dear! Is it "Mamma Mia!"? **That's my favorite**, but weren't those tickets expensive?
M: I got a 20% discount on them with my membership card. It **was originally $80** for two.
W: Thank you! When is the performance? Oh, it's Thursday the 17th.
M: Seven o'clock is all right with you, right? We don't have to rush after work.
W: Yes. Who will perform **the leading role** on that night?
M: Matilda Fletcher. She is one of the best musical singers.
W: Exactly. I'm a big fan of her. By the way, **how do we get to** the theater?
M: We can take a subway and transfer to a bus at City Hall Station.
W: Sounds good. I can't wait!

남: Isabella! 네가 보고 싶어 하던 뮤지컬의 티켓 두 장을 방금 샀어. 이걸 봐!
여: 아, 이런! '맘마미아'(① 뮤지컬 제목)니? 그거 내가 좋아하는 것이긴 한데 그 티켓 비싸지 않았니?
남: 내 회원카드로 20% 할인을 받았어. 원래 두 장에 80달러였어.(② 티켓 가격)
여: 고마워! 공연이 언제지? 아, 17일 목요일(③ 상연 일시)이구나.
남: 7시(③ 상연 일시)면 괜찮지, 그렇지? 우리가 퇴근 후에 서두를 필요가 없잖아.
여: 응. 그날 밤에는 주인공 역을 누가 공연할 거니?
남: Matilda Fletcher야(④ 주연 배우). 그녀는 최고의 뮤지컬 가수 중 한 명이야.
여: 정말 그래. 난 그녀의 열성 팬이야. 그런데. 우리 극장에 어떻게 가지?
남: 지하철을 타고 시청역에서 버스로 갈아탈 수 있어.
여: 그거 좋겠다. 너무 기다려져!

어휘 performance 공연, 연주; 수행; 성과 cf. perform 공연[연주]하다; 수행하다 rush 서두르다; 분주함; 돌진(하다) leading role 주연 transfer 갈아타다, 환승(하다); 이동(하다)

09 내용 불일치 ③

❋ 담화의 진행은 대개 선택지와 같은 순서이므로, 선택지를 보면서 일치하는 내용을 소거하는 식으로 푸는 것이 좋다. 같은 학생이 그린 다수의 그림도 허용될 것이라고 했

으므로 ③은 내용과 일치하지 않는다.

W: Could you go a day without water? What if we didn't have water to drink or shower with, or for firefighters to put out fires? Let your imagination run free, and put your ideas into a painting for the Knoxville Art Contest. The theme is "Imagine **a day without water**." This contest is open to all the students of Knoxville from grade 1 through grade 8. **Participants must submit** their artwork between April 3rd and April 7th. Paintings must be the work of one individual student, but **multiple paintings** from the same student will be accepted. Any medium, such as paint, colored pencils, or markers, can be used. However, paintings with **copyrighted characters** or images will not be accepted. For a full list of rules and information, please visit our website, www.knoxville.org/artcontest.

여: 물 없이 하루를 지낼 수 있습니까? 우리가 마시거나 샤워할, 또는 소방관이 불을 끌 물이 없다면 어떨까요? 여러분의 상상력을 자유롭게 발휘해서 Knoxville 미술 대회에 낼 그림에 여러분의 아이디어를 표현해보십시오. ① 주제는 '물 없는 하루를 상상해 보기'입니다. 이 대회는 1학년부터 8학년까지 Knoxville의 모든 학생이 참여할 수 있습니다. 참가자들은 ② 4월 3일과 7일 사이에 작품을 제출해야 합니다. 그림은 반드시 한 개인 학생의 작품이어야 하지만 ③ 같은 학생이 그린 다수의 그림은 허용될 것입니다. ④ 물감이나 색연필이나 마커 같은 어떤 재료든지 사용할 수 있습니다. 그러나 ⑤ 저작권이 있는 캐릭터나 이미지가 있는 그림은 허용되지 않을 것입니다. 규정과 정보에 관한 전체 목록을 보려면 저희 웹사이트 www.knoxville.org/artcontest에 방문해주십시오.

어휘 put out (불을) 끄다; 내놓다; 출시하다 theme 주제, 테마 participant 참가자 submit 제출하다; 복종[굴복]하다 multiple 다수의; 다양한 medium 재료; 도구; 중간의 copyrighted 저작권이 있는

10 도표 이해 ⑤

❋ 대화의 진행은 대개 도표 항목의 나열 순서대로 진행된다. 대화를 들으면서 도표의 각 항목 중 선택되지 않은 것을 소거하는 식으로 푸는 것이 좋다. 우선 공포 영화는 제외했고(① 소거) 청소년 관람 불가 영화도 제외했다(③ 소거). 또 오후 2시 이후에 시작하는 영화 중에서 골라야 한다고 했으므로(② 소거) ④와 ⑤가 남았는데 그중 평점이 높은 것을 선택했으므로 답은 ⑤이다.

M: Honey, let's go to see a movie with our kids tomorrow.
W: Good idea. Then we need to book tickets now. What should we watch?
M: Hmm, I don't think horror movies are good for our kids.
W: I agree. And we also should choose **a movie that's G-rated** since our kids are 8 and 12 years old.
M: You're right. Kids cannot see R-rated movies. So we can choose from among these three.
W: Why don't we go to see a movie **after having lunch** at a restaurant?
M: All right. There is a nice Italian restaurant near the cinema. Then we can see one that **starts at 2 or later**.
W: Yeah. Now we have these two options. Which one do you prefer?
M: Let's choose the one with **higher review scores**.
W: Okay. I'll book four tickets.

남: 여보, 내일 우리 애들하고 영화를 보러 갑시다.
여: 좋은 생각이에요. 그러면 지금 표를 예매해야 해요. 뭘 볼까요?
남: 음. 공포 영화는 우리 애들에게 좋지 않을 것 같아요.
여: 동의해요. 그리고 우리는 또 우리 애들이 8세와 12세이기 때문에 연령 제한이 없는 영화를 선택해야 해요.
남: 당신 말이 맞아요. 애들이 청소년 관람 불가 영화를 볼 수 없지요. 그러면 우리는 이 세 편 중에서 선택할 수 있어요.
여: 식당에서 점심을 먹고 나서 영화를 보러 가는 건 어때요?
남: 좋아요. 극장 근처에 멋진 이탈리아 음식점이 있어요. 그러면 2시 이후에 시작하는 걸 볼 수 있겠군요.
여: 네. 이제 우리는 이 두 개의 선택권이 있어요. 어떤 게 마음에 드나요?
남: 더 높은 평점을 받은 거로 선택하죠.
여: 좋아요. 내가 표 네 장을 예매할게요.

어휘 book 예매[예약]하다; 도서 G-rated ((영화)) 연령 제한이 없는 R-rated ((영화))

11 짧은 대화에 이어질 응답 ②

✱ 남자가 여동생의 케이크 장식을 하겠다고 부탁하자 어머니가 허락하면서 지시에 따를 것을 다짐시키고 있다. 이에 대한 응답으로는 ② '그럼요, 그렇게 할 것을 약속드려요.' 가 가장 적절하다.

① 와, 냄새가 정말 좋아요.
③ 고마워요. 우선 하트를 그려요.
④ 네, 그 애는 초콜릿 케이크를 좋아해요.
⑤ 멋져 보여요. 엄마가 자랑스러워요.

W: Sean, don't touch that! It's your sister's birthday cake.
M: It looks lovely. Mom, **can I decorate** the cake myself? Please! I'd really love to do it.
W: Hmm, it's a good idea. But you have to **follow my directions**, okay?
M: **Sure, I promise I'll do that.**

여: Sean, 그거 만지지 마! 그건 네 여동생 생일케이크야.
남: 예뻐 보여요. 엄마, 제가 케이크를 장식해도 돼요? 제발요! 정말 하고 싶어요.
여: 음, 좋은 생각이야. 하지만 내 지시에 따라야 한다, 알겠니?
남: 그럼요, 그렇게 할 것을 약속드려요.

어휘 decorate 장식하다, 꾸미다 follow (지시 등을) 따르다; 따라가다; 이해하다 direction 지시, 지휘; 명령; 방향; 감독

12 짧은 대화에 이어질 응답 ③

✱ 여자가 자동차 수리가 다 되었는지 묻자 남자가 다 되었다면서 오전 9시부터 오후 6시 사이에 언제든 가져가라고 했으므로 여자의 응답으로는 ③ '잘 되었군요! 내일 언젠가 들를게요.'가 적절하다.

① 전 가야 해서요. 나중에 이야기할게요.
② 미안해요. 다시는 늦지 않겠다고 약속드려요.
④ 다음에 하죠. 어쨌든 고마워요.
⑤ 알겠어요. 도서관 앞으로 데리러 갈게요.

[Telephone rings.]
M: Hello, Haynes Auto Repair. **How can I help you?**
W: This is Emma Clarks. I took my car in for repair yesterday. Is it ready?
M: Sure, Ms. Clarks. You can **pick it up** anytime between 9 a.m. and 6 p.m.
W: Great! I'll come by sometime tomorrow.

[전화벨이 울린다.]
남: 여보세요, Haynes 자동차 수리점입니다. 무엇을 도와드릴까요?
여: 저는 Emma Clarks예요. 어제 제 차를 수리하러 가져갔는데요, 다 됐나요?
남: 그럼요, Clarks 씨. 오전 9시와 오후 6시 사이에 언제든 가져가실 수 있습니다.
여: 잘 되었군요! 내일 언젠가 들를게요.

어휘 repair 수리(하다), 수선(하다) pick A up A를 찾아오다
| 선택지 어휘 | come by (잠깐) 들르다

13 긴 대화에 이어질 응답 ②

✱ 대화의 전체 맥락 하에 마지막 말의 의미나 의도를 정확히 파악하는 것이 좋다. 가기로 했던 카누 여행이 취소되면서 무엇을 할지를 의논하는 상황이다. 남자가 제안한 도보 여행과 여자가 제안한 쇼핑을 서로가 거절한 뒤 남자가 TV로 토크쇼 볼 것을 제안하고 있다. 이에 대한 여자의 응답으로는 동의하는 내용의 ② '그게 당신이 원하는 거라면 좋아요.'가 가장 적절하다.

① 그럼요, 우리가 필요한 것을 가서 찾아봅시다.
③ 당신이 그렇게 이해해줘서 기뻐요.
④ 경기는 오후 2시 정각에 시작할 거예요.
⑤ 네, 나는 그렇게 휴가를 갈 수 있었으면 좋겠어요.

W: Michael, look out the window. It's really cloudy outside.
M: Uh-oh! I don't think we can go on our canoe trip at the lake today.
W: That's too bad. I was really **looking forward to** our trip.
M: It'll be too difficult to take the canoe with all the fog.
W: You're right. What should we do then?
M: Should **we go hiking** instead?
W: It looks like it'll rain. I don't feel like **catching a cold** from the rain. How about going shopping?
M: You know how much I hate that. Oh, I have an idea. **Let's watch** a talk show on TV.
W: We do that all the time.
M: I heard Edward Robinson will appear on today's show. He is a terrific football player.
W: All right, if that's what you want.

여: Michael, 창밖을 봐요. 밖에 날씨가 정말 흐려요.
남: 이런! 오늘 우리가 호수 카누 여행을 갈 수 없을 것 같은데요.
여: 안타깝네요. 난 우리 여행을 정말 기대했었는데요.
남: 온통 안개가 싸여서 카누를 타기가 아주 힘들 거예요.
여: 당신 말이 맞아요. 그러면 우리 뭐를 할까요?
남: 대신에 도보 여행을 갈까요?
여: 비가 올 것 같은데요. 난 비 맞아서 감기에 걸리고 싶지는 않아요. 쇼핑가는 건 어때요?
남: 내가 그걸 얼마나 싫어하는지 알잖아요. 아, 좋은 생각이 있어요. TV로 토크쇼를 봅시다.
여: 우리가 늘 하는 거잖아요.
남: Edward Robinson이 오늘 토크쇼에 나올 거라고 들었어요. 그는 대단한 축구 선수예요.
여: 그게 당신이 원하는 거라면 좋아요.

어휘 look forward to A A를 기대하다 catch a cold 감기에 걸리다 appear 나오다, 나타나다; ~처럼 보이다 terrific 대단한, 아주 좋은 | 선택지 어휘 | sharp 정각에 get away 휴가를 가다; 탈출하다

14 긴 대화에 이어질 응답 ③

✱ 대화의 전체 맥락 하에 마지막 말의 의미나 의도를 정확히 파악하는 것이 좋다. 스페인어 연극을 하는 프로젝트에서 말하기에 자신 없어 하는 여자에게 남자가 서로 도와주면 해낼 수 있다고 말하고 있다. 여자가 정말 그렇게 생각하느냐고 확인했을 때 남자의 응답으로는 ③ '물론이지! 함께라면 우리는 더 잘할 수 있어.'가 가장 적절하다.

① 멋지다! 스페인은 큰 나라야.
② 좋아. 다음에는 내가 다른 주제를 시도할게.
④ 고마워. 네 대본 역시 훌륭했어.
⑤ 너를 연극에 초대하는 걸 잊다니 미안해.

M: Natalie, I'm happy you and I are a team for the Spanish class project.
W: So am I. I'll do my best.
M: We should make a five-minute play in Spanish by next Friday. Let's choose a topic first.
W: How about **making a story** that happens on an airplane?
M: Sounds interesting. Let's make a funny situation between a rude tourist and a smart flight attendant.
W: Um, Dylan, I'd rather **write the script** on my own, if you don't mind.
M: What do you mean?
W: I'm a terrible Spanish speaker, so I want to play **a minimal speaking** part.
M: That makes no sense! We're making a play, not a presentation.
W: I'm just worried I might make mistakes and ruin your grade.
M: Come on, Natalie. If I help you with speaking and you help me with writing, we can **get through it**.
W: Do you really think so?
M: **Of course! Together, we can do better.**

남: Natalie, 너하고 내가 스페인어 수업 프로젝트에서 한 팀이어서 기뻐.
여: 나도 그래. 최선을 다할게.
남: 우리는 다음 금요일까지 스페인어로 5분짜리 연극을 만들어야 해. 우선 주제를 정하자.

여: 비행기에서 일어나는 이야기를 만드는 건 어떨까?

남: 그거 재미있겠다. 무례한 관광객과 현명한 승무원 사이의 재미있는 상황을 만들어보자.

여: 음, Dylan, 네가 괜찮다면 내가 혼자서 대본을 썼으면 좋겠어.

남: 무슨 뜻이야?

여: 난 스페인어를 말하는 게 형편없어서 최소한으로 말하는 역할을 하고 싶어.

남: 그건 말도 안 돼. 우리는 연극을 하는 거지 발표를 하는 게 아니야.

여: 난 단지 내가 실수를 해서 네 성적을 망칠까 봐 걱정돼.

남: 이 봐, Natalie. 내가 말하는 것에서 너를 돕고 네가 글 쓰는 것에서 나를 도와준다면 우리는 해낼 수 있어.

여: 정말 그렇게 생각하니?

남: 물론이지! 함께라면 우리는 더 잘할 수 있어.

어휘 flight attendant 승무원   on one's own 혼자서, 단독으로   minimal 최소의, 아주 적은   ruin 망치다; 파괴하다; 폐허; 유적   get through ~을 해내대[끝내다]; 빠져나가다

15 상황에 적절한 말   ④

∗ 지시문을 통해 누가(A) 누구에게(B) 할 말인지를 우선 정확히 파악한다. 담화는 대개 A와 B에 대한 배경 설명과 B가 처한 문제 상황, 그리고 이에 대해 A가 어떤 말을 하려고 하는지에 대한 설명의 순서로 전개된다. 오케스트라 연습 중 실수한 학생이 사과하는 상황에서 지휘자 Brayden 선생님(A)은 연습 중이므로 실수가 별거 아니라고 생각해 Grace(B)의 기분을 나아지게 해주고 싶다. 이 상황에서 Brayden 선생님이 할 말로는 ④ '괜찮아. 넌 실수로부터 배울 수 있단다.'가 가장 적절하다.

① 넌 준비가 안 되었지만, 여전히 난 네가 자랑스럽단다.
② 미안하구나. 그게 내가 너를 위해 할 수 있는 최선이었어.
③ 고맙구나. 네가 내게 마음을 쓰는 걸 알게 되어 기쁘구나.
⑤ 걱정 말렴. 네 실패에 대해 누구에게도 말하지 않을게.

M: Grace is a high school student and a violinist in the community orchestra. The conductor of the orchestra is Mr. Brayden. The orchestra is having **their annual concert** next month, so they have to practice every day. Grace practices the violin for hours in the practice room every day. Because the violin has an important role in the piece they're playing, Grace wants to do **as well as she can**. But during practice today, Grace made **a few big mistakes** while playing. After the practice, she goes to Mr. Brayden and apologizes to him for her mistakes. Mr. Brayden thinks **it's no big deal** because they're still practicing. He wants to make her feel better. In this situation, what would Mr. Brayden most likely say to Grace?

Mr. Brayden: <u>It's all right. You can learn from your mistakes.</u>

남: Grace는 고등학생이자 지역 오케스트라의 바이올린 연주자이다. 오케스트라의 지휘자는 Brayden 선생님이다. 오케스트라는 다음 달에 연례 연주회가 있어서 매일 연습을 해야 한다. Grace는 매일 연습실에서 몇 시간씩 바이올린을 연습한다. 그들이 연주하는 작품에서 바이올린이 중요한 역할을 하기 때문에 Grace는 자신이 할 수 있는 한 잘하고 싶다. 하지만 오늘 연습 도중에 Grace는 연주하면서 몇 가지 큰 실수를 했다. 연습 후에 그녀는 Brayden 선생님께 가서 자신의 실수를 사과한다. Brayden 선생님은 그들이 아직 연습하는 중이기 때문에 그것이 별일 아니라고 생각한다. 그는 그녀의 기분을 나아지게 해주고 싶다. 이 상황에서 Brayden 선생님이 Grace에게 뭐라고 말하겠는가?

Brayden 선생님: <u>괜찮아. 넌 실수로부터 배울 수 있단다.</u>

어휘 conductor 지휘자; 안내원   annual 연례의, 매년의; 한 해의

16~17 세트 문항   16 ①   17 ③

∗ **16** 운동하면서 재미있게 노는 많은 방법이 있다고 하면서 예를 들고 있으므로 담화의 주제로는 ① '운동을 재미있게 하는 법'이 가장 적절하다. 담화 앞부분의 운동을 하지 않으면 몸이 엉망이 된다는 내용만으로 ④를 답으로 고르지 않도록 유의한다.

② 단체 활동의 혜택
③ 단체 경기를 개최하는 방법
④ 건강을 유지하기 위한 운동의 필요성
⑤ 친구를 만날 때 할 것

∗ **17** 해석 참조.
① 농구   ② 야구   ③ 수영   ④ 자전거 타기   ⑤ 춤추기

M: For many people, it is more fun to watch television than to run 5 miles. Yet, if you don't exercise, your body **gets out of shape**. You start to move, and maybe even think, more slowly. But why do something that isn't fun? Well, there are many ways to **exercise and have fun**. Many group activities can provide you with exercise and fun. Think of the times when you are just **hanging out** with your friends. You go outside and jump rope, play basketball or baseball, run races, and so on. Soon, you are all laughing and having a good time. But there are times when you are by yourself. Then what? You can **get plenty of exercise** just by walking, biking, or even dancing. For example, you can take an enjoyable morning walk with your dog in a park. You can ride your bike while listening to your favorite songs or practice the newest dance by yourself. Before long, you will be the fittest dancer of all your friends!

남: 많은 사람들에게 5마일을 달리는 것보다는 텔레비전을 보는 게 더 재미있습니다. 그러나 여러분이 운동하지 않는다면 여러분의 몸은 엉망이 됩니다. 여러분은 더 천천히 움직이기 시작하고 아마 심지어는 더 천천히 생각하게 됩니다. 하지만 재미있지 않은 것을 왜 합니까? 자, 운동하면서 재미있게 노는 많은 방법이 있습니다. 많은 단체 활동은 여러분에게 운동과 재미를 제공할 수 있습니다. 여러분이 그저 친구들과 어울려 시간을 보낼 때를 생각해보십시오. 여러분은 밖으로 나가서 줄넘기를 하거나 ① 농구나 ② 야구를 하고 경주를 달리고 등등을 합니다. 곧 여러분은 모두가 웃고 있고 즐거운 시간을 보내고 있습니다. 하지만 여러분 혼자일 때가 있습니다. 그러면 뭘 하나요? 여러분은 단지 걷거나 ④ 자전거를 타거나 심지어 ⑤ 춤을 추면서 수많은 운동을 할 수 있습니다. 예를 들면, 공원에서 여러분의 개와 즐거운 아침 산책을 할 수 있습니다. 여러분이 가장 좋아하는 노래를 들으면서 자전거를 타거나 혼자서 최신 춤을 연습할 수 있습니다. 머지않아 여러분은 모든 친구들 중에서 가장 건강한 댄서가 될 것입니다!

어휘 out of shape 몸[몸매]이 엉망인   hang out with ~와 시간을 보내다[어울리다]   jump rope 줄넘기를 하다   fit 건강한; 맞다; 어울리다; 어울리는
| 선택지 어휘 | organize (행사 등을) 개최하다; 조직[준비]하다; 정리하다   necessity 필요성; 필수품   get together 만나다; 모이다; 합치다

02회

01 화자가 하는 말의 목적　　　　　④

＊ 담화의 일부 내용이 아니라 중심 내용을 파악해야 한다. 자동차가 환경에 미치는 영향에 대해서 언급하면서 일주일에 한 번 차를 집에 두고 나오겠다는 공약을 하고 실천할 것을 제안하고 있으므로 담화의 목적은 ④이다. 대기 오염에 대한 언급은 있지만 주 1일 승용차 안 타기를 제안하기 위한 이유로 언급되고 있음에 유의한다.

M: Cars are one of the great mixed bags of our time. They are wonders of engineering and a serious threat to life on Earth at the same time. They create convenience and also **terrible traffic**. In the U.S., about 28% of all greenhouse gas emissions come from cars. If you are truly trying to lighten your environmental impact, the easiest thing to do is **get out of** your car once a week. If you leave your car at home one day a week, you prevent 55 pounds of pollution each year from **being emitted** into our air. Would you be willing to make a public commitment to leave your car at home and take a bus **once a week** for work? You'll not only save energy and your money but also get a chance to relax and exercise.

남: 자동차는 우리 시대의 굉장한 온갖 종류의 집합 중 하나입니다. 그것들은 공학의 경이로움이면서 동시에 지구상의 생명체에 대한 심각한 위협이기도 합니다. 그것들은 편리함과 또한 끔찍한 교통량을 만들어냅니다. 미국에서는 모든 온실가스 배출물의 약 28퍼센트가 차량에서 나옵니다. 여러분이 환경에 미치는 영향을 덜고자 진정으로 노력하고 있다면, 여러분이 해야 할 가장 쉬운 일은 일주일에 한 번 차에서 벗어나는 것입니다. 일주일에 한 번 차를 집에 둔다면, 여러분은 매년 55파운드의 오염 물질이 대기로 방출되는 것을 막는 것입니다. 일주일에 한 번 차를 집에 두고 직장에 버스를 타고 오겠다는 공약을 기꺼이 하시겠습니까? 여러분은 에너지와 돈을 절약할 뿐만 아니라 긴장을 풀고 운동할 기회를 얻게 될 것입니다.

어휘 wonder 경이로움; 불가사의   threat 위협, 협박   convenience 편리함, 편의; 이익   emission 배출(물), 배기가스 *cf.* emit 방출[배출]하다, 내뿜다   lighten 덜어주다; 가볍게 하다   prevent A from v-ing A가 v하는 것을 막다[예방하다]   pollution 오염 (물질), 공해   commitment 약속; 전념

02 의견　　　　　②

＊ 우선 지시문에서 명시한 화자의 성별을 보고 어느 화자의 말에 주목할지를 판단해야 한다. 특히 의견이나 주장을 표현하는 어구(I think ~, You should ~ 등)가 이끄는 내용을 잘 들어야 한다. 남자가 싹이 난 감자를 버리겠다고 하자 여자는 싹이 난 부분을 제거하면 먹기 안전하고 사용할 수 있어서 버릴 필요가 없다고 말하고 있다. 그러므로 여자의 의견으로는 ②가 가장 적절하다.

M: I bought three pounds of potatoes for a dollar at the grocery store.
W: That's **a good deal**. I don't know how that store makes money.
M: They were cheap, but some of the potatoes **had sprouted**.
W: Really? Potato sprouts are toxic and can give you a headache and other digestive symptoms.
M: Oh, then I should **throw them away**.
W: No need to throw them out. If you simply **cut away** any sprouts, the potatoes will be quite safe to eat.
M: Are you sure? I don't want to get sick after eating them.
W: Absolutely. **Just remove** the sprouts and any soft spots, and your potato should be fine to use.
M: Thanks for telling me. I'll make potato soup tonight.
W: Sounds delicious. Have a nice dinner.

남: 식료품점에서 1달러를 주고 감자 3파운드를 샀어.
여: 정말 싸게 샀네. 그 상점이 어떻게 돈을 버는지 모르겠어.
남: 감자가 싸긴 한데 일부가 싹이 났어.
여: 정말이야? 감자 싹은 독성이 있어서 두통과 다른 소화기 증상을 줄 수 있어.
남: 아, 그러면 저것들을 버려야겠군.

여: 버릴 필요는 없어. 간단하게 모든 싹을 잘라 버리면, 감자는 먹기 아주 안전할 거야.
남: 확실하니? 난 그것들을 먹고 아프고 싶지 않아.
여: 그렇고말고. 그냥 싹과 무른 부분을 제거해. 그러면 네 감자는 사용하기 괜찮을 거야.
남: 알려줘서 고마워. 오늘 밤 감자 수프를 만들어야겠다.
여: 맛있겠다. 근사한 저녁 먹어.

어휘 grocery store 식료품점   deal 거래; 대우   sprout 싹(이 나다)   toxic 독성의, 유독한   digestive 소화의   symptom 증상; (불길한) 징후   absolutely 그렇고말고, 정말 그래; 전적으로

03 관계　　　　　③

＊ 직업을 나타내거나 추론할 수 있는 힌트가 대화 전반에 걸쳐 드러나므로, 대화를 전체적으로 이해하는 것이 필요하다. 남자는 누구든 될 수 있는 직업을 갖고 있으며 가장 연기하기 좋은 배역에 대해서 이야기하고 있으므로 배우임을 알 수 있다. 여자는 남자를 인터뷰하고 있고 자신의 잡지 독자들을 위해 남자의 여가시간에 대해 질문하고 있는 것으로 보아 잡지 기자임을 알 수 있다. 그러므로 두 사람의 관계는 ③이 적절하다.

W: Next question, do you like your job?
M: Absolutely. I enjoy my job very much.
W: What do you like about your job?
M: I can be anybody. I can be a pilot, a police officer, or even a superhero. I feel like I'm living so **many different lives**.
W: That must be exciting. Which character do you like playing the best?
M: I especially like **playing a pilot** because that was my dream when I was young.
W: I understand. What do you do in your spare time?
M: Oh, I do many things.
W: Would you share them with the readers of our magazine?
M: I travel, read, and play basketball, and recently I've started to **do some volunteer work** for a children's hospital.
W: Sounds like you're really enjoying your life. Working hard, playing hard, and helping other people.
M: Well, I just try to **make the most of** this life.

여: 다음 질문입니다. 당신 직업을 좋아하나요?
남: 그렇고말고요. 전 제 일을 무척이나 즐깁니다.
여: 당신 직업에서 무엇을 좋아하나요?
남: 전 누구나 될 수 있어요. 비행기 조종사, 경찰관, 혹은 슈퍼 히어로도 될 수 있죠. 전 너무나 많은 다른 인생을 살고 있는 것처럼 느껴요.
여: 그건 분명히 흥미롭겠군요. 어떤 배역이 연기하기에 가장 좋은가요?
남: 어릴 적 제 꿈이었기 때문에 비행기 조종사를 연기하는 게 특히 좋습니다.
여: 그렇군요. 여가시간에는 뭘 하나요?
남: 아, 많은 걸 합니다.
여: 우리 잡지 독자들에게 그것들을 공유해주시겠어요?
남: 여행하고 독서하고 농구를 하죠. 그리고 최근에는 어린이 병원을 위한 자원봉사 일을 좀 시작했습니다.
여: 인생을 정말 즐기는 것 같군요. 열심히 일하고 열심히 놀고 다른 사람을 돕고요.
남: 글쎄요, 저는 단지 이 삶을 최대한 즐겁게 보내려고 해요.

어휘 character 배역; 특징; 성격   spare time 여가시간   make the most of ~을 최대한 즐기다[활용하다]

04 그림 불일치　　　　　④

＊ 대화가 나오기 전에 각 사물의 위치 관계와 외형(형태나 무늬, 개수 등)의 특징을 미리 확인하는 것이 좋다. 거리에서 살아있는 조각상 공연을 하는 행위 예술가를 보고 나누는 대화이다. ④의 남자는 발 옆 땅 위에 투구가 있다고 했는데 그림에는 투구를 머리에 쓰고 있으므로 대화의 내용과 일치하지 않는다.

W: Look over there. What are those people doing? They're all dressed in white with their hands and faces painted in white.
M: They're performing artists on the street. They look like living statues.
W: Oh, yes. That person who is sitting on a chair with his right hand **on his chin** looks like he's imitating Rodin's famous sculpture.
M: Right! *The Thinker*, I guess. I like the woman with wings next to *The Thinker*. She has **her hands together**.
W: She is a praying angel. The man next to her has the most difficult job out of them all.
M: Yes, he is **holding a round disk** in his right hand. He's trying to throw it.
W: Isn't he also imitating a famous sculpture?
M: I think so, and I think the man on the right **is dressed as** an old warrior.
W: He is holding a long sword with both hands, and there is **a helmet on the ground** beside his feet. By the way, what is that white jar in front of them for?
M: It's a tip jar. People **drop donations** in the jar. Why don't we tip them?
W: Okay, it's a good performance. I will.

여: 저길 봐요. 저 사람들 무얼 하고 있는 거죠? 모두 손과 얼굴을 하얗게 칠하고 흰옷을 입었어요.
남: 그들은 거리의 행위 예술가들이에요. 살아있는 조각상처럼 보이는군요.
여: 아, 그렇군요. 오른손을 턱에 대고 의자에 앉아있는 저 사람은 로댕의 유명한 조각상을 흉내 내고 있는 것처럼 보여요.
남: 맞아요! '생각하는 사람'인 것 같아요. 나는 '생각하는 사람' 옆의 날개를 단 여자가 좋군요. 그녀는 두 손을 함께 모으고 있네요.
여: 그녀는 기도하는 천사네요. 그녀 옆에 있는 남자는 저 사람들 모두 중에서 제일 어려운 일을 하고 있군요.
남: 네. 오른손으로 둥근 원반을 잡고 있군요. 그것을 던지려고 하고 있네요.
여: 그도 유명한 조각상을 흉내 내고 있는 거 아닌가요?
남: 그런 것 같아요. 그리고 오른쪽에 있는 남자는 옛 전사처럼 옷을 입은 것 같아요.
여: 그는 양손으로 긴 칼을 잡고 있고 그의 발 옆 땅 위에 투구가 있어요. 그런데 그들 앞에 있는 저 하얀 통은 무엇을 위한 거죠?
남: 팁을 넣는 통이에요. 사람들이 그 통에 기부금을 떨어뜨리는 거죠. 우리도 그들에게 팁을 주는 게 어때요?
여: 좋아요, 멋진 공연이니까요. 내가 줄게요.

어휘 statue 조각상, 상(像) imitate 흉내 내다; 모방하다 sculpture 조각(상) pray 기도[기원]하다, 빌다 warrior 전사, 무사 sword 칼, 검 donation 기부(금)

05 추후 행동 ④

＊ 대개 대화는 어떤 일을 하게 되는 상황이 먼저 제시된 뒤에 남자와 여자가 각각 할 일들과 이에 대한 수락/거절의 응답이 나열되는 식으로 전개된다. 여자가 할 일을 물었음에 유의한다. 저녁 설거지하기는 남자가 지금 하겠다고 한 일이고 차고 정리하기는 예정했던 일이지만 못하게 된 일이다. 자동차 전시회 방문 역시 남자가 앞으로 할 일이고 여자가 할 일은 토요일에 파마하기 위해 미용실 예약하기이다.

M: Mila, I'm going to San Francisco tomorrow and coming back on Sunday.
W: What are you talking about? We have to do a major house cleaning this Saturday.
M: Actually, Joel **was supposed to go** to the San Francisco Auto Show, but he got into an accident this morning.
W: You mean your co-worker Joel? Is he okay?
M: Yeah, but now I have to go there **instead of him**.
W: I understand. I was hoping you could clean the garage this Saturday.
M: I'll **take care of the dishes** tonight instead.
W: All right. Since you'll be out, I'll go to the beauty salon to get a perm this Saturday.
M: Sounds like a good idea. Why don't you **make a reservation** right now?
W: Thanks for reminding me. Otherwise, Saturday will be completely booked.

남: Mila. 내가 내일 샌프란시스코에 갔다가 일요일에 돌아와요.
여: 무슨 말이에요? 우리 이번 토요일에 대청소를 해야 하잖아요.
남: 사실, Joel이 샌프란시스코 자동차 전시회에 가기로 했는데 그가 오늘 아침 사고를 당했어요.

여: 당신 동료 Joel 말인가요? 그는 괜찮아요?
남: 네, 하지만 이제 내가 그 대신 거기 가야 해요.
여: 알겠어요. 이번 토요일에 당신이 차고를 치워줄 수 있기를 바랐는데요.
남: 대신 오늘 밤 설거지를 할게요.
여: 좋아요. 당신이 집을 비우니까 난 이번 토요일에 파마하러 미용실에 갈게요.
남: 그거 좋은 생각이네요. 지금 당장 예약을 하지 그래요?
여: 생각나게 해줘서 고마워요. 그러지 않다가는 토요일엔 완전히 예약이 찰 거예요.

어휘 be supposed to-v v하기로 되어 있다 accident 사고; 우연한 일 garage 차고, 주차장 make a reservation 예약하다(= book) remind 생각나게 하다, 상기시키다 otherwise 그렇지 않으면; (~와는) 달리 completely 완전히, 전적으로

06 금액 ④

＊ 여러 개의 수치 정보가 등장하므로 필요한 정보를 메모하면서 듣는 것이 좋다. 소파의 가격은 2,500달러인데 배달료가 추가된다. 배달료는 기본 200달러에 층마다 50달러의 추가 요금이 있고 여자의 집은 3층이므로 100달러가 추가되어 300달러가 나오므로 여자가 지불해야 하는 금액은 모두 2,800달러이다.

W: Excuse me. How much does this leather sofa cost? It looks great.
M: It's $2,500, **plus delivery charge**. It's a premium Italian leather sofa.
W: You mean the price doesn't include delivery charge?
M: No, it doesn't.
W: Oh, that seems kind of expensive.
M: It's **more expensive** than average — that's true. But this sofa will last longer, and you'll save money in the long run.
W: I see. Then how much is the delivery charge? I live in an apartment.
M: Does your building have elevators?
W: I'm afraid not. The only access is through a staircase. My apartment is on the 3rd floor.
M: The standard delivery charge is $200, but it's only for the first floor. There'll be an additional charge of $50 per floor.
W: Okay, so I'll have to pay **an additional $100**. How soon would you be able to deliver it?
M: Let's see... We could deliver it **in a week**.
W: All right. Here is my credit card.

여: 실례합니다. 이 가죽 소파가 얼마나 하는지요? 멋져 보이는데요.
남: 2,500달러에 배달료가 붙습니다. 최고급 이탈리아산 가죽 소파입니다.
여: 가격에 배달료가 포함되지 않는다는 말이죠?
남: 네, 포함되지 않습니다.
여: 아, 좀 비싼 것 같은데요.
남: 평균보다 좀 더 비싸죠, 그건 사실입니다. 하지만 이 소파는 더 오래 가니까 길게 보아서는 돈을 절약하실 것입니다.
여: 알겠어요. 그러면 배달료는 얼마인가요? 저는 아파트에 살고 있어요.
남: 건물에 엘리베이터가 있나요?
여: 유감이지만 없습니다. 유일한 접근이 계단을 통하는 거예요. 제 아파트는 3층이고요.
남: 기본 배달료는 200달러이지만 그건 1층에만 해당해요. 층마다 50달러의 추가 요금이 붙게 됩니다.
여: 좋아요. 그러면 제가 추가로 100달러를 더 지불해야 하는 거죠. 얼마나 빨리 배달해줄 수 있나요?
남: 어디 봅시다… 일주일 후에 배달할 수 있습니다.
여: 좋아요. 여기 제 신용카드요.

어휘 leather 가죽 delivery 배달, 전달 *cf.* deliver 배달[전달]하다 include 포함하다 charge 요금; 기소, 고발 average 평균(의); 보통의, 일반적인 in the long run 길게 보아서는, 결국에는 staircase 계단 standard 표준, 기준; 모범 additional 추가의

07 이유 ②

＊ 지시문을 통해 여자가 동백꽃을 살 수 없는 상황임을 파악한다. 여자는 동백꽃의 꽃말이 사랑과 아름다움이라서 약혼식 장식에 추가하고 싶어 하지만, 여름에는 동백꽃이 피는 철이 아니라서 구할 수 없는 상황이다. 그러므로 답은 ②가 적절하다.

M: When will you have your engagement party?
W: In two weeks. I have no idea **how I should decorate** for the occasion.
M: I'll do whatever I can for you. For engagement parties, I usually suggest classic flowers like roses and lilies for decorating.
W: Okay, and I love camellias. I'd like to add camellias to the selection.
M: Well, camellias **aren't available** at this time.
W: But these days so many flowers are imported into our country from all over the world. **I'm willing to** pay high prices.
M: You're right, but even these days, not every flower is available in all seasons.
W: Oh, that's so disappointing. I want them because they're **a symbol of** love and beauty.
M: I know what you mean. But the season for camellias is late winter to early spring. I'm afraid they aren't available in summer.
W: Oh, okay.
M: Let me show you other flowers that will **go with roses**.

남: 언제 약혼 파티가 있으신가요?
여: 이 주 후에요. 이 행사에 어떻게 장식해야 할지 모르겠어요.
남: 제가 손님을 위해 할 수 있는 건 뭐든지 해드릴게요. 약혼 파티를 위해 장식을 하려면 저는 보통 장미와 백합 같은 고전적인 꽃들을 권합니다.
여: 좋아요, 그리고 제가 동백꽃을 좋아하거든요. 구성에 동백꽃을 추가하고 싶어요.
남: 글쎄요. 동백꽃은 이 시기에 구할 수 없어서요.
여: 하지만 요즘은 아주 많은 꽃들이 세계 곳곳에서 우리나라로 수입되잖아요. 전 기꺼이 높은 가격을 지불하겠어요.
남: 맞습니다. 하지만 요즘조차도 모든 꽃이 모든 철에 구매 가능한 건 아닙니다.
여: 아, 그거 너무 실망스러운데요. 그 꽃이 사랑과 아름다움의 상징이라서 그걸 하고 싶거든요.
남: 무슨 말씀이신지 압니다. 하지만 동백꽃 철은 늦은 겨울부터 이른 봄까지입니다. 여름에는 구할 수 없을 것 같아요.
여: 아, 알겠어요.
남: 장미와 어울릴 다른 꽃들을 보여드릴게요.

어휘 engagement 약혼; 약속 occasion 행사, 의식; 때, 경우 classic 고전적인; 일류의; 대표적인 add 추가하다; 합하다 available 구할 수 있는 import 수입하다; 수입(품) be willing to-v 기꺼이 v하다 disappointing 실망스러운, 기대에 못 미치는 symbol 상징(물); 기호 go with ~와 어울리다; ~에 딸려 나오다

08 언급하지 않은 것 ⑤

※ 대화의 진행은 대개 선택지와 같은 순서이므로, 선택지를 보면서 언급된 내용을 소거하는 식으로 푸는 것이 좋다. 테니스 코치가 선수의 어머니에게 전화해서 주니어 테니스 대회에 대해 이야기를 나누고 있다. 우선 대회 일자와 참가비, 등록 마감일에 대해 언급하고 마지막으로 대회 장소에 대해 이야기하고 있다. 주최 기관에 대해서는 전혀 언급하지 않았으므로 답은 ⑤이다.

[Telephone rings.]
W: Hello, you've reached Caroline's house.
M: Hello, Mrs. Caroline. This is Henry O'Brien, Bret's tennis coach.
W: Oh, hello. How is Bret doing with his lessons?
M: He's doing very well. **That's why** I'm calling you. I asked him to participate in the Junior Tennis Tournament.
W: I heard that. **It'll be held from** October 28th **to** December 2nd.
M: Yes, there will be games for singles and doubles, and Bret will play in the doubles.
W: So, **how much is it** to register for the tournament?
M: It's $40 per player. He has to sign up **no later than** September 23rd. I'll give Bret the form tomorrow.
W: Okay. Oh, one more question. **Where are the games held**?
M: It's the Mesa Tennis Center, near Lawrence University.
W: All right. Thank you for calling.

[전화벨이 울린다.]
여: 여보세요, Caroline의 집입니다.
남: 여보세요, Caroline 부인. 저는 Bret의 테니스 코치인 Henry O'Brien입니다.

여: 아, 안녕하세요. Bret이 강습을 어떻게 하고 있나요?
남: 아주 잘 하고 있습니다. 그래서 전화 드렸는데요. 제가 그 애에게 주니어 테니스 대회에 참가하라고 했거든요.
여: 그 이야기 들었어요. 10월 28일부터 12월 2일까지(① 대회 일자) 열릴 거라고요.
남: 네, 단식과 복식 경기가 있는데 Bret은 복식을 뛸 겁니다.
여: 그러면 대회에 등록하려면 비용이 얼마나 드나요?
남: 선수당 40달러(② 참가비)입니다. 늦어도 9월 23일까지(③ 등록 마감일) 등록해야 해요. 제가 Bret에게 내일 신청서를 주겠습니다.
여: 알겠습니다. 아, 질문이 하나 더 있는데요. 경기가 어디서 열리나요?
남: Lawrence 대학 근처에 있는 Mesa 테니스 센터(④ 대회 장소)입니다.
여: 알겠습니다. 전화해 주셔서 감사합니다.

어휘 participate in ~에 참가[참여]하다 hold 열다, 개최하다 register for ~에 등록하다 sign up 등록하다 no later than 늦어도 ~까지는 form (문서의) 서식; 종류

09 내용 불일치 ⑤

※ 담화의 진행은 대개 선택지와 같은 순서이므로, 선택지를 보면서 일치하는 내용을 소거하는 식으로 푸는 것이 좋다. 수익금 모두가 아프리카의 가난한 지역에 책을 보내는 데 사용된다고 했으므로 ⑤는 내용과 일치하지 않는다.

W: This announcement is for all those attending the Timber Library Bazaar. If you would like to buy something, you must first **purchase coupons**. To prevent a lack of change, we ask that you buy all goods with these coupons. Any unused coupons **can be refunded** at the cashier. The food tables are still being set up. We will start selling food at 11:30 a.m. We will be selling used clothing on the right side of the library hall. New clothing will be sold on the left of the hall at greatly **discounted prices**. We are selling books and toys in front of the library. DVDs will be available there, too. **All profits will be used** to send books to poor regions of Africa. We thank you for coming to this bazaar and **contributing to sending books** to libraries in Africa. We hope you have a good time today.

여: 이 공지는 Timber 도서관 바자회에 참석하는 모든 분께 드리는 것입니다. 여러분이 무언가를 사고자 한다면, 먼저 반드시 쿠폰을 구매하셔야 합니다. 잔돈의 부족을 막기 위해서 ① 저희는 여러분이 모든 물품을 이 쿠폰으로 사시길 요청합니다. 사용하지 않은 쿠폰은 계산대에서 환불받으실 수 있습니다. 음식 테이블은 아직 설치 중입니다. ② 오전 11시 30분부터 음식을 팔기 시작할 것입니다. ③ 도서관 홀 오른편에서 중고 의류를 판매할 것입니다. 새 의류는 홀의 왼편에서 아주 많이 할인된 가격으로 판매될 것입니다. ④ 도서관 앞에서는 책과 장난감을 판매할 것입니다. DVD도 거기서 구매하실 수 있을 겁니다. ⑤ 모든 수익금은 아프리카의 가난한 지역에 책을 보내는 데 사용될 것입니다. 이 바자회에 오셔서 아프리카의 도서관에 책을 보내는 데 기여해주심에 감사드립니다. 오늘 여러분이 좋은 시간을 보내시길 바랍니다.

어휘 announcement 공지; 발표 (내용) attend 참석하다; 주의를 기울이다 bazaar 바자회 purchase 구매(하다), 구입(하다) lack 부족(하다), 결핍 goods 물품, 상품 set up 설치하다; 마련하다 discounted 할인된 profit 수익, 이익 region 지역, 지방 contribute 기여하다; 기부[기증]하다

10 도표 이해 ⑤

※ 대화의 진행은 대개 도표 항목의 나열 순서대로 진행된다. 대화를 들으면서 도표의 각 항목 중 선택되지 않은 것을 소거하는 식으로 푸는 것이 좋다. 우선 편도 4시간 넘게 쓰고 싶지 않다고 했으므로 ①은 제외된다. 그리고 하루는 텐트에서 자려고 호텔과 함께 캠핑장을 갖춘 곳을 원했으므로 ②가 제외된다. 나머지 중에서 어린이 프로그램이 있는 ③과 ⑤가 선택되었고 결국 가까운 곳보다는 가격이 싼 곳으로 결정했으므로 예약할 리조트는 ⑤이다.

M: Let's get away this weekend with the kids.
W: Good idea. How about staying at a resort? There is **a list of resorts** in this flyer.
M: Okay. But I don't want to spend **more than 4 hours driving** each day.
W: Me, neither. Let's choose a resort that's no more than a 4-hour drive away.

M: How about staying in a tent for a night?
W: I'd love to. I think it'll be a great experience for the kids.
M: All right. Then we'll choose a place that has **camping grounds**.
W: Good. We should also look for something that has a program for kids.
M: Well, it looks like there are two options. Let's go to the one that's closer. We don't want to **be stuck with** a long drive.
W: Wait a second. We should think about the price. I want **the cheaper one**.
M: That's a good point. I'll make reservations right now.

남: 이번 주말에 아이들과 함께 휴가를 떠납시다.
여: 좋은 생각이에요. 리조트에서 묵는 건 어때요? 이 광고 전단에 리조트 목록이 있어요.
남: 좋아요. 하지만 운전하는 데 하루에 4시간 넘게 쓰고 싶지는 않아요.
여: 나도 그래요. 자동차로 4시간 거리 이내의 리조트를 선택합시다.
남: 하룻밤은 텐트에서 지내는 게 어때요?
여: 그러고 싶어요. 그게 아이들에게 굉장한 경험이 될 것 같아요.
남: 좋아요. 그러면 캠핑장이 있는 곳을 선택할게요.
여: 좋아요. 우리는 또 아이들을 위한 프로그램이 있는 것을 찾아야 해요.
남: 음, 두 개의 선택권이 있는 것 같군요. 더 가까운 곳으로 합시다. 장거리 운전에 갇혀 있고 싶지 않아요.
여: 잠깐만요. 가격을 생각해봐야죠. 난 더 싼 것을 원해요.
남: 잘 지적했어요. 지금 당장 예약을 할게요.

어휘 **get away** 휴가를 가다; 탈출하다 **flyer** 광고 전단 **option** 선택(할 수 있는 것); (기기의) 옵션 **stuck** 갇힌; 움직일 수 없는

11 짧은 대화에 이어질 응답 ③

✱ 남편이 저녁 식사 요리를 해달라는 아내의 부탁을 흔쾌히 수락했다. 먹고 싶은 요리를 말하고 너무 귀찮게 하는 건 아닌지 묻는 아내에게 남편이 할 말로는 ③ '아니요, 그건 쉬워요. 오늘 밤 그걸 먹읍시다.'가 적절한 응답이다.

① 정말 멋지군요! 당신은 아주 멋진 아내예요.
② 천만에요. 그건 정말 내게 도움이 돼요.
④ 괜찮아요. 폐를 끼쳐 미안해요.
⑤ 당신이 좋다니 기쁘군요. 더 많이 맘껏 드세요.

W: Honey, would you **mind cooking dinner** tonight? It's my turn, but I'm very busy preparing for a presentation.
M: Sure. What would you like to have for dinner?
W: I really like your spaghetti with oil and garlic. Is it **too much trouble** for you?
M: No, that's easy. Let's have it tonight.

여: 여보, 오늘 밤 저녁 식사를 요리해주겠어요? 내 차례이지만, 발표를 준비하느라 너무 바빠요.
남: 그럼요. 저녁으로 뭘 먹고 싶어요?
여: 전 당신의 오일과 마늘 스파게티가 정말 좋아요. 그게 당신에게 너무 귀찮은가요?
남: 아니요, 그건 쉬워요. 오늘 밤 그걸 먹읍시다.

어휘 **turn** (무엇을 할) 차례, 순번 **presentation** 발표, 설명; 제출
| 선택지 어휘 | **awesome** 아주 멋진, 굉장한 **help yourself** 맘껏 드세요

12 짧은 대화에 이어질 응답 ④

✱ 여자가 허리케인 피해자들을 위해 헌혈하러 간다는 걸 듣고, 자기도 하고 싶다는 남자에게 여자가 할 말로는 같이 하러 가자는 내용의 ④ '너도 할 수 있어. 지금 나하고 같이 가지 않을래?'가 가장 적절하다.

① 꼭 그런 건 아니야. 그러면 넌 특별한 계획이 있니?
② 네 말이 맞아. 그들을 돕기 위한 최선의 것이 뭘까?
③ 난 모르겠어. 넌 얼마나 줄 여유가 있니?
⑤ 네가 존경스러워. 이 몇 년 동안 어떻게 그것을 한 거야?

M: I heard you're going to **donate blood** for the people who were injured by the hurricane.
W: Yes, I am. South Texas Blood Center is asking for **urgent blood donations**.

M: Sounds great. I'd also like to make a donation.
W: You can. Why don't you come along with me now?

남: 네가 허리케인으로 다친 사람들을 위해 헌혈을 할 거라고 들었어.
여: 응. 그래. South Texas 혈액 센터가 긴급한 헌혈을 요청하고 있거든.
남: 멋지다. 나도 헌혈을 하고 싶어.
여: 너도 할 수 있어. 지금 나하고 같이 가지 않을래?

어휘 **donate blood** 헌혈하다 *cf.* **blood donation** 헌혈 *cf.* **make a donation** 기증[기부]하다 **injured** 다친, 부상을 당한 **urgent** 긴급한, 시급한
| 선택지 어휘 | **afford to-v** v할 여유가 있다; v할 형편이 되다 **admire** 존경하다, 칭찬하다

13 긴 대화에 이어질 응답 ①

✱ 대화의 전체 맥락 하에 마지막 말의 의미나 의도를 정확히 파악하는 것이 좋다. 남자의 아들이 농구팀의 최고 슈팅가드이고 프로 농구인 NBA에 진출하라는 요청도 받았다는 것을 알게 된 상황이다. 헤어지면서 여자가 할 말로는 ① '알겠어요. 아드님에게 제가 응원한다고 말해주세요.'가 가장 적절하다.

② 알아요. 항상 제 기분을 좋게 해주시네요.
③ 그건 확실해요. 아드님이 더 좋아지기 시작하길 바라요.
④ 사실이에요. 그 학교 들어가기가 쉽지 않죠.
⑤ 네. 농구 경기 보는 걸 분명히 즐기시는군요.

M: Hello, Miss Lynn. It's a beautiful day, isn't it?
W: Oh, hello, Mr. Robinson. The weather is gorgeous. Are you on your way out?
M: I'm **on my way to** see a basketball game. I'm just waiting for my wife to come out.
W: I see. Well, I hope you have a wonderful time.
M: Thank you. I'm going to see the high school basketball finals. My son **will be playing**.
W: Oh, I had no idea your son was **such an athlete**!
M: He's one of the top shooting guards on his team.
W: Wow, very impressive. Is he planning to **play professionally** once he graduates?
M: Well, he was asked to join the NBA, but he plans to go to university first.
W: He sounds **very responsible for** his age. You must be proud of him. I'm sure he will be a wonderful person.
M: Thanks for saying so. Oh, there comes my wife. I should leave now.
W: Okay. Tell your son I'll cheer for him.

남: 안녕하세요, Lynn 씨. 날이 아름답죠, 그렇지 않나요?
여: 아, 안녕하세요, Robinson 씨. 날씨가 아주 좋네요. 나가시는 길인가요?
남: 농구 경기를 보러 가는 길이에요. 그냥 아내가 나오길 기다리고 있어요.
여: 알겠어요. 저, 즐거운 시간 보내시길 바라요.
남: 고마워요. 전 고등학교 농구 결승전을 보러 갈 거예요. 제 아들이 뛰거든요.
여: 아, 아드님이 그런 운동선수인지 몰랐어요!
남: 팀에서 아이가 최고의 슈팅가드랍니다.
여: 와, 아주 인상적인데요. 졸업한 후에 프로선수로 뛸 계획인가요?
남: 글쎄요, NBA에 진출하라는 요청을 받았지만 우선 대학에 가기로 계획하고 있어요.
여: 나이에 비해 무척 책임감이 있나 보군요. 자랑스러우시겠어요. 아드님이 훌륭한 사람이 될 거라고 믿어요.
남: 그렇게 말해줘서 고마워요. 아, 저기 제 아내가 오는군요. 지금 떠나야겠어요.
여: 알겠어요. 아드님에게 제가 응원한다고 말해주세요.

어휘 **gorgeous** 아주 좋은[아름다운/멋진] **on one's way** ~로 가는 길[도중]에 **final** 결승전; 기말시험 **athlete** 운동선수 **professionally** 프로(선수)로; 직업적으로 **graduate** 졸업하다 **responsible** 책임감 있는

14 긴 대화에 이어질 응답 ①

✱ 대화의 전체 맥락 하에 마지막 말의 의미나 의도를 정확히 파악하는 것이 좋다. 친구의 어머니에게 견학에 대해 문의했지만 모른다며 다른 친구에게 연락해보라고 한다. 이에 대한 응답으로는 ① '알겠어요, 다른 애에게 전화할게요. 어쨌든 고맙습니다.'가

가장 적절하다.

② 괜찮아요. 말씀하신 것을 가져오는 것 잊지 마세요.
③ 그럼요. 오늘 저녁에 당신에게 다시 전화하라고 그에게 말할게요.
④ 좋아요. 박물관에 방문하는 것을 기대하고 있어요.
⑤ 시간 내주셔서 감사합니다. 연락드릴게요.

[Telephone rings.]
W: Hello?
M: Hello. Can I talk to David? This is Julian, his friend.
W: David isn't home. **Why don't you call** his cell phone?
M: I did, but he didn't answer. His phone was off.
W: Maybe his phone's battery died. Do you want to **leave a message**?
M: Yes, please. I'm calling to ask him about our field trip tomorrow. Did you hear about the trip?
W: Ah, yes. I remember him talking about that.
M: We're going to the Museum of Science tomorrow. Do you happen to know **what we should bring** to the museum?
W: I'm sorry, but I don't know. David won't be home until late, so why don't you **contact another friend**?
M: Okay, I'll call someone else. Thanks anyway.

[전화벨이 울린다.]
여: 여보세요?
남: 여보세요, David와 통화할 수 있나요? 저는 그의 친구 Julian인데요.
여: David는 집에 없단다. 휴대전화로 전화하지 그러니?
남: 했지만 받지 않아요. 전화기가 꺼져 있었어요.
여: 아마 배터리가 떨어졌나 보다. 메시지를 남기고 싶니?
남: 네, 부탁드려요. 내일 저희 견학에 대해 물어보려고 전화했는데요. 견학에 대해 들으셨어요?
여: 아, 그래. 그것에 관해 이야기한 기억이 나는구나.
남: 저희가 내일 과학박물관을 가거든요. 박물관에 무엇을 가져가야 하는지 혹시 아세요?
여: 미안하지만 모르겠구나. David는 늦게까지 집에 오지 않을 텐데 다른 친구에게 연락해보지 그러니?
남: 알겠어요, 다른 애에게 전화할게요. 어쨌든 고맙습니다.

어휘 leave 남기다; 떠나다 **field trip** 견학, 현장 학습 contact 연락(하다); 접촉
| 선택지 어휘 | look forward to A A를 기대[고대]하다 be in touch with ~와 연락하다 [연락하고 지내다]

15 상황에 적절한 말 ⑤

＊ 지시문을 통해 누가(A) 누구에게(B) 할 말인지를 우선 정확히 파악한다. 담화는 대개 A와 B에 대한 배경 설명과 B가 처한 문제 상황, 그리고 이에 대해 A가 어떤 말을 하려고 하는지에 대한 설명의 순서로 전개된다. 주연 여배우가 급작스러운 사고로 교체된 상황이다. 제작자인 Justin(A)이 무대에서 관중(B)에게 교체된 배우도 잘 할 것이라면서 자신의 확신을 밝히려고 한다. 이 상황에서 할 말로는 ⑤ '저희는 그녀의 연기에 대해 여러분이 실망하지 않으실 것이라고 확신합니다.'가 가장 적절하다.

① 저희가 부주의했던 것에 대해 사과드립니다.
② 다행히도 그녀는 심하게 다치지 않았습니다.
③ 이것에 대해 꼭 갚아 줄 것을 약속합니다.
④ 그녀는 예술적 재능으로 몇 개의 상을 받았습니다.

W: Justin Kidwell is a producer of a local theater company. His theater company decided to **put on** the musical *Don Quixote*, and has been preparing for it. Finally, they will perform the musical at the community theater today. But unfortunately, Helen Myles, who plays **the leading female role**, fell down some stairs. It's not serious, but she is **in no condition** to perform tonight. So, Julia Smith will replace her. Since she has been practicing this role along with Helen, she will do fine. Now Justin goes onto the stage and informs the audience about the change. He says he is sure that Julia's performance will be just as good. He wants to **express his confidence** in tonight's performance. In this situation, what would Justin most likely say to the audience?

Justin: We're sure you won't be disappointed with her acting.

여: Justin Kidwell은 지역 극단의 제작자이다. 그의 극단은 뮤지컬 '돈키호테'를 상연하기로 결정했고 그 준비를 해오고 있다. 마침내 그들은 오늘 지역 극장에서 뮤지컬을 공연할 것이다. 그러나 불행하게도 여자 주인공 역을 맡은 Helen Myles가 계단에서 넘어졌다. 심각한 것은 아니지만 그녀는 오늘 밤 공연할 상태가 아니다. 그래서 Julia Smith가 그녀를 대신할 것이다. 그녀는 이 역할을 Helen과 같이 연습해왔기 때문에 잘 할 것이다. 이제 Justin은 무대에 올라가서 관중에게 교체에 대해 알린다. 그는 Julia의 공연이 똑같이 좋을 것이라 확신한다고 말한다. 그는 오늘 밤 공연에 대한 자신의 확신을 밝히고 싶다. 이 상황에서 Justin이 관중에게 뭐라고 말하겠는가?

Justin: 저희는 그녀의 연기에 대해 여러분이 실망하지 않으실 것이라고 확신합니다.

어휘 local 지역의, 현지의 put on (연극·쇼 등을) 상연하다; ~을 입다 perform 공연[연주/연기]하다; 행하다 *cf.* performance 공연, 연주, 연기; 수행 unfortunately 불행하게도, 유감스럽게도(↔ fortunately 다행히도, 운 좋게도) be in no condition to-v v할 상태가 아니다, v하기에 적합하지 않다 replace 대신[대체]하다 audience 관중, 청중
| 선택지 어휘 | carelessness 부주의; 무관심 disappointed 실망한, 낙담한 artistic 예술[미술]적인; 예술[미술](가)의

16~17 세트 문항 16 ④ 17 ④

＊ **16** 수면 부족이 가져오는 여러 가지 신체적, 정신적 문제에 대해 언급하고 있으므로 답은 ④ '수면 부족으로 일어나는 문제'가 적절하다. 근무 중 집중도가 떨어져 실수하는 문제와 기분에 미치는 영향도 이야기하고 있으므로 '수면과 건강의 관계'를 답으로 고르지 않도록 유의한다.

① 휴식을 취하는 것의 필요성
② 수면 부족이 능률에 미치는 영향
③ 수면과 건강의 관계
⑤ 수면 부족의 원인과 해결책

＊ **17** 해석 참조.
① 고혈압 ② 당뇨병 ③ 불규칙한 심장박동 ④ 혈액암 ⑤ 심장마비

W: How many hours did you sleep last night? These days, it seems most people aren't **sleeping enough**. This can be a real problem. Although it may not seem serious at first, lack of sleep can have side effects. Sleeping less can lead to **many illnesses**, including high blood pressure, stroke, and diabetes. In addition, frequent sleep loss can **put you at risk** for irregular heartbeat, or even a heart attack. Getting too little sleep can also affect how well we learn. Studies have shown that sleepy people **have trouble with** memory and concentration. Tired people also make mistakes on the job, which can cause injury. Perhaps even more importantly, **lack of sleep** affects your mood. Tired people are more nervous, less adaptable, and less flexible. What can you do to stay rested and cheerful? Go to bed at the same time every night. And remember, going to work **without proper sleep** is like starting your day with one foot in a hole.

여: 어젯밤에 몇 시간이나 잠을 주무셨습니까? 요즘 대부분의 사람들이 충분히 못 자는 것 같습니다. 이것은 정말 문제가 될 수 있습니다. 비록 처음에는 심각하지 않게 보여도, 수면 부족은 부작용이 있을 수 있습니다. 수면 부족은 ① 고혈압, 뇌졸중과 ② 당뇨병을 포함한 많은 질병으로 이어질 수 있습니다. 게다가 빈번한 수면 손실은 여러분을 ③ 불규칙한 심장박동이나 심지어 ⑤ 심장마비의 위험에 처하게 할 수 있습니다. 너무 적게 자는 것은 또한 우리가 얼마나 잘 배우는지에도 영향을 줄 수 있습니다. 연구에 의하면 졸린 사람은 기억력과 집중력에서 곤란을 겪습니다. 피곤한 사람은 또한 근무 중에 실수를 저지르고 그것은 부상을 일으킬 수 있습니다. 아마 훨씬 더 중요하게도, 수면 부족은 여러분의 기분에 영향을 줍니다. 피곤한 사람들은 더 신경질적이고 적응력이 떨어지고 유연성도 떨어집니다. 여러분이 원기를 회복하고 쾌활한 상태로 있기 위해 무엇을 할 수 있을까요? 매일 밤 같은 시간에 취침하십시오. 그리고 적절한 수면 없이 출근하는 것은 (여러분의) 한쪽 발이 구멍에 빠진 채로 하루를 시작하는 것과 같다는 것을 기억하십시오.

어휘 side effect 부작용 high blood pressure 고혈압 stroke 뇌졸중; 타법, 타격 diabetes 당뇨병 frequent 빈번한, 잦은 risk 위험; 모험; 도박 irregular 불규칙한; 비정상적인 affect 영향을 미치다; 발생하다 concentration 집중(력); 농도 injury 부상; 피해 adaptable 적응할 수 있는 flexible 유연한; 융통성 있는 rested 원기를 회복한, 활력이 넘치는 cheerful 쾌활한, 명랑한, 기운찬 proper 적절한, 올바른
| 선택지 어휘 | necessity 필요성; 필수품 efficiency 능률, 효율(성) solution 해결책, 해법

03회

| 01 ② | 02 ③ | 03 ④ | 04 ⑤ | 05 ② | 06 ③ | 07 ④ | 08 ⑤ | 09 ④ | 10 ③ |
| 11 ③ | 12 ② | 13 ① | 14 ① | 15 ③ | 16 ③ | 17 ④ | | | |

01 화자가 하는 말의 목적　　②

* 담화의 일부 내용이 아니라 중심 내용을 파악해야 한다. 본 담화는 절도 사건이 여러 번 일어나자 동네에 CCTV를 설치해달라는 편지를 시에 보낼 것인데 주민들에게 서명해 달라고 요청하고 있는 내용이다. 그러므로 말의 목적으로는 ②가 가장 적절하다.

W: Hello, community residents. Recently, there have been **a number of robberies** in our neighborhood, which has alarmed many residents. Our community has been known to be a very safe area, where children can walk alone during the day. But it seems that we are no longer safe. In order to prevent any further crimes, we have decided to ask the city to install **CCTV cameras** throughout our neighborhood. We strongly believe this will stop further criminal behavior and protect our streets. A letter asking the city to install CCTV cameras will be passed around the neighborhood, and we ask that you give us your full support **by signing** your name. We need your help to **make this happen**.

여: 안녕하세요, 지역 주민 여러분. 최근 우리 동네에 다수의 절도가 있었고 그것이 많은 주민들을 불안하게 했습니다. 우리 지역사회는 매우 안전한 구역으로 알려져 있고 아이들이 낮 동안 혼자 걸어 다닐 수 있는 곳입니다. 그러나 우리는 더 이상 안전하지 않은 것 같습니다. 더 이상의 범죄를 막기 위해서 우리 동네 전체에 CCTV 카메라를 설치해달라는 것을 시에 요청하기로 결정했습니다. 우리는 이것이 추가 범죄 행위를 막을 것이고 우리 거리를 보호할 것이라고 강하게 믿습니다. CCTV 카메라를 설치해달라고 시에 요청하는 편지를 동네에 돌릴 것인데 여러분의 이름을 서명해서 우리에게 전적인 지지를 보내주시길 부탁드립니다. 이것이 일어나게 하려면 여러분의 도움이 필요합니다.

어휘 resident 주민, 거주자 a number of 다수의 robbery 절도, 강도 (사건) neighborhood 동네, 근처; 이웃 alarm 불안하게 만들다 further 더 이상의, 추가의 crime 범죄, 범행 *cf.* criminal 범죄의; 죄악이 되는; 형사상의 install 설치[설비]하다 throughout 전체[도처]에; ~동안 죽 support 지지, 지원 sign 서명하다; 계약하다

02 의견　　③

* 우선 지시문에서 명시한 화자의 성별을 보고 어느 화자의 말에 주목할지를 판단해야 한다. 특히 의견이나 주장을 표현하는 어구(I think ~, You should ~ 등)가 이끄는 내용을 잘 들어야 한다. 지나치게 열심히 집을 청소하는 아내에게 남편은 너무 깨끗한 환경이 알레르기를 유발할 수 있다는 기사를 읽었다며 청소에 대해 너무 걱정하지 말라고 하고 있다. 그러므로 남자의 의견으로는 ③이 적절하다.

W: I need to clean the floor.
M: Amelia, you already did it this morning.
W: Think about our kids. **The cleaner** I keep my home, **the healthier** they will be.
M: I just read an article about that. It said environments that are too clean cause allergies.
W: Really? I can't believe that. You mean we should not clean our home?
M: They're not suggesting bringing harmful bacteria into the home, but data does suggest that being too clean **may not be good**.
W: Then I have been doing it wrong.
M: Maybe. They do say early exposure to bacteria or pet hair may be linked to **fewer allergies** later in life.
W: Oh, I've spent a great deal of time in cleaning.
M: I know. Of course we should clean our home, but don't be **too worried** about cleaning.
W: I'm confused. Let me read that article.

여: 바닥을 청소해야 해요.
남: Amelia, 당신은 오늘 아침에 이미 그걸 했잖아요.

여: 우리 애들을 생각해봐요. 내가 집을 더 깨끗이 유지할수록 아이들은 더 건강해질 거예요.
남: 그것에 대한 기사를 막 읽었어요. 기사에서 말하길 너무 깨끗한 환경이 알레르기를 유발한다고 하더군요.
여: 정말이요? 믿을 수가 없어요. 우리 집을 청소하지 말란 말인가요?
남: 집안으로 해로운 박테리아를 가지고 들어오라고 제안하고 있는 건 아니지만 너무 깨끗한 게 좋지 않을 수도 있다는 것을 자료가 정말로 보여주고 있어요.
여: 그러면 내가 잘못해오고 있는 거군요.
남: 어쩌면요. 박테리아나 애완동물 털에 일찍 노출되는 게 장래에 알레르기가 덜 일어나는 것과 연관될 수도 있다고 확실히 말하고 있어요.
여: 아, 난 청소하느라 엄청난 시간을 써왔어요.
남: 알아요. 물론 우리는 집을 청소해야 하지만 청소에 대해 지나치게 걱정하지 말아요.
여: 난 혼란스러워요. 그 기사를 읽어볼게요.

어휘 article (신문 등의) 기사; 물품 cause 유발하다, 초래하다; 원인 suggest 제안하다; 암시하다 exposure 노출; 폭로, 알려짐 linked to A A와 연관된[관계된]

03 관계　　④

* 직업을 나타내거나 추론할 수 있는 힌트가 대화 전반에 걸쳐 드러나므로, 대화를 전체적으로 이해하는 것이 필요하다. 남자는 한국에서 온 학생이며 여자는 그가 묵을 방을 보여주고 아침 식사 및 등교 시간과 학교 버스에 대해서 알려주고 있다. 또 한국의 부모님께 전화할 것도 챙기는 것으로 보아 여자는 홈스테이 보호자이고 남자는 유학생인 것을 알 수 있다.

W: Come here. This is your room, Minho.
M: Thank you. It's large and bright. I really like it.
W: Glad you like it. **Feel free to use** all of the closet and dresser space for your clothes.
M: I really appreciate it. May I ask **where the bathroom is**?
W: It's just down the hall. Oh, I'm afraid it's not the same as in Korea. There aren't any drains in the floor here.
M: I see. I'll try not to get any water on the floor.
W: Okay. What else? **We all get up** around seven, so we eat breakfast about 7:30 a.m. It'll give you plenty of time to catch the school bus.
M: When and where can I catch my school bus?
W: It's 8:30 a.m. at the corner across from our house, and your class starts at 9:30 a.m.
M: I see. I'm excited to see my new school.
W: Oh, if you want to **call your parents** in Korea, you can use the phone downstairs.
M: Thanks, but I can use my smartphone app to call them for free.

여: 이리로 오렴. 이게 네 방이란다. 민호야.
남: 고맙습니다. 크고 환하네요. 정말 좋아요.
여: 네가 좋다니 기쁘구나. 모든 옷장과 서랍장을 네 옷을 넣는 데 자유롭게 사용하렴.
남: 정말 고맙습니다. 욕실이 어딘지 여쭤봐도 될까요?
여: 바로 복도 끝이란다. 아, 그게 한국하고 똑같지 않은 것 같아. 여기 바닥에는 배수구가 없단다.
남: 알겠습니다. 바닥에 물이 들어가지 않도록 할게요.
여: 좋아. 또 뭐가 있지? 우리는 모두 일곱 시경에 일어나니까 오전 7시 30분쯤에 아침을 먹어. 그게 네가 학교 버스를 타는 데 충분한 시간을 줄 거야.
남: 언제 어디서 학교 버스를 탈 수 있나요?
여: 오전 8시 30분에 우리 집 건너편 모퉁이에서 타고, 네 수업은 오전 9시 30분에 시작한단다.
남: 알겠어요. 새 학교를 보는 게 너무 신나요.
여: 아, 한국에 계신 부모님께 전화하고 싶으면 아래층에서 전화를 사용해도 돼.
남: 고맙습니다. 하지만 전 부모님께 무료로 전화하는 제 스마트폰 앱을 사용할 수 있어요.

어휘 **drain** 배수구[관]; 물을 빼내다 **floor** 바닥; 층 **plenty of** 충분한; 많은 **downstairs** 아래층에서[으로] **for free** 무료로, 공짜로

04 그림 불일치 ⑤

✻ 대화가 나오기 전에 각 사물의 위치 관계와 외형(형태나 무늬, 개수 등)의 특징을 미리 확인하는 것이 좋다. 대화 내용에서는 남자의 아버지가 서서 파라솔을 펴려고 하고 있다고 했는데 그림에서는 파라솔 아래 앉아있으므로 ⑤가 내용과 일치하지 않는다.

W: What are you looking at? I want to see.
M: I took some photos from the barbecue party that my family had last weekend. Here, take a look.
W: Is that your grandfather who **is grilling** on the barbecue?
M: Yes, it is. And the girl who is holding the dishes next to him is my sister, Layla.
W: The girl with **a big ribbon** in her hair? She's so cute. How old is she?
M: She's 8 years old. She wanted to grill the meat, but she's too young to use the grill.
W: Who is the woman with a baby **in her arms**, to the right of your sister? She has a big smile.
M: That's my aunt, Angelina. Can you see the man who is holding a bucket near the table? He is her husband, my uncle Jerome.
W: Then who is the man with sunglasses on the right?
M: He is my father. **He was standing up** and trying to open the parasol since it was very hot.
W: It looks like you had a wonderful time.

여: 뭘 보고 있니? 나도 보고 싶어.
남: 우리 가족이 지난 주말에 한 바비큐 파티에서 사진을 좀 찍었어. 여기 있어. 봐.
여: 바비큐에서 굽고 있는 분이 네 할아버지시니?
남: 응, 맞아. 그리고 그분 옆에서 접시를 들고 있는 여자아이는 내 동생 Layla야.
여: 머리에 큰 리본을 단 여자아이 말이니? 너무 귀엽다. 몇 살이니?
남: 8살이야. 그 애는 고기를 굽고 싶어 했지만 그릴을 다루기에는 너무 어리지.
여: 네 여동생 오른편에 팔에 아기를 안고 있는 여자분은 누구니? 활짝 웃고 있네.
남: 그분은 내 숙모인 Angelina야. 식탁 근처에 양동이를 들고 있는 남자 보이니? 그가 숙모의 남편이자 내 삼촌인 Jerome이야.
여: 그러면 오른편에 선글라스를 쓴 남자는 누구니?
남: 우리 아버지셔. 날이 너무 더워서 아버지는 서서 파라솔을 펴려고 하고 계시지.
여: 너 멋진 시간 보낸 것 같구나.

어휘 **grill** (석쇠에) 굽다; 그릴, 석쇠 **bucket** 양동이; 많은 양 **parasol** 파라솔, 양산

05 추후 행동 ②

✻ 대개 대화는 어떤 일을 하게 되는 상황이 먼저 제시된 뒤에 남자와 여자가 각각 할 일들과 이에 대한 수락/거절의 응답이 나열되는 식으로 전개된다. 남자의 여동생이 연주회를 위해 머리에 파마할 예정이라고 하자 여자는 미용실을 소개해줬고 가격을 40%나 할인해주는 쿠폰을 주겠다고 하고 있다. 남자에게 기다리라고 하면서 가져오겠다고 하는 것으로 보아 여자의 할 일은 ②가 가장 적절하다.

M: Hi, Grace. Oh, you **got your hair cut**, didn't you? Your hair looks absolutely gorgeous!
W: Thanks. I found a really good hair stylist.
M: Great! Actually, my sister was looking for a good hair stylist. She needs to **get a perm** since she'll be playing the violin in a school concert.
W: Your younger sister? Wow! That's great! I'll tell you where my beauty salon is.
M: How much does a perm cost there?
W: I think it's more than 100 dollars.
M: It's so expensive! I guess it's **beyond her budget**.
W: Hold on. I'll give you the coupon I received. You **can get 40% off** the price with that coupon.
M: That's great. My sister will be very pleased.
W: Just wait here, and **I'll bring it** right now. It's in my backpack in the library.

M: Thank you, Grace.

남: 안녕, Grace. 아, 너 머리 커트했구나, 그렇지 않니? 네 머리 정말로 멋져 보인다!
여: 고마워. 아주 잘 하는 헤어 스타일리스트를 찾았어.
남: 잘됐다! 사실 내 여동생도 잘 하는 헤어 스타일리스트를 찾고 있었어. 그 애가 학교 연주회에서 바이올린을 연주할 거라서 파마를 해야 하거든.
여: 네 여동생 말이니? 왜! 그거 멋지다! 내가 내 미용실이 어디 있는지 알려줄게.
남: 거기 파마는 얼마나 하니?
여: 100달러가 넘는 것 같아.
남: 너무 비싸다! 내 동생 예산을 초과하는 것 같은데.
여: 잠깐만. 내가 받은 쿠폰을 네게 줄게. 그 쿠폰으로 가격의 40%를 할인받을 수 있어.
남: 그거 좋구나. 내 동생이 아주 기뻐할 거야.
여: 여기서 잠깐 기다려, 그러면 내가 그걸 바로 가지고 올게. 그게 도서관에 있는 내 가방 안에 있거든.
남: 고마워, Grace.

어휘 **absolutely** 굉장히, 극도로 **gorgeous** 아주 멋진 **perm** 파마; 파마를 해주다 **beyond** 넘어서는; ~ 이상 **budget** 예산; 예산을 세우다

06 금액 ③

✻ 여러 개의 수치 정보가 등장하므로 필요한 정보를 메모하면서 듣는 것이 좋다. 매달 200달러씩 12개월을 할부로 지불하거나, 매달 100달러씩 24개월을 할부로 지불하는 냉장고 가격은 2400달러이다. 일시불로 할 경우 10% 할인을 해준다고 했으므로 두 사람이 지불할 가격은 240달러를 뺀 2,160달러이다.

W: William, I think I found a great new refrigerator for us to use.
M: You know we don't have a lot of money right now.
W: They have very good payment plans where we can pay for it **in small amounts**. We can choose between 12-month and 24-month plans.
M: I think the interest must be very high.
W: No, they have an interest-free payment plan available on this refrigerator.
M: No interest? That's good. What's the payment each month?
W: We can either pay **$200 each month** for one year or pay $100 each month and finish in 2 years.
M: Well, if we pay all at once, is there any discount?
W: Yes, they offer **a 10% discount** for a one-off payment. It's quite a lot.
M: If we sell the old one at a used market, I think we can afford that. Let's pay all at once.
W: Okay! We really need a new refrigerator.

여: William, 우리가 사용할 멋진 새 냉장고를 찾은 것 같아요.
남: 지금 우리 돈이 그렇게 많지 않은 거 알잖아요.
여: 적은 금액으로 지불할 수 있는 아주 좋은 지불 방식이 있더라고요. 우리는 12개월과 24개월제 중에 고를 수 있어요.
남: 분명히 이자가 아주 높을걸요.
여: 아뇨, 이 냉장고에 적용 가능한 무이자 지불 방식이 있어요.
남: 무이자라고요? 그거 좋군요. 매달 지불금이 얼마인데요?
여: 일 년간 매달 200달러를 내거나 아니면 2년 동안 매달 100달러를 낼 수 있어요.
남: 음, 우리가 모두 한 번에 지불한다면 할인이 있나요?
여: 네, 일시불에는 10% 할인을 제공한대요. 상당히 많죠.
남: 우리가 오래된 냉장고를 중고시장에서 판다면 그걸 살 여유가 될 것 같은데요. 모두 한 번에 지불합시다.
여: 좋아요! 우린 정말로 새 냉장고가 필요해요.

어휘 **refrigerator** 냉장고 **payment** 지불 (금액) *cf.* **one-off payment** 일시불 **interest** 이자; 이익, 관심 **available** 이용할 수 있는 **at once** 한꺼번에; 즉시, 당장 **used** 중고의 **afford** ~할 여유가 되다

07 이유 ④

✻ 지시문을 통해 두 사람이 쿠키를 주문하지 못하는 상황임을 파악한다. 여자가 그 이유를 물어보면서 주문이 너무 많아서 그런지, 재료가 모자랐는지 아니면 아예 문을 닫은 건지 묻자 남자가 아니라고 함에 유의한다. Molly's Bakery는 새 점포로 이전하기

위해 임시로 문을 닫아 주문을 받지 않는 것이라고 했으므로 답은 ④이다.

M: Christie, **why don't we order** cookies from Molly's Bakery for Daniel's birthday party?
W: Good idea. Their cookies are fantastic! They use the best ingredients.
M: We can order their cookies online. Let's see.
W: I think we need a box of chocolate cookies and peanut butter cookies.
M: I see. Oh, no. They aren't taking **any orders** now.
W: Why? Do they have too many orders? Are they **lacking some ingredients**?
M: No, it's not that.
W: The bakery didn't close, did it?
M: No, it says they'll **move into** a new store on Anselmo Street, so the store is **temporarily closed** until this coming Sunday.
W: Oh, that's too bad. Our party is this Saturday.
M: Yeah, but I think we can order cookies from another bakery. I will search.

남: Christie, Daniel의 생일파티를 위해 Molly's Bakery에서 쿠키를 주문하는 게 어때요?
여: 좋은 생각이에요. 거기 쿠키는 환상적이죠! 최고의 재료를 사용하더군요.
남: 온라인으로 쿠키를 주문할 수 있어요. 어디 봅시다.
여: 우리는 초콜릿 쿠키하고 땅콩버터 쿠키 한 상자가 필요할 거예요.
남: 알았어요. 아, 이런. 지금 어떤 주문도 받지 않고 있네요.
여: 왜요? 너무 주문이 많아서요? 재료가 모자라서요?
남: 아니요, 그건 아니에요.
여: 제과점이 문을 닫은 건 아니죠, 그렇죠?
남: 아뇨, 여기에 쓰여 있기를 Anselmo 가에 있는 새 점포로 이사할 거라서 이번 다가오는 일요일까지 상점을 임시로 닫는다고 하네요.
여: 아, 그럼 어쩌죠. 우리 파티는 이번 토요일인데요.
남: 네, 하지만 다른 제과점에서 쿠키를 주문할 수 있을 거예요. 내가 찾아볼게요.

어휘 **order** 주문(하다); 명령(하다); 순서 *cf.* take an order 주문을 받다 **ingredient** 재료, 성분; 구성 요소 **temporarily** 임시로, 일시적으로

08 언급하지 않은 것 ⑤

✱ 대화의 진행은 대개 선택지와 같은 순서이므로, 선택지를 보면서 언급된 내용을 소거하는 식으로 푸는 것이 좋다. 여자의 고향 Spearfish에 대해 이야기를 나누고 있다. 인구수와 세워진 연도, 그리고 산과 개울이 있는 주변 경관에 대해 언급했고 이름의 유래에 대해서도 말했지만 ⑤ '관광 시설'에 대해서는 언급하지 않았다.

M: I heard you just moved here to our city. Where are you from?
W: I'm from Spearfish in South Dakota. It's a small town, so it's much different from this city.
M: Oh, really? **How is it different** from your hometown?
W: This city is so big and full of people. If you can believe it, Spearfish only had about 11,000 people living in it!
M: Wow, **that's tiny**. How old is your town?
W: It was founded in 1876. The town is surrounded **by three mountains**, and there are streams and canyons.
M: Sounds great. It must be very beautiful.
W: Yes. Actually, it got its name from the fact that it is on a stream where Indians **used to spear fish**.
M: Interesting. I'm sure the town attracts a lot of outdoor lovers.
W: That's right. Spearfish is ranked one of the best small towns.

남: 우리 도시로 막 이사 오셨다고 들었어요. 어디서 오셨나요?
여: 전 South Dakota에 있는 Spearfish에서 왔어요. 작은 마을이라서 이 도시와 아주 다르죠.
남: 아, 정말요? 당신의 고향과 어떻게 다른가요?
여: 이 도시는 매우 크고 사람이 많죠. 믿으실지 모르겠지만 Spearfish에는 단지 11,000명(① 인구수)이 살고 있어요!
남: 와, 아주 적군요. 마을이 얼마나 오래되었나요?
여: 1876년(② 세워진 연도)에 세워졌어요. 마을은 세 개의 산으로 둘러싸여 있고 개울과 협곡이 있답니다(③ 주변 경관).
남: 멋진 것 같군요. 분명히 아주 아름답겠는데요.

여: 네. 실은 인디언들이 작살로 물고기를 잡곤 했던 개울에 마을이 있다는 사실에서 이름을 따온 것이에요(④ 이름의 유래).
남: 재미있군요. 그 마을이 많은 야외활동 애호가들을 끌어들이겠군요.
여: 맞아요. Spearfish는 가장 좋은 작은 마을 중 하나로 평가되고 있어요.

어휘 **found** 세우다, 설립하다 **surround** 둘러싸다; 포위하다 **stream** 개울; 흐름 **canyon** 협곡 **spear** (물고기를) 작살로 잡다; 찌르다; 창 **attract** 끌어들이다; 마음을 끌다 **rank** 평가하다; (등급·순위를) 차지하다

09 내용 불일치 ④

✱ 담화의 진행은 대개 선택지와 같은 순서이므로, 선택지를 보면서 일치하는 내용을 소거하는 식으로 푸는 것이 좋다. 비가 오면 모든 장식과 축제 활동들이 학생식당 안으로 옮겨질 것이라고 했으므로 ④ '우천 시에는 행사가 취소된다.'는 내용과 일치하지 않는다.

M: Parents, I'm here to announce that Victorville Elementary School will be having its annual summer festival **one month later**. Our theme this year is "Under the Sea," **featuring ocean decorations** and activities. The festival will take place outside, right behind the cafeteria building. If it rains on that day, all the decorations and festival activities will be moved **inside the cafeteria**. You may take your children to any part of the festival you choose. But please stay with them at all times. Don't let them run off on their own! Our lunch will be served at 12:30 p.m. Our kitchen chefs have planned a fantastic meal of **shrimp and other seafoods**. I'm sure it's going to be a great day!

남: 부모님들. Victorville 초등학교가 ① 한 달 후에 연례 여름 축제를 가질 것을 공지하러 여기 섰습니다. ② 올해 우리의 주제는 바다 장식과 활동을 특색으로 하는 '바다 아래에서'입니다. 축제는 ③ 학생식당 건물 바로 뒤 야외에서 개최될 것입니다. ④ 그 날 비가 오면 모든 장식과 축제 활동들은 학생식당 안으로 옮겨질 것입니다. 여러분은 여러분이 선택하는 축제의 어느 곳에든 자녀를 데려갈 수 있습니다. 그러나 항상 그들과 함께 계시기 바랍니다. 아이들이 홀로 벗어나게 하지 마십시오! ⑤ 점심 식사는 오후 12시 30분에 제공될 것입니다. 저희 주방 요리사는 새우와 다른 해산물로 만든 환상적인 식사를 계획했습니다. 분명히 굉장한 날이 될 것이라고 믿습니다!

어휘 **announce** 공지하다, 알리다; 선언하다 **annual** 연례의, 매년의 **theme** 주제, 테마 **feature** 특징으로 하다; 특징 **take place** 개최되다, 일어나다 **cafeteria** 구내식당 **chef** 요리사

10 도표 이해 ③

✱ 대화의 진행은 대개 도표 항목의 나열 순서대로 진행된다. 대화를 들으면서 도표의 각 항목 중 선택되지 않은 것을 소거하는 식으로 푸는 것이 좋다. 우선 2세 연령에 맞는 걸 골라야 하니 ⑤는 제외되고 플라스틱이 아닌 것을 원한다고 했으므로 ① 또한 제외된다. 구성이 30조각 이상인 것을 원했으므로 ②와 ③ 중에서 고를 수 있는데, 남자는 값이 비싸도 유기농 재료를 사용한 것을 고르겠다고 했으므로 답은 ③이다.

M: I'm looking for a gift for my nephew's birthday. I want to get him something special. Can you recommend something for me?
W: Sure. I think he'd like toy blocks. Toy blocks **stimulate creativity** and develop important skills. Look here.
M: Good. Can you help me pick one?
W: How old is he? It's important to buy **age-appropriate toys** for kids.
M: He is two years old.
W: Then you can choose one among these four. Which material would you like?
M: Anything will be fine **except plastic**. And I think the block set should have more than 30 pieces.
W: You have these two options. Which would you like?
M: I'll take this one. It's more expensive, but it uses **organic materials**. It may be safer.
W: You're right. Kids often put toys in their mouth.

남: 제 조카의 생일선물을 찾고 있는데요. 뭔가 특별한 것을 사주고 싶어요. 제게 뭔가를

추천해주실 수 있나요?

여: 그럼요. 아이가 장난감 블록을 좋아할 거 같은데요. 장난감 블록은 창의성을 자극하고 중요한 기능을 발달시키거든요. 여기를 보세요.

남: 좋아요. 하나 고르도록 도와주시겠어요?

여: 조카가 몇 살이죠? 아이에게 연령에 맞는 장난감을 사주는 게 중요합니다.

남: 두 살이에요.

여: 그러면 이 네 개 중에서 고르실 수 있어요. 어떤 재료를 원하시나요?

남: 플라스틱 외에는 어떤 것이든 괜찮습니다. 그리고 블록 세트가 30조각 이상은 되어야 한다고 생각해요.

여: 이 두 개의 선택권이 있으십니다. 어떤 걸 원하세요?

남: 이걸 사겠어요. 더 비싸지만 유기농 재료를 사용했군요. 더 안전할 것 같아요.

여: 손님 말씀이 맞습니다. 아이들은 종종 장난감을 입에 넣거든요.

어휘 nephew 조카 (아들) stimulate 자극하다; 활발하게 하다 appropriate 알맞은, 적절한 material 재료, 재질; 물질적인 except 외에는, 제외하고는 organic 유기농의; 생물의

---

11 짧은 대화에 이어질 응답 ③

✱ 식당에 와서 예약 여부를 확인하고 좌석을 안내받는 상황이다. 손님이 예약자의 이름을 잘못 말했다가 정정한 후 식당 직원이 할 말로는 예약을 확인하고 좌석으로 안내하는 ③ '네, 세 분 좌석이죠. 이리로 오세요.'가 적절하다.

① 유감이지만 저는 이 자리가 마음에 안 듭니다.
② 제가 손님의 웨이터입니다. 여기 메뉴가 있습니다.
④ 죄송합니다. 제가 예약을 하지 못했어요.
⑤ 잠깐만요. 제가 주방에 확인해보겠습니다.

W: Excuse me. I have a reservation in the name of "Jones." We're **a party of three**.
M: Let me see... I'm sorry but the name is not on the list.
W: Are you sure? Oh, right! My friend made the reservation! Please check again with "Mason."
M: Yes, a table for three. Come this way.

여: 실례합니다. 'Jones'라는 이름으로 예약을 했는데요. 저희 일행은 세 명이에요.
남: 어디 봅시다… 죄송하지만 명단에 그 이름은 없는데요.
여: 정말요? 아, 맞아요! 제 친구가 예약했어요! 'Mason'으로 다시 확인해주세요.
남: 네, 세 분 좌석이죠. 이리로 오세요.

어휘 have[make] a reservation 예약하다 party 일행, 단체; 모임; 정당

---

12 짧은 대화에 이어질 응답 ②

✱ 남자가 자신이 찾는 사람이 언제 돌아올 것인지 묻고 있으므로 여자의 응답으로는 돌아올 시간을 알려주는 ② '아마 한 시간 후쯤이요. 당신이 전화했다고 그녀에게 알릴게요.'가 가장 적절하다.

① 잠깐만요. 미안하지만 그녀는 다른 전화를 받고 있어요.
③ 맞아요. 아마 전화기가 고장이 났나 봐요.
④ 고마워요. 하지만 난 그녀와 직접 통화하고 싶어요.
⑤ 통화상태가 좋지 않군요. 전화를 끊고 다시 걸게요.

[Telephone rings.]
M: Hello! This is Ryan Wilson. Can I speak to Jennifer Hume, please?
W: Hi, Ryan. Sorry, but **she's not in now**. Why don't you call her cell phone?
M: I tried, but she didn't answer. When is she expected back?
W: Maybe in an hour. I'll tell her you called.

[전화벨이 울린다.]
남: 여보세요! 저는 Ryan Wilson인데요. Jennifer Hume하고 통화할 수 있나요?
여: 안녕하세요, Ryan. 미안하지만 그녀는 지금 안 계세요. 그녀의 휴대전화로 전화하지 그래요?
남: 해봤지만 받지 않아서요. 언제 돌아올 거로 예상하나요?
여: 아마 한 시간 후쯤이요. 당신이 전화했다고 그녀에게 알릴게요.

어휘 | 선택지 어휘 | out of order 고장 난 hang up 전화를 끊다

---

13 긴 대화에 이어질 응답 ①

✱ 대화의 전체 맥락 하에 마지막 말의 의미나 의도를 정확히 파악하는 것이 좋다. 서로 음악 취향이 다른 남자와 여자의 대화이다. 남자가 자기가 좋아하는 음악을 들어보라고 추천하는 상황이므로 이에 대한 여자의 응답으로는 ① '모든 사람의 취향이 다르지만 시도해 볼게.'가 가장 적절하다.

② 음악을 제발 낮춰 줘. 너무 시끄러워.
③ 맞아. 고전 음악은 들을만한 가치가 있어.
④ 나는 더 잘하도록 노력해. 네가 날 이해할 수 있기를 바라.
⑤ 너한테 실망했어. 난 너를 믿을 수 있을 거라 생각했어.

M: What are you listening to, Abigail?
W: Oh, hi, Carter. I'm listening to Nirvana songs.
M: Nirvana? Is it a band?
W: Yes, Nirvana is a famous rock band. Do you want to listen together?
M: No, thanks. It was music for **my father's generation**, wasn't it?
W: No, they're in many top-ten lists of the best rock bands of all time.
M: They were, but I think rock music is **boring and outdated** now. Why don't you listen to the latest music?
W: **What kind of music** do you listen to?
M: I listen to only the latest hip hop music. Try it.
W: It's the latest, but I don't think it's the greatest. I have my own **likes and dislikes**.
M: Well... I'm sure you'll like it if you give it a chance. I really recommend it.
W: Everyone's tastes differ, but I will try.

남: 뭘 듣니, Abigail?
여: 아, 안녕, Carter. 난 Nirvana 노래를 듣고 있어.
남: Nirvana? 그거 밴드니?
여: 응. Nirvana는 유명한 록밴드야. 함께 들어볼래?
남: 아니, 괜찮아. 우리 아버지 세대의 음악이었지, 그렇지 않니?
여: 아니야. 그들은 역대 최고의 록밴드 상위 10위 리스트에 많이 올라 있어.
남: 그랬겠지만 록 음악은 이제 지루하고 구식 같아. 최신 음악을 듣지 그러니?
여: 넌 어떤 종류의 음악을 듣는데?
남: 난 최신 힙합 음악만 들어. 들어봐.
여: 그게 최신이기는 하지만 난 그게 가장 위대하다고는 생각하지 않아. 난 나 자신의 호불호가 있어.
남: 음… 네가 그것에게 기회를 준다면 좋아할 거라고 믿어. 정말 추천하는 거야.
여: 모든 사람의 취향이 다르지만 시도해 볼게.

어휘 generation 세대, 대 outdated 구식의, 시대에 뒤처진 | 선택지 어휘 | taste 취향, 기호; 맛 turn down (소리 등을) 낮추다; 거절[거부]하다 classical 고전의, 고전적인 worth 가치가 있는

---

14 긴 대화에 이어질 응답 ①

✱ 대화의 전체 맥락 하에 마지막 말의 의미나 의도를 정확히 파악하는 것이 좋다. 남자는 어두워져서 산에서 길을 잃을 것을 걱정하고 있다. 여자가 괜찮다고 말하지만, 남자의 응답으로는 빨리 내려가자는 내용의 ① '어쨌든 서둘러 내려가자. 안전한 게 좋은 거야.'가 가장 적절하다.

② 아, 이런. 넌 동화를 너무 많이 읽은 것 같다.
③ 네 말이 맞아. 어두워진 이후에 여기 있는 건 위험해.
④ 멋지다! 해가 산 너머로 졌어.
⑤ 응. 이 근처에 곰이 분명히 많이 있어.

M: Wow! This hiking is really difficult.
W: It's been a while since you've been hiking — that's why. You'll be all right.
M: I don't think I can go any further.
W: Okay. Let's **take a break**. Hmm, it's already six.
M: Really? Then it will **get dark soon**. How are you planning to get down in the dark?
W: We'll be all right. We can get down in about an hour.
M: I don't think so. We're going to have to run down.
W: Listen, Luke. There's no way we're going to **run down this trail**.
M: But it's getting really late. What if we **get hurt or lost** in the dark?

W: Hey, it's June. The sun won't go down for another couple of hours.
M: Anyway, let's hurry down. It's good to be safe.

남: 와! 이번 등산은 정말 힘들다.
여: 네가 등산한 지 꽤 되었잖아. 그래서 그런 거야. 괜찮아질 거야.
남: 더 이상 갈 수 없을 것 같아.
여: 좋아. 휴식을 취하자. 음, 벌써 여섯 시야.
남: 정말이야? 그러면 곧 어두워질 거야. 어둠 속에서 어떻게 내려갈 계획이야?
여: 우리는 괜찮을 거야. 한 시간 후면 내려갈 수 있어.
남: 난 그렇게 생각하지 않아. 우리는 빨리 내려가야 할 거야.
여: 들어봐, Luke. 우리가 이 산길을 빨리 내려갈 방법은 없어.
남: 하지만 정말 늦어질 거야. 우리가 어둠 속에서 다치거나 길을 잃으면 어떻게 할 거야?
여: 저기, 지금은 6월이야. 해가 두세 시간 동안은 지지 않을 거야.
남: 어쨌든 서둘러 내려가자. 안전한 게 좋은 거야.

어휘 trail 산길; 흔적, 자취 | 선택지 어휘 | fairy tale 동화 set (해·달이) 지다; 놓다

15 상황에 적절한 말 ③

* 지시문을 통해 누가(A) 누구에게(B) 할 말인지를 우선 정확히 파악한다. 보고서 마감 시간이 촉박해 서두르는 상황에서 마감일이 일주일 연기되었다고 알려주는 반 친구 Lucy(B)의 말에 대한 Oliver(A)의 응답으로는 안도를 표현하는 내용이 적절하다. 그러므로 ③ '정말 안심이야! 알려줘서 고마워.'가 가장 적절한 응답이다.

① 난 그걸 몰랐어. 하지만 상관없어.
② 넌 운이 좋구나. 이제 넌 충분한 시간이 있어.
④ 제발 부탁해. 네 보고서를 보여줘.
⑤ 늦지 마. 보고서를 여섯 시까지 꼭 제출해야 해.

M: Oliver is a college student. He is taking a religion and culture course this semester. In the class, he has to **submit a term paper**, and it's due today by six p.m. Unfortunately, his laptop is broken, so he has to go to the computer room to finish his paper. Oliver rushes to the computer room because he **doesn't have much time**. Then he runs into Lucy, his classmate. She asks him **why he is rushing**. When Oliver says why, Lucy tells him the due date for the paper has been postponed a week. The professor had e-mailed the announcement to all his students, but Oliver hadn't got it. He **feels relieved**. In this situation, what would Oliver most likely say to Lucy?

Oliver: <u>What a relief! Thanks for letting me know.</u>

남: Oliver는 대학생이다. 그는 이번 학기에 종교와 문화 수업을 듣고 있다. 수업에서 그는 학기말 리포트를 내야 하고 그것은 오늘 오후 6시까지 마감이다. 불행하게도, 그의 노트북 컴퓨터가 망가져서 그는 보고서를 마치기 위해 컴퓨터실로 가야 한다. Oliver는 시간이 많이 없어서 컴퓨터실로 서둘러 간다. 그때 그는 반 친구인 Lucy와 우연히 마주친다. 그녀는 그에게 왜 서두르냐고 묻는다. Oliver가 이유를 말하자 Lucy는 그에게 보고서 마감일이 한 주 연기되었다고 알려준다. 교수님이 모든 자신의 학생들에게 공지를 이메일로 보냈지만, Oliver가 받지 못한 것이었다. 그는 안도감을 느낀다. 이 상황에서 Oliver가 Lucy에게 뭐라고 말하겠는가?

Oliver: 정말 안심이야! 알려줘서 고마워.

어휘 religion 종교; 신앙(심) semester 학기 submit 제출하다; 항복하다 term paper 학기말 리포트 due 예정된; ~하기로 되어 있는 rush 서두르다; 급히 움직이다 run into ~와 우연히 마주치다 postpone 연기하다, 미루다 announcement 공지, 발표 relieved 안도하는 | 선택지 어휘 | beg 애원[간청]하다 make sure to-v 꼭[반드시] v하다 turn in ~을 제출하다[돌려주다]

16~17 세트 문항 16 ③ 17 ④

* **16** 시험 불안을 통제하기 위해 할 수 있는 간단한 일이 있다고 하면서 몇 가지 방법을 제시하고 있다. 그러므로 주제로 가장 적절한 것은 ③ '시험 불안을 다루는 효과적 방법'이다.

① 수험생의 스트레스의 원인
② 공부 습관과 기술을 증진하는 법

④ 불안한 개인을 위한 치료 방법
⑤ 시험 문제에 올바르게 답하는 비결

* **17** 해석 참조.
① 침실 ② 정원 ③ 공원 ④ 뒷마당 ⑤ 해변

W: If you feel nervous before an exam, you're not alone. This is test anxiety. In some ways, **a little anxiety** is a good thing. It helps to focus the mind and get the adrenaline going. Too much, though, is not so good. Fortunately, there are a couple of simple things you can do to control your test anxiety. First, eat regular, nutritious meals, and **avoid caffeine** wherever possible. This will keep your energy levels up. Exercise regularly, and **get lots of rest** so you can concentrate. Be positive. Instead of thinking that you are going to fail, imagine that you're not. Replace anxious, negative thoughts with positive ones. **Imagine a scene** or place that you remember as peaceful, restful, beautiful, and happy. It can be your bedroom or your garden. You can **picture riding your bike** in the park or walking on the beach. Remember that not every method is the perfect choice for every individual. Try several different techniques before you decide which ones are best for you.

여: 여러분이 시험 전에 초조하게 느낀다면, 그건 여러분 혼자만이 아닙니다. 이것은 시험 불안입니다. 여러 가지 점에서 약간의 불안은 좋은 것입니다. 그것은 정신을 집중하도록 도와주고 아드레날린을 나오게 합니다. 그러나 너무 지나치면 그다지 좋지 않습니다. 다행히도 여러분의 시험 불안을 조절하기 위해 여러분이 할 수 있는 간단한 일이 두세 개 있습니다. 우선 규칙적이고 영양가 높은 식사를 하고 가능하면 언제나 카페인을 피하십시오. 이것은 여러분의 기운을 상향 조정시킬 것입니다. 규칙적으로 운동하고 충분한 휴식을 취하면 집중할 수 있습니다. 긍정적으로 되십시오. 실패할 것이라는 생각 대신에 그러지 않을 거라고 상상하십시오. 불안하고 부정적인 생각을 긍정적인 것으로 대체하십시오. 여러분이 평화롭고 평온하고 아름답고 행복했다고 기억하는 장면이나 장소를 상상해보십시오. 그것은 여러분의 ① 침실이나 ② 정원일 수도 있습니다. ③ 공원에서 자전거를 타거나 ⑤ 해변을 걷는 것을 그려볼 수 있습니다. 모든 방법이 다 각각의 개인에게 완벽한 선택은 아니라는 걸 기억하십시오. 어떤 것이 여러분에게 최고일지 결정하기 전에 몇 가지 다른 기법들을 시도해 보십시오.

어휘 anxiety 불안, 염려 anxious 불안한, 염려하는; 열망하는 adrenaline 아드레날린 ((흥분·공포·분노 등의 감정을 느낄 때 분비되는 호르몬)) nutritious 영양가가 높은 concentrate 집중하다 negative 부정적인(↔ positive 긍정적인) replace A with B A를 B로 대체하다 individual 개인(의); 각각의 | 선택지 어휘 | improve 개선되다, 나아지다 manage 다루다; 처리[관리]하다; 경영하다 treatment 치료; 처리; 대우

04회

01 화자가 하는 말의 목적   ②

✽ 담화의 일부 내용이 아니라 중심 내용을 파악해야 한다. 본 담화는 자전거의 도난 방지뿐만 아니라 교정을 깨끗하게 하고 다른 사람을 불편하게 하지 않도록 자전거를 자전거 보관대에 자물쇠로 채워 두라고 이야기하고 있으므로 말의 목적은 ②가 적절하다. 자전거 자물쇠 사용이나 절도 방지, 보행자 보호 등은 언급되었지만 전체적 내용의 목적을 찾아야 함에 유의한다.

M: Hello, students. As you know, bicycles are **a popular means** of transportation around campus. You probably have also heard the news that there have been some bike robberies on campus. If you want to keep your bike safe, **lock your bike** to a bike rack. Bike racks are located near almost every building. In addition, **illegally parked bikes** block walkways and present serious danger for people who use wheelchairs or walking sticks. So, it's important to use the bicycle racks. Please don't park your bike **in the line** of travel to stairs, ramps, doorways, or door buttons. Furthermore, bikes locked to trees can cause **serious damage** to or even kill the trees. Please help keep the campus beautiful and keep your bikes safe by locking your bike to a bike rack.

남: 안녕하세요, 학생 여러분. 여러분도 알다시피, 자전거는 캠퍼스 주변의 인기 있는 교통수단입니다. 여러분도 아마 캠퍼스에서 일부 자전거 절도가 있었다는 소식을 들었을 겁니다. 여러분의 자전거를 안전하게 보관하길 원하신다면 자전거를 자전거 보관대에 자물쇠로 채워두십시오. 자전거 보관대는 거의 모든 건물 근처에 위치하고 있습니다. 게다가 불법적으로 주차된 자전거들은 보도를 막고 휠체어나 지팡이를 사용하는 사람들에게 심각한 위험을 줍니다. 그래서 자전거 보관대를 이용하는 게 중요합니다. 여러분의 자전거를 계단, 경사로, 출입구나 혹은 문 개폐 버튼으로 가는 진로에 주차하지 마십시오. 더 나아가 나무에 묶어둔 자전거는 나무에 심각한 손상을 주거나 심지어 나무를 죽게 할 수 있습니다. 여러분의 자전거를 자전거 보관대에 자물쇠로 채워둠으로써 교정을 아름답게 유지하는 데 도움을 주고 여러분의 자전거를 안전하게 보관하십시오.

어휘 means 수단, 방법 transportation 교통 (수단); 운송, 수송 robbery 절도; 도둑[강도][질] bike rack 자전거 보관대(= bicycle rack) illegally 불법적으로 walkway 보도, 인도 ramp 경사로, 비탈길

02 의견   ④

✽ 우선 지시문에서 명시한 화자의 성별을 보고 어느 화자의 말에 주목할지를 판단해야 한다. 특히 의견이나 주장을 표현하는 어구(I think ~, You should ~ 등)가 이끄는 내용을 잘 들어야 한다. 남자는 화성 탐사나 우주 탐험이 유용한 과학적 지식을 준다고 말하고 있지만, 여자는 일반적으로 그런 우주 탐사에 쓰이는 막대한 돈은 낭비하는 것이고 도움이 필요한 인류를 돕는 게 우선으로 해야 하는 일이라고 말하고 있다. 그러므로 여자의 의견으로는 ④가 적절하다.

M: Chelsea, I read about the coolest thing in the newspaper yesterday.
W: What was that?
M: It said humans could soon live inside Mars in underground caves. This project is really amazing, isn't it?
W: Well, that's cool, but I think it's better to use the money for humans **living on Earth**.
M: So you think it's a waste of money.
W: Yeah, I heard the budget to bring just 4 people to Mars was over $6 billion. Why should we spend so much money on that?
M: Well, it's important for our country to work with the newest technology.
W: Yeah, it **may well** give us good things. But why should we spend all this money exploring space and finding out **if there is water** on Mars?
M: You know, we do get useful scientific knowledge from space exploration.
W: Maybe, but I think the needs of common people should always **come first**. While there are people on Earth who need help, we should help them first.

M: I see what you're saying.
W: Common people on Earth are **the number one** priority. Keeping the human race alive is a necessity.

남: Chelsea, 나 어제 신문에서 가장 멋진 것에 대해 읽었어.
여: 그게 뭐였는데?
남: 인간이 곧 화성 내부 지하 동굴에서 살 수 있을 거라고 했어. 이 프로젝트는 정말로 놀라워, 그렇지 않니?
여: 음, 그거 멋지네. 하지만 난 지구에 사는 인간들을 위해 돈을 사용하는 게 더 좋다고 생각해.
남: 그러면 넌 그게 돈 낭비라고 생각하는구나.
여: 응, 난 단지 네 명의 사람을 화성에 보내는 데 드는 예산이 60억 달러가 넘었다고 들었어. 왜 우리가 그렇게 많은 돈을 거기 써야 하지?
남: 글쎄, 우리나라가 최신 과학기술을 가지고 일하는 게 중요하잖아.
여: 그래, 그게 우리에게 당연히 좋은 걸 주겠지. 하지만 왜 우리가 이 모든 돈을 우주를 탐험하고 화성에 물이 있는지 발견하는 데 써야 하는 거야?
남: 저기, 우리는 우주 탐험에서 유용한 과학 지식을 정말로 얻고 있어.
여: 그럴 수도 있지만 나는 보통 사람들의 필요가 항상 우선시되어야 한다고 생각해. 지구상에 도움이 필요한 사람들이 있는 동안은 우리는 그들을 먼저 도와줘야 해.
남: 네가 무엇을 말하는지 알겠어.
여: 지구상의 보통 사람들이 제일 우선순위라고. 인류를 살아있게 하는 게 필수적인 거야.

어휘 Mars 화성 underground 지하의; 지하에서 budget 예산(안); 예산을 세우다 explore 탐험[탐사]하다; 탐구하다 cf. exploration 탐험, 탐사; 탐구 priority 우선 (사항) human race 인류 necessity 필수, 필요(성)

03 관계   ③

✽ 직업을 나타내거나 추론할 수 있는 힌트가 대화 전반에 걸쳐 드러나므로, 대화를 전체적으로 이해하는 것이 필요하다. 본 대화에서는 티켓을 제시하고 신발을 벗고 보안 검색대를 지나는 상황이다. 다음번에는 주머니를 비우라고 당부하며 탑승권을 챙기라고 하는 내용으로 미루어 보아 공항 보안검색 요원과 탑승객의 관계임을 알 수 있다.

M: Next!
W: Here's my ticket.
M: Please **take your shoes off** and put them into a plastic bin. And step through the scanner.
W: Okay. [beep, beep, beep] What's wrong? I took off my watch and belt.
M: Please step to the side.
W: Certainly.
M: Do you have any coins or keys **in your pocket**?
W: No, but I just put my necklace into my pocket.
M: Ah, that might be **the problem**. Put your necklace in this basket and walk through the scanner again.
W: Okay.
M: [pause] Good. **Remember to** empty your pockets before you go through here next time. And **don't forget to** bring your boarding pass.
W: I'll keep your advice in mind. Thank you.

남: 다음 분이요!
여: 여기 제 티켓이 있습니다.
남: 신발을 벗고 그것들을 플라스틱 통 안에 넣으십시오. 그리고 검색대를 걸어서 지나가십시오.
여: 알겠어요. [삐, 삐, 삐] 뭐가 잘못된 거죠? 시계와 벨트를 풀었는데요.
남: 옆쪽으로 서십시오.
여: 그럼요.
남: 주머니에 동전이나 열쇠가 있습니까?
여: 아니요, 하지만 전 단지 주머니에 제 목걸이를 넣어두었는데요.
남: 아, 그게 문제였을 수도 있겠군요. 목걸이를 이 바구니에 넣으시고 검색대를 다시 걸어 지나가십시오.

여: 알겠습니다.

남: *[잠시 후]* 좋습니다. 다음번에 여기를 지나가시기 전에 주머니를 비우는 걸 명심하십시오. 그리고 탑승권을 가져가는 걸 잊지 마세요.

여: 충고 명심할게요. 고맙습니다.

어휘 empty 비우다; 비어 있는   boarding pass 탑승권   keep A in mind A를 명심하다

04 그림 불일치 ⑤

∗ 대화가 나오기 전에 각 사물의 위치 관계와 외형(형태나 무늬, 개수 등)의 특징을 미리 확인하는 것이 좋다. 대화에서는 말 두 마리가 울타리 오른쪽에서 풀을 먹으며 서 있었다고 했으므로 그림의 ⑤는 내용과 일치하지 않는다. 말 두 마리가 달리는 것을 봤냐는 여자의 질문을 두 사람이 보고 있는 사진의 내용으로 혼동하지 않도록 유의한다.

W: Kevin, how was your vacation to Bulgaria?
M: It was so amazing. I'll never forget it. Oh, I have a picture here.
W: Wow, it's a beautiful landscape. There are mountains in the background.
M: Yeah. You wouldn't believe **how high they were**! They're so tall, and some of them were covered by clouds!
W: Oh, there is a cute house on the left of the landscape.
M: Yes, it has a tall chimney!
W: I also like the tall tree next to the house. Do you know **who lives there**?
M: I never got to meet them. Oh, do you see the long fence in the center?
W: Yeah, there are two horses **eating grass** on the right side of the fence. They're lovely!
M: I think the owners of the house might have had a horse ranch.
W: I see. Did you see the horses run?
M: No, I didn't. They were **just standing there** eating grass. Anyway, it was really a great experience!

여: Kevin, 불가리아로 간 여행은 어땠니?
남: 아주 굉장했어. 난 결코 못 잊을 거야. 아, 여기 사진이 있어.
여: 와, 아름다운 풍경이구나. 배경에 산이 있네.
남: 응. 산이 얼마나 높은지 넌 믿을 수 없을 거야! 너무 높아서 그중에 몇몇은 구름에 덮여 있어!
여: 아, 풍경 왼쪽에 귀여운 집이 하나 있네.
남: 응, 높은 굴뚝을 갖고 있지!
여: 난 집 옆의 키 큰 나무도 마음에 든다. 누가 거기 사는지 아니?
남: 그들을 한 번도 만나 본 적이 없어. 아, 가운데 긴 울타리 보이니?
여: 응, 울타리 오른쪽에서 말 두 마리가 풀을 먹고 있구나. 아름다워!
남: 집 소유주가 말 목장을 가진 것 같아.
여: 그렇구나. 넌 말들이 달리는 걸 보았니?
남: 아니, 못 봤어. 말들은 그냥 풀을 먹으면서 거기 서 있었어. 어쨌든, 정말 멋진 경험이었어!

어휘 landscape 풍경, 경치   chimney 굴뚝   ranch (대규모) 목장, 농원, 사육장

05 추후 행동 ④

∗ 대개 대화는 어떤 일을 하게 되는 상황이 먼저 제시된 뒤에 남자와 여자가 각각 할 일들과 이에 대한 수락/거절의 응답이 나열되는 식으로 전개된다. 여자가 회의 문서를 10부씩 복사해달라고 했고 그걸 바로 하겠다고 했으므로 남자가 할 일은 ④이다. ⑤의 경우 여자가 부탁했다가 바로 자기가 처리하겠다고 취소했음에 유의한다.

W: Hey, Steven! Are you busy now?
M: Hi, Julia. I'm just finishing up some work. Can I help you with anything?
W: Actually, yes. I'm going into a meeting, but I don't have enough time **to prepare for it**. Can you help me?
M: Absolutely. What can I do for you?
W: I need **ten copies** of this document — one for each person who will be in the meeting.
M: All right. I'll do it right away. Anything else?
W: Please call Mr. Johnson and tell him that I won't be able to make it to our dinner appointment tonight.
M: I'll call him as soon as I finish the other job **you asked me to do**.
W: Oh, hold on. I forgot I had a question for him, so don't call Mr. Johnson. I'll just call him myself after my meeting.

M: Okay! I'll get going with that **meeting preparation**!
W: Thank you, Steven.

여: 저기, Steven! 지금 바빠요?
남: 안녕하세요, Julia. 전 막 일을 마무리하고 있어요. 제가 뭐 좀 도와드릴까요?
여: 사실, 그래요. 난 회의에 들어갈 건데 그걸 준비할 시간이 충분치 않아요. 날 도와줄 수 있어요?
남: 그럼요, 뭐를 해드릴까요?
여: 이 문서의 복사본 10장이 필요한데, 회의에 참석할 각 사람에게 한 장씩 줄 거예요.
남: 알겠어요. 바로 그걸 할게요. 다른 것도 있나요?
여: Johnson 씨에게 전화해서 오늘 밤 저녁 약속을 지킬 수 없을 것 같다고 말해줘요.
남: 제게 부탁하신 다른 일을 끝내자마자 그에게 전화할게요.
여: 아, 잠깐만요. 내가 그에게 물어볼 게 있는 걸 잊었어요. 그러니까 Johnson 씨에게 전화하지 마세요. 그냥 내가 회의 후에 직접 그에게 전화할게요.
남: 알겠습니다! 전 회의 준비를 하기 시작할게요!
여: 고마워요, Steven.

어휘 document 문서, 서류; 기록하다   appointment 약속; 임명, 지명

06 금액 ③

∗ 여러 개의 수치 정보가 등장하므로 필요한 정보를 메모하면서 듣는 것이 좋다. 일 인당 1,500달러짜리 여행상품을 두 사람이 예약했으므로 총액은 3,000달러이다. 그런데 10퍼센트 할인해주는 특가상품이므로 10퍼센트인 300달러를 뺀 2,700달러를 남자가 지불해야 하는 총액이다. 보증금 100달러도 지불 금액(2700달러)에 포함된 것이므로 그 금액을 지불 금액에서 더하거나 빼지 않도록 유의한다.

W: Hello, can I help you?
M: Oh, yes, I took this brochure yesterday, and now I'd like to take one of your holiday packages.
W: Okay. Which one **are you interested in**?
M: This one here, on page 36. I'd like to travel to Europe. How much is this fifteen-day tour?
W: It costs 2,000 dollars per person, and it's a five-nation trip.
M: Oh, that's a bit expensive. How about this nine-day tour which visits 3 countries?
W: That one's a special offer. It was originally **1,500 dollars per person**, but you can get a 10 percent discount. Is it what you want?
M: Yes, that's the one. I would like to book this tour for 2 people.
W: Good. Could you **fill out** this booking form? We need your full address and **a deposit of** 100 dollars. You can pay by credit card.
M: Oh, I see. **When do I have to pay** the rest of the money?
W: We need to receive the money at least ten days before the tour begins.

여: 안녕하세요, 제가 도와드릴까요?
남: 아, 네, 제가 어제 이 책자를 가져갔는데 지금 휴가 패키지 중 하나를 택하고 싶어서요.
여: 좋습니다. 어떤 것에 관심이 있으세요?
남: 36쪽에 있는 여기 이것이요. 유럽을 여행하고 싶어요. 이 15일짜리 여행은 얼마인가요?
여: 일 인당 2,000달러이고 5개국 여행입니다.
남: 아, 좀 비싸군요. 3개국을 가는 이 9일짜리 여행은 어떤가요?
여: 그건 특가품입니다. 원래 일 인당 1,500달러였지만 10퍼센트 할인을 받으실 수 있습니다. 이게 원하시는 건가요?
남: 네, 그거예요. 이 여행상품으로 두 사람 예약하고 싶습니다.
여: 좋습니다. 이 예약 서류에 기재해주시겠어요? 고객님의 전체 주소와 100달러의 보증금이 필요합니다. 신용카드로 지불하실 수 있습니다.
남: 아, 알겠습니다. 언제 나머지 돈을 지불해야 하나요?
여: 여행이 시작되기 적어도 열흘 전에 저희가 받아야 합니다.

어휘 brochure (안내·광고용) 책자, 브로셔   book 예약[예매]하다; 책, 도서 *cf.* booking 예약   fill out (서류 등을) 기재[작성]하다   deposit 보증금; 예금(하다)

07 이유 ③

∗ 지시문을 통해 남자가 학교 야구부원을 그만두려는 상황이며 남자의 말에 단서가 있을 가능성이 큼을 미리 파악한다. 남자는 주중에는 수업 전과 수업 후에 훈련이 있고

일요일도 경기를 해야 한다면서 프로 선수가 되려는 게 아니니 그만두겠다고 하고 있으므로 답은 ③ '너무 많은 시간을 빼앗겨서'가 적절하다.

W: Conner, I heard you are a member of the school baseball team.
M: Yes, I went to try out last month, and the coach said I was talented.
W: You're good at baseball! Your father must be proud of you.
M: Yes, he is, but I'm thinking of quitting the team.
W: Really? Is the coach too strict? Or don't you get on well with your teammates?
M: No, he is nice and my teammates are also okay.
W: Then why? You are talented, and the coach is nice. Now all you have to do is help them win as much as possible!
M: But I have to attend training at 7 a.m. every weekday morning before classes start.
W: That's not bad, I think.
M: Not only that. I have to train for three hours after school every day! And Sundays are spent playing other teams!
W: Oh, that sounds like hard work.
M: I just want to enjoy baseball. I'm not going to be a professional player.
W: I see, now I understand you.

여: Conner, 네가 학교 야구부원이라고 들었어.
남: 응, 지난달에 시험해 보러 갔는데 코치님이 내가 재능이 있다고 하셨어.
여: 너 야구 잘하는구나! 네 아버지가 분명 널 자랑스러워하시겠다.
남: 그래. 그러시지. 하지만 난 팀을 그만둘까 생각 중이야.
여: 정말? 코치가 너무 엄격하니? 아니면 동료들하고 잘 지내지 못하는 거야?
남: 아니야. 그분은 친절하고 동료들도 괜찮아.
여: 그런데 왜? 넌 재능이 있고 코치는 친절하잖아. 이제 네가 해야 할 일이라곤 가능한 한 그들이 승리하도록 돕는 거잖아!
남: 하지만 난 매일 주중 수업을 시작하기 전 아침 7시에 훈련에 참석해야 해.
여: 내 생각엔 나쁘지 않은 거 같은데.
남: 그뿐만이 아냐. 난 방과 후에 매일 3시간 동안 훈련해야 해! 그리고 다른 팀과 경기하면서 일요일을 보내!
여: 아, 그거 힘든 일 같구나.
남: 난 그냥 야구를 즐기길 원한 거야. 난 프로 선수가 될 게 아니야.
여: 알겠어, 이제 네가 이해되네.

어휘 talented (타고난) 재능이 있는   quit 그만두다, 중지하다   attend 참석[출석]하다; 주의를 기울이다; 돌보다   professional 프로의; 직업의, 전문직의

08 언급하지 않은 것   ⑤

＊ 대화의 진행은 대개 선택지와 같은 순서이므로, 선택지를 보면서 언급된 내용을 소거하는 식으로 푸는 것이 좋다. 섬의 위치와 소속 국가, 최초 발견 탐험가와 섬 이름의 유래는 언급했지만 석상을 세운 목적은 언급하지 않았다. 남자가 누가 석상을 만들었는지는 물었지만 만든 목적에 대해서는 질문도 답도 없었음에 유의한다.

W: Have you ever heard of Easter Island? It's an amazing island.
M: I've heard its name, but I don't know for sure. Where is it located?
W: It's a Polynesian island in the Pacific Ocean about 3,600 km off the coast of Chile.
M: Oh, I remember. It's part of Chile. Wasn't the island discovered by a Spanish navigator?
W: No, a Dutch sea captain, Jacob Roggeveen, was the first navigator to visit the Island in 1722 on Easter Day.
M: That's why it was named Easter Island. Anyway, what makes it so interesting?
W: One of the reasons is that it has 887 huge stone statues, called *moai*. Look at this picture.
M: Oh, yeah, I've seen them. Who made these stone statues?
W: We just know that the people who first inhabited the island were from Polynesia. But the mystery is yet to be solved.
M: I'd love to visit there sometime.

여: Easter 섬에 대해 들어본 적이 있니? 놀라운 섬이야.
남: 이름은 들어봤지만 확실히는 몰라. 어디에 위치하고 있어?

여: 칠레 해안에서 약 3,600킬로미터 떨어진 태평양(① 섬의 위치)에 있는 폴리네시아의 섬이야.
남: 아, 기억난다. 칠레(② 소속 국가)의 일부지. 그 섬을 스페인 항해사가 발견하지 않았어?
여: 아니야. 네덜란드 선장인 Jacob Roggeveen(③ 최초 발견 탐험가)이 1722년 부활절(Easter Day)에 그 섬을 찾아간 최초의 항해사야.
남: 그래서 Easter 섬이라는 이름이 지어졌구나(④ 섬 이름의 유래). 어쨌든 뭐가 그렇게 그 섬을 흥미롭게 하는데?
여: 그 이유 중 하나는 '모아이'라고 불리는 887개의 거대한 석상이 있다는 거야. 이 사진을 봐.
남: 아, 그래. 그걸 본 적이 있어. 누가 이 석상을 만들었니?
여: 우리는 섬에 처음 거주한 사람들이 폴리네시아에서 왔다는 것만 알고 있어. 하지만 미스터리는 아직 풀리지 않았어.
남: 나도 언젠가 거기 방문하고 싶다.

어휘 coast 해안 (지방)   navigator 항해사, 조종사   Dutch 네덜란드(인)의   Easter Day 부활절   statue 상(像), 조각상   inhabit 거주하다. 살다

09 내용 불일치   ⑤

＊ 담화의 진행은 대개 선택지와 같은 순서이므로, 선택지를 보면서 일치하는 내용을 소거하는 식으로 푸는 것이 좋다. 담화에서는 안내 데스크에서 무료 지도를 얻을 수 있다고 했으므로 일치하지 않는 것은 ⑤이다.

M: Welcome to the Skanes Zoo. The Skanes Zoo has been open for 28 years. We have about 20,000 animals here. I will tell you about the zoo and the animals while we ride on this small train. This train goes around the zoo. There are several stops where you can get on and off the train. Please use your cameras to take pictures if you want to, but you must not take pictures inside the buildings. To your left, you can see a movie theater which shows a movie about animals every two hours. To your right, there is the Visitors' Center. It has an information desk where you can get a free map of the zoo. It shows where all the animals are in the zoo. Today, you can all discover a wonderful world of animals. We hope you enjoy your visit.

남: Skanes 동물원에 오신 것을 환영합니다. ① Skanes 동물원은 문을 연 지 28년이 되었습니다. 여기에는 약 2만 마리의 동물들이 있습니다. 우리가 이 미니 기차를 타는 동안 제가 여러분에게 동물원과 동물에 관해 말씀드리겠습니다. 이 기차는 동물원 주변을 돕니다. 여러분이 ② 기차를 타고 내릴 수 있는 몇 개의 정거장이 있습니다. 원하시면 사진을 찍기 위해 카메라를 사용하십시오, 하지만 ③ 건물 안에서는 사진을 찍으면 안 됩니다. 여러분 왼편에는 ④ 두 시간마다 동물에 관한 영화를 상영하는 극장을 보실 수 있습니다. 오른편에는 방문자 센터가 있습니다. 그곳에는 여러분이 ⑤ 동물원의 무료 지도를 얻을 수 있는 안내 데스크가 있습니다. 그것은 모든 동물이 동물원 안 어디에 있는지 보여줍니다. 오늘, 여러분은 동물의 놀라운 세계를 모두 발견하실 수 있습니다. 여러분의 방문을 즐기시기를 바랍니다.

10 도표 이해   ①

＊ 대화의 진행은 대개 도표 항목의 나열 순서대로 진행된다. 대화를 들으면서 도표의 각 항목 중 선택되지 않은 것을 소거하는 식으로 푸는 것이 좋다. 우선 침실이 3개 이상, 욕실이 2개 이상인 집을 원하고 있으므로 ②는 제외된다. 한 달 임대료가 2,000에서 2,500달러 사이를 원했으므로 ⑤도 제외된다. 그리고 단층집을 원하므로 ③이 제외되고 남은 ①과 ④ 중에서 여자의 이사하려는 날짜인 9월에 이사가 가능한 집인 ①이 정답이다.

M: So, are you looking for a house on Westridge Drive?
W: Yes, it's near my office, and I hear there's a good school nearby.
M: That's right. We have 5 houses available for rent on Westridge Drive. How many bedrooms do you need?
W: We have two kids, so we want a house with at least 3 bedrooms and 2 bathrooms.
M: Okay. And what price range are you interested in?
W: Somewhere between $2,000-$2,500 a month including utilities.
M: Then you have these three options.

W: **I'm not a big fan** of stairs, because it's too easy for a child to slip and fall down the stairs.

M: So, you want a **one-story** home. You can choose one of these two. When would you like to move in?

W: Next month, around **September 15th**. Hmm, I think this one is exactly what I want. Can I go and see it now?

M: Sure.

남: 그러니까, Westridge Drive에 있는 집을 찾으시는 거죠?

여: 네, 그게 제 사무실에서 가깝고 근처에 좋은 학교가 있다고 들어서요.

남: 맞습니다. 저희는 Westridge Drive에 임대 가능한 5개의 주택이 있습니다. 침실이 몇 개나 필요하신지요?

여: 아이가 둘이라서 적어도 3개의 침실과 2개의 욕실이 있는 집을 원해요.

남: 알겠습니다. 그리고 어느 가격대에 관심이 있으신지요?

여: 공공요금을 포함해서 한 달에 2,000달러에서 2,500달러 사이쯤이요.

남: 그러시다면 선택하실 게 3개 있습니다.

여: 아이들이 계단에서 미끄러지거나 떨어지기가 너무 쉽기 때문에 전 계단을 별로 좋아하지 않아요.

남: 그러면 단층짜리 집을 원하시는군요. 이 둘 중 하나를 선택하실 수 있습니다. 언제 이사 오실 건가요?

여: 다음 달 9월 15일쯤이요. 음. 이 집이 바로 제가 원하는 집 같군요. 여길 지금 가서 볼 수 있을까요?

남: 그럼요.

어휘 available 구할[이용할] 수 있는; 시간[여유]이 있는   including 포함하여   utility (수도, 전기와 같은) 공공요금; 공공 서비스; 유용(성)   one-story 단층 ((층수가 하나인 건축물))

11   짧은 대화에 이어질 응답   ③

❋ 여자가 박물관 표를 사는 줄이 어디 있는지 묻고 있다. 이에 대한 응답으로는 ③ '그러면, 저기 있는 줄에 서셔야 합니다.'가 가장 적절하다.

① 그러니까, 저하고 교대 근무 시간을 바꾸고 싶다는 거죠.

② 죄송합니다만 일부러 그런 건 아니었어요.

④ 저기요, 새치기하지 마세요. 줄 뒤로 가세요.

⑤ 제가 화장실 가는 동안 제 자리를 좀 봐주세요.

W: Excuse me. Is this the line to buy tickets?

M: No. This is the line to get into Adele's concert. I'm afraid the tickets for her concert are **sold out**.

W: Oh, no. I want to buy tickets for the museum, not the concert. Do you happen to know **where to go**?

M: You have to stand in line over there, then.

여: 실례합니다. 이 줄이 표 사는 줄인가요?

남: 아니요. 이건 Adele의 콘서트로 들어가는 줄이에요. 그녀의 콘서트 표는 다 팔린 것 같은데요.

여: 아, 아니에요. 전 콘서트가 아니라 박물관 표를 사려고 해요. 어디로 가야 하는지 혹시 아세요?

남: 그러면, 저기 있는 줄에 서셔야 합니다.

어휘 sold out 다 팔린, 매진된, 품절의 | 선택지 어휘 | shift 교대 근무 (시간)   on purpose 일부러, 고의로   cut in line 줄에 새치기하다

12   짧은 대화에 이어질 응답   ⑤

❋ 내일 아침 회의에 참석하라는 상사의 말에 치과에 가야 해서 빠져도 되는지 묻자 어렵다고 하는 상황이다. 이에 대한 응답으로는 치과 예약을 바꾸겠다는 내용의 ⑤ '아, 알겠습니다. 예약을 다시 잡아야겠군요.'가 적절하다.

① 네, 그걸 하겠습니다. 도와줘서 고맙습니다.

② 시간을 변경해서 죄송해요. 거기서 봅시다.

③ 제게 이메일을 보내주세요. 기꺼이 도와드리겠어요.

④ 걱정 마세요. 회의에서 그걸 논의할게요.

M: Stephanie, you also need to attend the meeting tomorrow morning.

W: Really? Well, I have to go to the dentist tomorrow morning. **Can I be excused** from the meeting?

M: I'm sorry, but that's difficult. We really **need you** at the meeting.

W: **Oh, okay. I should reschedule the appointment.**

남: Stephanie, 당신도 내일 아침 회의에 참석해야 해요.

여: 정말요? 저, 제가 내일 아침 치과에 가야 해서요. 회의에 빠져도 될까요?

남: 미안하지만 그건 어렵네요. 우리는 회의에서 당신이 정말 필요해요.

여: 아, 알겠습니다. 예약을 다시 잡아야겠군요.

어휘 excuse 면제해 주다; 양해[용서]하다; 변명(하다) | 선택지 어휘 | reschedule 일정을 변경하다

13   긴 대화에 이어질 응답   ⑤

❋ 대화의 전체 맥락 하에 마지막 말의 의미나 의도를 정확히 파악하는 것이 좋다. 본 대화는 여자가 새로 산 포토 프린터를 사용하려 하는데 작동 방법을 몰라서 짜증이 난 상황이다. 남자가 고객 서비스 전화번호를 찾아내지만 여자는 시간이 늦어서 응답하지 않을 거라고 하고 있다. 이에 대한 응답으로는 ⑤ '걱정 마. 내일 아침에 전화해서 물어보자.'가 가장 적절하다.

① 그러지 마. 우리는 에너지를 절약해야 해.

② 나도 동감이야. 지금 당장 그걸 하자.

③ 진정해. 넌 지금 결정할 필요가 없어.

④ 그런 경우라면 넌 계획을 바꿔야 해.

M: Kaylee, you look really busy.

W: Yes, I am. Please **don't bother** me right now.

M: Hmm... What's wrong with you? You look upset.

W: Oh, I'm sorry, but I'm really annoyed. Why is this **so complicated**?

M: What are you trying to do?

W: Well, I'm just trying to use my new photo printer. There isn't any button! I can't **figure it all out**!

M: Why don't you look at the manual? I'm sure it'll help.

W: I've already studied the manual and followed the directions. But it still doesn't work.

M: Let me take a look. Oh! There is a phone number for **customer service** right here.

W: But it's already 11 p.m. **Nobody will answer now**.

M: **Don't worry. Let's call and ask tomorrow morning.**

남: Kaylee, 정말 바빠 보인다.

여: 응. 맞아. 지금 날 귀찮게 하지 말아줘.

남: 음… 뭐가 잘못되었니? 너 화가 나 보여.

여: 아, 미안해. 하지만 난 정말 짜증이 나. 왜 이것은 이렇게 복잡하니?

남: 뭘 하려고 하는데?

여: 저, 나는 그냥 내 새 포토 프린터를 사용하려고 하고 있어. 어떤 버튼도 없어! 난 모든 걸 알아낼 수가 없어!

남: 설명서를 보지 그러니? 그게 분명히 도와줄 거야.

여: 난 이미 설명서를 살펴봤고 지시대로 따랐어. 하지만 여전히 작동하지 않아.

남: 내가 볼게. 아! 바로 여기 고객 서비스의 전화번호가 있어.

여: 하지만 벌써 오후 11시야. 지금은 아무도 응답하지 않을 거야.

남: 걱정 마. 내일 아침에 전화해서 물어보자.

어휘 bother 귀찮게 하다; 귀찮은 일   annoyed 짜증이 난   complicated 복잡한   figure A out A를 알아내다[이해하다]   manual 설명서; 수동의   direction 지시; 방향

14   긴 대화에 이어질 응답   ④

❋ 대화의 전체 맥락 하에 마지막 말의 의미나 의도를 정확히 파악하는 것이 좋다. 서커스가 공연을 오는데 아이를 데려가지 못하는 여자에게 남자가 자기 아이와 함께 데려가 주겠다고 제안한다. 이에 대한 응답으로는 ④ '그렇다면 완벽하게 해결되는군요. 우리 애를 초대해줘서 고마워요!'가 가장 적절하다.

① 제발요! 내가 말을 끝낼 때까지 가로막지 말아요.

② 동의해요. 서커스는 아이들에게 굉장히 인기거리죠.

③ 좋은 생각이에요. 좋은 친구와 어울리는 것은 아주 중요해요.
⑤ 정말 친절하군요! 그런 사랑스러운 자녀가 있다니 행복하시겠어요.

M: Hailey, did you hear that the circus is coming to our town?
W: I did, and my daughter is so excited about it. She really wants to go, but my husband is **on a business trip**!
M: Oh, do you have any plans to take her?
W: I really want to, but I just learned that I have to work the night shift. I'm going to be working all the nights that the circus is here.
M: Oh, really? **That's a shame.**
W: I know. I wish I knew **a way for her to go**.
M: Well, here's an idea. I mean, I have a daughter, and I know she really wants to go.
W: Do you have time to take her?
M: Yes, I do. And I certainly **wouldn't mind** taking one extra kid.
W: Oh, that would be great! But I really don't want to bother you.
M: **It's no bother!** Plus, I'm sure my kid would love to meet your daughter.
W: **Then that works out perfectly. Thanks for inviting her!**

남: Hailey, 우리 도시에 서커스가 올 거라는 이야기 들었어요?
여: 들었어요. 그리고 제 딸아이가 그것에 대해 무척 신나있어요. 정말로 가고 싶어 하는데 제 남편이 출장 중이에요!
남: 아, 그 애를 데려갈 계획은 있나요?
여: 정말 그러고 싶지만 내가 야간 근무를 해야 한다는 걸 방금 알았어요. 서커스가 여기에 있는 모든 밤에 나는 일할 거예요.
남: 아, 정말이요? 그거 유감이군요.
여: 그래요. 딸애가 갈 방법을 알았으면 좋겠어요.
남: 음, 아이디어가 있는데요. 제 말은 저도 딸이 있고 그 애가 정말 가고 싶어 한다는 걸 알아요.
여: 아이를 데려갈 시간이 있어요?
남: 네, 있어요. 그리고 아이를 한 명 더 데려가는 게 분명 괜찮을 것 같아요.
여: 아, 그렇다면 너무 좋죠! 하지만 정말로 폐를 끼치고 싶지 않아요.
남: 귀찮지 않아요! 게다가 우리 애가 분명히 당신 딸을 만나고 싶어 할 거예요.
여: 그렇다면 완벽하게 해결되는군요. 우리 애를 초대해주셔서 고마워요!

어휘 night shift 야간 근무   bother 귀찮게 하다; 귀찮은 일 | 선택지 어휘 | interrupt 가로막다, 방해하다; 중단시키다   attraction 인기거리; 매력; 끌림; 명소, 명물   keep good company 좋은 친구와 어울리다   work out (일이) 잘 풀리다[진행되다]

15 상황에 적절한 말   ④

✽ 지시문을 통해 누가(A) 누구에게(B) 할 말인지를 우선 정확히 파악한다. 담화는 대개 A와 B에 대한 배경 설명과 B가 처한 문제 상황, 그리고 이에 대해 A가 어떤 말을 하려고 하는지에 대한 설명의 순서로 전개된다. Charlotte(A)가 친구 Gabriel(B)에게 기차 시간에 늦지 않게 나오라고 강조하는 말을 다시 하려고 한다. 그러므로 가장 적절한 말은 ④ '네가 제시간에 안 나타나면 우리는 기차를 놓칠 거야.'이다.

① 그건 걱정 마! 난 제시간에 거기 갈 거야.
② 넌 나를 믿어도 돼. 난 네 비밀을 지킬 수 있어.
③ 내가 너한테 다시 전화할게. 날 이해해줘서 고마워.
⑤ 늦어서 미안해. 난 더 일찍 잠자리에 들어야 했어.

W: Gabriel and Charlotte are friends. They plan to go hiking tomorrow. They are taking a trip to Copper Mountain, **located outside the city**. They decide to take the train to Copper Mountain. It will take about **a couple of hours** to get there. The train runs only **twice a day**, one in the morning and the other in the evening. If they miss the 7 o'clock morning train, their hiking plan will have to be canceled. Charlotte is very concerned because Gabriel is never on time. She warns Gabriel that their plans **will be ruined** if he's late and misses the train. She wants to remind him again that he has to **be on time**. In this situation, what would Charlotte most likely say to Gabriel?

Charlotte: **If you don't show up on time, we'll miss the train.**

여: Gabriel과 Charlotte은 친구이다. 그들은 내일 등산을 가기로 계획한다. 그들은 시 외곽에 위치한 Copper 산으로 여행을 갈 것이다. 그들은 Copper 산까지 기차를 타기

로 결정한다. 거기 가는 데는 약 두어 시간이 걸릴 것이다. 기차는 하루에 단 두 번, 한 번은 아침, 다른 한 번은 저녁에 운행한다. 그들이 7시 정각의 아침 기차를 놓친다면 그들의 등산 계획은 취소되어야 할 것이다. Gabriel이 결코 제시간에 오지 않기 때문에 Charlotte는 무척 걱정된다. 그녀는 Gabriel에게 그가 늦어서 기차를 놓치면 그들의 계획을 망칠 것이라고 경고한다. 그녀는 그에게 제시간에 와야 한다고 다시 상기시키고 싶다. 이 상황에서 Charlotte가 Gabriel에게 뭐라고 말하겠는가?

Charlotte: 네가 제시간에 안 나타나면 우리는 기차를 놓칠 거야.

어휘 run 운행하다; 운영하다   on time 시간을 어기지 않고, 정각에   ruin 망치다; 파괴하다   remind 상기시키다; 생각나게 하다 | 선택지 어휘 | rely on ~을 믿다[신뢰하다]; ~에 의지[의존]하다   show up (예정된 곳에) 나타나다

16~17 세트 문항   16 ④ 17 ②

✽ **16** 식물이 긍정적인 에너지의 수준을 증가시키는 것 이상의 효과가 있다는 걸 아는지 물으면서 학습 환경에서 식물의 역할에 대해 예를 들어 설명하고 있다. 그러므로 주제로는 ④ '수업 수행에서 식물의 긍정적인 영향'이 가장 적절하다.

① 실내 식물을 선택하고 보살피는 법
② 교실에서 인기 있는 화분에 담긴 식물의 종류
③ 주의력을 증진하는 데 끼치는 자연의 영향
⑤ 새로운 것을 학습하는 아이들의 능력을 증진하는 법

✽ **17** 해석 참조.
① 라벤더   ② 백합   ③ 로즈메리   ④ 자주달개비   ⑤ 금줄 범꼬리

M: You may have heard that having plants around the home and office greatly improves people's moods and reduces depression. But do you know plants can do **a lot more** than increase levels of positive energy? Recent research shows that children who spend time around plants **learn better**. For example, children with attention deficit disorder who learn in a natural environment engage more with classwork. In another experiment, keeping plants in children's learning environments enhanced learning capabilities by **helping them to focus**. For these benefits, some plants work better than others. Potted plants, such as lavender, rosemary, or aloe, in the classroom reduce children's tendency towards distraction and help them to better focus on schoolwork. Specifically for children with problems paying attention, spider plants or snake plants can have a dramatic positive effect on learning. In addition, **the soothing effects** of natural beauty help to minimize the anxiety that would otherwise occupy their minds. So if you want to help your children learn better, **try changing** their learning environment.

남: 여러분은 집과 사무실 주변에 식물을 두는 것이 사람들의 기분을 상당히 호전시키고 우울증을 줄여준다는 말을 들었을 겁니다. 그러나 식물이 긍정적 에너지의 수준을 증진하는 것보다 훨씬 더 많은 것을 할 수 있다는 것을 아십니까? 최근 연구는 식물 주변에서 시간을 보내는 아이들이 더 잘 배운다는 것을 보여줍니다. 예를 들면 자연의 환경에서 학습하는 주의력 결핍 장애가 있는 아이들이 교실학습에 더 몰두합니다. 또 다른 실험에서 보면 아이들의 학습 환경에 식물을 두는 것이 아이들이 집중하는 것을 도와줌으로써 학습 능력을 향상시켰습니다. 이러한 이로움에 있어서 일부 식물은 다른 것들보다 더 효과가 있습니다. 교실 안에 있는 ① 라벤더나 ③ 로즈메리나 알로에 같이 화분에 담긴 식물은 산만해지려는 아이들의 성향을 줄이고 학교 수업에 더 잘 집중하도록 돕습니다. 특히 집중하는 데 문제가 있는 아이들에게 ④ 자주달개비나 ⑤ 금줄 범꼬리가 학습에 극적인 긍정적 영향을 줄 수 있습니다. 게다가, 자연적 아름다움의 진정시키는 효과가 그렇지 않으면 아이들의 마음을 사로잡을 불안을 최소화하도록 돕습니다. 그러므로 여러분이 자녀가 더 잘 배우도록 돕고 싶다면 그들의 학습 환경을 바꾸도록 해보십시오.

어휘 mood 기분; 분위기   reduce 줄이다, 축소하다   depression 우울(증); 불경기   attention deficit disorder 주의력 결핍 장애 cf. attention 주의(력); 관심   engage 몰두하다; 약속하다   enhance 향상시키다, 높이다   capability 능력, 역량   work 효과가 있다   tendency 성향, 기질; 경향   distraction 주의 산만; 마음을 산만하게 하는 것   dramatic 극적인; 급격한; 연극의   soothing 마음을 진정시키는, 달래는   minimize 최소화하다   anxiety 불안(감), 염려   occupy (마음을) 사로잡다; (주의를) 끌다

05회

01 화자가 하는 말의 목적 ①

✻ 담화의 일부 내용이 아니라 중심 내용을 파악해야 한다. 초반부에 자신이 생태학 교수임을 밝히고 환경 운동가는 아니라고 말을 꺼냈지만, Gray 강의 안 좋은 상태를 발견하고 강을 살리기 위한 캠페인에 협력하기로 했다고 하면서 그 모임에 주민들이 참여하기를 촉구하고 있다. 그러므로 말의 목적은 ①이 가장 적절하다.

W: Hello, I'm Leah Andrews, an ecology professor at Stevenson University. I studied the condition of the environment for many years, but I was never an activist. I thought if I **got involved in** protecting the environment, I would see things less objectively during my research. However, as I was studying the Gray River, I found it was in a **very bad condition**. That's why I decided to **join hands with** the local residents to save Gray River. We all want to protect and **improve our river** so that we can safely use the water and swim in the river. We are planning to hold a meeting on July 12th at Stevenson Hall to start our campaign **to save the river**. There will be a lot of scientists there to tell you what's going on in the river. We hope to see all residents there.

여: 안녕하세요, 저는 Stevenson 대학의 생태학 교수인 Leah Andrews입니다. 저는 수년간 환경 실태를 연구했지만, 결코 (환경) 운동가는 아니었습니다. 저는 제가 환경을 보호하는 데 관여한다면 연구를 하는 동안 문제를 덜 객관적으로 볼 거라고 생각했습니다. 그러나 제가 Gray 강을 연구하고 있으면서 그것이 정말 안 좋은 상태임을 발견했습니다. 그것이 제가 Gray 강을 살리기 위해 지역 주민들과 협력하기로 결정한 이유입니다. 우리는 모두 물을 안전하게 사용하고 강에서 수영할 수 있도록 우리의 강을 보호하고 개선하기를 바랍니다. 우리는 강을 살리기 위한 우리의 캠페인을 시작하기 위해 7월 12일 Stevenson 홀에서 모임을 할 계획입니다. 여러분에게 강에서 무슨 일이 벌어지고 있는지 알려줄 많은 과학자들이 그곳에 올 것입니다. 그곳에서 모든 주민들을 뵙기를 바랍니다.

어휘 ecology 생태학: 생태(계) activist 운동가, 행동주의자 get involved in ~에 관여하다 objectively 객관적으로 research 연구(하다), 조사(하다) join hands with ~와 협력하다[손을 잡다] resident 주민: 거주자 improve 개선하다: 나아지게 하다 campaign 캠페인, (사회·정치적 목적을 위한) 운동[활동]

02 의견 ⑤

✻ 우선 지시문에서 명시한 화자의 성별을 보고 어느 화자의 말에 주목할지를 판단해야 한다. 특히 의견이나 주장을 표현하는 어구(I think ~, You should ~ 등)가 이끄는 내용을 잘 들어야 한다. 이 대화에서 남자는 여자가 사진을 찍으면서 실제의 순간을 놓치고 있고 사진을 찍는 것이 휴가를 망치고 있다고 생각한다. 또한, 자신의 눈으로 풍경을 봐야 한다고 말하는 것으로 보아 남자의 의견으로는 ⑤가 가장 적절하다.

M: Oh, look at the Alhambra Palace in the sunset! It's breathtaking!
W: Wow! I should take some pictures. *[Snap! Snap!]* These are beautiful!
M: Amelia, there's **nothing compared** to the sunset that is right in front of you.
W: Of course. But I want to capture the moment. I take photos for the memories. *[Snap! Snap!]*
M: Don't you think you're missing the **actual moment** while taking all those pictures?
W: I just want to preserve the beauty forever.
M: You always take so many pictures wherever we visit. I think your desire to capture the moment actually **ruins the vacation**.
W: What do you mean by that?
M: I mean we should see the sunset **with our own eyes**. Just enjoy the scenery and this moment.
W: I understand, but don't push me too much. You like seeing scenery, and I like **taking pictures**.

남: 오, 석양의 Alhambra 궁전을 봐! 숨 막히게 아름다워!
여: 왜! 사진을 찍어야겠어. *[찰칵! 찰칵!]* 이거 아름답다!
남: Amelia, 네 눈 바로 앞에 있는 석양과 비교할 수 있는 건 아무것도 없어.
여: 물론이지. 하지만 난 순간을 포착하고 싶어. 난 추억을 위해 사진을 찍는 거야. *[찰칵! 찰칵!]*
남: 네가 그 모든 사진을 찍는 동안 실제의 순간을 놓치고 있다고 생각하지 않니?
여: 난 그냥 아름다움을 영원히 보존하고 싶어.
남: 넌 언제나 우리가 방문하는 곳마다 너무 많은 사진을 찍어. 나는 순간을 포착하려는 네 욕망이 실제로는 휴가를 망치고 있다고 생각해.
여: 그게 무슨 뜻이야?
남: 우리가 우리 자신의 눈으로 석양을 봐야 한다는 말이야. 풍경과 이 순간을 그냥 즐겨.
여: 알아, 하지만 나한테 너무 강요하지 마. 넌 풍경을 보는 걸 좋아하는 것이고 나는 사진 찍기를 좋아하는 거야.

어휘 palace 궁전 sunset 석양, 일몰 breathtaking (너무 아름답거나 놀라워서) 숨이 막히는 compare to A A와 비교하다 capture 포착하다; 붙잡다 preserve 보존하다; 보호하다 desire 욕망; 바라다 ruin 망치다, 엉망으로 만들다 scenery 풍경, 경치

03 관계 ②

✻ 직업을 나타내거나 추론할 수 있는 힌트가 대화 전반에 걸쳐 드러나므로, 대화를 전체적으로 이해하는 것이 필요하다. 감독이 남자를 여자에게 보냈고 남자는 연극에서 마술사 배역을 맡았다. 여자는 배역을 위한 의상을 만들기 위해 대본을 읽고 배역을 이해하고 배우의 치수를 재는 것으로 보아 두 사람의 관계는 ② '배우 ─ 의상 디자이너'임을 알 수 있다.

M: Excuse me, are you Leah Jones?
W: That's me! What can I help you with?
M: I'm David Clark. Mr. Miller, the director, told me I could meet you here.
W: Nice to meet you, David. You'll be **playing the magician** in the play, right?
M: Exactly. This is **my first big role**, so I'm very nervous.
W: I'm sure you'll do a great job. Now, the magician should be an attractive character, so I'll make a fancy costume.
M: The makeup designer said something similar. Did you already read the script?
W: Of course. We need to understand the roles to make the costumes. Now I'll **take your measurements**.
M: Okay. I'm looking forward to seeing **the costumes you will make**.
W: I'll do my best.

남: 실례합니다. Leah Jones 신가요?
여: 저예요! 뭘 도와드릴까요?
남: 저는 David Clark입니다. 감독인 Miller 씨가 제게 여기서 당신을 만날 수 있다고 말씀하셨거든요.
여: 만나서 반가워요, David. 연극에서 마술사를 연기하실 거죠, 맞죠?
남: 맞습니다. 이게 제 첫 큰 배역이라서 무척 떨리네요.
여: 아주 잘 하실 거라 믿어요. 자, 마술사는 매력적인 인물이어야 해서 전 화려한 의상을 만들 거예요.
남: 분장사도 비슷한 말을 했어요. 벌써 대본을 읽으셨어요?
여: 물론이죠. 의상을 만들려면 배역을 이해해야 하거든요. 이제 제가 치수를 잴게요.
남: 알겠습니다. 만드실 의상을 보기를 기대해요.
여: 최선을 다할게요.

어휘 play 연기하다; 연극 role 배역, 역할 attractive 매력적인, 마음을 끄는 fancy 화려한; 값비싼 costume 의상, 복장 script 대본, 원고 take (one's) measurements 치수를 재다 look forward to v-ing v하기를 기대하다 do one's best 최선을 다하다

04 그림 불일치   ⑤

✲ 대화가 나오기 전에 각 사물의 위치 관계와 외형(형태나 무늬, 개수 등)의 특징을 미리 확인하는 것이 좋다. 여자가 원래는 서랍 세 개짜리 옷장을 사려다가 물건을 더 많이 보관하려고 네 개짜리로 바꿨다고 했다. 그러나 그림의 옷장은 서랍이 세 개뿐이므로 ⑤가 대화의 내용과 일치하지 않는다.

M: Honey, I'm home! What are you doing?
W: William, look! I just decorated our baby's room.
M: Oh, how lovely! You put the baby bed near the wall between the windows.
W: Yes, and I **hung** the bird mobile **over the bed**.
M: It's nice! I heard mobiles help the baby's brain to develop.
W: That's right. And I put an armchair beside the bed near the window.
M: Wow! It's a good place for you to play with the baby. I also like **the round carpet** on the floor.
W: I put it on the floor for safety. I also bought the chest of four drawers on the right.
M: Perfect! You can keep all the baby supplies in it.
W: I was planning to buy a chest of three drawers, but I **changed my mind** because I guessed four drawers would hold more things.
M: That was a good purchase. Three drawers **wouldn't be enough**.

남: 여보, 나 집에 왔어요! 뭐 하고 있나요?
여: William, 봐요! 내가 방금 우리 아기방을 꾸몄어요.
남: 아, 정말 사랑스러워요! 아기 침대를 창문 사이 벽 근처에 두었군요.
여: 네, 그리고 침대 위에 새 모빌을 매달았어요.
남: 멋져요! 모빌이 아기들의 두뇌 발달을 돕는다고 들었어요.
여: 맞아요. 그리고 창문 근처 침대 옆에 안락의자를 두었어요.
남: 왜! 당신이 아기와 함께 놀기 좋은 장소군요. 나는 바닥에 있는 둥근 카펫도 마음에 들어요.
여: 안전을 위해 바닥에 그걸 두었어요. 나는 또 오른편에 서랍이 네 개 있는 옷장을 샀어요.
남: 완벽해요! 아기용품을 거기 보관할 수 있겠어요.
여: 서랍 세 개짜리 옷장을 사려 했지만 서랍 네 개짜리가 물건을 더 많이 보관할 것 같아서 마음을 바꿨어요.
남: 잘 샀어요. 서랍 세 개는 충분하지 않을 거예요.

어휘 hang 매달다: 걸다 chest of drawers 옷장 cf. drawer 서랍

05 추후 행동   ④

✲ 대개 대화는 어떤 일을 하게 되는 상황이 먼저 제시된 뒤에 남자와 여자가 각각 할 일들과 이에 대한 수락/거절의 응답이 나열되는 식으로 전개된다. 호텔 직원과 투숙객의 대화로 남자가 여러 가지를 묻고 있다. 택시를 예약해달라는 남자의 부탁을 여자가 수락했으므로 여자가 할 일은 ④ '택시 회사에 전화하기'이다.

W: Good morning, sir. How can I help you?
M: Hi. Where is the restaurant for breakfast?
W: It's right over there, sir.
M: Thanks. I also have some laundry that needs **to be done**. When will the clothes be returned if I send them this evening?
W: Well, it usually takes a day. What is your room number? I'll send someone to **pick them up** this evening.
M: Thank you. It's 809. And I have to be at a business conference at 10 o'clock at Plaza Hotel. Can I take the subway to get there?
W: Well, yes, but you need to transfer twice. I think it's better **to take a taxi**.
M: Isn't it far away from here?
W: No. It's only a 20-minute drive from this hotel.
M: That's good. Could you **make a booking** for me at 9:20 a.m.?
W: Sure, sir. **I'll take care of it** right away.

여: 안녕하세요, 손님. 무엇을 도와드릴까요?
남: 안녕하세요. 아침 식사를 할 식당이 어디 있나요?
여: 바로 저기 있습니다, 손님.
남: 고맙습니다. 또 세탁해야 할 게 좀 있는데요. 오늘 저녁에 옷을 보내면 언제 그것들을 돌려받나요?

여: 음, 보통 하루가 걸립니다. 방 호수가 어떻게 되세요? 제가 오늘 저녁에 그것들을 수거할 사람을 보내겠습니다.
남: 고마워요. 809호예요. 그리고 10시 정각에 Plaza 호텔에서 있는 업무 회의에 가야 하거든요. 거기 가는 데 지하철을 탈 수 있나요?
여: 음, 네, 하지만 두 번 갈아타셔야 해요. 택시를 타시는 게 더 나을 것 같습니다.
남: 여기서 멀지 않나요?
여: 아뇨. 이 호텔에서 자동차로 단지 20분 거리입니다.
남: 그거 좋군요. 오전 9시 20분에 예약을 해줄 수 있나요?
여: 그럼요, 손님. 바로 처리해드리겠습니다.

어휘 laundry 세탁물 conference 회의: 학회 transfer 갈아타다. 환승하다 make a booking 예약을 하다

06 금액   ②

✲ 여러 개의 수치 정보가 등장하므로 필요한 정보를 메모하면서 듣는 것이 좋다. 한 달에 30달러인 달리기 강좌를 신청했는데 석 달 치를 미리 내면 10% 할인을 해준다고 해서 세 달 치를 지불하려고 한다. 따라서 90달러에 9달러 할인을 받았으므로 답은 ②이다.

M: Good afternoon! Do you want to sign up for a class?
W: Yes. **What sort of class** would you recommend?
M: What is the goal of your workout? If you want to build muscle, I suggest taking the body building class. It's 60 dollars a month.
W: No, I don't want to exercise too hard. I want something to **keep me fit**, and that's all.
M: Well... Do you like running? We have a special class on Mondays and Fridays for runners.
W: Sounds good. How much is the fee?
M: It costs **30 dollars a month**. This class usually runs outdoors but runs indoors on rainy days.
W: I think that sounds good. I'd like to sign up now.
M: If you pay for **3 months in advance**, you can receive **a 10% discount**.
W: Sounds great. Then I'll pay for 3 months in advance. Here's my credit card.
M: Okay. Hold on, please.

남: 안녕하세요! 강좌에 등록하시려고요?
여: 네. 어떤 종류의 강좌를 추천해주겠어요?
남: 운동 목표가 무엇인지요? 근육을 만들고 싶다면 보디빌딩 강좌를 택하실 것을 권합니다. 한 달에 60달러입니다.
여: 아뇨, 너무 힘들게 운동하고 싶지는 않아요. 전 건강을 유지하게 하는 걸 원하고, 그게 다예요.
남: 음… 달리기를 좋아하시나요? 월요일과 금요일에 달리는 사람들을 위한 특별 강좌가 있어요.
여: 그거 좋군요. 수강료가 얼마인가요?
남: 한 달에 30달러입니다. 이 강좌는 보통 야외에서 달리지만 비가 오는 날에는 실내에서 달립니다.
여: 그거 좋은 것 같군요. 지금 등록하고 싶어요.
남: 석 달 치를 미리 지불하시면 10% 할인을 받으실 수 있습니다.
여: 그거 좋군요. 그러면 석 달 치를 미리 지불할게요. 여기 제 신용카드요.
남: 알겠습니다. 잠시만 기다려주세요.

어휘 sign up (for) (~에) 등록[가입]하다 sort 종류. 유형 muscle 근육: 힘 fit 건강한. 탄탄한 fee 수강료: 요금: 수수료 in advance 미리. 사전에

07 이유   ③

✲ 지시문을 통해 여자가 전화를 걸려는 상황임을 파악한다. 주차 장소를 찾는 데 어려움을 겪을까 봐 걱정하는 여자에게 남자는 Stephanie의 남편에게 전화해 미리 주차 장소에 대해 문의하라고 했고 여자가 알겠다고 했으므로 답은 ③이 적절하다.

W: Jack, what time is it? We are going to be late for the party!
M: No. It's around six. **We are on time**.
W: But I think we have to be at Stephanie's house by 6:30 for her surprise birthday party.

M: Don't worry. We're not going to be late.

W: I don't think we can make it because there is a lot of **rush-hour traffic** at this time of day.

M: I'm sure **we'll make it**. We're not far away now.

W: Are you sure? We'll probably spend more than 10 minutes to find a parking place.

M: You're right. Then why don't you call Stephanie's husband and ask him **where we can park** our car?

W: Okay. I'll call him now.

M: Don't worry. Anyway, the party starts at 7.

여: Jack, 몇 시예요? 우리 파티에 늦겠어요!

남: 아뇨. 6시쯤 되었어요. 제시간이에요.

여: 하지만 Stephanie의 깜짝 생일 파티를 위해서는 6시 30분까지는 그녀의 집에 도착해야 할 것 같은데요.

남: 걱정 말아요. 우리가 늦지는 않을 거예요.

여: 하루 중 이 시간에 교통 체증이 심하기 때문에 우리가 제시간에 갈 수 있을 것 같지 않아요.

남: 분명히 우리는 제시간에 도착할 수 있어요. 지금 멀리 있지 않거든요.

여: 확실해요? 우리는 아마 주차 장소를 찾기 위해 10분 넘게 써야 할 거예요.

남: 맞아요. 그러면 Stephanie의 남편에게 전화해서 우리가 차를 어디에 주차할 수 있는지 물어보지 그래요?

여: 알았어요. 지금 그에게 전화할게요.

남: 걱정 말아요. 어쨌든 파티는 7시에 시작하니까요.

어휘 rush-hour (출퇴근) 혼잡 시간대   make it (제시간에) 도착하다: 성공하다   probably 아마

08 언급하지 않은 것 ④

※ 대화의 진행은 대개 선택지와 같은 순서이므로, 선택지를 보면서 언급된 내용을 소거하는 식으로 푸는 것이 좋다. 11권의 책은 Stephen King의 출간 작품 수가 아니라 여자가 읽은 책의 수임에 유의한다. 수많은 소설을 썼다는 언급은 있지만 구체적인 작품 수를 언급하지 않았으므로 답은 ④이다.

M: Hi, Sophia. What are you reading?

W: Hi, Brandon. I'm reading this book I just bought. Have you ever heard of the author Stephen King?

M: Yeah, he is a very famous author of horror fiction. He is quite old, I guess.

W: Right. He **was born in** 1947. And did you know 350 million copies of his books have been sold?

M: That's amazing. Why the sudden interest in Stephen King?

W: Well, I read his **first published** novel, *Carrie*, and I found it very interesting. So I kept on reading his books.

M: He has written numerous novels. Did you read all of them?

W: No, I've only **read eleven books**. I also saw some movies made from his work.

M: Wow! You are a big fan of him! By the way, it's almost 1:30. We have English class now!

W: Okay. Oh, that reminds me, Stephen King was once **an English teacher** in a high school.

M: Really? Anyway, let's hurry. We don't want to be late for class.

남: 안녕, Sophia. 뭐 읽고 있니?

여: 안녕, Brandon. 난 방금 산 이 책을 읽고 있어. 작가 Stephen King에 대해 들어본 적 있니?

남: 응. 공포 소설의 아주 유명한 작가잖아. 굉장히 나이가 있는 것 같은데.

여: 맞아. 1947년(① 출생연도)에 태어났어. 그리고 그의 책이 3억 5천만 부(② 책 판매 부수)가 팔렸다는 걸 알았니?

남: 그거 굉장하다. 갑자기 Stephen King에 대한 관심은 왜?

여: 음. 그의 첫 번째 출간 소설인 'Carrie'(③ 최초 출간 소설)를 읽었는데 너무 재미있었어. 그래서 계속해서 그의 소설을 읽었어.

남: 수많은 소설을 썼다. 그걸 모두 읽은 거야?

여: 아니. 단지 11권만 읽었어. 난 또 그의 작품으로 만든 영화도 몇 편 보았어.

남: 왜! 너는 그의 열렬한 팬이구나! 그런데 1시 30분이 거의 다 되었어. 우리 지금 영어 수업이 있어!

여: 알았어. 아, 그러니까 생각나는 건데 Stephen King은 한때 고등학교 영어 선생님(⑤ 이전 직업)이었어.

남: 정말이야? 어쨌든 서두르자. 우린 수업에 늦고 싶지는 않잖아.

어휘 author 작가, 저자   fiction 소설, 허구   sudden 갑작스러운, 급작스러운   interest 관심, 흥미: 이자   publish 출간[발표]하다   keep on v-ing 계속 v하다   numerous 수많은   that reminds me ((구어)) 그러고 보니 생각난다   once 한때: 한 번

09 내용 불일치 ⑤

※ 담화의 진행은 대개 선택지와 같은 순서이므로, 선택지를 보면서 일치하는 내용을 소거하는 식으로 푸는 것이 좋다. 수상 여부에 상관없이 이야기가 마음에 든다면 Jackson County Times에 게재할 가능성이 있다고 했으므로 ⑤는 담화의 내용과 일치하지 않는다.

M: Welcome to the Halloween Scary Story Contest. It's our biggest contest. You already know the basic rules. Your story must be **500 words or under**, and be an original. Stories should be typed or **neatly handwritten**. Stories have to be in before our deadline. The deadline is September 30th. First place wins a $1,000 gift card, second place wins a $500 gift card, and third place wins a $250 gift card. We will announce and post the winners on **October 30th**! And, if we like your story, **regardless of** winning or not, you have a chance of being published in our Halloween print issue of *Jackson County Times*. We are looking for **the scariest of the scary** this time. Please scare us!

남: 핼러윈 무서운 이야기 대회에 오신 걸 환영합니다. 이것은 우리의 가장 큰 대회입니다. 여러분은 이미 기본 규칙은 알고 있습니다. ① 여러분의 이야기는 500단어 이하여야 하고 원문이어야 합니다. ② 이야기는 타자로 치거나 깔끔하게 손글씨로 써야 합니다. 이야기는 우리의 마감 시간 전에 들어와야 합니다. 마감 일자는 9월 30일입니다. ③ 1등은 1,000달러짜리 상품권을 받고 2등은 500달러짜리 상품권을 받고, 그리고 3등은 250달러짜리 상품권을 받습니다. 우리는 ④ 10월 30일에 입상자를 발표하고 게시할 것입니다! 그리고, 우리가 여러분의 이야기가 마음에 든다면 ⑤ 입상하거나 못하거나에 상관없이 우리의 'Jackson County Times' 핼러윈 인쇄판에 게재할 가능성이 있습니다. 이번 무서운 이야기 중 가장 무서운 것을 기대하고 있습니다. 우리를 놀라게 해주세요!

어휘 scary 무서운, 겁나는 cf. scare 놀라게[겁먹게] 하다   original 원문: 독창적인; 원래의   neatly 깔끔하게   deadline 마감 시간[일자]   announce 발표하다. 알리다   post 게시[공고]하다   regardless of ~에 상관없이   publish 발행[출판]하다   issue (정기 간행물의) 판[호]; 발행(물); 주제, 쟁점

10 도표 이해 ⑤

※ 대화의 진행은 대개 도표 항목의 나열 순서대로 진행된다. 대화를 들으면서 도표의 각 항목 중 선택되지 않은 것을 소거하는 식으로 푸는 것이 좋다. 우선 예약 청소 기능이 있는 것을 원했고(② 소거) HEPA 필터가 있는 것을 원했다(③ 소거). 나머지 중에서 가격이 600달러가 넘는 ①을 제외하고 남은 둘 중 리모컨이 있는 것을 골랐으므로 답은 ⑤이다.

W: I'm so busy these days, so I'm thinking of getting a robotic vacuum cleaner.

M: Good idea. Robot vacuum cleaners are a convenient way to **get your cleaning done**.

W: I want a cleaner that can clean my house while I'm out.

M: Then you should get one that has a **scheduled-cleaning** function.

W: Great. My child has allergies, so is there a vacuum cleaner that has a special filter?

M: Of course. You should get something that has a HEPA filter. It **filters out** all micro dust.

W: I definitely like that. His allergies have been getting worse.

M: I see. How much are you willing to spend?

W: I don't want to spend more than $600.

M: Then you can choose between these two.

W: I'll take the one that has **a remote control**. That will be more convenient.

여: 요즘 매우 바빠서 로봇 진공청소기를 하나 살까 생각 중이에요.
남: 좋은 생각입니다. 로봇 진공청소기는 청소를 끝내는 편리한 방식이죠.
여: 난 내가 외출했을 때 집을 청소할 수 있는 청소기를 원해요.
남: 그러면 예약 청소 기능이 있는 걸 사셔야겠군요.
여: 좋아요. 우리 애가 알레르기가 있는데 특수 필터가 있는 진공청소기가 있나요?
남: 물론입니다. HEPA 필터가 있는 것을 사셔야 합니다. 그건 모든 미세먼지를 걸러내거든요.
여: 난 확실히 그게 좋네요. 우리 애 알레르기가 점점 심해지고 있거든요.
남: 알겠습니다. 얼마 정도 쓰려고 하십니까?
여: 600달러 넘게 쓰고 싶진 않아요.
남: 그러면 이 둘 중 고르실 수 있습니다.
여: 리모컨이 있는 걸 살게요. 그게 더 편리하겠어요.

어휘 vacuum cleaner 진공청소기　function 기능(하다)　filter 필터, 여과 장치: 거르다
cf. filter out ~을 걸러내다　micro dust 미세먼지, 황사　definitely 확실히, 틀림없이
remote control 리모컨

11 짧은 대화에 이어질 응답　　　　　　　　　　②

✽ 후식 추천을 부탁받은 식당 종업원인 여자가 후식을 추천하고 있다. 이에 대한 남자의 응답으로는 ② '그거 좋겠군요. 그걸 좀 원합니다.'가 가장 적절하다.

① 좋아하신다니 기쁩니다. 다시 오십시오.
③ 여기 샐러드가 있습니다. 손님의 생선은 오는 중입니다.
④ 죄송합니다. 저희는 오늘 딸기가 없습니다.
⑤ 알겠습니다. 저는 레몬을 곁들인 구운 생선을 추천합니다.

W: And would you like a dessert?
M: Yes, please. **Could you recommend** anything?
W: Well, today we have strawberry cheesecake. It's **one of** our best desserts.
M: That sounds good. I'd like some of that.

여: 그럼 후식을 드시겠습니까?
남: 네, 부탁드립니다. 무엇이든 추천해주시겠어요?
여: 음, 오늘 저희는 딸기 치즈케이크가 있습니다. 저희 최고의 후식 중 하나입니다.
남: 그거 좋겠군요. 그걸 좀 원합니다.

어휘 recommend 추천하다, 권장하다　| 선택지 어휘 | on one's[the] way 오는[가는] (중인), 도중에　grilled 구운

12 짧은 대화에 이어질 응답　　　　　　　　　　⑤

✽ 남자가 여자에게 비행편의 도착 시각에 대해서 물었으므로 가장 적절한 응답은 ⑤ '잘 모르겠어요. 안내센터에 물어보지 그러세요?'이다.

① 여기 있습니다. 여권을 보여주시겠어요?
② 맞습니다. 그건 악천후로 인해 연착했어요.
③ 죄송합니다. 지금은 모든 좌석이 찼습니다.
④ 알겠습니다. 도착순으로 줄을 서주실 수 있나요?

M: Excuse me. This is terminal C, right?
W: Yes, that's right.
M: Do you know **what time** United Airlines flight 235 **arrives**?
W: I'm not sure. Why don't you ask at the information center?

남: 실례합니다. 이곳이 C 터미널이죠, 맞죠?
여: 네, 맞아요.
남: 언제 United Airlines 235 비행편이 도착하는지 아시나요?
여: 잘 모르겠어요. 안내센터에 물어보지 그러세요?

어휘 | 선택지 어휘 | passport 여권　due to A A 때문에　take 차지하다: 가지고 가다
at the moment 지금(은), 현재　line up 줄을 서다

13 긴 대화에 이어질 응답　　　　　　　　　　③

✽ 대화의 전체 맥락 하에 마지막 말의 의미나 의도를 정확히 파악하는 것이 좋다. 본 대화는 오랜만에 우연히 친구를 만난 상황이다. 서로 반가워하며 남자가 여자의 전화번호를 저장한다고 했을 때 여자가 할 말로는 ③ '나한테 전화 줘. 언제 저녁 식사할 수 있잖아.'가 가장 적절하다.

① 잘 되었구나! 하지만 난 널 그리워할 거야.
② 그거 좋은 생각이야. 우리는 당장 그걸 시작할 수 있어.
④ 죄송합니다. 전화 잘못 거셨습니다.
⑤ 정말 친절하구나. 하지만 난 갈 수 없을 것 같아.

W: Hello, there! You're Julian! Wow! It's great to see you here again.
M: Sarah! Hello! **What a coincidence**! I haven't seen you in ages.
W: Yeah, what are you doing here in Louisville? Are you just visiting?
M: I just got a new job here in accounting, so I'm shopping for some new clothes.
W: That's great! Where do you live now?
M: I'm renting an apartment on Kent Street. Well, this is a small world.
W: Really! Oh, I have to go back to work. We must **keep in touch**.
M: Okay, but I don't have your phone number now. **Do you still have** my cell phone number?
W: No, I lost my phone. Here is my new number.
M: Okay. I'll save your number.
W: Give me a call. We can have dinner sometime.

여: 저기, 안녕! 너 Julian이지! 왜! 널 여기서 다시 보다니 반갑다.
남: Sarah야! 안녕! 정말 우연이다! 굉장히 오랜만이야.
여: 응, 여기 Louisville에서 뭘 하는 거야? 그냥 방문한 거니?
남: 그냥 여기서 회계 분야의 새 직장을 얻어서 새 옷을 좀 사려고 쇼핑 중이야.
여: 굉장하다! 지금 어디 사니?
남: Kent 가에 있는 아파트를 임대했어. 이거 참, 세상 좁다.
여: 정말 그래! 아. 난 직장으로 돌아가야 해. 우리 연락하고 지내야지.
남: 좋아. 그런데 지금 네 전화번호가 없어. 넌 아직 내 휴대전화 번호를 갖고 있니?
여: 아니, 난 내 전화기를 잃어버렸거든. 여기 내 새 번호야.
남: 알았어. 네 번호를 저장할게.
여: 나한테 전화 줘. 언제 저녁 식사할 수 있잖아.

어휘 coincidence 우연의 일치　accounting 회계 (업무)　rent 임대하다, 빌리다　keep in touch 연락하고 지내다

14 긴 대화에 이어질 응답　　　　　　　　　　④

✽ 대화의 전체 맥락 하에 마지막 말의 의미나 의도를 정확히 파악하는 것이 좋다. 본 대화는 비행기를 타야 하는데 지각해서 오지 않는 친구를 기다리는 상황이다. 마지막 탑승 안내 방송이 나오니 가야 한다고 하자 여자 역시 게이트가 닫힐 거라면서 떠나지 않을 수가 없다고 하고 있다. 이에 대한 남자의 응답은 ④ '네 말이 맞아. 우리는 할 수 있는 모든 걸 다 했어.'가 가장 적절하다.

① 서둘러. 우리 비행기는 한 시간 후에 떠나.
② 걱정 마. 우리는 쇼핑하러 갈 시간이 있어.
③ 미안해. 하지만 모든 이용 가능한 좌석이 다 찼어.
⑤ 그가 잘 할 거라고 생각해. 그는 주차하는 곳을 알고 있어.

M: It's 5:20. We should board the plane now.
W: But Tim **hasn't arrived yet**. Why don't you call him again?
M: I just did, but he didn't answer. He is impossible. He promised me not to be late, but he is late again.
W: He probably had a hard time finding a parking space.
M: No, he said he would take an airport limousine. He has **a habit of being late**.
W: Oh, really?
M: Yes. I **wouldn't be surprised** even if he missed the plane.
W: We've been waiting for him for almost an hour.
M: Oh, there is the last announcement for our flight. I think we should go.
W: I think so. The gate will be closing soon. We **can't help leaving** now.

M: You're right. We've done everything we can.

남: 5시 20분이야. 우리는 지금 비행기에 탑승해야 해.
여: 하지만 Tim이 아직 도착하지 않았어. 그에게 다시 전화해보지 그러니?
남: 방금 했지만, 받지 않았어. 그를 참을 수 없어. 나한테 늦지 않겠다고 약속했는데, 다시 늦잖아.
여: 아마 주차장을 찾느라 고생했을 거야.
남: 아니야, 그는 공항버스를 탈 거라고 말했어. 그는 지각하는 습관이 있어.
여: 아, 정말 그래?
남: 응. 난 그가 비행기를 놓친다고 해도 놀라지 않을 거야.
여: 우리 그를 거의 한 시간째 기다리고 있어.
남: 아, 우리 비행기의 마지막 (탑승) 안내 방송이야. 우리 가야 할 것 같아.
여: 나도 그렇게 생각해. 게이트가 곧 닫힐 거야. 우리는 지금 떠나지 않을 수가 없어.
남: 네 말이 맞아. 우리는 할 수 있는 모든 걸 다 했어.

어휘 board 탑승하다; 게시판 impossible (사람·상황 등이) 참을 수 없는; 믿기 어려운 announcement 발표, 공고 can't help v-ing v하지 않을 수 없다
| 선택지 어휘 | available 이용할 수 있는

15 상황에 적절한 말 ③

✱ 지시문을 통해 누가(A) 누구에게(B) 할 말인지를 우선 정확히 파악한다. 담화는 대개 A와 B에 대한 배경 설명과 B가 처한 문제 상황, 그리고 이에 대해 A가 어떤 말을 하려고 하는지에 대한 설명의 순서로 전개된다. 슈퍼마켓 계산대 줄에서 Jessica(A)가 앞의 남자(B)에게 자신이 먼저 계산을 해도 되는지 양해를 구하는 상황이다. 그러므로 가장 적절한 응답은 ③ '미안하지만 제가 먼저 해도 될까요? 제가 급해서요.'이다.

① 계산원이 어디 있나요? 이걸 사고 싶은데요.
② 언제 그게 끝나나요? 난 애들을 데리러 가야 해요.
④ 여기서 얼마나 오래 기다렸나요? 오랜 시간이 걸리네요.
⑤ 제가 어디서 이런 카트를 찾을 수 있을까요? 사용하기 좋아 보이는데요.

M: Jessica has two children who are both elementary school students. She always has to pick up her children from school at 3:30. Today, she **stops by** a supermarket to do some grocery shopping. She picks up a few things she needs and goes to the counter to **pay for them**. Unfortunately, the line at the counter is very long. It's almost 3 o'clock and there is still one person in front of her. Jessica **has to leave now** to pick her children up. The man before her in line has a lot of stuff in his cart. It will surely take a long time. Jessica wants to ask the man if she can pay **before him**. In this situation, what would Jessica most likely say to the man?

Jessica: Sorry, but could I go first please? I'm in a hurry.

남: Jessica는 모두 초등학생인 두 자녀가 있다. 그녀는 언제나 3시 30분에 학교로 아이들을 데리러 가야 한다. 오늘, 그녀는 식료품을 조금 사려고 슈퍼마켓에 들른다. 그녀는 필요한 몇 가지를 골라 계산을 하러 계산대로 간다. 불행히도 계산대의 줄이 매우 길다. 거의 3시 정각이 다 되어 가는데 그녀 앞에는 여전히 한 사람이 있다. Jessica는 아이들을 데리러 지금 떠나야 한다. 그녀 앞에 줄 서 있는 남자는 카트에 많은 물건이 있다. 그것은 분명히 시간이 오래 걸릴 것이다. Jessica는 그 남자에게 자신이 그보다 먼저 계산할 수 있는지 부탁하고자 한다. 이 상황에서 Jessica가 남자에게 뭐라고 말하겠는가?

Jessica: 미안하지만 제가 먼저 해도 될까요? 제가 급해서요.

어휘 pick up (~을) 차에 태우러 가다; ~을 고르다 stop by ~에 (잠시) 들르다 grocery 식료품 stuff 물건, 것

16~17 세트 문항 16 ④ 17 ⑤

✱ **16** 각 문화에서 무례하고 불쾌한 것으로 여겨질 수 있는 선물을 예를 들어 설명하고 있으므로 담화의 주제로는 ④ '다양한 나라의 선물 주기에서 금기시되는 것'이 가장 적절하다.

① 사업상 선물을 주는 예의에 대한 조언
② 선물 교환에서 따라야 할 규칙들
③ 모든 경우에서의 선물 주는 기술
⑤ 다른 문화권에서 적절한 선물 고르는 방법

✱ **17** 해석 참조.
① 시계 ② 고기 ③ 와인 ④ 장미 ⑤ 인형

W: Giving gifts is a popular way to show affection all around the world. However, certain gifts are viewed by people in other cultures as **rude or unpleasant**. For example, clocks are not good gifts to give to your Chinese friends, because the word in Chinese for "clock" is very similar to the word for "death." The Japanese are a little picky about **the number of gifts**; giving nine of anything is considered bad luck, and therefore it's recommended that you always give **in pairs**. Meat and leather goods are not good in India, where people never eat cows. Also remember that many Muslims don't drink alcohol, so purchasing a bottle of wine for them is probably not the best idea. Flowers are welcomed in many cultures around the world, but they have some different meanings **depending on the situation**. For instance, red roses, a traditional lovers' gift, would appear **out of place** at a business meeting. Yellow roses commonly suggest mistrust in France, and death in Mexico.

여: 선물을 주는 것은 전 세계적으로 애정을 보여주는 일반적인 방식입니다. 그러나 어떤 선물은 다른 문화의 사람들에게는 무례하고 불쾌한 것으로 보입니다. 예를 들어 ① 시계는 중국어의 '시계'라는 단어가 '죽음'이라는 단어와 아주 유사하기 때문에 여러분의 중국인 친구들에게 주기에 좋은 선물이 아닙니다. 일본인은 선물의 숫자에 좀 까다로워서 어떤 것이든 아홉 개를 주는 것은 불운으로 여겨지므로 항상 둘씩 짝으로 주는 것이 추천됩니다. ② 고기와 가죽제품은 인도에서는 좋은 것이 아닌데, 그곳의 사람들은 절대로 소를 먹지 않습니다. 또한, 많은 무슬림교도가 술을 마시지 않는다는 것을 기억하세요. 따라서 그들을 위해 ③ 와인 한 병을 사는 것은 아마도 가장 좋은 생각이 아닐 겁니다. 꽃은 전 세계적으로 많은 문화에서 환영 됩니다만 상황에 따라 좀 다른 의미가 있습니다. 예를 들어 전통적인 연인들의 선물인 붉은 ④ 장미는 업무 회의에서는 부적절한 것으로 보일 것입니다. 노란 장미는 일반적으로 프랑스에서는 불신을, 멕시코에서는 죽음을 나타냅니다.

어휘 popular 일반적인; 대중적인 affection 애정; 보살핌 picky 까다로운 in pairs 둘씩 짝을 지어 leather 가죽 purchase 사다, 구입(하다) out of place 부적절한, (상황에) 맞지 않는 suggest 나타내다; 제안하다 mistrust 불신 | 선택지 어휘 | exchange 교환(하다) occasion 경우, 때 taboo 금기시되는 것, 터부 proper 적절한

06 회

| 01 ④ | 02 ② | 03 ③ | 04 ⑤ | 05 ③ | 06 ④ | 07 ⑤ | 08 ④ | 09 ④ | 10 ⑤ |
| 11 ② | 12 ② | 13 ② | 14 ⑤ | 15 ③ | 16 ③ | 17 ④ | | | |

01 화자가 하는 말의 목적 ④

✱ 담화의 일부 내용이 아니라 중심 내용을 파악해야 한다. 본 담화는 어린이들에게 놀이터에서 놀면서 안전하게 정해진 규칙에 따를 것을 당부하고 있다. 줄을 서기와 미끄럼틀을 탈 때 주의할 점을 이야기하고 시소와 그네 탈 때 주의할 내용을 언급하면서 기본적인 규칙을 지키라고 하고 있으므로 담화의 목적은 ④가 적절하다.

W: Hello, guys! It's nice weather, so I hope you have a good time here on the playground. You can run, slide, climb, and jump! But if you don't **follow certain rules**, this can be a very dangerous place. First, you need to **stand in line** before using the equipment. People should slide down the slide one person at a time. You must use the stairs **when going up** the slide. Also, your feet must come first when riding down the slide. Do not slide down standing up or on your stomach. When using the swing, you must tightly hold onto the handles. In addition, **do not stand** or jump on the seesaw. If you follow all of these basic rules, you can really enjoy yourself here. Now have fun!

여: 안녕하세요, 여러분! 좋은 날씨예요. 그래서 여러분이 여기 놀이터에서 즐거운 시간 보내기를 바라요. 여러분은 달리고 미끄럼타고 오르고 뛸 수 있어요! 하지만 여러분이 정해진 규칙을 따르지 않으면 이곳은 아주 위험한 장소가 될 수 있어요. 우선, 시설을 이용하기 전에 일렬로 나란히 줄을 서야 해요. 한 번에 한 사람씩 미끄럼틀을 타고 내려와야 해요. 미끄럼틀로 올라갈 때는 반드시 계단을 이용해야 해요. 또 미끄럼틀을 타고 내려올 때는 반드시 발이 먼저 와야 해요. 일어서거나 배를 대고 엎드려서 내려오면 안 돼요. 그네를 이용할 때는 손잡이를 꽉 잡아야 해요. 덧붙여서 시소에서 서 있거나 뛰지 마세요. 이 모든 기본적인 규칙을 지킨다면 여러분은 여기서 정말 즐겁게 보낼 수 있을 거예요. 이제 재미있게 보내요!

어휘 certain 정해진; 특정한; 확실한   stand in line 일렬로 나란히 서다   equipment 기기, 설비; 장치   swing 그네; 흔들리다   tightly 꽉, 단단히; 빽빽이   hold onto ~을 꼭 잡다; 고수하다

02 의견 ②

✱ 우선 지시문에서 명시한 화자의 성별을 보고 어느 화자의 말에 주목할지를 판단해야 한다. 특히 의견이나 주장을 표현하는 어구(I think ~, You should ~ 등)가 이끄는 내용을 잘 들어야 한다. 여자는 어린이의 TV 시청의 부정적인 영향에 대해 이야기하고 있다. 하지만 남자는 어린이 프로그램이 교육적일 수 있고 아이들의 TV 시청을 감시한다면 긍정적인 영향을 준다고 말하고 있으므로 남자의 의견으로는 ②가 적절하다.

W: Honey! Can you **take care of** Lily tonight? I have a dinner appointment with Carrie.
M: Well, actually, I need to send e-mails to my clients, but it'll be okay. I'll let Lily watch TV while I work.
W: Hmm, I don't think it's a good idea.
M: Don't worry. I'll put on a children's program.
W: I heard watching TV can be bad for kids' brain development.
M: I don't think so. TV is not all that bad for kids. Children's programs can even be **educational for kids**.
W: But if kids watch TV, they won't want to read books or exercise.
M: I read an article about it in the newspaper. If you monitor their viewing, you will find TV has a **positive influence on** children.
W: All right. It's up to you tonight.
M: Don't worry. I've got it under control.

여: 여보! 오늘 밤 Lily를 돌봐줄 수 있어요? 나는 Carrie하고 저녁 약속이 있어요.
남: 음, 사실 나는 내 고객들에게 이메일을 보내야 하지만 괜찮을 거예요. 내가 일하는 동안 Lily가 TV를 보게 할게요.
여: 음, 그건 좋은 생각 같지 않아요.
남: 걱정 말아요. 어린이 프로그램을 틀게요.

여: TV를 보는 게 아이의 두뇌발달에 나쁠 수 있다고 들었어요.
남: 난 그렇게 생각하지 않아요. TV가 아이들에게 다 그렇게 나쁜 건 아니에요. 어린이 프로그램은 심지어 아이들에게 교육적일 수 있다고요.
여: 하지만 아이들이 TV를 본다면 책을 읽거나 운동을 하고 싶어 하지 않을 거예요.
남: 신문에서 그것에 관한 기사를 봤어요. 아이들의 시청을 감시한다면 TV가 아이들에게 긍정적인 영향을 준다는 걸 알게 될 거예요.
여: 좋아요. 오늘 밤은 당신이 알아서 하는 거니까요.
남: 걱정 말아요. 내가 잘 관리할게요.

어휘 take care of ~을 돌보다; ~에 주의하다[신경을 쓰다]   appointment 약속; 임명   client 고객, 의뢰인   put on (TV·테이프 등을) 틀다; ~을 입다   development 발달, 성장   educational 교육적인   article 기사, 글   positive 긍정적인   influence 영향(을 주다)

03 관계 ③

✱ 직업을 나타내거나 추론할 수 있는 힌트가 대화 전반에 걸쳐 드러나므로, 대화를 전체적으로 이해하는 것이 필요하다. 본 대화에서 두 사람은 응급실은 언제나 바쁘지만 오늘 더 바빴다는 이야기를 하고 있고 남자가 여자에게 Johnson 씨에게 약과 주사를 주었는지 묻고 여자가 체온을 보고하는 것으로 보아 ③ '의사 – 간호사'의 관계임을 알 수 있다.

M: You look so tired.
W: Yes, **I'm exhausted**. It's been a very busy day.
M: The emergency room is always busy, but today seemed busier than ever.
W: I know... Anyway, you must be hungry, right? I have some sandwiches. Would you like some?
M: No, thanks. I don't feel like eating now. By the way, do I have more patients to check on?
W: No, but Mr. Johnson, who came in **with a headache**, is still complaining about the pain.
M: How about his temperature? Did you give him his medicine and a shot?
W: Yes, I did. His temperature has gone down to normal, 37℃. But he appears very anxious.
M: Have we received his scan results?
W: No, **we haven't received** them yet.
M: Well, I'll see him shortly.

남: 무척 피곤해 보이는군요.
여: 네, 완전히 지쳤어요. 정말 바쁜 날이었어요.
남: 응급실은 언제나 바쁘지만 오늘은 어느 때보다 바쁜 것 같았어요.
여: 맞아요… 그나저나 배가 고프시죠, 그렇죠? 제게 샌드위치가 좀 있어요. 좀 드실래요?
남: 아니요, 괜찮습니다. 지금 먹고 싶은 기분이 아니에요. 그런데, 제가 살펴볼 환자가 더 있나요?
여: 아니요, 하지만 두통으로 들어온 Johnson 씨가 아직도 고통을 호소하고 있어요.
남: 그의 체온은 어떤가요? 그에게 약과 주사를 주었나요?
여: 네, 줬어요. 그의 체온은 37℃로 정상으로 내려갔어요. 하지만 무척 불안해 보여요.
남: 그의 검사 결과를 우리가 받았나요?
여: 아니요, 아직 받지 않았어요.
남: 음, 제가 곧 그를 볼게요.

어휘 exhausted 완전히 지친; 다 써버린, 소모된   emergency room 응급실   appear ~인 것 같이 보이다; 나타나다, 출현하다   anxious 불안해하는, 염려하는   shortly 곧; 간단히

04 그림 불일치 ⑤

✱ 대화가 나오기 전에 각 사물의 위치 관계와 외형(형태나 무늬, 개수 등)의 특징을 미리

확인하는 것이 좋다. 마지막에 가장 오른쪽에 있는 소년이 두 팔을 모두 공중으로 들고 있다고 했는데 그림에서는 왼팔만 들고 있으므로 ⑤는 내용과 일치하지 않는다.

M: Olivia, look at this paper. This article is about my son's basketball team winning the championship.
W: Oh, it's Miller Grove High School's basketball team. Is your son holding up the championship trophy?
M: The boy in the far left? No. Try to guess **where my son is**. People say that my son resembles me.
W: It's **hard to figure out** from this picture. Well, is he the boy who is holding a basketball?
M: No, you're wrong again. My son is holding a banner in the center.
W: Oh, he's so good-looking. It says "2018 Boys Basketball Champions" on the banner. You must be proud of him!
M: Yes. And the man with a striped shirt and a tie is their head coach. I've met him several times. He's very good with the students.
W: That's great. By the way, why is the coach holding up 7 fingers?
M: Because it's their 7th championship win.
W: That's amazing! That's why the boy **in the far right** is raising **both his arms up** in the air.
M: Maybe. They do look happy with their victory.

남: Olivia, 이 신문을 봐요. 이 기사는 내 아들의 농구팀이 선수권 대회에서 우승한 것에 관한 거예요.
여: 아, Miller Grove 고등학교 농구팀이군요. 당신 아들이 우승 트로피를 들고 있나요?
남: 가장 왼쪽에 있는 애 말이죠? 아니요. 내 아들이 어디 있는지 맞혀 보세요. 사람들은 내 아들이 나를 닮았다고들 해요.
여: 이 사진으로 알아보기가 어려운데요. 음. 농구공을 잡고 있는 소년인가요?
남: 아뇨. 또 틀렸군요. 내 아들은 중앙에서 깃발을 들고 있어요.
여: 아, 아주 잘 생겼군요. 깃발에 '2018 소년 농구 우승팀'이라고 쓰여 있군요. 정말 아들이 자랑스럽겠어요!
남: 네. 그리고 줄무늬 셔츠를 입고 넥타이를 한 남자는 그들의 수석 코치예요. 그를 몇 번 만났거든요. 학생들과 아주 잘 지낸답니다.
여: 그거 잘 되었군요. 그런데 왜 코치가 7개의 손가락을 들고 있나요?
남: 왜냐하면 그것이 그들의 7번째 선수권 대회 우승이거든요.
여: 그거 굉장하군요! 그래서 가장 오른쪽에 있는 소년이 두 팔을 모두 공중으로 들고 있는 거군요.
남: 아마도 그럴 거예요. 그들은 승리해서 정말로 행복해 보여요.

어휘 championship 선수권 (대회); 우승 resemble 닮다, 비슷[유사]하다 figure out ∼을 알아내다[이해하다] striped 줄무늬가 있는 several (몇)몇의; 각각[각자]의 victory 승리, 전승

05 추후 행동 ③

✻ 대개 대화는 어떤 일을 하게 되는 상황이 먼저 제시된 뒤에 남자와 여자가 각각 할 일들과 이에 대한 수락/거절의 응답이 나열되는 식으로 전개된다. 어머니가 동생의 바자회를 위해 만들어둔 파이를 아들이 먹고 싶어 하면서 자신에게도 복숭아 파이를 만들어 달라고 했고 어머니가 승낙하고 있다. 그러므로 어머니의 할 일은 ③ '파이 만들기'이다. 숙제는 아들이 할 일이고 복숭아는 남아 있다고 했고 조리법은 이미 찾았음에 유의한다.

M: Mom, I am home. What are you cooking? It smells so good.
W: I am cooking dinner. This is your favorite, baked salmon.
M: It looks really yummy. And I see some pie over there, too. Is it our dessert?
W: No, your sister has to take it to the school bazaar tomorrow. I found **a new recipe for pie** on Today's Cooking's website.
M: Oh, what is it? Did you try the new recipe?
W: Yes, it's a recipe for peach pie. Since this is **peach season**, I thought it would be a good choice.
M: I want to try some. Can you bake one for me? I'll go to the supermarket and buy some peaches now.
W: You don't have to. There are some peaches left. I'll **make it for you** now.
M: That's great. Do you need any help, Mom?
W: No, you can go do your homework and leave it to me.
M: Thanks, Mom. Call me whenever it's ready.

남: 엄마, 저 집에 왔어요. 뭘 요리하고 계세요? 냄새가 너무 좋아요.
여: 저녁 식사를 요리하고 있단다. 이건 네가 아주 좋아하는 구운 연어야.
남: 정말 맛있어 보여요. 그리고 저기 파이도 좀 보이네요. 우리 디저트인가요?
여: 아니야. 네 여동생이 내일 학교 바자회에 저걸 가져가야 해. 오늘의 요리 웹사이트에서 파이 만드는 새로운 조리법을 찾았거든.
남: 아, 그게 뭔데요? 새로운 조리법을 시도해 보셨어요?
여: 응. 그건 복숭아 파이 조리법이란다. 복숭아 철이기 때문에 그게 좋은 선택이라고 생각했어.
남: 저도 좀 먹고 싶어요. 저를 위해서 하나 구워주실 수 있어요? 지금 슈퍼마켓에 가서 복숭아를 좀 사 올게요.
여: 그럴 필요 없단다. 복숭아가 좀 남았거든. 지금 너에게 복숭아 파이를 만들어줄게.
남: 정말 좋아요. 도움이 필요하신가요, 엄마?
여: 아니야. 넌 숙제하러 가도 되니 내게 맡기렴.
남: 고마워요, 엄마. 준비되면 언제든 저를 불러주세요.

어휘 recipe 조리법 whenever ∼할 때는 언제든지; ∼할 때마다 (매번)

06 금액 ④

✻ 여러 개의 수치 정보가 등장하므로 필요한 정보를 메모하면서 듣는 것이 좋다. 남자의 병원비 2,200달러와 약값 500달러를 100% 보상해주고 2,700달러에 특별 보상으로 500달러를 더 준다고 했으므로 남자가 받게 될 보상 금액은 총 3,200달러이다.

W: Good afternoon, Mr. Brown. Have a seat.
M: Good afternoon, Ms. Thomas. I've brought all the documents you asked.
W: Okay. Would you like **something to drink**?
M: No, thanks. As I told you over the phone, I broke my arm and had an operation.
W: Yes, so you want to **make a claim** on your insurance.
M: My medical bill came to $2,200, and my medicine bill was $500. Will you pay for everything?
W: Yes, your insurance plan **covers you 100%**. And you can get an extra $500.
M: Really? That's great news.
W: Yes, because you hurt yourself in a car accident, you can get extra money from our special coverage.
M: Good. I'm glad I have insurance.
W: This is why our customers are **so satisfied with** Pacific Insurance. We'll pay you in ten days.

여: 안녕하세요, Brown 씨. 앉으세요.
남: 안녕하세요, Thomas 씨. 요청하신 서류들을 모두 가져왔습니다.
여: 좋습니다. 마실 것 좀 드릴까요?
남: 아니요, 괜찮습니다. 전화로 이야기했다시피, 제가 팔이 부러져서 수술을 받았어요.
여: 네, 그래서 보험 청구를 하는 걸 원하시는 거지요.
남: 제 병원비가 2,200달러이고 약값이 500달러였어요. 모두 지불해주는 건가요?
여: 네, 고객님의 의료 보험이 100% 보상해드립니다. 그리고 추가로 500달러를 받으실 수 있어요.
남: 정말요? 그거 굉장한 소식인데요.
여: 네, 자동차 사고로 다치셨기 때문에 특별 보상으로 추가의 돈을 받으실 수 있습니다.
남: 좋군요. 제가 보험을 들어서 기뻐요.
여: 이것이 저희 고객분들이 Pacific 보험에 그토록 만족해하시는 이유랍니다. 열흘 후에 지불해드리겠습니다.

어휘 document 서류, 문서 operation 수술; 작전 claim (보상금 등에 대한) 청구; 주장 insurance 보험 *cf.* insurance plan 의료 보험 medical 의료[의학]의 bill 청구서, 고지서 cover 보상하다; 덮다 *cf.* coverage 보상; 보도, 방송 accident 사고, 재해 be satisfied with ∼에 만족하다

07 이유 ⑤

✻ 지시문을 통해 여자가 나비 장식 머리띠를 구입하지 않은 상황이며 여자의 말에 단서가 있을 가능성이 큼을 미리 파악한다. 여자가 머리띠 디자인을 보고 원하던 것이라고 했고 가격도 좋다고 했지만 착용해 보니 귀 바로 뒤쪽에 통증을 일으켜서 구입하지 않겠다고 했으므로 구입하지 않은 이유는 ⑤ '착용 시 귀 뒤쪽이 아파서'이다.

W: I'd like to get a hair band. Are these all on sale?

M: No, there are a few that __are not on sale__. Which one would you like?

W: Hmm, I'd like something simple with a small decoration.

M: Let me see... Then what about this band with a butterfly decoration? This butterfly is decorated with pearls and crystals.

W: Wow, it looks pretty. That's __exactly what I want__. How much is it?

M: It was originally $35, but now it's on sale for $22.

W: Sounds great. Can I see it?

M: Sure. Here it is. It's very flexible and soft. Simple but fancy. Would you like to __try it on__?

W: Okay. *[pause]* Hmm... Oh, I don't think I can wear it for a long time. __It causes pain__ just behind my ears.

M: Then why don't you try another one?

W: No, thanks. I have to go now. I'll come back another time.

여: 헤어밴드를 사고 싶은데요. 이게 다 할인 중인가요?

남: 아니요, 할인하지 않는 게 몇 개 있습니다. 어떤 걸 원하세요?

여: 음, 작은 장식이 있는 단순한 걸 원해요.

남: 글쎄요… 그러면 나비 장식이 있는 이 밴드는 어떠신가요? 이 나비는 진주와 크리스털로 장식되어 있어요.

여: 와, 예뻐 보이는데요. 바로 제가 원하던 거예요. 얼마인가요?

남: 원래 35달러였지만 지금 22달러로 할인하고 있습니다.

여: 좋은 것 같아요. 제가 볼 수 있을까요?

남: 그럼요. 여기 있습니다. 무척 유연하고 부드러워요. 단순하지만 고급스럽죠. 써보시겠어요?

여: 좋아요. *[잠시 후]* 음… 아, 제가 이걸 오래 쓸 수 있을 것 같지 않군요. 제 귀 바로 뒤에 통증을 일으키네요.

남: 그러면 다른 걸 써보시겠어요?

여: 아니요, 괜찮아요. 제가 지금 가야 해서요. 다음번에 다시 올게요.

어휘 on sale 할인 중인 decoration 장식(품) *cf.* decorate 장식하다, 꾸미다 exactly 바로, 꼭; 정확하게 flexible 유연한; 신축성[융통성] 있는 fancy 고급의; 공상, 몽상

08 언급하지 않은 것 ④

＊ 대화의 진행은 대개 선택지와 같은 순서이므로, 선택지를 보면서 언급된 내용을 소거하는 식으로 푸는 것이 좋다. 우선 수영장이 있다고 했고 어린이 놀이 시설에 대해서도 언급했으며, 공항까지 운행하는 셔틀버스와 호텔 내 인터넷 사용에 대해서도 이야기했다. 비즈니스 센터 사용 금액에 대해서는 대략 말해줬으나 하루 숙박비용에 대해서는 언급하지 않았으므로 답은 ④이다.

[Telephone rings.]

M: Hello. This is Marina Hotel. How can I help you?

W: Yes, I'm thinking of __bringing my family__ to your hotel for our summer holiday. But first, can you tell me about your facilities?

M: Certainly, ma'am. We have two swimming pools and saunas.

W: I have two children. Is there any __place to take them__? I'm worried they'll get bored.

M: Sure. Lots of kids seem to have a great time at our go-cart track. We also have a games room.

W: That's wonderful. We'll be coming by airplane. Do you run a bus from the airport to the hotel?

M: Yes, we run a shuttle bus every half hour.

W: Okay. And I need to check my e-mail. Is there __an Internet cafe__ there?

M: Certainly, ma'am. We offer Wi-Fi all around the hotel. And there is also the Business Center.

W: Do you know what it costs to use __the Business Center__?

M: I'm not quite sure, but it costs less than $30 a day.

W: Okay. Thanks.

[전화벨이 울린다.]

남: 여보세요. Marina 호텔입니다. 무엇을 도와드릴까요?

여: 네, 여름휴가 때 거기 호텔로 가족들을 데리고 갈까 합니다. 하지만 먼저 시설에 대해 알려주실 수 있나요?

남: 그럼요, 손님. 저희는 2개의 수영장(① 수영장 시설)과 사우나가 있습니다.

여: 제가 아이가 둘이라서요. 아이들을 데려갈 만한 장소가 있나요? 아이들이 지루해할까 걱정되어서요.

남: 물론이죠. 많은 아이들이 저희의 고카트 트랙(② 어린이 놀이 시설)에서 즐거운 시간을 보내는 것 같습니다. 게임룸(② 어린이 놀이 시설)도 있습니다.

여: 그거 멋지군요. 우리는 비행기로 갈 건데요. 공항에서 호텔까지 버스를 운행하나요?

남: 네, 저희는 30분마다 셔틀버스를 운행합니다(③ 공항 셔틀 버스 제공).

여: 알겠어요. 그리고 제 이메일을 확인해야 하는데요. 거기 인터넷 카페가 있나요?

남: 그럼요, 손님. 저희는 호텔 전체에 와이파이를 제공합니다(⑤ 인터넷 사용 가능 여부). 그리고 비즈니스 센터도 있습니다.

여: 비즈니스 센터를 이용하기 위한 비용이 얼마인지 아시나요?

남: 확실히는 모르지만 하루에 30달러 미만입니다.

여: 알겠어요. 고맙습니다.

어휘 facility 시설; 기능 certainly 그럼요, 물론이죠; 틀림없이, 분명히 go-cart 고카트 ((지붕·문이 없는 작은 경주용 자동차)) track 트랙, 경주로; 길 run (서비스·강좌 등을) 운영[제공]하다

09 내용 불일치 ④

＊ 담화의 진행은 대개 선택지와 같은 순서이므로, 선택지를 보면서 일치하는 내용을 소거하는 식으로 푸는 것이 좋다. 미리 등록할 필요가 없이 그냥 책을 읽고 토론할 준비를 하고 오라고 했으므로 ④는 내용과 일치하지 않는다.

M: Welcome to Columbus County Library. The Columbus County Library offers a book discussion group called Book Talk. Book Talk is a book discussion group that __meets every month__. Book Talk is open to adults from Columbus County. The group generally meets at 7 p.m. on the last Wednesday of every month in the library's conference room. Sarah Wise, the librarian, selects books for discussion. The title for the discussion on Wednesday, December 27 is a historical fiction, *Salt to the Sea* by Ruta Sepetys. There is no need __to register in advance__ to join Book Talk. Just read the book and come to the group ready to talk about it. After the meeting, __light refreshments__ are provided. For more information about Book Talk, contact Sarah Wise at 940-782-5280.

남: Columbus County 도서관에 오신 것을 환영합니다. Columbus County 도서관은 Book Talk라고 하는 독서 토론 그룹을 제공하고 있습니다. Book Talk는 매달 만나는 독서 토론 그룹입니다. Book Talk는 ① Columbus County의 성인들에게 열려 있습니다. 그룹은 보통 ② 매달 마지막 수요일 오후 7시에 도서관 회의실에서 만납니다. 사서인 Sarah Wise가 토론할 책을 선정합니다. ③ 12월 27일 수요일에 토론할 책 제목은 Ruta Sepetys가 쓴 역사 소설인 'Salt to the Sea'입니다. ④ Book Talk에 참여하기 위해서 미리 등록할 필요는 없습니다. 그냥 책을 읽고 그것에 대해 이야기 나눌 준비를 하고 그룹으로 오십시오. ⑤ 모임 후에는 가벼운 다과가 제공됩니다. Book Talk에 대해 더 많은 정보를 원하시면 940-782-5280으로 Sarah Wise에게 연락하십시오.

어휘 offer 제공하다; 제안[제의]하다 discussion 토론, 토의 generally 보통; 일반적으로 conference 회의; 협의 librarian 사서; 도서관 직원 historical 역사(상)의, 역사적인 register 등록[기재]하다; 기록하다 in advance 미리, 앞서 refreshment 다과; 가벼운 식사, 음료 contact 연락(하다); 접촉(하다)

10 도표 이해 ⑤

＊ 대화의 진행은 대개 도표 항목의 나열 순서대로 진행된다. 대화를 들으면서 도표의 각 항목 중 선택되지 않은 것을 소거하는 식으로 푸는 것이 좋다. 우선 과일과 채소가 모두 포함된 형태를 원했으므로 ①이 제외된다. 그다음에 주 1회 배달을 원했으므로 또 ③이 제외된다. 상자 크기는 큰 것으로 선택했으므로 이제 ④와 ⑤가 남는데 과일과 채소 모두 유기농으로 원했으므로 여자가 선택한 농산물 상자는 ⑤이다.

M: How can I help you?

W: I'd like to __sign up for__ your produce delivery service.

M: Thanks. You have several options to choose from. Would you like fruit and vegetables, or just vegetables?

W: I would like fruit and vegetables, please. __How often can I__ get the delivery box?

M: We can send it to you once a week or twice a week.

W: I prefer once-a-week delivery. Can I have them delivered on Mondays?

M: Sure. And we have small, medium, and large boxes, so you can **choose the quantity**. Which one do you want?

W: Since I have a large family, I definitely need the large boxes.

M: Would you like your fruit and vegetables both to be organic or just the vegetables?

W: I definitely want **all of them** to be organic.

M: Okay. Can you fill out this form?

남: 무엇을 도와드릴까요?
여: 거기 농산물 배달 서비스를 신청하고 싶어서요.
남: 고맙습니다. 고를 수 있는 몇 가지 선택권이 있습니다. 과일과 채소를 원하시나요, 아니면 그냥 채소만 원하시나요?
여: 과일과 채소를 원해요. 얼마나 자주 배달 상자를 받을 수 있죠?
남: 일주일에 한 번이나 일주일에 두 번 보내드릴 수 있습니다.
여: 전 주 1회 배달이 더 좋아요. 월요일에 배달받을 수 있나요?
남: 그럼요. 그리고 저희는 소, 중, 대 상자가 있어서 양을 선택하실 수 있습니다. 어떤 것을 원하시나요?
여: 대가족이라서 우리는 확실히 큰 상자가 필요해요.
남: 과일과 채소 둘 다 유기농이기를 원하시나요, 아니면 그냥 채소만 유기농이길 원하시나요?
여: 전 확실히 그것들 모두가 유기농이기를 바라요.
남: 알겠습니다. 이 양식을 작성해주시겠어요?

어휘 **sign up for** ~을 신청[가입]하다 **produce** 농산[생산]물; 생산하다 **delivery** 배달(물) **option** 선택권; 옵션, 선택(할 수 있는 것) **medium** 중간의; 매체, 수단 **quantity** 양, 수량 **definitely** 확실히, 분명히; 절대(로) **organic** 유기농의, 화학 비료를 쓰지 않는 **fill out** (서류 등을) 작성[기재]하다

11 짧은 대화에 이어질 응답   ②

❋ 여자가 출근길에 대해 물으면서 지하철을 얼마나 타느냐고 질문했을 때 그에 대한 응답은 걸리는 시간을 말해주는 ② '음, 30분 이동이에요.'가 가장 적절하다.

① 네, 저는 직장까지 지하철을 탑니다.
③ 맞아요. 걷기에 좀 멀죠.
④ 아뇨, 전 20마일을 더 가야 해요.
⑤ 사실, 앞쪽에 교통이 혼잡해요.

W: So, Mr. Philips, how do you **get to work**?

M: I take the ferry to Manhattan. It's a beautiful ride, and it's free! After that, I take the subway and get off at 72nd Street Station.

W: Sounds great. **How long** is your ride on the subway?

M: Well, it's half an hour's journey.

여: 그러면, Philips 씨, 출근은 어떻게 하세요?
남: Manhattan까지 페리를 타고 갑니다. 아름다운 길이고 무료예요! 그러고 나서, 지하철을 타고 72번가 역에서 내립니다.
여: 멋진 것 같군요. 지하철을 얼마나 타시나요?
남: 음, 30분 이동이에요.

어휘 | 선택지 어휘 | **journey** 이동, 여정, 여행

12 짧은 대화에 이어질 응답   ②

❋ 바지에 거대한 구멍이 났다고 새 바지를 사야 한다는 아들에게 어머니가 할 말로는 구멍을 수선해주겠다는 내용의 ② '난 그렇게 생각하지 않아. 내가 구멍을 수선해주마.'가 가장 적절하다.

① 물론이지. 다른 바지를 입어보렴
③ 맞아. 네 바지는 좀 끼더라.
④ 안 돼. 그것들은 너무 일이 많아.
⑤ 동의해. 그게 주머니가 있는 이유지.

M: Mom, the pocket in my pants has **a huge hole** in it.

W: You just bought those pants a month ago. I said you shouldn't carry your keys and pens in your pocket.

M: I see. You're right. Anyway, I think I need to **buy another pair** this weekend.

W: I don't think so. I'll fix the hole.

남: 엄마, 제 바지 주머니에 거대한 구멍이 났어요.
여: 그 바지 겨우 한 달 전에 샀잖아. 내가 주머니에 열쇠와 펜을 넣고 다니지 말라고 했지.
남: 알겠어요. 엄마 말이 맞아요. 어쨌든, 이번 주말에 새 바지를 사야 할 것 같아요.
여: 난 그렇게 생각하지 않아. 내가 구멍을 수선해주마.

어휘 **huge** 거대한, 막대한, 엄청난 | 선택지 어휘 | **tight** 몸에 꼭 끼는, 꼭 맞는; 단단한

13 긴 대화에 이어질 응답   ②

❋ 대화의 전체 맥락 하에 마지막 말의 의미나 의도를 정확히 파악하는 것이 좋다. 친구 간의 대화로 휴대폰을 잃어버렸는데 롤러코스터를 타면서 운동복 상의 작은 주머니에 넣었다가 떨어뜨린 것으로 추정하고 있는 상황이다. 작은 주머니에 휴대폰을 넣은 것을 자책하는 남자에게 여자가 할 말로는 ② '너무 자책하지 마. 그냥 잊어버려.'가 가장 적절하다.

① 난 나 자신이 너무 싫어. 난 아무짝에도 쓸모가 없어.
③ 누구나 실수를 할 수 있어. 그러니 나는 그를 용서해.
④ 미안해. 난 어젯밤에 네 휴대폰을 충전해놓지 않았어.
⑤ 네가 최선을 다했다는 걸 알아. 내가 다른 걸 네게 사줄게.

W: You look upset. Is something wrong?

M: I think I **lost my new smartphone**.

W: Are you sure? You just bought it a month ago. Did you call your phone?

M: Yes. I keep calling my phone, but no one is answering.

W: Where do you think you lost it?

M: Maybe… I think I lost it **while I was riding** a roller coaster over there. I couldn't find my phone after riding it.

W: Really? You mean that crazy roller coaster?

M: Yes, I put the phone in my sweatshirt pocket, but the pocket is really small.

W: Too bad. If that's the case, there's **no way to find** it, and even if you did, the phone is probably ruined.

M: I don't understand why I put it in this pocket. I'm such an idiot.

W: Don't be hard on yourself. Just forget about it.

여: 너 화가나 보여. 뭐가 잘 못 되었니?
남: 내 새 휴대폰을 잃어버린 것 같아.
여: 정말이야? 바로 한 달 전에 그걸 샀잖아. 네 전화로 전화해봤어?
남: 응, 계속 전화하고 있지만 아무도 받지 않아.
여: 어디서 잃어버린 것 같니?
남: 아마… 내가 저기서 롤러코스터를 타면서 잃어버린 것 같아. 그걸 탄 뒤로 내 전화기를 찾을 수가 없었어.
여: 정말? 저 말도 안 되는 롤러코스터 말하는 거야?
남: 응. 내 운동복 상의 주머니에 전화기를 넣어두었는데 주머니가 정말 작거든.
여: 어쩔 수 없지 뭐. 그런 경우라면 찾을 방법이 없고 설사 찾더라도 전화기가 아마 손상됐을 거야.
남: 내가 왜 이 주머니에 그걸 넣었는지 모르겠어. 난 정말 바보야.
여: 너무 자책하지 마. 그냥 잊어버려.

어휘 **sweatshirt** 운동복[추리닝] 상의 **ruin** 손상시키다: 파산시키다 | 선택지 어휘 | **be hard on A** A를 심하게 나무라다[대하다] **charge** 충전하다: 청구하다: 기소하다

14 긴 대화에 이어질 응답   ③

❋ 대화의 전체 맥락 하에 마지막 말의 의미나 의도를 정확히 파악하는 것이 좋다. 학기가 시작될 텐데 수영팀에 들어갔고 인류를 위한 해비타트 회원으로 주말에 집을 짓는 것을 돕고 노인복지관까지 방문한다고 말하는 여자에게 남자가 할 말로는 ③ '와! 네가 바쁠 거라는 게 당연하구나.'가 가장 적절하다.

① 알았어! 진정하고 나한테 천천히 이야기해봐.

② 기운 내! 넌 다음에 그곳을 방문할 수 있어.
④ 너 지쳐 보인다. 너 자신을 돌보렴!
⑤ 맞아! 가을은 언제나 바쁜 시기인 것 같아.

W: Oh, no! I can't believe summer's over, can you?
M: **Neither can I.** I had a really good time this summer vacation, but now we have to go back to school.
W: I know, but I'm excited now because I **have a lot planned** for this semester.
M: I'm going to join the golf team. Do you want to join with me?
W: I'd **consider doing that**, but I'm already on the swim team, so I don't think I would have time.
M: You can do both if you change your swimming schedule.
W: I don't think so. I need to do a lot of volunteer work, too.
M: **What kinds of** volunteer work are you involved in?
W: I'm a member of the local "Habitat for Humanity," so I'll spend all of my weekends to help build houses. And I'll also visit the local senior center.
M: Wow! No wonder you're going to be busy.

여: 아, 안 돼! 여름이 끝난다는 걸 믿을 수 없어. 넌 안 그러니?
남: 나도 그래. 난 이번 여름 방학에 정말 좋은 시간을 보냈지만 이제 우리는 학교로 돌아가야 하잖아.
여: 알아, 하지만 내가 이번 학기에 많은 것을 계획했기에 지금은 신이 나.
남: 난 골프팀에 가입할 거야. 너도 나하고 같이 가입할래?
여: 그걸 고려해봤지만 벌써 난 수영팀에 들었으니까 시간이 없을 것 같아.
남: 네가 수영 일정을 바꾼다면 둘 다 할 수 있어.
여: 그럴 수 없을 거야. 난 자원봉사도 많이 해야 하거든.
남: 어떤 종류의 자원봉사에 관여하는 거니?
여: 난 지역 '인류를 위한 해비타트'의 회원이라서 주말 모두 집을 짓는 걸 돕는 데 보낼 거야. 그리고 지역 노인복지관도 방문할 거야.
남: 왜! 네가 바쁠 거라는 게 당연하구나.

어휘 semester 학기 consider 고려[숙고]하다 involve 관여[관련]하다; 수반[포함]하다 local 지역[현지]의; 주민 humanity 인류; 인간성 senior center 노인복지관 | 선택지 어휘 | (it's) no wonder (that) ~하는 것도 당연하다. ~은 놀랄 일이 아니다

15 상황에 적절한 말 ③

* 지시문을 통해 누가(A) 누구에게(B) 할 말인지를 우선 정확히 파악한다. 담화는 대개 A와 B에 대한 배경 설명과 B가 처한 문제 상황, 그리고 이에 대해 A가 어떤 말을 하려고 하는지에 대한 설명의 순서로 전개된다. 노래를 가수처럼 잘 부르는 직장 동료 Michael(B)은 가수의 꿈을 가지고 있지만, 자신이 가수 되기에는 나이가 너무 많다고 한다. 이러한 동료에게 Nora(A)가 꿈을 위해 시도해보라고 격려하고 싶을 때 할 말로는 ③ '시도해 봐요! 시작하기에 충분히 젊으니까요.'가 가장 적절하다.

① 그거 놀랍군요! 행운을 빌어요.
② 꿋꿋이 버텨요! 실망하지 말아요.
④ 좋아요! 계획을 잘 세우고 꿈을 이뤄요.
⑤ 고마워요! 난 오디션 프로그램을 준비하고 있어요.

W: Michael is a coworker of Nora. They work in a small trading company. Today their company has a picnic to help strengthen teamwork and have fun. There is a song competition in the program. Michael participates in the song competition and wins first prize. He sings so well, just **like a professional.** Nora is amazed and tells him that if she could sing like him, she would be a singer. Michael says he once thought about becoming a singer. But he thinks he's a little **too old to become** a singer now even though it has always been his dream. Nora doesn't think so. There are some audition programs on TV, and she thinks it's not too late **for him to try.** She wants to encourage him to share his talent. In this situation, what would Nora most likely say to Michael?

Nora: Try it! You're young enough to start.

여: Michael은 Nora의 직장 동료이다. 그들은 작은 무역회사에서 일한다. 오늘 그들의 회사는 팀워크를 강화하는 것을 돕고 즐기기 위해 야유회를 갖는다. 프로그램에 노래 대회가 있다. Michael은 노래 대회에 참가해 1등 상을 받는다. 그는 노래를 마치 전

문가처럼 너무도 잘 한다. Nora는 깜짝 놀라서 그에게 자기가 그처럼 노래를 부를 수 있다면 가수가 될 거라고 말한다. Michael은 그도 한때 가수가 되는 것을 생각했다고 말한다. 하지만 그는 그것이 항상 자신의 꿈이긴 했지만 이제 가수가 되기에는 나이가 조금 지나치게 많다고 생각한다. Nora는 그렇게 생각하지 않는다. TV에는 몇 개의 오디션 프로그램이 있고 그녀는 그가 시도하기에 너무 늦지 않다고 생각한다. 그녀는 그의 재능을 공유하라고 그를 격려하고 싶다. 이 상황에서 Nora가 Michael에게 뭐라고 말하겠는가?

Nora: 시도해 봐요! 시작하기에 충분히 젊으니까요.

어휘 coworker 동료 strengthen 강화하다. 더 튼튼하게 하다 competition (경연) 대회; 경쟁 participate in ~에 참가[참여]하다 professional 전문가, 프로; 직업[직종]의 amazed (대단히) 놀란 once (과거) 한때; 한 번 encourage 격려[고무]하다. 용기를 북돋우다 | 선택지 어휘 | hang in there 꿋꿋이 버티다[견디다] disappointed 실망한, 낙담한 achieve 이루다; 달성하다

16~17 세트 문항 16 ③ 17 ④

* **16** 독서를 하면 능동적 상상력을 이용하여 상상력이 더 진보하므로 이를 최대한 활용하기 위해 가장 잘 팔리는 책을 확인하라고 하고 있다. 그러므로 담화의 주제는 ③ '상상력 증진의 도구로서의 독서'이다.

① 독서의 효과적인 기법
② 상상력과 창의력을 향상시키는 법
④ 다양한 종류의 책을 읽는 것의 이점
⑤ TV 시청과 독서의 차이점

* **17** 해석 참조.
① 추리 소설 ② 스파이 소설 ③ 역사책 ④ 공포 소설 ⑤ 전기

M: How often do you watch television? Do you know that you're using your imagination while watching TV? Yes, you are! Watching television does use your imagination, but it's only **passive imagination.** When reading, however, you use active imagination. Why? When you read, your mind tends to **see what you read.** Suppose you are reading a mystery or a spy novel. Your mind will imagine a mysterious setting that matches what you have **read and understood.** A good science fiction writer creates a picture with the characters, scenes, and settings in his or her story. But that is all a writer can give you. The rest is **up to you.** The more you read, the more your imagination improves. If you read different types of books, such as history books, biographies, and romance novels, you will start to **come up with** more creative ideas. To get the most out of your imagination, don't forget to check out the bestselling books online or at a bookstore.

남: 여러분은 얼마나 자주 텔레비전을 봅니까? TV를 보는 동안 여러분은 상상력을 이용하고 있다는 것을 아십니까? 네, 그렇습니다! 텔레비전을 보는 것은 여러분의 상상력을 정말로 이용하지만 그것은 그저 수동적인 상상력입니다. 그러나 책을 읽을 때 여러분은 능동적인 상상력을 사용합니다. 왜일까요? 여러분이 책을 읽을 때 여러분의 마음은 읽고 있는 것을 보고자 하는 경향이 있습니다. 여러분이 ① 추리 소설이나 ② 스파이 소설을 읽고 있다고 가정해봅시다. 여러분의 마음은 여러분이 읽고 이해하고 있던 것과 일치하는 미스터리한 배경을 상상할 것입니다. 훌륭한 공상과학소설 작가는 자기 이야기의 인물들과 장면들과 배경으로 그림을 만들어냅니다. 그러나 그것이 작가가 여러분에게 줄 수 있는 전부입니다. 나머지는 여러분에게 달려 있습니다. 더 읽으면 읽을수록 여러분의 상상력은 더 진보합니다. 여러분이 ③ 역사책, ⑤ 전기와 연애 소설 같은 다양한 종류의 책을 읽는다면 여러분은 더 창의적인 아이디어를 생각해내기 시작할 것입니다. 여러분의 상상력을 최대한 활용하기 위해서 온라인이나 서점에서 가장 잘 팔리는 책을 확인하는 걸 잊지 마십시오.

어휘 imagination 상상력, 상상 passive 수동적인, 소극적인; 수동태(↔ active 능동적인, 활발한) tend to-v v하는 경향이 있다 suppose 가정[추측]하다 novel 소설; 새로운, 신기한 setting 배경; 설정 scene 장면; 현장; 풍경 rest 나머지; 휴식 improve 진보하다; 증진[향상]시키다 biography (인물의) 전기 come up with ~을 생각해내다 get the most out of ~을 최대한 활용하다 | 선택지 어휘 | effective 효과적인 benefit 이로움, 이익; 혜택

07회

| 01 ⑤ | 02 ④ | 03 ② | 04 ⑤ | 05 ④ | 06 ④ | 07 ③ | 08 ④ | 09 ③ | 10 ④ |
| 11 ② | 12 ③ | 13 ⑤ | 14 ① | 15 ③ | 16 ② | 17 ⑤ | | | |

01 화자가 하는 말의 목적   ⑤

＊ 담화의 일부 내용이 아니라 중심 내용을 파악해야 한다. 건물의 화재 경보 시스템 테스트를 한다고 알리면서 단지 시스템 테스트이므로 건물을 떠날 필요는 없다고 하고 있다. 그러므로 여자의 말의 목적으로는 ⑤가 가장 적절하다.

W: This is an announcement from your maintenance office. I'm sorry to interrupt your working day by shouting over the building's sound system like this. But I wanted to **let everyone know** that we will be conducting a test of the building's **fire-alarm system** shortly. These frequent tests are essential to your well-being in the event of an emergency. We urge you **to be patient** during this test so that we can ensure your safety in the future. This is only a test of the system, **not a real emergency**, so there will be no need to leave the building at this time. However, if you need or want to leave the building, you are **free to do so**. Thank you again for your patience.

여: 이것은 관리실로부터 공지입니다. 이렇게 건물의 음향 시스템으로 시끄러운 소리를 내서 여러분의 근무일을 방해해서 죄송합니다. 그러나 우리가 건물의 화재 경보 시스템 테스트를 곧 시행할 것을 모든 분께 알리고자 합니다. 이러한 자주 있는 테스트는 비상시에 여러분의 안녕에 아주 중요합니다. 우리가 미래에 여러분의 안전을 보장할 수 있도록 이 테스트를 하는 동안 참아주시기를 간청합니다. 이것은 단지 시스템에 대한 테스트이며 실제 비상상황이 아니므로 이번에는 건물을 떠나실 필요가 없을 것입니다. 그러나 여러분이 건물을 떠날 필요가 있거나 원하신다면 자유로이 그렇게 하십시오. 다시 한번 여러분의 인내에 감사드립니다.

어휘 announcement 공지; 발표 (내용)   maintenance office 관리실   interrupt 방해하다; 중단시키다   conduct 수행(하다); 행동(하다)   shortly 곧; 간단히   frequent 잦은, 빈번한   essential 극히 중요한, 필수적인; 본질적인   emergency 비상(사태)   urge 간청하다; 강력히 권고하다; (강한) 욕구[충동]   patient 참을성[인내심] 있는; 환자 *cf.* patience 인내(심). 참을성   ensure 보장하다

02 의견   ④

＊ 우선 지시문에서 명시한 화자의 성별을 보고 어느 화자의 말에 주목할지를 판단해야 한다. 특히 의견이나 주장을 표현하는 어구(I think ~, You should ~ 등)가 이끄는 내용을 잘 들어야 한다. 이 대화에서 남자는 자외선 차단제가 화학물질 혼합체라고 하면서 해로운 화학물질을 포함하고 있어 암으로 이어질 수도 있다고 말한다. 그러므로 남자의 의견으로는 ④가 가장 적절하다. ③은 여자의 의견임에 유의한다.

M: Jennifer, why don't we go out for a walk?
W: Good idea, but hold on. I have to **put on some sunscreen** before I leave the house.
M: It's cloudy, so don't worry about it too much.
W: You must wear sunscreen any time you'll be out. **You can't escape** the UV rays even on cloudy days. We just can't see them.
M: Isn't that what cosmetic companies want you to believe?
W: But it's true that getting a sunburn can increase your risk for skin cancer.
M: Well, I think that **putting stuff** on your face is worse for you. It's **just a mix** of chemicals.
W: UV rays can make your skin older and even give you skin cancer!
M: Actually, sunscreen itself **can lead to cancer** because it contains harmful chemicals. You should think about that.
W: Oh, I hadn't heard that. I can't believe sunscreen itself is harmful.
M: I'll send you an article about that. Then you'll be convinced.

남: Jennifer, 산책하러 나가지 않을래요?
여: 좋은 생각이에요. 하지만 잠시만요. 집을 나서기 전에 자외선 차단제를 발라야 해요.
남: 날이 흐리니까 그건 너무 걱정하지 말아요.

여: 외출할 때는 언제든지 자외선 차단제를 발라야 해요. 흐린 날조차도 자외선을 피할 수 없거든요. 우리는 단지 그것을 보지 못할 뿐이에요.
남: 그건 화장품 회사가 당신에게 믿게 하려는 것 아니에요?
여: 하지만 햇볕에 타는 게 피부암의 위험을 증가시킬 수 있다는 건 사실이에요.
남: 음. 난 당신 얼굴에 뭔가를 바르는 게 더 안 좋다고 생각해요. 그건 그냥 화학물질 혼합체잖아요.
여: 자외선은 피부를 늙게 하고 심지어 피부암을 생기게 할 수 있다니까요!
남: 사실 자외선 차단제는 해로운 화학물질을 포함하고 있기 때문에 그 자체가 암으로 이어질 수도 있어요. 그것에 대해 생각해봐야 해요.
여: 아, 그런 말은 들어본 적이 없어요. 자외선 차단제 자체가 해롭다는 건 믿을 수 없어요.
남: 내가 그것에 관한 기사를 보내줄게요. 그러면 납득하게 될 거예요.

어휘 put on (얼굴·피부 등에) ~을 바르다(= wear)   sunscreen 자외선 차단제   escape 피하다; 도망치다   UV rays 자외선   cosmetic 화장품   sunburn 햇볕에 탐   chemical ((주로 복수형)) 화학물질   contain 포함하다; 억누르다   article (신문, 잡지의) 기사   convince 납득[확신]시키다; 설득하다

03 관계   ②

＊ 직업을 나타내거나 추론할 수 있는 힌트가 대화 전반에 걸쳐 드러나므로, 대화를 전체적으로 이해하는 것이 필요하다. 보이스피싱 전화를 받은 여자는 은행 계좌를 확인하기 위해 왔고, 남자는 신분증과 계좌번호를 묻고 계좌의 인출 내역을 확인해주고 있다. 그러므로 두 사람의 관계는 은행원과 은행 고객임을 알 수 있다. 세무서나 경찰서는 여자가 가야 할지 생각해봤다는 장소라고 했음에 유의한다.

M: Good afternoon. How can I help you?
W: I got a call and was told that I had a problem with my personal **income tax**.
M: Your income tax?
W: Yes, and they asked my account number and PIN number over the phone.
M: You didn't give them the numbers, did you?
W: Well, I gave the first number but stopped. It didn't feel right.
M: Good for you! It sounds like voice phishing.
W: Yes, I wasn't sure if **I was supposed to go** to the tax office or to the police. So I decided to come here first to check **my bank account**.
M: Good. Can I have your ID card and account number, please?
W: Here's my ID and account number.
M: Hmm... **Let me check**. Well, no one withdrew any money from your account today. If you get another phone call like that, please **contact us immediately**.
W: I see. I'm so relieved. That really scared me. I don't know how these people knew my name and phone number.

남: 안녕하세요. 무엇을 도와드릴까요?
여: 전화를 받았는데 내 개인 소득세에 문제가 있다는 말을 들었어요.
남: 고객님의 소득세요?
여: 네, 그리고 그들이 전화로 내 계좌번호와 비밀번호를 물었어요.
남: 그 번호를 주지 않았죠, 그렇죠?
여: 음, 첫 번째 숫자를 주었지만 멈췄어요. 그게 잘못된 느낌이 들어서요.
남: 잘하셨어요! 그거 보이스피싱 같군요.
여: 네, 제가 세무서나 경찰서로 가야 할지 모르겠더라고요. 그래서 제 은행 계좌를 확인하기 위해 여기 먼저 오기로 결정했죠.
남: 좋습니다. 신분증과 계좌번호를 주시겠어요?
여: 여기 제 신분증과 계좌번호가 있습니다.
남: 음… 확인해보겠습니다. 저, 오늘 고객님 계좌에서 어떤 돈도 인출되지 않았군요. 그것과 같은 다른 전화를 받으면 저희에게 바로 연락해주세요.
여: 알겠습니다. 정말 안심이에요. 그게 나를 정말 겁나게 했거든요. 그 사람들이 어떻게 내 이름과 전화번호를 알았는지 모르겠어요.

04 그림 불일치   ⑤

✻ 대화가 나오기 전에 각 사물의 위치 관계와 외형(형태나 무늬, 개수 등)의 특징을 미리 확인하는 것이 좋다. 책상 옆에 있는 두 개의 의자에 검진받을 순서의 두 아이를 앉혀 기다리게 하라고 했는데, 그림에는 하나의 의자밖에 없으므로 ⑤가 내용과 일치하지 않는다.

M: Hi, Ms. Moore. Mr. Wilson asked me to help you with the student physical checkups.
W: Hi, James. Thanks. You **need to guide** the kids through their checkups.
M: All right. Should I line the kids up in front of this room?
W: Yes. And bring kids **one by one** to the scale on the left side of the room.
M: I see. You'll measure their heights and weights with it.
W: Right. And they'll have their eye exams.
M: Oh, there is an eye chart on the wall above the bed. By the way, what will you use the bed for?
W: We won't use it this time. Oh, when you bring kids, you **should confirm** their names on the charts which are placed on the desk.
M: Do you mean the desk on the right?
W: Yeah. And while I examine a kid, have two kids wait **on the two chairs** next to the desk.
M: Okay. I can do that.

남: 안녕하세요, Moore 선생님. Wilson 선생님께서 저더러 학생들 신체검사하는 데 선생님을 도우라고 부탁하셨어요.
여: 안녕, James. 고맙구나. 넌 검사 내내 아이들을 안내해야 해.
남: 알겠습니다. 제가 이 방 앞에 아이들을 줄 세워야 하나요?
여: 그래. 그리고 방 왼쪽에 있는 체중계로 아이들을 한 명씩 데려오렴.
남: 알겠습니다. 그걸로 신장과 체중을 측정하실 거군요.
여: 맞아. 그리고 아이들은 시력검사도 하게 될 거야.
남: 아, 침대 위 벽에 시력 검사표가 있군요. 그런데 침대를 뭐에 쓰실 건가요?
여: 이번에는 그걸 사용하지 않을 거란다. 아, 네가 아이들을 데려올 때 책상 위에 놓여 있는 진료 차트에서 아이들 이름을 확인해야 한다.
남: 오른쪽의 책상 말씀인가요?
여: 그래. 그리고 내가 한 아이를 진찰하는 동안 책상 옆 두 개의 의자에 두 아이가 기다리도록 해주렴.
남: 알겠습니다. 할 수 있어요.

어휘   physical checkup 신체검사   through 내내, 줄곧; 지나서   line up ~을 한 줄[일렬]로 세우다   scale 저울; 규모   measure 측정하다; 평가[판단]하다   confirm 확인[확정]하다   examine 진찰하다; 검사[조사]하다

05 추후 행동   ④

✻ 대개 대화는 어떤 일을 하게 되는 상황이 먼저 제시된 뒤에 남자와 여자가 각각 할 일들과 이에 대한 수락/거절의 응답이 나열되는 식으로 전개된다. 어둠이 무서워서 잠자리에 들지 않으려는 딸아이에게 동화책을 읽어주기로 했는데 남편은 보고서를 끝내야 해서 아내가 읽어주기로 했다. 그러므로 여자가 할 일은 ④ '아이에게 동화책 읽어주기'이다.

W: Honey, I'm worried about Chloe. She doesn't want to go to bed tonight.
M: It's almost 11 p.m. Doesn't she feel well?
W: No, she is healthy. Recently she gets so worried before going to sleep at night.
M: Really? Do you know the reason why **she's so worried**?
W: Hmm... I don't know exactly, but I think she's just **afraid of the dark**.
M: It's quite common at her age. How about buying some stuffed animal toys for her?
W: She already has **several stuffed animals**, such as teddy bears and cuddly

rabbits.
M: Oh! **Why don't we** read her a storybook before she goes to sleep?
W: That's great. Will you do it now?
M: I'm afraid I can't do it now. I've got to finish this report. What about you?
W: Okay. I'll **give it a try** while you finish your work.
M: That's good. I think it will make her feel much more safe and relaxed.

여: 여보, 난 Chloe가 걱정돼요. 그 애는 오늘 밤 잠자리에 들려고 하지 않아요.
남: 거의 오후 11시인데요. 몸이 안 좋은 건가요?
여: 아니요. 건강해요. 최근에 그 애는 밤에 잠자리에 들기 전에 굉장히 불안해해요.
남: 정말이요? 그 애가 그렇게 불안해하는 이유가 뭔지 알아요?
여: 음... 정확히는 모르지만 그냥 어둠을 무서워하는 것 같아요.
남: 그 애 나이에 아주 흔한 것이죠. 아이에게 봉제 동물 인형을 좀 사주는 건 어때요?
여: 벌써 테디 베어하고 껴안을 수 있는 토끼 인형 같은 봉제 동물 인형이 몇 개 있어요.
남: 아! 잠자기 전에 아이에게 동화책을 읽어주는 건 어때요?
여: 그거 좋군요. 지금 당신이 할래요?
남: 난 지금 할 수 없을 것 같아요. 이 보고서를 끝내야 하거든요. 당신은 어때요?
여: 알았어요. 당신이 일을 끝내는 동안 내가 해보도록 할게요.
남: 좋아요. 그게 그 애를 훨씬 더 안전하고 편안한 기분이 들게 할 것 같아요.

어휘   stuffed animal (toys) 봉제 동물 인형   cuddly 껴안을 수 있게 만든   give it a try 한번 해보다, 시도하다

06 금액   ④

✻ 여러 개의 수치 정보가 등장하므로 필요한 정보를 메모하면서 듣는 것이 좋다. 남자가 사려고 결정한 코트는 원래 가격이 1,000달러이고 20% 할인하는 것이다. 그러므로 지불할 금액은 800달러이다. 1,500달러짜리는 비싸서, 또한 500달러이지만 20% 할인해 400달러인 코트는 넓은 깃이 마음에 안 들어서 사지 않았음에 유의한다.

W: Do you need any help?
M: Yes. How much is this wonderful coat?
W: It's $1,500. It's made of all cashmere wool.
M: Wow! It's way above **what I can afford**.
W: There are some nice coats which are being sold at a 20% discount. How about this one? It was originally $500, but it's now 20% off.
M: That's a good price, but I don't like **its wide collar**.
W: Then you'll like this coat. It was originally $1,000, but you can also get a 20% discount on it. Why don't you try it on?
M: *[pause]* Looks good, but it's also **beyond my budget**.
W: May I ask what price range you have in mind?
M: I'm hoping to spend no more than $700.
W: Well, it is really warm and lightweight. I think you **shouldn't mind paying** a little extra **for better quality**.
M: Hmm... Okay. I'll take it.

여: 도움이 필요하신가요?
남: 네, 이 아주 멋진 코트는 얼마인가요?
여: 1,500달러입니다. 모두 캐시미어 울로 만들어졌죠.
남: 왜! 제가 쓸 수 있는 걸 훨씬 넘어서는군요.
여: 20% 할인해서 판매하고 있는 멋진 코트가 몇 개 있습니다. 이건 어떠세요? 원래 500달러였는데 지금은 20% 할인합니다.
남: 좋은 가격이지만 난 이 넓은 깃이 마음에 들지 않아요.
여: 그러면 이 코트를 좋아하시겠군요. 원래 1,000달러였는데 이것 역시 20% 할인받으실 수 있습니다. 입어보지 그러세요?
남: [잠시 후] 좋아 보이는군요. 하지만 이것도 제 예산을 초과하네요.
여: 손님께서 생각하시는 가격대는 얼마 정도인지 여쭤봐도 될까요?
남: 저는 단지 700달러 정도만 쓰고 싶어요.
여: 음. 이건 정말 따뜻하고 가벼워요. 더 좋은 품질을 위해 약간 더 지불하시는 걸 꺼리지 않으셔야 한다고 생각해요.
남: 음... 좋아요. 이걸로 하겠습니다.

어휘   way above 훨씬 위쪽에; 먼 옛날   afford 여유[형편]가 되다   collar 깃, 칼라   beyond ~을 초과하는[넘어서는]   budget 예산(안)   lightweight 가벼운

07 이유 ③

✻ 지시문을 통해 남자가 네팔 여행을 가지 못하는 상황이며 남자의 말에 단서가 있을 가능성이 큼을 미리 파악한다. 남자의 네팔 여행이 취소되었다는 말을 들은 여자가 부모님이 허락하지 않으셨는지, 여름 학기를 듣게 된 건지 물었지만 남자는 모두 아니라고 답했다. 경비는 충분하지만 비행기 표가 이미 완전히 다 팔렸고 대기자 명단에 너무 많은 사람들이 있어 못 가게 되었다고 하고 있다. 그러므로 답은 ③이다.

W: Hi, Jeremy. I heard you're going to Nepal this summer. When are you leaving?
M: Unfortunately, my trip's been canceled.
W: Oh, sorry to hear that. Your parents didn't want you to travel, right?
M: No, they said I could go, and I've worked at a restaurant every weekend.
W: You must have saved **enough money** then.
M: Yes, but it is useless now. I can't make the trip this summer after all.
W: Why? Do you have to take summer school?
M: No, I don't. When I tried to **book a flight**, I found all the tickets to Nepal were completely **sold out**.
W: That's too bad. Why don't you put your name on the waiting list?
M: I already did, but there are **so many people** on the list ahead of me. So I gave up.
W: How about going somewhere else? There are a lot of beautiful countries you can go to.
M: No, going to Nepal has been my dream. I just decided I would go there next time.

여: 안녕, Jeremy. 네가 이번 여름에 네팔로 갈 거라고 들었어. 언제 떠나니?
남: 유감스럽게도 내 여행이 취소되었어.
여: 아, 그렇다니 안됐다. 네 부모님이 네가 여행하는 걸 원하지 않으셨구나, 맞지?
남: 아니야. 부모님은 내가 갈 수 있다고 하셨고 그래서 난 주말마다 식당에서 일했어.
여: 그러면 분명히 돈을 충분히 모았겠구나.
남: 응. 하지만 이제 소용없어. 난 이번 여름에 어쨌든 여행을 가지 못해.
여: 왜? 여름 학기를 들어야만 하니?
남: 아니, 그렇지 않아. 내가 비행기를 예약하려고 했는데 네팔로 가는 모든 비행기 표가 완전히 다 팔렸어.
여: 그거 안됐다. 네 이름을 대기자 명단에 올리지 그러니?
남: 벌써 했지만 내 앞에 너무 많은 사람들이 명단에 있어. 그래서 포기했어.
여: 다른 데 가는 게 어때? 네가 갈 수 있는 아름다운 나라가 많잖아.
남: 아니야. 네팔에 가는 게 내 꿈이었어. 난 그냥 거길 다음번에 가기로 결정했어.

어휘 useless 소용[쓸모]없는 after all 어쨌든; 결국에는 book 예약하다 sold out 다 팔린, 매진된 waiting list 대기자 명단 give up 포기하다; 그만두다

08 언급하지 않은 것 ④

✻ 대화의 진행은 대개 선택지와 같은 순서이므로, 선택지를 보면서 언급된 내용을 소거하는 식으로 푸는 것이 좋다. 화재가 시작된 날, 피해 면적, 피해 가옥 수와 동원된 소방대원 수에 대해서는 언급했지만 발화 원인에 대해서는 언급하지 않았다. 그러므로 답은 ④이다.

M: There was a huge wildfire in Douglas County.
W: Yes, I saw it on the news.
M: **The fire began** on Friday, October 5th and quickly spread across the county.
W: I heard it **burned** across 1,400 acres. I think that's because it's very dry in October.
M: Right. One of my friends lives there, and he said he's never seen anything like that.
W: Oh, really? I think lots of people were harmed. Is he safe?
M: Yeah, he and his house are safe, but about 40 houses **burned to the ground**.
W: I feel so sorry for those people.
M: They are not sure **what started this fire** in the first place, but we always should be careful in the forest.
W: They must have needed a lot of firefighters to put out the fires.

M: I heard there were about **900 firefighters** on scene, but more firefighters should have been there.

남: Douglas 카운티에 큰 산불이 났어.
여: 응. 뉴스에서 봤어.
남: 화재가 10월 5일 금요일에(① 시작된 날) 시작되었고 빠르게 카운티 전역으로 퍼져나갔어.
여: 1,400에이커에 걸쳐서(② 피해 면적) 타버렸다고 들었어. 10월이 아주 건조하기 때문에 그런 것 같아.
남: 맞아. 내 친구 한 명이 거기 사는데 그와 같은 건 전혀 본 적이 없다고 말했어.
여: 아, 정말? 많은 사람들이 다쳤을 것 같다. 그는 안전하니?
남: 응. 그와 그의 집은 안전해. 하지만 약 40채의 집(③ 피해 가옥 수)이 전소되었어.
여: 그 사람들이 너무 안됐다.
남: 처음에 무엇이 화재를 냈는지 모른다고 해. 하지만 우리는 숲에서 항상 주의를 기울여야 해.
여: 불을 끄느라 소방대원이 많이 필요했음에 틀림없어.
남: 현장에 약 900명의 소방대원(⑤ 동원된 소방대원 수)이 있었다고 들었지만 더 많은 소방대원이 거기 있어야 했는데 말이야.

어휘 spread 퍼지다, 확산(되다) burn to the ground 전소하다, 완전히 타버리다 put out (불을) 끄다; 출시하다 on scene 현장[현지]의

09 내용 불일치 ③

✻ 담화의 진행은 대개 선택지와 같은 순서이므로, 선택지를 보면서 일치하는 내용을 소거하는 식으로 푸는 것이 좋다. 담화에서는 등산화를 3달러에 빌릴 수 있다고 했는데 ③에서는 무료로 빌릴 수 있다고 했으므로 내용과 일치하지 않는다.

M: The Big Rock Youth Climbing Competition is back! The Big Rock Youth Climbing Competition is an opportunity for you to test your climbing ability and have fun in a friendly atmosphere. It'll **take place on Friday**, November 17th in the Big Rock Climbing Center. Since it was started in 2010, this is the 9th competition this year. It's **open to all climbers** from age 8 to 18. No experience is necessary, and you can **rent climbing shoes** for $3. There will be 12 routes to choose from. Registration is needed to participate. You must register online by November 10th. The entry fee is $15, but it will be reduced to $10 if you **register early** by October 30th. For more information, please contact Joe Mason at 405-992-3746.

남: Big Rock 청소년 등반 대회가 돌아왔습니다! Big Rock 청소년 등반 대회는 여러분이 자신의 등반 능력을 시험하고 친근한 분위기에서 재미있게 놀 수 있는 기회입니다. ① 그것은 11월 17일 금요일, Big Rock 등반 센터에서 개최될 것입니다. 2010년부터 시작되었기에 올해가 9번째 대회입니다. ② 8세부터 18세 연령까지의 모든 등반가들이 참여할 수 있습니다. 경험은 필요하지 않으며, ③ 등산화를 3달러에 빌릴 수 있습니다. 선택할 수 있는 12개의 (등반) 경로가 있을 것입니다. 참가하려면 등록이 필요합니다. 11월 10일까지 ④ 온라인으로 등록해야 합니다. 참가비는 15달러입니다만 여러분이 10월 30일까지 ⑤ 일찍 등록하면 10달러로 할인될 것입니다. 더 많은 정보를 원하시면 405-992-3746으로 Joe Mason에게 연락하십시오.

어휘 climbing 등반, 등산 cf. climber 등반가 competition 대회, 시합; 경쟁 opportunity 기회 atmosphere 분위기; 대기, 공기 take place 개최되다, 일어나다 registration 등록 cf. register 등록하다 entry fee 참가비

10 도표 이해 ④

✻ 대화의 진행은 대개 도표 항목의 나열 순서대로 진행된다. 대화를 들으면서 도표의 각 항목 중 선택되지 않은 것을 소거하는 식으로 푸는 것이 좋다. 우선 트럭을 원하지 않았고(⑤ 소거) 2리터 이하를 원했다(① 소거). 그리고 차 문의 개수가 두 개인 것은 싫다고 했고(③ 소거) ②와 ④가 남은 가운데 남자는 액수가 조금 초과하더라도 좌석이 더 많은 것을 사겠다고 했으므로 남자가 구매할 차는 ④이다.

W: Can I help you find something?
M: Yes, I'm looking for a used car. We need a family car.
W: May I ask what kind of car you're looking for?

M: We don't need a truck, since **I have one already**.
W: Okay. What size engine do you want?
M: I don't want anything **bigger than** 2 liters.
W: I understand. The bigger ones drink far more fuel.
M: Certainly. And I don't like 2-door cars because **it's not convenient** to ride in the back seat.
W: Then you can choose between these two. How much is your budget?
M: Well, I'd like to stay under $5,000. Oh, I like this one.
W: Oh, well, this one is just a little bit over $5,000, so it doesn't really **fit into your budget**.
M: But I think such a small amount over is okay. And **it has more seats**, so my family will really like this one. I'll take it.

여: 찾으시는 걸 도와드릴까요?
남: 네, 중고차를 찾고 있는데요. 우리는 가족 차가 한 대 필요해서요.
여: 어떤 종류의 차를 찾고 계시는지 여쭤봐도 될까요?
남: 우리는 벌써 트럭 한 대를 갖고 있기 때문에 트럭은 필요 없어요.
여: 알겠습니다. 어떤 크기의 엔진을 원하시나요?
남: 2리터보다 더 큰 건 원하지 않아요.
여: 알겠습니다. 더 클수록 연료를 더 많이 먹죠.
남: 그럼요. 그리고 전 문 두 개짜리 차는 뒷좌석에 타기가 편하지 않기 때문에 좋아하지 않아요.
여: 그러면 이 둘 중에서 선택하실 수 있습니다. 예산이 얼마인가요?
남: 음. 5,000달러 미만이면 좋겠어요. 아, 전 이게 마음에 듭니다.
여: 아, 글쎄요. 이건 5,000달러를 약간 넘어서 손님의 예산에 꼭 들어맞지는 않는데요.
남: 하지만 그런 적은 액수 초과는 괜찮은 것 같습니다. 그리고 이건 좌석이 더 많아서 우리 가족이 정말로 좋아할 것 같군요. 이걸 사겠어요.

어휘 used 중고의 fuel 연료 convenient 편리한; 접근이 편한 fit into ~에 꼭 들어맞다[적합하다]; 어울리다

11 짧은 대화에 이어질 응답　　②

✱ 주차할 수 있는 장소를 찾는 여자가 근처에 주차장이 있는지 묻고 있다. 이에 대한 남자의 응답으로는 주차장의 위치를 알려주는 ② '그럼요. 저 건물 뒤에서 하나 발견할 수 있습니다.'가 적절하다.

① 그렇고말고요. 오후 6시에 그걸 찾으실 수 있습니다.
③ 네, 주차장보다 조금 더 쌉니다.
④ 여기 티켓이 있습니다. 차가 필요하시면 저희에게 전화해 주십시오.
⑤ 아니요. 그것들은 주민을 위해 지정된 주차장소입니다.

W: Excuse me. Can I **park my car** on this side of the street?
M: No, you can't. It's a No-Parking Zone until 6 p.m.
W: Well, then where can I park until 6? Are there **any parking lots** around here?
M: **Sure. You can find one behind that building.**

여: 실례합니다. 거리 이쪽에 제 차를 주차할 수 있나요?
남: 아니요, 안 됩니다. 오후 6시까지는 주차 금지 구역입니다.
여: 음, 그러면 6시까지 어디에 주차할 수 있나요? 이 근처에 주차장이 있나요?
남: 그럼요. 저 건물 뒤에서 하나 발견할 수 있습니다.

어휘 park 주차하다 cf. No-Parking Zone 주차 금지 구역 cf. parking lot 주차장 | 선택지 어휘 | reserved 지정의, 예약된; 보류한 resident 주민, 거주자

12 짧은 대화에 이어질 응답　　③

✱ 남자가 TV로 농구 경기를 보는 여자에게 다른 채널로 돌려 자신이 좋아하는 TV 프로그램을 보자고 하고 있다. 이에 대한 여자의 응답으로는 ③ '경기는 10분 후에 끝날 거야. 기다려줘.'가 가장 적절하다.

① 그는 훌륭한 배우야. 난 그의 열렬한 팬이야.
② 이제 TV를 꺼. 공부할 시간이야.
④ 경기를 다시 하자. 이번에는 내가 너를 이길 거야.
⑤ 너무 기분 나빠 하지 마. 그건 네 잘못이 아니야.

M: Sue, can I **turn it to** another channel? I'd like to watch my favorite TV show.
W: No. I'm watching a basketball game now. **Why don't you watch** your show online? It's a rerun, isn't it?
M: My laptop monitor is too small. I'd like to watch it on TV.
W: The game will be over in 10 minutes. Please wait.

남: Sue. 내가 다른 채널로 돌려도 되겠니? 내가 제일 좋아하는 TV 프로그램을 보고 싶어.
여: 안 돼. 난 지금 농구 경기를 보고 있어. 네 프로그램을 온라인으로 보지 그러니? 그거 재방송이잖아, 그렇지 않아?
남: 내 노트북의 모니터가 너무 작아. 난 TV로 그걸 보고 싶어.
여: 경기는 10분 후에 끝날 거야. 기다려줘.

어휘 rerun 재방송(하다) laptop 노트북 | 선택지 어휘 | terrific 훌륭한, 아주 좋은 beat 이기다; 두드리다; 박자 fault 잘못; 책임; 단점

13 긴 대화에 이어질 응답　　⑤

✱ 대화의 전체 맥락 하에 마지막 말의 의미나 의도를 정확히 파악하는 것이 좋다. 남자가 여자에게 일상 활동에 대한 피드백을 줘서 운동하게 돕는 앱을 알려주고 있다. 이에 대한 여자의 응답으로는 좋아하면서 해보겠다고 하는 내용의 ⑤ '마치 나만의 트레이너를 갖는 것 같겠구나. 그걸 시도해볼게.'가 가장 적절하다.

① 맞아. 규칙적으로 운동하는 걸 잊지 마.
② 너 먼저 보여. 나도 좋은 몸매를 유지하고 싶어.
③ 내가 그걸 할 수 없을 것 같아. 난 일찍 일어나는 사람이 아니야.
④ 좋아. 그냥 편한 운동복을 입고 와.

M: You look serious. What's wrong?
W: I'm trying to lose weight, but I **don't have much time**.
M: You look good. But if you want to be in better shape and you're too busy, find other ways to include activity **in your daily routine**.
W: Like what?
M: You can walk quickly to the office or climb up and down the stairs instead of taking the elevator.
W: That sounds like a good idea. But I don't think I'd be encouraged to keep going.
M: I use a fitness app on my smartphone. It'll encourage you to walk more.
W: What's that? And how does it help me **to work out**?
M: It can track your activities, like steps, distance walked, and calories burned, using your phone.
W: That's cool! What's the name of the app? Do I have to pay for it?
M: No, it's a free app called the Daily Fitness App. It **gives you feedback on** your daily activities.
W: It sounds like having my own trainer. I'll try that.

남: 너 심각해 보인다. 뭐가 잘못된 거야?
여: 체중을 줄이려고 노력하고 있는데 시간이 별로 없어.
남: 너 좋아 보여. 하지만 네가 더 좋은 체형이 되기를 원하는데 너무 바쁘다면 네 일과에 신체 활동을 포함시킬 다른 방법을 찾아봐.
여: 예를 들면?
남: 사무실까지 빠르게 걷거나 엘리베이터를 타는 대신에 계단을 오르내릴 수도 있어.
여: 그거 좋은 생각 같아. 하지만 계속하게끔 힘을 얻게 될 것 같지 않아.
남: 난 내 스마트폰에 있는 신체 단련 앱을 사용해. 그게 너를 더 걷게 힘을 줄 거야.
여: 그게 뭔데? 그리고 그게 어떻게 내가 운동하게 돕는다는 거니?
남: 그건 네 휴대폰을 이용해서 발걸음과 걸은 거리, 그리고 소모한 열량 같은 네 활동을 추적할 수 있어.
여: 그거 멋지다! 그 앱 이름이 뭐야? 내가 돈을 지불해야 하니?
남: 아니. 그건 Daily Fitness App이라고 하는 무료 앱이야. 그건 네 일상 활동에 대한 피드백을 네게 줘.
여: 마치 나만의 트레이너를 갖는 것 같겠구나. 그걸 시도해볼게.

어휘 encourage A to-v A가 v하도록 격려[장려]하다 keep v-ing 계속해서 v하다 fitness 신체 단련, 건강; 적합함 work out 운동하다 cf. workout 운동 track 추적하다: 흔적 | 선택지 어휘 | get in shape 좋은 몸매를 유지하다

14 긴 대화에 이어질 응답 ①

✽ 대화의 전체 맥락 하에 마지막 말의 의미나 의도를 정확히 파악하는 것이 좋다. 아내가 어떤 선물을 원하는지 남편에게 묻자 남편이 목공을 하기 위한 공구 세트를 이야기하며 뒷마당에 테이블을 만들겠다고 했고, 아내가 멋진 아이디어라며 휴가 동안 자기도 돕겠다고 한다. 이에 대한 응답으로는 ① '훌륭한 계획이에요! 당신은 정말 다정해요!'가 가장 적절하다.

② 당신은 숙련된 목수예요. 존경스러워요!
③ 그렇게 생각해요. 난 우선 더 작은 물건을 세울 거예요.
④ 네, 이 책이 그것을 어떻게 만드는지를 가르쳐줘요.
⑤ 맞아요. 좋은 공구 세트를 찾는 건 정말로 어려워요.

W: Honey, is there anything you've been wanting to buy lately?
M: Hmm... I don't know. Why do you ask?
W: Christmas is coming up, and I want to know the things I could **get for you**.
M: That's so sweet of you, honey! But you've already given me far too much.
W: Just tell me, please. Can you think of anything you'd want?
M: Hmm... Well, you know I'm **interested in woodworking**.
W: Certainly. You said you wanted **to be a carpenter** when you were young.
M: I found a nice tool kit for woodworking at K Mart the other day. If I had it, I'd like to make **a barbecue table** for our backyard.
W: That sounds like a great idea for Christmas! Maybe I can help you **make a table** during the holiday!
M: **What a great plan! You're so sweet!**

여: 여보, 최근에 당신이 사고 싶었던 것 있어요?
남: 음… 모르겠어요. 왜 묻죠?
여: 크리스마스가 다가오고 있어서 내가 당신에게 사줄 수 있는 것을 알고 싶어요.
남: 여보, 정말 다정하군요! 하지만 당신은 내게 이미 너무 많이 줬어요.
여: 제발 내게 말해줘요. 원하는 것에 대해 생각해 볼 수 있어요?
남: 음… 저, 내가 목공에 관심이 있다는 걸 알죠.
여: 그럼요. 당신은 어렸을 때 목수가 되고 싶어 했다고 말했잖아요.
남: 저번에 K 마트에서 목공을 하는 데 아주 좋은 공구 세트를 발견했어요. 내가 그걸 갖는다면 우리 뒷마당에 바비큐 테이블을 만들고 싶어요.
여: 그거 크리스마스를 위한 멋진 아이디어 같아요! 아마 내가 휴가 동안 당신이 테이블을 만드는 걸 도울 수도 있을 거예요!
남: <u>훌륭한 계획이에요! 당신은 정말 다정해요!</u>

어휘 woodworking 목공 carpenter 목수 tool kit 공구 세트
| 선택지 어휘 | admire 존경[칭찬]하다

15 상황에 적절한 말 ③

✽ 지시문을 통해 누가(A) 누구에게(B) 할 말인지를 우선 정확히 파악한다. 담화는 대개 A와 B에 대한 배경 설명과 B가 처한 문제 상황, 그리고 이에 대해 A가 어떤 말을 하려고 하는지에 대한 설명의 순서로 전개된다. Owen의 어머니(A)가 Owen(B)이 상을 받았다는 결과보다는 그것을 위해 애쓴 아들의 노력을 칭찬하고자 한다고 했으므로 Owen의 어머니가 할 말로는 ③ '이걸 위해 네가 얼마나 열심히 노력했는지 알아. 네가 자랑스럽구나.'가 가장 적절하다.

① 굉장하구나. 내 모든 노력이 보상받는 기분이구나.
② 축하한다. 네가 수상했다고 네게 알려주게 되어 기쁘구나.
④ 좋아. 다른 계획들처럼 넌 목표를 세우고 그걸 향해 달려가는 게 필요해.
⑤ 그건 사실이야. 가장 중요한 것은 네 일을 즐기는 거야.

W: Owen is a high school student, and he wants to major in photography at an art school. In the hopes of **achieving his dream**, he decides to enter an international photography competition which is open for students. Owen always takes a camera with him and takes **as many photos as** he can. He gets up early in the morning at 5 a.m. to take pictures of the sunrise. He tries to put emotion and feelings in his photographs. Finally, he sends his photos to the competition organizers. And today he **is informed that** he will receive third prize. When his mother hears the news, she is very pleased and wants to **praise his effort** rather than the outcome. In this situation, what would Owen's mother most likely say to Owen?

Owen's mother: <u>I know how hard you've worked for this. I'm proud of you.</u>

여: Owen은 고등학생이고 그는 예술학교에서 사진을 전공하고 싶어 한다. 그의 꿈을 이루려는 희망으로 그는 학생을 대상으로 하는 국제 사진 대회에 참가하기로 결심한다. Owen은 항상 카메라를 들고 다니면서 가능한 한 많은 사진을 찍는다. 그는 일출 사진을 찍으려고 아침 오전 5시에 일찍 일어난다. 그는 자신의 사진에 감정과 정서를 넣으려고 애쓴다. 마침내 그는 자신의 사진을 대회 주최자에게 보낸다. 그리고 오늘 그는 자신이 3등 상을 받을 것이라는 통지를 받는다. 그의 어머니가 그 소식을 듣자 무척 기뻐하면서 결과보다는 그의 노력을 칭찬하고자 한다. 이 상황에서 Owen의 어머니가 Owen에게 뭐라고 말하겠는가?

Owen의 어머니: <u>이걸 위해 네가 얼마나 열심히 노력했는지 알아. 네가 자랑스럽구나.</u>

어휘 major in ~을 전공하다 achieve 이루다, 성취하다 inform 통지하다, 알리다 effort 노력, 수고 outcome 결과, 성과 | 선택지 어휘 | reward 보상(하다), 보상금

16~17 세트 문항　　16 ② 17 ⑤

✽ **16** 요즘 가정에서 가장 흔하게 사용되는 기구는 전자레인지라는 설명 뒤에 널리 쓰이고 있는 전자레인지의 예시와 그것의 편리성을 차례로 나열하고 있으므로 담화의 주제로는 ② '전자레인지는 어디서나 왜 그렇게 인기가 많은가'가 가장 적절하다.

① 전자레인지를 효과적으로 사용하는 법
③ 전자레인지를 사용하는 것의 건강상 영향
④ 사람들이 전자레인지 사용을 선호하지 않는 이유
⑤ 전자레인지와 일반적인 오븐의 차이

✽ **17** 해석 참조.
① 식당　② 기차　③ 구내식당　④ 슈퍼마켓　⑤ 빵집

M: What do you think is the most commonly used device in homes today? As you may have guessed, it is the microwave. Because using a microwave can cut **dinner preparation time**, they are used by many families. But microwaves aren't just used in the home. They're everywhere — in restaurants, trains, cafeterias, college dormitories, and break rooms in workplaces. It's not surprising that microwaves are popular. Workers and students can **put leftovers** from last night's dinner in the microwave, heat them for a few minutes, and eat a delicious lunch. Supermarkets also **add to the convenience** of microwaves because they sell different types of "microwaveable" meals. Some people say that using a microwave **takes away** from the pleasure of cooking. But, for many modern people who do not believe cooking is fun, microwaves are a wonderful device to make their lives **a lot easier**.

남: 요즘 가정에서 가장 흔하게 사용되는 기구는 무엇이라고 생각하시나요? 여러분이 짐작했듯이, 그건 전자레인지입니다. 전자레인지를 사용하는 것은 저녁 식사 준비 시간을 줄일 수 있기 때문에 그것은 많은 가정에서 사용됩니다. 하지만 전자레인지는 가정에서만 사용되는 것은 아닙니다. 그것들은 ① 식당, ② 기차, ③ 구내식당과 대학의 기숙사, 그리고 직장의 쉼터 등 모든 곳에 있습니다. 전자레인지가 인기 있는 것은 놀랄 일이 아닙니다. 근로자들과 학생들은 어제 저녁 식사에서 남은 음식을 전자레인지에 넣어 몇 분 동안 데워 맛있는 점심을 먹을 수 있습니다. ④ 슈퍼마켓 또한 다양한 종류의 '전자레인지 조리가 가능한' 음식을 팔기 때문에 전자레인지의 편리함을 증가시킵니다. 일부 사람들은 전자레인지를 사용하는 것이 요리의 기쁨을 빼앗아간다고 말합니다. 그러나 요리가 즐거움이라고 생각하지 않는 많은 현대인들에게 전자레인지는 그들의 삶을 무척 쉽게 만들어주는 훌륭한 기구입니다.

어휘 device 기구, 장치 dormitory 기숙사 leftover (먹다) 남은 음식; 나머지의 add to A A를 증가시키다[늘리다] convenience 편리(함), 편의 take away from ~을 빼앗아가다 | 선택지 어휘 | effectively 효과적으로; 사실상 cf. effect 영향; 효과

08회

01 화자가 하는 말의 목적   ④

✱ 담화의 일부 내용이 아니라 중심 내용을 파악해야 한다. 본 담화는 방과 후 운동장에 아이들을 돌볼 선생님이나 교직원도 없고 담장도 없어 안전하지 않고, 또 아이들이 심각하게 다칠 수도 있어 방과 후 운동장을 비우는 규칙을 세웠다고 말하고 있다. 새로운 학교의 규칙과 위반 시 처벌에 대해서 알리는 내용이므로 여자가 하는 말의 목적으로는 ④가 적절하다.

W: Hello. Recently, it has come to my attention that there have been several students staying and playing in the schoolyard after school. The schoolyard is not safe after school because there are no teachers or school staff **to look after children**. Besides, as there is no fence around the yard, anyone can enter the yard. And school property might be damaged, or worse, children could even be seriously injured. So our school has decided that **no children are to be** on the schoolyard after school. This is now **a school rule**. Once school finishes, the yard must **be empty of** students until the next day. If we find anyone after school, they'll be punished and their parents will be notified.

여: 안녕하세요. 최근, 방과 후에 몇몇 학생들이 학교 운동장에 남아서 노는 것을 알게 되었습니다. 방과 후에는 아이들을 돌볼 선생님이나 교직원이 없기 때문에 학교 운동장은 안전하지 않습니다. 게다가, 운동장 주변에는 담장이 없어서 누구나 운동장으로 들어올 수 있습니다. 그리고 학교 소유물이 망가질 수도 있고 더 나쁜 것은 아이들이 심지어 심각하게 다칠 수도 있습니다. 그래서 우리 학교는 방과 후에 학교 운동장에 어떤 아이들도 (남아) 있지 않도록 결정했습니다. 이것은 이제 학교 규칙입니다. 일단 학교가 끝나면 운동장에는 다음날까지 학생들이 없어야 합니다. 만일 우리가 방과 후 누군가를 발견한다면 그들은 처벌받을 것이고 학부모들에게 통지할 것입니다.

어휘 (school)yard (학교) 운동장   look after ~을 돌보다[맡다]   besides 게다가   fence 담장; 울타리   property 소유물; 부동산   injure 다치게 하다   empty 없는; 비어 있는   punish 처벌하다   notify 통지하다, 알리다

02 의견   ③

✱ 우선 지시문에서 명시한 화자의 성별을 보고 어느 화자의 말에 주목할지를 판단해야 한다. 특히 의견이나 주장을 표현하는 어구(I think ~, You should ~ 등)가 이끄는 내용을 잘 들어야 한다. 남자는 사냥으로 사슴의 개체 수를 조절하는 게 효과적인 방법이고 또한 이것이 사슴이 식량을 바닥내는 것을 막아줄 수 있다고 하고 있다. 그러므로 남자의 의견은 ③이 적절하다. 사슴을 막아줄 전기 철조망에 대한 언급은 남자가 아닌 여자가 했음에 유의한다.

M: Did you hear that a deer destroyed a vegetable garden in our neighborhood?
W: Yes, I heard that. There are so many deer around here.
M: There has been **a lot of damage** caused by them on farms and in gardens.
W: They're harmful animals to us now. I think the government should do something to control their population.
M: You're right. I think hunting is **a very effective way** to solve this problem.
W: But isn't it too cruel? I believe it's better to build electric fences around neighborhoods. They're effective for keeping out deer.
M: It costs way too much. We can control the deer population **by hunting**. This also prevents deer from **running out of** food.
W: Well, I think electric fences are safer. Maybe the government can help pay for electric fences.
M: Hmm... Maybe... But I think the cheaper and easier solution is best.
W: It still seems kind of cruel to me, but I see your point.

남: 사슴이 우리 동네의 채소밭을 망가뜨렸다는 이야기 들었어요?
여: 네, 그 이야기 들었어요. 이 주변에 사슴이 너무 많아요.
남: 농장과 정원에 그것들이 일으킨 피해가 아주 많아요.

여: 지금 그들은 우리에게 해로운 동물이에요. 난 정부가 그 개체 수를 조절하기 위해 뭔가를 해야 한다고 생각해요.
남: 당신 말이 맞아요. 사냥이 이 문제를 해결할 아주 효과적인 방법이라고 생각해요.
여: 하지만 그건 너무 잔인하지 않아요? 난 동네 주변에 전기 철조망을 세우는 게 더 낫다고 생각해요. 전기 철조망은 사슴을 쫓아내는 데 효과적이거든요.
남: 그건 비용이 엄청나게 들어요. 우리는 사냥으로 사슴 개체 수를 조절할 수 있어요. 이것은 또한 사슴이 식량을 바닥내는 것을 막아줘요.
여: 음, 난 전기 철조망이 더 안전하다고 생각해요. 아마 정부가 전기 철조망에 대한 비용을 지불하는 것을 도와줄 수 있을 거예요.
남: 음… 어쩌면요… 하지만 난 더 저렴하고 더 쉬운 해결책이 최선이라고 생각해요.
여: 그건 내게 여전히 좀 잔인한 것 같지만 당신이 무슨 말을 하는지는 알겠어요.

어휘 destroy 망치다; 파괴하다   neighborhood 동네, 근처; 이웃   damage 피해, 손상   harmful 해로운, 유해한   government 정부   population 개체 수; 인구   cruel 잔인한, 잔혹한   electric fence 전기 철조망   keep out ~을 들어오지 못하게 하다   prevent A from B A가 B하는 것을 막다   run out of ~을 바닥내다; ~이 없어지다

03 관계   ③

✱ 직업을 나타내거나 추론할 수 있는 힌트가 대화 전반에 걸쳐 드러나므로, 대화를 전체적으로 이해하는 것이 필요하다. 본 대화에서 처음에는 와이파이 연결이 안 된다는 내용으로 인해 통신회사 직원과 이용자의 관계인 것으로 오해할 수 있다. 그러나 여자가 라운지에 무료 와이파이가 있으니 와서 사용하라고 제안하고, 남자는 방으로 기술자를 보내 달라고 하며 또한 아침 식사를 방으로 배달해달라고 요청하고 있다. 따라서 이들은 ③ '호텔 직원 – 투숙객'의 관계임을 알 수 있다.

[Telephone rings.]
W: Good evening. How can I help you?
M: I've got some network problems. I can't connect to your Wi-Fi. The login screen doesn't appear.
W: Oh, I see. We'll send someone **as soon as possible**.
M: Can you send him immediately? I have to send an e-mail now.
W: If it's urgent, why don't you **come to the lounge**? There is free Wi-Fi in the lounge.
M: No, I'll wait for the technician in my room. How long **should I wait**?
W: It will be about 20 minutes.
M: That'll be okay. And I'd like to have some breakfast and coffee delivered to my room tomorrow morning at 7 o'clock.
W: **Which breakfast** would you like, the English or continental breakfast?
M: Continental, please. I'll pay my bill when I check out.
W: All right, sir. I'm arranging everything right now.

[전화벨이 울린다.]
여: 안녕하세요. 무엇을 도와드릴까요?
남: 네트워크 문제가 좀 있는데요. 여기 와이파이에 연결할 수가 없어요. 로그인 화면이 나타나지 않아요.
여: 아, 알겠습니다. 가능한 한 빨리 사람을 보내겠습니다.
남: 사람을 즉시 보내줄 수 있나요? 전 지금 이메일을 보내야 해서요.
여: 급하시면 라운지로 오시는 건 어떠신가요? 라운지에 무료 와이파이가 있습니다.
남: 아니요, 제 방에서 기술자를 기다릴게요. 제가 얼마나 기다려야 하나요?
여: 20분쯤 될 겁니다.
남: 그러면 괜찮아요. 그리고 내일 아침 7시 정각에 제 방으로 아침 식사와 커피를 배달해 주면 좋겠어요.
여: 영국식 또는 유럽식 아침 식사 중 어떤 아침 식사를 원하시나요?
남: 유럽식으로 부탁해요. 체크아웃할 때 계산하겠습니다.
여: 알겠습니다, 손님. 즉시 모든 것을 처리하겠습니다.

어휘 connect 연결하다   immediately 즉시   urgent 긴급한, 시급한   technician 기술자   continental 유럽식의; (유럽) 대륙의   bill 계산서; 고지서   arrange (일을) 처리하다; 배열하다

04 그림 불일치 ④

＊ 대화가 나오기 전에 각 사물의 위치 관계와 외형(형태나 무늬, 개수 등)의 특징을 미리 확인하는 것이 좋다. 나뭇가지 끝의 나뭇잎을 호박과 옥수수 그림으로 바꾸자고 남자가 제안하고 있으므로 두 사람이 보는 포스터에는 나뭇잎이 그려져 있는 상황이다. 그러나 그림에는 나뭇잎이 아닌 호박과 옥수수가 나뭇가지 끝에 놓여 있으므로 ④는 대화의 내용과 일치하지 않는다.

W: This is the initial draft of the poster for our Thanksgiving dinner. What do you think?
M: Well, it looks great. I like **the way you wrote** the words, "HAPPY THANKSGIVING" on the banner at the top!
W: Thanks, and I drew two owls on the branch.
M: They're really cute! The owl on the left is wearing a black hat with a buckle on the front.
W: Yes, **that's what we call** a pilgrim's hat. And the owl on the right is wearing an Indian feather hat.
M: Great. They're both symbols of Thanksgiving. But it looks like we need to **make a change** here at the bottom.
W: What do you want to change?
M: You drew some leaves at the end of the branch. Why don't you draw a pumpkin and some corn **instead of leaves**?
W: Good idea. I'll change them. How about the time and location of the dinner at the far right?
M: I like it. I think it's the most important information on the poster. Thank you. It's really great.

여: 이건 우리 추수감사절 저녁 식사를 위한 포스터의 초안이에요. 어떻게 생각해요?
남: 음. 먼저 보이는군요. 맨 위의 현수막에 있는 '행복한 추수감사절'이라고 말을 쓴 방식이 마음에 들어요!
여: 고마워요. 그리고 나는 나뭇가지 위에 두 마리의 부엉이를 그렸어요.
남: 정말 귀엽네요! 왼쪽 부엉이는 앞에 버클이 있는 검은 모자를 쓰고 있군요.
여: 네, 저것은 우리가 순례자 모자라고 부르는 거예요. 그리고 오른쪽 부엉이는 인디언 깃털 모자를 쓰고 있어요.
남: 좋아요. 그것들 모두 추수감사절의 상징이죠. 하지만 우리가 여기 아래쪽은 바꿔야 할 것 같아요.
여: 어떤 걸 바꾸고 싶어요?
남: 나뭇가지 끝에 나뭇잎을 몇 개 그렸잖아요. 나뭇잎 대신에 호박 하나하고 옥수수 몇 개를 그리는 건 어때요?
여: 좋은 생각이에요. 그걸 바꿀게요. 맨 오른쪽에 있는 저녁 식사의 시간과 장소는 어때요?
남: 마음에 들어요. 그게 포스터의 가장 중요한 정보라고 생각해요. 고마워요. 정말 멋져요.

어휘 initial 처음의; 초기의 draft 도안; 초안; 원고 Thanksgiving 추수감사절 banner 현수막, 플래카드 branch 나뭇가지 owl 부엉이, 올빼미 pilgrim 순례자 feather 깃털 symbol 상징 pumpkin 호박

05 추후 행동 ⑤

＊ 대개 대화는 어떤 일을 하게 되는 상황이 먼저 제시된 뒤에 남자와 여자가 각각 할 일들과 이에 대한 수락/거절의 응답이 나열되는 식으로 전개된다. 할아버지는 이메일로 사진 보내는 방법을 설명해주기를 요청했고 손녀인 여자가 알려 드리겠다고 했으므로 여자의 할 일은 ⑤ '이메일로 사진 보내는 법 알려주기'이다. ③은 할아버지가 할 일임에 유의한다.

M: Becky! Can you give me a hand?
W: Sure, Grandpa. What do you need?
M: I've just started to take a free computer course at the senior center.
W: Wow! Good for you! But is your laptop **working well**? It's been more than ten years, I guess.
M: Don't worry. I bought a used tablet PC. By the way, you're a computer expert, aren't you?
W: Well, no, I wouldn't call myself a computer expert, but I think **I can help you**.

M: Okay. My computer teacher asked me to **send one of my pictures** to his e-mail, but I forgot how to do it. Can you explain it for me?
W: Sure. It's very easy once you know how. Is your picture you want to send to him on your tablet PC?
M: No, it's on my smartphone. I feel embarrassed about forgetting.
W: Grandpa, I'm proud of you. Most people at your age hardly try to learn about technology, so don't feel discouraged.
M: Thank you. Anyway, I'm going to **bring my smartphone** in my room.

남: Becky! 날 도와줄 수 있니?
여: 그럼요, 할아버지. 뭐가 필요하세요?
남: 내가 노인복지관에서 무료 컴퓨터 강좌 수강을 막 시작했단다.
여: 왜! 잘 되었네요! 하지만 할아버지 노트북이 잘 작동하나요? 10년 이상 된 것 같은데요.
남: 걱정 말아라. 난 중고 태블릿 PC를 샀다. 그런데 너 컴퓨터 전문가지, 그렇지 않니?
여: 음, 아니에요, 저 자신을 컴퓨터 전문가라고 부르지는 않겠지만 할아버지를 도와드릴 수 있을 것 같아요.
남: 좋아. 내 컴퓨터 선생님이 내게 자기 이메일로 내 사진 하나를 보내라고 하셨지만 어떻게 하는지 잊어버렸구나. 내게 그걸 설명해줄 수 있겠니?
여: 그럼요. 일단 어떻게 하는지 아시면 아주 쉬워요. 할아버지가 선생님에게 보내고 싶은 사진이 태블릿 PC에 있나요?
남: 아니, 그건 내 스마트폰에 있어. 잊어버린 게 창피한 생각이 드는구나.
여: 할아버지, 전 할아버지가 자랑스러워요. 할아버지 연세의 대부분의 사람들은 기술을 배우려고 거의 노력하지 않으니까 낙담하지 마세요.
남: 고맙다. 어쨌든, 내 방에서 스마트폰을 가져올게.

어휘 give A a hand A를 도와주다 course 강좌, 강의 senior center 노인복지관 used 중고의 expert 전문가; 숙련된 embarrassed 창피한, 당황스러워 하는 hardly 거의 ~않다 discouraged 낙담[낙심]한

06 금액 ④

＊ 여러 개의 수치 정보가 등장하므로 필요한 정보를 메모하면서 듣는 것이 좋다. 커피숍을 북카페로 바꾸는 데 드는 예상 금액은 리모델링 3,000달러에 책 등 물품비용 2,400달러, 그리고 마케팅과 광고 비용 800달러이다. 이 셋을 합친 금액은 6,200달러이므로 답은 ④이다. 마케팅 비용으로 1,000달러를 언급한 것은 여자가 그 정도 비용이 드는지 질문한 금액임을 유의한다.

M: Carla, I've got an idea for getting more customers to come to our coffee shop.
W: What's that?
M: There are many coffee shops including ours around here, right? But there aren't any book cafes here.
W: So are you suggesting **starting a book cafe** of our own?
M: Definitely. I'm sure there are people who want to read books with coffee and tea.
W: That's a good idea, but I'm not sure **we have the money** for that right now.
M: I have a business plan. We need $3,000 for the remodeling costs.
W: We also need to buy books and other stuff.
M: That will be **about $2,400**. I think we can afford it.
W: Don't forget we'll need money for marketing and advertising. How much do you think it costs? Around $1,000?
M: I already thought about that. **I'm guessing $800** for that.
W: Not bad. I agree with you. We can do this.

남: Carla, 우리 커피숍에 더 많은 손님을 오게 할 아이디어가 있어요.
여: 그게 뭔데요?
남: 이 근처에 우리 것을 포함해서 커피숍이 많이 있어요. 맞죠? 하지만 여긴 어떤 북카페도 없어요.
여: 그래서 우리가 북카페를 시작하자고 제안하는 건가요?
남: 그럼요. 커피와 차를 마시면서 책을 읽고 싶어 하는 사람들이 있을 거라고 확신해요.
여: 좋은 생각이지만 우리가 당장 그걸 할 돈이 있는지 모르겠어요.
남: 나한테 사업계획이 있어요. 우리는 리모델링 비용으로 3,000달러가 필요해요.
여: 우리는 또 책하고 다른 것들을 사야 해요.

남: 그게 약 2,400달러 될 거예요. 난 우리가 여유가 있다고 생각해요.

여: 우리가 마케팅하고 광고하는 데 돈이 필요할 거라는 걸 잊지 말아요. 얼마나 비용이 들 거 같아요? 1,000달러쯤이요?

남: 내가 이미 그걸 생각했어요. 그 비용으로 800달러를 생각하고 있어요.

여: 괜찮아요. 당신에게 동의해요. 우리가 할 수 있을 거예요.

어휘 including 포함하여　suggest 제안하다; 추천하다　definitely 그럼, 물론; 분명히　cost 비용, 값; (값·비용이) 들다, (얼마)이다　stuff 것(들), 물건; 재료　afford 여유[형편]가 되다　advertise 광고하다

07 이유　　　　　　　　　　　③

※ 지시문을 통해 두 사람이 집을 구매하지 않으려는 상황이며 여자와 남자의 말 모두에 단서가 있을 가능성이 큼을 미리 파악한다. 여자는 집을 살 여유가 없다고 하면서 집을 사게 되면 집 부자이지만 현금 거지가 될 거라고 했고 남자가 이에 동의하며 더 싼 집을 찾자고 했으므로 답은 ③이다. 자동차 소음 문제는 남자가 언급했지만, 여자가 교통량이 많지 않다고 했으므로 답이 아니다.

W: Robert, look at this house for sale. I really like this house.
M: Yes, it's a beautiful house.
W: It's in a great neighborhood, and the beach is **within walking distance**.
M: But the house is on the corner. That means it gets twice as much traffic and noise.
W: Don't worry. There is **not much traffic** in this area. Best of all, it's got a big backyard.
M: I'm sure our kids would love to play basketball in the backyard.
W: Let me see its price. Uh, oh. **We can't afford** this house.
M: Are you sure? I think we can afford it.
W: If we buy this house, we'll be house rich, but cash poor. Think about the monthly payment.
M: Hmm... You're right. We have to find a **cheaper house**.

여: Robert, 팔려고 내놓은 이 집을 봐요. 난 이 집이 정말 마음에 들어요.
남: 네, 아름다운 집이군요.
여: 아주 좋은 지역에 있고 해변도 걸어서 갈 수 있는 거리에 있어요.
남: 하지만 집이 모퉁이에 있군요. 그건 교통량과 소음이 두 배라는 뜻이잖아요.
여: 걱정 말아요. 이 지역은 교통량이 그렇게 많지 않아요. 무엇보다도 큰 뒷마당이 있어요.
남: 우리 애들이 뒷마당에서 농구 하는 걸 좋아할 게 틀림없어요.
여: 가격을 봅시다. 아, 이런. 우린 이 집을 살 여유가 없어요.
남: 확실해요? 우린 살 여유가 있는 것 같은데요.
여: 우리가 이 집을 사면 우리는 집 부자이지만 현금 거지가 될 거예요. 매달 지불 금액을 생각해 봐요.
남: 음… 당신 말이 맞아요. 우리는 더 싼 집을 찾아야 해요.

어휘 for sale 팔려고 내놓은　within ~이내에　traffic 교통(량), 차량들　backyard 뒷마당; 뒤뜰　monthly 매달의, 한 달에 한 번의　payment 지불[납입] 금액

08 언급하지 않은 것　　　　　　⑤

※ 대화의 진행은 대개 선택지와 같은 순서이므로, 선택지를 보면서 언급된 내용을 소거하는 식으로 푸는 것이 좋다. 근무 장소, 근무 시간, 건강 보험 혜택과 유급 휴가 일수에 대해선 언급했지만, 연봉 액수는 말하지 않았으므로 답은 ⑤이다. 연봉에 대한 이야기가 있었지만 구체적인 연봉 액수는 언급하지 않은 것을 유의한다.

W: By the way sir, can you tell me a little about the position?
M: Sure. What do you want to know?
W: If I get this job, will I be working at the office or at the stores?
M: You'll be spending most of your time **in the office**.
W: I see. And when are the office hours? Is it from nine to five?
M: No, it'll be **from eight to five**. If you have more questions, please ask me freely.
W: Thanks. I'd like to know more about **health insurance**.
M: The company pays for 90% of your health insurance for you and your family. But you have to pay your medical bills until the total reaches

$1,500.
W: Okay. I heard that I'll get 10 days of vacation a year. Is it paid vacation?
M: Yes, you get a 10-day **paid vacation** each year. And you already know about the annual salary for this job, right?
W: Yes, I'm satisfied with the salary. Thank you.
M: We'll be contacting you soon. It was nice meeting you, Ms. Johnson.

여: 그런데요, 직책에 관해 좀 말씀해주실 수 있나요?
남: 물론이죠. 뭘 알고 싶은가요?
여: 제가 이 직업을 얻는다면 사무실에서 일하나요, 아니면 상점에서 일하나요?
남: 대부분의 시간을 사무실(① 근무 장소)에서 보내게 될 겁니다.
여: 알겠습니다. 그리고 근무 시간이 언제인가요? 9시부터 5시까지인가요?
남: 아니요, 8시부터 5시까지(② 근무 시간)입니다. 질문이 더 있으면 자유로이 물어보세요.
여: 고맙습니다. 전 건강 보험에 대해 더 알고 싶습니다.
남: 회사는 당신과 당신 가족을 위해 건강 보험의 90%를 지불합니다(③ 건강 보험 혜택). 하지만 병원비 총액이 1,500달러에 이를 때까지는 당신이 지불해야 합니다.
여: 알겠습니다. 제가 일 년에 10일 휴가를 얻게 될 거라고 들었어요. 유급 휴가인가요?
남: 네, 매년 10일간의 유급 휴가(④ 유급 휴가 일수)를 받습니다. 그리고 이 직업의 연봉에 대해서는 이미 알고 있죠, 그렇죠?
여: 네, 급여에 대해서는 만족합니다. 고맙습니다.
남: 곧 연락드리겠습니다. 만나서 반가웠어요, Johnson 씨.

어휘 position 직위, (일)자리　health insurance 건강 보험　total 총, 전체의　paid vacation 유급 휴가　annual 연간의; 매년의　salary 급여, 월급　contact 연락(하다); 접촉(하다)

09 내용 불일치　　　　　　　④

※ 담화의 진행은 대개 선택지와 같은 순서이므로, 선택지를 보면서 일치하는 내용을 소거하는 식으로 푸는 것이 좋다. 캠프 비용에 매일의 간식과 음료가 포함되어 있다고 했으므로 ④는 담화의 내용과 일치하지 않는다.

W: Trinity School will have its Championship Chess Camp, starting from June 21st to the 25th, for 5 days from 8 a.m. to noon. This annual tradition is open for **first through sixth graders**, and it has always proved fun and a great learning experience for them. All students, from **the first-time player** to the experienced competitor, are welcome to join. There will be **pre-chess games** for beginners, guided play, and game play. A mini-tournament will make a fun and exciting conclusion to this camp. The cost for the camp is $210 and includes **daily snacks and drinks**. You can register for it either online, www.trinityatl.org, or by contacting Anna Lewis at 910-287-4468. Don't miss out on this great opportunity to have fun, learn, and play more chess.

여: Trinity 학교는 ① 6월 21일부터 시작해서 25일까지 5일 동안 오전 8시부터 정오까지 Championship Chess Camp를 가질 것입니다. 이 연례 전통은 ② 1학년부터 6학년 학생들이 참여할 수 있고 그들을 위한 즐거움과 커다란 학습 경험을 언제나 입증해왔습니다. ③ 처음 하는 선수부터 숙련된 참가자에 이르기까지 모든 학생들이 함께하는 것을 환영합니다. 초보자들을 위한 예비 체스 게임과 지도 대국, 경기 대국이 있을 것입니다. 미니 토너먼트가 이 캠프에 즐거움과 신나는 결말을 만들어줄 것입니다. ④ 캠프 비용은 210달러이고 매일의 간식과 음료를 포함합니다. 여러분은 ⑤ www.trinityatl.org 온라인으로, 혹은 910-287-4468로 Anna Lewis에게 연락해서 등록할 수 있습니다. 재밌게 놀고 배우고 체스를 더 두기 위한 이 놀라운 기회를 놓치지 마십시오.

어휘 prove 입증하다; (~임이) 판명되다　experienced 숙련된; 경험 있는[많은]　competitor 참가자; 경쟁자　conclusion 결말; 결론, (최종적인) 판단　include 포함[포괄]하다　register for ~에 등록하다　opportunity 기회　have fun 재미있게 놀다

10 도표 이해　　　　　　　　⑤

※ 대화의 진행은 대개 도표 항목의 나열 순서대로 진행된다. 대화를 들으면서 도표의 각 항목 중 선택되지 않은 것을 소거하는 식으로 푸는 것이 좋다. 플라밍고 쇼를 보러 가야 해서 6시 이전에 돌아와야 하므로 오후 6시 이후까지 관광이 있는 ②가 제외된다.

그다음에 대성당과 궁전 관광을 제외하면 ①, ④, ⑤가 남는데, 그중 가격이 더 싼 ④와 ⑤ 중에서 점심을 제공하는 것으로 선택했으므로 답은 ⑤이다.

M: What should we do tomorrow?
W: I walked more than 6 hours today, so I'm tired of walking. Let's take a bus tour tomorrow. I got this brochure in the hotel lobby.
M: Good idea. We can choose **one of these tours**. What would you like to choose?
W: We reserved a flamingo show at 7 p.m. tomorrow. We have to choose one which finishes **before 6 p.m.**
M: That's right. Which course are you interested in?
W: We already saw so many historic sites such as cathedrals and palaces. I'd like to do **something outdoors** tomorrow.
M: Then it looks like we have these three options. Let's choose one of the cheaper ones.
W: I'd like a tour **that includes lunch** if they're the same price.
M: You have a point. We won't need to spend time to search for restaurants. Let's take this one.
W: Okay. I'll call and reserve it.

남: 내일 우리 뭐 할까요?
여: 난 오늘 6시간 이상 걸어서 걷는 데 지쳤어요. 내일은 버스 관광을 합시다. 호텔 로비에서 이 책자를 가져왔어요.
남: 좋은 생각이에요. 우리는 이 관광 중 하나를 선택할 수 있겠군요. 어떤 걸 선택하고 싶어요?
여: 우리는 내일 오후 7시에 플라밍고 쇼를 예약했어요. 오후 6시 전에 끝나는 걸 골라야 해요.
남: 맞아요. 당신은 어떤 코스에 관심이 있나요?
여: 우린 이미 대성당과 궁전 같은 유적지를 너무 많이 봤어요. 내일은 야외에서 뭔가를 하고 싶어요.
남: 그러면 우린 이 세 가지 선택권이 있는 것 같군요. 더 싼 것 중 하나를 고릅시다.
여: 난 같은 가격이라면 점심 식사가 포함된 관광이 좋아요.
남: 당신 말이 맞아요. 우리는 식당을 찾으러 시간을 보낼 필요가 없을 거예요. 이걸로 합시다.
여: 좋아요. 내가 전화해서 예약할게요.

어휘 be tired of v-ing v하는 데 싫증이 나다   brochure 책자   reserve 예약하다
historic site 유적지 cathedral 대성당 palace 궁전, 왕실 outdoor 야외에서

11 짧은 대화에 이어질 응답   ③

✽ 치과의사가 환자에게 충치가 아주 심해져 몇 주에 걸쳐 치료해야 한다면서 괜찮겠냐고 묻고 있다. 이에 대한 응답으로는 ③ '음, 선택의 여지가 없는 것 같군요.'가 가장 적절하다.

① 죄송합니다만 고의는 아니었어요.
② 아니요, 그건 전적으로 선생님께 달려 있습니다.
④ 맞아요. 그게 바로 제가 생각하던 것입니다.
⑤ 좋습니다. 오늘 오후 1시 이후는 언제든 좋습니다.

W: Your cavity has gotten so bad. It looks pretty serious. You **should have come** earlier.
M: I've been so busy with work.
W: I won't be able to treat it in one visit. I'll have to **work on it** for several weeks. Is that okay with you?
M: **Well, I guess I have no choice.**

여: 충치가 아주 심해졌군요. 꽤 심각해 보입니다. 더 일찍 오셨어야 했어요.
남: 전 일이 너무 바빴어요.
여: 한 번 방문해서는 치료할 수 없을 거예요. 몇 주 동안 이것에 노력을 들여야겠어요. 괜찮으신가요?
남: 음, 선택의 여지가 없는 것 같군요.

어휘 cavity 충치; 구멍   serious 심각한; 진지한   treat 치료하다; 다루다   work on
～에 노력을 들이다[착수하다] | 선택지 어휘 | totally 전적으로, 완전히   exactly 바로, 꼭

12 짧은 대화에 이어질 응답   ③

✽ 여자가 기차표를 예매하려고 하는데 매표원이 원하는 시간에 페리를 타려면 적어도 30분 일찍 도착하는 기차를 타라고 조언하고 있다. 이에 대한 응답으로는 ③ '그건 몰랐네요. 알려주셔서 감사해요.'가 가장 적절하다.

① 저를 재촉하지 마세요. 생각할 시간이 필요해요.
② 시간을 잘 지킬 것을 약속해요. 걱정하실 필요가 없어요.
④ 기차로 거기에 갈 수 있어요. 여기 기차 시간표가 있어요.
⑤ 죄송합니다. 연착한 기차 때문에 페리를 놓쳤어요.

M: How can I help you?
W: I'd like an 8:30 a.m. train ticket to Green Harbor. I have to take the morning ferry, **which leaves** at 10 a.m. there.
M: Then I recommend the 8:00 a.m. train because you need to arrive at the harbor at least **30 minutes before** the ferry.
W: **I didn't know that. Thanks for the information.**

남: 무엇을 도와드릴까요?
여: Green 항구로 가는 오전 8시 30분 기차표를 원해요. 아침 페리를 타야 하는데, 거기서 아침 페리가 오전 10시에 떠나거든요.
남: 그렇다면 페리를 타기 전 적어도 30분 전에 항구에 도착해야 하므로 오전 8시 기차를 추천해 드립니다.
여: 그건 몰랐네요. 알려주셔서 감사해요.

어휘 harbor 항구, 항만   ferry 페리, 연락선   at least 적어도, 최소한
| 선택지 어휘 | rush 재촉하다; 서두르다   on time 시간을 어기지 않고; 정각에   schedule
시간표; 목록   delay 지연시키다; 연기하다

13 긴 대화에 이어질 응답   ③

✽ 대화의 전체 맥락 하에 마지막 말의 의미나 의도를 정확히 파악하는 것이 좋다. 친구 간의 대화로 추운 날씨에 하이킹을 갔다가 돌아가는 길에 커피숍을 발견한 상황이다. 여자가 들어가서 따뜻한 커피를 마시자고 제안하자 남자가 동의한다. 이에 대한 여자의 응답으로는 ③ '좋아. 추위를 좀 피하자.'가 가장 적절하다.

① 좋은 생각이야. 내일은 맑을 거야.
② 환상적이야! 벌써 크리스마스 같아.
④ 응. 난 하이킹을 좋아하지만 집에 있는 게 정말 좋아.
⑤ 알았어. 내 의자를 벽난로로 가져올게.

M: Are you all right, Ella?
W: Actually, no. It's really cold outside! The weatherman was wrong again.
M: Yes, they said the cold weather **was supposed to finish** yesterday.
W: They never get the weather right. If they said it would be cold like this, we wouldn't have gone hiking today.
M: You're right, and this strong wind is making it feel so much colder.
W: I feel like my toes are freezing.
M: We're nearly to the town. **Hang in there.**
W: Look! There is a coffee shop over there. Do you mind **if we go there**? We can have some warm coffee.
M: Sounds great. It seems that there is a fireplace inside.
W: **All right. Let's get out of the cold for a bit.**

남: 괜찮니, Ella?
여: 사실 괜찮지 않아. 밖이 너무 추워! 일기 예보관이 또 틀렸네.
남: 그래, 추운 날씨가 어제 끝날 거라고 말했지.
여: 그들은 결코 날씨를 정확하게 맞히지 않아. 이렇게 추울 거라고 했으면 우리는 오늘 하이킹을 오지 않았을 거야.
남: 맞아, 그리고 이 강한 바람이 훨씬 더 춥게 느껴지게 하고 있어.
여: 내 발가락이 어는 느낌이야.
남: 우리 마을에 거의 다 왔어. 힘내.
여: 봐! 저기 커피숍이 있어. 저기 가도 될까? 우리 따뜻한 커피를 마실 수 있어.
남: 좋은 생각이야. 안쪽에 벽난로가 있는 것 같아.
여: 좋아. 추위를 좀 피하자.

어휘 weatherman 일기 예보관   be supposed to-v v하기로 되어 있다   freeze 얼다;

얼리다 **hang in there** 힘내; 꿋꿋이 버티다[견디다] **fireplace** 벽난로

14 긴 대화에 이어질 응답 ②

✻ 대화의 전체 맥락 하에 마지막 말의 의미나 의도를 정확히 파악하는 것이 좋다. 본 대화는 잠을 잘 자지 못하는 여자에게 남자가 카페인을 피하고 잠자기 전 따뜻한 우유를 마시라고 조언한다. 이에 대해 여자가 정말로 효과가 있을 것 같은지 질문했을 때 남자의 응답으로는 해 볼 만하다는 내용의 ② '확실하지는 않지만 시도해 볼 만하다고 생각해.'가 가장 적절하다.

① 넌 너 자신을 더 잘 보살펴야 해.
③ 그게 나한테 기회를 주기 때문에 난 그걸 해.
④ 내 문제에 귀를 기울여줘서 정말 고마워.
⑤ 네가 건강해지고 싶다면 더 잘 먹어야 해.

M: Hi, Hannah. How's it going?
W: Hi, Carter. Not so good.
M: You look really tired. Are you sick?
W: No, I'm not getting much sleep these days.
M: Is something **bothering you**?
W: Not really. I don't really have a serious problem. I just can't get a good night's rest.
M: Hmm... Getting plenty of sleep is so important to our health.
W: I know. So **I started working out**, but it makes me even more tired.
M: Well, I suggest you avoid caffeine in the afternoon and evening. Instead, drink some warm milk before you go to bed.
W: Do you think **that will really work**?
M: I'm not sure, but I guess it's worth a try.

남: 안녕, Hannah. 어떻게 지내니?
여: 안녕, Carter. 그다지 좋지 않아.
남: 너 정말 피곤해 보인다. 아픈 거야?
여: 아니야. 요즘 잠을 충분히 못 자고 있어.
남: 신경 쓰이게 하는 게 있어?
여: 꼭 그런 건 아니야. 정말로 심각한 문제는 없어. 난 그냥 밤에 푹 쉬지 못하는 거야.
남: 음… 충분한 잠을 자는 건 건강에 아주 중요해.
여: 알아. 그래서 운동을 시작했지만 그게 날 훨씬 더 피곤하게 만들어.
남: 음, 오후와 저녁에 카페인을 피하는 걸 권해. 대신에 잠자기 전에 따뜻한 우유를 좀 마셔.
여: 그게 정말로 효과가 있을 것 같니?
남: 확실하지는 않지만 시도해 볼 만하다고 생각해.

어휘 **these days** 요즘에는 **bother** 신경 쓰이게 하다; 괴롭히다 **plenty** 충분한, 많은 **work out** 운동하다 | 선택지 어휘 | **worth** ~해 볼 만한, ~할 가치가 있는

15 상황에 적절한 말 ②

✻ 지시문을 통해 누가(A) 누구에게(B) 할 말인지를 우선 정확히 파악한다. 담화는 대개 A와 B에 대한 배경 설명과 B가 처한 문제 상황, 그리고 이에 대해 A가 어떤 말을 하려고 하는지에 대한 설명의 순서로 전개된다. Dominic(A)이 커다란 상자를 나르는 데 어려움을 겪고 있는 Green 부인(B)에게 상자를 나르는 일을 도와도 되겠냐고 먼저 물어보려는 상황이다. 이런 상황에서 적절한 말은 ② '제가 그 상자를 들어드려도 될까요?'이다.

① 제가 이 상자를 여기 놓아도 괜찮나요?
③ 그걸 혼자 하실 수 있는 게 확실한가요?
④ 괜찮으시다면 저를 차에 태워주실 수 있나요?
⑤ 그걸 도와달라고 누군가에게 요청하지 그러세요?

M: Dominic is a high school student. Today, he is on his way home from school. Since he knows almost **all of the neighbors** on his block, he greets everyone he meets as he's walking along. As he comes near his house, he sees Mrs. Green, **who lives next door** to him, walking out of her front door. She is carrying a big box from the house to her car in the driveway. Mrs. Green is an elderly woman at the age of 65, and she is having difficulty carrying the box. Dominic would like to help her to carry

the box. But he knows Mrs. Green is a very independent woman, so he wants to **ask her permission first**. In this situation, what would Dominic most likely say to Mrs. Green?

Dominic: Could I give you a hand with that box?

남: Dominic은 고등학생이다. 오늘 그는 학교에서 집으로 가는 중이다. 그가 자기 단지에 있는 거의 모든 이웃을 알기 때문에 그는 걸어가면서 만나는 모든 사람과 인사한다. 집 근처에 왔을 때 그는 옆집에 사는 Green 부인이 그녀의 집 앞문에서 걸어 나오는 것을 본다. 그녀는 집에서부터 차도에 있는 자기 차로 커다란 상자를 나르고 있다. Green 부인은 나이가 65세 된 노인이고 상자를 나르는 데 어려움을 겪고 있다. Dominic은 그녀가 상자를 나르는 것을 돕고 싶다. 하지만 그는 Green 부인이 매우 독립적인 여성인 걸 알아서 우선 그녀의 허락을 얻고자 한다. 이 상황에서 Dominic이 Green 부인에게 뭐라고 말하겠는가?

Dominic: 제가 그 상자를 들어드려도 될까요?

어휘 **on one's way** ~하는 중에; ~으로 가는 길에 **driveway** 차도, 진입로 **elderly** 연세가 드신 **have a difficulty (in) v-ing** v하는 데 어려움을 겪다 **independent** 독립적인, 자립심이 강한 **permission** 허락, 허가 | 선택지 어휘 | **give A a ride** A를 태워주다

16~17 세트 문항 16 ③ 17 ④

✻ 16 많은 사람들이 장르에 상관없이 다양한 노래로 기분을 북돋울 수 있고, 특정한 시간에 노래를 재생하면서 원하는 것에 성공하는 자신을 상상하면 노래가 힘과 행복의 기분을 준다고 하고 있다. 그러므로 담화의 주제로 ③ '기분을 북돋우기 위한 노래의 효용'임을 알 수 있다.

① 노래의 부정적 효과
② 다양한 종류의 최신 노래
④ 의사소통 수단으로서의 노래
⑤ 일상생활에서 노래의 중요성

✻ 17 해석 참조.

① 민요 ② 재즈 ③ 발라드 ④ 록 음악 ⑤ 힙합

M: What do you usually do when you feel down? Some people might eat delicious food, and others might go on a trip. But many people would agree that the easiest way to cheer up is **by listening to music**. The genre of music doesn't really matter. There are lots of great pop and folk songs that can touch you with beautiful stories. Jazz, ballads, and hip hop songs can also **boost your mood** with sweet rhymes and smooth rhythms. CD players, smartphones, and YouTube enable you to **surround yourself with** the particular kind of song that you like most. Make a list of the songs that you love most. **Play these songs** at a specific time, such as on your way to work or just when you want to be motivated. As you listen, imagine yourself succeeding in what is most important to you right now. You will find that songs automatically give you **a feeling of power** and well-being.

남: 여러분은 우울할 때, 보통 무엇을 하나요? 어떤 사람들은 맛있는 음식을 먹을지도 모르고, 다른 사람들은 여행을 떠날지도 모릅니다. 그러나 많은 사람들이 기운을 나게 하는 가장 쉬운 방법은 음악을 듣는 것이라는 데 동의할 것입니다. 음악의 장르는 사실 중요하지 않습니다. 아름다운 이야기로 여러분을 감동시킬 수 있는 많은 훌륭한 팝송과 ① 민요가 있습니다. ② 재즈, ③ 발라드, ⑤ 힙합 또한 감미로운 운과 부드러운 리듬으로 여러분의 기분을 북돋울 수 있습니다. CD 플레이어와 스마트폰과 유튜브가 여러분을 여러분이 가장 좋아하는 특정한 종류의 노래로 둘러싸이게 할 수 있습니다. 가장 좋아하는 노래의 목록을 만드십시오. 이런 노래들을 직장에 가는 길이나 단지 동기를 부여받고 싶을 때와 같은 특정한 시간에 재생하십시오. 노래를 들으면서 지금 당장 여러분에게 가장 중요한 것에서 성공하는 자신을 상상하십시오. 여러분은 노래가 자동으로 힘과 행복의 기분을 준다는 것을 발견할 것입니다.

어휘 **genre** 장르, 유형 **folk song** 민요 **touch** 감동시키다 **boost** 북돋우다 (시 등의) 운(韻); 운을 맞추다 **enable A to-v** A가 v할 수 있게 하다 **surround** 둘러싸다, 에워싸다 **motivate** 동기를 부여하다 **succeed** 성공하다 **automatically** 자동으로, 무의식적으로 | 선택지 어휘 | **various** 다양한, 여러 가지의 **means** 수단, 방법

09 회

01 화자가 하는 말의 목적　②

＊ 담화의 일부 내용이 아니라 중심 내용을 파악해야 한다. 본 담화는 더 깨끗한 물을 위해 오래된 수도관 교체 공사를 알리면서 공사 당일 단수가 될 것이므로 물을 충분히 저장해 놓을 것을 권하고 있다. 그러므로 담화의 목적은 ② '수도관 교체로 인한 단수를 공지하려고'이다.

M: The Westville Apartment Management Office would like to make an announcement to all Westville residents. We have good news for those of you who have complained about the yellow water that flows through our old water pipes. As you know, the pipes are nearly 40 years old. In order to provide you with cleaner water, we will **replace our old water pipes** with new ones. The construction will start from Apartment B. The water **will be shut off** on Apartment B most of the day on March 19th starting at 8 a.m. We apologize for the inconvenience but ask for your cooperation, as we will provide you with cleaner water. We suggest that you **store as much water as** you need before the construction. Please call 751-907-9589 for further questions.

남: Westville 아파트 관리소가 Westville 주민 모두에게 공지 말씀드립니다. 오래된 수도관을 통해서 흘러나오는 누런 물에 대해 불평하셨던 분들에게 좋은 소식입니다. 여러분도 아시다시피, 파이프는 거의 40년이 되었습니다. 여러분에게 더 깨끗한 물을 공급하기 위해서 오래된 수도관을 새것으로 교체할 것입니다. 공사는 아파트 B동부터 시작할 것입니다. 3월 19일 오전 8시부터 시작해서 거의 온종일 아파트 B동에서 단수가 될 것입니다. 불편을 끼쳐 죄송하지만 여러분에게 더 깨끗한 물을 공급할 것이므로 협조를 부탁드립니다. 공사 전에 필요한 만큼 충분한 물을 저장하실 것을 권합니다. 추가 질문이 있으시면 751-907-9589로 전화해 주십시오.

어휘　management office 관리소　announcement 공지; 발표 (내용)　resident 주민, 거주자; 투숙객　provide A with B A에게 B를 공급[제공]하다　replace 교체하다; 대체[대신]하다　construction 공사, 건설　shut off 차단하다　inconvenience 불편, 애로; 불편한[귀찮은] 것　cooperation 협조; 협력, 합동　suggest 권하다; 시사[암시]하다　store 저장[보관]하다; 백화점　further 추가의, 더 이상의

02 의견　③

＊ 우선 지시문에서 명시한 화자의 성별을 보고 어느 화자의 말에 주목할지를 판단해야 한다. 특히 의견이나 주장을 표현하는 어구(I think ~, You should ~ 등)가 이끄는 내용을 잘 들어야 한다. 페이스북을 시작하고 싶어 하는 아들에 관해 부부가 나누는 대화이다. 남자는 페이스북이 끼칠 영향을 걱정하면서 아이가 페이스북 사용에 많은 시간을 쓰는 것, 항상 감시가 어려워 해로울 수도 있다는 것을 지적하고 있다. 그러므로 남자의 의견으로는 ③이 적절하다.

W: Alex, Joshua really **wants to create** a Facebook account.
M: Really? I heard there is a Facebook age limit.
W: It's 13, and Joshua will be 13 years old next month. He said many of his friends have already opened Facebook accounts.
M: Well, that's not really a good reason to do something.
W: But at his age, doing something together is very important to make friends.
M: Maybe. But I'm worried about the effect Facebook will have. He will probably spend a lot of **time using it**.
W: You're right. He needs to play outdoors instead of spending time posting on his Facebook.
M: I think Facebook itself is okay, but it's hard for us to monitor him all the time. It could be **harmful for him**.
W: I understand. Why don't you talk to Joshua about it?
M: Yes, I will.

여: Alex, Joshua가 페이스북 계정을 무척 만들고 싶어 해요.

남: 정말이요? 페이스북에 연령 제한이 있다고 들었는데요.

여: 13세인데 Joshua는 다음 달에 13세가 돼요. 그 애가 말하길 자기 친구 중 많은 수가 이미 페이스북 계정을 열었다고 해요.

남: 음, 그건 정말로 뭔가를 하는 좋은 이유가 되지 않아요.

여: 하지만 그 애의 나이에서는 함께 뭔가를 한다는 건 친구를 사귀는 데 아주 중요해요.

남: 그럴 수도 있죠. 하지만 난 페이스북이 끼칠 영향을 걱정하는 거예요. 그 애는 아마 그걸 사용하는 데 많은 시간을 쓸 거예요.

여: 맞아요. 그 애가 자기 페이스북에 게시하는 데 시간을 보내는 대신에 밖에서 노는 게 필요하죠.

남: 난 페이스북 자체는 괜찮다고 생각하지만 우리가 그 애를 항상 감시하기가 어렵잖아요. 그건 아이에게 해로울 수 있어요.

여: 이해해요. 당신이 그것에 관해 Joshua와 이야기해보는 건 어때요?

남: 그래요, 그럴게요.

어휘　account 계정; 계좌; (회계) 장부　probably 아마　post 게시[공고]하다; 우편(물)　monitor 감시[관리]하다; 모니터하다　harmful 해로운, 유해한

03 관계　④

＊ 직업을 나타내거나 추론할 수 있는 힌트가 대화 전반에 걸쳐 드러나므로, 대화를 전체적으로 이해하는 것이 필요하다. 본 대화에서 여자는 문제를 맞혀야 하고 우승하면 10,000달러의 상금을 받게 되며 남자는 진행을 하면서 문제를 내고 있다. 그러므로 두 사람의 관계는 ④ '퀴즈쇼 진행자 – 출전자'임을 알 수 있다.

M: Great, Rebecca! You've just entered our bonus round. How do you feel?
W: Thank you. I'm so nervous.
M: Who did you come here with?
W: My husband and my two children. They're over there.
M: Let's say hello to Rebecca's family! Now you're **trying to win** the $10,000 cash prize. If you win, what will you do with all that money?
W: I really don't know at this moment.
M: All right. When the buzzer goes off, you must **give your answer** within 5 seconds. Are you ready?
W: Yes, I'm ready.
M: Gandhi was often called "Mahatma" by the Indian people. What does **this word mean**?
W: *[buzz]* That means "Great Soul."
M: You are correct!

남: 훌륭합니다. Rebecca! 보너스 라운드에 막 들어섰습니다. 기분이 어떠세요?

여: 고맙습니다. 너무 떨려요.

남: 누구와 함께 여기 왔나요?

여: 제 남편과 두 아이들이요. 저기 있어요.

남: Rebecca의 가족에게 안녕이라고 인사합시다! 이제 당신은 10,000달러의 상금을 받으려고 도전하고 있습니다. 획득하면 그 돈으로 다 뭘 할 건가요?

여: 지금은 정말 모르겠어요.

남: 좋습니다. 버저가 울리면 5초 이내에 답을 해야 합니다. 준비되었나요?

여: 네, 준비되었습니다.

남: 간디는 인도 사람들에게 종종 '마하트마'라고 불렸습니다. 이 단어의 뜻은 무엇일까요?

여: *[버저를 울리다]* 그 뜻은 '위대한 영혼'입니다.

남: 맞았습니다!

어휘　go off (경보 등이) 울리다; 자리를 뜨다; 발사[폭발]하다; (불, 전기 등이) 나가다　within ~이내에[안에]

04 그림 불일치　④

＊ 대화가 나오기 전에 각 사물의 위치 관계와 외형(형태나 무늬, 개수 등)의 특징을 미리

확인하는 것이 좋다. 여자는 캡틴 아메리카 코스튬을 입은 남자의 마스크에 B가 프린트되어 있어 이상하다고 말하지만 그림에서는 A가 프린트되어 있으므로 ④는 대화의 내용과 일치하지 않는다.

M: Do you want to see pictures of me in a costume? Here, look at this picture.
W: Oh, you took it at Comic Con. There is a big monitor **on the wall** behind you guys.
M: Yes, it showed an animated UFO. We took this picture in front of an animation booth.
W: Yeah, there is a signboard standing on the left. I like this comic character, one of the Ghostbusters.
M: I like him, too. Can you guess who I am?
W: Hmm, are you the one who is wearing a black mask and has a long sword in his hand?
M: No, that's not me. I'm the one **holding a shield** with a big star in the center.
W: Wow, you're Captain America! But it's a bit strange. Why did you print the letter B on your mask? Shouldn't it be the letter A?
M: **I printed the B** because my name is Brandon, which begins with B. And the man on the right is my friend, Sean.
W: He is holding **a big hammer**. He must be Thor! You guys had a lot of fun!
M: Absolutely! It was a great experience.

남: 코스튬을 입은 내 사진을 볼래? 여기, 이 사진을 봐.
여: 오, 너 코믹 콘에서 이걸 찍었네. 너희들 뒤쪽의 벽에 커다란 모니터가 있구나.
남: 응. 그게 만화영화로 만들어진 UFO를 보여주었어. 우리는 만화영화 부스 앞에서 이 사진을 찍었지.
여: 그래. 왼쪽에 서 있는 간판이 있네. 난 고스트버스터즈 중 하나인 이 만화 캐릭터가 좋아.
남: 나도 그것을 좋아해. 너 내가 누군지 알아맞힐 수 있니?
여: 음, 검은 마스크를 쓰고 손에 긴 검을 든 사람이니?
남: 아니. 그건 내가 아니야. 난 가운데 커다란 별이 있는 방패를 들고 있는 사람이야.
여: 와, 너 캡틴 아메리카구나! 하지만 좀 이상해. 왜 네 마스크에 문자 B를 프린트한 거야? 그거 문자 A여야 하지 않니?
남: 내 이름이 Brandon인데, 그게 B로 시작되기 때문에 내가 B를 프린트했어. 그리고 오른쪽에 있는 남자는 내 친구 Sean이야.
여: 그는 커다란 망치를 들고 있네. 그는 분명히 토르겠구나! 너희들 무척 재미있었겠어!
남: 그럼! 굉장한 경험이었어.

어휘 animate 만화영화로 만들다: 생기를 불어넣다 cf. animation 만화영화: 생기, 활기 signboard 간판 sword 검, 칼 shield 방패: 보호하다, 가리다 absolutely 그럼, 물론이지: 전적으로, 틀림없이

05 부탁한 일 ②

☀ 부탁하는 사람이 어떤 상황에 처해 있는지와 부탁하는 사람과 그 일을 하는 사람이 누구인지 정확히 구분하여 부탁하는 사람의 말에 집중해야 한다. 본 대화에서는 남자가 내일 수업에 필요한 책을 찾으러 서점에 가야 하는데 스마트폰이 물에 빠져 급하게 수리하러 가야 하는 상황이다. 남자가 여자에게 자기를 위해 책을 찾아올 수 있는지 묻고 있으므로 남자가 부탁하는 일은 ② '서점에서 책 찾아오기'이다.

[Telephone rings.]
M: Hello, is Carrie there?
W: Yes, this is she speaking. **Who's calling**, please?
M: It's me, Carlos. Do you have plans to go downtown today by any chance?
W: Actually, I'm already in the downtown area to meet some friends. Do you want to join us?
M: Thanks, but I can't. I just dropped my smartphone in some water so I **should go** to the service center now.
W: Sorry to hear that. That's why you didn't call with your phone.
M: Yes. The problem is that I have to pick up a book I ordered for my history class at the Stanley Bookstore. But I don't have enough time.
W: Oh, the one near Union Plaza?
M: Yes, so I was wondering **if you could** pick it up for me. I really need that book for tomorrow's class.
W: Okay. **I'll pick it up** and stop by your place on the way home.

M: Thanks a million.

[전화벨이 울린다.]
남: 여보세요, 거기 Carrie 있나요?
여: 네, 접니다. 전화 거신 분은 누구신가요?
남: 나야, Carlos. 혹시 오늘 시내에 갈 계획이 있니?
여: 사실 난 벌써 친구를 만나려고 시내에 있어. 우리와 함께하기를 바라니?
남: 고마워, 하지만 못 해. 난 방금 물에 스마트폰을 떨어뜨려서 지금 서비스 센터에 가야 해.
여: 그거 유감이구나. 그래서 네가 네 전화로 전화하지 않았구나.
남: 응. 문제는 내가 Stanley 서점에서 역사 수업을 위해 주문한 책을 찾아와야 한다는 거야. 하지만 난 시간이 충분치 않아.
여: 아, Union 광장 근처에 있는 거지?
남: 응. 그래서 네가 나를 위해 그걸 찾아올 수 있는지 물어보려고. 난 내일 수업을 위해 그 책이 정말로 필요하거든.
여: 좋아. 내가 책을 찾아서 집에 가는 길에 네 집에 들를게.
남: 정말 고마워.

어휘 downtown 시내에[로] by any chance 혹시 pick up 찾아오다 order 주문하다: 명령[지시]하다 stop by (~에) (잠시) 들르다 | 선택지 어휘 | repair 수리, 보수, 수선 check out (도서관 등에서) 대출하다 appointment 약속: 임명, 지명

06 금액 ②

☀ 여러 개의 수치 정보가 등장하므로 필요한 정보를 메모하면서 듣는 것이 좋다. 남자는 왕복 항공권으로 450달러를 지불했고 호스텔은 1박에 45달러인 곳에서 10박을 했으므로 450달러를 썼으므로 합쳐서 남자가 항공권과 숙박비로 쓴 금액은 900달러이다. 1박에 65달러인 1인용 침실은 여자에게 정보로 주기 위해 이야기한 것이므로 오해하지 않도록 유의한다.

W: Julian, I heard you recently traveled to New York.
M: Yes, it was just great. **Have you ever been** there?
W: No, but I'm planning to visit there next month. How much did you pay for your flights and hotel?
M: Well, I spent $450 for **round-trip tickets**.
W: Oh, it's quite cheap. Where did you stay?
M: I stayed at the Chelsea Hostel **for 10 nights**, and that was **$45 a night**. It's clean and located in one of the safest neighborhoods in New York.
W: Sounds great. Did you have your own room?
M: No, it was a dormitory room. If you want a single room, you have to pay $65 a night.
W: I don't mind dormitories. If I save some money on hotels, I can watch a Broadway musical.
M: Good idea. But there is no elevator in the hostel, so you should ask for a room **on a lower floor**.
W: That's good to know. Thanks for the information.

여: Julian, 최근에 네가 뉴욕을 여행했다고 들었어.
남: 응. 정말 굉장했어. 너 거기 가본 적 있니?
여: 아니, 하지만 다음 달에 거기 가려고 계획 중이야. 항공권과 호텔에 얼마나 지불했니?
남: 음, 왕복 티켓에 450달러를 썼어.
여: 아, 그거 꽤 싸다. 어디에서 묵었니?
남: 난 Chelsea 호스텔에서 10박을 했는데 1박에 45달러였어. 거기는 깨끗하고 뉴욕에서 가장 안전한 동네 중 한 곳에 위치해 있어.
여: 좋은 것 같다. 너 혼자 쓰는 방이었니?
남: 아니야. 공동침실 방이었어. 네가 1인용 침실을 원한다면 1박에 65달러는 내야 해.
여: 난 공동침실은 괜찮아. 호텔에서 돈을 절약할 수 있다면 브로드웨이 뮤지컬을 볼 수 있을 거야.
남: 좋은 생각이야. 하지만 호스텔에 엘리베이터가 없으니까 낮은 층 방을 요청해야 해.
여: 그거 알게 되어 좋다. 알려줘서 고마워.

어휘 flight 항공편, 항공기: 여행, 비행 round-trip 왕복 여행: 왕복의 locate 위치하다: 위치를 찾아내다 neighborhood 동네: 근처, 이웃 dormitory 공동침실: 기숙사 floor 층: 바닥

07 이유   ④

✻ 지시문을 통해 남자가 여름방학에 집에 돌아가지 않는 상황이며 남자의 말에 단서가 있을 가능성이 큼을 미리 파악한다. 대학 박물관에서 일하는 것은 여자이고 남자가 집에 돌아가지 않는 이유는 수학과 물리학에서 나쁜 성적을 받아 여름학기를 듣기 위해서이므로 답은 ④ '성적이 나빠 여름학기를 신청해서'이다.

W: Chris! Why haven't you gone home yet?
M: I'm not going home this summer. What about you?
W: I've got **a part-time job** at the University Museum until next week. So, I'll leave next Saturday. But what's going on with you?
M: Well, something happened.
W: What is it? Is it because of summer training for the school's football team?
M: No. I quit the team two months ago. It's nothing **to do with that**.
W: Hmm... Are your parents going on an overseas trip?
M: No. Well, it's **because of my grades**. I got two D's in math and physics.
W: I can't believe it! You always get good grades. What happened?
M: I've been lazy about studying these days. So I decided to **take summer school** to focus on my studying.
W: I understand. But your parents are going to miss you.
M: I miss them, too. But I have no choice.

여: Chris! 너 왜 아직 집에 가지 않니?
남: 이번 여름엔 집에 가지 않아. 넌 어때?
여: 난 다음 주까지 대학 박물관에서 아르바이트를 해. 그래서 다음 토요일에 떠날 거야. 하지만 넌 무슨 일이니?
남: 음. 뭔가 일이 생겼어.
여: 뭔데? 학교 축구팀의 여름 훈련 때문이니?
남: 아니야. 난 두 달 전에 그 팀을 그만두었어. 그거하고는 아무 관련이 없어.
여: 음... 부모님이 해외여행을 가시는 거야?
남: 아니야. 저, 내 성적 때문이야. 난 수학하고 물리학에서 D를 받았어.
여: 믿을 수가 없어! 넌 항상 좋은 성적을 받잖아. 무슨 일이야?
남: 요즘 공부하는 데 게을렀어. 그래서 공부에 집중하기 위해 여름학기를 듣기로 결정했어.
여: 알겠어. 하지만 네 부모님이 널 그리워하실 텐데.
남: 나도 그리워. 하지만 선택의 여지가 없어.

어휘   quit 그만두다; 떠나다; 중지하다   be[have] nothing to do with ~와 아무 관련이 없다   overseas 해외[외국/국외]의   physics 물리학   focus on ~에 집중하다

08 언급하지 않은 것   ④

✻ 대화의 진행은 대개 선택지와 같은 순서이므로, 선택지를 보면서 언급된 내용을 소거하는 식으로 푸는 것이 좋다. 온라인으로 참가비를 지불하는 것에 대해서는 이야기했지만 참가 신청 방법에 대해서는 언급하지 않았으므로 답은 ④이다.

[Telephone rings.]
W: Hello, this is the Junior Chef Academy. How can I help you?
M: **I'm calling about** your Junior Cooking Competition held on November 11. I'd like to ask a few questions about it.
W: Sure. What do you want to know?
M: Is there an age limit **to participate in** the competition?
W: Yes, the age limit will range from 8 to 17.
M: Okay. And I'd like to know the entry fee.
W: It's $50. You can pay it online.
M: I see. Can my friends and family **attend and watch** the competition?
W: Yes, of course! There are 500 **seats for family**, and their admission is free.
M: Sounds good. Thank you.
W: My pleasure. You can find further information on our website.

[전화벨이 울린다.]
여: 여보세요, Junior 셰프 아카데미입니다. 무엇을 도와드릴까요?
남: 11월 11일(① 대회 개최 일자)에 열리는 Junior 요리 대회에 관해서 전화했습니다. 그것에 관해 몇 가지 질문을 하고 싶어서요.
여: 네. 무엇을 알고 싶으신가요?

남: 대회에 참가하는 데 연령 제한이 있나요?
여: 네. 연령 제한은 8세부터 17세까지(② 참가 가능 연령)일 것입니다.
남: 알겠습니다. 그리고 참가비에 대해 알고 싶어요.
여: 50달러(③ 대회 참가비)입니다. 온라인으로 지불하실 수 있습니다.
남: 알겠어요. 제 친구들과 가족이 대회에 동행해서 관람할 수 있습니까?
여: 네, 물론이죠(⑤ 가족 참관 가능 여부)! 가족을 위한 500석이 있고 가족 입장은 무료입니다.
남: 그거 좋군요. 고맙습니다.
여: 천만에요. 우리 웹사이트에서 추가 정보를 찾으실 수 있습니다.

어휘   competition 대회, 시합; 경쟁   participate in ~에 참가[참여]하다   range from A to B (범위가) A에서 B 사이이다   entry fee 참가비; 입장료   attend 동행[동반]하다; 참석[출석]하다   admission 입장(료); 가입; 입학

09 내용 불일치   ③

✻ 담화의 진행은 대개 선택지와 같은 순서이므로, 선택지를 보면서 일치하는 내용을 소거하는 식으로 푸는 것이 좋다. 입장권은 5달러인데 UMC 학생의 경우 무료라고 했으므로 ③은 내용과 일치하지 않는다.

W: Attention, students! You are all invited to our **9th Annual Culture Night**. Culture Night is the biggest event on campus. Last year we hosted more than 1,400 students and community members. It'll be **held on Saturday**, April 21st from 5 p.m. to 9 p.m. This event is also open to the public. Admission tickets are $5, but **it's free for** UMC students. You can taste a variety of free foreign food and learn about cultures and traditions at multiple student exhibits. From 7 o'clock, there will be cultural performances and **a fashion show** of traditional costumes from around the world. We also need volunteers to help with setting up, decorating, and serving and organizing food. To volunteer, please register online through our Facebook.

여: 주목하십시오, 학생 여러분! ① 제9회 연례 문화의 밤에 여러분 모두를 초대합니다. 문화의 밤은 캠퍼스에서 가장 큰 행사입니다. 작년에 우리는 1,400명 이상의 학생과 지역 구성원을 손님으로 맞이했습니다. ② 4월 21일 토요일에 오후 5시부터 9시까지 열릴 것입니다. 이 행사는 일반인도 참석할 수 있습니다. ③ 입장권은 5달러이지만 UMC 학생은 무료입니다. 여러분은 여러 가지의 무료 외국 음식을 맛볼 수 있고 다양한 학생 전시회에서 문화와 전통에 대해 배울 수 있습니다. ④ 7시 정각부터 문화 행사와 전 세계의 전통 의상 패션쇼가 있을 겁니다. 우리는 또한 무대 설치, 장식과 음식을 차려내고 준비하는 것을 도울 자원봉사자를 필요로 합니다. ⑤ 자원봉사를 하려면 우리 페이스북을 통해 온라인으로 등록하십시오.

어휘   annual 연례의, 매년의   host (손님을) 접대하다; 주최하다; 주인   community 지역 사회; 공동체 사회   hold 개최하다; 쥐다   public 일반 사람들, 대중   a variety of 여러 가지의, 다양한   multiple 다양한; 다수[복수]의   set up 설치하다; 세우다   organize 준비하다; 조직하다; 정리하다   register 등록[기재]하다; 신고하다

10 도표 이해   ④

✻ 대화의 진행은 대개 도표 항목의 나열 순서대로 진행된다. 대화를 들으면서 도표의 각 항목 중 선택되지 않은 것을 소거하는 식으로 푸는 것이 좋다. 우선 서랍이 있는 것을 선택했으므로 ⑤는 제외되고 프레임은 나무로 된 것으로 결정했으므로 ① 역시 제외된다. 100달러 이하를 원했으므로 ③이 제외되고 남은 ②와 ④중에서 밝은색의 책상을 사겠다고 했으므로 두 사람이 구매할 책상은 ④이다.

W: David, Ashley is starting elementary school this year, so we need to get a desk for her.
M: Yes, I know. Let's order it online since they offer the best prices.
W: Okay. Let's do it now.
M: Do you think she needs **a desk with drawers**?
W: Absolutely. She needs drawers to store and organize her stuff.
M: Okay. What sort of frame will be good for her? I think metal frames are strong.
W: I don't think Ashley would like it. She is a young girl. A desk with a metal frame looks like office furniture.

M: You're right. Then we'll choose **a wooden frame**. Now we have these three options. I don't want to **spend over** $100.

W: I agree with you. And dark colors won't match with her room's atmosphere. **Light colors are better**.

M: Got it. Then let's get this one.

여: David, Ashley가 올해 초등학교에 입학하니까 그 애를 위해서 책상을 사야 할 필요가 있어요.

남: 네, 알아요. 온라인이 가장 좋은 가격을 제공하니 거기에서 주문합시다.

여: 좋아요. 지금 해요.

남: Ashley에게 서랍이 있는 책상이 필요하다고 생각해요?

여: 그렇고말고요. 물건들을 보관하고 정리하는 데 서랍이 필요해요.

남: 알았어요. 어떤 종류의 프레임이 그 애에게 좋을까요? 난 금속 프레임이 튼튼하다고 생각해요.

여: Ashely가 그걸 좋아하지 않을 것 같아요. 어린 소녀잖아요. 금속 프레임이 있는 책상은 사무실 가구 같아 보여요.

남: 당신 말이 맞아요. 그러면 나무로 된 프레임을 선택하도록 하죠. 이제 이 세 가지 옵션이 있어요. 난 100달러가 넘게 쓰고 싶지 않아요.

여: 동의해요. 그리고 어두운색은 그 애 방의 분위기와 어울리지 않을 거예요. 밝은색이 더 좋아요.

남: 알았어요. 그러면 이걸로 삽시다.

어휘 offer 제공하다: 제의, 제안 drawer 서랍 stuff 물건, 것(들) sort 종류, 유형 frame (가구 · 건물 등의) 프레임[뼈대] furniture 가구 atmosphere 분위기, 기운: (지구의) 대기

11 짧은 대화에 이어질 응답 ③

※ 아내가 아기를 가졌다고 좋아하는 남자에게 여자가 축하 인사를 건넸다. 이에 대한 응답으로는 감사를 표하고 기분이 좋아 소식을 함께 나누고 싶었다는 내용의 ③ '고마워요. 그냥 좋은 소식을 공유해야 했어요.'가 적절하다.

① 와, 아기가 막 걷기 시작했어요.
② 그럼요. 그건 내가 얼마나 열심히 일하느냐에 달렸어요.
④ 너무 절 칭찬하지 마세요. 그 말을 들으니 얼굴이 붉어져요.
⑤ 맞아요. 그녀는 다른 사람의 감정에 예민해요.

W: You look happy, Andrew. What's new?
M: Maria is going to have a baby! I can't believe we're going to **have a baby**!
W: Oh my, that's great news! Congratulations. I'm really happy for you two.
M: Thanks. I just had to share the good news.

여: 행복해 보이네요, Andrew. 잘 지내요?
남: Maria가 아기를 가졌어요! 우리가 아기를 갖다니 믿을 수가 없어요!
여: 어머, 굉장한 소식이네요! 축하해요. 두 사람 덕분에 정말 기뻐요.
남: 고마워요. 그냥 좋은 소식을 공유해야 했어요.

어휘 | 선택지 어휘 | certainly 그럼요, 물론이지요: 틀림없이, 분명히 flatter 칭찬하다: 추켜세우다: 아첨하다 blush 얼굴을 붉히다: 얼굴이 빨개지다 sensitive 예민한, 민감한: 세심한

12 짧은 대화에 이어질 응답 ④

※ 남자가 극장에서 좌석을 뒤쪽으로 옮기고 싶고 이것이 가능한지 묻고 있다. 이에 대해 극장 직원인 여자가 할 말로는 가능하다거나 안 된다는 내용이 나와야 할 것이다. 그러므로 여자의 응답으로는 ④ '영화가 시작한 후에 빈 좌석으로 옮기실 수 있습니다.'가 가장 적절하다.

① 저하고 좌석을 바꾸실 수 있는지 궁금해요.
② 좌석을 발로 찬 것을 사과드리고 싶어요.
③ 이리로 오시면 제가 안내해드리겠습니다.
⑤ 극장 안으로 어떤 음료든 들여올 수 없습니다.

M: Excuse me, I'd like to **move to a seat** in the back since it's better to see a movie from farther away.
W: What's your seat number?
M: It's 11E. Is that **possible to arrange**?

W: You can move to a vacant seat after the movie begins.

남: 실례합니다. 영화를 더 멀리 떨어져 보는 게 더 좋기 때문에 뒤쪽에 있는 좌석으로 옮기고 싶은데요.
여: 좌석 번호가 뭔가요?
남: 11E예요. 조정하는 게 가능한가요?
여: 영화가 시작한 후에 빈 좌석으로 옮기실 수 있습니다.

어휘 arrange 조정하다: 정리[정돈]하다 | 선택지 어휘 | vacant 빈: 공석의 allow 허락하다: 가능하게 하다

13 긴 대화에 이어질 응답 ④

※ 대화의 전체 맥락 하에 마지막 말의 의미나 의도를 정확히 파악하는 것이 좋다. 교수님께 보고서를 제날짜에 제출하지 못하는 상황에서 여자가 걱정하고 있고, 남자는 미리 보고서를 제출하라고 조언하고 있다. 이에 대한 응답으로는 ④ '네 말이 맞아! 교수님께 내가 그걸 일찍 제출할 수 있는지 여쭤볼게.'가 가장 적절하다.

① 미안해. 난 지금 당장 그걸 할 시간이 없어.
② 지금 그걸 알았어. 너한테 먼저 물어봤어야 했는데.
③ 정말 안심이다! 그분이 내게 며칠 더 연장을 해주셨어.
⑤ 서둘러! 아니면 넌 보고서를 제시간에 끝낼 수 없을 거야.

M: Stephanie, how's it going?
W: Oh, I'm okay. How about you?
M: Very good. It's Friday! But you look worried.
W: Yes, I'm worried about my paper for Professor O'Hara's sociology class.
M: What's the problem? We have plenty of time left before the deadline.
W: Yes, the paper is **due next Friday**, but I'm leaving next Wednesday to go to Santa Barbara and coming back on Saturday. My cousin is getting married there.
M: Did you tell Professor O'Hara about it?
W: Yes, but he said I should **turn it in** on Friday.
M: Then why don't you turn in your paper **before you leave**? I think it'll be fine.
W: You're right! I'll ask him if I can submit it early.

남: Stephanie, 어떻게 지내니?
여: 아, 괜찮아. 넌 어때?
남: 아주 좋아. 금요일이잖아! 하지만 넌 걱정스러워 보이는데.
여: 응, O'Hara 교수님의 사회학 수업에 낼 보고서가 걱정스러워.
남: 뭐가 문제인데? 우리는 마감 전에 충분한 시간이 남아 있잖아.
여: 응, 보고서가 다음 금요일까지이지만 난 다음 주 수요일에 Santa Barbara로 떠나서 토요일에 돌아와. 사촌이 거기서 결혼을 하거든.
남: 그것에 관해 O'Hara 교수님께 말씀드렸니?
여: 응, 하지만 교수님께서는 내가 금요일에 그걸 제출해야 한다고 하셨어.
남: 그러면 떠나기 전에 네 보고서를 제출하지 그러니? 그건 괜찮을 것 같은데.
여: 네 말이 맞아. 교수님께 내가 그걸 일찍 제출할 수 있는지 여쭤볼게.

어휘 professor 교수 sociology 사회학 plenty of 충분한: 풍부한 deadline 마감 시간[일자], 기한 due ~하기로 되어있는, 예정된 turn A in A를 제출하다 | 선택지 어휘 | relief 안심, 안도, 완화, 경감 extension (기간의) 연장: 확대 submit 제출하다: 항복[굴복]하다 on time 제시간에

14 긴 대화에 이어질 응답 ③

※ 대화의 전체 맥락 하에 마지막 말의 의미나 의도를 정확히 파악하는 것이 좋다. 아동 노동 반대 캠페인을 하는 친구를 만나 아동 노동에 대해 알게 된 남자가 기부하겠다고 하자 여자가 기부 양식 서류를 주며 감사를 표한다. 이에 대한 남자의 응답으로는 돕게 되어 기쁘다는 내용의 ③ '어떤 식으로든 내가 도울 수 있다는 걸 알게 되어 기뻐.'가 적절하다.

① 우리는 네 기부를 유효하게 이용할 거야.
② 우리가 그들을 어렵게 만들까 걱정스러워.
④ 넌 이 양식을 가져가서 빈칸에 기재해야 해.
⑤ 네 관심 때문에 이 아이들을 구할 수 있어.

W: Hi, Jacob.
M: Oh, Vivien. What are you doing here? A campaign **against child labor**?
W: Yes, more than 200 million children between 5 and 17 are employed.
M: Really? That's a lot! That doesn't include house chores or part time jobs, does it?
W: No. Listen, you might have an after-school job, or maybe you help out with chores around the house. That's not child labor.
M: Oh, I see. Then it's much more serious.
W: Yes. They can't go to school, and many are **put in danger**. Every year a lot of children die from accidents related to their work.
M: That's awful. I didn't know that.
W: This pamphlet will tell you more about child labor.
M: Can I offer **you a donation** of some kind?
W: Sure. Please fill out this form to make a donation. I'd really appreciate it.
M: I'm glad to know that I can help in some way.

여: 안녕, Jacob.
남: 아, Vivien. 너 여기서 뭐하니? 아동 노동에 반대하는 캠페인?
여: 응. 5세부터 17세 사이의 2억 명 이상의 아동들이 고용되어 있어.
남: 정말이야? 그거 많은데! 그게 집안일이나 아르바이트를 포함하는 건 아니지, 그렇지?
여: 아니야. 들어봐. 너는 학교가 끝난 후에 일할 수도 있고 집에서 집안일을 도울 수도 있어. 그건 아동 노동이 아니야.
남: 아, 알았어. 그러면 그건 훨씬 더 심각한 거지.
여: 응. 그들은 학교에 갈 수 없고 많은 아이들이 위험에 처해 있어. 매년 수많은 아이들이 그들이 하는 일과 관련된 사고로 사망해.
남: 그거 끔찍하다. 난 몰랐어.
여: 이 팸플릿이 네게 아동 노동에 대해 더 많이 알려줄 거야.
남: 내가 일종의 기부를 제공할 수 있니?
여: 그럼. 기부하겠다는 이 양식을 기재해 줘. 정말 고마워.
남: 어떤 식으로든 내가 도울 수 있다는 걸 알게 되어 기뻐.

어휘 **labor** 노동, 근로 **include** 포함하다 **chore** 일; 허드렛일 **accident** 사고, 재해; 우연 **related to A** A와 관련된[관련이 있는] **awful** 끔찍한, 지독한; 엄청 **donation** 기부, 기증 *cf.* **make a donation** 기부[기증]하다 **fill out** (서류 등을) 기재[작성]하다 **appreciate** 고마워하다; 이해하다; 진가를 인정하다
| 선택지 어휘 | **put A to good use** A를 유효하게 이용하다 **blank** 빈칸, 여백; 빈

15 상황에 적절한 말 ⑤

＊ 지시문을 통해 누가(A) 누구에게(B) 할 말인지를 우선 정확히 파악한다. 담화는 대개 A와 B에 대한 배경 설명과 B가 처한 문제 상황, 그리고 이에 대해 A가 어떤 말을 하려고 하는지에 대한 설명의 순서로 전개된다. 일이 안 풀리는 날에 우울해하는 동료 Olivia(B)에게 Daniel(A)이 할 수 있는 위로의 말로는 ⑤ '네 기분이 어떤지 알아. 그 일로 우울해하지 마.'가 적절하다.

① 신경 쓰지 마. 넌 언제나 그걸 다시 시도할 수 있어.
② 미안해. 난 그것에 관해 다른 어떤 것도 할 수 없어.
③ 확실히는 모르겠어. 하지만 그건 네 잘못이야.
④ 잘 되었다. 넌 실수로부터 배울 수 있어.

W: Olivia and Daniel are co-workers. Today, Olivia is late to work, and their boss is angry with her because there is an important meeting in the morning. Olivia looks sad, so Daniel gives her a cup of coffee with warm words. Olivia tells him that she is having **a really bad day** today. She says that her car stopped in the middle of the street. And then she had to have it taken to a repair shop. **To make matters worse**, when she tried to call the office, she dropped her cell phone and broke the screen. And her boss never listened to why she was late and got angry with her. She is very depressed. Daniel wants to **comfort her**. In this situation, what would Daniel most likely say to Olivia?

Daniel: I know how you feel. Don't let it get you down.

여: Olivia와 Daniel은 직장 동료이다. 오늘 Olivia는 직장에 지각하고 그들의 상사는 아침에 중요한 회의가 있기 때문에 그녀에게 화가 나 있다. Olivia가 슬퍼 보여서 Daniel은 그녀에게 따뜻한 말과 함께 커피 한 잔을 건넨다. Olivia는 그에게 오늘이

자신에게 정말 일이 안 풀리는 날이라고 말한다. 그녀는 자신의 차가 길 가운데에서 멈췄다고 말한다. 그러고는 그녀는 차를 정비소까지 이동시켜야 했다. 엎친 데 덮친 격으로 그녀가 사무실로 전화를 걸려고 할 때 휴대폰을 떨어뜨려 스크린이 깨졌다. 그리고 상사는 그녀가 왜 늦었는지 이유를 전혀 듣지 않고 그녀에게 화를 냈다. 그녀는 아주 우울하다. Daniel은 그녀를 위로하고 싶다. 이 상황에서 Daniel이 Olivia에게 뭐라고 말하겠는가?

Daniel: 네 기분이 어떤지 알아. 그 일로 우울해하지 마.

어휘 **repair shop** 정비소 **to make matters worse** 엎친 데 덮친 격으로, 설상가상으로 **depressed** 우울한; 우울증을 앓는 **comfort** 위로[위안]하다; 안락, 편안
| 선택지 어휘 | **never mind** ~은 신경 쓰지 마라 **for sure** 확실히 **fault** 잘못, 책임; 단점 **get A down** A를 우울하게 만들다

16~17 세트 문항 16 ② 17 ③

＊ **16** 명상이 정신과 신체에 주는 긍정적 영향에 대해 예를 들어 이야기하며 명상을 할 것을 권하고 있다. 그러므로 담화의 주제는 ② '명상의 치유력'이다. 운동을 빗대어 명상의 역할을 설명했지만 둘을 비교하는 것은 아님에 유의한다.

① 초보자들을 위한 명상하는 법
③ 강력한 동기부여로서의 명상
④ 운동과 명상의 비교
⑤ 신체적 정신적 건강의 균형을 잡는 법

＊ **17** 해석 참조.
① 불면증 ② 우울증 ③ 폐암 ④ 보통 감기 ⑤ 심장병

M: Good morning, everyone. I'm Chris from the Johnsville Meditation Center. Are you looking for something better in life? Then meditation can help. Just as you can train your body through exercise, you can train your mind through meditation. Meditation **helps you build** the mental and emotional muscle you need to live a happier, more positive life. When you meditate, the mind becomes calm and relaxed. Several studies have shown that just 30 minutes of meditation daily **can improve symptoms** of anxiety, sleeplessness, or depression. On top of that, we now know that the mind has a direct impact on the body. You might have noticed that the health of some people gets worse when they are stressed out for a long time. Meditation helps in improving **overall health**. In fact, the practice of meditation for a period of time can even help cure the common cold, a severe headache, or heart disease. Now that you have meditation as **a natural healer** to all your big and small problems, why worry? Just meditate!

남: 안녕하세요, 여러분. 저는 Johnsville 명상 센터에서 온 Chris입니다. 삶에서 더 나은 무언가를 찾고 있습니까? 그러면 명상이 도와줄 수 있습니다. 여러분이 운동을 통해서 신체를 훈련할 수 있듯이 명상을 통해서 마음을 수련할 수 있습니다. 명상은 여러분이 더 행복하고 더 긍정적인 삶을 사는 데 필요한 정신적, 정서적 근육을 만드는 것을 도와줍니다. 여러분이 명상하면 마음은 고요해지고 편안해집니다. 몇몇 연구는 매일 단지 30분의 명상이 불안이나 ① 불면증, 혹은 ② 우울증의 증상을 개선할 수 있다는 것을 보여주었습니다. 무엇보다도, 우리는 이제 정신이 신체에 직접적인 영향을 준다는 걸 알고 있습니다. 여러분은 오랜 기간 스트레스를 받을 때 어떤 사람들의 건강이 나빠진다는 것을 알아챘을 것입니다. 명상은 전반적 건강을 개선하는 데 도움을 줍니다. 사실 일정 기간의 명상 수행은 심지어 ④ 보통 감기나 심한 두통이나 ⑤ 심장병을 치료하는 데 도움을 줄 수 있습니다. 여러분의 크고 작은 문제의 자연적 치유자로서 명상이 있는데 왜 걱정하십니까? 그저 명상하십시오!

어휘 **meditation** 명상; 숙고 *cf.* **meditate** 명상[숙고]하다 **emotional** 정서의, 감정의; 감정적인 **several** (몇)몇의; 각각[각자]의 **improve** 개선하다; 향상시키다 **symptom** 증상; 징후, 조짐 **anxiety** 불안(감); 걱정거리 **depression** 우울(증) **impact** 영향; 충돌 **notice** 알아채다; 인지하다; 주의하다 **overall** 전반적인; 전체의 **severe** 극심한; 가혹한
| 선택지 어휘 | **motivator** 동기를 부여하는 것[사람] **comparison** 비교, 대조; 비유

10 회

01 화자가 하는 말의 목적　　②

✳ 담화의 일부 내용이 아니라 중심 내용을 파악해야 한다. 10년이 되었고 동창생들이 참석했고 마지막에 08년도 졸업생의 동창회에 온 것을 환영하며 축하하자는 말을 하는 것으로 보아 담화의 목적은 ② '동창회 개최 환영사를 하려고'이다.

M: Good evening, ladies and gentlemen! I'm Timothy Whittier. Sorry for the delay. We are all so excited to meet each other, and we've been absorbed **in small talk**. I'm so glad to see all of you here. It already has been 10 years. This must be a very special and **meaningful evening** for all of us. And there are many more **who couldn't be here** today but wanted to. Among us who are here, we have classmates like Edward, who flew back all the way from Singapore. My classmate Jonathan gave me a card some 10 or 11 years ago with a little children's poem on it that goes: "There are big ships; There are small ships; But there is **no ship like friendship**." Welcome to the AAHS Class of '08, 10 year reunion! Let's celebrate!

남: 안녕하세요, 신사 숙녀 여러분! 저는 Timothy Whittier입니다. 지연되어서 죄송합니다. 우리는 모두 서로를 만나서 매우 신이 나 있고 수다에 빠져 있습니다. 여기서 여러분 모두를 보게 되어 무척 기쁩니다. 벌써 10년이 되었습니다. 이것은 우리 모두에게 분명히 아주 특별하고 의미 있는 저녁입니다. 그리고 오늘 여기 오지 못했지만 오고 싶어 하던 더 많은 이들이 있습니다. 여기 온 우리 중에서 Edward와 같은 동창생이 있는데, 그는 싱가포르에서부터 여기까지 날아왔습니다. 제 반 친구였던 Jonathan은 어린아이의 시가 적힌 카드를 약 10년이나 11년 전에 제게 주었는데 거기에는 '큰 배(big ship)가 있다; 작은 배(small ships)가 있다; 하지만 우정(friendships) 같은 배는 없다.'라고 적혀있습니다. AAHS 08년도 졸업생의 10주년 동창회에 오신 것을 환영합니다. 축하합시다!

어휘 be absorbed in ~에 몰두[열중]하다　small talk 수다; 잡담　meaningful 의미 있는, 중요한　reunion 동창회; 재결합

02 의견　　①

✳ 우선 지시문에서 명시한 화자의 성별을 보고 어느 화자의 말에 주목할지를 판단해야 한다. 특히 의견이나 주장을 표현하는 어구(I think ~, You should ~ 등)가 이끄는 내용을 잘 들어야 한다. 여자는 고래에 관한 다큐멘터리를 보고 고래 사냥이 금지되어야 한다고 말하고 있으므로 여자의 의견은 ①임을 알 수 있다.

W: Christian, have you ever seen that documentary about whales?
M: No, I haven't. Did you see it?
W: Yes, I saw it yesterday. It's a good documentary, but so sad.
M: I heard whales are **becoming endangered**.
W: Yeah, every year Japan, Norway, and Iceland kill around 1,500 whales.
M: Well, I saw an interview with a Japanese whale hunter. He said it's a cultural thing.
W: It's different. We **do not depend on** whale meat to live, as we have farm animals such as pigs and cows that provide plenty of food.
M: Oh, I agree. We certainly don't need to eat whale meat these days.
W: Actually, in Japan, whales are even **used in pet food**. About three million whales were killed in the 20th century alone.
M: That many? That's a lot more than I'd guessed.
W: Plus, whale hunting is really cruel. There is no kind way to kill a whale at sea. Many die a slow, painful death. **It should be banned**.
M: I should watch the documentary.

여: Christian, 고래에 관한 저 다큐멘터리를 본 적 있니?
남: 아니, 없어. 넌 봤어?
여: 응, 어제 봤어. 훌륭한 다큐멘터리인데 너무 슬퍼.
남: 고래가 멸종위기에 처해가고 있다고 들었어.
여: 응, 매년 일본과 노르웨이와 아이슬란드가 약 1,500마리의 고래를 죽인대.

남: 음, 난 일본 고래잡이 어부의 인터뷰를 봤어. 그가 말하기를 그건 문화적인 문제래.
여: 그건 달라. 우리는 충분한 식량을 제공하는 돼지와 소 같은 가축이 있기 때문에 생존하기 위해 고래 고기에 의존하는 건 아니야.
남: 아, 동의해. 요즘 우리가 분명히 고래 고기를 먹을 필요가 없지.
여: 사실, 일본에서는 고래가 심지어 애완동물 먹이로도 사용돼. 20세기에만 약 300만 마리의 고래가 죽임을 당했어.
남: 그렇게 많아? 그거 내가 추측했던 것보다 훨씬 더 많구나.
여: 게다가 고래 사냥은 정말로 잔인해. 바다에 있는 고래를 친절하게 죽일 방법이 없거든. 많은 수가 서서히 고통스럽게 죽어가. 그건 금지되어야 해.
남: 그 다큐멘터리를 봐야겠다.

어휘 endangered 멸종위기에 처한　cruel 잔인한, 잔혹한　painful 고통스러운, 아픈　ban (공식적으로) 금지(하다)

03 관계　　④

✳ 직업을 나타내거나 추론할 수 있는 힌트가 대화 전반에 걸쳐 드러나므로, 대화를 전체적으로 이해하는 것이 필요하다. 여자가 남자에게 주차장의 전구가 나간 것을 알려주며 고쳐달라고 요구하고 또 아파트에 사는 다른 사람에게 음악 소리를 낮추도록 이야기해달라고 하는 것으로 보아 아파트 관리인과 주민의 관계임을 알 수 있다. 주차 문제를 이야기하는 전반부만 보고 주차장 경비원과 주차인으로 답을 고르지 않도록 유의한다.

M: Good afternoon. Can I help you?
W: Good afternoon. I'd like to speak to you about **a safety issue** I noticed last night.
M: What was the problem that you experienced?
W: I was parking my car in the parking lot in the back of the building.
M: Did somebody park their car in your designated parking space?
W: No, I had no trouble parking in my space. But it was very dark out there.
M: Oh, maybe some of the bulbs **have burned out**.
W: Right. They need to be fixed because a dark parking lot can be a dangerous place.
M: I agree. I'll go out there after dark and **check it out**.
W: Thanks. And would you mind talking to the person in apartment 2C and asking him to **keep his music down** after 10 at night? I can't sleep at night.
M: Oh, okay. I'll talk to him about that.

남: 안녕하세요. 도와드릴까요?
여: 안녕하세요. 어젯밤 제가 알게 된 안전 문제에 관해 말씀드리려고요.
남: 어떤 문제를 겪으셨습니까?
여: 제가 건물 뒤쪽 주차장에 제 차를 주차하고 있었거든요.
남: 지정 주차 장소에 누군가가 자기 차를 주차해놨나요?
여: 아니요, 제 장소에 주차하는 데 문제는 없었어요. 하지만 그곳이 아주 어둡더군요.
남: 아, 아마 전구 몇 개가 나갔나 보군요.
여: 맞아요. 어두운 주차장이 위험한 장소가 될 수 있기 때문에 그것들을 고쳐야 하겠어요.
남: 동의합니다. 어두워진 후에 제가 나가서 확인해보겠습니다.
여: 고맙습니다. 그리고 아파트 2C호에 있는 사람에게 말해서 밤 10시 이후에 음악 소리를 낮춰달라고 요청해주시겠어요? 제가 밤에 잠을 잘 수 없어서요.
남: 아, 알겠습니다. 그분께 그것에 대해 이야기하겠습니다.

어휘 issue 문제; 쟁점; 발표하다　notice (보거나 듣고) 알다　park 주차하다 cf. parking lot 주차장　designated 지정된　burn out (다 타고) 꺼지다; (에너지를) 소진하다

04 그림 불일치　　④

✳ 대화가 나오기 전에 각 사물의 위치 관계와 외형(형태나 무늬, 개수 등)의 특징을 미리

확인하는 것이 좋다. 대화에서는 테이블 위가 지금은 비어 있지만, 오늘 저녁에 쿠키와 컵케이크를 올려놓을 것이라고 했다. 그러므로 지금 테이블 위는 비어있어야 하는데 그림에서는 간식이 놓여 있으므로 ④가 대화의 내용과 일치하지 않는다.

M: You look tired, Madison. What's wrong?
W: My daughter planned a slumber party in our house this evening, so I was very **busy preparing** for it yesterday.
M: What is a slumber party?
W: It's a party where young girls spend the night together at one of their houses. Look at this photo in my cell phone. My daughter and I decorated her room.
M: Fantastic! There are two tents on each side of the room. You **decorated the tents** with flowers on top.
W: Can you see a teddy bear in the tent on the left side? It's my daughter's favorite.
M: How cute! You **hung** a big picture with a moon and stars **on the wall**. It's lovely. Is the table under the picture for snacks?
W: Yes, there's **nothing on the table** now, but I'll put some cookies and cupcakes on it this evening.
M: Oh, I like the cushion in the tent on the right side. I like **the floral pattern** on it. How many friends did your daughter invite?
W: She invited five friends.
M: I hope they'll have a great party. You're the best mom.

남: 피곤해 보이는군요. Madison. 무슨 일이에요?
여: 딸애가 오늘 저녁 우리 집에서 파자마 파티를 계획해서 어제 그걸 준비하느라고 매우 바빴어요.
남: 파자마 파티가 뭐죠?
여: 어린 소녀들이 그들 중 한 집에서 함께 밤을 보내는 파티예요. 내 휴대폰에 있는 이 사진을 봐요. 딸과 내가 그 애 방을 장식했어요.
남: 굉장히 멋지네요! 방의 양쪽에 2개의 텐트가 있네요. 텐트 꼭대기를 꽃으로 장식했군요.
여: 왼쪽 텐트 안에 테디베어가 보여요? 그게 우리 애가 가장 좋아하는 거예요.
남: 정말 귀여워요! 달하고 별이 있는 큰 그림을 벽에 걸었군요. 사랑스러워요. 그림 아래 테이블은 간식을 놓기 위한 건가요?
여: 네, 지금은 테이블 위에 아무것도 없지만 오늘 저녁에 쿠키하고 컵케이크를 좀 그 위에 둘 거예요.
남: 아, 오른쪽 텐트 안의 쿠션이 마음에 드는군요. 난 그것의 꽃무늬가 좋아요. 따님이 몇 명의 친구를 초대했나요?
여: 다섯 명의 친구를 초대했어요.
남: 그들이 멋진 파티를 하기를 바라요. 당신은 최고의 엄마군요.

어휘 **slumber party** 파자마 파티 ((친구 집에 모여 잠옷을 입고 밤새워 노는 파티)) **floral** 꽃의; 꽃무늬의

05 추후 행동 ③

❋ 대개 대화는 어떤 일을 하게 되는 상황이 먼저 제시된 뒤에 남자와 여자가 각각 할 일들과 이에 대한 수락/거절의 응답이 나열되는 식으로 전개된다. 본 대화는 헤어디자이너와 손님이 머리를 어떻게 할지 의논하는 상황이다. 남자가 여자에게 최신 헤어스타일이 실린 잡지를 원하는지 물으면서 자신이 가서 가져오겠다고 하고, 여자가 그렇게 해달라고 부탁했으므로 남자가 할 일은 ③ '잡지 가져다주기'이다. 헤어스타일을 검색하는 것은 여자가 할 일임에 유의한다.

M: Good afternoon, Mrs. Stuart. Have a seat.
W: Good afternoon. Mr. Glenn.
M: Would you like some coffee or orange juice?
W: No, thanks. I already drank some coffee.
M: Okay. **How would you like** your hair done? Would you like it a bit shorter today?
W: Yes, my hairstyle is **too plain**. I'm ready for a new image, but I don't want too much cut off.
M: Okay, then I could just cut a little. Do you **have** a particular style **in mind**?
W: Well, actually I'm not sure. Can you recommend one?
M: How about putting some color in your hair?

W: I think it'll damage my hair.
M: Don't worry. These days coloring doesn't damage your hair as much. Do you want to **see some magazines** that feature the latest hairstyles? I'll go get them.
W: Yes, please. I'll also **search for some images** with my smartphone.
M: Okay. Wait a second.

남: 안녕하세요, Stuart 씨. 앉으세요.
여: 안녕하세요. Glenn 씨.
남: 커피나 오렌지 주스를 좀 드시겠어요?
여: 아니요, 괜찮습니다. 이미 커피를 좀 마셨어요.
남: 알겠습니다. 머리를 어떻게 하고 싶으세요? 오늘은 좀 더 짧게 하시겠어요?
여: 네, 제 헤어스타일이 너무 평범해서요. 새로운 이미지를 할 준비가 되었지만, 너무 많이 자르는 건 원하지 않아요.
남: 알겠습니다. 그러면 그냥 약간만 자를 수 있겠군요. 특별히 원하시는 스타일이 있으신가요?
여: 음, 사실 잘 모르겠어요. 하나 추천해주실 수 있어요?
남: 머리카락에 염색을 약간 하는 건 어떠세요?
여: 그건 내 머리카락을 상하게 할 것 같아요.
남: 걱정하지 마세요. 요즘 염색은 머리카락을 그렇게 상하게 하지 않는답니다. 최신 헤어스타일이 특별히 나오는 잡지를 좀 보고 싶으신가요? 제가 가서 가져올게요.
여: 네, 부탁드려요. 저도 스마트폰으로 이미지를 좀 검색해볼게요.
남: 알겠습니다. 잠깐만요.

어휘 **plain** 평범한; 꾸미지 않은, 소박한   **damage** 손상시키다; 손상, 피해   **feature** 특별히 포함하다. 특징으로 삼다

06 금액 ④

❋ 여러 개의 수치 정보가 등장하므로 필요한 정보를 메모하면서 듣는 것이 좋다. 남자는 우선 30달러짜리 1주 승차권을 원했다. 12세 미만의 어린이들을 위한 1주 승차권은 20달러인데, 남자가 어린이 1주 승차권 3장과 어른 1주 승차권 1장을 구매했으므로 지불할 금액은 90달러(20달러×3+30달러×1)이다.

M: Excuse me. Does that bus go to Greenville?
W: Yes, you need to buy a bus pass here.
M: Okay. How much does it cost for a bus pass?
W: It depends on **what you want**. There are passes for a day, a week, and a month.
M: How much are the day pass and the weekly pass?
W: The day pass is $5, and the weekly pass is $30.
M: I'd like some weekly passes, then.
W: Sure. **How many do you need**?
M: I have three children. Is there **any discount** on them?
W: Yes, the weekly pass for **a child under 12** is $20.
M: Then I'd like to buy three child passes and one adult pass.
W: Here you go. Thank you for your purchase.

남: 실례합니다. 저 버스가 Greenville로 가나요?
여: 네. 여기서 버스 승차권을 구매하셔야 합니다.
남: 알겠습니다. 버스 승차권은 얼마나 하나요?
여: 무엇을 원하시는가에 달렸습니다. 1일 승차권하고 1주 승차권, 그리고 1개월 승차권이 있습니다.
남: 1일 승차권과 1주 승차권은 얼마나 하나요?
여: 1일 승차권은 5달러이고 1주 승차권은 30달러입니다.
남: 그러면 1주 승차권을 주세요.
여: 물론이죠. 얼마나 필요하세요?
남: 아이가 세 명인데요. 아이들에게 할인이 있나요?
여: 네, 12세 미만의 어린이를 위한 1주 승차권은 20달러입니다.
남: 그러면 어린이 승차권 세 장하고 어른 승차권 한 장 주세요.
여: 여기 있습니다. 구매해주셔서 감사합니다.

어휘 **depend on** ~에 달려있다; ~에 의존하다   **pass** 승차권, 통행증; 합격   **purchase** 구매(하다)

07 이유 ④

✻ 지시문을 통해 여자가 영화를 보러 갈 수 없는 상황이며 여자의 말에 단서가 있을 가능성이 큼을 미리 파악한다. 여자는 이번 토요일에 친구와 함께 가난한 나라의 사람들을 돕기 위해 자선 음악회를 열어 영화를 보러 가지 못한다고 하므로 답은 ④이다. 여자의 전공이 바이올린이어서 음악회를 여는 것이며 바이올린 연주회에 가는 것은 아님에 유의한다.

M: Chloe, **I was wondering** if we could go to see a movie this Saturday.
W: That sounds like fun, but I can't.
M: Are you busy with your homework?
W: No, actually, I'm planning to help people **in poor countries**.
M: Sounds great! Do you plan to go to one of those countries?
W: No, my friends and I are planning to **raise some money** this weekend.
M: Oh, how will you raise money? Are you going to sell something?
W: No. You know my major is violin. We'll **hold a little concert** in front of the Evergreen Shopping Mall this Saturday.
M: I admire you. There are always plenty of people passing by.
W: Yes, **that's why I'm busy** this Saturday.
M: Oh, okay. I'll go there to see you then.
W: I really appreciate it.

남: Chloe, 이번 토요일에 우리가 영화를 보러 갈 수 있을지 알고 싶어.
여: 그거 재미있을 것 같은데 난 안 돼.
남: 숙제하느라 바쁘니?
여: 아니, 사실은, 난 가난한 나라에 있는 사람들을 도울 계획을 하고 있어.
남: 그거 굉장한데! 그런 나라들 중 하나에 가려고 계획하는 거니?
여: 아니야, 내 친구하고 내가 이번 주말에 돈을 좀 모금하려고 계획 중이야.
남: 아, 어떻게 돈을 모금할 건데? 뭔가를 팔 거니?
여: 아니야. 내 전공이 바이올린인 거 알지. 우리는 이번 토요일에 Evergreen 쇼핑몰 앞에서 작은 음악회를 열 거야.
남: 네가 존경스러워. 거긴 언제나 많은 사람이 지나다니지.
여: 응, 그래서 내가 이번 토요일에 바쁜 거야.
남: 아, 알았어. 그러면 내가 너를 보러 거기 갈게.
여: 정말 고마워.

어휘 raise money 돈을 모금[마련]하다 hold 열다: 잡고 있다 admire 존경하다: 칭찬하다 appreciate 감사하다: 감상하다: 이해하다

08 언급하지 않은 것 ④

✻ 대화의 진행은 대개 선택지와 같은 순서이므로, 선택지를 보면서 언급된 내용을 소거하는 식으로 푸는 것이 좋다. 우선 주차 공간에 대해 문의했고 그다음 탈의실과 사물함 제공에 대해 질문했다. 그리고 강좌를 등록하는 방법과 월 회비에 대해 언급했다. 그러나 운동 시설에 대해서는 전혀 언급하지 않았으므로 답은 ④이다.

[Telephone rings.]
M: Hello, Anytime Fitness.
W: Hello, I'd like to ask a few questions about your fitness club.
M: Sure. What can I do for you?
W: I'd like to **sign up for a class** there. Where can I park my car while I'm exercising?
M: We have a large, **free parking lot** in front of the building.
W: Good. Do you provide changing rooms and lockers?
M: Of course. We offer **separate changing rooms** and lockers for men and women, free of charge. We recommend that you bring your own lock.
W: That's great. How do I sign up for the classes?
M: You need to come here and **fill out** an application form. Then you can choose the class you want.
W: Okay. Can you tell me how much **the monthly membership fee** is?
M: It's 40 dollars a month.
W: Thanks! I can't wait to get started.
M: No problem. I'll see you soon!

[전화벨이 울린다.]
남: 여보세요, Anytime Fitness입니다.

여: 여보세요, 거기 피트니스 클럽에 관해 몇 가지 질문을 하고 싶은데요.
남: 그럼요. 무엇을 도와드릴까요?
여: 그곳의 강좌에 등록하고 싶은데요. 운동하는 동안 어디에 차를 주차할 수 있나요?
남: 저희는 건물 앞에 커다란 무료 주차장(① 주차 공간)이 있습니다.
여: 좋군요. 탈의실과 사물함을 제공하나요?
남: 물론이죠. 남성과 여성을 위한 구분된 탈의실과 사물함을 무료로 제공(② 사물함 제공)합니다. 저희는 본인의 자물쇠를 가져오시기를 권장합니다.
여: 좋아요. 강좌에 어떻게 등록하나요?
남: 여기 오셔서 신청서를 기재하셔야 합니다(③ 등록 방법). 그러고 나서 원하는 강좌를 선택하실 수 있습니다.
여: 알겠어요. 한 달 회비가 얼마인지 알려주실 수 있나요?
남: 한 달에 40달러(⑤ 월 회비)입니다.
여: 고마워요! 빨리 시작하고 싶군요.
남: 그럼요. 곧 뵙겠습니다!

어휘 sign up for ~에 등록[가입]하다 separate 구분[분리]된: 분리하다 changing room 탈의실 fill out 기재하다: 작성하다 application 신청(서), 지원(서): 응용 membership fee 회비

09 내용 불일치 ③

✻ 담화의 진행은 대개 선택지와 같은 순서이므로, 선택지를 보면서 일치하는 내용을 소거하는 식으로 푸는 것이 좋다. 신선한 해산물은 폭풍우로 구매가 어렵지만, 냉동 해산물은 할인된 가격에 구매할 수 있다고 했으므로 ③ '냉동 해산물은 폭풍우로 공급이 어렵다.'는 내용과 일치하지 않는다.

M: Good evening, ladies and gentlemen! This week is a special week at Foodtown because we are celebrating our first anniversary. All fruits and vegetables are **at least 10 percent off**, and meat products are at least 20 percent off. We have special buys on beef steaks for grilling and imported legs of lamb. We regret that our fresh seafood is **in short supply**, due to continuing storms off the coast. But frozen seafood **is available** at bargain prices. While you shop at Foodtown, please enjoy **a free cup of** coffee in the bakery department. You are also **invited to sample** our many delicious local and imported speciality foods. Thank you for shopping at Foodtown.

남: 안녕하세요, 신사 숙녀 여러분! 이번 주는 저희가 1주년을 기념하고 있기 때문에 Foodtown에서의 특별한 주간입니다. ① 모든 과일과 채소가 최소한 10퍼센트 할인되고 식육 가공품은 최소한 20퍼센트 할인됩니다. 구워 드실 ② 소고기 스테이크와 수입 양 다리의 특별 판매가 있습니다. 연안에서의 계속되는 폭풍우 때문에 저희의 신선한 해산물의 공급이 부족하게 되어 유감스럽게 생각합니다. 그러나 ③ 냉동 해산물은 할인된 가격에 구매하실 수 있습니다. 여러분이 Foodtown에서 쇼핑하시는 동안 ④ 베이커리 매장에서 무료 커피 한 잔을 즐기십시오. 또한, 저희의 많고 맛있는 ⑤ 지역 특산 식품과 수입 특산 식품을 시식하시기를 권합니다. Foodtown에서 쇼핑해주셔서 감사합니다.

어휘 anniversary 기념일 at least 최소한, 적어도 import 수입하다 supply 공급(량) bargain price 할인 가격 department 매장: 부서: 학과 sample 시식[시음]하다: 샘플 speciality (지역의) 특산물

10 도표 이해 ⑤

✻ 대화의 진행은 대개 도표 항목의 나열 순서대로 진행된다. 대화를 들으면서 도표의 각 항목 중 선택되지 않은 것을 소거하는 식으로 푸는 것이 좋다. 우선 4구짜리 토스터는 필요 없으므로 ①을 제외하고, 색은 검은색이나 은색 아닌 다채로운 것을 원했으므로 ② 역시 제외된다. 가격은 50달러 미만을 원했으므로 ④가 제외되면 남는 것은 ③과 ⑤인데 덮개가 있는 것을 원했으므로 여자가 구매할 토스터는 ⑤이다.

W: Hi, I'm looking for a toaster.
M: We have a great selection here. Which type of toaster are you looking for?
W: Well, I'm not quite sure. What could you recommend?
M: How big is your family? If you have a big family, I'd recommend this 4-slice model.
W: No, I have **a small family** of three. I don't need a 4-slice toaster. How

about the extra features?

M: Actually, all of these have basic functions; timer, a cancel function, and bagel settings.

W: If so, I'd like one of **these colorful toasters**. I don't like silver or black colors.

M: Okay, and **what price range** do you have in mind?

W: I'd like to stay under $50.

M: Then you can choose between these two.

W: Hmm... Then I'll take the one with a cover. **It'll prevent dust** while it's not in use.

M: Good choice. It also prevents children's hands **from entering inside**.

여: 안녕하세요, 토스터를 찾고 있는데요.
남: 여기 아주 좋은 제품이 있습니다. 어떤 종류의 토스터를 찾고 계시나요?
여: 음, 확실히 모르겠어요. 뭘 추천해주시겠어요?
남: 가족이 얼마나 많으십니까? 대가족이시면 이 4구짜리 모델을 추천합니다.
여: 아니요, 세 명인 작은 가족이에요. 전 4구짜리 토스터는 필요하지 않아요. 추가 기능은 어떤가요?
남: 사실 이 모든 게 다 기본적인 기능. 그러니까 타이머, 취소 기능과 베이글 세팅을 갖고 있습니다.
여: 그렇다면 나는 이 다채로운 토스터 중 하나를 원해요. 은색이나 검은색은 마음에 안 들어요.
남: 알겠습니다. 그리고 가격대는 얼마 정도를 생각하고 계시나요?
여: 50달러 미만으로 하고 싶어요.
남: 그러면 이 둘 사이에서 선택하실 수 있습니다.
여: 음… 그러면 저는 덮개가 있는 걸 사겠어요. 사용하지 않을 때 그게 먼지를 막아줄 거예요.
남: 좋은 선택이에요. 그건 또한 아이들의 손이 안으로 들어가는 걸 막아줍니다.

어휘 extra 추가의; 여분의 function 기능(하다) prevent (A from v-ing) (A가 v하는 것을) 막다[예방하다] dust 먼지; 가루

11 짧은 대화에 이어질 응답 ⑤

＊ 부모님의 결혼기념일에 포토북을 선물하자고 하는데 남자는 가격이 비쌀까 봐 망설이고 있고 여자가 100달러보다 비용이 덜 든다고 하고 있다. 가격이 그렇게 비싸지 않다는 걸 확인했을 때 이어질 응답으로는 ⑤ '그렇다면 우리가 그걸 살 여유가 있어. 부모님을 위해 그걸 주문하자.'가 적절하다.

① 동의해. 그게 돈을 절약할 좋은 방법이 될 거야.
② 멋지다. 부모님에게 내 축하를 전해줘.
③ 미안해. 난 부모님의 기념일에 갈 수 없어.
④ 비싸지만 우리 미래의 목표를 위해서는 가치 있어.

W: Dylan, our parents' 20th wedding anniversary is next month. What do you think of **ordering a photo book** for them?

M: That sounds great, but it must be very expensive.

W: Not really. Actually, **it costs less than** a hundred dollars.

M: Then we can afford that. Let's order it for them.

여: Dylan, 다음 달이 우리 부모님의 결혼 20주년이야. 부모님을 위해 포토북을 주문하는 거에 대해 어떻게 생각해?
남: 그거 좋은 것 같아. 하지만 분명히 무척 비쌀 거야.
여: 꼭 그런 건 아니야. 사실, 100달러보다 비용이 더 적게 들어.
남: 그렇다면 우리가 그걸 살 여유가 있어. 부모님을 위해 그걸 주문하자.

어휘 order 주문(하다); 명령(하다) | 선택지 어휘 | costly 값비싼, 비용이 많이 드는 worth 가치가 있는; 가치 afford (금전적, 시간적) 여유가 되다; 형편이 되다

12 짧은 대화에 이어질 응답 ⑤

＊ 의사가 체중 감량을 권하자 매일 달리고 설탕을 줄이고 채소를 많이 먹으며 최선을 다하겠다는 남자에게 할 말로는 ⑤ '행운을 빌어. 네가 목표를 이루기를 바라.'가 가장 적절하다.

① 바로 그거야. 그래서 내가 그걸 하는 거야.
② 맞아. 아무도 네가 하는 일에 신경 쓰지 않아.

③ 넌 잘 해냈어. 네가 자랑스러워.
④ 걱정하지 마. 네 기분이 어떨지 이해해.

M: My doctor advised that I **should lose weight** for my health. I'll run for an hour every day.

W: Good for you! You'll feel much better if you do.

M: I'm going to **cut back on sugars** and eat more vegetables. I'll do my best to lose weight.

W: Good luck. I hope you achieve your goal.

남: 의사 선생님께서 내 건강을 위해서 체중을 줄여야 한다고 권했어. 난 매일 한 시간씩 달릴 거야.
여: 잘 되었다! 네가 그런다면 훨씬 더 좋아질 거야.
남: 난 설탕을 줄이고 채소를 더 많이 먹을 거야. 체중을 줄이기 위해 최선을 다할 거야.
여: 행운을 빌어. 네가 목표를 이루기를 바라.

어휘 advise 권고[조언/충고]하다 cut back on ~을 줄이다 | 선택지 어휘 | exactly (맞장구치는 말로) 바로 그거야; 정확히 achieve 이루다, 성취하다

13 긴 대화에 이어질 응답 ②

＊ 대화의 전체 맥락 하에 마지막 말의 의미나 의도를 정확히 파악하는 것이 좋다. 집을 사려는 여자가 남자의 친구인 부동산 중개인을 소개해 달라고 하자 남자가 흔쾌히 승낙한다. 이에 대한 여자의 응답으로는 감사를 표하면서 도움이 필요하다고 말하는 ② '고마워요. 난 정말로 전문가의 도움이 필요해요.'가 가장 적절하다.

① 절대 아니에요. 난 그걸 살 여유가 없다고 생각해요.
③ 그건 잘 작동하지 않을 수도 있어요. 하지만 난 다시 시도해볼게요.
④ 그거 아주 좋겠는데요. 내 모든 돈을 투자할게요.
⑤ 그는 아직 준비되지 않았어요. 내일 그가 당신에게 전화할 거예요.

W: I'm thinking of **buying a house**.

M: Good idea. Where do you want to live?

W: I want a house near Orchard Street and Oxford Street.

M: I know where that is. It's **a nice place** to live.

W: Absolutely. And that area is really good for children, since there are many good schools in the neighborhood.

M: Did you find a house that you really like?

W: Not yet. I'll visit a real estate agent next week. Do you happen to know any **real estate agents** around there?

M: One of my friends is a real estate agent.

W: That's great. Can you **introduce him to me**?

M: Sure. If you want, I'll call him right now.

W: Thanks. I really need an expert's help.

여: 집을 살까 생각 중이에요.
남: 좋은 생각이에요. 어디서 살고 싶으세요?
여: 난 Orchard 가와 Oxford 가 근처의 집을 원해요.
남: 거기가 어디인지 알아요. 살기 좋은 곳이죠.
여: 그렇고말고요. 그리고 그 지역은 근처에 좋은 학교가 많기 때문에 아이들에게도 정말 좋아요.
남: 마음에 꼭 드는 집을 찾았나요?
여: 아직 못 찾았어요. 다음 주에 부동산 중개인을 만날 거예요. 혹시 그 근처의 부동산 중개인을 알고 있나요?
남: 내 친구 중 하나가 부동산 중개인이에요.
여: 그거 군요. 나에게 그를 소개해줄 수 있어요?
남: 그럼요. 원한다면 그에게 당장 전화할게요.
여: 고마워요. 난 정말로 전문가의 도움이 필요해요.

어휘 neighborhood 지역; 근처 real estate agent 부동산 중개인 | 선택지 어휘 | expert 전문가 invest 투자하다

14 긴 대화에 이어질 응답 ③

＊ 대화의 전체 맥락 하에 마지막 말의 의미나 의도를 정확히 파악하는 것이 좋다. 남자는 버려진 고양이를 보고 바로 집에 데려가자고 하고 여자는 주인이 있을 수도 있다며 동

물 보호소에 연락하자고 한다. 주인을 찾는 동안이라도 집에 두고 주장하는 남자에게 여자가 갑작스럽다면서 망설이고 있다. 이에 대한 남자의 응답으로는 ③ '우리는 적어도 고양이를 기를 수 있는 누군가를 찾도록 노력해야 해요.'가 가장 적절하다.

① 우리가 야생동물을 보호할 방법을 찾아야 해요.
② 내일 지역 동물 보호소에서 고양이를 입양할게요.
④ 애완동물을 기르는 것은 아이에게 아주 좋은 학습 경험이에요.
⑤ 애완동물을 버리는 사람에게 벌금을 물려야 한다고 생각해요.

M: Emily, look! There's a kitten in this box!
W: It's very cute. But why is it here?
M: Someone **must have abandoned** it here! Who would do such a thing?
W: That might not be the case. It could just be lost.
M: I don't think so, since it's in a box. Oh, poor thing. **Let's take it home**. It could die in this cold weather.
W: Let's call the **animal shelter** first. They might be able to find its owner.
M: Well, I'd like to keep it at home while we search for its owner.
W: Charles, we don't have anything that **the cat needs** in our home.
M: We can go buy a few things. If it doesn't have an owner, let's raise it. Otherwise, it might **freeze to death**.
W: I know, but it's all very sudden.
M: We should at least try to find someone who can keep it.

남: Emily, 봐요! 이 상자 안에 새끼고양이가 있군요!
여: 너무 귀엽군요. 하지만 왜 여기 있는 거죠?
남: 누군가가 여기 버린 게 분명해요! 누가 이런 일을 했을까요?
여: 그런 경우가 아닐 수도 있어요. 그냥 길을 잃었을 수도 있고요.
남: 상자 안에 있는 걸 보니 그건 아닌 것 같아요. 아, 불쌍한 것. 집으로 데려갑시다. 이런 추운 날씨에 죽을 수 있어요.
여: 우선 동물 보호소에 전화해요. 그들이 고양이의 주인을 찾아줄 수 있을지도 몰라요.
남: 음, 우리가 주인을 찾는 동안 집에 두고 싶어요.
여: Charles, 우리 집에는 고양이에게 필요한 게 아무것도 없어요.
남: 몇 가지를 사러 갈 수 있어요. 주인이 없다면 기릅시다. 그렇지 않으면 고양이가 얼어 죽을지도 몰라요.
여: 알아요, 하지만 모든 게 너무 갑작스러워서요.
남: 우리는 적어도 고양이를 기를 수 있는 누군가를 찾도록 노력해야 해요.

어휘 abandon 버리다, 유기하다; 포기하다   animal shelter 동물 보호소   raise 기르다; 올리다   freeze to death 얼어 죽다 | 선택지 어휘 | adopt 입양하다; 택하다   fine ((수동태로)) 벌금을 물리다

15 상황에 적절한 말 ⑤

* 지시문을 통해 누가(A) 누구에게(B) 할 말인지를 우선 정확히 파악한다. 담화는 대개 A와 B에 대한 배경 설명과 B가 처한 문제 상황, 그리고 이에 대해 A가 어떤 말을 하려고 하는지에 대한 설명의 순서로 전개된다. Katie(B)의 수학 성적이 좋지 않은 이유가 주말마다 일하기 때문이라는 것을 알게 된 상담 선생님(A)이 공부할 시간을 놓치지 말라고 말하고 싶은 상황에서 할 말로는 ⑤ '일을 그만두는 게 좋겠구나. 중요한 일을 먼저 하렴.'이 가장 적절하다.

① 그건 전적으로 네게 달렸어. 난 전혀 상관하지 않아.
② 인생이 네게 교훈을 가르쳐줄 거야. 넌 그걸 기억할 거야.
③ 네가 찾는 것을 항상 가질 수는 없어.
④ 지금까지는 잘해온 것 같구나. 그걸 망치지 말렴.

M: Katie is a high school student. She took a math exam last week but didn't get a good score. Today, Katie visits the school counselor's office **to get some advice** about university. Since her math grade was really bad, the counselor asks her why. Katie says she couldn't study much because she's been **working in** a clothing store every weekend. The counselor asks her what she wants to do after high school. She wants to major in computer science and become a computer technician. The counselor says she needs **a high grade** in math to get into the computer science department. The counselor wants to tell her **not to lose time** for studying. In this situation, what would the counselor most likely say to Katie?

The counselor: <u>You'd better quit working. Do the important thing first.</u>

남: Katie는 고등학생이다. 그녀는 지난주 수학 시험을 봤지만 좋은 성적을 받지 못했다. 오늘 Katie는 대학에 관한 조언을 구하려고 학교 상담실을 방문한다. 그녀의 수학 성적이 정말 안 좋았기 때문에 상담 선생님은 그녀에게 이유를 묻는다. Katie는 주말마다 옷가게에서 일하고 있기 때문에 공부를 많이 하지 못했다고 말한다. 상담 선생님은 그녀에게 고등학교를 나온 후에 무엇을 하고 싶은지 묻는다. 그녀는 컴퓨터 공학을 전공해서 컴퓨터 기술자가 되고 싶다. 상담 선생님은 컴퓨터 공학과에 들어가려면 수학에서 높은 성적이 필요하다고 말한다. 상담 선생님은 그녀에게 공부할 시간을 놓치지 말라고 말하고 싶다. 이 상황에서 상담 선생님이 Katie에게 뭐라고 말하겠는가?

상담 선생님: 일을 그만두는 게 좋겠구나. 중요한 일을 먼저 하렴.

어휘 major in ~을 전공하다   technician 기술자; 전문가
| 선택지 어휘 | entirely 전적으로, 완전히   spoil 망치다, 못쓰게 만들다   quit 그만두다, 중지하다

16~17 세트 문항 16 ② 17 ②

* 16 미래에 가장 인기 있는 직업에 관해 이야기하고 있으므로 담화의 주제는 ② '미래의 가장 유망한 직업들'이다.

① 미래에 사라질 직업들
③ 미래의 직업을 준비하는 법
④ 숙련된 노동자의 수요와 공급
⑤ 로봇 산업의 성장과 인기

* 17 해석 참조.
① 간호사   ② 약사   ③ 치과의사   ④ 식품공학자   ⑤ 로봇 조종 기사

M: Every year, the United States government issues a report on what **the "hottest" jobs** will be in the future. Based on information provided by the biggest industries, this report predicts how quickly these industries will need new employees. Recently, the reports have said that some of the "hottest" jobs are in the **service industry**. Jobs in the service industry include jobs in health care, medical technology, and food services, for example. There are many reasons why certain industries will have more jobs available in the future. One reason is that people are **living longer** nowadays. This means more people are needed to take care of the old. Therefore, nurses, dentists, and food engineers **are expected to** be some of the "hottest" jobs in the near future. In addition, with robots slowly **taking over** manual labor jobs, robot operators will be needed in specific industries. Will you be ready for one of the "hottest" jobs in the future?

남: 매년 미국 정부는 미래에 '가장 인기 있는' 직업이 무엇이 될 것인지에 관한 보고서를 발표합니다. 가장 규모가 큰 산업들이 제공한 정보에 근거해서 이 보고서는 얼마나 빨리 이런 산업들이 새로운 직원을 필요로 하는지 예측합니다. 최근, 보고서는 '가장 인기 있는' 직업 중 일부가 서비스 산업에 있다고 합니다. 서비스 산업의 직업은 예를 들면 보건, 의료 기술, 외식 산업 분야의 직업을 포함합니다. 특정 산업이 미래에 더 많은 직업을 가능하게 할 것인지에 대한 많은 이유가 있습니다. 한 가지 이유는 요즘 사람들이 더 오래 살고 있다는 점입니다. 이것은 노인을 보살피기 위해 더 많은 사람이 필요하다는 것을 의미합니다. 그러므로 ① 간호사, ③ 치과의사와 ④ 식품공학자가 가까운 미래에 '가장 인기 있는' 직업 중 일부가 될 것으로 기대됩니다. 게다가 로봇이 서서히 육체노동을 대신하고 있으므로 ⑤ 로봇 조종 기사가 특정 산업에서 필요하게 될 것입니다. 여러분은 미래에 '가장 인기 있는' 직업 중 하나를 위한 준비를 하겠습니까?

어휘 industry 산업; 근면   predict 예측[예견]하다   employee 직원   nowadays 요즘   take over ~을 대신하다[인수하다]   manual labor 육체노동, 수공일   operator (기계, 장치 등의) 조작자, 기사 | 선택지 어휘 | promising 유망한, 촉망되는   skilled 숙련된, 능숙한   popularity 인기; 대중성   pharmacist 약사

11회

01 화자가 하는 말의 목적 ④

✻ 담화의 일부 내용이 아니라 중심 내용을 파악해야 한다. 본 담화는 취업이 힘들다는 이유로 포기하지 말고 실패하더라도 계속 노력하는 것이 중요하다고 하고 있다. 그러므로 담화의 목적은 ④ '취업 면접을 계속 시도할 것을 조언하려고'이다.

W: We all know that the economy these days isn't good. It's very hard to find a job. However, many young people use this as an excuse to stay home and not go out and look for a job. It's important **to keep trying no matter what happens**, even if you fail a few times before you succeed. Even if it takes you a long time to find a job, you'll meet a lot of great people along the way. It will also give you useful experience. As you do **more and more** job interviews, you'll learn what interviewers are looking for in people. You'll get **better and better at doing** those interviews! Plus, although it might take a few tries to find that perfect job, you'll feel that much more proud when you finally get a job you love.

여: 우리는 모두 요즘 경제가 좋지 않다는 것을 압니다. 직장 구하기가 무척 어렵습니다. 그러나 많은 젊은이는 이것을 집에 머물면서 나가서 직장을 구하지 않는 핑계로 사용합니다. 비록 성공하기 전 몇 번 실패하더라도 무슨 일이 있든지 계속 노력하는 것이 중요합니다. 비록 직장을 찾는 것이 오래 걸린다 하더라도 여러분은 그 과정에서 많은 좋은 사람들을 만날 것입니다. 이것은 또한 여러분에게 유용한 경험을 줄 것입니다. 여러분이 취업 면접을 더 많이 보면 볼수록, 면접관이 사람들에게서 찾는 것이 무엇인지 알게 될 것입니다. 여러분은 그 면접을 점점 더 잘 보게 될 것입니다! 게다가, 비록 그 완벽한 직장을 찾기 위해서 몇 번의 시도가 필요할지도 모르지만 여러분은 마침내 좋아하는 직장을 구했을 때 그만큼 더 자부심을 느낄 것입니다.

어휘 excuse 핑계; 변명   no matter what happens 무슨 일이 있든지   succeed 성공하다; 뒤를 잇다

02 의견 ②

✻ 우선 지시문에서 명시한 화자의 성별을 보고 어느 화자의 말에 주목할지를 판단해야 한다. 특히 의견이나 주장을 표현하는 어구(I think ~, You should ~ 등)가 이끄는 내용을 잘 들어야 한다. 여자가 때에 따라 적절하게 옷을 입는 것이 중요하다며 교향악연주회에는 더 격식을 차려입으라고 권하는 것으로 보아 여자의 의견으로는 ② '상황에 따른 적절한 옷차림을 해야 한다.'가 가장 적절하다.

M: Mom! Hurry up! We're going to be late for the concert.
W: Don't worry. I'm almost done. Oh, Leon! Look at you! Please **change your clothes**.
M: Why? I like this sweatshirt and jeans.
W: If you plan to go to a baseball game, a sweatshirt and jeans are perfect. But it's a symphony orchestra concert!
M: What do you want me to wear?
W: Well, I want you to dress more formally. It's important **to dress properly for the occasion**.
M: You mean I should wear a tuxedo?
W: No, you don't need to dress as if you **were attending a dinner** at the White House. But you need to dress more formally than now.
M: But I want to listen to music in comfort.
W: A symphony concert **is different from** a concert of popular music. Here are your jacket and shirt. Please hurry up!
M: Okay. Okay.

남: 엄마! 서두르세요! 연주회에 늦겠어요.
여: 걱정 마라. 거의 다 했어. 아, Leon! 너를 보렴! 제발 옷을 갈아입어라.
남: 왜요? 전 이 운동복 상의하고 청바지가 좋아요.
여: 네가 야구 경기에 가기로 한다면 운동복 상의하고 청바지는 완벽하지. 하지만 이건 교

향악단 연주회야!
남: 제가 뭘 입기 바라시는 거예요?
여: 음. 더 격식을 갖춰 입기를 바란다. 때에 따라 적절하게 옷을 입는 건 중요해.
남: 제가 턱시도를 입어야 한다는 말씀이에요?
여: 아니야, 넌 백악관에서 하는 만찬에 참석하는 것처럼 입을 필요는 없어. 하지만 지금보다는 더 격식을 갖춰 입어야 해.
남: 하지만 전 편안하게 음악을 듣고 싶어요.
여: 교향악연주회는 대중음악 연주회와는 달라. 여기 네 재킷과 셔츠가 있다. 제발 서둘러라!
남: 알았어요, 알았어.

어휘 sweatshirt 운동복 상의   symphony orchestra 교향악단 cf. symphony concert 교향악연주회   formally 격식을 차려; 공식적으로, 정식으로   properly 적절히, 제대로; 올바로   occasion 때, 경우; 특별한 일, 행사   attend 참석하다, ~에 다니다
comfort 편안, 안락; 위로, 위안

03 관계 ④

✻ 직업을 나타내거나 추론할 수 있는 힌트가 대화 전반에 걸쳐 드러나므로, 대화를 전체적으로 이해하는 것이 필요하다. 본 대화에서 두 사람이 거실의 벽지와 바닥 색을 정하고 조명을 결정하면서 나중에 아이 방의 세부사항에 대해 이야기하자고 하는 것으로 보아 인테리어 디자이너와 의뢰인의 관계임을 알 수 있다. 따라서 답은 ④이다.

M: Mrs. Wilson. I'd like to talk about the living room now.
W: All right. I have some time to talk.
M: **Which color would you like** for the wallpaper?
W: I'd like my living room to be warm and inviting **as well as elegant**.
M: How about putting in maple floors and cream colored wallpaper?
W: Maple? What color is that?
M: It's a light brown color. I have some pictures of some samples here.
W: Let me see. [pause] I like it. And as for the lighting, I'd prefer LED lighting.
M: Got it. **Considering total energy costs**, LED lighting is more practical than others. How about this pendant lighting?
W: That's very nice. It's very unique. Oh, I'm afraid I have to leave now. I have a meeting with a real estate agent.
M: Okay. We'll talk about the details for the children's rooms later.
W: Thanks.

남: Wilson 부인. 이제 거실에 대해서 이야기를 나누고 싶은데요.
여: 좋아요. 이야기할 시간이 좀 있어요.
남: 벽지로 어떤 색을 원하십니까?
여: 전 거실이 우아하면서도 따뜻하고 매력적이기를 바라요.
남: 단풍색 바닥하고 크림색 벽지를 하는 게 어떤가요?
여: 단풍색이요? 그게 무슨 색이죠?
남: 밝은 갈색이에요. 여기 몇 가지 견본 사진이 있습니다.
여: 어디 봅시다. [잠시 후] 좋아요. 그리고 조명에 대해서 이야기하자면, 전 LED 조명이 좋아요.
남: 알겠습니다. 전체 에너지 비용을 고려하면, LED 조명이 다른 것들보다 더 실용적이죠. 이 펜던트식 조명은 어떤가요?
여: 아주 멋져요. 아주 독특하고요. 아, 지금 제가 나가야 할 것 같아요. 부동산 중개인하고 회의가 있어서요.
남: 알겠습니다. 나중에 아이 방의 세부사항에 대해 이야기를 나누죠.
여: 고마워요.

어휘 inviting 매력적인, 솔깃한; 초대하는   elegant 우아한, 품격 있는   considering ~을 고려[감안]하면   practical 실용적인, 유용한; 알맞은; 현실적인   real estate agent 부동산 중개인

04 그림 불일치 ④

✱ 대화가 나오기 전에 각 사물의 위치 관계와 외형(형태나 무늬, 개수 등)의 특징을 미리 확인하는 것이 좋다. 테라스 오른쪽에 소파가 놓여 있다고 이야기하면서 Victoria의 아이들은 거기에 그네 벤치를 놓고 싶어 했지만, Victoria가 소파를 놓기로 결정했다고 말하고 있다. 그러나 그림에서는 그네 벤치가 있으므로 ④는 내용과 일치하지 않는다.

W: I visited Victoria's house yesterday. It has a really nice terrace.
M: Was it her housewarming party? A house with a terrace is my dream house.
W: Yes, I took a picture of her terrace with my phone. Do you want to see it?
M: Sure. Oh, it has a roof and looks fancy. I like this lamp **hanging from the ceiling**.
W: It looks like there are three candlesticks on it. Can you see these two armchairs on the left?
M: Yes, they look comfortable. Wow! There is a fireplace in the center! Fantastic!
W: Yeah, she made a fireplace in the stone wall. That's the best part of it.
M: Yeah, I agree. She also **put a sofa on the right**.
W: Yes. She said her kids really wanted to put a swinging bench there, but she decided to put a sofa because **it would be better for relaxing** on the terrace.
M: A swinging bench might be dangerous for kids anyway. There is a round table in front of the fireplace.
W: Victoria put a flower vase on it. She really has **an eye for interior design**.
M: She really does!

여: 어제 Victoria의 집을 방문했어요. 정말 멋진 테라스가 있더군요.
남: 집들이였어요? 테라스가 있는 집은 내가 꿈꾸던 집인데요.
여: 네, 내 휴대폰으로 그녀의 테라스 사진을 찍었어요. 볼래요?
남: 그럼요. 아, 지붕이 있고 고급스러워 보이는군요. 천장에 매달린 이 등이 마음에 들어요.
여: 세 개의 촛대가 등에 있는 것 같아요. 왼쪽에 이 두 개의 안락의자가 보여요?
남: 네, 편안해 보이는군요. 왜 가운데에 벽난로가 있군요! 환상적이에요!
여: 맞아요. 그녀가 돌벽에 벽난로를 만들었더군요. 그게 제일 좋은 부분이에요.
남: 네, 동의해요. 그녀는 오른쪽에 또 소파를 두었군요.
여: 맞아요. 그녀가 말하길 아이들이 그곳에 그네 벤치를 놓기를 정말 원했지만, 테라스에서 휴식을 취하는 게 더 좋을 거라서 소파를 놓기로 결정했대요.
남: 어쨌든 그네 벤치는 아이들에게 위험할 수도 있겠네요. 벽난로 앞에 둥근 테이블이 있군요.
여: Victoria가 거기에 꽃병을 두었어요. 그녀는 정말로 인테리어 디자인을 보는 눈이 있어요.
남: 정말 그렇군요!

어휘 housewarming party 집들이 fancy 고급의, 값비싼; 공상, 상상 hang 매달다, 걸다 ceiling 천장 armchair 안락의자 fireplace 벽난로 interior 인테리어; 내부의, 안에 있는

05 추후 행동 ②

✱ 대개 대화는 어떤 일을 하게 되는 상황이 먼저 제시된 뒤에 남자와 여자가 각각 할 일들과 이에 대한 수락/거절의 응답이 나열되는 식으로 전개된다. 타이어가 펑크 나서 여자의 차가 꼼짝 못 하고 있는 상황이다. 남자가 여자에게 여분의 타이어가 있냐고 묻고 자기가 대신 교체해주겠다고 했으므로 남자가 할 일은 ② '자동차 타이어 교체하기'이다. 주의 표지판을 두는 것은 여자가 할 일임에 유의한다.

M: Excuse me! Ma'am! **You're not supposed to park** here. You could get a parking ticket if you leave your car here.
W: I know that, but I have a flat tire so I'm stuck.
M: Oh, really? Why don't you call a repair shop or your insurance company?
W: I'd like to call a repair shop, but I don't know their phone number. **Do you happen to know** the number of one?
M: No, I don't. Well, do you have a spare tire in your car's trunk?
W: Yes, but I'm not sure of how to change it. Besides, I don't have the proper tools.

M: I have some tools on hand, so I can change the tire for you.
W: Oh, are you sure? It's very kind of you. I really hope I'm not bothering you too much.
M: It's no problem at all. Could you place this "caution" sign behind your car **while I'm working on your tire**?
W: Yes, I will. Thanks a million.

남: 실례합니다! 부인! 여기에 주차하시면 안 됩니다. 차를 여기 두면 주차 위반 딱지를 받을 수 있습니다.
여: 알지만, 타이어가 펑크 나서 꼼짝할 수 없어요.
남: 아, 정말이요? 정비소나 보험회사에 전화하시지 그러세요?
여: 정비소에 전화하고 싶지만, 그들 전화번호를 몰라요. 혹시 거기 전화번호 아세요?
남: 아니요, 모릅니다. 음. 당신 자동차 트렁크에 여분의 타이어가 있나요?
여: 네, 하지만 어떻게 교체하는지 몰라요. 게다가 적절한 연장도 없고요.
남: 제가 가지고 있는 연장이 좀 있으니까 대신 타이어를 교체해줄 수 있어요.
여: 아, 정말이요? 정말 친절하시군요. 제가 너무 많이 귀찮게 하는 건 아니길 정말 바라요.
남: 정말 괜찮습니다. 제가 타이어 작업을 하는 동안 이 '주의' 표지판을 당신 차 뒤에 놓아주시겠어요?
여: 네, 그럴게요. 정말 고맙습니다.

어휘 be supposed to-v v해야 한다 parking ticket 주차 위반 딱지 flat 펑크 난; 평평한, 편평한 stuck 꼼짝 못 하는, 움직일 수 없는 repair shop 정비소 insurance 보험; 보험료 spare 여분의, 예비용의 proper 적절한, 제대로 된 bother 귀찮게 하다; 괴롭히다 caution 주의[경고](문); 조심

06 금액 ②

✱ 여러 개의 수치 정보가 등장하므로 필요한 정보를 메모하면서 듣는 것이 좋다. 20달러짜리 책을 100권 주문했으니 총액이 2,000달러인데 20% 할인을 받았으므로 지불할 금액은 1,600달러이다. 처음에는 10% 할인을 해주겠다고 했지만 여자가 설득하여 최종적으로 20% 할인으로 조정되었음에 유의한다.

[Telephone rings.]
M: Hello, Green Publishing Company.
W: Hi, I'm Mila Hamilton from Westville University Bookstore.
M: Okay. How can I help you?
W: **I'd like to place an order** for one of your books, *A-Level Biology*. How much is it?
M: Its original price is twenty dollars.
W: Can you offer me a discount? I'd like to get one hundred copies.
M: Let me see. Yes, we can offer you a discount. **It's 10% off** the original price.
W: Just 10%? Can I get a 20% discount? We're a regular customer and plan to place a big order next semester.
M: Hmm... Okay. **You can get 20% off.** But this is an exception.
W: Thank you very much. I'll send you an e-mail with the delivery address.
M: All right.

[전화벨이 울린다.]
남: 여보세요, Green 출판사입니다.
여: 안녕하세요, 저는 Westville 대학 서점의 Mila Hamilton입니다.
남: 네, 무엇을 도와드릴까요?
여: 그쪽 출판사 책 중 하나인 'A-Level Biology'를 주문하고 싶어요. 얼마인가요?
남: 원래 가격은 20달러입니다.
여: 할인을 해 주실 수 있나요? 100권을 사고 싶어요.
남: 어디 봅시다. 네, 할인을 해드릴 수 있습니다. 원래 가격에서 10% 깎아드립니다.
여: 겨우 10%요? 20% 할인받을 수 있나요? 저희는 단골 고객이고 다음 학기에 대량 주문을 하려고 하는데요.
남: 음… 좋습니다. 20% 할인을 받으실 수 있습니다. 하지만 이번은 예외입니다.
여: 정말 고맙습니다. 배달 주소를 이메일로 보내드리겠습니다.
남: 알겠습니다.

어휘 publishing 출판, 출판업 place an order 주문하다 discount 할인(하다) semester 학기 exception 예외; 이례 delivery 배달, 인도, 전달

07 이유 ④

✻ 지시문을 통해 남자가 자전거를 사지 않은 상황이며 남자의 말에 단서가 있을 가능성
이 큼을 미리 파악한다. 남자가 자전거를 사려고 돈을 모았는데 자전거 상점에서 개최
한 미술 대회에서 상품으로 자전거를 받아 사지 않게 되었다고 말하고 있다. 그러므로
답은 ④ '미술 대회 상품으로 받게 되어서'이다.

W: You look really excited. What's going on?
M: Yeah! I'm going to Miami next week.
W: Sounds great! But I think the trip will cost a lot. How did you get the
money? Did your parents give you some?
M: No, I've been saving my money **for the past couple of months**.
W: But you've saved that for a bike, haven't you?
M: Yes! But **I don't need to buy the bike** anymore.
W: Do you mean that you gave up the bike to go to Miami?
M: No. Do you remember the drawing contest the Cube Bike Shop was
holding last month?
W: Yes, I heard about that. The prize was a bicycle. Oh, my goodness! Did you
win?
M: Yes. **I won the bicycle** from that drawing contest! So I can go to Miami,
also.
W: I didn't know you could draw so well. This is amazing!

여: 너 정말 신나 보인다. 무슨 일이 있니?
남: 응! 나 다음 주에 마이애미에 갈 거야.
여: 그거 좋겠다! 하지만 여행에 비용이 많이 들 것 같은데. 어떻게 돈을 구했니? 부모님
이 좀 주셨어?
남: 아니, 지난 두 달 동안 돈을 저축했어.
여: 하지만 그건 자전거를 사려고 저축한 거잖아, 그렇지 않아?
남: 응! 하지만 더 이상 자전거를 살 필요가 없어.
여: 마이애미로 가기 위해 자전거를 포기했다는 뜻이야?
남: 아니야. 너 Cube 자전거 상점이 지난달에 개최한 미술 대회를 기억하니?
여: 응, 그 대회에 관해 들어봤어. 상품이 자전거였지. 아, 이런! 네가 우승했던 거야?
남: 응. 난 그 미술 대회에서 자전거를 받았어! 그래서 마이애미도 갈 수 있어.
여: 난 네가 그림을 그렇게 잘 그리는지 몰랐어. 놀라워!

어휘 cost (값·비용이) 들다[이다]; 값, 비용   hold 개최하다; 잡고 있다

08 언급하지 않은 것 ④

✻ 대화의 진행은 대개 선택지와 같은 순서이므로, 선택지를 보면서 언급된 내용을 소거
하는 식으로 푸는 것이 좋다. 맞벌이 부모를 위해서 학교에서 어린이들에게 아침 식사
를 제공해 주는 서비스인 Breakfast Club에 관한 대화이다. 참여 대상과 운영 시간,
제공 메뉴와 등록 방법에 대해서는 언급했으나 ④ '등록비'는 언급하지 않았다.

W: Honey, I finally got a job. But I have to go to work at 8 in the morning.
M: Congratulations! Then both of us **leave for work early**. Then we should
think about Melissa. Her school starts at 9 a.m.
W: Don't worry. There is Breakfast Club in her school. It's a service that
provides a breakfast for children in the morning. It's open **to all students**.
M: That's a good service. Does it run every weekday?
W: Yes. It's open from 7:15 to 8:45 a.m. each day.
M: Sounds great. **What do they serve for breakfast**?
W: They provide a variety of cereals, hot foods, toast, fruit, and milk. After
breakfast, there is time to play with friends.
M: That's perfect!
W: I'd like Melissa to attend Breakfast Club. Do you agree with me?
M: Absolutely. Should we **book and pay in advance**?
W: Yes, we can book through the online booking system on the school's
website.
M: Let's do it right now.

여: 여보, 내가 마침내 일자리를 얻었어요. 하지만 아침 8시에 출근해야 해요.
남: 축하해요! 그러면 우리 둘 다 일찍 일을 나가는군요. 그러면 Melissa에 대해 생각해봐
야겠군요. 그 애 학교가 오전 9시에 시작하잖아요.

여: 걱정 말아요. 그 애 학교에 Breakfast Club이 있어요. 그건 아침에 아이들에게 아침
식사를 제공하는 서비스예요. 모든 학생(① 참여 대상)이 참여할 수 있어요.
남: 그거 좋은 서비스군요. 주중에 매일 운영하나요?
여: 네. 매일 오전 7시 15분부터 8시 45분까지 문을 열어요(② 운영 시간).
남: 그거 아주 좋군요. 아침으로 뭘 주나요?
여: 다양한 시리얼, 뜨거운 요리, 토스트, 과일과 우유(③ 제공 메뉴)를 제공해요. 아침 식
사 후에는 친구들과 노는 시간이 있어요.
남: 완벽하군요!
여: 난 Melissa가 Breakfast Club을 다녔으면 해요. 당신도 동의하죠?
남: 그렇고말고요. 우리가 예약하고 비용을 선불로 내야 하나요?
여: 네, 학교 웹사이트의 온라인 예약 시스템을 통해 예약할 수 있어요(⑤ 등록 방법).
남: 지금 당장 그걸 합시다.

어휘 provide 제공[공급]하다   a variety of 여러 가지의   absolutely 그렇고말고, 정말
그래; 틀림없이   book 예약하다   in advance 미리, 앞서; 사전에

09 내용 불일치 ③

✻ 담화의 진행은 대개 선택지와 같은 순서이므로, 선택지를 보면서 일치하는 내용을 소
거하는 식으로 푸는 것이 좋다. 플래시를 끄라고 했지만 사진 촬영은 모든 구역에서
가능하다고 했으므로 ③은 내용과 일치하지 않는다.

M: Welcome to a tour of the Paradise Nuclear Generating Station. During the
tour, we will pass through a restricted area. While you are in that area,
we ask that you remain **within the yellow lines** painted on the walkway.
Children 12 years and under must stay with their parents at all times. You
may take photographs in all areas. We do ask, however, that you turn
off your flash; you won't need it because there is plenty of light. **Food
and drink are prohibited** at all points on the tour. Experienced guides
lead each group of 15 visitors and teach you about nuclear generating
facilities. Visitors are advised that anyone not obeying these rules will be
escorted to a waiting area. Shall we begin?

남: Paradise 원자력 발전소 관광에 오신 것을 환영합니다. 관광하는 동안 우리는 제한 구
역을 통과할 것입니다. 여러분이 ① 그 구역에 있는 동안 보도에 칠해진 란색 선 안에
있으시도록 요청드립니다. ② 12세 이하 어린이는 항상 부모와 함께 있어야 합니다.
③ 모든 구역에서 사진을 찍으실 수 있습니다. 그러나 플래시는 꺼주시기를 부탁드립
니다. 빛이 밝기 때문에 플래시가 필요하지는 않으실 겁니다. ④ 음식과 음료는 관광
에서 완전히 금지됩니다. ⑤ 숙련된 가이드가 방문객 집단을 15명씩 인솔하고 원자력
발전 설비에 대해 가르쳐드릴 겁니다. 이 규칙을 따르지 않는 사람은 대기 지역으로
호송될 것임을 방문객들에게 알려드립니다. 시작해 볼까요?

어휘 Nuclear Generating Station 원자력 발전소 *cf.* nuclear 원자력의; 핵(무기)의
cf. generate 발생시키다, 만들어 내다   restricted 제한된, 제약을 받는   remain 머무르다;
여전히 ~이다   plenty of 많은   prohibit 금(지)하다   at all points 완전히; 모든 점에서
experienced 숙련된, 경력[경험]이 있는[많은]   facility 설비, 시설   obey 따르다, 지키다,
순종[복종]하다   escort 호송[호위]하다

10 도표 이해 ④

✻ 대화의 진행은 대개 도표 항목의 나열 순서대로 진행된다. 대화를 들으면서 도표의 각
항목 중 선택되지 않은 것을 소거하는 식으로 푸는 것이 좋다. 우선 150달러가 넘는 ⑤
는 선택에서 제외되고 그다음에 스크린 크기는 6인치를 원했으므로 ②가 제외된다. 무
게가 200그램보다 덜 나가는 ③과 ④ 중 배터리 수명이 더 긴 것을 원했으므로 여자가
구매할 전자책 리더기는 ④이다.

W: Hi, Chris. I'd like to buy an e-book reader. I heard the screens look like
paper, so **it's easy on the eyes**.
M: Exactly. I have used one for several months. It weighs about one tenth of
paper books but can store thousands of full books.
W: Great. Can you help me choose the best one? I can pay **up to 150 dollars**.
M: Okay. Look at this site. They compare the top 5 best e-book readers.
W: Great. I can make a decision after comparing.
M: There are **two types of screen size**: 6-inch and 8-inch. Which one would
you like?

W: I want a 6-inch screen because **a smaller one is easier to carry**.
M: Then you also want the lighter one. I think one which weighs less than 200 grams would be all right. Now you have these two options.
W: I'll take this one **with longer battery life** even if it's a bit expensive.
M: Good choice.
W: Thanks for helping me.

여: 안녕, Chris. 나 전자책 리더기를 사고 싶어. 스크린이 종이 같아서 눈에 편안하다고 들었어.
남: 맞아. 나도 하나를 몇 달 동안 사용하고 있어. 종이 책의 10분의 1의 무게지만 수천 권의 책 전권을 저장할 수 있어.
여: 멋지다. 내가 가장 좋은 걸 고르도록 도와줄 수 있니? 난 150달러까지 지불할 수 있어.
남: 좋아. 이 사이트를 봐. 그들이 상위 5개의 최고의 전자책 리더기를 비교하고 있어.
여: 멋지다. 비교한 다음에 결정을 내릴 수 있겠구나.
남: 스크린 크기가 6인치와 8인치로 두 가지 종류가 있어. 어떤 걸 원하니?
여: 더 작은 게 가지고 다니기 더 쉬우니 6인치 스크린을 원해.
남: 그러면 넌 더 가벼운 것도 좋아하겠구나. 200그램보다 무게가 덜 나가는 게 괜찮을 것 같아. 이제 넌 이 두 가지 선택권이 있어.
여: 난 좀 비싸더라도 배터리 수명이 더 긴 이걸 선택할게.
남: 잘 선택했어.
여: 도와줘서 고마워.

어휘 easy 편안한, 안락한; 쉬운   store 저장하다; 보관하다   up to A A까지   compare 비교하다; ~에 필적하다

11 짧은 대화에 이어질 응답   ⑤

※ 대회에서 우승한 남자에게 여자가 계속 잘하라고 하면서 올림픽에서 좋은 결과를 얻을 것을 믿는다고 하고 있다. 이에 대한 응답으로는 ⑤ '제가 기대에 부응할 수 있기를 바라요.'가 가장 적절하다.

① 그것은 굉장한 배드민턴 경기였어요.
② 우리는 당신 없이 이 경기에서 이길 수 없어요.
③ 길잡이가 되어주셔서 감사합니다.
④ 당신의 공연에 감명 받았어요.

W: I'm proud of you! You're the winner of the BWF World Championships.
M: Thank you very much.
W: Keep up the good work. I believe **you'll get good results** in the next Olympic Games.
M: **I hope I can live up to your expectations.**

여: 네가 자랑스럽구나! 넌 BWF 세계 선수권 대회의 우승자야.
남: 정말 고맙습니다.
여: 앞으로도 계속 잘 하렴. 네가 다음 올림픽에서 좋은 결과를 얻으리라고 믿는다.
남: 제가 기대에 부응할 수 있기를 바라요.

어휘 championship 선수권 (대회); 우승 | 선택지 어휘 | impressed 감명[감동]을 받은, 인상 깊게 생각하는   live up to A A에 부응[합당]하다   expectation 기대; 예상

12 짧은 대화에 이어질 응답   ⑤

※ 남자가 사려고 하는 영화 회차의 티켓이 모두 다 팔려서 다른 시간의 티켓을 구할 수 있는지 여자에게 묻고 있다. 이에 대한 응답으로는 다른 시간의 티켓에 대한 정보를 주는 ⑤ '확인해보겠습니다. 6시 15분에 다섯 좌석이 가능하군요.'가 적절하다.

① 물론이죠. 총액은 45달러입니다.
② 아직 시작하지 않았습니다. 영화 보기에 늦지 않으셨어요.
③ 여기 티켓이 있습니다. 7관으로 가셔야 합니다.
④ 맞습니다. 이 영화는 두 달간 상영되고 있습니다.

M: I'd like to buy five tickets for *Kingsman* at 5:20, please.
W: Sorry, we don't have any seats available for that show. They're sold out.
M: Oh, that's too bad. What about other times? **Are there any other tickets available**?
W: Please let me check. We have 5 seats available at 6:15.

남: 5시 20분에 '킹스맨' 티켓 다섯 장을 사려고 하는데요.
여: 죄송합니다. 그 회차에는 구할 수 있는 자리가 없습니다. 모두 다 팔렸어요.
남: 아, 곤란하군요. 다른 시간은 어떤가요? 다른 티켓을 구할 수 있나요?
여: 확인해보겠습니다. 6시 15분에 다섯 좌석이 가능하군요.

어휘 available 구할[이용할] 수 있는 | 선택지 어휘 | in time (~에) 늦지 않게, 시간 맞춰

13 긴 대화에 이어질 응답   ③

※ 대화의 전체 맥락 하에 마지막 말의 의미나 의도를 정확히 파악하는 것이 좋다. 환자와 병원 직원 간의 대화로 병원에서 진료 후 다음 진료 예약을 위해 날짜를 잡는 상황이다. 날짜가 결정된 후 환자인 남자가 인사를 하고 나서 여자가 할 말로는 ③ '그때 뵙겠습니다. 저기 있는 출납직원에게 지불하십시오.'가 적절하다.

① 죄송합니다만 의사 선생님이 신규 환자는 받고 있지 않으세요.
② Harris 의사 선생님은 안 계십니다. 대신에 지금은 Jones 의사 선생님을 보실 수 있습니다.
④ 괜찮습니다. 저희는 다음 목요일 3시 정각에 개원합니다.
⑤ 기다려주셔서 감사합니다. 10분 후에 Harris 의사 선생님을 만나실 수 있습니다.

M: Excuse me. Dr. Harris said to me that I need to make the next appointment here.
W: Yes, you need to see him in January. What day would be good for you?
M: Well, Tuesdays or Fridays are good.
W: Why don't you come on Tuesday, January 9th at 10 in the morning?
M: I'm afraid I'm working at 10. **Is there anything available** after 3 p.m.?
W: Dr. Harris doesn't take any appointments on Tuesday and Friday afternoons.
M: Then on what days does he take afternoon appointments?
W: Mondays and Thursdays. **Would you like to make an appointment** on Monday, January 15th?
M: I'd prefer Thursday, if that's all right. **How about January 18th**?
W: That's fine. How does 3 p.m. sound?
M: That would be great. Thanks for your help.
W: **We'll see you then. Please pay at the cashier over there.**

남: 실례합니다. Harris 의사 선생님께서 제게 다음 예약을 여기서 해야 한다고 말씀하셨는데요.
여: 네, 환자분은 1월에 선생님을 만나셔야 합니다. 무슨 요일이 좋으시겠어요?
남: 음, 화요일이나 금요일이 좋습니다.
여: 1월 9일 화요일, 오전 10시에 오시는 게 어떠신지요?
남: 제가 10시에는 일을 해서요. 오후 3시 이후에 가능한 건 없나요?
여: Harris 의사 선생님은 화요일하고 금요일 오후에는 어떠한 예약도 받지 않으세요.
남: 그러면 어느 요일에 오후 예약을 받으시나요?
여: 월요일과 목요일이요. 1월 15일 월요일에 예약하시겠어요?
남: 괜찮다면 전 목요일이 더 좋습니다. 1월 18일은 어떤가요?
여: 괜찮습니다. 오후 3시는 어떠신 것 같아요?
남: 아주 좋습니다. 도와주셔서 감사합니다.
여: 그때 뵙겠습니다. 저기 있는 출납직원에게 지불하십시오.

어휘 make an appointment (진료·상담 등을) 예약하다 cf. appointment 예약   prefer 더 좋아하다. 선호하다 | 선택지 어휘 | patient 환자; 참을성[인내심] 있는

14 긴 대화에 이어질 응답   ②

※ 대화의 전체 맥락 하에 마지막 말의 의미나 의도를 정확히 파악하는 것이 좋다. 본 대화는 여자가 입사 시험은 좋은 성적으로 통과했지만 면접에서 너무 긴장해 일자리를 얻지 못해 우울해하고 있는 상황이다. 이러한 여자에게 남자가 할 말은 위로와 격려의 ② '걱정 마. 넌 분명히 다음에 더 잘 해낼 거야.'가 적절하다.

① 난 내일 취업 면접이 있어. 행운을 빌어줘.
③ 그런 것 같아. 이건 네게 아주 좋은 기회가 될 거야.
④ 도와줘서 고마워. 난 이걸 찾고 있었어.
⑤ 너도 그것을 할 수 있어. 포기하지 말고 계속 시도해.

M: Jasmine, why do you look so down?

W: Oh, nothing is working out these days. I'm so depressed.

M: What's wrong?

W: **I applied for a job** at Louisville Company in Langford.

M: Oh, I guess you didn't pass the company exam. I heard their exam is quite difficult.

W: Actually, I passed the examination with a high score. I studied really hard.

M: Then what was the problem?

W: The problem was the interview. It was my first interview, and I was **too nervous to speak**. I could barely breathe. So, I didn't get the job.

M: That's really too bad. I'm sorry to hear that.

W: I was **so disappointed in myself**. I really wanted to get the job.

M: Don't worry. I'm sure you'll do better next time.

남: Jasmine, 왜 그렇게 기운이 없어 보이니?

여: 아, 요즘 아무 일도 풀리지 않아서. 난 너무 우울해.

남: 무슨 일이야?

여: Langford에 있는 Louisville 사의 일자리에 지원했어.

남: 아, 입사 시험을 통과하지 못한 것 같구나. 거기 시험이 꽤 어렵다고 들었어.

여: 사실 높은 성적으로 시험을 통과했어. 난 정말 열심히 공부했거든.

남: 그러면 뭐가 문제였어?

여: 문제는 면접이었어. 첫 번째 면접이라 말하는 데 너무 긴장했어. 거의 숨을 쉬지 못했어. 그래서 그 일자리를 얻지 못했어.

남: 정말 안타깝다. 그렇다니 유감이야.

여: 나 자신에게 너무 실망스러워. 난 그 일자리를 정말 원했거든.

남: 걱정 마. 넌 분명히 다음에 더 잘 해낼 거야.

어휘 depressed 우울한, 암울한 apply for ~에 지원하다 barely 거의 ~ 않다; 간신히
| 선택지 어휘 | opportunity 기회

15 상황에 적절한 말　⑤

＊ 지시문을 통해 누가(A) 누구에게(B) 할 말인지를 우선 정확히 파악한다. 담화는 대개 A와 B에 대한 배경 설명과 B가 처한 문제 상황, 그리고 이에 대해 A가 어떤 말을 하려고 하는지에 대한 설명의 순서로 전개된다. 어머니가 생일 선물로 사주며 잃어버리지 말라고 주의를 준 시계를 잃어버린 친구 Michael(B)이 차마 어머니에게 그 사실을 말하지 못하겠다고 하는데 Kevin(A)은 사실대로 말해야 한다고 생각한다. 이 상황에서 Kevin이 할 말로는 ⑤ '어머니께 사실대로 말씀드려. 나중에 아시면 더 나빠질 거야.' 가 가장 적절하다.

① 괜찮아. 너는 실수로부터 배울 수 있어.

② 내가 네 시계 찾는 걸 도울게. 도서관으로 가자.

③ 너 큰일 났다. 이번에 너는 너무 지나쳤어.

④ 모두 실수는 해. 난 네가 왜 그랬는지 이해해.

M: Michael has a nice watch. He got it as a birthday gift from his mother. Since he often loses things, his mother has warned him **not to lose it**. Today, **he loses the watch** somewhere in the library. He looks everywhere in the library for it, but he can't find it. He goes to the lost-and-found, but it hasn't been turned in. Then he runs into his friend, Kevin. He tells Kevin that **he can't bear** to tell his mother that he lost her gift. Actually, his mother didn't want to buy him that fancy watch because he is careless, but he asked her to buy it. Kevin thinks that Michael should tell his mother what happened **because honesty is the best policy**. In this situation, what would Kevin most likely say to Michael?

Kevin: Tell her the truth. It will be worse if she finds out later.

남: Michael은 멋진 시계를 가지고 있다. 그는 어머니로부터 생일선물로 그 시계를 받았다. 그가 종종 물건을 잃어버리기 때문에 어머니는 그에게 시계를 잃어버리지 말라고 주의를 주셨다. 오늘 그는 도서관 어딘가에서 그 시계를 잃어버린다. 그는 그것을 찾느라고 도서관 곳곳을 보지만 찾을 수 없다. 그는 유실물 보관소에 가지만 그것은 들어오지 않았다. 그때 그는 친구 Kevin을 우연히 만난다. 그는 어머니가 주신 선물을 잃어버린 것을 어머니께 차마 말씀드릴 수 없다고 Kevin에게 말한다. 사실 그의 어머니는 그가 부주의하기 때문에 그렇게 고급의 시계를 그에게 사주는 것을 원하지 않으셨는데 그가 사달라고 부탁했던 것이다. Kevin은 정직이 최선의 방책이기 때문에 Michael이 어머니께 무슨 일이 일어났는지 말씀드려야 한다고 생각한다. 이 상황에

서 Kevin이 Michael에게 뭐라고 말하겠는가?

Kevin: 어머니께 사실대로 말씀드려. 나중에 아시면 더 나빠질 거야.

어휘 warn 주의를 주다, 경고하다 lost-and-found 유실물 보관소 run into ~을 우연히 만나다 fancy 고급의, 값비싼; 공상, 상상 careless 부주의한, 조심성 없는 honesty 정직(성), 솔직함 policy 방책; 정책, 방침 | 선택지 어휘 | go too far 지나치다, 도를 넘다

16~17 세트 문항　16 ⑤　17 ⑤

＊ **16** 예술이 우리 삶의 모든 부분에 있고 우리가 일상의 활동에서 그런 종류의 예술을 만들어 낸다고 하면서 예를 들어 설명하고 있다. 그러므로 담화의 주제로는 ⑤ '우리 일상생활 속에 살아있는 예술'이 가장 적절하다.

① 예술의 다양한 형태　　　　② 집을 장식하는 방법

③ 예술의 기능과 가치　　　　④ 의사전달 도구로서의 예술

＊ **17** 해석 참조.

① 바구니 만들기　② 꽃꽂이　③ 자동차 장식　④ 케이크 장식　⑤ 종이접기

M: Many people think that art is created by really talented people **who just sit down** and produce it. But most of us have always played with and created art. Art is in every part of our lives; what we wear, the design of our homes we live in, and even what our cars look like. We ourselves produce those kinds of art in everyday activities. For example, **making baskets and arranging flowers** are ways of expressing our feelings in an artistic way. A taxi driver hangs a decoration like a dancing toy on the cab dashboard to give pleasure to passengers during the hours of work. A chef may carefully arrange **slices of meat** on a dish and pile different colored vegetables around the edges. When we throw a housewarming party, we may decorate our rooms by choosing a wallpaper color and arranging furniture and other home decorations. We also make cake decorations for our children's birthday parties. Like this, we often **create art without even realizing it**. It even happens each morning when we choose our clothes and matching accessories for the day.

남: 많은 사람들이 예술은 그저 앉아서 그것을 만들어 내는 진짜 재능 있는 사람들이 창조한다고 생각합니다. 그러나 우리 대부분은 항상 예술을 가지고 놀고 창조해 왔습니다. 예술은 우리가 입는 것, 우리가 사는 집의 설계와 심지어 우리 차가 어떻게 보이는지와 같은 우리 삶의 모든 부분에 있습니다. 우리 자신들은 일상의 활동에서 그런 종류의 예술을 만들어 냅니다. 예를 들면, ① 바구니를 만들고 ② 꽃꽂이를 하는 것은 예술적 방식으로 우리 감정을 표현하는 방식입니다. 택시 기사는 일하는 동안 승객들에게 즐거움을 주기 위해 ③ 택시 계기판에 춤추는 인형 같은 장식을 매답니다. 요리사는 접시 위에 정성스럽게 얇은 고기 조각을 배열하고 가장자리에 다른 색깔의 채소를 쌓아 올릴 수도 있습니다. 집들이할 때 우리는 벽지 색깔을 고르고 가구와 다른 실내 장식을 배치해서 우리 방들을 꾸밀 수도 있습니다. 우리는 또한 자녀의 생일 파티를 위해 ④ 케이크 장식을 만듭니다. 이와 같이 우리는 그것을 인식하지도 못하고 자주 예술을 창조합니다. 그것은 심지어 우리가 하루를 위해 옷과 그에 어울리는 액세서리를 고르는 매일 아침 일어납니다.

어휘 talented (타고난) 재능[재주]이 있는 arrange flowers 꽃꽂이하다 *cf.* arrange 배열하다, 배치하다; 마련하다 *cf.* flower arrangement 꽃꽂이 decoration 장식(품) *cf.* decorate 꾸미다, 장식하다 dashboard (승용차의) 계기판 pile 쌓다, 포개다; 더미 edge 가장자리, 모서리 furniture 가구 realize 인식[자각]하다, 깨닫다
| 선택지 어휘 | function 기능(하다) value 가치; 평가하다, 값을 매기다

12회

01 화자가 하는 말의 목적　②

✽ 담화의 일부 내용이 아니라 중심 내용을 파악해야 한다. 본 담화는 이 자리에 있게 되어 기쁘다고 하면서 참가자들과 체육 선생님을 환영하고 연례 운동회에 대한 이야기를 하고 있다. 마지막으로 연례 운동회의 개회를 선언하게 되어 기쁘다고 말을 맺었으므로 담화의 목적은 ②가 가장 적절하다.

M: Ladies and Gentlemen. Boys and Girls. It gives me great pleasure to be here. This is truly a wonderful opportunity. And I want to **give a warm welcome** to all the participants and physical education teachers. This event shows just how much we all respect and admire our athletes. I am sure that we will witness some amazing performances of athletic skill over the course of this championship. Do your best and compete **in the spirit of** sportsmanship and fair play. And take the opportunity to **come closer to each other**. Indeed, the Annual Sports Meet is incredibly important to our school's image and our students' reputation. In closing, I wish you every success and good health. I am so happy to **declare the Annual Sports Meet open**.

남: 신사 숙녀 여러분. 청소년 여러분. 저는 이 자리에 있게 되어 대단히 기쁩니다. 이것은 참으로 멋진 기회입니다. 그리고 저는 모든 참가자들과 체육 선생님들을 따뜻하게 환영하고자 합니다. 이 행사는 우리 모두가 운동선수들을 얼마나 존중하고 존경하는지를 보여줍니다. 저는 우리가 이 우승의 과정 동안 운동 기술의 놀라운 수행을 목격하게 될 것을 확신합니다. 최선을 다하고 스포츠맨십과 정정당당한 경기 태도의 정신으로 경쟁하십시오. 그리고 서로 더 가까워질 기회를 잡으십시오. 정말로 연례 운동회는 우리 학교의 이미지와 우리 학생들의 명성에 엄청나게 중요합니다. 마지막으로 여러분에게 모든 성공과 건강을 바랍니다. 연례 운동회 개회를 선언하게 되어 무척 기쁩니다.

어휘 pleasure 기쁨, 즐거움　opportunity 기회　participant 참가자　admire 존경하다: 감탄하다　athlete 운동선수 cf. athletic 운동 (경기)의: 탄탄한　witness 목격하다: 목격자　championship 우승: 선수권 대회　compete 경쟁하다　spirit 정신: 기분　indeed 정말로: 사실　annual 연례의, 매년의　incredibly 엄청나게. 믿을 수 없을 정도로　reputation 명성. 평판　declare 선언하다: (과세 물품을) 신고하다

02 의견　④

✽ 우선 지시문에서 명시한 화자의 성별을 보고 어느 화자의 말에 주목할지를 판단해야 한다. 특히 의견이나 주장을 표현하는 어구(I think ~, You should ~ 등)가 이끄는 내용을 잘 들어야 한다. 여자는 원자력이 안전하지 않고 폐기물도 위험하며 테러의 표적이 될 수도 있다면서 원자력 발전소의 사용을 멈춰야 한다고 말하고 있다. 그러므로 여자의 의견으로는 ④가 적절하다.

W: Lucas, please set the air conditioner on low. In summer, people use a lot of electricity, and this can cause power failures.
M: I see. I think we **need to build more** nuclear power plants.
W: What are you talking about?
M: I heard that power plants using fossil fuels cause global warming. Nuclear energy is relatively **cleaner and safer**.
W: That's not true. Think about the 2011 disaster in Japan. It's clearly unsafe.
M: But that kind of accident doesn't happen often. And I think it's getting safer.
W: What about **the waste products from nuclear power**? They are highly dangerous, too.
M: We can find a good way to deal with the waste.
W: It sounds almost impossible. Moreover, nuclear power plants can be a target for terrorism. **We should stop using it**.
M: Well, nuclear power may not be good, but it's a realistic choice.

여: Lucas, 에어컨을 약하게 맞춰두세요. 여름엔 사람들이 전기를 많이 써서 이게 정전을

일으킬 수 있어요.
남: 알았어요. 난 우리가 더 많은 원자력 발전소를 지어야 한다고 생각해요.
여: 무슨 말이에요?
남: 화석 연료를 쓰는 발전소가 지구 온난화를 일으킨다고 들었어요. 원자력은 비교적 더 깨끗하고 더 안전하잖아요.
여: 그건 사실이 아니에요. 2011년 일본의 재난을 생각해봐요. 그건 분명히 안전하지 않아요.
남: 하지만 그런 종류의 사고는 자주 일어나진 않죠. 그리고 나는 그게 더 안전해지고 있다고 생각해요.
여: 원자력 발전에서 나오는 폐기물은 어떻고요? 그것들 역시 매우 위험해요.
남: 우리는 폐기물을 처리할 좋은 방법을 찾을 수 있어요.
여: 그건 거의 불가능한 것 같아요. 게다가 원자력 발전소는 테러의 표적이 될 수도 있어요. 우리는 그걸 사용하는 걸 멈춰야 해요.
남: 글쎄요, 원자력이 안 좋을 수도 있지만 그것은 현실적인 선택이에요.

어휘 set (시계·기기를) 맞추다　electricity 전기, 전력　power failure 정전　nuclear power plant 원자력 발전소 cf. power plant 발전소 cf. nuclear 원자(력)의, 핵의 cf. nuclear power 원자력 (발전)　fossil fuel 화석 연료　global warming 지구 온난화　relatively 비교적, 상대적　disaster 재난, 재해　clearly 분명히: 또렷하게　accident 사고, 우연　waste products 폐기물, 쓰레기　highly 매우　deal with (문제를) 처리하다: 다루다　moreover 게다가, 더욱이　target 표적: 목표　terrorism 테러: 테러리즘 realistic 현실적인: 현실에 맞는

03 관계　③

✽ 직업을 나타내거나 추론할 수 있는 힌트가 대화 전반에 걸쳐 드러나므로, 대화를 전체적으로 이해하는 것이 필요하다. 본 대화에서 여자가 남자에게 물리학을 가르쳐 주고 과학자가 되도록 용기를 주었다고 하고, 여자는 남자에게 가장 똑똑한 제자 중 하나였다고 말하고 있다. 또한, 남자의 고교 동창들이 여자를 모임에 초대하면서 많은 것을 가르쳐 주셨다고 말하는 것으로 보아 ③ '물리학 교사 – 졸업생'의 관계임을 알 수 있다.

W: Come on in, Mason. It's been a long time. You look great!
M: Thanks, Ms. Baker. You haven't changed a bit in the last 20 years.
W: Really? What have you been doing?
M: I became **a chief scientist** of NASA. How about you?
W: Very good. Congratulations! I'm very proud of you.
M: Thanks. You taught me **how interesting physics can be** and encouraged me to be a scientist. I really appreciate it.
W: I was very happy to teach you. You were indeed one of the brightest students I had. By the way, **what brings you here**?
M: Some of my high school classmates planned a get-together, so I was wondering **if you could join us**.
W: Really? Are you sure you want me there?
M: Yes, we'd like to invite you. When we were high school students, **you taught us many things**, including how to live and how to dream.
W: I'd be happy to. Let me check my schedule.

여: 어서 오렴, Mason. 오랜만이구나. 너 멋져 보인다!
남: 감사합니다. Baker 선생님. 지난 20년 동안 조금도 변하지 않으셨네요.
여: 정말이니? 어떻게 지내니?
남: 저는 NASA의 수석 과학자가 되었습니다. 선생님은 어떠세요?
여: 아주 좋아. 축하한다! 네가 무척 자랑스럽구나.
남: 고맙습니다. 선생님이 제게 물리학이 얼마나 흥미로울 수 있는지 가르쳐 주시고 과학자가 되도록 용기를 주셨어요. 정말 감사합니다.
여: 너를 가르쳐서 무척 행복했단다. 정말로 가장 똑똑한 내 제자 중 하나였지. 그런데 여긴 어쩐 일이니?
남: 제 고등학교 동창 몇몇이 모임을 계획했어요. 그래서 선생님이 저희와 함께 해주실 수 있을지 궁금해서요.
여: 정말? 내가 거기에 있길 원하는 게 확실하니?
남: 네, 저희는 선생님을 초대하고 싶습니다. 저희가 고등학생이었을 때 선생님은 저희에

게 살아가는 법과 꿈꾸는 법을 포함해서 많은 것을 가르쳐 주셨잖아요.
여: 기쁘구나. 내 일정을 확인해볼게.

어휘 chief 최고(위의): 최고위자; 주된 physics 물리학 encourage A to-v A가 v하도록 용기[기운]를 북돋우다 appreciate 감사하다; 인식하다; 감상하다 get-together 모임; 친목회 wonder 궁금해하다 including ~을 포함하여

04 그림 불일치 ⑤

✽ 대화가 나오기 전에 각 사물의 위치 관계와 외형(형태나 무늬, 개수 등)의 특징을 미리 확인하는 것이 좋다. 피크닉 테이블 뒤의 바닥에 깃발이 두 개가 꽂혀 있다고 했는데 그림에서는 세 개가 있으므로 ⑤는 내용과 일치하지 않는다. 원래 세 개를 가져왔다는 말을 듣고 꽂혀 있는 깃발을 세 개로 오해하지 않도록 한다.

W: Hey, Oliver! What's that picture on your desk?
M: It was taken when I went Boy Scout camping last month.
W: It looks like a great time. There are **two tents under the tree**. Did you set up those tents?
M: Yes, after setting up the tents, we prepared lunch.
W: I see you here near the campfire. You're **the one holding a stick** in your hand, right?
M: Right. I tried to make a fire for cooking.
W: I see the big pot near the campfire. What is this boy sitting at the picnic table doing?
M: He is Matthew, the leader of the Boy Scouts. **He was reading a map**.
W: He looks focused! Oh, there are **two flags stuck in the ground** behind the table.
M: Yes, actually we took three flags there. But somebody **left one flag in** the car.
W: I see. Anyway, it must have been great fun.

여: 이봐, Oliver! 네 책상에 저 사진 뭐니?
남: 내가 지난달 보이스카우트 캠핑 갔을 때 찍은 거야.
여: 아주 좋은 시간이었던 것 같구나. 나무 아래 텐트가 두 개 있네. 네가 저 텐트를 세웠니?
남: 응. 텐트를 세운 다음에 우리는 점심을 준비했어.
여: 여기 모닥불 근처에 네가 있는 게 보이네. 손에 막대기를 들고 있는 사람이 너지, 맞지?
남: 맞아. 난 요리를 하려고 불을 피우려고 했어.
여: 모닥불 근처에 커다란 냄비가 보이네. 피크닉 테이블에 앉아 있는 이 소년은 뭐 하고 있는 거니?
남: 그는 보이스카우트 리더인 Matthew야. 그는 지도를 읽고 있어.
여: 집중하는 것처럼 보인다! 아. 테이블 뒤의 땅에 깃발 두 개가 꽂혀 있구나.
남: 응. 사실 우리는 그곳에 깃발 세 개를 가져갔어. 하지만 누군가가 차에 깃발 하나를 두고 왔어.
여: 그렇구나. 어쨌든 분명 정말 재미있는 시간을 보냈겠구나.

어휘 set up 세우다; 설치하다 stick 막대기; 박다; 붙이다 focus 집중하다; 초점을 맞추다

05 추후 행동 ⑤

✽ 대개 대화는 어떤 일을 하게 되는 상황이 먼저 제시된 뒤에 남자와 여자가 각각 할 일들과 이에 대한 수락/거절의 응답이 나열되는 식으로 전개된다. 남자가 무료 전자책을 볼 수 있는 웹사이트를 여자에게 알려주겠다고 했으므로 남자가 할 일은 ⑤ '무료 전자책 제공 사이트 알려주기'이다. 노트북 컴퓨터 꺼내기는 여자가 할 일임에 유의한다.

M: Elizabeth, did you finally borrow the book for your history class?
W: No, not yet. The school library didn't have it.
M: You said you need it **urgently**.
W: Yeah, so I was thinking of going down to the public library this afternoon. Can you **give me a ride** there?
M: Sorry, I have a dentist appointment this afternoon. By the way, you can use free books on the Internet.
W: Really? I didn't know that. How can I use them?
M: There are some websites **where you can find free e-books**. They have

tons of free books for you **to read online** or download to your computer.
W: Wow! That sounds great.
M: Yeah, **I'll let you know** some of them.
W: Thank you! Let me take out my laptop.

남: Elizabeth, 역사 수업을 위한 책을 결국 빌렸니?
여: 아니, 아직 아냐. 학교 도서관에 없었어.
남: 너 급하게 필요하다고 했잖아.
여: 응, 그래서 오늘 오후에 공공 도서관에 가볼까 생각 중이었어. 거기까지 나를 태워줄 수 있니?
남: 미안하지만 오늘 오후에 치과 예약이 있어. 그런데 너는 인터넷에서 무료 책을 이용할 수 있어.
여: 정말이니? 그건 몰랐어. 어떻게 그것들을 이용할 수 있니?
남: 무료 전자책을 찾을 수 있는 웹사이트가 몇 개 있어. 거기에는 네가 온라인으로 읽거나 네 컴퓨터로 다운받을 수 있는 수많은 무료 책들이 있어.
여: 와! 그거 굉장하다.
남: 그래. 네게 그것들 중 몇 개를 알려줄게.
여: 고마워! 내 노트북 컴퓨터를 꺼낼게.

어휘 urgently 급히 give A a ride A를 태워주다 appointment 예약; 약속; 임명

06 금액 ④

✽ 여러 개의 수치 정보가 등장하므로 필요한 정보를 메모하면서 듣는 것이 좋다. 매달 30달러씩 30개월 동안 지불하거나 40달러씩 24개월 동안 지불할 수 있는데, 여자는 24개월짜리 계획을 선택했다. 따라서 960달러에 스크린 보호 필름 10달러를 추가하면 여자가 지불하게 될 총금액은 ④ '$970'이다.

M: Hello. How can I help you?
W: I'd like to get a new smartphone, the Sky Phone advertised on TV.
M: Good choice. It has a super HD touch screen and 64 gigabytes of internal memory.
W: I see. Are you offering **any special discounts**?
M: Well, yes, but it depends on **how long you'll use** this phone.
W: What's the best plan?
M: There are two pricing options: a 30-month plan and a 24-month plan.
W: How much should I pay each month?
M: You need to pay $30 per month for **30 months** or $40 per month for **24 months**.
W: Hmm... I'll sign up for a 24-month plan.
M: Okay. **Do you need anything else?**
W: I need a phone case and a protective film for the screen.
M: The phone case is free, but you need to pay for **the protective film**. It is $10.
W: Okay. I'll buy it.

남: 안녕하세요? 뭘 도와드릴까요?
여: TV에서 광고하는 새 스마트폰인 Sky Phone을 사려고요.
남: 잘 선택하셨습니다. 초고화질 터치스크린과 64기가바이트의 내장 메모리를 갖고 있죠.
여: 알겠습니다. 특별 할인을 해주시나요?
남: 음, 네, 하지만 그건 손님이 이 휴대전화를 얼마나 오래 사용하실지에 달려 있습니다.
여: 가장 좋은 계획이 무엇인가요?
남: 두 개의 가격 선택이 있습니다. 30개월짜리 계획과 24개월짜리 계획이 있어요.
여: 매달 제가 얼마를 내야 하나요?
남: 30개월 동안 매달 30달러를 지불하시거나 24개월 동안 매달 40달러를 내셔야 해요.
여: 음… 전 24개월 계획으로 신청할게요.
남: 알겠습니다. 다른 건 필요하지 않으신가요?
여: 휴대전화 케이스와 스크린에 붙일 보호 필름이 필요해요.
남: 휴대전화 케이스는 무료지만 보호 필름은 비용을 지불하셔야 합니다. 10달러입니다.
여: 좋아요. 그걸 사겠어요.

어휘 advertise 광고하다 internal 내부의; 체내의 offer 제공하다; 내놓다 depend on ~에 달려있다[의존하다] sign up for ~을 신청[등록]하다 protective 보호하는; 방어적인

07 이유 ④

* 지시문을 통해 남자가 오늘 저녁 식사를 함께하지 못하는 상황이며 남자의 말에 단서가 있을 가능성이 큼을 미리 파악한다. 남자가 초과 근무를 해야 하는 건 아니라고 했고 동료가 다쳐 그를 집에 데려다줘야 한다고 말하고 있다. 그러므로 답은 ④이다. 다친 사람은 본인이 아닌 남자의 동료임에 유의한다.

[Telephone rings.]
W: Hello?
M: Hello, Jennifer. It's Gabriel speaking.
W: Gabriel! Are you still in the office? I'm waiting for you.
M: Jennifer, that's why I'm calling. We were supposed to eat out tonight, but I **won't be able to make it.**
W: Oh, why? I've been looking forward to this dinner.
M: I'm really sorry I have to miss it.
W: Do you **have to work overtime**?
M: No, do you know my co-worker, Benjamin? He **fell down the stairs** when he left the office, and I had to take him to the hospital.
W: Oh, dear! Is he okay?
M: Yes, he is okay now. I'm waiting for him to be treated. He lives alone, so I **have to take him home.**
W: If that's the case, that's okay. By the way, my mother called me and said she'll visit me next month. Would you like to meet her?
M: Certainly. I'd love to see her. Let's talk about it later.

[전화벨이 울린다.]
여: 여보세요?
남: 여보세요, Jennifer. Gabriel이에요.
여: Gabriel! 아직 사무실에 있는 거예요? 당신을 기다리고 있어요.
남: Jennifer, 그래서 전화했어요. 우리 오늘 밤 외식하기로 했잖아요. 하지만 난 못 갈 거예요.
여: 아, 왜요? 이번 저녁 식사를 기대했는데요.
남: 못 가게 돼서 정말 미안해요.
여: 초과 근무를 해야 하는 건가요?
남: 아니요. 내 동료 Benjamin 알아요? 그가 퇴근하면서 계단에서 넘어졌고 그를 병원으로 데려와야 했어요.
여: 아, 이런! 그는 괜찮나요?
남: 네, 지금은 괜찮아요. 나는 그가 치료받는 걸 기다리고 있어요. 그가 혼자 살아서 내가 그를 집까지 데려다줘야 해요.
여: 그런 경우라면 괜찮아요. 그런데 우리 어머니가 전화하셔서 다음 달에 방문하겠다고 말씀하셨어요. 어머니를 만나겠어요?
남: 그럼요. 뵙고 싶어요. 나중에 그것에 관해 이야기해요.

어휘 be supposed to-v v하기로 되어있다   eat out 외식하다   make it (모임 등에) 가다[참석하다]   look forward to A A를 기대[고대]하다   overtime 초과 근무; 야근   co-worker 동료   leave 떠나다, 출발하다   take 데리고 가다; 가져다 주다   treat 치료하다; 대하다   certainly 그럼요, 틀림없이

08 언급하지 않은 것 ②

* 대화의 진행은 대개 선택지와 같은 순서이므로, 선택지를 보면서 언급된 내용을 소거하는 식으로 푸는 것이 좋다. 여름에는 보통 날씨가 덥다고 했지만 어떤 옷차림을 하라는 언급은 없었으므로 답은 ②이다.

[Telephone rings.]
M: Hello, Sequoia Sightseeing Tours. How can I help you?
W: Hello. I'd like to ask something about the tour. How long is the tour?
M: Our full-day tour is generally **8 hours long**, and the half-day tour is 3 and half hours long.
W: **What will the weather be like** during the tour in this season of the year?
M: Well, it's very difficult to predict. But as you know, it's usually very hot in the summer.
W: Okay. Can you tell me what I should bring?
M: **We recommend you to bring** your camera, water, snacks to eat, and sunscreen.
W: Oh, thanks. Does the tour include lunch?

M: Yes, **we stop for lunch** at Wuksachi Lodge.
W: I see. How do I book a tour?
M: **You can book the tour online** through our website or call us at this number.
W: Thank you. Let me think about it and call back to you.

[전화벨이 울린다.]
남: 여보세요, Sequoia 관광 투어입니다. 무엇을 도와드릴까요?
여: 여보세요. 투어에 대해 좀 물어보려고요. 투어는 얼마나 걸리나요?
남: 저희 종일 투어는 보통 8시간 걸리고 반나절 투어는 3시간 반 걸립니다(① 소요 시간).
여: 매년 이 무렵에 투어하는 동안 날씨는 어떨까요?
남: 음, 예측하기가 아주 어렵습니다. 하지만 아시다시피, 여름에는 보통 아주 덥죠.
여: 알겠어요. 뭘 가져가야 하는지 알려주실 수 있나요?
남: 카메라와 물, 먹을 간식과 자외선 차단제를 가져오실 것(③ 준비물)을 권합니다.
여: 아, 고마워요. 투어에 점심이 포함되나요?
남: 네, 저희는 점심을 먹으러 Wuksachi 산장에 들릅니다(④ 점심 제공 여부).
여: 그렇군요. 어떻게 투어를 예약하나요?
남: 저희 웹사이트를 통해 온라인으로 투어를 예약하실 수도 있고 아니면 이 번호로 저희에게 전화해 주실 수 있습니다(⑤ 예약 방법).
여: 고맙습니다. 생각해보고 다시 전화할게요.

어휘 sightseeing 관광   generally 보통; 일반적으로   predict 예측[예상]하다   recommend 권하다, 추천하다   lodge 산장, 오두막   book 예약하다

09 내용 불일치 ⑤

* 담화의 진행은 대개 선택지와 같은 순서이므로, 선택지를 보면서 일치하는 내용을 소거하는 식으로 푸는 것이 좋다. 시의 웹사이트에서 작년 수상자들의 의상을 찾아볼 수 있다고 했으므로 ⑤는 내용과 일치하지 않는다.

W: If you've ever dreamed about dressing up as your favorite movie or TV character, this is your chance! Our town will hold a Fall Costume Contest in the town square next Saturday, **October 15th.** Any costume is welcome, whether you're dressing as a real or **fictional character**. The costumes **will be judged by** our mayor, Sarah Turner, and business owners in town. Prizes will be given for the top costume of **each of four categories**. The categories are the most creative costume, funniest costume, most beautiful costume, and scariest costume. You can find last year's winners on the City's website. But it's not permitted to imitate past winners' costumes. The costume you dress up in **should be original**. Give it a try and come to see everyone's costumes!

여: 여러분이 좋아하는 영화나 TV 인물처럼 옷을 입는 것에 대해 꿈꿔본 적 있다면 이번이 여러분의 기회입니다! 우리 마을이 다음 토요일인 ① 10월 15일에 마을 광장에서 Fall Costume 대회를 열 것입니다. 여러분이 실제 인물처럼 입든 ② 가상 인물처럼 입든 어떤 의상이든지 환영합니다. 의상은 ③ 우리 시장님인 Sarah Turner와 마을의 기업가들이 심사할 것입니다. ④ 상은 각기 4개 부문의 최고 의상에 주어질 것입니다. 부문은 가장 창의적인 의상, 가장 웃긴 의상, 가장 아름다운 의상과 가장 무서운 의상입니다. 여러분은 ⑤ 시 웹사이트에서 작년 수상작들을 찾아볼 수 있습니다. 그러나 지난 수상자의 의상을 모방하는 것은 허용되지 않습니다. 여러분이 입는 의상은 독창적이어야 합니다. 시도해보시고 모든 이들의 의상을 보러 오십시오!

어휘 hold 열다, 개최하다   costume 의상, 복장   square 광장; 정사각형(의)   judge 심사하다; 판단하다   mayor 시장   category 부문, 범주   creative 창의[창조]적인   permit 허용[허락]하다   imitate 모방하다; 흉내 내다   original 독창적인; 원래의

10 도표 이해 ④

* 대화의 진행은 대개 도표 항목의 나열 순서대로 진행된다. 대화를 들으면서 도표의 각 항목 중 선택되지 않은 것을 소거하는 식으로 푸는 것이 좋다. 우선 공기 정화 기능이 없는 ①을 제외하고 그다음에는 물을 매일 줘야 하는 ②를 제외시킨다. 그다음 조건으로 키가 큰 식물인 ③을 제외시키면 ④와 ⑤가 남는데, 80달러 미만의 가격을 원했으므로 남자가 구매할 식물은 ④이다.

W: How can I help you?

M: I'd like to get a nice plant for my mother for Mother's Day. Do you deliver?

W: Of course. Is there a particular plant you're interested in?

M: Honestly, I don't know much about plants, but I'd like to get her **something that cleans the air**.

W: We have houseplants that clean the air. Anything else?

M: I think a plant that **doesn't need a lot of watering** would be good for her.

W: All right. We have plants that only need to be watered once a week or even once a month.

M: Both are good. And my mother **doesn't like tall plants** because they can cover the windows and block the light.

W: That narrows down your choices to these two. How much **were you planning** to spend?

M: No more than $80.

W: Well, I think this is what you want.

M: Great. Please deliver it to this address.

여: 무엇을 도와드릴까요?

남: 어머니날에 어머니께 멋진 식물을 사드리고 싶어요. 배달됩니까?

여: 물론입니다. 관심을 갖고 계신 특정한 식물이 있으신가요?

남: 솔직히, 식물에 대해서 잘 모릅니다만 어머니께 공기를 정화하는 것을 사드리고 싶습니다.

여: 우리는 공기를 정화하는 실내용 식물이 있습니다. 다른 건 또 없습니까?

남: 물을 많이 줄 필요가 없는 식물이 어머니께 좋을 것 같군요.

여: 알겠습니다. 단지 일주일에 한 번이나 심지어 한 달에 한 번 물을 줘야 하는 식물이 있습니다.

남: 둘 다 좋습니다. 그리고 제 어머니는 창문을 가리고 빛을 막을 수 있기 때문에 키 큰 식물을 좋아하지 않으세요.

여: 그건 이 둘로 선택 범위를 줄여주는군요. 얼마나 쓸 계획이셨어요?

남: 80달러가 넘지 않게요.

여: 음, 이게 당신이 원하시는 거 같군요.

남: 좋습니다. 그걸 이 주소로 배달해주세요.

어휘 particular 특정한; 특별한 honestly 솔직히; 정말로, 진짜로 cover 가리다; 덮다 block 막다, 차단하다 narrow down 줄이다, 좁히다

11 짧은 대화에 이어질 응답 ③

✳ 여자가 약을 건네줄 수 있는지 물었고, 이에 남자가 할 적절한 응답은 ③ '알았어요! 내가 물도 좀 가져올게요.'이다.

① 그럼요. 내가 약국에 잠시 들르게요.

② 좋습니다. 이 약을 매끼 식사 후 복용하십시오.

④ 그건 맞습니다. 그게 곧 당신에게 효과가 있을 것입니다.

⑤ 네. 의사가 내게 처방전을 주었어요.

W: Aiden, can you get me my medicine? It is **in the pill box**.

M: Sure. Is it an oval or round shaped tablet?

W: The pill I need is a round one. **Can you hand me the pill?**

M: All right! Let me get some water, too.

여: Aiden, 내 약 좀 가져다주겠어요? 약 상자 안에 있어요.

남: 그럼요. 타원형 모양인가요, 아니면 둥근 모양의 정제인가요?

여: 내가 필요한 약은 둥근 것이에요. 약을 건네주겠어요?

남: 알았어요! 내가 물도 좀 가져올게요.

어휘 pill 알약 oval 타원형의 tablet 정제 ((둥글넓적한 모양의 약제)) | 선택지 어휘 | stop by 잠시 들르다 pharmacy 약국 work 효과가 있다 prescription 처방(전), 처방된 약

12 짧은 대화에 이어질 응답 ④

✳ 여자가 저녁 식사 초대에 대해 가겠다고 한 상황에서 남자가 구체적인 시간이 괜찮은지를 물었으므로 이에 대한 응답으로는 ④ '물론 괜찮지요. 저희가 토요일에 거기 갈 것을 기대하셔도 돼요.'가 가장 적절하다.

① 와주셔서 감사합니다. 언제든 환영입니다.

② 그냥 몸만 오세요. 필요한 건 다 있답니다.

③ 아주 좋아요. 음료수를 가져오신다면 너무 좋을 것 같아요.

⑤ 그거 재미있겠군요. 제게 초대장만 갖다 주세요.

M: Hi, Eliana. **I'm dropping by** to invite you and your husband to our place this Saturday night.

W: It's so kind of you to stop by. We would love to come and join you.

M: The dinner starts at about 6 o'clock. **Is that okay with you?**

W: It sure is. You can expect us there on Saturday.

남: 안녕, Eliana. 이번 토요일 저녁에 우리 집으로 당신 부부를 초대하려고 들렀어요.

여: 들러주다니 너무 감사해요. 저희는 가서 함께 하고 싶어요.

남: 저녁 식사는 6시 정각쯤 시작해요. 괜찮으세요?

여: 물론 괜찮지요. 저희가 토요일에 거기 갈 것을 기대하셔도 돼요.

어휘 drop by ~에 들르다(= stop by) | 선택지 어휘 | invitation 초대(장)

13 긴 대화에 이어질 응답 ②

✳ 대화의 전체 맥락 하에 마지막 말의 의미나 의도를 정확히 파악하는 것이 좋다. 브라질리안 주짓수를 수강하자는 여자의 권유에 남자는 망설이면서 어려워 보인다고 주저하고 있다. 이에 대한 여자의 응답으로는 ② '네가 원하는 대로 할 수 있어. 강요하지 않을게.'가 가장 적절하다.

① 그건 걱정 마. 넌 아주 잘 했어.

③ 나를 믿어. 제시간에 거기 갈게.

④ 네 말이 맞아. 그 강좌에 우리 둘 다 등록할게.

⑤ 아니, 괜찮아. 난 더 신나는 걸 하고 싶어.

W: Thomas, I want to learn a new sport!

M: Sounds great. What do you want to learn?

W: I'm going to take a Brazilian Jiujitsu class. **Would you like to take it** with me?

M: Brazilian Jiujitsu? Isn't it a martial art?

W: Yes, it is. I really want to **be more athletic**.

M: Then why don't you try swimming or tennis?

W: Brazilian Jiujitsu will help me get in shape. Plus, the way you earn different levels of belts is exciting!

M: It sounds fun, but **I don't enjoy fighting against** others.

W: You don't have to worry about that. In the beginning, you don't fight at all!

M: Well, **I doubt that** I'd be very good. It seems too difficult.

W: You can do as you want. I won't force you.

여: Thomas, 난 새로운 스포츠를 배우고 싶어!

남: 그거 좋겠다. 뭘 배우고 싶니?

여: 난 브라질리안 주짓수 강좌를 수강할 거야. 나하고 같이 수강할래?

남: 브라질리안 주짓수라고? 그거 무술 아니니?

여: 응. 맞아. 난 정말 더 탄탄해지고 싶어.

남: 그러면 수영이나 테니스를 하지 그러니?

여: 브라질리안 주짓수는 내가 좋은 몸매를 유지하도록 도울 거야. 게다가, 다른 단계의 벨트를 얻는 방식이 흥미로워!

남: 그거 재미있겠구나, 하지만 난 다른 사람과 싸우는 걸 즐기지 않아.

여: 그건 걱정할 필요가 없어. 처음에는 전혀 싸우지 않아!

남: 글쎄, 내가 정말 잘할지 의심스러워. 아주 어려워 보이거든.

여: 네가 원하는 대로 할 수 있어. 강요하지 않을게.

어휘 Brazilian Jiujitsu 브라질리안 주짓수 ((일본의 유술 기법을 브라질 격투술과 접목한 무술)) martial art 무술 athletic (몸이) 탄탄한; (운동) 경기의 get in shape 좋은 몸매 [상태]를 유지하다 earn 얻다, 받다; 벌다 doubt 의심(하다), 의혹(을 품다) | 선택지 어휘 | force 강요하다, (어쩔 수 없이) ~하게 만들다; 힘 count on ~을 믿다 [확신하다]; ~에 의지하다 register 등록하다; 신고하다

14 긴 대화에 이어질 응답 ①

✳ 대화의 전체 맥락 하에 마지막 말의 의미나 의도를 정확히 파악하는 것이 좋다. 본 대화는 경기에서 공을 떨어뜨리는 실수를 해서 자기 팀이 지게 되었다고 생각하는 여자

를 남자가 위로하고 있다. 여자가 계속 자책하는 상황에서 남자가 할 말로는 ① '스스로 비하하는 걸 그만하고 그냥 넘겨.'가 가장 적절하다.

② 그 일을 끝내는 데 시간이 좀 걸린다는 걸 알아.
③ 넌 잘 해냈으니까 정말 자부심을 가져야 해.
④ 멍청하게 굴지 말고 너무 늦기 전에 그걸 포기해.
⑤ 내가 너한테 진정하고 너무 흥분하지 말라고 말했잖아.

M: Madison, cheer up. Want some tea?
W: No, thanks.
M: A cup of tea will give you relief. Why don't you try some?
W: No, **I don't feel like it**. I can't believe I dropped the ball.
M: It's just one of those things.
W: I **should have held onto** the ball, but I dropped it. If I hadn't, we would have won the game.
M: You did your best. That's enough.
W: No, **I spoiled everything**. I'm sure the coach must be very angry with me.
M: No, he isn't. **It could happen to anyone**.
W: I hate myself. I feel so stupid.
M: **Stop putting yourself down and let it go.**

남: Madison, 기운 내. 차를 좀 마실래?
여: 아니, 괜찮아.
남: 차 한 잔이 너에게 안도감을 줄 거야. 좀 마시지 그러니?
여: 아니, 그럴 기분이 아니야. 내가 공을 떨어뜨렸다는 걸 믿을 수 없어.
남: 그건 그냥 어쩔 수 없는 일이야.
여: 공을 꼭 잡았어야 했는데 떨어뜨렸어. 내가 그러지 않았다면 우리가 경기에서 이겼을 거야.
남: 넌 최선을 다했어. 그거면 충분해.
여: 아니야, 내가 모든 걸 망쳤어. 코치님은 분명 내게 화가 아주 많이 나셨을 거야.
남: 아니, 그렇지 않아. 그건 누구에게나 일어날 수 있어.
여: 나 자신이 싫어. 너무 바보같이 느껴져.
남: 스스로 비하하는 걸 그만하고 그냥 넘겨.

어휘 relief 안도, 안심 (just) one of those things (그냥) 어쩔 수 없는 일 hold onto ～을 꼭 잡다; ～에 매달리다 spoil (일을) 망치다; (아이를) 버릇없게 키우다 stupid 바보 같은; 어리석은 | 선택지 어휘 | put oneself down 자기 비하하다 give A up A를 포기하다[그만두다] calm down 진정하다

15 상황에 적절한 말 ③

＊ 지시문을 통해 누가(A) 누구에게(B) 할 말인지를 우선 정확히 파악한다. 담화는 대개 A와 B에 대한 배경 설명과 B가 처한 문제 상황, 그리고 이에 대해 A가 어떤 말을 하려고 하는지에 대한 설명의 순서로 전개된다. 여행을 가게 되었는데 자신의 개를 맡기지 못해서 걱정하고 있던 Maria(B)에게 Natalie(A)가 개를 맡아주겠다고 자원하자 Maria는 감사를 표한다. 이 상황에서 Natalie가 할 말로는 ③ '천만예요. 난 개를 좋아하고 당신을 돕게 되어 기뻐요.'가 가장 적절하다.

① 어떻게 감사를 해야 할지 모르겠어요. 당신은 생명의 은인이세요.
② 제 여행을 취소해야 할 것 같아요. 선택의 여지가 없어요.
④ 그건 죄송합니다. 다시는 그런 일이 일어나지 않도록 확실히 하겠습니다.
⑤ 그건 맞아요. 저를 도와주시면 은혜 갚을 것을 약속드려요.

W: Maria lives with two dogs. She is planning to travel Eastern Europe with her friends for a month this summer. But **she can't take them** on her trip. She also can't put her dogs in a shelter for dogs because her dogs don't like to stay in shelters. And her other friends can't help her because they live in a "no pets" apartment. So **she puts an advertisement** in the newspaper in hopes to find someone who will look after her dogs. Unfortunately, **no one responds to** the advertisement. She is really worried about it. Today, she **happens to meet** her neighbor, Natalie, and tells her about it. Natalie **volunteers to look after** her dogs for a month. Maria deeply thanks Natalie. But Natalie thinks it's no big deal because she likes pets. In this situation, what would Natalie most likely say to Maria?

Natalie: **It's my pleasure. I love dogs, and I'm glad to help you out.**

여: Maria는 두 마리의 개와 함께 산다. 그녀는 이번 여름에 한 달 동안 친구들과 동유럽을 여행할 계획이다. 그러나 그녀는 개들을 여행에 데려갈 수 없다. 그녀의 개들이 개 보호소에 머물기를 싫어하기 때문에 개들을 보호소에 맡길 수도 없다. 그리고 그녀의 다른 친구들은 '애완동물 금지' 아파트에 살기 때문에 그녀를 도울 수 없다. 그래서 그녀는 자신의 개를 돌봐줄 사람을 찾으려는 희망으로 신문에 광고를 낸다. 유감스럽게도 아무도 광고에 답하지 않는다. 그녀는 정말 걱정한다. 오늘 그녀는 우연히 이웃인 Natalie를 만나 그녀에게 그 일에 관해 이야기한다. Natalie는 한 달 동안 그녀의 개를 돌봐주겠다고 자원한다. Maria는 Natalie에게 깊이 감사를 표한다. 그러나 Natalie는 자신이 애완동물을 좋아하기 때문에 별일 아니라고 생각한다. 이 상황에서 Natalie가 Maria에게 뭐라고 말하겠는가?

Natalie: 천만예요. 난 개를 좋아하고 당신을 돕게 되어 기뻐요.

어휘 shelter 보호소; 대피처 advertisement 광고 look after ～을 돌보다; 맡다 volunteer 자원하다; 자원봉사자 | 선택지 어휘 | make sure 확실히 하다 return the favor 은혜를 갚다

16~17 세트 문항 16 ① 17 ④

＊ **16** 빠른 결과를 얻으려고 운동을 너무 심하게 하면 도리어 신체에 안 좋을 수 있으므로 운동 속도를 서서히 올리라고 하면서 몸이 안 좋으면 휴식을 취하라고 조언하고 있다. 그러므로 담화의 주제는 ① '운동할 때 몸을 소중히 하기'이다.

② 운동을 하는 것의 이점과 위험
③ 운동하지 않고 열량을 소모하는 법
④ 운동을 통해 건강을 유지하는 것의 이로움
⑤ 규칙적인 운동과 좋은 식이요법의 필요성

＊ **17** 해석 참조.
① 걷기 ② 자전거 타기 ③ 하이킹 ④ 하키 ⑤ 야구

M: Hello, everyone. I'm Daniel, a fitness trainer. You may think that the harder you exercise, the stronger you become. But you should know exercising can **have some bad effects** if you are not careful. When you **work out too much all at once** to get fast results, your body can easily get injured. So, start slowly and build up gradually. **Give yourself plenty of time** to warm up with easy walking or gentle stretching. Then speed up to a pace you can maintain for five to ten minutes. As your stamina improves, gradually increase the amount of time you exercise. Work your way up to 30 to 60 minutes of exercise most days of the week. Your workout routine can include various light activities, such as walking, or bicycling. You can go hiking or play baseball with your family on weekends. But **always listen to your body**. If you feel pain, shortness of breath, or dizziness from exercising too much, take a break. **Be flexible about your schedule**. If you're not feeling good, give yourself a day or two off.

남: 안녕하세요, 여러분. 저는 피트니스 트레이너인 Daniel입니다. 여러분은 아마 운동을 열심히 하면 할수록 여러분이 더 튼튼하게 될 것이라고 생각하실 수 있습니다. 그러나 여러분이 주의를 기울이지 않으면 운동이 나쁜 영향을 줄 수 있다는 것을 아셔야 합니다. 빠른 결과를 얻기 위해 갑자기 너무 심하게 운동하면 여러분의 신체는 쉽게 부상을 입을 수 있습니다. 그러므로 천천히 시작하고 서서히 강화해 가십시오. 쉬운 걷기나 가벼운 스트레칭으로 여러분 자신에게 몸을 풀 충분한 시간을 주십시오. 그러고 나서 여러분이 5분에서 10분 동안 지속할 수 있는 속도로 올리십시오. 여러분의 체력이 향상되면서 운동 시간의 양을 점진적으로 늘리십시오. 일주일의 대부분을 30분에서 60분 운동으로 차근차근 늘려가십시오. 여러분의 운동 일과는 ① 걷기나 ② 자전거 타기 같은 다양한 가벼운 활동을 포함할 수 있습니다. 여러분은 주말에 ③ 하이킹을 가거나 가족과 함께 ⑤ 야구를 할 수 있습니다. 그러나 항상 여러분의 신체에 귀 기울이십시오. 너무 심하게 운동하여 고통을 느끼거나 숨이 가쁘거나 어지러우면 휴식을 취하십시오. 여러분의 일정을 자율적으로 하십시오. 몸이 안 좋으면 하루나 이틀 쉬십시오.

어휘 all at once 갑자기 injure 부상을 입히다; 손상시키다 gradually 서서히, 점진적으로 plenty of 많은 pace 속도; 속도를 유지하다 maintain 지속[유지]하다 stamina 체력 routine 일과; 틀에 박힌 (일) flexible 융통성 있는; 잘 구부러지는
| 선택지 어휘 | advantage 이점, 장점 risk 위험 benefit 이로움; 혜택 necessity 필요(성); 필수품

13 회

01 ④	02 ④	03 ③	04 ④	05 ③	06 ④	07 ⑤	08 ③	09 ④	10 ⑤
11 ②	12 ③	13 ①	14 ④	15 ④	16 ④	17 ③		

01 화자가 하는 말의 목적 ④

✻ 담화의 일부 내용이 아니라 중심 내용을 파악해야 한다. 본 담화는 정규 프로그램을 중단하고 뉴스 속보를 알리고 있다. 강풍과 폭설을 동반한 큰 폭풍이 접근해 오니 대비할 것을 안내하며 이에 대비해 충분한 식량과 연료를 준비하라고 알리고 있다. 그러므로 담화의 목적은 ④이다.

M: We interrupt regular programming for this breaking news. We have been informed by the National Weather Office that a big storm is moving in. It is bringing **high winds and heavy snow**. City officials have been advised to close down all public buildings, including schools. We must ensure that everyone is prepared for heavy snow. The storm **will last three days** and will bring at least two meters of snow. So do not expect to follow **your regular schedule** for a minimum of six days or more. Everyone should have on hand plenty of food and fuel. **Stay tuned to this station** for further instructions. We now return to our regular programming.

남: 이 뉴스 속보로 정규 프로그램을 중단합니다. 국립 기상청에서 큰 폭풍이 접근해오고 있다고 알려왔습니다. 그것은 강풍과 폭설을 동반하고 있습니다. 시 공무원들은 학교를 포함해 모든 공공건물을 폐쇄할 것을 권고받았습니다. 우리는 반드시 모든 사람이 폭설에 대비하게 해야 합니다. 폭풍은 3일간 계속될 것이고 적어도 2미터의 눈을 가져올 것입니다. 그러므로 최소한 6일 이상 정규 일정을 따르는 것을 기대하지 마십시오. 모두 구할 수 있는 충분한 식량과 연료를 가지고 계셔야 합니다. 추가적인 지시를 (듣기) 위해 이 방송국에 주파수를 고정해 주십시오. 이제 정규 프로그램으로 돌아갑니다.

어휘 interrupt 중단시키다; 방해하다 regular 정규의; 규칙적인 breaking news 뉴스 속보 official 공무원, 임원 advise 권고하다, 충고하다 including ~을 포함하여 ensure 반드시 ~하게 하다; 보장하다 last 계속되다, 지속되다 on hand 구할[얻을] 수 있는 further 추가의, 더 이상의 instruction 지시; 설명

02 의견 ④

✻ 우선 지시문에서 명시한 화자의 성별을 보고 어느 화자의 말에 주목할지를 판단해야 한다. 특히 의견이나 주장을 표현하는 어구(I think ~, You should ~ 등)가 이끄는 내용을 잘 들어야 한다. 여자는 바이올린 연주가 아이들의 집중력과 기억력을 향상시킨다면서 조기 교육이 아주 중요하다고 이야기하는 것으로 보아 여자의 의견은 ④ '어린이 조기 교육은 미래의 성공을 위해 필요하다.'임을 알 수 있다.

W: I want to give Camilla violin lessons. Music School at Ohio University has just opened a violin class for kids.
M: Violin? Camilla is already taking soccer class and drawing class.
W: Playing the violin improves children's concentration and memory.
M: Since she's still young, **keeping her healthy** is enough, don't you think?
W: **Early childhood education** is so important. During that time, the human brain develops rapidly.
M: I know, but that doesn't mean we have to force it.
W: What you need to succeed in life is established before **you enter kindergarten**. Research has shown that.
M: Well, Camilla is very active. For a girl like her, all these classes can be very stressful.
W: I don't think so. The violin class will be just once a week.
M: It'll put too much pressure on her. I know she'd rather do something physical.
W: Actually, I think she would probably **enjoy violin lessons**. Besides, I'm sure they'll be good for her.
M: Hmm... Okay. I'll consider your suggestion.

여: 난 Camilla에게 바이올린 강습을 시키고 싶어요. Ohio 대학의 음악학교에서 아이들

을 위한 바이올린 수업을 막 열었어요.
남: 바이올린이요? Camilla는 이미 축구 수업과 그림 수업을 듣고 있잖아요.
여: 바이올린 연주하기는 아이들의 집중력과 기억력을 향상시키거든요.
남: 아직 애가 어려서 아이의 건강을 유지하는 것으로 충분해요. 그렇게 생각하지 않아요?
여: 조기 교육은 아주 중요해요. 그 시기 동안 인간 두뇌가 급속하게 발달하잖아요.
남: 알아요, 하지만 그게 우리가 억지로 시켜야 한다는 뜻은 아니에요.
여: 인생에서 성공하는 데 필요한 것은 유치원에 들어가기 전에 확립돼요. 연구들이 그걸 보여주고요.
남: 음. Camilla는 아주 활동적이에요. 그 애 같은 여자아이에게 이 모든 강좌는 스트레스를 많이 줄 수 있어요.
여: 난 그렇게 생각하지 않아요. 바이올린 수업은 단지 일주일에 한 번일 거예요.
남: 그건 그 애에게 너무 많은 압박을 가할 거예요. 난 그 애가 신체적인 무언가를 하는 편이 낫다는 걸 알아요.
여: 사실 그 애는 아마 바이올린 강습을 즐길 것 같아요. 게다가 난 그것들이 그 애에게 좋을 거라고 확신해요.
남: 흠… 좋아요. 당신 제안을 고려해볼게요.

어휘 concentration 집중(력); 농도 rapidly 급속히, 빨리 force 억지[강제]로 ~시키다 succeed 성공하다 establish 확립하다; 설립하다 kindergarten 유치원 put pressure on A A에게 압박을 가하다 physical 신체[육체]적인 consider 고려하다; 여기다 suggestion 제안, 제의

03 관계 ③

✻ 직업을 나타내거나 추론할 수 있는 힌트가 대화 전반에 걸쳐 드러나므로, 대화를 전체적으로 이해하는 것이 필요하다. 본 대화에서 여자는 대학원생으로 Herold 박사의 연구를 돕고 있다고 했으므로 연구 조교임을 알 수 있다. 남자는 실험실 건물로 들어오려는 사람이 여기서 일하는지 아닌지 확인하는 일을 하고 있으므로 실험실 경비원이다. 그러므로 둘의 관계는 ③이다.

[beep, beep, beep]
M: Is there a problem?
W: This ID scanner can't read my ID card. The door isn't opening.
M: Hold on. **Let me check my monitor**. Do you work here?
W: Yes, I am a graduate student and **help the research** of Dr. Herold here. I didn't have a problem yesterday.
M: Your personal information isn't coming up on my monitor. You have to go to the office over there and ask about it.
W: I already went there, but no one is in the office right now.
M: I'm afraid there's nothing I can do at the moment. I have to be able to check **if you're working here or not**.
W: Here's my ID card with photo. Can't you **just let me in** this one time?
M: Sorry, I can't do that. It's a laboratory safety policy. Why don't you call a researcher in your lab and ask for help?
W: Okay. I'll call.

[삐, 삐, 삐]
남: 문제가 있습니까?
여: 이 신분 확인 장치가 제 ID 카드를 읽지 못하네요. 문이 열리지 않아요.
남: 잠깐만요. 제 모니터를 확인해볼게요. 여기서 일하십니까?
여: 네, 저는 대학원생이고 여기서 Herold 박사님의 연구를 돕고 있어요. 어제는 문제가 없었는데요.
남: 개인 정보가 제 모니터에 뜨지 않는군요. 저기 있는 사무실로 가서 물어보셔야겠어요.
여: 이미 거기 갔었는데 지금 사무실에 아무도 없어요.
남: 유감이지만 지금 제가 해드릴 수 있는 게 아무것도 없는 것 같군요. 여기서 일하는지 아닌지 제가 확인할 수 있어야 합니다.
여: 여기 사진이 있는 제 ID 카드가 있어요. 이번 한 번만 들어가게 해줄 수 없나요?
남: 죄송합니다만 그렇게 할 수 없습니다. 실험실 안전 방침입니다. 그쪽 실험실에 있는 연구원에게 전화해서 도움을 요청하지 그래요?

여: 알겠어요. 전화할게요.

어휘 ID card ID 카드, 신분증   graduate student 대학원생   personal 개인의, 개인적인
at the moment 지금   laboratory 실험실, 연구소(= lab)   policy 방침; 방책

04 그림 불일치   ④

✻ 대화가 나오기 전에 각 사물의 위치 관계와 외형(형태나 무늬, 개수 등)의 특징을 미리
확인하는 것이 좋다. 대화에서는 책 세 권 근처에 헤드셋을 그려 넣었다고 했는데 그
림에서는 안경이 놓여 있으므로 ④는 내용과 일치하지 않는다. 안경은 여자가 바꿔 그
리겠다고 한 것임에 유의한다.

W: Justin, I made the poster for opening our library. Would you like to take a
look?
M: Let me see. You drew a big tree in the center. It creates **a relaxing
atmosphere**.
W: Yeah, and it symbolizes growth and development. I also drew two birds in
the tree.
M: Good. But there's one thing I'd like to change.
W: Don't you like the three books under the tree?
M: I like them. The image of the books **represents the library**. But you drew a
headset near the books. I think this headset looks strange.
W: Really? Why?
M: Well, I think putting a pair of **eyeglasses would be better** than a headset
because the poster is for a library.
W: Okay. **I'll change it** right away.
M: But I like the way you wrote the title "READ" in the bottom center.
W: I think too many words are not effective, so I just wrote "The Parkville
Library Opens" and "Monday, August 27" under the title.
M: That looks impressive.

여: Justin, 우리 도서관 개관을 위한 포스터를 만들었어요. 살펴보겠어요?
남: 어디 봅시다. 가운데 큰 나무를 그렸군요. 그게 편안한 분위기를 만들어내요.
여: 네, 그리고 그건 성장과 발달을 상징해요. 나는 또 나무에 두 마리의 새를 그렸어요.
남: 좋아요. 하지만 바꾸고 싶은 게 하나 있어요.
여: 나무 아래 책 세 권이 마음에 안 드나요?
남: 그건 마음에 들어요. 책의 이미지가 도서관을 나타내니까요. 하지만 책 근처에 헤드셋
을 그렸군요. 이 헤드셋이 이상해 보여요.
여: 정말요? 왜죠?
남: 음, 난 이 포스터가 도서관을 위한 것이기 때문에 헤드셋보다는 안경 한 개를 놓는 게
더 좋을 것 같아요.
여: 알겠어요. 바로 바꿀게요.
남: 하지만 아래쪽 가운데에 제목인 'READ'를 쓴 방식은 좋아요.
여: 너무 많은 단어는 효과적이지 않을 것 같아서 'Parkville 도서관 개관'과 '8월 27일 월
요일'만 제목 아래 써넣었어요.
남: 인상적으로 보여요.

어휘 atmosphere 분위기; 대기   symbolize 상징하다   growth 성장; 증가
development 발달, 성장   represent 나타내다; 대표하다   effective 효과적인; 시행되는
impressive 인상적인; 감명 깊은

05 추후 행동   ③

✻ 대개 대화는 어떤 일을 하게 되는 상황이 먼저 제시된 뒤에 남자와 여자가 각각 할 일
들과 이에 대한 수락/거절의 응답이 나열되는 식으로 전개된다. 남자의 어지럽혀진 책
상을 보면서 여자가 정리 요령을 조언하고 있다. 여자는 연필과 펜을 모두 머그잔에
보관하라고 제안하면서 자신에게 여분의 머그잔이 있으니 가져다주겠다고 하고 있다.
그러므로 여자가 할 일은 ③ '머그잔 가져다주기'이다.

W: Austin! Can I borrow a pencil knife?
M: Sure. It's somewhere on my desk.
W: On your desk? Oh, Austin! **Your desk is too messy.** I can't find it.
M: Then I'm going to find it for you. I need to organize my desk. Oh, here it is.
W: You need to clean up your desk soon.
M: No problem. It's easy. First, I'll move all my books here to the bookshelf.

W: There are so many pencils and pens all over your desk.
M: I'm thinking of putting them into one of the desk drawers.
W: Hmm, no. Why don't you **keep them in a mug**? That way you can find
them easily, but they won't make a mess.
M: I don't have an extra mug. I should **go to the store to buy one**.
W: You don't have to. I have one. **I'll bring it** right now.
M: Thanks.

여: Austin! 연필 칼을 빌릴 수 있을까요?
남: 그럼요. 내 책상 어딘가에 있을 거예요.
여: 책상 위요? 아, Austin! 책상이 너무 지저분해서 찾을 수가 없어요.
남: 그러면 내가 찾을게요. 내 책상을 정리해야 해요. 아, 여기 있군요.
여: 바로 책상을 청소해야겠어요.
남: 문제없어요. 쉬워요. 우선 여기 있는 내 책 모두를 책꽂이로 옮길 거예요.
여: 책상 위에 온통 너무나 많은 연필하고 펜이 널려 있군요.
남: 그것들을 책상 서랍 하나 안으로 넣을까 생각 중이에요.
여: 음, 아니요. 그것들을 머그잔에 보관하지 그래요? 그런 식으로 그것들을 쉽게 찾을 수
있지만 어지럽혀지지는 않을 거예요.
남: 난 여분의 머그잔이 없어요. 하나 사러 가게에 가야겠군요.
여: 그럴 필요 없어요. 내게 하나 있어요. 지금 바로 그걸 가져올게요.
남: 고마워요.

어휘 messy 지저분한, 엉망인 cf. make a mess 어질러 놓다; 망쳐놓다   organize
정리하다; 준비[조직]하다   bookshelf 책꽂이   drawer 서랍   extra 여분[추가]의

06 금액   ④

✻ 여러 개의 수치 정보가 등장하므로 필요한 정보를 메모하면서 듣는 것이 좋다. 두 사
람이 사기로 한 갈색 아기 침대는 300달러이지만 10% 할인을 해서 270달러이고 서랍
장은 100달러인 4개짜리 서랍장을 사기로 했으므로 총액은 370달러이다.

W: Honey, I can't believe we're having a baby in just three months.
M: I can't believe it at all. We've got to prepare baby furniture. I've found a
nice online store. Look here!
W: Great. **Let's start with a baby bed.** What do you think of this grey one?
M: It costs $200. But this brown one looks better.
W: Its price is $300. It's a little more expensive than the grey one.
M: But they're having **a 10% sale on** this brown baby bed. I think we can
afford it.
W: All right. Let's order the brown baby bed. And we need a dresser.
M: How about this 5-drawer dresser? It's $200.
W: It's too high. I want to use it as **a diaper-changing table**.
M: You mean you'll change our baby's diapers on it?
W: Right. So I think **a 4-drawer dresser** should be enough. It's just $100.
M: I see. Let's order them now.

여: 여보, 우리가 단지 삼 개월 뒤에 아기를 낳는다니 믿을 수가 없어요.
남: 나도 전혀 믿어지지 않아요. 우리 아기 가구를 준비해야 하잖아요. 멋진 온라인 상점
을 찾아냈어요. 여기 봐요!
여: 멋져요. 아기 침대부터 시작해요. 이 회색 침대는 어떻게 생각해요?
남: 200달러 하는군요. 하지만 이 갈색이 더 좋아 보여요.
여: 그건 300달러예요. 회색보다 조금 더 비싸네요.
남: 하지만 이 갈색 아기 침대는 10% 할인을 하고 있어요. 우리가 그것을 살만한 여유가
있다고 생각해요.
여: 좋아요. 갈색 아기 침대를 주문합시다. 그리고 우리는 서랍장이 필요해요.
남: 이 5개짜리 서랍장은 어때요? 200달러군요.
여: 서랍이 너무 높아요. 난 그걸 기저귀 가는 탁자로 사용하고 싶거든요.
남: 그 위에서 아기 기저귀를 갈 것이라는 말이죠?
여: 맞아요. 그래서 난 이 4개짜리 서랍장이 충분하다고 봐요. 단지 100달러고요.
남: 알았어요. 그것들을 지금 주문합시다.

어휘 furniture 가구   afford ~할 여유가 되다, 형편이 되다   diaper 기저귀

07 이유 ⑤

* 지시문을 통해 여자가 수영 수업을 택할 수 없는 상황이며 여자의 말에 단서가 있을 가능성이 큼을 미리 파악한다. 여자는 수영장 물에 알레르기가 있어서 수영을 못한다고 하므로 답은 ⑤이다. 다른 수업을 듣고 있지만 수업 시간이 겹친다는 언급은 없었고 가격이 비싸다고 한 것은 회원권임에 유의한다.

M: What's up, Laura? I didn't know you're a member of this fitness club.
W: Hi, Eric! I just joined here today. It's a very good place to exercise.
M: It's nice to see you here. Aren't these facilities really nice?
W: Yeah, but **the price of membership** is so high.
M: It's worth it. By the way, what class are you taking?
W: I'm taking aerobics and yoga. How about you?
M: I'm taking tennis and swimming. There are very nice tennis courts here.
W: I know, but **I'm not good at** tennis.
M: Oh, how about swimming? There is an Olympic size swimming pool.
W: Sorry, but I can't. I enjoyed swimming when I was young, but now **I'm allergic to the water** in swimming pools.
M: That's too bad. I'd hoped **we could enjoy** the same class.
W: That would be fun. Anyway, I'm glad we bumped into each other.

남: 무슨 일이니, Laura? 난 네가 이 헬스클럽의 회원인 줄 몰랐어.
여: 안녕, Eric! 여기에 오늘 방금 가입했어. 운동하기 아주 좋은 장소구나.
남: 너를 여기서 보다니 반가워. 이 시설들이 정말 훌륭하지 않니?
여: 그래, 하지만 회원권 가격이 너무 높아.
남: 이건 그만한 가치가 있어. 그런데 어떤 강좌를 수강하니?
여: 에어로빅하고 요가를 수강하고 있어. 너는?
남: 난 테니스하고 수영을 듣고 있어. 여기 아주 훌륭한 테니스 코트가 있거든.
여: 알아, 하지만 난 테니스를 잘 하지 못해.
남: 아, 수영은 어때? 올림픽 규격의 수영장이 있어.
여: 미안하지만 못해. 내가 어렸을 때 수영을 즐겼지만 지금은 수영장 물에 알레르기가 있어.
남: 그거 안 됐구나. 우리가 같은 강좌를 즐길 수 있기를 바랐는데.
여: 그렇게 해도 재미있을 텐데. 어쨌든, 우리가 서로 우연히 만나서 기뻐.

어휘 worth ~할 만한 가치가 있는   be allergic to A A에 알레르기가 있다   bump into ~와 우연히 만나다

08 언급하지 않은 것 ③

* 대화의 진행은 대개 선택지와 같은 순서이므로, 선택지를 보면서 언급된 내용을 소거하는 식으로 푸는 것이 좋다. 감독과 시사회의 시작 시간, 사진 촬영 장소와 영화의 장르에 대해서는 이야기했지만 주연 배우에 대해서는 언급하지 않았다. 많은 배우들이 올 것이라는 언급만 있었음에 유의한다.

W: Hi, I'm Alyssa. I'm the photographer for *Film News*.
M: Hello, Alyssa. It's nice to meet you. So, you're here for the movie preview?
W: Yes, I am. My boss wants me to take pictures of all the famous actors and actresses who come down the red carpet for the preview.
M: As you know, there will be a lot of actors and actresses **because the director is** Christopher Martin. He is a genius.
W: I think so. Do you know **when they'll arrive here**?
M: The show starts at 7 p.m. They usually start to arrive about 30 minutes before the show.
W: Okay, I'll be ready for it. Where is the photo spot?
M: Over there, by the door. All of the actors and actresses will **walk by that spot**, so you can get some great photos from there.
W: Thank you. I'll move there.
M: Since it's an action movie, I think a lot of people will **find it very enjoyable**.
W: I see. Thanks for your advice. You've been a great help.

여: 안녕하세요, 저는 Alyssa입니다. 'Film News'의 사진기자예요.
남: 안녕하세요, Alyssa. 만나서 반가워요. 그러면 영화 시사회 때문에 여기 오신 거죠?
여: 네, 그렇습니다. 제 상사가 시사회를 위해 레드 카펫을 걸어 내려오는 모든 유명한 배우들의 사진을 찍길 바라서요.

남: 아시다시피 감독이 Christopher Martin(① 영화감독)이기 때문에 수많은 배우들이 올 겁니다. 그는 천재예요.
여: 저도 그렇게 생각해요. 그들이 여기 언제 도착하는지 아시나요?
남: 행사가 오후 7시에 시작하거든요(② 시작 시간). 보통 행사 약 30분 전에 도착하기 시작해요.
여: 알겠어요. 난 그 준비를 할 거예요. 어디가 사진 찍는 장소인가요?
남: 저기 문 옆이요.(④ 사진 촬영 장소) 모든 배우들이 그 지점을 지나칠 거니까 거기서 멋진 사진을 찍으실 수 있을 거예요.
여: 고맙습니다. 그리로 옮겨가겠어요.
남: 액션 영화(⑤ 영화의 장르)이기 때문에 많은 사람들이 영화가 아주 재미있다는 걸 알게 될 것 같아요.
여: 알겠습니다. 조언 감사해요. 큰 도움이 되었습니다.

어휘 preview 시사회   director 감독; 지휘자; 책임자   spot 장소; 지점; 발견하다   enjoyable 재미있는, 즐거운

09 내용 불일치 ④

* 담화의 진행은 대개 선택지와 같은 순서이므로, 선택지를 보면서 일치하는 내용을 소거하는 식으로 푸는 것이 좋다. 약 15분 후에 터널로 들어가며 그 15분이 장비를 착용하는 시간을 줄 것이라고 했다. 15분은 터널로 들어가기 전까지의 시간이지 터널 탐방 시간이 아님에 유의한다. 따라서 답은 ④이다.

M: May I have your attention, please? Welcome to the Diamond Mine Tour! We **are about to enter** our first tunnel. Safety helmets and safety shoes are required beyond this point. If you go through the entrance on the right, you will be provided with helmets and shoes. I see some children in the group. I am sorry, but for safety reasons, **no children under 12 are permitted** on the mine tour. They can wait in the waiting area. **Cameras are not permitted**, so please leave your cameras in a locker. We will be entering the underground facility **in about 15 minutes**, which will allow you time to put on all the equipment. You can also put any inconvenient large-size bags in a locker before entering the tunnel. Thank you.

남: 주목해주시겠습니까? Diamond 광산 투어에 오신 것을 환영합니다! 우리의 첫 번째 터널로 막 들어가려고 합니다. 이 지점 너머에서는 ① 안전모와 안전화가 필요합니다. 오른쪽 입구를 지나가면 여러분에게 헬멧과 신발이 제공될 것입니다. 단체에서 어린 아이 몇 명이 보이는군요. 죄송합니다만 안전상의 이유로 ② 12세 미만 어린이는 광산 투어에 허용되지 않습니다. 그 아이들은 대기 구역에서 기다릴 수 있습니다. ③ 카메라는 허용되지 않으므로 여러분의 카메라를 사물함에 넣어두십시오. ④ 약 15분 후에 우리는 지하 시설로 들어갈 건데, 그 시간이 여러분에게 모든 장비를 착용하는 시간을 줄 것입니다. 여러분은 또한 터널에 들어가기 전에 ⑤ 불편한 큰 크기의 가방을 사물함에 넣어둘 수 있습니다. 감사합니다.

어휘 attention 주목; 관심   mine 광산; 나의 것   be about to-v 막 v하려는 참이다   beyond ~ 너머; ~ 이상   entrance (출)입구; 입장   permit 허용[허가]하다   underground 지하의   facility 시설; 기관   inconvenient 불편한

10 도표 이해 ⑤

* 대화의 진행은 대개 도표 항목의 나열 순서대로 진행된다. 대화를 들으면서 도표의 각 항목 중 선택되지 않은 것을 소거하는 식으로 푸는 것이 좋다. 우선 가격은 800달러 이하를 원했으므로 ①이 제외되고 청소 서비스를 원했으므로 ②, ③도 제외된다. ④와 ⑤중에서 가격은 ④가 싸지만 사업 운영 연수와 고객평이 더 좋은 회사를 원했으므로 두 사람이 선택한 카펫 회사는 ⑤이다.

W: Carlos, I've contacted five different carpet companies since we have to replace our carpet.
M: Did you find a company that **you're interested in**?
W: I wanted to discuss it with you first. Let's take a look at this list.
M: Wow, excellent! I think the price is the most important factor for us. I don't want to pay more than $800.
W: I agree.
M: Why don't we go with the company that offers us the cheapest price?
W: I want the carpet cleaning service, but the company that offers the

cheapest price doesn't offer this service.
M: Then choose the one that gives us the best offer and provides **the cleaning service**, too.
W: Well, this company has only been in business for 3 years. I can't trust them.
M: **How about checking** some customer reviews?
W: They don't have good reviews. I'd like to choose this company that has more experience and better reviews.
M: Okay. Let's choose that. **The price is within our budget**.

여: Carlos, 우리 카펫을 교체해야 해서 다섯 군데의 다른 카펫 회사와 연락했어요.
남: 관심이 가는 회사를 발견했나요?
여: 우선 당신하고 그걸 의논하고 싶었어요. 이 리스트를 살펴봐요.
남: 와, 훌륭해요! 가격이 우리에게 가장 중요한 요소라고 생각해요. 난 800달러 넘게 지불하고 싶지 않아요.
여: 동의해요.
남: 가장 저렴한 가격을 제공하는 회사로 하는 게 어떤가요?
여: 난 카펫 청소 서비스를 원하는데 하지만 가장 싼 가격을 제공하는 회사는 이 서비스를 제공하지 않아요.
남: 그러면 가장 좋은 가격을 제시하고 청소 서비스도 제공하는 곳을 선택합시다.
여: 음, 이 회사는 사업을 한 지 겨우 3년이에요. 난 그들을 신뢰할 수 없어요.
남: 고객평을 확인하는 건 어때요?
여: 좋은 평이 없어요. 더 경력이 많고 더 좋은 평이 있는 이 회사를 선택하고 싶어요.
남: 좋아요. 그곳으로 선택합시다. 가격이 우리 예산 내에 있군요.

어휘 contact 연락(하다); 접촉(하다)   replace 교체하다; 대신하다   discuss 의논[토론]하다   factor 요소   offer 제공(하다); 제안, 제의   provide 제공[공급]하다   experience 경력, 경험; 체험   budget 예산(안)

11 짧은 대화에 이어질 응답 ②

✻ 무대에 올라갈 차례가 되어 불안해하는 여자에게 남자가 할 말로는 ② '괜찮아. 그냥 긴장을 풀고 너 자신을 믿으렴.'이 가장 적절하다.

① 아니. 난 실수하는 걸 두려워하지 않아.
③ 알아. 넌 첫 번째에 아주 잘했어.
④ 문제없어. 용기를 줘서 고맙구나.
⑤ 물론이지. 이것이 끝이 아니란 걸 기억하렴.

W: Oh, there are so many people in the audience. It's **my turn to go** onto the stage, right?
M: Yes, but don't worry. You had plenty of practice. Are you ready, Sophia?
W: I'm not sure. **I'm getting nervous**, and my legs are shaking.
M: It's okay. Just relax and trust in yourself.

여: 아, 너무 많은 청중들이 왔네요. 제가 무대에 올라갈 차례인 거죠, 맞죠?
남: 맞아, 하지만 걱정하지 마라. 넌 많이 연습했어. 준비되었니, Sophia?
여: 모르겠어요. 불안해지면서 다리가 떨리네요.
남: 괜찮아. 그냥 긴장을 풀고 너 자신을 믿으렴.

어휘 audience 청중, 관중   turn 차례, 순번   plenty of 많은
| 선택지 어휘 | encourage 용기를 북돋우다, 격려[고무]하다

12 짧은 대화에 이어질 응답 ③

✻ 시험 한 달 전부터 공부한다는 여자에게 남자가 이유를 묻고 있다. 이에 대한 적절한 응답은 ③ '난 그냥 좋은 성적을 얻기 위해 최선을 다하고 싶어.'이다.

① 난 그때 다른 약속이 있는 것 같아.
② 난 내일 친구를 데려오고 싶어.
④ 난 금요일에는 어떤 시험도 예정되어 있지 않아.
⑤ 난 항상 학교와 공부로 무척 스트레스를 받아.

M: Do you think you'll be able to make it to my party this weekend?
W: Sorry, I can't. I have to **study all weekend**. I have an important final exam coming up!

M: Really? You still **have one month** before final exams! Why are you studying so early?
W: I just want to do my best to get good grades.

남: 너 이번 주말에 우리 파티에 올 수 있을 것 같니?
여: 미안하지만 안 돼. 주말 내내 공부해야 해. 중요한 기말시험이 다가오고 있어!
남: 정말? 넌 기말시험 전까지 아직 한 달 남았잖아! 왜 그렇게 일찍부터 공부하는 거야?
여: 난 그냥 좋은 성적을 얻기 위해 최선을 다하고 싶어.

어휘 make it (모임 등에) 가다, 참석하다 | 선택지 어휘 | appointment 약속; 임명   scheduled 예정된

13 긴 대화에 이어질 응답 ①

✻ 대화의 전체 맥락 하에 마지막 말의 의미나 의도를 정확히 파악하는 것이 좋다. 자원봉사하러 온 남자에게 도움을 받는 할머니가 감사의 표시로 머플러를 선물했고 남자가 감사와 기쁨을 표시하고 있다. 이에 대한 할머니의 응답으로는 ① '네가 좋다니 기쁘구나. 널 위해 만들었단다.'가 적절하다.

② 고맙구나. 난 파티를 열 것이란다.
③ 내가 그 머플러를 가져갈게. 나는 그 초록색이 마음에 든단다.
④ 아름답구나. 그 색은 나한테 더 잘 어울린다.
⑤ 그렇게 머플러를 만드는 법을 배우고 싶구나.

M: Mrs. Campbell. How are you feeling today?
W: Oh, Daniel. You've come again. I'm doing well, thank you.
M: You mentioned that your legs **were bothering you** last week. Is everything all right?
W: They feel much better now. It's so wonderful of you to see me every Friday like this.
M: It's my pleasure, and **it's only once a week**.
W: But it's not easy cleaning and looking after a disabled elderly woman.
M: Mrs. Campbell, I come here because I really enjoy the visits.
W: You're so kind! Daniel, I want to give you this muffler. Please take it.
M: Oh, my! Thank you so much. I don't know what to say. It's lovely!
W: You don't have to say anything. I just wanted to show my appreciation.
M: It feels warm, and it's my favorite color. **I'll wear it on my way home** tonight.
W: I'm glad you like it. I made it for you.

남: Campbell 부인. 오늘 건강은 어떠신가요?
여: 아, Daniel. 다시 왔구나. 난 건강하단다. 고맙구나.
남: 지난주에 다리가 아프다고 말씀하셨어요. 다 괜찮은 건가요?
여: 이제 훨씬 좋아졌단다. 매주 금요일 이렇게 나를 만나러 와주니 무척 고맙구나.
남: 제가 좋아서 하는 거고 일주일에 한 번뿐인데요.
여: 하지만 청소하고 장애가 있는 노인을 돌보는 건 쉬운 일이 아니지.
남: Campbell 부인, 저는 오는 게 정말 좋기 때문에 여기 와요.
여: 너무 친절하구나! Daniel, 네게 이 머플러를 주고 싶구나. 부디 가져가렴.
남: 아, 이런! 정말 고맙습니다. 뭐라고 말씀드려야 할지 모르겠어요. 멋져요!
여: 아무 말도 할 필요가 없단다. 난 그냥 내 감사를 표시하고 싶었을 뿐이야.
남: 따뜻하고 제가 아주 좋아하는 색이에요. 오늘 밤 집에 가는 길에 이걸 두를게요.
여: 네가 좋다니 기쁘구나. 널 위해 만들었단다.

어휘 bother 괴롭히다; 귀찮게 하다   look after ~을 돌보다   disabled 장애가 있는   appreciation 감사; 감상; 이해, 평가   on one's way (to) (~로 가는) 길[도중]에
| 선택지 어휘 | throw a party 파티를 열다

14 긴 대화에 이어질 응답 ④

✻ 대화의 전체 맥락 하에서 마지막 말의 의미나 의도를 정확히 파악하는 것이 좋다. 두 사람이 수족관에 와서 감탄하는 상황이다. 계속 아름다운 광경에 대해 서로 이야기하던 상황이므로 여자가 감탄하면서 오게 되어 기쁘다고 했을 때 남자의 응답으로는 동의하는 내용인 ④ '동의해. 난 이렇게 아름다운 광경을 본 적이 없어.'가 적절하다.

① 천만에. 시간을 내줘서 고마워.
② 그게 내가 생각하는 바야. 넌 주의를 해야 해.

③ 우리는 물고기를 물로 돌려보내야 해.
⑤ 응, 바다를 소중히 돌보는 게 중요해.

W: This aquarium is amazing! Look over there, Pablo!
M: Where? Wow! It's like being under the sea.
W: Yes, and doesn't **she look like a mermaid**?
M: What? Weren't you pointing to that colorful fish?
W: I was talking about the female diver next to the fish. She looks like a mermaid.
M: What is a mermaid?
W: It's a legendary creature **with the head** and upper body of a female human and the tail of a fish.
M: Ah, I knew that. But that diver doesn't have a fish tail. Anyway, she looks like the queen of the underwater world.
W: She is swimming with sharks and **other friends of the sea**.
M: Wow! It's like a rainbow with all these colorful fish.
W: It's amazing. They all look like they're dancing. I'm glad we came here to this aquarium.
M: I agree. I've never seen such a beautiful sight.

여: 이 수족관은 굉장하다! 저기를 봐, Pablo!
남: 어디? 와! 바다 밑에 있는 것 같아.
여: 그래, 그리고 저 여자 인어 같지 않니?
남: 뭐가? 저 다채로운 물고기를 가리키는 거 아니었어?
여: 난 그 물고기 옆의 여성 잠수부에 대해 이야기하고 있었어. 그녀가 인어 같아 보여.
남: 인어가 뭐니?
여: 그건 인간 여성의 머리와 상체 그리고 물고기 꼬리를 가진 전설의 생명체야.
남: 아, 그거 알고 있어. 하지만 저 잠수부는 물고기 꼬리가 없잖아. 어쨌든 그녀는 물속 세상의 여왕 같아 보여.
여: 상어하고 다른 바다 친구들하고 함께 헤엄치고 있잖아.
남: 와! 이 모든 색색의 물고기가 무지개 같아.
여: 놀라워. 그것들 모두가 춤추고 있는 것 같아. 우리가 이 수족관에 오게 되어 기뻐.
남: 동의해. 난 이렇게 아름다운 광경을 본 적이 없어.

어휘 **aquarium** 수족관   **mermaid** 인어   **female** 여성의   **legendary** 전설(상)의, 전설적인; 아주 유명한

15 상황에 적절한 말 ④

* 지시문을 통해 누가(A) 누구에게(B) 할 말인지를 우선 정확히 파악한다. Dylan(A)이 두 회사로부터 입사 제의를 받아 어디를 선택할지 고민하는 상황에서 아버지(B)에게 조언을 구하려고 한다. 이때 할 말로는 ④ '제가 어떤 제안을 받아들여야 한다고 생각하세요?'가 가장 적절하다.
① 제가 이 직장을 그만두어야 한다고 생각하세요?
② 면접을 어떻게 준비해야 할까요?
③ 지금 저를 위해 만남을 주선해주실 수 있나요?
⑤ 아버지 회사에 일자리가 있나요?

W: Dylan has been looking for a job for the past several months. He's been to several job interviews. And today **he is offered a position** by two companies. Dylan is very happy because he had been out of work for such a long time. But now he has to choose **which company to work for**. However, it's very difficult to choose because both are excellent companies which offer great benefits and salary. Dylan **has a hard time deciding** which to accept. He finally calls his father. Dylan explains to his father why he can't make up his mind. He's **hoping to get some advice** from his father. In this situation, what would Dylan most likely say to his father?

Dylan: **Which offer do you think I should accept?**

여: Dylan은 지난 몇 달간 구직해 오고 있다. 그는 몇 군데 취업 면접을 보았다. 그리고 오늘 그는 두 회사로부터 일자리를 제안받는다. Dylan은 너무 오랫동안 직업이 없었기 때문에 무척 기쁘다. 하지만 이제 그는 어떤 회사에서 일할지를 선택해야 한다. 그러나, 둘 다 좋은 복리 후생 혜택과 급여를 제공하는 훌륭한 회사이기 때문에 선택하

기가 무척 어렵다. Dylan은 어떤 것을 받아들일지 결정하는 데 어려움을 겪는다. 그는 마침내 아버지에게 전화한다. Dylan은 아버지에게 왜 자기가 결정할 수 없는지 설명한다. 그는 아버지로부터 조언을 얻기를 바라고 있다. 이 상황에서 Dylan이 그의 아버지에게 뭐라고 말하겠는가?

Dylan: 제가 어떤 제안을 받아들여야 한다고 생각하세요?

어휘 **benefit** 복리 후생 혜택; 이익   **salary** 급여, 월급   **make up one's mind** 결정[결심]하다 | 선택지 어휘 | **quit** 그만두다; 떠나다   **set up** 마련하다; 설치하다   **opening** 빈자리, 공석; 개막식

16~17 세트 문항   16 ④ 17 ③

* **16** 소설을 읽는 것을 부정적으로 보는 사람들의 말로 담화를 시작했지만, 다섯 번째 문장(But ~ entertainment)부터 소설을 읽는 것의 장점에 대해 차례로 나열하고 소설의 읽는 것이 사회성 기술을 발전시키는 훌륭한 방법이 될 수 있다는 말로 마무리하므로 담화의 주제는 ④ '사회성 기술을 배우기 위한 도구로서 소설의 가치'임을 알 수 있다.
① 소설을 읽는 것의 장단점
② 독서 능력을 향상하기 위한 방법으로서 소설 읽기
③ 영웅담을 통한 인간 본성의 이해
⑤ 어린이의 읽고 쓰는 능력을 발전시키기 위한 비결

* **17** 해석 참조.
① 동화 ② 영웅담 ③ 판타지 소설 ④ 전설 ⑤ 신화

W: Do you remember the very first book you read? Probably it was a short story with a fictional character. Some people claim that reading fiction such as fairy tales or hero stories is a waste of time. They say, "Those stories usually begin with a perfect world. The ending is always happy for the one who has overcome failure. It's false and unreal!" But reading fiction can do more than provide relaxation and entertainment. Reading fiction allows us **to learn about our social world** and, as a result, helps us behave properly. One study showed that children ages 4-6 who read a lot of children's storybooks had a significantly stronger ability to read **the mental and emotional states** of other people. Similarly, psychologists have found that traditional tales, from legends to myths, perform the essential work of **defining group identity** and act as a kind of social glue. Thus, reading fiction can be a great way of learning to **deal with other people**.

여: 여러분이 맨 처음 읽었던 책을 기억합니까? 아마 그것은 허구적 인물이 나오는 단편이었을 겁니다. 어떤 사람들은 ① 동화나 ② 영웅담 같은 소설을 읽는 것이 시간 낭비라고 주장합니다. 그들은 "그런 이야기들은 보통 완벽한 세상으로 시작한다. 실패를 극복한 사람에게 결말은 항상 행복하다. 그건 거짓이고 비현실적이다!"라고 말합니다. 하지만 소설을 읽는 것은 휴식과 오락을 제공하는 이상의 것을 할 수 있습니다. 소설 읽기는 우리에게 우리의 사회 세계에 대해 알도록 하고 그 결과 우리가 적절하게 행동하도록 돕습니다. 한 연구는 많은 어린이 이야기책을 읽은 4세에서 6세 연령의 어린이가 다른 사람들의 정신적, 정서적 상태를 읽는 상당히 더 강력한 능력을 갖추고 있다는 것을 보여주었습니다. 비슷하게 심리학자들은 ④ 전설부터 ⑤ 신화에까지 이르는 전통 설화가 집단 정체성을 규정하는 근본적인 일을 수행하고 일종의 사회적 접착제(유대감)로서 작용한다는 것을 발견했습니다. 그러므로 소설을 읽는 것은 타인을 대하는 것을 배우는 훌륭한 방법이 될 수 있습니다.

어휘 **probably** 아마   **fictional** 허구적인, 소설의 cf. **fiction** 소설   **claim** 주장하다; 요구하다   **fairy tale** 동화 cf. **tale** 설화, 이야기   **overcome** 극복하다; 이기다   **significantly** 상당히, 크게; 중요하게   **emotional** 정서의, 감정의   **state** 상태   **myth** 신화   **perform** 수행하다, 행하다   **essential** 근본적인, 필수적인   **define** 규정하다; 정의하다   **identity** 정체성; 신원   **glue** 접착제; 붙이다   **deal with** ~을 대하다[다루다]; (문제 등을) 처리하다 | 선택지 어휘 | **advantage** 장점(↔ **disadvantage** 단점)   **nature** 본성; 본질   **value** 가치; 평가(하다)

14회

01 ④   02 ③   03 ②   04 ④   05 ②   06 ③   07 ②   08 ⑤   09 ⑤   10 ①
11 ②   12 ④   13 ②   14 ③   15 ③   16 ④   17 ④

01 화자가 하는 말의 목적   ④

✷ 담화의 일부 내용이 아니라 중심 내용을 파악해야 한다. 여자는 리허설을 끝내고 떨지 말라고 하면서 독무를 추는 사람에게 주의를 주는 등 공연 전 전반적으로 주의와 당부를 하고 있다. 또한, 대회에 좋은 시간을 보내려고 왔다고 했으므로 댄스 대회에 출전하는 상황임을 알 수 있다. 그러므로 담화의 목적은 ④ '댄스 대회 출전 전 최종 당부를 하려고'이다.

W: We're finally finished with rehearsals. We've practiced for six months, and our dance performance will be evaluated sometime later. Don't be too nervous. Think of this performance as just another one of our rehearsals. When you **get on stage**, don't think of this as your first performance. Most importantly, you must make sure that **each of you harmonizes perfectly**. Just as we've done before, you must not only concentrate on your movement but the entire group's. Emma, don't forget to take a step forward when you're doing your solo. Also, always listen to the music and try to get into the rhythm of it. We are not here to win a contest but to have a good time. All right, **it's time to get on stage**. Is everyone in line?

여: 우리는 마침내 리허설을 끝냈어요. 우리는 여섯 달 동안 연습했고 우리 댄스 공연은 얼마 후에 평가될 거예요. 너무 떨지 말아요. 이 공연을 단지 또 다른 우리 리허설 중 하나로 생각해요. 여러분이 무대에 설 때 이것을 여러분의 첫 공연이라고 생각하지 말아요. 가장 중요한 건, 여러분 각자가 반드시 완벽하게 조화를 이루어야 한다는 거예요. 꼭 우리가 전에 해왔던 것처럼 자신의 동작에 집중할 뿐만 아니라 전체 집단의 동작에도 집중해야 합니다. Emma, 독무를 출 때 한 발자국 앞으로 나오는 걸 잊지 말아요. 또한, 항상 음악을 듣고 그 리듬을 타려고 노력하도록 해요. 우리는 대회에 우승하기 위해서가 아닌 좋은 시간을 보내려고 여기에 온 거예요. 좋아요, 무대에 올라갈 시간이에요. 모두 줄을 섰죠?

어휘 rehearsal 리허설, 예행연습 evaluate 평가[감정]하다 think of A as B A를 B로 생각하다[여기다] make sure (that) 반드시 (~하도록) 하다 harmonize 조화를 이루다 concentrate on ~에 집중하다 movement 동작, 움직임 entire 전체의, 온 get into the rhythm 리듬을 타다

02 의견   ③

✷ 우선 지시문에서 명시한 화자의 성별을 보고 어느 화자의 말에 주목할지를 판단해야 한다. 특히 의견이나 주장을 표현하는 어구(I think ~, You should ~ 등)가 이끄는 내용을 잘 들어야 한다. 여자가 남자 나라의 엄격한 성별 규칙에 따른 조언에 대해 타당하지 않다고 말하자 남자가 그건 나라의 문화이고 환영받는 손님이 되기 위해서는 존중해야 한다고 말하고 있다. 그러므로 남자의 의견은 ③ '여행자는 그 나라 문화를 존중해야 한다.'이다.

W: Asad, I'll travel to your country next month.
M: That's great. I'm sure you'll like its beautiful scenery and kind people.
W: Yeah, I'm very excited. **Do you have any advice** for me?
M: Well, one of the most important things is **not to make direct eye contact** with local men.
W: Really? In my culture, it's basic etiquette to make eye contact when I'm speaking to someone.
M: In my culture, there are strict gender rules. Women should not make too much eye contact with men.
W: Oh, then I should wear dark sunglasses.
M: That's a good idea. And don't wear short pants or a tight top. Those clothes will send the wrong message to local men.
W: That's not fair! Think about the temperature in the desert in your country!
M: Well, I understand. But fair or not, it's our culture. **You need to respect it** to be a welcome guest.
W: I see. I'll keep that in mind. Thanks for your advice.

여: Asad, 나 다음 달에 너희 나라로 여행 갈 거야.
남: 그거 아주 좋은데. 분명히 넌 그곳의 아름다운 풍경과 친절한 사람들을 좋아하게 될 거야.
여: 응. 너무 신이 나. 나한테 조언해 줄 거 있니?
남: 음. 가장 중요한 것 중 하나는 현지 남자들과 직접 눈을 마주치지 않는 거야.
여: 정말이야? 우리 문화에서는 누군가와 이야기할 때 눈을 쳐다보는 게 기본예절이야.
남: 우리 문화에서는 엄격한 성별 규칙이 있어. 여성들은 남성들과 너무 많이 눈을 마주치면 안 돼.
여: 아, 그러면 어두운 선글라스를 껴야겠다.
남: 좋은 생각이야. 그리고 짧은 바지나 딱 들러붙는 상의를 입지 마. 그런 의상은 현지 남자들에게 잘못된 메시지를 줄 거야.
여: 그건 타당하지 않아! 너희 나라의 사막 기온을 생각해 봐!
남: 음, 이해해. 하지만 타당하든 그렇지 않든, 그건 우리 문화야. 네가 환영받는 손님이 되기 위해서는 그걸 존중해야 해.
여: 알았어. 그걸 명심할게. 조언해줘서 고마워.

어휘 scenery 풍경, 경치 eye contact 눈[시선]을 마주침 local 현지[지역]의; 현지인 gender 성별 fair 타당한; 공정한 temperature 기온; 온도 respect 존중[존경](하다) keep A in mind A를 명심하다

03 관계   ②

✷ 직업을 나타내거나 추론할 수 있는 힌트가 대화 전반에 걸쳐 드러나므로, 대화를 전체적으로 이해하는 것이 필요하다. 여자는 오늘 밤이 공연이라 무대에 올라 노래를 불러야 하고 남자는 여자의 건강을 돌보고 프로그램을 챙겨주며 스케줄을 관리하고 있다. 그러므로 두 사람의 관계는 ② '가수 – 매니저'임을 알 수 있다.

W: Donald, can I have some water?
M: Here it is. How do you feel? Don't you think you should see a doctor?
W: No, I'm not that sick. I feel better after getting some rest.
M: **You have to go on stage** this evening. Will you be all right?
W: Sure. Don't worry about that.
M: Here's tonight's performance program. This is the final performance. You can take a rest tomorrow.
W: Okay. Anyway, what are all those flowers for? There are so many.
M: **Your fans sent them to you.** They also sent you some chocolate. Do you want some?
W: No, thanks. But I'm grateful. Let's have a rehearsal. I'll get makeup after the rehearsal.
M: Okay. If it's too hard, why don't you **lip sync instead of singing live**?
W: I don't want to do that. It's so unprofessional. Is the band here?
M: Of course. They're all waiting for you.

여: Donald, 물을 좀 주겠어요?
남: 여기 있어요. 몸 상태가 어때요? 의사를 만나야 할 것 같지 않아요?
여: 아뇨, 그렇게 아프지는 않아요. 좀 쉬었더니 한결 나아졌어요.
남: 오늘 저녁에 무대에 올라야 해요. 괜찮겠어요?
여: 그럼요. 그건 걱정 말아요.
남: 여기 오늘 밤 공연 프로그램이에요. 이게 마지막 공연이에요. 내일은 쉴 수 있어요.
여: 알았어요. 그건 그렇고, 저 모든 꽃은 뭐죠? 매우 많군요.
남: 팬들이 당신에게 보낸 거예요. 그들이 초콜릿도 좀 보냈어요. 좀 먹을래요?
여: 아니요, 괜찮아요. 하지만 고맙네요. 리허설을 하죠. 리허설 후에 분장을 할게요.
남: 알았어요. 너무 힘들면 라이브로 노래하는 대신에 립싱크를 하지 그래요?
여: 그렇게 하고 싶지는 않아요. 그건 너무 프로답지 않아요. 밴드가 여기 있나요?
남: 물론이죠. 그들 모두 당신을 기다리고 있어요.

어휘 lip sync 립싱크를 하다 unprofessional 프로답지 않은; 전문가가 아닌

04 그림 불일치 ④

✻ 대화가 나오기 전에 각 사물의 위치 관계와 외형(형태나 무늬, 개수 등)의 특징을 미리 확인하는 것이 좋다. 대화에서는 탁자에 의자 세 개가 있다고 했는데 그림에서는 네 개가 있으므로 ④가 대화의 내용과 일치하지 않는다. 남자가 디자인을 바꿔 나중에 의자 네 개를 두겠다고 했으므로 현재 디자인에는 의자가 세 개임을 유의한다.

M: This is the design for our company booth for the State Fair.
W: You placed the information counter on the left side. Good.
M: How about the flower vase on the counter? It'll **create a brighter atmosphere**.
W: Good idea. And I like the name of our company, "Zamil," on the banner on the left side of the wall.
M: It's for balance because there is a large monitor **on the right side of the wall**.
W: Okay. We can also play our company's promotional video clip throughout the day.
M: Yes. And I put a round table under the monitor.
W: Perfect. It's for our booth visitors, right? **There are three chairs**. Hmm...
M: Do you think we need more chairs?
W: Yes, I think four chairs will be better than three.
M: Okay! I'll change the design. How about **this tall tree in a pot** near the table?
W: I like it. You did a good job.

남: 이건 주 박람회를 위한 우리 회사 부스의 디자인이에요.
여: 왼쪽에 안내카운터를 두었군요. 좋아요.
남: 카운터 위의 꽃병은 어때요? 그게 더 밝은 분위기를 만들어낼 거예요.
여: 좋은 아이디어예요. 그리고 나는 벽 왼쪽의 현수막에 있는 우리 회사 이름인 'Zamil'이 마음에 들어요.
남: 그건 벽 오른쪽에 커다란 모니터가 있기 때문에 균형을 맞추기 위한 거예요.
여: 좋아요. 우리는 종일 우리 회사의 홍보 비디오 영상을 상영할 수도 있군요.
남: 네. 그리고 나는 모니터 아래에 둥근 탁자를 두었어요.
여: 완벽해요. 우리 부스 방문객을 위한 거죠, 맞죠? 의자가 세 개 있군요. 음…
남: 의자가 더 필요하다고 생각하세요?
여: 네, 의자 네 개가 세 개보다 더 좋을 것 같군요.
남: 알겠어요! 디자인을 변경할게요. 탁자 근처의 화분에 있는 이 키가 큰 식물은 어떤가요?
여: 좋아요. 잘 했어요.

어휘 flower vase 꽃병 atmosphere 분위기; (지구의) 대기 banner 현수막 promotional 홍보[판촉]의 throughout ~동안 죽, 내내; 도처에

05 추후 행동 ②

✻ 대개 대화는 어떤 일을 하게 되는 상황이 먼저 제시된 뒤에 남자와 여자가 각각 할 일들과 이에 대한 수락/거절의 응답이 나열되는 식으로 전개된다. 남자는 숙제를 하고 있고 숙제가 끝난 후 친구 집에 책을 돌려주러 가야 하지만, 엄마의 부탁으로 지금 하겠다고 한 일은 ② '쓰레기 버리기'이다. 설거지나 야구는 서로 추측으로 한 이야기이고 저녁 식사는 엄마가 준비하겠다고 했음에 유의한다.

W: Alex, what are you doing? **Do you have a minute**?
M: I'm sorry, Mom. I have to hurry up and finish my homework. After that I'm going over to Blake's house.
W: Are you going over there to play baseball?
M: No. I borrowed his book yesterday, and **I have to return it** this evening.
W: I guess that means you can't help me for five minutes.
M: Five minutes? Then I can help you. I thought you wanted me to wash the dishes.
W: No. I just finished cleaning the kitchen, and there's a lot of trash.
M: Do you want me **to take out the trash**?
W: Can you? It's quite heavy, so I don't think I can carry it.
M: All right. **I'll take care of it** right away.
W: Good. I'll prepare dinner.

여: Alex, 뭐 하니? 잠깐 시간 좀 내줄 수 있니?

남: 죄송해요, 엄마. 전 서둘러 숙제를 끝내야 해요. 그다음에 Blake네 집에 갈 거예요.
여: 야구 하러 거기 가는 거니?
남: 아뇨. 어제 그 애의 책을 빌렸는데 오늘 저녁에 그걸 돌려줘야 해요.
여: 그건 5분도 나를 도울 수 없다는 말 같구나.
남: 5분이요? 그렇다면 도와드릴 수 있어요. 전 엄마께서 제가 설거지하기를 원하신다고 생각했어요.
여: 아니야. 난 방금 부엌 청소를 끝냈는데 쓰레기가 아주 많구나.
남: 제가 쓰레기를 버리길 바라세요?
여: 그래 줄 수 있니? 꽤 무거워서 내가 그걸 들 수 없을 것 같구나.
남: 알겠어요. 당장 그걸 처리할게요.
여: 좋아. 난 저녁 식사를 준비할게.

어휘 return 돌려주다; 돌아오다[가다] wash the dishes 설거지하다 take care of ~을 처리하다; ~을 돌보다[신경 쓰다]

06 금액 ③

✻ 여러 개의 수치 정보가 등장하므로 필요한 정보를 메모하면서 듣는 것이 좋다. 사무실 파티를 위해 200달러짜리 방을 빌리는 대신 사무실에서 무료로 하기로 했고, 장식에 50달러, 간식에 100달러, 마지막으로 음료에 80달러를 쓰기로 했으므로 총비용은 230 달러이다.

W: Jonathan, I need your help. I'm **trying to plan an office party**, but I don't even know where to begin.
M: I planned last year's office party; maybe I can help you out. First, what do you have in mind for the location?
W: Well, there's a room at the community center that we could rent, but it's going to cost $200 for the night.
M: I can save you that money pretty easily. Why don't we have the party here at the office? **That would be completely free**.
W: Then what about decorations? We need balloons and banners.
M: Don't worry. If you go to the decorations store, you can find "Party in a Box." It's $50 **for everything you could need**!
W: I think I'll do that! Then, the last thing is refreshments.
M: Snacks usually run $100 for a party package, and drinks usually run $80 on K-mart's website. They also offer free delivery.
W: Okay, **I'll order both of them**. Thanks for helping me.
M: My pleasure. Just tell me if you need any help.

여: Jonathan, 도움이 필요해요. 사무실 파티를 계획하려고 하는데 어디서 시작해야 할지조차 모르겠어요.
남: 작년 사무실 파티를 내가 계획했어요. 어쩌면 내가 도울 수 있겠군요. 우선 장소는 어디를 마음에 두고 있나요?
여: 음, 우리가 빌릴 수 있는 주민 센터에 방이 있지만 하룻밤에 200달러가 들 거예요.
남: 내가 그 돈을 아주 쉽게 절약하게 해줄 수 있어요. 여기 사무실에서 파티를 하는 건 어때요? 완전히 무료잖아요.
여: 그러면 장식은요? 우리는 풍선과 현수막이 필요해요.
남: 걱정 말아요. 장식 전문점에 가면 '상자 하나에 든 파티'를 찾을 수 있어요. 필요한 모든 게 50달러예요!
여: 그걸 해야겠어요! 그러면 마지막은 다과예요.
남: K-mart 웹사이트에서 간식은 보통 파티 꾸러미 하나에 100달러이고 음료수는 보통 80달러 해요. 그들은 또 무료로 배송해줘요.
여: 좋아요, 둘 다 주문할게요. 도와줘서 고마워요.
남: 천만에요. 언제든 도움이 필요하면 내게 말만 해요.

어휘 cost (값·비용이) 들다[~이다]; 값, 비용 completely 완전히 decoration 장식(품) refreshment 다과; 가벼운 식사, 음료 package 꾸러미; 소포

07 이유 ②

✻ 지시문을 통해 남자가 이전 직장을 그만둔 상황이고 남자의 말에 단서가 있을 가능성이 큼을 미리 파악한다. 남자는 이전 직장에서 상사와 문제도, 건강 문제도 없었다고 한다. 봉급도 이전 직장이 더 높았지만 일이 너무 많아 매일 야근을 해야 해서 그만두었다고 말하고 있다. 그러므로 남자가 이전 직장을 그만둔 이유는 ② '일이 너무 많아서'이다.

W: Hi, Sam! Good to see you here. Are you jogging?

M: Yes, actually I'm preparing for the Phoenix Half Marathon.

W: Wow! That sounds great! But aren't you busy? You said you've been terribly busy since you became a manager.

M: Actually, **I quit my job** last October.

W: Really? Did you have some problem with your boss or some health problems?

M: Not at all. My decision to quit **had nothing to do with** those things. By the way, I got a new job.

W: Good. You changed jobs because the new job pays you more money, right?

M: No, actually not. I got paid better in the previous job.

W: Oh, I see. **Were you overworked** at your previous job?

M: Yeah, **I had to work overtime** every day. I felt like I was a machine.

W: I understand why you quit. You look happy now.

M: Yes, I'm happy. I work eight to four, and I can enjoy running.

여: 안녕, Sam! 여기서 보다니 반가워요. 조깅하는 거예요?

남: 네, 사실 난 Phoenix 하프 마라톤을 준비하고 있어요.

여: 왜! 그거 굉장한데요! 하지만 바쁘지 않아요? 관리자가 된 이후로 몹시 바쁘다고 했잖아요.

남: 사실은 지난 10월에 일을 그만두었어요.

여: 정말요? 상사하고 문제가 좀 있거나 건강 문제가 좀 있었던 거예요?

남: 전혀 아니에요. 그만두기로 한 내 결정은 그런 것들과 전혀 상관이 없었어요. 그런데 새 직장을 구했어요.

여: 좋은데요. 새 직장이 돈을 더 많이 줘서 직장을 바꿨군요, 맞죠?

남: 아뇨, 사실 아니에요. 난 이전 직장에서 더 높은 봉급을 받았어요.

여: 아, 알겠어요. 이전 직장에서 일이 너무 많았죠?

남: 네, 난 매일 야근을 해야 했어요. 내가 기계 같다는 느낌이었죠.

여: 왜 그만두었는지 이해해요. 지금은 행복해 보이네요.

남: 네, 행복해요. 난 8시부터 4시까지 일하고 달리기를 즐길 수 있어요.

어휘 terribly 몹시, 극심하게   quit 그만두다   decision 결정, 판단; 결단력   previous 이전의

08 언급하지 않은 것   ⑤

* 대화의 진행은 대개 선택지와 같은 순서이므로, 선택지를 보면서 언급된 내용을 소거하는 식으로 푸는 것이 좋다. 영업시간과 휴무일에 대해 언급하고 서점의 위치를 알려준 다음 주차 공간을 문의했으므로 언급되지 않은 것은 ⑤ '웹사이트 주소'이다.

[Telephone rings.]

M: Good afternoon, Evans Used Bookstore. How can I help you?

W: Hello, I'd like to sell some of my used books. Can I ask you **how to price my books**?

M: The price is decided based on the type of book and **how damaged it is**.

W: Then I should bring the books there. I'd like to visit your store this evening. When do you close?

M: We are open from 10 a.m. to 7 p.m.

W: Oh, I don't think I can make it this evening. Do you open on Saturday?

M: Yes, we're open until 3 p.m. on Saturdays, but **we close on Sundays**.

W: **Where is your store located**, exactly?

M: It's 198 Luis Street, near Union Square.

W: Thanks. Is there any place I can park my car around your bookstore?

M: We don't have a parking lot, but you can use street parking.

W: Okay. Thank you.

[전화벨이 울린다.]

남: 안녕하세요, Evans 중고 서점입니다. 무엇을 도와드릴까요?

여: 여보세요, 제 중고 책 몇 권을 팔고 싶은데요. 제 책 가격을 어떻게 매기는지 여쭤볼 수 있을까요?

남: 가격은 책의 종류와 책이 얼마나 손상되었는지에 근거해 결정됩니다.

여: 그러면 거기로 책을 가져가야겠군요. 오늘 저녁에 서점을 방문하고 싶은데요. 언제 문을 닫나요?

남: 저희는 오전 10시부터 오후 7시까지 영업합니다(① 영업시간).

여: 아, 오늘 저녁은 맞춰 갈 수 없겠군요. 토요일에 문을 여나요?

남: 네, <u>토요일에는 오후 3시까지 영업합니다만(① 영업시간)</u> <u>일요일에는 문을 닫습니다(② 휴무일)</u>.

여: 정확하게 서점이 어디 위치해 있나요?

남: <u>Union 광장 근처 Luis 가 198번지(③ 위치)</u>입니다.

여: 고맙습니다. 서점 근처에 제 차를 주차할 수 있는 장소가 있나요?

남: <u>주차장은 없습니다만 노상 주차를 하실 수 있습니다(④ 주차 공간)</u>.

여: 알겠습니다. 고맙습니다.

어휘 price 가격을 매기다; 값   make it 시간 맞춰 가다; 해내다

09 내용 불일치   ⑤

* 담화의 진행은 대개 선택지와 같은 순서이므로, 선택지를 보면서 일치하는 내용을 소거하는 식으로 푸는 것이 좋다. 야영객은 캠프 사무실에서 장작을 구매해야 한다고 했으므로 ⑤ '야영객에게 장작이 무료로 제공된다.'는 내용과 일치하지 않는다.

M: Hello, I'm Robert Moore, manager of Bruce Canyon Park. The park has a wide variety of wild plants and animals **which are rare in Europe**. It also has clear mountain streams, and you can enjoy fishing and swimming on a hot summer day. The park is open all year **except on Christmas Day**. The park is open from 9 a.m. to 6 p.m. for day visitors. There is **no fee in the daytime**, but there are fees for overnight camping. Each campsite is limited to 2 tents and begins at a base rate of $15.00 per night. Fires are permitted in grills, but **campers must purchase wood** at the camp office. Please come out and enjoy nature in Bruce Canyon Park.

남: 안녕하세요. 저는 Bruce Canyon 공원의 관리인 Robert Moore입니다. 공원에는 ① <u>유럽에서 드문 매우 다양한 야생 동물</u>이 있습니다. 또한, 맑은 산 속의 개울이 있어 여러분은 ② <u>더운 여름날 낚시와 수영</u>을 즐기실 수 있습니다. 공원은 ③ <u>크리스마스 날을 제외하고 1년 내내 문을 엽니다</u>. 주간 방문객에게는 오전 9시부터 오후 6시까지 개방합니다. ④ <u>낮 동안에는 요금이 없</u>지만 밤에 숙박하는 야영에는 요금이 있습니다. 각각의 캠프 장소는 2개의 텐트로 제한되고 하룻밤에 15달러의 기본요금에서 시작합니다. 그릴 안에서 불 사용은 허용되지만 ⑤ <u>야영객은 캠프 사무실에서 장작을 구매해야 합니다</u>. 나오셔서 Bruce Canyon 공원의 자연을 즐기십시오.

어휘 a wide variety of 매우 다양한   rare 드문, 희귀한   stream 개울, 시내; 흐름   except ~을 제외하고, ~외에는   fee 요금, 회비; 수수료   permit 허용[허락]하다   purchase 구매[구입](하다)

10 도표 이해   ①

* 대화의 진행은 대개 도표 항목의 나열 순서대로 진행된다. 대화를 들으면서 도표의 각 항목 중 선택되지 않은 것을 소거하는 식으로 푸는 것이 좋다. 우선 재질이 플라스틱인 제품을 제외했고(② 소거) 동물 모양의 병따개도 제외했다(④ 소거). 남은 ①, ③, ⑤ 중에서 열쇠고리 형태의 ③도 제외되고 나머지 둘 중 가격이 더 싼 것으로 결정했으므로 두 사람이 구매할 병따개는 ①이다.

W: Let's give away bottle openers as promotional gifts for the grand opening of our store.

M: Good idea. How about this plastic bottle opener? It is owl-shaped. Isn't it cute?

W: It's cute, but it doesn't fit the image of our store. **Let's go with metal**.

M: Okay. Do you like any of the animal-shaped openers, like the bear?

W: No, I'd like to go with a simple design.

M: Then let's choose among these three. There is a key-ring type opener. **Hanging it on the wall** would be good advertising.

W: I don't think people would like it. I've never seen key rings hanging on the wall.

M: Then **you want one with a magnet** on the back of it.

W: Yes, I think it's better and more useful. People can attach it on the refrigerator.

M: Okay. Now which one do you prefer? Would you like the cheaper one?

W: Absolutely. Let's go with the cheaper one.

여: 우리 상점 개점을 위한 판촉 선물로 병따개를 증정합시다.
남: 좋은 아이디어예요. 이 플라스틱 병따개는 어때요? 부엉이 모양인데요. 귀엽지 않아요?
여: 귀엽지만 우리 상점의 이미지에 맞지 않아요. 금속으로 선택하죠.
남: 알았어요. 곰과 같은 동물 모양의 병따개는 마음에 들어요?
여: 아뇨, 난 단순한 디자인으로 하고 싶어요.
남: 그러면 이 셋 중에서 선택합시다. 열쇠고리 형태의 병따개가 있군요. 벽에 그걸 걸어 두는 건 좋은 광고가 될 거예요.
여: 사람들이 그걸 좋아할 것 같지 않아요. 벽에 열쇠고리가 걸린 걸 본 적이 없어요.
남: 그러면 뒤에 자석이 있는 걸 원하는군요.
여: 네, 그게 더 좋고 더 유용하다고 생각해요. 사람들이 그걸 냉장고에 붙여둘 수 있잖아요.
남: 좋아요. 이제 어떤 게 더 좋은가요? 가격이 더 싼 걸 원해요?
여: 그렇고말고요. 더 싼 거로 선택합시다.

어휘 give away ~을 증정하다[선물로 주다] owl 부엉이, 올빼미 go with ~을 선택하다[받아들이다] hang 걸다, 매달다 advertising 광고(업) attach 붙이다, 첨부하다 absolutely 그렇고말고, 정말 그래; 전적으로, 틀림없이

11 짧은 대화에 이어질 응답 ②

✻ 어머니가 해변에 가려는 아들에게 짐을 잘 쌌는지 확인하는 상황이다. 어머니가 가장 중요한 수영복을 넣었는지 물었을 때 아들의 응답으로는 ② '아, 그걸 잊었어요! 저 정말 멍청한가 봐요!'가 가장 적절하다.

① 저, 저는 그걸 원하지 않아요. 그만 하세요.
③ 끔찍하네요! 제 선글라스를 잃어버렸어요.
④ 네. 수영할 때 주의할게요.
⑤ 걱정 마세요. 수영한 후에 그걸 세탁할게요.

W: Sam, **did you pack everything**? Check if you forgot anything.
M: Don't worry, Mom. I've got an extra pair of underwear, sunglasses, and a long sleeve shirt, **just in case**.
W: Okay, have fun at the beach. Oh, one more thing, Sam. You did **pack your swimsuit**, didn't you?
M: Oh, I forgot it! How stupid of me!

여: Sam, 짐을 모두 다 쌌니? 잊어버린 게 있는지 확인하렴.
남: 걱정 마세요, 엄마. 여분의 속옷, 선글라스와 만약의 경우에 대비해서 긴 소매 셔츠를 가져가요.
여: 좋아, 해변에서 재미있게 놀렴. 아, 한 가지 더 있구나. Sam. 너 정말로 수영복 챙겼지, 그렇지 않니?
남: 아, 그걸 잊었어요! 저 정말 멍청한가 봐요!

어휘 pack (짐을) 싸다[챙기다] underwear 속옷 just in case 만약의 경우를 대비해서 | 선택지 어휘 | stupid 멍청한; 어리석은

12 짧은 대화에 이어질 응답 ④

✻ 바라던 새 프로젝트를 맡아서 설레지만 잘 해낼 수 있을지 모르겠다는 남자에게 여자가 할 말로는 격려의 내용을 담은 ④ '당신은 자격이 있어요. 분명히 아주 잘 해낼 거예요.'가 가장 적절하다.

① 기운 내요! 당신은 다음엔 더 잘할 거예요.
② 미안해요. 당신이 해낼 수 있을 거라고 생각하지 않아요.
③ 환영해요. 당신이 여기서 일하는 걸 즐기길 바라요.
⑤ 그건 걱정 말아요. 당신이 관여할 일이 아니에요.

M: I'm really excited about my new project at work. It's something I'd hoped **to be involved in**.
W: Good for you. It sounds like a great opportunity for you.
M: That's right. I don't know **if I can do well**, but this is something I've wanted for a while.
W: You deserve it. I'm sure you'll do a great job.

남: 직장에서의 나의 새 프로젝트가 정말 설레요. 내가 참여하기를 바랐던 것이에요.
여: 잘되었군요. 당신에게 아주 좋은 기회 같아요.

남: 맞아요. 내가 잘 해낼 수 있을지는 모르지만 이건 내가 한동안 바라 왔던 것이에요.
여: 당신은 자격이 있어요. 분명히 아주 잘 해낼 거예요.

어휘 be involved in ~에 참여하다[개입되다] for a while 한동안; 잠시(동안) | 선택지 어휘 | deserve 누릴 자격이 있다, 받을 만하다

13 긴 대화에 이어질 응답 ②

✻ 대화의 전체 맥락 하에 마지막 말의 의미나 의도를 정확히 파악하는 것이 좋다. 아파서 일주일간 결석해 기말고사를 걱정하는 여자에게 남자가 도와주겠다면서 노트를 모두 빌려주겠다고 한다. 이에 대한 여자의 응답으로는 ② '넌 은인이야. 난 벌써 안심이 된다.'가 가장 적절하다.

① 그건 맞아. 넌 더 열심히 공부해야 해.
③ 내가 뭘 해야 하는지 알아. 하지만 쉽지 않아.
④ 괜찮아. 난 그것들이 더 이상 필요한 것 같지 않아.
⑤ 너 창백해 보인다. 집에 가서 쉬어야겠어.

M: Hello, Ashley. **What have you been up to**? Were you on a trip? I haven't seen you around.
W: No, I've been sick.
M: I'm sorry to hear that. What was wrong?
W: I've been seeing my doctor **on a regular basis** because of bad headaches.
M: That's terrible.
W: I'm okay now. But I have a lot of stress these days.
M: Why is that? I guess **it has to do with school**.
W: Yes, I haven't been able to attend any of my classes for a week. My final exams are coming up, and I don't know what to do.
M: Oh, don't worry about it. I can help you if you want.
W: I don't want to bother you. Are you sure?
M: Yeah. What are friends for? I'll **let you borrow** all my notes.
W: You're a lifesaver. I feel relieved already.

남: 안녕, Ashley. 지금까지 어떻게 지냈어? 여행했니? 오랜만이다.
여: 아니야, 난 아팠어.
남: 그렇다니 안됐구나. 뭐가 문제였니?
여: 심한 두통으로 정기적으로 진찰을 받아왔어.
남: 그거 심하구나.
여: 지금은 괜찮아. 하지만 요즘 스트레스가 많아.
남: 왜 그러니? 학교와 관련된 것 같은데.
여: 응, 일주일 동안 어떤 수업도 출석하지 못했어. 기말고사가 다가오고 있는데 뭘 해야 할지 모르겠어.
남: 아, 그건 걱정 마. 네가 원한다면 내가 도울 수 있어.
여: 널 귀찮게 하고 싶지는 않은데. 정말이니?
남: 응. 친구 좋다는 게 뭐야? 내가 내 모든 노트를 빌려줄게.
여: 넌 은인이야. 난 벌써 안심이 된다.

어휘 on a regular basis 정기적으로 attend 출석[참석]하다 bother 귀찮게 하다; 신경 쓰이게 하다 | 선택지 어휘 | relieved 안심[안도]하는 pale 창백한; (색이) 연한

14 긴 대화에 이어질 응답 ③

✻ 대화의 전체 맥락 하에 마지막 말의 의미나 의도를 정확히 파악하는 것이 좋다. 아내의 허락도 없이 동료를 위한 송별회를 집에서 하기로 한 남자가 뒤늦게 아내의 양해를 구하고 있다. 아내가 이번에는 해주지만 다음번에는 미리 묻지 않으면 아무것도 하지 않겠다고 했을 때 남자의 응답으로는 ③ '다음번에는 당신에게 묻겠다고 약속해요. 고마워요.'가 가장 적절하다.

① 당신 말이 맞아요. 그는 내 오랜 친구예요.
② 그거 좋은 것 같은데요. 확실히 그는 이 파티를 즐겼을 거예요.
④ 현실적으로 됩시다. 당신은 모든 걸 가질 순 없어요.
⑤ 진정해요. 화낸다고 문제가 해결되는 건 아니에요.

M: Honey, what's your schedule like next weekend?
W: I'll have to check my planner. [pause] Well, I'm planning to go shopping.
M: Uh, well, you can go shopping sometime later, can't you?

W: Yeah. Why are you asking?

M: Well, it's just that I've invited some people over from work.

W: What? To our house? **What's the occasion**?

M: Thomas is leaving the company next week. So I'm throwing him a farewell party.

W: You decided to do this without asking me?

M: I'm very sorry. He looked so depressed, so **I made the suggestion unexpectedly**. I think about seven people are coming.

W: Charles! **You should have told me**.

M: I'm really sorry. We'll have a barbecue. So, I'd really appreciate it if you made some salad for us.

W: Hmm... All right. But if you don't ask me in advance next time, I'm **not doing anything**.

M: I promise to ask you next time. Thank you.

남: 여보, 다음 주말 당신 일정이 어떻게 돼요?

여: 내 일정표를 확인해봐야 해요. [잠시 후] 음, 쇼핑을 갈 계획이에요.

남: 어, 저, 쇼핑은 나중에 언제나 갈 수 있죠, 그렇지 않아요?

여: 그렇죠, 왜 묻는 거예요?

남: 음, 단지 내가 직장에서 몇 사람을 초대해서 그래요.

여: 뭐라고요? 우리 집으로요? 무슨 일이죠?

남: Thomas가 다음 주에 회사를 그만두거든요. 그래서 그에게 송별회를 해주려고요.

여: 나한테 묻지 않고 이걸 결정했다고요?

남: 정말 미안해요. 그가 너무 우울해 보여서 뜻밖에 제안을 했어요. 일곱 명 정도 올 것 같아요.

여: Charles! 나한테 말했어야죠.

남: 정말 미안해요. 우리는 바비큐를 할 거예요. 그러니까 당신이 우리를 위해 샐러드를 좀 만들어주면 정말 고맙겠어요.

여: 음… 좋아요. 하지만 다음번에 나한테 미리 묻지 않는다면 난 아무것도 하지 않을 거예요.

남: 다음번에는 당신에게 묻겠다고 약속해요. 고마워요.

어휘 occasion (특별한) 일, 행사   farewell party 송별회   depressed 우울한   suggestion 제안, 제의   unexpectedly 뜻밖에, 예상외로, 갑자기   appreciate 고마워하다; 감상하다; 진가를 인정하다; 평가하다   in advance 미리, 사전에
| 선택지 어휘 | practical 현실적인; 실용적인

15 상황에 적절한 말 ③

✽ 지시문을 통해 누가(A) 누구에게(B) 할 말인지를 우선 정확히 파악한다. 담화는 대개 A와 B에 대한 배경 설명과 B가 처한 문제 상황, 그리고 이에 대해 A가 어떤 말을 하려고 하는지에 대한 설명의 순서로 전개된다. 룸서비스를 이용하지 않은 투숙객의 계산서에 그 금액을 포함한 실수를 했으므로 Robert(A)가 투숙객(B)에게 할 말로는 ③ '실수를 사과드립니다. 그 요금을 삭제하겠습니다.'가 가장 적절하다.

① 사과드립니다. 손님 방은 10층에 있습니다.
② 네. 룸서비스는 9시 정각까지 이용 가능합니다.
④ 물론입니다. 하지만 3시 정각까지는 가방을 가져가셔야 합니다.
⑤ 실례합니다. 손님 앞에 다른 손님이 계십니다.

W: Robert works at a small hotel. He takes reservations at the front desk as well as handles check-ins for hotel guests. As usual, he's at the front desk today. He's very busy with a large tour group **that has just arrived**. At this time, a female guest wishes to check out. She also asks if the front desk can hold her bag until 3 o'clock after check-out. Robert says it's possible and **calculates her charges**. The guest stayed in a standard room for three nights. Robert sees that she's also used room service. As soon as she looks at her charges, she tells him that she's never used room service. After double checking, Robert realizes that he's **confused her bill** with another guest's and that she is right. In this situation, what would Robert most likely say to the guest?

Robert: **I'm sorry for the mistake. I'll remove the charge.**

여: Robert는 작은 호텔에서 일한다. 그는 호텔 투숙객을 위해 체크인을 처리할 뿐만 아니라 프런트에서 예약을 받는다. 늘 그렇듯이 오늘 그는 프런트에 있다. 그는 방금 도착한 많은 단체 여행객들로 매우 바쁘다. 이때 한 여성 투숙객이 퇴실하기를 바란다.

그녀는 또한 퇴실 후 3시 정각까지 프런트에서 자기 가방을 맡아줄 수 있는지 묻는다. Robert는 그것이 가능하다고 말하고 그녀의 요금을 계산한다. 그 투숙객은 일반실에서 3일간 묵었다. Robert는 그녀가 또한 룸서비스를 이용했음을 본다. 그녀가 자신의 계산서를 보자마자 그녀는 그에게 자신이 룸서비스를 이용한 적이 전혀 없다고 말한다. 다시 한번 확인한 후에 Robert는 자신이 그녀의 계산서를 다른 투숙객의 것과 혼동했고 그녀 말이 맞다는 것을 깨닫는다. 이 상황에서 Robert가 투숙객에게 뭐라고 말하겠는가?

Robert: 실수를 사과드립니다. 그 요금을 삭제하겠습니다.

어휘 reservation 예약; 보류   handle 처리하다, 다루다   as usual 늘 그렇듯이, 평상시처럼   calculate 계산하다; 추정[추산]하다   charge 요금; 청구하다   standard 일반적인; 기준(의), 표준(의)   realize 깨닫다, 인식[자각]하다   confuse A with B A를 B와 혼동하다
| 선택지 어휘 | available 이용 가능한; 시간[여유]이 있는

16~17 세트 문항   16 ④ 17 ④

✽ **16** 식이요법을 언급하며 말을 시작했지만 체중 문제의 원인을 아는 것이 중요하다고 하면서 몇 가지 원인을 꼽고, 이를 관리하기 위한 조언을 하고 있다. 그러므로 담화의 주제는 ④ '비만의 원인과 치료법'이다.

① 효과적이고 간단한 다이어트 계획
② 다이어트를 시작하는 효과적인 방법
③ 비만으로 야기되는 문제들
⑤ 비만이 건강에 미치는 해로운 영향

✽ **17** 해석 참조.
① 우유   ② 청량음료   ③ 초콜릿   ④ 파이   ⑤ 감자 칩

M: Are you thinking about dieting to lose weight? Before you start, it's important to learn **the cause of your weight problems**, since there can be many factors. For example, you may have bad food habits. Foods that are high in fat, sugar, and salt provide more energy than the body needs. Do you have easy access to food? Many stay-at-home moms **are likely to overeat** since they have more access to food at home. Another reason to overeat is an inactive lifestyle. Many people are not physically active enough for good health and spend too much time sitting. So, **how can you manage your weight**? To begin, eat the right amount of the right stuff. Try to drink milk instead of soft drinks. Don't have chocolate, potato chips, or cookie jars around you. Don't stay up late playing computer games or watching TV. Eating out on a regular basis is also something you should avoid. I hope you keep all these points in mind and **start to control your weight**.

남: 체중을 줄이기 위해 다이어트를 할 것을 생각하고 계십니까? 시작하기 전에 여러분의 체중 문제의 원인을 아는 것이 중요한데, 거기에는 많은 요인이 있을 수 있기 때문입니다. 예를 들어 여러분은 나쁜 식습관을 가지고 있을지 모릅니다. 지방과 당과 염분이 높은 음식은 신체가 필요로 하는 것보다 더 많은 에너지를 제공합니다. 음식에 접근하기 쉬운가요? 많은 집에서 머무는 어머니들이 집에서 음식에 접근하기 더 쉽기 때문에 과식할 가능성이 있습니다. 과식의 또 다른 이유는 활동하지 않는 생활방식입니다. 많은 사람들이 건강할 만큼 충분히 신체적으로 활동하지 않고 너무 많은 시간을 앉아서 보냅니다. 그렇다면 어떻게 체중을 관리할 수 있을까요? 우선, 올바른 것을 적당량 드십시오. ② 청량음료 대신에 ① 우유를 마시려 노력하십시오. ③ 초콜릿, ⑤ 감자 칩, 혹은 쿠키 병을 주변에 두지 마십시오. 컴퓨터 게임을 하거나 TV를 보면서 늦게까지 깨어있지 마십시오. 정기적으로 외식을 하는 것 또한 여러분이 피해야 할 것입니다. 여러분이 이 모든 점을 명심하고 여러분의 체중을 조절하는 것을 시작하기를 바랍니다.

어휘 factor 요인, 요소   access 접근(권); 접근하다   be likely to-v v할 가능성이 있다, v할 것 같다   inactive 활동하지 않는; 소극적인(↔ active 활동하는; 적극적인)   physically 신체[육체]적으로; 물리적으로   manage 관리하다; 경영하다   control 조절[조정]하다; 통제[지배]하다 | 선택지 어휘 | effective 효과적인; 실질적인, 사실상의   cause 야기하다; 초래하다; 원인   obesity 비만   treatment 치료(법); 대우

15회

01 화자가 하는 말의 목적　②

✽ 담화의 일부 내용이 아니라 중심 내용을 파악해야 한다. 본 담화는 Rosie와 Chris의 특별한 날이라고 하면서 두 사람을 위해 축하하며 마지막에 신부와 신랑을 위해 건배를 하는 것으로 보아 남자는 결혼식에서 축하의 말을 하고 있음을 알 수 있다. 그러므로 답은 ②이다.

M: Good afternoon, ladies and gentlemen. Thank you for sharing this very special day with Rosie and Chris. For those of you who don't know me, I'm Brandon. I've known Chris since middle school. Chris is really the best friend I've ever had. I'm very proud to stand by his side today. Rosie, I think we can all agree that you're beautiful this afternoon and that Chris **won the lottery**. Rosie and Chris, this afternoon **we celebrate you**. We all wish you a lifetime of happiness, love, health, success, and laughter. I hope you can always find humor in the bad and appreciation for the good. And I hope your love continues to grow throughout all the years to come. **To the bride and groom**. Cheers!

남: 안녕하세요, 신사 숙녀 여러분. Rosie와 Chris의 이 매우 특별한 날을 함께 해주셔서 감사합니다. 저를 모르시는 분들에게 말씀드리자면 저는 Brandon입니다. 저는 중학교 때부터 Chris를 알아왔습니다. Chris는 정말로 지금껏 제 가장 친한 친구입니다. 오늘 저는 그의 옆에 서게 되어 무척 자랑스럽습니다. Rosie, 오늘 오후 당신이 아름다우며 Chris가 복권에 당첨되었다는 데 우리가 모두 동의할 것으로 생각합니다. Rosie와 Chris, 오늘 오후 우리는 당신들을 축하합니다. 우리 모두는 당신들에게 평생의 행복, 사랑, 건강, 성공과 웃음을 기원합니다. 당신들이 나쁠 때 유머를, 좋을 때 감사를 항상 찾을 수 있기를 바랍니다. 그리고 당신들의 사랑이 앞으로 다가올 세월 동안 계속 커지기를 바랍니다. 신부와 신랑을 위해. 건배!

어휘 lottery 복권: 추첨　appreciation 감사: 감상: 이해, 평가　continue to-v 계속해서 v하다　throughout ~동안 죽: 내내　bride 신부 cf. groom 신랑

02 의견　④

✽ 우선 지시문에서 명시한 화자의 성별을 보고 어느 화자의 말에 주목할지를 판단해야 한다. 특히 의견이나 주장을 표현하는 어구(I think ~, You should ~ 등)가 이끄는 내용을 잘 들어야 한다. 남자가 시험 전 2주 동안 열심히 공부했는데도 수학 성적이 안 좋았다고 침울해하자 여자는 수학 공부를 매일 하면서 튼튼한 기초를 세우고 차근차근 쌓아나가라고 하고 있다. 그러므로 여자의 의견은 ④ '수학 실력은 장기간에 걸쳐 쌓이는 것이다.'가 적절하다.

W: Nick, are you okay? You look so down.
M: I received my report card today. I really studied math hard, but I got a terrible grade anyway.
W: Have you thought about **why your grades haven't improved**?
M: I don't know. I stopped playing computer games and playing baseball for two weeks. I really did my best this time.
W: I know that you tried hard this time. But studying hard just for **a couple of weeks** won't improve your math grades.
M: What do I need to do?
W: Studying for math is like a marathon. **You need to do it every day** instead of cramming right before an exam.
M: Are you saying that I should study at a steady pace?
W: Exactly. Don't expect quick results but set a strong foundation and build **step by step**.
M: I see. It sounds difficult, but I'll try.

여: Nick, 너 괜찮니? 너무 침울해 보인다.
남: 오늘 성적표를 받았어. 수학을 정말 열심히 공부했지만 결국 형편없는 성적을 받았어.
여: 왜 네 성적이 향상하지 않았는지에 대해 생각해 봤니?
남: 모르겠어. 난 2주 동안 컴퓨터 게임하고 야구 경기하는 것을 하는 걸 그만두었어. 이번에는 정말로 최선을 다했어.
여: 네가 이번에 열심히 노력한 건 알아. 하지만 단지 2주 동안 열심히 공부하는 거로는 네 수학 성적을 향상시킬 수 없을 거야.
남: 내가 뭘 해야 할까?
여: 수학 공부는 마라톤과 같아. 시험 바로 전에 벼락치기 공부를 하는 거 대신 매일 그걸 해야 해.
남: 내가 꾸준한 속도로 공부해야 한다는 말이니?
여: 바로 그거야. 빠른 결과를 기대하지 말고 튼튼한 기초를 세우고 차근차근 쌓아나가.
남: 알겠어. 어려운 것 같지만 노력해볼게.

어휘 report card 성적표　improve 향상시키다, 개선되다　cram 벼락치기 공부를 하다; 밀어 넣다　steady 꾸준한; 한결같은　pace 속도　foundation 기초; 설립; 재단

03 관계　②

✽ 직업을 나타내거나 추론할 수 있는 힌트가 대화 전반에 걸쳐 드러나므로, 대화를 전체적으로 이해하는 것이 필요하다. 본 대화에서 외국인 학생인 남자에게 뚜껑이 없는 음료수를 들고 들어올 수 없다고 제지하고 책을 찾는 방법을 알려주며 도서 대출 등에 대해 알려주는 것으로 보아 여자는 도서관 사서임을 알 수 있다. 그러므로 둘의 관계는 ② '도서관 사서 – 학생'이 적절하다.

W: Excuse me. You're **not allowed to bring** your drink here.
M: Oh, really? But the woman over there also brought her drink.
W: She's got a tumbler with a cap. Covered drinks are allowed.
M: Oh, I see. I'm a foreign student and this is my first time here, so I didn't know that. Umm, could you tell me **how I can search for a book**?
W: Tell me which book you want, or you can use the computers over there.
M: Can I use those computers for free?
W: Sure. Just type keywords from the title or the author's name into the search box.
M: Thanks. **How many books can I borrow** at a time?
W: If you're a student here, you can check out 10 books for 2 weeks.
M: I see. One more question: Are there copy machines inside?
W: Of course. You need to buy a copy card to photocopy materials.
M: Thank you. I'll go out to drink this and come back again.

여: 실례합니다. 여기 음료수를 가져오는 건 허용되지 않아요.
남: 아, 정말이요? 하지만 저기 있는 여자도 음료수를 가져왔는데요.
여: 그 사람은 뚜껑이 있는 텀블러를 갖고 있어요. 뚜껑이 덮인 음료수는 허용됩니다.
남: 아, 알겠어요. 전 외국인 학생이고 이번이 여기 처음이라서 그걸 몰랐어요. 음, 제가 어떻게 책을 찾을 수 있는지 알려주실 수 있나요?
여: 원하는 책을 저한테 말하시거나 저기 있는 컴퓨터를 사용하실 수 있어요.
남: 저 컴퓨터들을 무료로 사용할 수 있나요?
여: 그럼요. 그냥 검색창에 제목의 키워드나 저자 이름을 입력하세요.
남: 고맙습니다. 제가 한 번에 몇 권의 책을 빌릴 수 있나요?
여: 여기 학생이라면 2주 동안 10권의 책을 대출하실 수 있어요.
남: 알겠습니다. 질문이 하나 더 있는데요. 안에 복사기가 있나요?
여: 물론이죠. 자료를 복사하시려면 복사 카드를 사야 해요.
남: 고맙습니다. 이걸 마시기 위해 나갔다 다시 오겠습니다.

어휘 be allowed to-v v하는 것이 허용되다　author 저자　check out (도서관에서 책을) 대출하다　copy machine 복사기　photocopy 복사하다　material 자료; 재료; 물질

04 그림 불일치　③

✽ 대화가 나오기 전에 각 사물의 위치 관계와 외형(형태나 무늬, 개수 등)의 특징을 미리 확인하는 것이 좋다. 대화에서 사각형 상자는 초콜릿만 있어서 남자는 초콜릿과 사탕 조합이 있는 하트 모양 상자를 택했으므로 그림에서의 사각형 상자는 대화의 내용과

일치하지 않는다. 그러므로 답은 ③이다.

M: I'd like to get some chocolate and candy for my little sister. She just graduated from kindergarten.
W: If you want something special, why don't you make your own gift basket?
M: Good idea. I'd like that. Can you help me to make it?
W: Sure. First, you need to choose a basket. I recommend this basket **with heart decorations**.
M: Great. And a teddy bear is the first thing to put in the basket. My sister really likes teddy bears.
W: Okay. I'll put a teddy bear in the middle of the basket. And which chocolate box do you want?
M: Does this square box have chocolates and candy?
W: No, it only has chocolates. This heart-shaped box has **a combination** of chocolates and candy.
M: Then I'd like **the heart-shaped one**. Put it on the left side of the teddy bear.
W: Sure. How about putting these three roses in the basket?
M: Good idea. She loves roses. And could you decorate **the top of the basket** with a big ribbon?
W: Certainly. Here you go. How do you like it?
M: It looks great. Thank you.

남: 저의 여동생을 위해 초콜릿과 사탕을 사주고 싶은데요. 유치원을 막 졸업했거든요.
여: 특별한 것을 원하신다면 손님 자신만의 선물 바구니를 만드는 게 어떠세요?
남: 좋은 생각이에요. 그걸 원해요. 만드는 걸 도와주실 수 있나요?
여: 그럼요. 우선 바구니를 선택하셔야 해요. 이 하트 장식이 있는 바구니를 추천합니다.
남: 좋아요. 그리고 테디 베어가 바구니에 제일 먼저 넣을 것이죠. 제 동생이 테디 베어를 정말로 좋아하거든요.
여: 알겠습니다. 제가 테디 베어를 바구니 가운데 넣을게요. 그리고 어떤 초콜릿 상자를 원하시나요?
남: 이 사각형 상자에 초콜릿과 사탕이 있나요?
여: 아니요, 그건 초콜릿만 있습니다. 이 하트 모양 상자에 초콜릿과 사탕 조합이 있습니다.
남: 그러면 하트 모양 상자를 원해요. 테디 베어 왼쪽에 그것을 넣어주세요.
여: 그럼요. 이 세 송이의 장미를 바구니에 넣는 건 어떠세요?
남: 좋은 생각이에요. 그 애는 장미를 좋아하거든요. 그리고 바구니 맨 위를 큰 리본으로 장식해주실 수 있나요?
여: 물론이죠. 여기 있습니다. 어떠신가요?
남: 멋져 보여요. 고맙습니다.

어휘 kindergarten 유치원   decoration 장식(품) cf. decorate 장식하다. 꾸미다
combination 조합[결합](물)   certainly 물론이지요. 그럼요; 틀림없이

05 추후 행동   ④

* 대개 대화는 어떤 일을 하게 되는 상황이 먼저 제시된 뒤에 남자와 여자가 각각 할 일 들과 이에 대한 수락/거절의 응답이 나열되는 식으로 전개된다. 면세점 쇼핑은 남자가 거절해서 안 하게 되었고 커피숍에서 커피를 마시는 데 동의했으나 남자가 우선 서점 에 들르기를 원했다. 따라서 남자가 할 일로는 ④ '서점에서 잡지 구매하기'가 적절하 다. 은행에서 환전하는 것은 여자가 할 일임을 유의한다.

M: Okay. Now we've finished our flight check-in.
W: Honey, you got our boarding passes, right?
M: Yeah, here's yours and here's mine. Our flight leaves in two hours.
W: We don't need to wait at the boarding gate, do we?
M: Of course not. It's okay to be there an hour before the departure time.
W: Since we still have some time, **how about doing some duty-free shopping**?
M: To tell you the truth, I hate shopping. It's so boring!
W: Then what do you want to do? Would you like to get some coffee at the coffee shop?
M: That sounds good. But before we do that, **can we stop by the bookstore**? I'd like to get a magazine.
W: Okay. Oh, hold on. **I forgot to exchange my money**. I need to go to the bank first.
M: Then let's do what we each want and meet at the information desk later.

W: Good idea. Let's meet there later.

남: 좋아요. 이제 우리는 비행기 탑승수속이 끝났어요.
여: 여보, 우리 탑승권 당신이 가지고 있죠, 맞아요?
남: 그래요, 이건 당신 것이고 이건 내 것이에요. 우리 비행기는 2시간 후에 떠나요.
여: 탑승구에서 기다릴 필요는 없죠, 그렇죠?
남: 물론 없죠. 출발 시간 한 시간 전에 거기 가도 괜찮아요.
여: 우리 아직 시간이 좀 있으니까 면세점 쇼핑을 좀 하는 건 어때요?
남: 사실을 말하자면 난 쇼핑이 싫어요. 그건 너무 지루해요!
여: 그러면 뭘 하고 싶어요? 커피숍에서 커피를 좀 마시고 싶어요?
남: 그거 좋겠군요. 하지만 그걸 하기 전에 서점에 잠시 들를 수 있을까요? 잡지를 사고 싶어요.
여: 좋아요. 아, 잠깐만요. 난 돈을 환전하는 걸 잊었어요. 난 우선 은행에 가야 해요.
남: 그럼 각자 원하는 걸 하고 나중에 안내 데스크에서 만나요.
여: 좋은 생각이에요. 나중에 거기서 봐요.

어휘 flight 항공기, 항공편; 여행, 비행   check-in (공항의) 탑승수속; (호텔의) 투숙 절차
boarding pass (여객기의) 탑승권   departure 출발, 떠남   duty-free shop 면세점
stop by ~에 잠시 들르다   exchange 환전(하다); 교환(하다)

06 금액   ③

* 여러 개의 수치 정보가 등장하므로 필요한 정보를 메모하면서 듣는 것이 좋다. 소포를 보내는 비용으로 85달러에 국제 등기 서비스로 20달러를 추가했으므로 남자가 지불 해야 하는 금액은 ③ '$105'이다. 70달러는 남자가 내야 할 돈이 아니라 운송 중 사고 가 날 때 보상받을 수 있는 금액의 상한선임에 유의한다.

M: Good morning. I have to send this package to Brazil.
W: OK, could you put it on the scale? Let's see **how much it weighs**.
M: Sure. I want to send it by airmail. How long does it take to get there?
W: It'll take about 7 days.
M: How much is it?
W: It weighs 5 kilograms, so **it costs $85**. You also have the option of using "International Signed For."
M: What is that? I've never heard of it.
W: Your item will be fully tracked. And the person in Brazil has to **sign for it** when the postman delivers it to them.
M: It sounds much safer. How much does that cost?
W: An extra $20. You will receive up to $70 **if an accident happens** during shipping.
M: That's good. I'd like International Signed For service.
W: Do you need anything else?
M: No, thanks.

남: 안녕하세요. 이 소포를 브라질로 보내야 하는데요.
여: 알겠습니다. 그걸 저울 위에 놓으시겠어요? 무게가 얼마나 나가는지 봅시다.
남: 좋아요. 항공우편으로 보내고 싶어요. 거기 가는 데 얼마나 걸리나요?
여: 약 7일 걸릴 겁니다.
남: 얼마인가요?
여: 무게가 5킬로그램 나가니까 85달러네요. 또 '국제 등기'를 이용할 선택권이 있습니다.
남: 그게 뭐죠? 들어본 적이 없는데요.
여: 손님 물품이 완전히 추적될 것입니다. 그리고 배달원이 그걸 브라질에 있는 사람에게 배달하면 그들이 그것을 수령했다고 서명해야 합니다.
남: 훨씬 더 안전할 것 같군요. 그건 얼마나 하나요?
여: 추가로 20달러입니다. 운송 중에 사고가 일어나면 70달러까지 받으실 겁니다.
남: 그거 좋군요. 국제 등기 서비스로 하겠어요.
여: 다른 필요하신 거 있나요?
남: 아니요, 괜찮습니다.

어휘 package 소포; 포장물   scale 저울; 규모, 범위   track 추적하다; 길, 자취   shipping (해상) 운송; 선박, 배

07 이유   ④

* 지시문을 통해 남자가 Jack에게 화가 난 상황이며 남자의 말에 단서가 있을 가능성이

큼을 미리 파악한다. 남자가 Jack에게 화가 난 이유는 Jack이 책을 빌려 가서 포도 주스를 쏟아 책을 읽지도 못하게 해놓고는 미안하다는 말만 하고 피해 다녀서이다. 그러므로 답은 ④ '책을 망가뜨리고 피해 다녀서'이다.

W: Oh, there's Jack. Hi, Jack!
M: Jack? You mean Jack Tylor? Where is he?
W: Oh, he just walked away. Maybe he didn't see us.
M: I'm sure **he pretended he didn't see me**.
W: Why? What has he got against you? Did you guys have a fight or something?
M: No, we didn't fight. I just got angry with him. He borrowed my book and **spilled sticky grape juice** all over it.
W: Oh, my goodness!
M: I had to read the book for a report, but I couldn't read **more than half of the pages**.
W: That's too bad. Did he apologize and buy you a new book?
M: He just said, "I'm sorry!" and **he's been avoiding me**. I should buy the book again.
W: Oh. I think he should make a sincere apology to you.

여: 아, 저기 Jack이 있다. 안녕, Jack!
남: Jack이라고? Jack Tylor 말이니? 그가 어디 있니?
여: 아, 그냥 걸어가 버렸어. 아마 우리를 못 봤나 봐.
남: 그가 나를 못 본 척했던 게 분명해.
여: 왜? 그가 널 싫어하는 이유가 뭐야? 너희들 싸우거나 뭐 그런 거야?
남: 아니. 우리는 싸우지 않았어. 난 단지 그에게 화가 났어. 그는 내 책을 빌려 가서는 책 전체에 끈적거리는 포도 주스를 쏟았어.
여: 아, 저런!
남: 보고서를 내기 위해 그 책을 읽어야 했지만, 책 페이지의 절반 이상을 읽지 못했어.
여: 그거 안됐다. 그가 사과하고 너한테 새 책을 사줬니?
남: 단지 "미안해!"라고만 말했고 계속 나를 피하고 있어. 나는 그 책을 다시 사야 해.
여: 아. 난 그가 너에게 진심 어린 사과를 해야 한다고 생각해.

어휘 pretend ~인 척하다 spill 쏟다, 흘리다 apologize 사과하다 cf. apology 사과 sincere 진심 어린, 진실한

08 언급하지 않은 것 ④

※ 대화의 진행은 대개 선택지와 같은 순서이므로, 선택지를 보면서 언급된 내용을 소거하는 식으로 푸는 것이 좋다. 자리에 앉는 올바른 자세와 손목 받침대, 수직 모양의 마우스, 모니터와의 거리에 대해 언급했지만, 모니터의 각도에 대해서는 언급하지 않았다. 그러므로 답은 ④이다.

M: Megan, aren't you tired?
W: Yes, I'm tired. I've been on the computer for a long time.
M: I noticed your posture **while you use the computer**. You look so uncomfortable.
W: I was so focused on writing a paper that I didn't realize what I was doing.
M: You need to sit up straight. Push your hips **back as far as they can go** in the chair.
W: I'll be careful about that. And my wrists really hurt, too.
M: How about using a wrist pad when you're using the mouse? It'll support your wrist, and you'll feel less pain.
W: Thanks for pointing that out.
M: And you can change your mouse to a vertical mouse. **With a vertical mouse**, you can move your hand without a problem.
W: I've heard about that. I'll think about it.
M: And make sure to **keep a healthy distance from the monitor**. You should keep yourself at least 40cm from the monitor.
W: I got it. Thanks for your good advice.

남: Megan, 너 피곤하지 않니?
여: 응. 피곤해. 오랫동안 컴퓨터를 했거든.
남: 네가 컴퓨터를 사용하는 동안 네 자세를 주의해서 봤어. 너무 불편해 보이더라.
여: 보고서 쓰는 데 너무 집중해서 내가 뭘 하고 있는지 깨닫지 못했어.
남: 넌 똑바로 앉을 필요가 있어. 엉덩이를 가능한 한 의자 뒤로 깊이 밀어 넣어(① 올바른

자세).
여: 그것에 대해 신경 쓸게. 그리고 내 손목도 정말 아파.
남: 네가 마우스를 사용할 때 손목 받침대(② 손목 받침대)를 사용하는 건 어때? 그게 네 손목을 받쳐주고 넌 덜 아플 거야.
여: 그걸 언급해줘서 고마워.
남: 그리고 넌 네 마우스를 수직 마우스(③ 마우스 모양)로 바꿀 수 있어. 수직 마우스로 문제없이 네 손을 움직일 수 있어.
여: 수직 마우스에 대해 들었어. 그것을 생각해볼게.
남: 그리고 반드시 모니터와 건강한 거리를 유지해야 해. 너 자신을 모니터로부터 적어도 40cm(⑤ 모니터와의 거리) 떨어지게 유지해야 하지.
여: 알았어. 좋은 충고 고마워.

어휘 notice 주목하다, 관심을 기울이다 posture 자세; 태도 uncomfortable 불편한 realize 깨닫다, 인식[자각]하다 wrist 손목, 팔목 support 떠받치대[받치다]; 지지하다 point out 언급하다, 지적하다 vertical 수직의, 세로의 make sure 반드시 (~하도록) 하다 distance 거리

09 내용 불일치 ⑤

※ 담화의 진행은 대개 선택지와 같은 순서이므로, 선택지를 보면서 일치하는 내용을 소거하는 식으로 푸는 것이 좋다. 연주회 시작 한 시간 전부터 입장할 수 있다고 했으므로 ⑤ '연주회 시작 두 시간 전부터 입장할 수 있다.'는 내용과 일치하지 않는다.

M: If you're dreaming of a musical Christmas, don't miss the Wichita Symphony's Annual Holiday Concert! The concert will open up with a choir, directed by Jay Decker. And **as always**, the concert will include our popular audience sing-along. The concert will be held on Friday, December 14, 7:30 p.m., at Wichita University Auditorium. **You can't reserve tickets in advance**, and they can only be purchased individually on the night of the concert. Tickets will be $25 for adults and $10 for children under 12. Wichita University students **get in free** with student ID. Doors open at 6:30 p.m. So, **you can enter from up to an hour** before the start of the concert. For more ticket information, please visit the Wichita Symphony's website.

남: 여러분이 음악이 있는 크리스마스를 꿈꾸고 있다면 Wichita 교향악단의 연례 연말연시 연주회를 놓치지 마십시오! 연주회는 Jay Decker가 지휘하는 합창단과 함께 시작될 것입니다. 그리고 늘 그렇듯이 ① 연주회에는 우리의 인기 있는 청중과 함께 노래 부르기가 포함될 것입니다. ② 연주회는 12월 14일 금요일 오후 7시 30분에 Wichita 대학 강당에서 열릴 것입니다. ③ 티켓을 미리 예약할 수 없으며 연주회를 하는 당일 밤에 개별적으로만 구매할 수 있습니다. 티켓은 성인은 25달러이고 ④ 12세 미만 아동은 10달러일 것입니다. Wichita 대학 학생들은 학생증이 있으면 무료로 입장합니다. 문은 오후 6시 30분에 엽니다. 그러므로 ⑤ 연주회 시작 한 시간 전부터 입장할 수 있습니다. 티켓에 대한 더 많은 정보를 원하면 Wichita 교향악단 웹사이트를 방문해 주십시오.

어휘 symphony 교향악(단); 교향곡 annual 연례의, 매년의 holiday 연말연시; 휴가 choir 합창단, 성가대 direct 지휘[감독]하다; 명령하다; 직접적인 audience 청중, 관객 auditorium 강당; 객석 reserve 예약하다; 보유하다 in advance 미리, 사전에 purchase 구매(하다), 사다 individually 개별적으로, 각각 따로

10 도표 이해 ⑤

※ 대화의 진행은 대개 도표 항목의 나열 순서대로 진행된다. 대화를 들으면서 도표의 각 항목 중 선택되지 않은 것을 소거하는 식으로 푸는 것이 좋다. 우선 체중 감량을 목표로 했으므로 ③이 제외된다. 그리고 주중에는 오후 6시 이후인 저녁 시간만 가능하다고 했으므로 오후 3시인 ① 또한 제외된다. 남은 것 중 수강료가 50달러를 넘는 ②를 제외하면 ④와 ⑤가 남는데 여성 강사를 원했으므로 여자가 택할 강좌는 ⑤이다.

W: Excuse me. I want to sign up for one of your classes.
M: Some classes are already full, but several classes are still open. Here's the list of all the classes you can register for.
W: **I want to lose some weight**.
M: Then I recommend this swimming class.

W: Oh, but it's on Tuesday and Thursday afternoon. I can't take it since I work 9 to 6. I'm only free weekday evenings.

M: Then you can choose one of the evening classes.

W: Okay. Why is this class so expensive **among the remaining classes**?

M: It's because it offers private lessons. I'm sure this will be very effective.

W: But **it's beyond my budget**. As for the fee, I'd like to stay under 50 dollars a month.

M: Then it looks like you have two options. Which one do you prefer?

W: I'd like to **learn from a female instructor**.

M: All right. Then this is what you want.

여: 실례합니다. 여기 강좌 중 하나를 신청하고 싶은데요.

남: 일부 강좌는 이미 꽉 찼지만 몇몇 강좌는 아직 자리가 있습니다. 여기 등록하실 수 있는 모든 강좌의 목록이 있습니다.

여: 저는 체중을 좀 감량하고 싶은데요.

남: 그러면 이 수영 강좌를 추천해 드립니다.

여: 아, 하지만 그건 화요일과 목요일 오후군요. 저는 9시부터 6시까지 일하기 때문에 그걸 들을 수 없어요. 저는 주중 저녁에만 시간이 있어요.

남: 그러면 저녁 강좌 중 하나를 선택하실 수 있죠.

여: 알겠어요. 남아있는 강좌 중 이 강좌는 왜 이렇게 비싼가요?

남: 그건 개인 강습을 제공하기 때문입니다. 분명히 이것이 아주 효과적일 것이라고 확신합니다.

여: 하지만 제 예산을 초과하네요. 수강료에 대해서 말하자면 한 달에 50달러 미만이면 좋겠어요.

남: 그러면 두 가지 선택이 있으신 것 같군요. 어느 것이 더 좋으신가요?

여: 여성 강사에게 배우고 싶어요.

남: 알겠습니다. 그러면 이게 원하시는 것이군요.

어휘 **sign up for** ~에 신청[가입]하다　**register** 등록하다　**private** 개인의; 사적인　**effective** 효과적인　**beyond** 넘어서는; 저편에　**fee** 요금; 수수료　**prefer** (더) 좋아하다. 선호하다　**instructor** 강사

11 짧은 대화에 이어질 응답　　　　①

＊ 동아리 회장에 출마한 여자는 경쟁자가 경험이 많아 자신이 이길 것 같지 않다고 말했다. 이에 대한 남자의 응답으로는 ① '시도해보기 전에는 결코 알 수 없는 거야.'가 가장 적절하다.

② 나는 훌륭한 회장이 될 거야.

③ 선거에 도움이 좀 필요해.

④ 우리는 누군가 다른 후보자를 지지할 거야.

⑤ 너는 네 선거운동 예산을 줄일 수 있어.

W: I've been really busy these days. **I'm going to run for president** of my club.

M: That's great. I hope you get elected.

W: I don't think I can win. My rival has **a lot of experience** with this kind of thing.

M: **You never know until you try.**

여: 요즘 나는 너무 바빠. 우리 동아리 회장에 출마할 거거든.

남: 그거 굉장하다. 네가 선출되기를 바라.

여: 난 내가 이길 거 같지 않아. 내 경쟁자는 이런 종류의 일에 경험이 많거든.

남: 시도해보기 전에는 결코 알 수 없는 거야.

어휘 **run for** ~에 출마[입후보]하다　**president** 회장; 대통령　**elect** 선출[선거]하다; 선택하다 *cf.* election 선거; 당선　| 선택지 어휘 | **candidate** 후보자; 지원자　**budget** 예산(안)

12 짧은 대화에 이어질 응답　　　　③

＊ 시간이 있냐는 남자의 질문에 여자는 내야 하는 영어 에세이가 있어 시간이 없다고 했지만, 재차 남자가 힙합 콘서트에 가자고 권유한다. 이에 대한 응답으로는 ③ '좋겠다. 하지만 난 못 갈 것 같아.'가 적절하다.

① 네 말이 맞아. 제일 중요한 걸 먼저 해야지.

② 이건 내가 낼게. 내가 너를 위해 지불할게.

④ 잘했어. 훨씬 나아졌구나.

⑤ 도와줘서 고마워. 내일 보자.

M: Sarah, are you free tomorrow?

W: No. Actually, I have **an English essay** due next Friday.

M: **You have plenty of time**. Let's go to the Hip Hop concert tomorrow evening. I have tickets.

W: **Sounds great. But I'm afraid I can't.**

남: Sarah, 내일 시간 있니?

여: 아니. 사실 다음 금요일까지 내야 하는 영어 에세이가 있어.

남: 시간이 충분히 있잖아. 내일 저녁 힙합 콘서트에 가자. 내게 티켓이 있어.

여: 좋겠다. 하지만 난 못 갈 것 같아.

어휘 **essay** 에세이, 과제물; 수필　**due** (언제) ~하기로 되어 있는　**plenty of** 충분[풍부]한, 많은　| 선택지 어휘 | **improvement** 향상; 개선

13 긴 대화에 이어질 응답　　　　②

＊ 대화의 전체 맥락 하에 마지막 말의 의미나 의도를 정확히 파악하는 것이 좋다. 본 대화에서 여자가 취직을 간절히 바라고 있던 상황에서 합격자 명단에서 자신의 이름을 발견했다. 남자가 축하의 인사를 건넸을 때 여자의 응답으로는 기쁨을 표시하는 ② '꿈만 같아! 드디어 취직했어!'가 가장 적절하다.

① 잘했어! 네가 해낼 수 있다니 너무 기뻐!

③ 이건 너무 어려워. 하지만 분명히 그만한 가치가 있을 거야.

④ 도움이 필요해. 내게 무슨 잘못이 있는지 모르겠어.

⑤ 걱정 마. 넌 많은 다른 선택권이 있어.

M: Miranda, what are you doing? **Are you surfing the Internet**?

W: I applied at Soft Tech Company, and they're announcing the people who are hired today.

M: **What's the result**? Do you see your name?

W: I can't find my name. I really thought I was going to get this job. Soft Tech is hiring a lot of new employees, and I was hoping to be one of them.

M: Let me see. The names are all **in alphabetical order**.

W: [pause] Oh, my! I'm not on the list.

M: Wait a minute! The last names are in alphabetical order, not first names.

W: You're right. Let's see. T... Townshend.

M: Look! I see Townshend! There you are, Townshend, Miranda!

W: Really! Are you sure? Oh, Tim! Thanks a million.

M: **No need to thank me**. It's your doing. Congratulations!

W: It seems like a dream! I finally got a job!

남: Miranda, 뭐 하니? 인터넷 검색을 하고 있니?

여: 내가 Soft Tech 사에 지원했는데 그들이 오늘 고용된 사람을 발표하고 있어.

남: 결과가 어떠니? 네 이름이 보이니?

여: 내 이름을 찾을 수 없어. 난 정말로 이 일자리를 얻게 될 거라고 생각했어. Soft Tech는 많은 신입직원을 고용할 거라서 내가 그들 중 하나가 되기를 바라고 있었어.

남: 내가 볼게. 이름이 모두 알파벳 순서구나.

여: [잠시 후] 아, 이런! 난 명단에 없어.

남: 잠깐 기다려! 성이 알파벳 순서지 이름은 아니야.

여: 맞아. 어디 보자. T… Townshend.

남: 봐! Townshend가 보여! 여기 있구나, Townshend, Miranda!

여: 정말 그래! 확실한 거지? 아, Tim! 정말 고마워.

남: 나한테 고마워할 필요 없지. 네가 한 거야. 축하해!

여: 꿈만 같아! 드디어 취직했어!

어휘 **apply** 지원[신청]하다　**announce** 발표하다, 알리다; 선언하다　**hire** 고용하다　**alphabetical order** 알파벳 순서　| 선택지 어휘 | **make it** (바라던 일을) 해내다; 성공하다; (장소에) 이르다　**be worth it** 그만한 가치가 있다

14 긴 대화에 이어질 응답　　　　③

＊ 대화의 전체 맥락 하에 마지막 말의 의미나 의도를 정확히 파악하는 것이 좋다. 여자는 많은 사람들이 버스보다 가격이 비싼데도 불구하고 페리를 이용하는 이유를 묻고

있다. 이에 대한 남자의 응답으로는 ③ '많은 사무실이 강을 따라 있어서 그들은 시간을 절약할 수 있거든.'이 가장 적절하다.

① 대부분의 사람들이 운전하기 때문에 페리는 그렇게 인기가 없거든.
② 페리는 주말에는 운항하지 않거든.
④ 그들은 다리에서 아름다운 야경을 즐길 수 있거든.
⑤ 그건 그것이 도시의 명소로 여겨지기 때문이야.

W: This river **that goes through the city** is really awesome.
M: Isn't it? I don't think this city would be here without this river.
W: The trees on the riverside are beautiful.
M: Yes, it's even more beautiful at night when the bridge and **riverside are lit up**.
W: I should come here at night one day. There are a lot of tourists this morning.
M: Those people aren't tourists. They're people who are going to work across the river.
W: Really? I thought this ferry was for tourists.
M: Yeah, you would think so. But many people save time going to work by taking the ferry in the morning. If they didn't, **they would be stuck in traffic jams**.
W: That's a good idea. Is the fare cheap?
M: Not really. It's much more expensive than the bus.
W: Really? Then **why do they use the ferry**?
M: They can save time since many offices are along the river.

여: 도시를 통과해 흐르는 이 강은 정말 놀라워.
남: 그렇지 않니? 이 강이 없다면 이 도시가 여기 있지 않을 거라고 생각해.
여: 강가의 나무들이 아름다워.
남: 그래, 다리와 강변에 불이 켜지는 밤에 훨씬 더 아름답지.
여: 언젠가 밤에 여기 와야겠다. 오늘 아침엔 관광객이 많구나.
남: 저 사람들은 관광객이 아니야. 그들은 강을 건너 출근하려는 사람들이야.
여: 정말이야? 난 이 페리가 관광객을 위한 건 줄 알았어.
남: 그래, 그렇게 생각할 거야. 하지만 많은 사람들은 아침에 페리를 타면서 출근하는 시간을 절약해. 그렇지 않다면 그들은 교통 체증에 걸려 꼼짝 못할 거야.
여: 그거 좋은 아이디어구나. 페리 요금은 싸니?
남: 꼭 그런 건 아니야. 버스보다는 훨씬 더 비싸지.
여: 그래? 그러면 왜 사람들이 페리를 이용하는 거야?
남: 많은 사무실들이 강을 따라 있어서 그들은 시간을 절약할 수 있거든.

어휘 be stuck in ~에 갇히다 traffic jam 교통 체증 fare (교통) 요금
| 선택지 어휘 | along ~을 따라 consider 여기다, 생각하다 landmark 명소, 랜드마크

15 상황에 적절한 말   ③

* 지시문을 통해 누가(A) 누구에게(B) 할 말인지를 우선 정확히 파악한다. 담화는 대개 A와 B에 대한 배경 설명과 B가 처한 문제 상황, 그리고 이에 대해 A가 어떤 말을 하려고 하는지에 대한 설명의 순서로 전개된다. Jerry(B)의 사정을 들은 교수님(A)이 늦게 제출하게 된 Jerry의 보고서를 받아들일 수 있다고 생각하는 상황이다. 그러므로 교수님이 할 말로는 ③ '이 경우에는 어떠한 불이익 없이 보고서를 받아들일게.'가 가장 적절하다.

① 걱정 마라. 너만을 위해 시험을 연기해줄게.
② 미안하지만, 네 늦은 보고서를 받을 수 없을 것 같구나.
④ 그렇다니 유감이구나. 할머니가 곧 회복되시길 바란다.
⑤ 그렇다면 난 네가 할머니를 방문할 것을 제안해.

W: Jerry is a college student. He's taking Professor Walker's biology class this semester. He had to **hand in a paper** for his biology class last week. But his grandmother in Boston had a heart attack and was taken to the hospital. Jerry had to stay with his grandmother for a week. Fortunately, **his grandmother got better**, but Jerry's paper for the biology class is now a week late. Today, Jerry wants to give the paper to the professor, so he explains to the professor **why it's late**. Normally, the professor doesn't accept late papers, but she thinks **she can accept Jerry's paper** because of what happened to him. In this situation, what would the professor most likely say to Jerry?

Professor: In this case, I'll accept the paper without any penalty.

여: Jerry는 대학생이다. 그는 이번 학기에 Walker 교수님의 생물학 수업을 수강하고 있다. 그는 지난주에 생물학 수업에 낼 보고서를 제출해야 했다. 그러나 Boston에 계신 그의 할머니가 심장마비를 일으켜 병원에 실려 가셨다. Jerry는 일주일 동안 할머니와 함께 있어야 했다. 다행히도 Jerry의 할머니는 회복하셨지만, 그의 생물학 수업 보고서는 이제 일주일이 늦는다. 오늘 Jerry는 교수님께 보고서를 드리려고 하고, 그래서 왜 늦은 건지 교수님께 설명한다. 보통 그 교수님은 늦게 내는 보고서를 받지 않지만, Jerry에게 일어난 일 때문에 그의 보고서를 받아들일 수 있다고 생각한다. 이 상황에서 교수님이 Jerry에게 뭐라고 말하겠는가?

교수님: 이 경우에는 어떠한 불이익 없이 보고서를 받아들일게.

어휘 professor 교수 biology 생물학 semester 학기 hand in ~을 제출하다 paper 보고서; 시험지; 서류 accept 받다, 받아들이다; 수락하다
| 선택지 어휘 | postpone 연기하다, 미루다 penalty 불이익; 벌금; 처벌 recover (건강이) 회복되다 suggest 제안[제의]하다

16~17 세트 문항   16 ① 17 ②

* **16** 반려동물을 기르는 것이 아이들을 가르칠 수 있다고 하면서 예를 들어 설명하고 있다. 그러므로 담화의 주제로는 ① '반려동물이 아이들에게 미치는 교육적 효과'가 가장 적절하다.

② 반려동물을 안전하고 건강하게 기르는 법
③ 반려동물을 기르는 것의 장단점
④ 아이들의 신체적 성장에 미치는 반려동물의 영향
⑤ 아이들을 위해 반려동물을 입양하기 위한 조언

* **17** 해석 참조.
① 개 ② 거북이 ③ 뱀 ④ 물고기 ⑤ 햄스터

M: Did you care for a pet in childhood? The excitement of raising another being creates lifelong memories. While it's clear that **having a pet is entertaining**, did you know it can also teach your child in a positive and meaningful way? Having a pet in the family home brings great joy but also creates additional household chores. These chores are where children can learn important values and virtues **when raising pets**. For example, dogs can teach children to be responsible. Children who have to feed a dog, give a dog water, and walk a dog **learn to be responsible for** the life of another being. Cats also teach children responsibility, and also, children who own a cat learn about independence. Snakes, fish, and hamsters are also good **for teaching children** about cleanliness and proper bathing habits. Thus, adopting a pet is a huge responsibility and shouldn't be taken lightly, but it might be **the best thing you could ever do** for your kids' childhood.

남: 어린 시절에 반려동물을 돌보았습니까? 다른 존재를 기르는 즐거움은 평생의 기억을 만들어냅니다. 반려동물을 기르는 게 즐겁다는 것이 명백한 반면 그것이 또한 긍정적이고 의미 있는 방식으로 여러분의 자녀를 가르칠 수 있다는 것을 아셨습니까? 가정에서 반려동물을 기르는 것은 큰 즐거움을 가져오지만, 또한 부가적인 집안일을 만들어냅니다. 이러한 집안일들은 아이들이 반려동물을 기르면서 중요한 가치와 덕목을 배울 수 있는 부분입니다. 예를 들어, ① 개는 아이들에게 책임감을 갖도록 가르칠 수 있습니다. 개에게 먹이를 주고 물을 주고 개를 산책시켜야 하는 아이들은 다른 존재의 생명에 대해 책임감을 갖는 것을 배우게 됩니다. 고양이 역시 아이들에게 책임감을 가르칠 수 있고 또한 고양이를 가진 아이들은 독립심에 대해 배웁니다. ③ 뱀, ④ 물고기와 ⑤ 햄스터 역시 아이들에게 청결과 적절한 목욕 습관을 가르치는 데 좋습니다. 그러므로 반려동물을 입양하는 것은 커다란 책임감이고 가볍게 받아들여서는 안 되지만 여러분 자녀의 어린 시절을 위해 여러분이 할 수 있는 가장 최고의 일일지도 모릅니다.

어휘 care for 돌보다; 좋아하다 raise 기르다; 올리다; 모으다 lifelong 평생의, 일생의 meaningful 의미 있는 additional 부가적인, 추가의 household chores 집안일, 허드레 가사일 virtue 덕목, 미덕 responsible 책임감을 가진; 책임이 있는 cf. responsibility 책임, 책무 independence 독립(심); 자립정신 proper 적절한, 올바른 adopt 입양하다; 채택하다 | 선택지 어휘 | educational 교육적인; 교육의 influence 영향(력); 영향을 끼치다

16회

01 화자가 하는 말의 목적 ④

✻ 담화의 일부 내용이 아니라 중심 내용을 파악해야 한다. 본 담화는 미술관에 들어가기 전 명심해야 할 몇 가지 주의사항을 알려주고 있다. 그러므로 담화의 목적은 ④ '미술관 관람 주의사항을 알리려고'이다.

W: Hey, guys! Welcome to ZQ Art Gallery. Before we enter the gallery, I'm going to tell you some things that you should **keep in mind**. First, respect the place we are going to visit. It's not a playground, so don't shout or run around. And make sure to only look at works of art **with your eyes**, not with your hands. Everyone has oils on their hands that can damage the art. So please don't touch. Just look and appreciate the works of art. **Keep a safe distance from the art**, about one meter away. You can take photos, but **make sure your flash is off**. You can feel hungry while exploring art, but you should enjoy your drinks and snacks only in the lobby and third-floor cafe. Now, are you ready to find a work of art that tells a story? OK! Let's go!

여: 얘들아! ZQ 미술관에 온 걸 환영한다. 우리가 미술관으로 들어가기 전에 너희들이 명심해야 할 몇 가지 것들을 알려줄게. 우선 우리가 방문할 장소를 소중히 여겨라. 놀이터가 아니니까 소리치거나 뛰어다니지 마라. 그리고 예술 작품을 반드시 너희들 손이 아니라 눈으로만 보도록 해야 해. 모든 사람들은 손에 예술 작품에 손상을 줄 수 있는 기름기가 있단다. 그러니 제발 손대지 말렴. 그저 예술 작품을 보면서 감상해. 예술 작품으로부터 약 1미터 정도 떨어져 안전거리를 유지해. 너희는 사진을 찍을 수 있지만 플래시는 꼭 꺼두도록 해. 예술을 탐구하면서 허기를 느낄 수 있겠지만 음료수와 간식은 로비와 3층 카페에서만 즐겨야 해. 이제 이야기를 들려주는 예술 작품을 찾을 준비가 되었니? 좋아! 가자!

어휘 keep in mind ~을 명심하다 respect 소중히 여기다, 존중하다 make sure 반드시[꼭] (~하도록) 하다, (~을) 확실히 하다 damage 손상(을 주다), 피해(를 입히다) appreciate 감상하다; 감사하다; 진가를 인정하다 distance 거리 explore 탐구[답사/탐험]하다

02 의견 ④

✻ 우선 지시문에서 명시한 화자의 성별을 보고 어느 화자의 말에 주목할지를 판단해야 한다. 특히 의견이나 주장을 표현하는 어구(I think ~, You should ~ 등)가 이끄는 내용을 잘 들어야 한다. 여자는 아들이 안에 모피를 댄 모자가 있는 재킷을 사는 것을 반대하며 과거와는 달리 현재는 다른 의류를 선택할 수 있고 난방 시스템이 잘 되어있으니 모피를 입는 것을 그만두어야 한다고 주장하고 있다. 그러므로 여자의 의견은 ④ '의류에 모피 사용을 중지해야 한다.'이다.

M: Mom, I'd like to get that jacket with a fur-lined hood. It looks very warm and comfortable.
W: Is the fur real or fake?
M: The clerk said it's real fox fur. Doesn't it look fancy?
W: Josh, I don't want you to wear anything with real fur.
M: I know **you're against wearing fur**, but it's just a small amount of decoration. And fur has been worn for centuries.
W: Yes, people have traditionally worn fur to survive cold winters, but they had no choice. But today we have **other clothing options**.
M: Oh, yeah. I understand.
W: And modern technology provides us with good heating systems. Even worse is that **animals are killed cruelly** to keep their fur at the best quality.
M: Really? That's terrible.
W: **Humans should stop wearing it**. Killing animals for fashion is wrong.
M: I see. I'll choose another jacket.

남: 엄마, 난 안에 모피를 댄 모자가 있는 저 재킷을 사고 싶어요. 아주 따뜻하고 편해 보

여요.
여: 모피가 진짜니 아니면 인조니?
남: 점원이 말하길 진짜 여우 모피라고 했어요. 고급스러워 보이지 않으요?
여: Josh, 난 네가 진짜 모피가 있는 어떤 것도 입지 않기를 바라.
남: 엄마가 모피를 입는 것에 반대하시는 건 알아요. 하지만 저건 단지 적은 양의 장식이에요. 그리고 모피는 수 세기 동안 입어왔고요.
여: 그래, 사람들은 추운 겨울을 견디기 위해 전통적으로 모피를 입었지만, 그들은 선택의 여지가 없었단다. 하지만 오늘날 우리는 다른 의류 선택권이 있어.
남: 아, 네. 알아요.
여: 그리고 현대 기술은 우리에게 좋은 난방 시스템을 제공하잖아. 더 나쁜 건 모피를 최상의 품질로 유지하기 위해 동물들을 잔혹하게 죽인다는 거야.
남: 정말이요? 그건 끔찍하네요.
여: 인간들은 그걸 입는 걸 그만둬야 해. 패션을 위해 동물을 죽이는 것은 나쁜 거야.
남: 알겠어요. 다른 재킷을 고를게요.

어휘 fake 인조[모조]의; 거짓된 against ~에 반대하여; ~을 대비하여 decoration 장식(품) modern 현대의, 근대의 provide A with B A에게 B를 제공[공급]하다 cruelly 잔혹하게, 무참하게 quality 질(質); 우수함, 고급

03 관계 ⑤

✻ 직업을 나타내거나 추론할 수 있는 힌트가 대화 전반에 걸쳐 드러나므로, 대화를 전체적으로 이해하는 것이 필요하다. 본 대화에서 여자가 911에 전화한 이유를 말하고 남자는 여자의 딸에게 산소마스크를 씌우고 병원에 데려가겠다고 하는 것으로 보아 ⑤ '구급 대원 – 환자 보호자'의 관계임을 알 수 있다.

M: Where is your daughter?
W: She's in the living room. Please follow me.
M: Is she still **having trouble breathing**?
W: She's getting better but still having trouble. Here she is.
M: What's her name?
W: Amber.
M: OK, Amber. I'm going to **put an oxygen mask on you**. It'll help you breathe. Just relax. How long has she been this way?
W: It started around 8 o'clock, after dinner. She didn't have anything unusual for dinner. Will she be okay?
M: The oxygen mask is helping.
W: Oh, I know I shouldn't panic, but it really scared me. **That's why I called 911**.
M: Don't worry. She's breathing normally now. But we really should **take her to the hospital** for some tests.
W: Okay. I'll prepare to leave right now.

남: 따님이 어디 있나요?
여: 거실에 있어요. 저를 따라오세요.
남: 여전히 숨쉬기 어려운가요?
여: 좋아지고 있지만 여전히 문제가 있어요. 여기 있어요.
남: 아이 이름이 뭐죠?
여: Amber요.
남: 좋아, Amber. 내가 너한테 산소마스크를 씌울게. 그게 네가 숨 쉬는 걸 도울 거야. 그냥 긴장을 풀렴. 아이가 얼마나 오래 이런 식으로 있었나요?
여: 저녁 먹고 8시 정각쯤 시작되었어요. 저녁으로 별다른 것을 먹지 않았어요. 애는 괜찮을까요?
남: 산소마스크가 도움을 주고 있습니다.
여: 아, 제가 겁에 질리면 안 된다는 걸 알지만 정말 무서웠어요. 그래서 911에 전화했던 거예요.
남: 걱정 마세요. 아이는 이제 정상적으로 호흡하고 있습니다. 하지만 몇 가지 검사를 받기 위해 아이를 꼭 병원으로 데려가야 합니다.
여: 좋아요. 저는 당장 떠날 준비를 할게요.

어휘 breathe 숨을 쉬다, 호흡하다 put on ~을 쓰다[입다] oxygen 산소 unusual 유다른; 드문 panic 겁에 질려 어쩔 줄 모르다, 공황 상태에 빠지다

04 그림 불일치 ⑤

* 대화가 나오기 전에 각 사물의 위치 관계와 외형(형태나 무늬, 개수 등)의 특징을 미리 확인하는 것이 좋다. 대화에서는 탑 꼭대기에 깃발이 있다고 했는데 그림에서는 깃발이 없으므로 ⑤가 대화의 내용과 일치하지 않는다. 딸이 아버지에게 깃발을 지울지 물은 것으로 보아 딸이 그린 그림에서는 깃발이 있던 상황임에 유의한다.

W: Dad, I've just finished my drawing for the art contest.
M: Oh, let me see. Wow, it's a lovely drawing! This drawing seems to tell a story.
W: Yes, it's a story about a princess and a dragon.
M: Oh, it's a dragon! Right. It has **wings and a long pointy tail**. It's sitting on a chair.
W: Yes, the dragon wants to have a cup of tea with the princess.
M: So there's a tea pot and **a cup on the table**. I like this table cloth with a flowery pattern. What is **under the table**?
W: It's a mouse. This mouse wants to rescue the princess from the dragon.
M: What a great story! That's why the princess doesn't look so happy. Oh, **she is holding a cup** to drink some tea.
W: Yes. Can you see the tall tower on the right? She has been locked up there.
M: Oh, I see **a flag on top of the tower**. Does that have some meaning?
W: No, I just drew it. Should I remove it?
M: No, no. You really did a good job. I love this drawing.

여: 아빠, 제가 미술대회에 낼 그림을 방금 다 그렸어요.
남: 아, 어디 보자꾸나. 와, 사랑스러운 그림이구나! 이 그림은 이야기를 말해주는 것 같구나.
여: 네, 이건 공주와 용에 대한 이야기예요.
남: 아, 용이구나! 맞아. 용은 날개와 길고 뾰족한 꼬리를 갖고 있네. 의자에 앉아있구나.
여: 네, 용이 공주하고 차를 한잔하고 싶어 해요.
남: 그래서 테이블 위에 찻주전자 하나와 컵 하나가 놓여 있구나. 난 꽃무늬가 있는 이 테이블보가 마음에 드는구나. 테이블 아래에 뭐가 있는 거니?
여: 그건 생쥐예요. 이 생쥐는 용에게서 공주를 구하고 싶어 해요.
남: 정말 멋진 이야기구나! 그래서 공주가 행복해 보이지 않는구나. 아, 공주가 차를 좀 마시려고 컵을 들고 있네.
여: 네. 오른쪽에 높은 탑 보이세요? 그녀는 거기 갇혀 있었어요.
남: 아, 탑 꼭대기에 깃발이 보이는구나. 그게 어떤 의미가 있니?
여: 아니요, 그냥 그렸어요. 그걸 지울까요?
남: 아니, 아니야. 정말로 잘 했다. 이 그림이 너무 좋구나.

어휘 tea pot 찻주전자 rescue 구하다, 구조[구출]하다 lock 꼭 잡혀 있다; 잠그다; 고정되다 remove 없애다; 쫓아내다

05 추후 행동 ⑤

* 대개 대화는 어떤 일을 하게 되는 상황이 먼저 제시된 뒤에 남자와 여자가 각각 할 일들과 이에 대한 수락/거절의 응답이 나열되는 식으로 전개된다. 남자가 여자에게 식당 안내 앱을 소개해주면서 리뷰가 좋은 곳을 선택하라고 조언했다. 여자가 그 앱이 혼란스럽지 않을까 걱정하자 남자가 식당 리뷰를 확인해주겠다고 하므로 남자가 할 일은 ⑤ '앱에서 식당 리뷰 조사하기'이다. 앱을 다운받는 것은 여자가 할 일임에 유의한다.

M: Sarah, I'm going to see a movie this Saturday with Bruce and Scarlet. Do you want to join us?
W: I can't. It's my mother's birthday this Saturday. **I need to find a nice restaurant** and order a birthday cake.
M: You're a nice daughter. Oh, I've been to Yang's Kitchen downtown. They serve nice Chinese food.
W: Sounds great, but my mother doesn't like Chinese food. She likes Italian food.
M: I see. Why don't you look at **the city restaurant guide app**?
W: Oh, that's a good idea. **I'll download the app**. I hope it's not too confusing.
M: Just choose one that has good reviews. I'm sure the reviews will help you decide. If you're busy, **I'll check them** for you.
W: How nice of you! That would be great.
M: Okay. I'll call you soon.

남: Sarah, 내가 이번 토요일에 Bruce와 Scarlet하고 영화를 보러 갈 거야. 우리와 함께 갈래?
여: 나는 못 가. 이번 토요일이 우리 엄마 생신이거든. 멋진 식당을 찾고 생일 케이크를 주문해야 해.
남: 넌 좋은 딸이구나. 아, 내가 시내의 Yang's Kitchen에 간 적이 있어. 훌륭한 중국 음식을 제공하더라.
여: 좋은 것 같은데, 하지만 우리 엄마는 중국 음식을 좋아하지 않으셔. 엄마는 이탈리아 음식을 좋아하셔.
남: 그렇구나. 도시 식당 안내 앱을 보지 그러니?
여: 아, 그거 좋은 생각이야. 그 앱을 다운받을게. 그게 너무 혼란스럽지 않기를 바라.
남: 그냥 좋은 리뷰가 있는 곳을 골라. 분명히 리뷰들이 네가 결정하는 데 도움이 될 거야. 네가 바쁘면 내가 너를 위해 그걸 확인해줄게.
여: 정말 친절하다! 그렇게 해주면 좋겠어.
남: 좋아. 내가 곧 전화할게.

어휘 order 주문하다; 명령[지시]하다 downtown 시내에[로] serve 내다[차려 주다]; 제공하다 confusing 혼란스러운

06 금액 ③

* 여러 개의 수치 정보가 등장하므로 필요한 정보를 메모하면서 듣는 것이 좋다. 좌석당 100달러짜리 티켓 두 장으로 200달러인데 20% 할인을 받으면 160달러이다. 여기에 예약 수수료가 티켓당 3달러씩이므로 두 장의 수수료인 6달러를 더하면 총액은 ③ '$166'이다.

M: Kaitlyn, how about going to the musical, *Chicago*? Our local theater is performing it next month.
W: Sounds fantastic! I've always wanted to see it.
M: I'll get the tickets then.
W: How much are the tickets for that?
M: The most expensive seats are $150, and the cheapest ones are $50.
W: Wow, **the prices are rather expensive**.
M: Let's get **the seats for $100**. They're rear orchestra seats, so they should be nice.
W: The total for both is $200. That's too expensive!
M: Don't worry. I got **a 20-percent-discount** coupon.
W: Really? That's great. But there should be a reservation fee, I guess.
M: That's right. But it's only a **$3 reservation fee for each ticket**. I'll reserve the tickets now.
W: Thank you so much. I'll treat you to dinner then.

남: Kaitlyn, 뮤지컬 'Chicago'를 보러 가는 거 어때요? 우리 시역 극장에서 다음 달에 그걸 공연할 거예요.
여: 환상적인데요! 항상 그걸 보길 바라 왔어요.
남: 그러면 내가 티켓을 살게요.
여: 그 티켓이 얼마인가요?
남: 가장 비싼 좌석은 150달러이고 가장 싼 것은 50달러예요.
여: 와, 가격이 꽤 비싸군요.
남: 100달러짜리 좌석을 삽시다. 그건 1층 뒤쪽 좌석이라서 좋을 거예요.
여: 둘의 총액이 200달러네요. 너무 비싸요!
남: 걱정 말아요. 내가 20퍼센트 할인 쿠폰을 얻었어요.
여: 정말이요? 그거 아주 좋은데요. 하지만 예약 수수료가 있을 것 같은데요.
남: 맞아요. 하지만 티켓당 3달러의 예약 수수료가 있을 뿐이에요. 지금 티켓을 예약할게요.
여: 너무 고마워요. 그러면 내가 저녁 식사를 대접할게요.

어휘 perform 공연[연주/연기]하다 rather 꽤; 약간 rear 뒤쪽의 orchestra seat 1층의 관객석 fee 수수료; 요금 treat 대접하다, 한턱내다; 대하다

07 이유   ④

✱ 지시문을 통해 남자가 제시간에 출근할 수 없는 상황이며 남자의 말에 단서가 있을 가능성이 큼을 미리 파악한다. 남자가 회사에 늦겠다고 전화했는데 교통 체증 때문도 아니고 자동차 문제도 아니라고 했다. 남자의 어머니가 탄 비행기가 늦게 도착해 어머니를 모시러 공항에 갔다 와서 늦게 출근한다고 했으므로 답은 ④ '공항으로 어머니 마중을 가서'이다.

[Telephone rings.]
W: Hello. You've reached Watson Company. Jennifer Rubin speaking.
M: Hello, Jennifer. It's Simon Kien. I'm afraid I'm going to be late today.
W: **Are you stuck in traffic**, or is your car having trouble?
M: No, it's not that. My mother **was supposed to arrive** at the airport last night, but she arrived this morning.
W: I guess **the flight was delayed**.
M: Yes. Due to weather conditions, the flight couldn't take off on time.
W: All right. Oh, your mother lives in Vietnam, doesn't she?
M: Yes, she flew out to visit me. So I had to be there **to pick her up**.
W: I see. You must be excited. And you have a meeting at 10 a.m. Will you be able to attend the meeting?
M: Sure. I just arrived home now. So **I'll be there no later than** 9:30 a.m.
W: Okay. If you can't make it, just call me.
M: Thanks, Jennifer.

[전화벨이 울린다.]
여: 여보세요. Watson 사입니다. Jennifer Rubin입니다.
남: 여보세요, Jennifer. Simon Kien이에요. 미안하지만 오늘 제가 늦을 것 같아요.
여: 교통 체증에 갇혔나요, 아니면 차에 문제가 있는 거예요?
남: 아니요. 그런 건 아니에요. 제 어머니께서 어젯밤에 공항에 도착하시기로 되어있는데 오늘 아침에 도착하셨어요.
여: 항공편이 지연됐나 보군요.
남: 네. 기상 상태 때문에 비행기가 제시간에 이륙하지 못했어요.
여: 알겠어요. 아, 당신 어머니께서는 베트남에서 사시죠, 그렇지 않아요?
남: 네, 절 만나러 날아오셨어요. 그래서 거기로 어머니를 모시러 가야 했어요.
여: 그렇군요. 분명히 들떴겠군요. 그리고 오전 10시에 회의가 있는데요. 그 회의에 참석할 수 있어요?
남: 그럼요. 지금 막 집에 도착했어요. 그래서 늦어도 오전 9시 30분까지는 거기 갈 거예요.
여: 알았어요. 못 오면 저한테 전화만 하세요.
남: 고마워요, Jennifer.

어휘 be stuck in ~에 갇히다 be supposed to-v v하기로 되어있다 flight 항공편; 여행, 비행 delay 지연시키다, 지체하게 하다 take off 이륙하다 on time 제시간에 pick A up A를 태우러 가다 attend 참석하다; 다니다

08 언급하지 않은 것   ④

✱ 대화의 진행은 대개 선택지와 같은 순서이므로, 선택지를 보면서 언급된 내용을 소거하는 식으로 푸는 것이 좋다. 수강 대상은 모든 학생이고 담당 교수의 이름, 수업 방식이 토론에 기반을 둔다는 것, 그리고 두 번의 시험과 최종 에세이로 성적을 평가한다는 것에 대해서는 이야기를 나누었지만 수업 교재명은 언급하지 않았다.

W: Marcus, did you take the class, History of Food?
M: Yes, I took that class last semester. It's a freshmen class, isn't it?
W: No, **it's open for all students to take**. The professor is James Mayers, right?
M: Yes, that's right. His class was interesting, and I liked the way he taught. And the class was **discussion based**.
W: How are discussions held?
M: He gave students the reading list for the class. We had to read the books before the class so that **we could freely discuss** in class.
W: That sounds a bit tough. What about the exams and grading?
M: There will be two tests, a mid-term and final, and a final essay. The professor evaluates your grade **based on the two tests** and the essay.
W: Okay. Thanks for the information. I'll think about taking this class. See you.

M: I recommend it. It was a very worthwhile experience.
W: I'll keep that in mind.

여: Marcus, 너 음식의 역사라는 수업 수강했니?
남: 응. 지난 학기에 그 수업을 수강했어. 그거 1학년 수업이지, 그렇지 않아?
여: 아니야. <u>모든 학생이 수강하도록(① 수강 대상)</u> 개방되어 있어. <u>교수님이 James Mayers지(② 담당 교수)</u>, 맞아?
남: 응. 맞아. 그분의 수업이 재미있었고 가르치시는 방식도 좋았어. 그리고 <u>수업은 토론을 기반으로 했어(③ 수업 방식)</u>.
여: 어떻게 토론이 열리니?
남: 교수님이 학생들에게 수업을 위한 독서 목록을 주셨어. 우리는 수업에서 자유롭게 토론할 수 있도록 수업 전에 그 책들을 읽어야 했어.
여: 그거 좀 어려울 것 같아. 시험하고 성적 매기기는 어떠니?
남: 중간고사하고 기말고사인 두 번의 시험과 최종 에세이가 있을 거야. 교수님은 <u>두 번의 시험과 에세이에 근거해서 네 성적을 평가하셔(⑤ 평가 방법)</u>.
여: 알았어. 정보 고마워. 이 수업을 수강하는 걸 생각해봐야겠어. 나중에 보자.
남: 난 추천해. 굉장히 보람 있는 경험이었어.
여: 유념할게.

어휘 semester 학기 freshmen 1학년생, 신입생 professor 교수 discussion 토론, 토의 cf. discuss 토론[토의]하다 freely 자유롭게 evaluate 평가하다, 감정하다 recommend 추천하다 worthwhile 보람[가치] 있는, 할 가치가 있는

09 내용 불일치   ⑤

✱ 담화의 진행은 대개 선택지와 같은 순서이므로, 선택지를 보면서 일치하는 내용을 소거하는 식으로 푸는 것이 좋다. 텐트와 식탁은 제공하지만 침낭과 랜턴 같은 개인 트레킹 장비는 가져오라고 했으므로 ⑤ '트레킹 장비를 모두 제공한다.'는 내용과 일치하지 않는다.

M: Do you want to go hiking in green forests and visit a clear blue lake? Join us on this 2-day hike to Blue Lake, at the base of Mount Lapa. This is a tour **for beginning to advanced hikers**. On the first day, we will begin to hike at Santiago Village at nine. After hiking **about five hours**, we will reach Blue Lake (4,350m) at the base of Mt. Lapa. Later, we will camp **by this amazing lake**. After breakfast, on Day 2, we will guide you to a small lookout to enjoy some special views. Later, we will go back down to Santiago Village. We will provide tents and tables. But you need to **bring your personal trekking gear**, such as sleeping bags and lanterns. Don't miss this amazing experience!

남: 초록빛 숲속으로 하이킹을 가서 맑고 푸른 호수를 방문하고 싶나요? Lapa 산의 기슭에 있는 Blue Lake로 가는 <u>① 이 2일 동안의 하이킹</u>에 우리와 함께하십시오. 이것은 <u>② 초보에서 상급 도보 여행자를 위한</u> 여행입니다. ③ 첫째 날에 우리는 9시에 Santiago 마을에서 하이킹을 시작할 것입니다. <u>③ 약 5시간 하이킹을 한 후에</u> 우리는 Lapa 산의 기슭에 있는 4,350미터의 Blue Lake에 도달할 것입니다. 후에 우리는 이 놀라운 <u>④ 호수 옆에서 야영</u>할 것입니다. 둘째 날 아침 식사 후에 우리는 몇몇 특별한 풍경을 즐기기 위해 여러분을 작은 전망대로 안내할 것입니다. 후에 Santiago 마을로 다시 내려올 것입니다. 우리가 텐트와 식탁을 제공해드릴 것입니다. <u>⑤ 하지만 침낭과 랜턴 같은 여러분의 개인 트레킹 장비는 가져오셔야 합니다.</u> 이 놀라운 경험을 놓치지 마십시오!

어휘 advanced 상급[고급]의; 선진의 lookout 전망; 망보는 곳; 감시 provide 제공[공급]하다, 주다 personal 개인의, 개인적인 trekking ((등산)) 트레킹; 여행 gear 장비, 복장

10 도표 이해   ⑤

✱ 대화의 진행은 대개 도표 항목의 나열 순서대로 진행된다. 대화를 들으면서 도표의 각 항목 중 선택되지 않은 것을 소거하는 식으로 푸는 것이 좋다. 우선 6월 22일에 예약이 가능하지 않은 ①은 제외된다. 좌석은 150석보다 더 많고 250석보다 더 적은 홀을 원했으므로 ③이 제외되고 대여료가 500달러 미만인 곳을 원했으므로 ④ 역시 제외된다. 남은 ②와 ⑤ 중에서 위치가 학교 근처인 곳을 선택했으므로 남자가 예약할 홀은 ⑤이다.

M: Hey, Jane. We have to find a hall to rent for our band's 3rd concert. Could you help me out?

W: Sure. First, when are you planning to hold the concert?

M: I'm planning to hold it **on June 22nd**.

W: Okay. How many people are you expecting?

M: I'd like a place that holds more than 150 people.

W: If you're looking at more than 150, how about getting a bigger place?

M: Well, if **it holds more than 250**, it'll be too big. There'll be too many empty seats.

W: All right. What about your budget? How much can you spend?

M: We'd like to **stay under $500**. We're trying to save money.

W: Then you have these two options. Look here. Which one do you like?

M: I like this one. Since **it's located close to our school**, it'll be more convenient.

W: Sounds great. Then let's make a reservation.

남: 이봐, Jane. 우리 밴드의 세 번째 콘서트를 위해 대여할 홀을 찾아야 해. 날 도와줄 수 있니?

여: 그럼. 우선 언제 콘서트를 열 계획이니?

남: 6월 22일에 열 계획이야.

여: 좋아. 얼마나 많은 사람을 예상하고 있어?

남: 150명보다 더 많이 수용하는 장소를 원해.

여: 150명보다 더 많이 생각하고 있다면 더 큰 장소를 얻는 건 어때?

남: 음, 250을 넘게 수용하면 그건 너무 클 거야. 너무나 많은 빈자리가 있을 거야.

여: 알았어. 예산은 어떠니? 얼마나 쓸 수 있어?

남: 우리는 500달러 미만으로 하고 싶어. 돈을 절약하려고 하거든.

여: 그러면 넌 이 두 가지 선택권이 있어. 여길 봐. 어떤 게 좋니?

남: 이게 좋아. 여기가 우리 학교에서 가깝게 위치하고 있어서 더 편리할 거야.

여: 그거 좋겠네. 그러면 예약하자.

어휘 hold 열다; (사람·사물을) 수용하다   expect 예상[기대]하다   empty 비어 있는; 공허한   budget 예산(안), 비용   convenient 편리한   make a reservation 예약하다

11 짧은 대화에 이어질 응답 ④

* 여자가 공항 리무진과 지하철 중 어느 것을 타면 Grand 호텔까지 더 빨리 갈 수 있는지 묻고 있다. 그러므로 남자의 응답으로는 ④ '둘 다 거의 똑같이 걸릴 거예요.'가 적절하다.

① 그건 우리가 어디 가고자 하는지에 달렸어요.
② 제 여행용 왕복표를 원해요.
③ 전에 공항 리무진을 탄 적이 있어요.
⑤ 지하철역은 여기서 멀지 않아요.

W: Now **how should we get to** the downtown Grand Hotel from here?

M: We have two options. **We can take either** the airport limousine **or** the subway.

W: Which one will get us there faster?

M: **It'll take about the same time for both.**

여: 이제 우리가 여기서 시내의 Grand 호텔로 어떻게 가야 하나요?

남: 두 가지 선택권이 있어요. 공항 리무진을 타거나 지하철을 탈 수 있어요.

여: 어떤 게 더 빨리 우리가 거기로 도착하게 할까요?

남: 둘 다 거의 똑같이 걸릴 거예요.

어휘 | 선택지 어휘 | depend on ~에 달려 있다, ~에 의해 결정되다   return ticket 왕복표   journey 여행, 여정, 이동

12 짧은 대화에 이어질 응답 ②

* 출석도 잘하고 시험도 잘 봤는데 성적이 너무 안 좋게 나와 받아들이기 어렵다는 남자에게 여자가 조언할 말로는 ② '내가 너라면 교수님께 말해보겠어.'가 적절하다.

① 반드시 네 모든 과제를 끝내도록 해.
③ 네가 그걸 안 했다면 그러면 그걸로 신경 쓰지 마.
④ 요행에 의존하지 말고 네가 할 수 있는 최선을 다해.

⑤ 네가 좋은 성적을 원한다면 근면해야 해.

M: I got a D in History 201. I don't understand **why my grade is so low**.

W: Really? There must be something wrong. You had good attendance, and you did well on your exams.

M: That's exactly my point. **This is unacceptable**.

W: If I were you, I would talk to the professor.

남: 나 역사 201에서 D를 받았어. 왜 내 성적이 이렇게 낮은지 이해할 수 없어.

여: 정말? 뭔가 잘못된 게 분명해. 넌 출석률도 좋고 시험도 잘 봤잖아.

남: 내 말이 바로 그거야. 이건 받아들이기 어려워.

여: 내가 너라면 교수님께 말해보겠어.

어휘 attendance 출석률; 출석, 참석   unacceptable 받아들이기[용납하기] 어려운 | 선택지 어휘 | make sure (that) 반드시 (~하도록) 하다, (~을) 확실히 하다   assignment 과제, 임무   bother 신경 쓰이게 하다, 애를 쓰다   rely on ~에 의존[의지]하다; ~을 필요로 하다   diligent 근면한, 성실한

13 긴 대화에 이어질 응답 ②

* 대화의 전체 맥락 하에 마지막 말의 의미나 의도를 정확히 파악하는 것이 좋다. 여자가 도서관에서 책을 대출할 수 있는지 묻자 남자는 참고 도서라 빌릴 수 없다고 한다. 이에 대한 응답으로는 ② '알겠습니다. 그러면 여기서 읽어야겠군요.'가 가장 적절하다.

① 그건 공평하지 않아요. 그렇게 말씀하실 순 없죠.
③ 알려주셔서 고마워요. 이제 이해합니다.
④ 그렇군요. 이 두 권을 대출하고 싶습니다.
⑤ 죄송합니다. 지금 빌리실 수 있는 게 아무것도 없습니다.

W: Excuse me, **could you do me a favor?** Where can I find books about Old English?

M: Go to Section L over there. Can you see the sign?

W: Yes, I see. Thanks.

M: [pause] Excuse me. You **shouldn't step on the shelf**. It can be dangerous.

W: I'm sorry, but I couldn't find a ladder around here.

M: Do you want to get a book from **the top shelf**?

W: Yes, the book I want is on the top shelf, but I can't reach it.

M: I'll get it for you. Which one do you want?

W: The thick green book, titled "A Dictionary of the Old English Language."

M: Wait a second. [pause] Here you go.

W: **Could I check out** this book?

M: I'm sorry, but you can't. It's a reference book, so **it can't be borrowed**.

W: Okay. I'll have to read it here, then.

여: 실례합니다만 부탁 좀 들어주실 수 있나요? 제가 고대 영어에 관한 책을 어디서 찾을 수 있을까요?

남: 저쪽 L 섹션으로 가세요. 표지판이 보이세요?

여: 네, 보입니다. 고맙습니다.

남: [잠시 후] 죄송합니다. 책꽂이들 밟고 올라가면 안 됩니다. 위험할 수 있어요.

여: 죄송합니다만 여기 근처에선 사다리를 찾을 수 없어서요.

남: 맨 위 칸에서 책을 꺼내려고 하세요?

여: 네, 제가 원하는 책이 맨 위 칸에 있는데 그곳에 손이 닿지 않아서요.

남: 제가 꺼내드리죠. 어떤 걸 원하세요?

여: '고대 영어 사전'이라는 제목의 두꺼운 초록 책이요.

남: 잠깐 기다리세요. [잠시 후] 여기 있습니다.

여: 제가 이 책을 대출할 수 있나요?

남: 죄송하지만 하실 수 없습니다. 참고 도서라서 빌리실 수 없어요.

여: 알겠습니다. 그러면 여기서 읽어야 하겠군요.

어휘 shelf 책꽂이, 칸; 선반   ladder 사다리   check out (도서관 등에서) 대출하다   reference book 참고 도서 | 선택지 어휘 | fair 공평[공정]한; 박람회

14 긴 대화에 이어질 응답 ⑤

✱ 대화의 전체 맥락 하에 마지막 말의 의미나 의도를 정확히 파악하는 것이 좋다. 여자는 집이 마음에 들지만 예산을 조금 초과하는 가격에 사는 것을 망설이며 생각할 시간을 줄 수 있는지 묻고 있다. 이에 대한 남자의 응답으로는 ⑤ '그럼요. 당장 결정하실 필요는 없습니다.'가 적절하다.

① 네, 있습니다. 그건 우리에게 충분히 커요.
② 걱정 말아요. 우리가 지금 그걸 보러 갈 거예요.
③ 훌륭한 것 같군요. 계약서에 서명합시다.
④ 그러면 이게 바로 당신이 원하던 것 같군요.

M: Come in, please. As I said, this is the biggest house on Maple Street.
W: Oh, **how wonderful**! The living room is bright and spacious.
M: Right. It's got three bedrooms and two bathrooms.
W: First I'd like to see the kitchen.
M: It's right here. It's quite modern and **fully equipped** — dishwasher, oven, microwave, and refrigerator.
W: That's very good. Is there a washing machine?
M: Yes, there's a washing machine and a dryer in the basement.
W: The house is perfect, but it's a little **beyond my budget**.
M: You'll never find a house like this anywhere around here.
W: I know. Can you give me **more time to think about this**?
M: Sure. You don't have to decide right away.

남: 들어오십시오. 말씀드렸다시피 이건 Maple 가에서 가장 큰 집입니다.
여: 아, 정말 멋지군요! 거실이 환하고 넓어요.
남: 그렇습니다. 세 개의 침실과 두 개의 욕실이 있습니다.
여: 우선 부엌을 보고 싶어요.
남: 바로 여기 있습니다. 꽤 현대적이고 식기세척기, 오븐, 전자레인지하고 냉장고가 있어서 완전히 장비가 갖춰져 있죠.
여: 아주 좋군요. 세탁기가 있나요?
남: 네, 세탁기와 건조기는 지하실에 있습니다.
여: 집은 완벽하지만 제 예산을 좀 넘어서네요.
남: 이 근처 어디에서도 여기 같은 집을 결코 찾으실 수 없을 겁니다.
여: 알아요. 이것에 대해 생각할 시간을 좀 더 주실 수 있나요?
남: 그럼요. 당장 결정하실 필요는 없습니다.

어휘 spacious 넓은; 거대한 fully 완전히, 충분히 equipped 장비를 갖춘 dishwasher 식기세척기 microwave 전자레인지 refrigerator 냉장고 basement 지하실[층] beyond ~을 넘어서; 너머에 | 선택지 어휘 | contract 계약(서); 계약하다

15 상황에 적절한 말 ②

✱ 지시문을 통해 누가(A) 누구에게(B) 할 말인지를 우선 정확히 파악한다. 담화는 대개 A와 B에 대한 배경 설명과 B가 처한 문제 상황, 그리고 이에 대해 A가 어떤 말을 하려고 하는지에 대한 설명의 순서로 전개된다. Paul(B)은 상점에서 구매한 신발로 발이 몹시 검게 되어 분명히 교환을 받아야 하는 상황인데, 이를 상점 점원에게 거절당했다. 이에 비슷한 경험이 있는 Tiffany(A)가 조언할 말로는 ② '고객 서비스 센터에 전화해. 분명히 그들은 너를 도와줄 수 있을 거야.'가 적절하다.

① 내가 네 구두를 닦아줄게. 그러면 더 좋아 보일 거야.
③ 똑바로 가. 오른쪽에서 신발 상점을 발견할 수 있어.
④ 신발 상점으로 전화해. 그들이 더 큰 치수의 신발을 찾을 수 있어.
⑤ 그것들은 너에게 정말 잘 어울려 보여. 검은색이 너한테 잘 어울리는구나.

W: Paul bought a pair of shoes cheap at a shoe store last week. He goes to school wearing those shoes this morning. When he takes off his shoes in the evening, he finds his feet are **extremely black** from the color in the shoes. He calls the store **to complain and asks for** an exchange. But the salesclerk **refuses his request**. The salesclerk says there is no refund or **exchange on sale items**. Paul is upset and asks his friend, Tiffany, for some advice. Tiffany feels that the store should change Paul's shoes with another pair. She had a similar situation before and dealt with the same problem. Tiffany wants to tell Paul **how he can solve the problem**. In this situation, what would Tiffany most likely say to Paul?

Tiffany: Call customer service. I'm sure they can help you.

여: Paul은 지난주에 신발 상점에서 신발 한 켤레를 싸게 구매했다. 그는 오늘 아침에 그 신발을 신고 학교로 간다. 그가 저녁에 신발을 벗자 자신의 발이 신발의 색으로 몹시 검게 된 것을 발견한다. 그는 항의하려고 상점에 전화해 교환을 요구한다. 그러나 점원은 그의 요구를 거절한다. 점원은 할인 물품에 대해서는 환불이나 교환이 없다고 말한다. Paul은 화가 나서 자신의 친구 Tiffany에게 조언을 좀 요청한다. Tiffany는 그 상점이 Paul의 신발을 다른 것으로 교환해주어야 한다고 생각한다. 그녀는 전에 비슷한 상황을 겪었고 같은 문제를 처리했다. Tiffany는 Paul에게 문제를 해결할 수 있는 방법을 알려주고 싶다. 이 상황에서 Tiffany가 Paul에게 뭐라고 말하겠는가?

Tiffany: 고객 서비스 센터에 전화해. 분명히 그들은 너를 도와줄 수 있을 거야.

어휘 extremely 몹시, 아주; 극도로 complain 항의[불평]하다 exchange 교환(하다), 바꾸다 salesclerk 점원, 판매원 refuse 거절[거부]하다 refund 환불(하다) deal with 처리하다; 다루다 | 선택지 어휘 | polish 닦다. 윤[광]을 내다 suit 어울리다; 맞다

16~17 세트 문항 16 ⑤ 17 ④

✱ **16** 우리가 십 대에 평생 지속되어야 하는 뼈 대부분을 만들므로 이때 뼈 형성이 중요하다고 하면서 뼈가 약해졌을 때의 문제점과 뼈를 튼튼하게 만드는 방법도 소개하고 있다. 그러므로 담화의 주제로는 ⑤ '십 대에 튼튼한 뼈를 형성하는 것의 중요성'이 적절하다.

① 골밀도를 향상하기 위한 방법
② 십 대에 규칙적인 운동의 필요성
③ 튼튼한 뼈를 유지하는 데 칼슘의 역할
④ 좋은 뼈 건강을 유지하는 습관을 개발하기

✱ **17** 해석 참조.
① 춤 ② 하이킹 ③ 조깅 ④ 요가 ⑤ 걷기

W: You may not think much about your bones, but you can't make a move without them. Strong bones help you look good, stay active, and feel your best. During the teen years, we make most of the bone that must **last our lifetime**. Bone building is so important for teens because the teen years are **the only years of life** when new bone growth occurs faster than bone loss. If you don't gain sufficient bone strength as a teen, your bones are more likely to **become weak and break** later in life. Moreover, those with weak bones are unlikely to recover quickly from injury. **To make your bones strong** as a teenager, you can take part in a variety of fun activities, such as dancing or hiking with your friends. Or you can even go jogging or walking by yourself. Getting enough calcium is also critical. The important thing is that you should build bones that are **as strong as possible** during this time.

여: 여러분은 여러분의 뼈에 대해 많이 생각해보지 않았을 수 있겠지만 그것들 없이는 움직일 수 없습니다. 튼튼한 뼈는 여러분을 좋아 보이고 활발하게 지내고 자신을 최고로 느끼게 돕습니다. 십 대에 우리는 평생 지속되어야 하는 뼈의 대부분을 만듭니다. 십 대는 새로운 뼈 성장이 뼈 손실보다 더 빠르게 일어나는 인생의 유일한 시기이기 때문에 십 대들에게 뼈 형성은 아주 중요합니다. 여러분이 십 대에 충분한 뼈 강도를 얻지 못한다면 나중에 여러분의 뼈는 약해지고 부러질 가능성이 더 높습니다. 게다가, 약한 뼈를 가진 사람들은 부상으로부터 빠르게 회복되지 않을 수 있습니다. 십대로서 뼈를 튼튼하게 만들기 위해 여러분은 친구들과 함께 ① 춤이나 ② 하이킹 같은 다양한 재밌는 활동에 참여할 수 있습니다. 또는 혼자서 ③ 조깅이나 ⑤ 걷기를 하러 갈 수도 있습니다. 충분한 칼슘을 얻는 것 또한 대단히 중요합니다. 가장 중요한 것은 여러분이 이 기간 동안에 가능한 한 튼튼한 뼈를 형성해야 한다는 것입니다.

어휘 last 지속되다; 계속되다 occur 일어나다, 발생하다 sufficient 충분한 be likely to-v v할 가능성이 있다[것 같다] cf. be unlikely to-v v할 가능성이 낮다 recover 회복되다; 되찾다 take part in ~에 참여[참가]하다 a variety of 다양한 critical 대단히 중요한; 비판적인 | 선택지 어휘 | bone density 골밀도 cf. density 밀도, 농도; 짙음 maintain 유지하다 necessity 필요성, 필수품

| 본문 p.104 |

17회

| 01 ③ | 02 ② | 03 ④ | 04 ④ | 05 ⑤ | 06 ⑤ | 07 ④ | 08 ④ | 09 ④ | 10 ① |
| 11 ⑤ | 12 ⑤ | 13 ② | 14 ② | 15 ③ | 16 ② | 17 ④ | | | |

01 화자가 하는 말의 목적 ③

* 담화의 일부 내용이 아니라 중심 내용을 파악해야 한다. 본 담화는 여자가 Wipe All이라는 청소 도구의 기능을 설명하면서 30% 할인한 특별 가격에 판매하니 서둘러 주문하라고 하고 있다. 그러므로 담화의 목적은 ③ '청소 도구 판매를 광고하려고'임을 알 수 있다.

W: Yes! The famous blogger Masha Wells strongly recommended Wipe All. Its stainless steel handle and frame makes your cleaning easier and faster. It includes 2 wet mop pads and 1 dust mop pad **which clean more thoroughly** and effectively than cotton mops. When you clean your house, **just attach** the mop pads here and gently wipe. Take a look. Isn't the floor completely clean? Wipe All **collects all the dirt and leaves** the floor perfectly clean. This is the time you've all been waiting for. We're giving you this great product **at a special price** of $36, 30% off the original price! Call us at 080-244-2290. Please hurry and order Wipe All now.

여: 그렇습니다! 유명 블로거 Masha Wells는 Wipe All을 강력하게 추천했습니다. 그것의 스테인리스 강철 손잡이와 뼈대는 여러분의 청소를 더 쉽고 더 빠르게 만들어줍니다. 그것은 면 대걸레보다 더 철저하고 효과적으로 청소하는 2개의 젖은 대걸레용 패드와 1개의 먼지 대걸레용 패드를 포함하고 있습니다. 여러분이 집을 청소할 때 대걸레용 패드를 여기 붙이고 부드럽게 닦기만 하세요. 보세요. 바닥이 완전히 깨끗하지 않습니까? Wipe All은 모든 먼지를 모아서 바닥을 완벽히 깨끗하게 만듭니다. 지금이 여러분 모두가 기다려 온 시간입니다. 여러분에게 이 굉장한 제품을 원래 가격에서 30% 할인한 특별 가격 36달러에 드리고 있습니다! 080-244-2290으로 전화하세요. 서두르셔서 지금 Wipe All을 주문하세요.

어휘 wipe 닦다, 훔치다 frame 뼈대, 프레임 mop 대걸레 thoroughly 철저히; 대단히 effectively 효과적으로 attach 붙이다; 첨부하다 completely 완전히, 전적으로 dirt 먼지, 때

02 의견 ②

* 우선 지시문에서 명시한 화자의 성별을 보고 어느 화자의 말에 주목할지를 판단해야 한다. 특히 의견이나 주장을 표현하는 어구(I think ~, You should ~ 등)가 이끄는 내용을 잘 들어야 한다. 아들의 여행 가방을 싸주는 아내에게 남편은 아이가 실수로부터 배운다고 말하며 아이 스스로 여행 가방을 싸게 하라고 권유하고 있다. 그러므로 남자의 의견은 ② '자녀가 스스로 자기 일을 하게 해야 한다.'가 가장 적절하다.

M: Honey, what are you doing?
W: **I'm packing a suitcase** for Blake. He is going on a trip to New York.
M: Sophia, our son is old enough to pack his stuff for a trip.
W: But he's careless and always forgets something.
M: I understand it's hard to sit back and watch him make mistakes. But he'll **learn from his mistakes**.
W: But if I don't pack his stuff, he'll be in trouble in New York.
M: I don't think so. By the way, where is he now?
W: He is reading a comic book in his room.
M: If he can't do his own packing, what can he do **on his own later in life**?
W: Okay. I'll **tell him to pack** his suitcase now.
M: Yeah. We're just a guide. In life, there are no mistakes, only lessons.

남: 여보, 뭐 하고 있어요?
여: Blake를 위해 여행 가방을 싸고 있어요. 그 애가 뉴욕으로 여행을 가잖아요.
남: Sophia, 우리 아들은 여행을 가기 위해 자기 물건을 싸기에 충분한 나이예요.
여: 하지만 그 애는 부주의하고 언제나 뭔가를 잊어요.
남: 가만히 앉아서 우리 애가 실수하는 걸 보는 게 어렵다는 건 이해해요. 하지만 그 애는 자신의 실수로부터 배울 거예요.

여: 하지만 내가 그 애 물건을 싸주지 않으면 그 애는 뉴욕에서 어려움에 처할 거예요.
남: 난 그렇게 생각하지 않아요. 그런데 지금 아이는 어디 있죠?
여: 자기 방에서 만화책을 읽고 있어요.
남: 우리 애가 자기 자신의 짐을 쌀 수 없다면 장래 인생에 혼자서 뭘 할 수 있겠어요?
여: 알았어요. 내가 그 애에게 지금 여행 가방을 싸라고 말할게요.
남: 그래요. 우리는 그저 안내자예요. 인생에서는 실수란 없고 오직 교훈만 있어요.

어휘 pack (짐을) 싸다, 꾸리다 suitcase 여행 가방 stuff 물건, 것 careless 부주의한, 조심성 없는 be in trouble 어려움[곤경]에 처한 on one's own 혼자서, 단독으로 guide 안내인; 지도자, 인도자 lesson 교훈; 가르침; 수업

03 관계 ④

* 직업을 나타내거나 추론할 수 있는 힌트가 대화 전반에 걸쳐 드러나므로, 대화를 전체적으로 이해하는 것이 필요하다. 본 대화에서 남자는 편집부의 다른 부서원들과 함께 여자가 작성한 유명 배우와의 인터뷰 기사를 재확인하고, 기사의 내용은 좋지만 사진이 안 좋다고 지적하는 것으로 보아 ④ '잡지 기자 – 편집장'의 관계임을 알 수 있다.

W: Mr. Martin, I heard you wanted to see me.
M: Ah, Nicole. Have a seat here, please.
W: Sure.
M: It's about your article. I **double-checked** your article with other members of the editing department.
W: You mean **my article with the interview** with Conner McCarthy?
M: Yes, Conner McCarthy, the famous actor.
W: Is there anything wrong with it?
M: No, it's well-written, but **the photos wouldn't look good** in the magazine. The actor's face should be clearer and more natural.
W: I got it. I have several other photos. I'll send them to you as soon as possible.
M: All right. Then we can choose the proper photos among them. And you know **the deadline for this issue** is the 20th. Please send them soon.
W: Don't worry. I'll send them tomorrow morning.

여: Martin 씨, 저를 보자고 하셨다고 들었어요.
남: 아, Nicole. 여기 앉으세요.
여: 그래요.
남: 당신 기사에 관한 거예요. 내가 편집부의 다른 부서원들과 함께 당신의 기사를 재확인했어요.
여: Conner McCarthy와의 제 인터뷰 기사 말씀이신가요?
남: 네, 유명 배우인 Conner McCarthy요.
여: 기사에 뭐가 잘못 된 게 있나요?
남: 아니요, 잘 썼어요. 하지만 사진이 잡지에 좋아 보이지 않아서요. 배우의 얼굴이 더 선명하고 더 자연스러워야 하겠어요.
여: 알겠습니다. 제가 다른 사진 몇 장을 갖고 있어요. 그것들을 가능한 한 빨리 보내드릴게요.
남: 좋아요. 그러면 우리가 그것들 중에서 적절한 사진을 선택할 수 있겠어요. 그리고 이번 호의 마감 일자가 20일인 거 알죠. 그것들을 빨리 보내주세요.
여: 걱정 마세요. 내일 아침에 그걸 보낼게요.

어휘 double-check 재확인하다 article 기사 edit 편집[교정]하다 department 부서; 학부; 분야 deadline 마감 일자[시간], 기한 issue (정기 간행물의) 호

04 그림 불일치 ④

* 대화가 나오기 전에 각 사물의 위치 관계와 외형(형태나 무늬, 개수 등)의 특징을 미리 확인하는 것이 좋다. 대화에서는 식당 앞에 의자가 두 개 있다고 했는데 그림에서는 벤치 하나가 있으므로 ④가 일치하지 않는다. 벤치는 남자가 의자 대신 제안한 것이며

실제 견본 디자인에서는 의자 두 개가 있었음에 유의한다.

M: Congratulations on opening your restaurant!
W: Thanks. I can't believe it. I just got the sample design of the exterior now.
M: Is this the sample? I like **the plant box next to** the main entrance.
W: I love how it goes so well with our door.
M: The sign board **above the door** is excellent.
W: The designer drew a fork, a spoon, and a knife on it. I really like them.
M: The chalkboard sign near the door is a great idea. You can **write down** the day's specials and prices.
W: What about **these two chairs in front of** the restaurant's front window?
M: It's a great idea for customers who are waiting. But I think a long bench would be better.
W: That's a good idea. They can wait on it together. Oh, what about the parasol on the right?
M: Nice idea. **Waiting customers can hide** from strong sunlight.
W: I'm glad you like it.

남: 레스토랑 개업을 축하해요!
여: 고마워요. 믿을 수가 없어요. 난 지금 외관의 견본 디자인을 막 받았어요.
남: 이게 그 견본인가요? 정문 옆의 식물 박스가 마음에 드는군요.
여: 그게 우리 문하고 얼마나 잘 어울리는지 마음에 들어요.
남: 문 위의 간판이 훌륭하네요.
여: 디자이너가 거기에 포크하고 숟가락하고 나이프를 그렸어요. 난 그것들이 정말 좋아요.
남: 문 근처에 있는 칠판 표지판은 아주 좋은 생각이에요. 그날의 특별식과 가격을 써넣을 수 있잖아요.
여: 식당 앞유리창 앞에 있는 이 두 개의 의자는 어때요?
남: 기다리는 손님들을 위한 훌륭한 생각이에요. 하지만 긴 벤치가 더 좋을 거라는 생각이 드네요.
여: 그거 좋은 생각이에요. 그들이 거기서 함께 기다릴 수 있겠군요. 아, 오른쪽의 파라솔은 어때요?
남: 멋진 생각이에요. 기다리는 고객들이 강한 햇빛을 피할 수 있겠어요.
여: 마음에 드신다니 기뻐요.

어휘 sample 견본, 샘플   exterior 외관, 외부   main entrance 정문, 중앙 출입구   go well with ~와 잘 어울리다   sign board 간판   chalkboard 칠판

05 추후 행동 ⑤

✻ 대개 대화는 어떤 일을 하게 되는 상황이 먼저 제시된 뒤에 남자와 여자가 각각 할 일들과 이에 대한 수락/거절의 응답이 나열되는 식으로 전개된다. 남자가 여자에게 교수님의 전화번호를 찾아서 문자로 보내달라고 한다. 이에 여자가 수락하므로 여자의 할 일은 ⑤ '교수님 전화번호 찾아 보내주기'이다. 교수님에게 사정을 대신 이야기해주겠다고 여자가 제안했지만 남자가 거절하며 자기가 말씀드리겠다고 했음에 유의한다.

W: Tristan, you look worried. What's wrong?
M: I just got a phone call from my neighbor, and she said my mom **fell down the stairs** and got hurt.
W: How awful! Then you need to go home and take her to the hospital, don't you?
M: She called 911 for an ambulance, but I have to go to the hospital.
W: Oh, you should. I hope it's not serious.
M: Well, but **I have a math test** this afternoon. It's an important test.
W: Don't worry. If that's the case, I'm sure the professor will understand and you can take it another time. Who is your professor?
M: Dr. Heywood. Philip Heywood.
W: I know him. I think he can understand. If you want, I'll **tell him about your story**.
M: Well, no, I think I should tell him myself. Diana, could you find his phone number and **text it to me**? I have to go to the hospital now.
W: Okay. I will. Go ahead.

여: Tristan, 너 걱정스러워 보인다. 뭐가 문제니?
남: 방금 이웃 아주머니에게서 전화를 받았는데 우리 엄마가 계단에서 넘어져서 다쳤다고 말씀하셨어.

여: 끔찍해라! 그러면 넌 집에 가서 어머니를 병원으로 모시고 가야겠다. 그렇지 않니?
남: 이웃 아주머니가 구급차를 부르려고 911에 전화하셨지만 내가 병원으로 가야 해.
여: 아, 그래야지. 심각한 게 아니기를 바라.
남: 음, 하지만 내가 오늘 오후에 수학 시험이 있어. 중요한 시험이거든.
여: 걱정 마. 그런 경우라면, 분명히 교수님이 이해하실 거고 넌 다른 때에 시험을 칠 수 있을 거야. 교수님이 누구시니?
남: Heywood 박사님이야. Philip Heywood.
여: 그분을 알아. 이해해주실 거라고 생각해. 네가 원한다면, 내가 네 이야기를 교수님께 알릴게.
남: 음, 아니야. 내가 직접 교수님께 말씀드려야 한다고 생각해. Diana, 그분 전화번호를 찾아서 나한테 문자로 보내줄 수 있니? 지금 나는 병원에 가야 해.
여: 좋아. 그럴게. 어서 가.

어휘 neighbor 이웃 (사람)   awful 끔찍한, 지독한   ambulance 구급차   professor 교수

06 금액 ⑤

✻ 여러 개의 수치 정보가 등장하므로 필요한 정보를 메모하면서 듣는 것이 좋다. 15달러짜리 머그잔이 아니라 머그잔과 차가 함께 들어 있는 20달러짜리 차 세트를 사기로 했음에 유의한다. 선물할 직원 숫자 역시 5명이 아닌 시간제 직원을 포함한 총 8명이다. 그러므로 지불할 금액은 ⑤ '$160(20×8)'이다.

W: Michael, look at that mug. It looks like a ceramic mug, but it's a stainless steel mug.
M: Wow, great. It's been made specifically to keep coffee warm.
W: And it's lighter than ceramic mugs.
M: That's true. Should we give this mug as a gift for all our employees? They're only 15 dollars each.
W: It's been a year since our store's opening, and I think it's a good idea.
M: Oh, there are **mugs that come with tea**. Each set includes one mug and ten tea bags. **It's 20 dollars**.
W: They're more expensive, but I think our staff would like them better. Let's get some tea sets then.
M: We have **a total of five employees**, right?
W: No, we can't forget the part-time employees.
M: That's right. We have **three part-time employees**, right?
W: Yes. Let's get them.

여: Michael, 저 머그잔을 봐요. 도자기 머그잔 같아 보이지만 스테인리스 강철 머그잔이에요.
남: 와, 멋지군요. 그건 커피를 따뜻하게 유지하려고 특별히 만들어진 거네요.
여: 그리고 도자기 머그잔보다 가볍고요.
남: 맞아요. 이 머그잔을 우리 전 직원에게 선물로 줄까요? 하나에 15달러밖에 안 하는데요.
여: 우리 가게를 개업한 지 일 년이 되었으니 좋은 생각인 것 같아요.
남: 아, 차가 딸린 머그잔이 있군요. 각 세트가 머그잔 하나와 티백 10개를 포함하네요. 20달러군요.
여: 더 비싸지만 우리 직원이 그걸 더 좋아할 것 같아요. 그러니 차 세트로 삽시다.
남: 우리 직원이 총 5명이죠, 맞죠?
여: 아니요, 시간제 직원들을 잊으면 안 돼요.
남: 맞아요. 3명의 시간제 직원이 있죠, 그렇죠?
여: 그래요. 저걸 삽시다.

어휘 ceramic 도자기   employee 직원, 종업원   come with ~이 딸려있다   include 포함하다   part-time 시간제의

07 이유 ④

✻ 지시문을 통해 남자가 축구 동아리를 그만둔 상황이며 남자의 말에 단서가 있을 가능성이 큼을 미리 파악한다. 남자에게 축구를 그만둔 이유를 묻자 심장병이 있어서 의사가 축구를 하는 대신 수영을 권했다고 말한다. 그러므로 답은 ④ '의사가 그만두라고 조언해서'이다.

W: Oh, hi, Stephen. I didn't expect to see you here.

M: Hi, Jasmine. We seem to be running into each other everywhere.

W: I know. What brings you here? It's Friday, and your soccer club practices every Friday, doesn't it?

M: Yeah, but **I gave up soccer club**.

W: Why? Was it too tough?

M: Actually, I have heart problems. **My doctor suggested** that I should swim **instead of playing soccer**.

W: Oh, is it serious?

M: No, but my doctor said the best thing is to **work out in the water**. How about you?

W: I just love the water because I was raised by the beachside. After moving to the city, I've tried to come to the swimming pool as often as I can.

M: Anyway, how about having lunch with me?

W: Sounds good. There's a restaurant that has great pasta around here.

여: 아, 안녕, Stephen. 여기서 보리라고 예상하지 못했어요.

남: 안녕, Jasmine. 우리는 어디를 가든지 서로 우연히 만나는 것 같군요.

여: 맞아요. 여긴 무슨 일이에요? 오늘은 금요일이고 당신은 금요일마다 축구 동아리 연습이 있잖아요, 그렇지 않아요?

남: 네, 하지만 축구 동아리를 그만뒀어요.

여: 왜요? 너무 힘들었어요?

남: 사실 난 심장병이 있어요. 의사가 축구를 하는 대신에 수영을 해야 한다고 권했어요.

여: 아, 심각한가요?

남: 아니요, 하지만 의사가 말하길 가장 좋은 게 물속에서 운동하는 것이라고 하더군요. 당신은 어때요?

여: 난 해변에서 자랐기 때문에 그저 물을 좋아해요. 도시로 이사한 후에 가능한 한 자주 수영장에 오려고 노력해왔어요.

남: 어쨌든, 나와 같이 점심을 먹는 것이 어떤가요?

여: 그거 좋네요. 이 근처에 굉장한 파스타를 하는 식당이 있어요.

어휘 expect 예상[기대]하다 run into ~을 우연히 만나다[마주치다] suggest 권하다; 제안[제의]하다; 시사[암시]하다 work out 운동하다 raise 키우다; 일으키다

08 언급하지 않은 것　　④

✽ 대화의 진행은 대개 선택지와 같은 순서이므로, 선택지를 보면서 언급된 내용을 소거하는 식으로 푸는 것이 좋다. 콜로라도에 있는 통나무집의 숙박 요금은 하룻밤에 120달러이고 애완동물이 허용되고 도보 10분 거리에 식료품점이 있고 전기는 있지만 인터넷 접속은 안 된다고 했다. 그러므로 언급하지 않은 것은 ④ '수도 시설'이다.

M: I'm here to find out some information for my summer vacation.

W: Please have a seat. Where are you planning to go?

M: I'm **interested in staying in** a log cabin in Colorado for a week from June 12th.

W: Then we have a good place. Look at this photo. This Westside Log Cabin is located near Pikes Park. It's priced **at $120 per night**.

M: It looks great. Oh, I have a dog. Can I take my dog?

W: Sure. **Pets are allowed** in this log cabin. It has two bedrooms and a kitchen.

M: Good. Are there grocery stores in the area for me to pick up food?

W: Of course. It's just **a 10-minute walk from** the grocery store.

M: Does it have Wi-Fi service or Internet access?

W: No, the log cabin has electricity **but no Wi-Fi or** Internet service.

M: No problem. I'll just leave my laptop at home then. It's not a big deal. Can you make the arrangements for me?

남: 여름휴가를 위한 정보를 좀 찾으려고 여기 왔는데요.

여: 앉으십시오. 어디 가실 계획이신가요?

남: 6월 12일부터 일주간 콜로라도에 있는 통나무집에서 묵는 데 관심이 있어요.

여: 그러면 저희에게 좋은 장소가 있습니다. 이 사진을 보세요. 이 Westside 통나무집은 Pikes 공원 근처에 위치하고 있는데요. 가격은 하룻밤에 120달러입니다(① 숙박 요금).

남: 좋아 보이는군요. 아, 제가 개가 있어요. 개를 데려갈 수 있나요?

여: 그럼요. 이 통나무집에는 애완동물이 허용됩니다(② 애완동물 허용 여부). 침실 두 개와 부엌이 있고요.

남: 좋아요. 그 지역에 제가 식품을 살 식료품점이 있나요?

여: 물론이죠. 여긴 식료품점으로부터 도보로 단지 10분 거리(③ 근처 상점과의 거리)입니다.

남: 와이파이 서비스나 인터넷 접속이 되나요?

여: 아니요. 통나무집은 전기는 있지만 와이파이나 인터넷 접속은 안 됩니다(⑤ 인터넷 가능 여부).

남: 괜찮습니다. 그러면 내 노트북을 집에 두면 될 테니까요. 별일 아니에요. 그 준비를 해주실 수 있나요?

어휘 log cabin 통나무집　grocery store 식료품점　pick up ~을 사다[찾다]　access 접속(하다); 접근(하다)　electricity 전기, 전력　arrangement 준비, 마련; 배치

09 내용 불일치　　④

✽ 담화의 진행은 대개 선택지와 같은 순서이므로, 선택지를 보면서 일치하는 내용을 소거하는 식으로 푸는 것이 좋다. 질문에 바르게 답하면 5점을 얻고 답을 틀리면 2점을 잃는다고 했다. 그러므로 ④ '질문에 대한 답이 틀리면 5점을 잃는다.'는 내용과 일치하지 않는다.

M: Hello and welcome to our game show, Trivia Track! Now **four people are trying to win** our grand prize. As you know, **the winner will receive** $50,000 in cash and a six-day vacation to Bali! The rules are very simple. The first round is basic question and answer. I'll ask a question, and whoever knows the answer **should push the buzzer** in front of them. The person who answers the question correctly gets five points. If the answer is wrong, you lose two points. If you don't know an answer, say "pass." **The first player to get thirty points** wins the first round. Have you got it? Now, for the first question. Listen carefully and push the buzzer as soon as you know the answer. Which European river flows through six different countries?

남: 안녕하세요, 우리 게임 쇼, Trivia Track에 오신 걸 환영합니다! ① 이제 네 분이 1등을 차지하기 위해 도전하고 계십니다. 여러분도 아시다시피 ② 우승자는 현금 5만 달러와 6일간의 발리행 휴가를 받게 될 것입니다! 규칙은 아주 간단합니다. 첫 번째 라운드는 기본적인 질문과 답변입니다. 제가 질문을 드릴 거고 ③ 답을 아는 누구든 앞에 있는 버저를 누르셔야 합니다. 질문에 바르게 답한 사람은 5점을 얻습니다. ④ 답이 틀리면 2점을 잃습니다. 답을 모르시면 "통과"라고 말씀하세요. ⑤ 30점을 얻는 첫 번째 참가자가 1라운드에서 승리합니다. 아셨습니까? 이제 첫 번째 질문입니다. 잘 듣고 답을 알자마자 버저를 누르십시오. 어떤 유럽의 강이 여섯 개의 다른 나라를 통과해 흐르나요?

어휘 receive 받다, 받아들이다　correctly 바르게; 정확하게　flow 흐르다; 흐름

10 도표 이해　　①

✽ 대화의 진행은 대개 도표 항목의 나열 순서대로 진행된다. 대화를 들으면서 도표의 각 항목 중 선택되지 않은 것을 소거하는 식으로 푸는 것이 좋다. 자원봉사할 그룹을 고르는 상황이다. 우선 건축 전공을 필요로 하는 ④가 제외되고 건강관리 프로그램인 ③도 제외된다. 스페인어를 요구하는 ⑤를 제외하고 남은 ①과 ②중에서 봉사를 6개월간 할 수 있다고 했으므로 여자가 선택한 그룹은 ①이다.

W: I saw your advertisement in the newspaper for various volunteer programs, and I'd like to sign up for something.

M: Thanks for coming. What type of work would you like to do?

W: I'm not quite sure. **I'm majoring in science**.

M: Then you can choose these four groups.

W: All right, but I don't think I can do healthcare work. I'm **already participating in** another healthcare program.

M: Oh, okay. Can you speak Spanish by any chance?

W: No, I'm afraid not.

M: Okay. Then you can't choose this one because they want volunteers **who can speak Spanish**. How long could you volunteer?

W: I'd like to volunteer **for six months**. I'm going to join a camp this winter, so I can't work any longer than that.

M: Okay. I guess this is your only option, then.

W: Thanks. I'd like to sign up now.

여: 신문에서 이곳의 다양한 자원봉사 프로그램 광고를 봤는데 하나 신청하고 싶어서요.
남: 와주셔서 고맙습니다. 어떤 종류의 일을 하고 싶나요?
여: 확실히 모르겠어요. 전 과학을 전공하고 있어요.
남: 그러면 이 4개의 그룹 중에서 선택할 수 있어요.
여: 알겠어요. 하지만 건강관리 일은 할 수 없을 것 같아요. 전 벌써 다른 건강관리 프로그램에 참여하고 있거든요.
남: 아, 알겠습니다. 혹시 스페인어를 할 줄 아세요?
여: 아니요, 할 수 없어요.
남: 알겠습니다. 그러면 이건 스페인어를 할 줄 아는 자원봉사자를 원하기 때문에 선택할 수 없습니다. 얼마나 오래 봉사할 수 있나요?
여: 6개월 동안 봉사하고 싶어요. 제가 이번 겨울에 캠프에 참가할 거라서 그보다 더 길게 일할 수는 없어요.
남: 알겠습니다. 그러면 이게 유일한 선택지 같은데요.
여: 고맙습니다. 지금 신청하고 싶어요.

어휘 advertisement 광고 various 다양한, 여러 가지의 sign up for ~을 신청[가입]하다 major 전공하다; 주요한, 중대한 participate in ~에 참여하다 by any chance 혹시라도

11 짧은 대화에 이어질 응답 ⑤

✻ 학생이 교수님에게 보고서 마감 일자의 연장을 부탁하고 있다. 이에 대한 교수님의 응답으로는 ⑤ '유감이지만 난 늦게 낸 어떠한 숙제도 받지 않는단다.'가 가장 적절하다.

① 왜? 넌 3일 이상 남았잖니.
② 내가 늦게 낸 숙제에 대해 대단히 미안하구나.
③ 그 일이 다신 일어나지 않도록 열심히 일하자.
④ 네가 또 한 번의 연장이 필요하면 내게 알려주렴.

W: Excuse me, professor. I have to talk to you about my biology homework. I wasn't able to finish it.
M: **It's due tomorrow morning**, isn't it?
W: Yes, it is. But I was sick. Could you **extend the deadline for** my paper until Thursday?
M: I'm afraid I don't accept any late homework.

여: 죄송합니다. 교수님. 제 생물학 숙제에 대해 말씀드려야 할 게 있어요. 전 그 숙제를 끝낼 수가 없었어요.
남: 그건 내일 아침까지잖니, 그렇지 않니?
여: 네, 그래요. 하지만 제가 아팠어요. 제 보고서 마감 일자를 목요일까지 연장해주실 수 있나요?
남: 유감이지만 난 늦게 낸 어떠한 숙제도 받지 않는단다.

어휘 biology 생물학 extend 연장하다; 더 길게 만들다 cf. extension 연장; 확대, 확장
| 선택지 어휘 | accept 받아들이다

12 짧은 대화에 이어질 응답 ⑤

✻ 여자는 프린터가 고장 난 줄 알고 수리 센터에 전화하려 했지만, 남자가 프린터의 코드가 전원에 연결되어 있지 않았다고 말하므로 이에 대한 여자의 응답으로는 ⑤ '정말이야? 난 그걸 확인해 볼 생각조차 하지 못했어!'가 적절하다.

① 걱정 마. 이제 시도하고 작동하는지 봐.
② 응. 그것들이 연결되지 않으면 켜지지 않을 거야.
③ 그거 안타깝다. 내가 새 걸 주문할게.
④ 그건 충분히 진하지 않아. 잉크가 다 떨어진 것 같아.

M: Natalie, what's wrong with the computer? Let me take a look at it.
W: The printer isn't working. **Should I call** the repair center?
M: No, there's nothing wrong with the printer. **The cord wasn't plugged in.**
W: **Really? I'd never even thought to check that!**

남: Natalie. 컴퓨터에 무슨 문제라도 있니? 내가 살펴볼게.
여: 프린터가 작동하지 않아. 수리 센터에 전화해야 할까?

남: 아니야. 프린터에는 잘못된 게 아무것도 없어. 코드가 전원에 연결되어 있지 않았어.
여: 정말이야? 난 그걸 확인해 볼 생각조차 하지 못했어!

어휘 repair 수리[보수](하다) plug in 전원을 연결하다
| 선택지 어휘 | connect 연결하다; 이어지다 run out 다 떨어지다[써버리다]

13 긴 대화에 이어질 응답 ②

✻ 대화의 전체 맥락 하에 마지막 말의 의미나 의도를 정확히 파악하는 것이 좋다. 여자는 사이즈가 맞는 샌들을 신어보지만 가격이 높아 언제 할인을 할지 묻고 있다. 남자는 연례 여름 할인 계획을 대답하므로 이에 대한 여자의 응답으로는 ② '그때 사겠어요. 지금은 살 여유가 없군요.'가 적절하다.

① 10%를 더 할인해주면 그걸 살게요.
③ 그게 더 싼 가격에 그 물건을 살 수 있는 방법입니다.
④ 그건 괜찮을 거예요. 하지만 오래 기다리셔야 할 거예요.
⑤ 그때쯤 그게 없을지도 몰라요. 지금 사야 해요.

M: Hello. How can I help you?
W: I'd like to get a pair of sandals.
M: How about these white sandals? I guess you're a size 7 or 8. Would you like to try them on?
W: Yes, my size is 8. [pause] **They fit really well**.
M: They look great on you.
W: Oh, dear! Is the price $189 like it says here on the price tag? Are you offering any discounts by any chance?
M: **Nothing is on sale** right now.
W: Oh, I see. That would definitely be **out of my price range**. When do you plan to have a sale?
M: The department store will have **its annual summer sale** on the 11th of this month.
W: **I'll buy them then. I can't afford them right now.**

남: 안녕하세요. 무엇을 도와드릴까요?
여: 샌들 한 켤레를 사고 싶어요.
남: 이 하얀 샌들은 어떠신가요? 손님은 사이즈가 7이나 8일 것 같은데요. 신어보시겠어요?
여: 네, 제 사이즈는 8이에요. [잠시 후] 정말 잘 맞네요.
남: 아주 잘 어울리십니다.
여: 아, 이런! 여기 가격표에 쓰여 있는 것처럼 가격이 189달러인가요? 혹시 할인해 주나요?
남: 지금은 어떤 것도 할인 판매하지 않습니다.
여: 아, 그렇군요. 그건 분명히 제 가격 범위를 벗어나는군요. 언제 할인할 계획이 있나요?
남: 백화점이 이번 달 11일에 연례 여름 할인을 할 거예요.
여: 그때 사겠어요. 지금은 살 여유가 없군요.

어휘 fit (모양·크기가) 맞다 offer 제공하다; 제의[제안]하다 by any change 혹시라도 on sale 할인[세일] 중인 definitely 분명히, 틀림없이; 절대(로) range 범위 department store 백화점 annual 연례의, 매년의
| 선택지 어휘 | afford (~을 살) 여유[형편]가 되다

14 긴 대화에 이어질 응답 ②

✻ 대화의 전체 맥락 하에 마지막 말의 의미나 의도를 정확히 파악하는 것이 좋다. 본 대화는 두 사람이 영화를 보고 실망스러워하는 상황이다. 영화의 내용뿐만 아니라 극장의 난방 시스템까지 끔찍했다는 여자의 말에 남자의 응답으로는 ② '네 말에 동의해. 그건 정말 짜증 났어.'가 적절하다.

① 너무 시끄러워서 잠을 푹 잘 수 없었어.
③ 넌 날 믿어도 돼. 난 널 다시는 실망시키지 않을 거야.
④ 나도 마찬가지야. 내가 그것을 더 따뜻하게 해달라고 요청해야 했어.
⑤ 놀라웠어. 그건 멋지고 역동적인 소리를 만들어냈어.

M: How did you like the movie?
W: Actually, it was a little disappointing.

M: I agree. **It fell short of** my expectations.

W: I think I expected too much from the movie because of the reviews. This movie got such good reviews, didn't it?

M: Yeah, right. But **it wasn't as good as the reviews**.

W: The storyline was bad. I didn't understand why the main character refused to explain anything to his friends.

M: Exactly! That **didn't make any sense at all**.

W: Also, the heating system in the theater was awful. **It sounded like** a bunch of bees buzzing and was far too hot.

M: I agree with you. That was really irritating.

남: 영화는 어땠니?

여: 사실 좀 실망스러웠어.

남: 동의해. 내 기대에 못 미쳤어.

여: 평론 때문에 영화에 너무 많이 기대했던 것 같아. 이 영화는 정말 좋은 평론을 받았잖아, 그렇지 않니?

남: 응, 맞아. 하지만 평론만큼 좋지는 않았어.

여: 줄거리가 형편없었어. 왜 주인공이 자기 친구들에게 무엇이든 설명하는 걸 거부하는지 이해하지 못했어.

남: 정말 그래! 그건 전혀 말이 안 됐어.

여: 또 극장의 난방 시스템은 끔찍했어. 그건 다수의 벌들이 윙윙거리는 것 같은 소리를 냈고 너무 지나치게 더웠어.

남: 네 말에 동의해. 그건 정말 짜증 났어.

어휘 disappointing 실망스러운, 기대에 못 미치는 *cf.* disappoint 실망시키다, 실망을 안겨 주다 ｜ fall short of A A에 미치지 못하다 ﹡ review 평론, 비평; 재조사 storyline 줄거리 make sense 말이 되다; 이해가 되다 a bunch of 다수의 buzz 윙윙거리다 ｜ 선택지 어휘 ｜ irritating 짜증나게 하는; 화나게 하는 rely on ~을 믿다; ~에 의존하다 dynamic 역동적인; 활발한

15 상황에 적절한 말 ③

﹡ 지시문을 통해 누가(A) 누구에게(B) 할 말인지를 우선 정확히 파악한다. 담화는 대개 A와 B에 대한 배경 설명과 B가 처한 문제 상황, 그리고 이에 대해 A가 어떤 말을 하려고 하는지에 대한 설명의 순서로 전개된다. Alex(A)는 길을 물어보자는 Caroline(B)의 말을 듣지 않다가 결국 저녁 약속에 늦고 고집부린 것에 대해 사과를 하려는 상황이다. 그러므로 Alex가 할 말로는 ③ '미안해요. 당신 말을 들었어야 했어요.'가 가장 적절하다.

① 일부러 늦은 건 아니었어요. 극심한 교통량이 있어서요.

② 제발 나한테 화내지 말아요. 난 솔직해지고 싶어요.

④ 당신은 너무 완고했어요. 당신이 우리를 저녁 식사에 늦게 만들었어요.

⑤ 그 말을 들으니 유감이군요. 분명히 실망했겠어요.

M: Caroline and Alex are a couple, and they've been invited to one of their friends' houses. The dinner is at 6 o'clock, and they leave their home early. Unfortunately, their GPS isn't working. They try to call their friend, but his phone is turned off. Caroline **tells Alex to stop the car** at a gas station and **ask for directions**, but Alex refuses to ask for help. He says he can **find the house on his own** since he's been in this area before. But they get lost. Finally, Caroline finds someone who gives clear directions. Still, they are late for the dinner appointment in the end. When they arrive at the friend's house, Alex **wants to apologize to** Caroline for what he did. In this situation, what would Alex most likely say to Caroline?

Alex: I'm sorry. I should have listened to what you said.

남: Caroline과 Alex는 부부이고 그들은 친구 중 한 명의 집에 초대받았다. 저녁 식사는 6시 정각이라서 그들은 일찍 집을 떠난다. 불행히도 그들의 GPS가 작동하지 않는다. 그들은 친구에게 전화를 걸려고 하지만 친구의 전화가 꺼져있다. Caroline은 Alex에게 차를 주유소에 세워 가는 길을 묻자고 말하지만, Alex는 도움을 요청하는 것을 거절한다. 그는 자기가 전에 이 지역에 와봤기 때문에 혼자서 집을 찾을 수 있다고 말한다. 하지만 그들은 길을 잃는다. 마침내 Caroline이 명확하게 가는 길을 알려주는 사람을 찾는다. 그러나 그들은 결국 저녁 약속에 늦는다. 그들이 친구 집에 도착할 때, Alex는 Caroline에게 자신이 한 일에 대해 사과하고 싶다. 이 상황에서 Alex는 Caroline에게 뭐라고 말하겠는가?

Alex: 미안해요, 당신 말을 들었어야 했어요.

어휘 refuse 거절[거부]하다 appointment 약속; 임명; 지명 apologize 사과하다, 사죄하다 ｜ 선택지 어휘 ｜ heavy traffic 극심한 교통량 honest 솔직한; 정직한 stubborn 완고한, 고집스러운 frustrated 실망한, 좌절당한

16~17 세트 문항 16 ② 17 ④

﹡ **16** 십 대들 사이에서 근시가 증가하고 있다는 내용으로 시작하여 근시를 막기 위해 해야 할 일을 열거하고 있다. 따라서 담화의 주제는 ② '근시를 예방하는 것을 돕는 방법'이다. ③ '식습관이 눈 건강에 미치는 효과'는 담화의 일부 내용임을 유의한다.

① 우리 시력을 보호하기 위한 운동

③ 식습관이 눈 건강에 미치는 효과

④ 근시의 증가 이유

⑤ 독서 시 적절한 조명의 중요성

﹡ **17** 해석 참조.

① 당근 ② 시금치 ③ 브로콜리 ④ 아몬드 ⑤ 딸기

W: Hello, class. Do you wear glasses? More and more teenagers wear glasses because they can't see far objects easily. What can you do to prevent this condition? First and foremost, doctors strongly suggest you get **a yearly eye exam** for possible signs of near-sightedness. Early detection is crucial. Also, **maintaining the natural balance** of moisture within your eyes is one of the most important things you can do to keep your eyes healthy. Make sure **you have enough lighting** when reading a book. You can also help your eyes by getting plenty of vitamins A and C. Some foods containing vitamin A are sweet potatoes, carrots, and spinach. Broccoli, strawberries, and oranges have a lot of vitamin C. Since your eyes are put under constant strain and stress while watching TV and staring at computer screens and smartphones, you must **give your eyes a break** from time to time. You should treat your eyes like you do your body by exercising them and giving them rest. I hope you keep these points in mind to maintain good eye health.

여: 안녕하세요, 여러분. 여러분은 안경을 쓰나요? 점점 더 많은 십 대들이 멀리 있는 물체를 쉽게 볼 수 없어서 안경을 쓰고 있어요. 이런 상태를 막기 위해 여러분이 뭘 할 수 있을까요? 다른 무엇보다도 의사들은 여러분이 근시의 가능성 있는 조짐을 찾기 위해 매년 시력 검사를 받기를 강력하게 권고하고 있어요. 조기 발견이 아주 중요해요. 또한, 여러분 눈 속의 수분의 자연적인 균형을 유지하는 것이 여러분의 눈을 건강하게 유지하기 위해 할 수 있는 가장 중요한 일 중 하나예요. 책을 읽을 때는 반드시 충분한 조명이 있도록 해야 해요. 여러분은 또한 비타민 A와 C를 많이 먹어서 눈을 도울 수 있어요. 비타민 A를 포함한 몇몇 음식은 고구마, ① 당근과 ② 시금치예요. ③ 브로콜리와 ⑤ 딸기와 오렌지는 비타민 C가 많아요. 여러분이 TV를 시청하고 컴퓨터 화면과 스마트폰을 응시하는 동안 여러분의 눈이 끊임없는 압박과 스트레스를 받기 때문에 때때로 눈에 휴식을 줘야 해요. 여러분은 운동하고 휴식을 주면서 여러분의 신체에 하는 것처럼 눈을 대해야 해요. 좋은 눈 건강을 유지하기 위해 이 점을 명심하길 바라요.

어휘 prevent 막다, 예방[방지]하다 first and foremost 다른 무엇보다도 near-sightedness 근시 detection 발견; 탐지 crucial 아주 중요한, 결정적인 maintain 유지하다, 지키다 moisture 수분, 습기 contain 포함 [함유]하다 spinach 시금치 constant 끊임없는; 거듭되는 strain 압박; 부담 stare at ~을 응시하다 keep A in mind A를 명심[유념]하다 ｜ 선택지 어휘 ｜ protect 보호하다 eyesight 시력 effect 효과; 결과 proper 적절한; 제대로 된

18회

01 화자가 하는 말의 목적   ⑤

✱ 담화의 일부 내용이 아니라 중심 내용을 파악해야 한다. 본 담화는 일 년 전 이날 강에 빠진 두 소년을 구하고 목숨을 잃은 Jonathan Adams를 기리는 장학금을 제정한다고 했으므로 담화의 목적은 ⑤ '의사자 추모 장학금 제정을 기념하려고'이다.

M: We are gathered here today to remember a special person. Jonathan Adams was an Asher High School student. He was a basketball player, and he was **a person who would help anybody** whenever he could. A year ago on this day, Jonathan was running along a riverbank. When he saw two boys fall into the river, he jumped into the water immediately and saved them. But after rescuing them, he was swept away by the river. Today, Asher High School has set up **a scholarship in honor of** Jonathan Adams. This scholarship will help students who are not financially able to go to college. This is **our way to honor** and remember him the best way we can.

남: 우리는 오늘 한 특별한 사람을 기억하기 위해 여기 모였습니다. Jonathan Adams는 Asher 고등학교 학생이었습니다. 그는 농구 선수였고 할 수 있을 때마다 누구든지 도우려는 사람이었습니다. 일 년 전 이날 Jonathan은 강둑을 따라 달리고 있었습니다. 그가 두 소년이 강에 빠진 것을 보았을 때 그는 즉시 물속으로 뛰어들어 그들을 구조했습니다. 하지만 그들을 구조한 후에 그는 강에 휩쓸려버리고 말았습니다. 오늘 Asher 고등학교는 Jonathan Adams를 기리는 장학금을 제정합니다. 이 장학금은 재정상 대학에 갈 수 없는 학생들을 도울 것입니다. 이것이 우리가 할 수 있는 최선의 방식으로 그에게 경의를 표하고 그를 기억하는 방법입니다.

어휘 **gather** 모으다, 모이다   **riverbank** 강둑   **immediately** 즉시, 바로; 직접적으로   **rescue** 구조[구제]하다, 구하다   **sweep away** ~을 휩쓸다   **scholarship** 장학금; 학문   **in honor of** ~을 기념하여, ~에 경의를 표하여 *cf.* **honor** 경의를 표하다, 존중하다; 명예, 영예   **financially** 재정상, 재정적으로

02 의견   ②

✱ 우선 지시문에서 명시한 화자의 성별을 보고 어느 화자의 말에 주목할지를 판단해야 한다. 특히 의견이나 주장을 표현하는 어구(I think ~, You should ~ 등)가 이끄는 내용을 잘 들어야 한다. 여자는 폭력적인 영화가 사회에 악영향을 주고 현실에서의 범죄로 이어질 수 있어 위험하다고 말하고 있다. 그러므로 여자의 의견은 ② '지나치게 폭력적인 영화는 사회에 해로운 영향을 준다.'이다.

W: What did you think of the movie?
M: I liked it. I like these kinds of movies.
W: Really? I didn't like it. I don't know **what they want to say**.
M: They probably want to show how cruel humans can be.
W: Then, they should do it in a more artistic way, not this way of just showing blood.
M: Well, just enjoy it. You're too serious sometimes.
W: But it is serious. Violent movies can affect people.
M: Do you really think so?
W: Yes! Some movie producers make these kinds of movies for money, but they really **have a bad influence on society**.
M: I don't think so. People like violent movies because violence is part of human nature.
W: These movies **can lead to real-life crimes**. They're very dangerous.

여: 그 영화 어땠니?
남: 좋았어. 이런 종류의 영화를 좋아해.
여: 정말이야? 난 별로였어. 그들이 말하고자 하는 게 뭔지 모르겠어.
남: 그들은 아마 인간이 얼마나 잔인해질 수 있는지 보여주길 원한 걸 거야.
여: 그러면, 그걸 그냥 피를 보여주는 이런 방식이 아니라 좀 더 예술적 방식으로 해야지.

남: 음, 그냥 즐겨. 넌 가끔은 너무 진지하더라.
여: 하지만 이건 심각해. 폭력적인 영화가 사람들에게 영향을 줄 수 있잖아.
남: 너 정말 그렇게 생각하니?
여: 응! 일부 영화 제작자는 돈을 벌려고 이런 종류의 영화를 만드는데, 하지만 그것들은 정말로 사회에 악영향을 주고 있어.
남: 난 그렇게 생각하지 않아. 사람들은 폭력이 인간 본성의 일부이기 때문에 폭력적인 영화를 좋아하는 거야.
여: 이런 영화들은 현실에서의 범죄로 이어질 수 있어. 그것들은 아주 위험해.

어휘 **probably** 아마   **cruel** 잔인한, 잔혹한   **artistic** 예술적인; 예술의   **serious** 진지한; 심각한   **violent** 폭력적인 *cf.* **violence** 폭력, 폭행; 격렬함   **affect** 영향을 주다   **influence** 영향(력); 영향을 끼치다   **nature** 본성; 자연   **crime** 범죄, 범행

03 관계   ②

✱ 직업을 나타내거나 추론할 수 있는 힌트가 대화 전반에 걸쳐 드러나므로, 대화를 전체적으로 이해하는 것이 필요하다. 본 대화에서 여자는 26마일을 달리는 것을 앞두고 있고 지난 몇 달간 이것을 위해 연습해왔다고 한다. 남자는 여자를 격려하면서 어떻게 달려야 할지 알려주고 있으므로 두 사람의 관계는 ② '마라톤 코치 – 선수'임을 알 수 있다.

M: Are you ready, Erin?
W: I'm not sure.
M: **Believe in yourself**. You've had plenty of practice for the past few months.
W: I just hope I can do what I did during my practice sessions.
M: I'm sure you'll do even better. Just remember **not to run too fast** in the beginning. Twenty-six miles is a long run.
W: I know. I'll keep that in mind.
M: You already know the course. When you're running, try to hold the same pace.
W: Got it. Do you think I can break my own record?
M: I trust you. **You're in good condition**, so all you have to do is do your best.
W: I'll take your word for it. I guess that's all I can do.
M: Now, let's do some warming up.

남: 준비됐니, Erin?
여: 모르겠어요.
남: 너 자신을 믿으렴. 넌 지난 몇 달간 연습을 많이 했어.
여: 전 단지 제가 연습 기간 동안 했던 걸 할 수 있기를 바라요.
남: 분명히 넌 훨씬 더 잘할 거야. 처음에 너무 빨리 달려가지 않는 것만 기억해라. 26마일은 장거리야.
여: 알아요. 그걸 명심할게요.
남: 넌 이미 코스를 알고 있어. 달릴 때 같은 속도를 유지하도록 노력하렴.
여: 알았어요. 저 자신의 기록을 깰 수 있을 거라고 생각하세요?
남: 난 널 믿어. 넌 컨디션이 좋으니까 네가 해야 할 모든 건 최선을 다하는 거야.
여: 말씀을 그대로 믿을게요. 그게 제가 할 수 있는 전부인 것 같아요.
남: 자, 준비 운동을 좀 하자.

어휘 **plenty of** 많은   **session** 기간, 시간   **keep A in mind** A를 명심하다[기억해 두다]   **take one's word for it** ~의 말을 그대로 받아들이다   **warming up** 준비 운동

04 그림 불일치   ③

✱ 대화가 나오기 전에 각 사물의 위치 관계와 외형(형태나 무늬, 개수 등)의 특징을 미리 확인하는 것이 좋다. 사진을 찍은 여자는 사진에서 장군 옆에 서서 왼손에는 가방을 들고 있어서 한 손만 들고 있다고 했는데 그림에서는 두 손을 다 들고 있으므로 ③이 내용과 일치하지 않는다. 여자가 원래는 두 손을 들고 싶었지만 그러지 못했다는 말을 유의해 들어야 한다.

M: What is this picture? It looks like a wax museum.
W: Yes, a wax museum in Seoul. It's the room of "Great Men of Korea."
M: Who is this woman on the left? She is sitting **in front of a big pine tree**.
W: She was a famous artist. And the man next to her was a great general.
M: Oh, he is wearing a hat with feathers and holding a stick.
W: Can you see me near him?
M: Yes, you're standing next to him and **raising your hand**.
W: Actually, I wanted to raise both my hands, but I couldn't because of the bag in my left hand.
M: You look good. Is the man on the right a king? He is sitting on a large chair.
W: Yes, he is King Sejong the Great. He created the Korean alphabet, Hangeul. **That's why he's holding a book**.
M: Oh, there's a big book behind him, too!

남: 이 사진은 뭐니? 밀랍 박물관 같아 보인다.
여: 응, 서울에 있는 밀랍 박물관이야. '한국의 위인들'이라는 방이야.
남: 왼쪽에 있는 이 여자는 누구니? 커다란 소나무 앞에 앉아 있는데.
여: 그분은 유명한 화가셨어. 그리고 그분 옆에 있는 남자는 위대한 장군이셨지.
남: 아, 그분은 깃털이 달린 모자를 쓰고 지휘봉을 들고 있구나.
여: 그분 근처에 내가 보이니?
남: 응, 너는 그분 옆에 서서 손을 올리고 있잖아.
여: 사실 난 두 손을 올리고 싶었지만 왼손에 있는 가방 때문에 그러지 못했어.
남: 좋아 보인다. 오른쪽의 남자는 왕이니? 그는 커다란 의자에 앉아 있네.
여: 응, 그분은 세종대왕이야. 한글이라는 한국의 글자를 발명하셨어. 그래서 그분께서 책을 들고 있는 거야.
남: 아, 그분 뒤에 큰 책도 있어!

어휘 wax 밀랍, 왁스 pine tree 소나무 general 장군; 일반[보편]적인 feather 깃털

05 추후 행동 ③

✻ 대개 대화는 어떤 일을 하게 되는 상황이 먼저 제시된 뒤에 남자와 여자가 각각 할 일들과 이에 대한 수락/거절의 응답이 나열되는 식으로 전개된다. 빵집을 개업하려고 하는 여자가 장소를 찾고 있다고 하자 남자가 부동산 중개인인 자신의 사촌을 소개해줄 수 있다고 한다. 여자가 소개를 부탁했고 남자가 당장 그에게 전화하겠다고 했으므로 남자의 할 일은 ③ '사촌에게 전화하기'이다.

W: Greg, you'll never believe this. I just got the most amazing news!
M: What? What happened?
W: I just got the money I needed to open my own bakery!
M: Really? That's great news. Congratulations!
W: I **will specialize in** pies and cupcakes since those are my favorite things to bake!
M: That sounds like a wonderful idea. And now **it has come true**!
W: It has! Now I need to find the location for my bakery. It's the most difficult thing for me.
M: Do you need professional help? My cousin is **a real estate agent**. If you want, **I'll introduce you to him**.
W: Can you do that? I really need some advice.
M: Sure. **I'll call him right now**. I'm sure he can be very helpful to you.
W: That sounds good.

여: Greg, 넌 절대 이거 믿지 못할 거야. 내게 가장 놀랄만한 소식이 있어!
남: 뭔데? 무슨 일이야?
여: 방금 내 빵집을 개업하는 데 필요한 돈이 생겼어!
남: 정말? 굉장한 소식이다. 축하해!
여: 파이와 컵케이크가 내가 가장 굽기 좋아하는 것들이어서 그것들을 전문으로 할 거야!
남: 훌륭한 생각 같아. 그리고 이제 이루어졌구나!
여: 그래! 이제 난 빵집을 할 장소를 찾아야 해. 그게 나한테는 가장 어려운 일이야.
남: 전문가의 도움이 필요하니? 내 사촌이 부동산 중개인이야. 네가 원하면 너를 그에게 소개시켜줄게.
여: 그렇게 해줄 수 있어? 난 정말 조언이 좀 필요해.
남: 그럼. 내가 당장 사촌에게 전화할게. 분명히 그가 너한테 아주 도움이 될 수 있을 거야.
여: 그거 좋다.

어휘 specialize in ~을 전문으로 하다[전공하다] professional 전문가의; 전문적인; 직업의 real estate agent 부동산 중개인

06 금액 ③

✻ 여러 개의 수치 정보가 등장하므로 필요한 정보를 메모하면서 듣는 것이 좋다. 남자가 한 상자에 10달러 하는 카드를 5상자 사고 추가로 3상자를 더 샀으므로 남자가 지불할 금액은 ③ '$80(10×8)'이다. 상자 안에 들어있는 12개의 카드의 숫자를 구매 숫자로 오해하지 않도록 유의한다.

[Telephone rings.]
W: Hello. I'm calling from "Angel Covers" foundation.
M: I don't want to buy that. I'm busy.
W: No, I'm not a telemarketer. We're **a charity organization**.
M: Oh, you're doing fine work.
W: I'm calling you to ask if you would like to **buy our greeting cards**. They're $10 per box.
M: Well, can I ask what you do exactly?
W: We work to provide food, health care, and education to people in need.
M: Oh, I see. How many cards are in the box?
W: Each box includes 12 different cards. And these are designed just for Angel Covers.
M: Oh, then I'd like **to order 5 boxes**.
W: Thanks. Most of the purchase price goes to people in need.
M: That sounds great. **Then I'd like to order 3 more boxes**.
W: Thanks a lot.

[전화벨이 울린다.]
여: 여보세요, 'Angel Covers' 재단에서 전화드리는데요.
남: 그거 사고 싶지 않습니다. 바빠요.
여: 아니요, 전 텔레마케터가 아닙니다. 저희는 자선 단체예요.
남: 아, 좋은 일을 하는군요.
여: 저희 신년카드를 사주실 수 있는지 여쭤보려고 전화했어요. 한 상자에 10달러예요.
남: 음, 정확히 무슨 일을 하는지 물어봐도 될까요?
여: 저희는 어려움에 처한 사람들에게 음식과 의료와 교육을 제공하기 위해 일합니다.
남: 아, 알겠어요. 그 상자에 카드가 몇 개나 들었나요?
여: 각각의 상자에는 12개의 다른 카드가 들어 있습니다. 그리고 이것들은 오직 Angel Covers를 위해 디자인된 것입니다.
남: 아, 그러면 5상자를 주문하고 싶어요.
여: 감사합니다. 구매 가격의 대부분이 어려움에 처한 분들에게 갑니다.
남: 그거 좋군요. 그러면 3상자 더 구매하겠어요.
여: 정말 감사합니다.

어휘 foundation 재단; 설립; 기초 charity organization 자선 단체 in need 어려움에 처한 purchase 구매(하다)

07 이유 ③

✻ 지시문을 통해 남자가 책을 할인해 준 상황이며 남자의 말에 단서가 있을 가능성이 큼을 미리 파악한다. 중고 책은 아니지만 표지가 손상되어서 할인해주겠다고 했으므로 할인 이유는 ③ '표지가 손상되어서'이다.

M: Can I help you? Are you looking for something?
W: Yes, **I'm looking for** the foreign language section.
M: Oh, it's right above you. That is the foreign language section up there.
W: I'm looking for Garcia Marquez's novel. Oh, it's on the top shelf. Can you get the red book **from the top shelf** for me?
M: [pause] This one? Here it is.
W: Thanks. It's 26 dollars. Oh, **the cover is damaged**. Do you have another copy?
M: No, that's the last one.
W: What should I do? It looks like a used book.
M: It's not a used book, but **we can give you** a 50% discount because its cover is damaged.

W: Really? That would be great. I'll take it.
M: Okay. Please follow me.

남: 도와드릴까요? 어떤 걸 찾으시나요?
여: 네, 저는 외국어 부문을 찾고 있어요.
남: 아, 바로 손님 위에 있습니다. 저기 위가 외국어 부문입니다.
여: 저는 Garcia Marquez의 소설을 찾고 있어요. 아, 맨 위 칸에 있군요. 꼭대기 칸에서 빨간 책을 꺼내주실 수 있나요?
남: [잠시 후] 이거요? 여기 있습니다.
여: 고맙습니다. 26달러군요. 아, 표지가 손상되었는데요. 다른 책은 없나요?
남: 없습니다. 그게 마지막 책이에요.
여: 어떡하죠? 이건 중고 책 같아 보여요.
남: 그건 중고 책이 아니지만, 표지가 손상되었기 때문에 50% 할인을 해드릴 수 있어요.
여: 정말요? 그러면 좋죠. 이걸 살게요.
남: 좋습니다. 저를 따라오세요.

어휘 section 부문, 부분 novel (장편) 소설; 새로운 shelf (책장의) 칸; 선반 cover 표지; 덮개, 커버

08 언급하지 않은 것   ②

✻ 대화의 진행은 대개 선택지와 같은 순서이므로, 선택지를 보면서 언급된 내용을 소거하는 식으로 푸는 것이 좋다. 기니피그의 크기에 대해 이야기한 후 평균 수명과 보충 영양제로 비타민 C가 필요하다는 이야기도 했으며, 마지막으로 성향도 언급했지만 먹이에 대해서는 언급하지 않았다. 그러므로 답은 ②이다.

W: Patrick, do you have a pet?
M: Yes, I have two guinea pigs. I have a picture of them in my cell phone. Look!
W: Oh, how cute they are! **How big are they**?
M: They are about 10 inches long and weigh 2 to 3 pounds.
W: Their cage is pretty big.
M: Yes, they need a lot of room to run, so I made a large homemade cage for them.
W: That's very good. How long do guinea pigs live?
M: On average, they live about 5 to 7 years. Do you know they need to **get vitamin C from their diet** like humans?
W: Really? That's interesting! So do you give them vitamin C tablets?
M: Yes. Also, they are very **social animals** and **very active**.

여: Patrick, 너 애완동물 있니?
남: 응, 난 두 마리의 기니피그가 있어. 내 휴대폰에 그것들 사진이 있지. 봐!
여: 아, 정말 귀엽구나! 크기가 얼마나 되니?
남: 약 10인치 길이에 무게는 2에서 3파운드 나가(① 크기).
여: 기니피그의 우리가 꽤 크다.
남: 그래, 그것들이 달리도록 많은 공간이 필요해서 내가 그것들을 위해 커다란 우리를 집에서 만들었어.
여: 그거 아주 좋다. 기니피그는 얼마나 오래 사니?
남: 평균 5년에서 7년 정도 살아(③ 평균 수명). 그것들이 인간처럼 음식으로부터 비타민 C를 얻어야 한다는 거 아니?
여: 정말? 그거 흥미롭다! 그래서 비타민 C 정제(④ 보충 영양제)를 그들에게 주는 거야?
남: 그래. 또한, 그것들은 아주 사회적인 동물이고 무척 활발해(⑤ 성향).

어휘 on average 평균적으로 tablet 정제 ((둥글넓적한 모양의 약제))

09 내용 불일치   ⑤

✻ 담화의 진행은 대개 선택지와 같은 순서이므로, 선택지를 보면서 일치하는 내용을 소거하는 식으로 푸는 것이 좋다. 스포츠 센터 시설을 이용하려면 반드시 발급받은 스포츠 카드를 가져오라고 했으므로 ⑤ '시설 이용 시 학생증을 지참해야 한다.'는 내용과 일치하지 않는다. 학생증은 스포츠 카드를 발급받기 위해 필요한 것임에 유의한다.

W: Thank you. Welcome to the Green Sports Center. I'm happy that so many of you have been coming here to use **our sports facilities** since

we opened 5 years ago. All students at the college can be members of this sports center for an annual fee of $37. To register, you need to **come to reception** in the lobby, between 2 and 6 p.m., Monday to Thursday. Now, there are two things that you must remember **to bring with you** when you come to register. These are your student card and a recent photograph of yourself. After registering, you will receive a sports card, and **you must bring this sports card** with you whenever you use the Sports Center facilities.

여: 고맙습니다. Green 스포츠 센터에 오신 것을 환영합니다. ① 우리가 5년 전 개장한 이후 우리 스포츠 시설을 이용하러 아주 많은 분들이 여기로 오고 계셔서 기쁩니다. ② 모든 대학생분들은 37달러의 연회비로 이 스포츠 센터의 회원이 되실 수 있습니다. ③ 등록하려면 로비에 있는 접수처로 월요일부터 목요일, 오후 2시에서 6시 사이에 오셔야 합니다. 이제 ④ 등록하러 올 때 반드시 가져올 것을 기억해야 하는 두 가지가 있습니다. 이것들은 여러분의 학생증과 여러분의 최근 사진입니다. 등록한 후에 여러분은 스포츠 카드를 받게 될 것인데 ⑤ 스포츠 센터 시설을 이용할 때마다 반드시 이 스포츠 카드를 함께 가져오셔야 합니다.

어휘 facility 시설, 설비 annual fee 연회비 register 등록하다 reception 접수처

10 도표 이해   ③

✻ 대화의 진행은 대개 도표 항목의 나열 순서대로 진행된다. 대화를 들으면서 도표의 각 항목 중 선택되지 않은 것을 소거하는 식으로 푸는 것이 좋다. 제일 먼저 4도어 형은 여자가 싫다고 했으므로 ①은 제외하고 가격은 2,000달러 이하를 원했으므로 ④ 역시 제외된다. 가장 가격이 싸지만, 고객평가 별의 개수가 2.5개인 ⑤도 제외하면 남은 2개 중에서 보증 기간이 긴 것을 사기로 했으므로 두 사람이 살 냉장고는 ③이다.

W: Honey, what about buying a new refrigerator? Ours is so old.
M: Yeah, we really need a new refrigerator. **Let's check for one** online. How about this one?
W: I don't like the 4-door type. They don't have much room inside.
M: Then let's choose a 3-door or 2-door type.
W: Okay, and I think we can pay up to 2,000 dollars. But **the cheaper, the better**.
M: I agree. But the cheapest one got bad customer reviews. It received 2.5 out of 5 stars.
W: I don't want to buy it. Let's choose one which got 4 or 4.5 stars **in the customer reviews**.
M: Then there are two options we can choose from.
W: I think a warranty is very important. Let's choose the one **with a longer warranty**.
M: I agree. Let's order this one right now.

여: 여보, 새 냉장고를 사는 건 어때요? 우리 것은 너무 오래되었어요.
남: 맞아요. 우리는 정말로 새 냉장고가 필요해요. 온라인에서 하나 확인해봅시다. 이건 어때요?
여: 난 4도어 형은 좋아하지 않아요. 그건 안에 공간이 많지 않아요.
남: 그러면 3도어 형이나 2도어 형에서 고릅시다.
여: 좋아요. 그리고 우리가 2,000달러까지 지불할 수 있다고 생각해요. 하지만 더 쌀수록 더 좋죠.
남: 동의해요. 하지만 가장 싼 것은 고객평가를 나쁘게 받았어요. 별 5개 중에서 2.5개를 받았네요.
여: 난 그건 사고 싶지 않아요. 고객평가에서 별 4개나 4.5개를 받은 것을 고릅시다.
남: 그러면 우리가 고를 수 있는 건 이 두 개의 선택권이에요.
여: 보증 기간이 아주 중요하다고 생각해요. 보증 기간이 더 긴 걸 선택합시다.
남: 동의해요. 이걸 당장 주문합시다.

어휘 refrigerator 냉장고 up to A A까지; A에 달려 있는 warranty 품질 보증(서)

11 짧은 대화에 이어질 응답   ①

✻ 시험공부를 하라는 어머니에게 아들의 응답으로 나올만한 말은 ① '그건 걱정 마세요. 제가 알아서 할게요.'가 가장 적절하다.

② 그런 것 같아요. 새로운 걸 시도할 시간이에요.
③ 정확히 그래요. 저도 시험에서 꽤 좋은 성적을 받았어요.
④ 언제나 그렇게 말씀하시죠. 그건 그냥 핑계예요.
⑤ 화가 났어요. 전 시험에서 큰 실수를 했어요.

W: You're late again, Steve. I think you need to do some studying and prepare for the final exam.
M: Mom, I can't study all the time. I need a break once in a while.
W: If you want to get a good grade, you need to **prepare yourself for the exam**.
M: Don't worry about it. I'll take care of it.

여: 또 늦었구나, Steve. 난 네가 공부를 좀 해서 기말시험을 준비해야 한다고 생각하는데.
남: 엄마. 전 항상 공부만 할 수는 없어요. 가끔은 휴식이 필요해요.
여: 네가 좋은 성적을 받고 싶다면 시험 준비를 해야 해.
남: 그건 걱정 마세요. 제가 알아서 할게요.

어휘 once in a while 가끔, 이따금 | 선택지 어휘 | excuse 핑계, 변명

12 짧은 대화에 이어질 응답   ②

※ 교실을 찾지 못해 어디인지 알려달라는 질문에 대한 응답으로는 ② '제가 안내해 드릴 수 있어요. 그 근처에서 수업이 있거든요.'가 가장 적절하다.

① 미안해요. 하지만 전 그 수업을 전에 들었던 적이 없어요.
③ 알겠어요. 월요일에 그 수업을 신청할게요.
④ 괜찮아요. 그냥 그것이 어느 건물에 있는지 말해주세요.
⑤ 아주 좋아요. 아직 자리가 있는 두 개의 수업이 있어요.

M: Excuse me. I can't find my class. Could you **tell me where it is**?
W: Of course, what room number is it?
M: It's room 612 in the Pearson building.
W: I can show you. I have a class around there.

남: 실례합니다. 제 교실을 찾을 수 없어서요. 어디인지 알려주실 수 있나요?
여: 물론이죠, 교실 번호가 뭐가요?
남: Pearson 빌딩 612호예요.
여: 제가 안내해 드릴 수 있어요. 그 근처에서 수업이 있거든요.

어휘 | 선택지 어휘 | sign up for ~을 신청[가입]하다

13 긴 대화에 이어질 응답   ①

※ 대화의 전체 맥락 하에 마지막 말의 의미나 의도를 정확히 파악하는 것이 좋다. 첫 영화부터 팬이었던 여자가 휴가지에서 배우인 남자를 우연히 만나 사인을 받고 함께 사진을 찍은 후 할 말로는 ① '정말 고맙습니다. 이날을 결코 잊지 못할 거예요.'가 가장 적절하다.

② 천만에요. 저도 당신을 만나게 되어 정말 반가웠습니다.
③ 그게 맞아요. '치즈'라는 소리는 당신을 미소 짓게 만들죠.
④ 조금 진정할 필요가 있으시군요. 너무 흥분하셨어요.
⑤ 정말 부럽군요. 저도 그를 직접 만나고 싶어요!

W: Excuse me, but are you Mr. Downey?
M: Yes, that's right. Are you a tourist?
W: Yes, I'm here in Bali on vacation. I can't believe **I ran into you** here.
M: [laughing] Well, it's really me.
W: I'm a huge fan of yours. I've been a fan since your first movie.
M: Really? Then **it's been a long time**.
W: Yeah, I've sent you many fan letters in the past. Meeting you here is like a dream come true.
M: It's a pleasure to meet you, too.
W: Oh, can I **get your autograph** here? My name is Anne Palmer.
M: I'd be honored to, Anne.
W: Would you mind **if we took a picture together**?
M: Of course not. Say "cheese!"
W: Thank you so much. I'll never forget this day.

여: 실례하지만, Downey 씨죠?
남: 네, 맞습니다. 여행객이세요?
여: 네, 여기 발리에 휴가 차 왔어요. 여기서 당신을 우연히 만나다니 믿을 수가 없군요.
남: [웃음] 음, 진짜 저입니다.
여: 전 당신의 열렬한 팬이에요. 첫 영화부터 당신의 팬이었어요.
남: 정말요? 그러면 오래되었군요.
여: 네, 예전에는 팬레터도 많이 보냈어요. 여기서 당신을 만나다니 꿈이 이루어진 것 같아요.
남: 저도 만나게 되어 기쁩니다.
여: 아, 제가 여기에 당신의 사인을 받을 수 있을까요? 제 이름은 Anne Palmer예요.
남: 영광이에요, Anne.
여: 제가 함께 사진을 찍어도 될까요?
남: 그럼요. '치즈' 하세요!
여: 정말 고맙습니다. 이날을 결코 잊지 못할 거예요.

어휘 run into ~와 우연히 만나다   autograph 사인(을 해주다)
| 선택지 어휘 | calm down 진정하다   envy 부러워하다; 부러움   in person 직접

14 긴 대화에 이어질 응답   ②

※ 대화의 전체 맥락 하에 마지막 말의 의미나 의도를 정확히 파악하는 것이 좋다. 본 대화는 박사인 남자가 도서관에서 빌린 책을 반납하지 않아 도서관 사서인 여자가 이메일을 보낸 상황이며 전화로 다시 한번 반납을 요청하고 있다. 이에 대한 남자의 응답으로는 ② '미안합니다. 가능한 한 빨리 반납할게요.'가 가장 적절하다.

① 그게 맞아요. 그것들은 한 달 안에 반납하셔야 해요.
③ 그게 작동하지 않으면 내가 할 수 있는 게 아무것도 없어요.
④ 반납하지 않은 책에는 연체료가 있기 때문입니다.
⑤ 걱정 마세요. 이메일로 도서 목록을 보낼게요.

[Telephone rings.]
M: Hello? This is Dr. Russell.
W: Dr. Russell, this is Jessica Blower in the Central Library.
M: Oh, hi. I was trying to call you. **Have the books I ordered arrived**?
W: Let's see. Uh... They will arrive in two weeks. Is that okay with you?
M: Yeah, it will be all right.
W: By the way, Dr. Russell, did you receive the list of books that **you need to return**?
M: List? No, I don't think so.
W: We e-mailed an individual list to each professor. We hope that you will return **your unreturned books** by July 10th.
M: Just a moment. I'll open my e-mail. [pause] Yes, I got the mail.
W: There are many books that have not been returned. So we ask all professors **to bring them back** by July 10th.
M: I'm sorry. I'll return them as soon as possible.

[전화벨이 울린다.]
남: 여보세요? Russell 박사입니다.
여: Russell 박사님, 저는 중앙 도서관의 Jessica Blower입니다.
남: 아, 안녕하세요. 내가 전화 걸려고 하고 있었어요. 내가 주문했던 책들이 도착했나요?
여: 볼게요. 어… 2주 후에 도착할 거예요. 괜찮으신지요?
남: 네, 괜찮을 거예요.
여: 그런데요, Russell 박사님, 반납하셔야 할 도서 목록을 받으셨는지요?
남: 목록이요? 아니요, 안 받은 것 같은데요.
여: 저희가 각 교수님께 개별적인 목록을 이메일로 보내드렸어요. 7월 10일까지 반납하지 않은 책들을 반납하시기를 바라요.
남: 잠깐만요. 내 이메일을 열어볼게요. [잠시 후] 네, 메일을 받았군요.
여: 반납되지 않은 책들이 많아요. 그래서 모든 교수님들께 7월 10일까지 그것들을 가져오시라고 요청하는 거예요.
남: 미안합니다. 가능한 한 빨리 반납할게요.

어휘 order 주문하다; 명령[지시]하다   return 반납하다, 돌려주다 cf. unreturned 되돌려지지 않은   individual 개별적인; 각각의   professor 교수 | 선택지 어휘 | late fee 연체료

15 상황에 적절한 말 ③

* 지시문을 통해 누가(A) 누구에게(B) 할 말인지를 우선 정확히 파악한다. 담화는 대개 A와 B에 대한 배경 설명과 B가 처한 문제 상황, 그리고 이에 대해 A가 어떤 말을 하려고 하는지에 대한 설명의 순서로 전개된다. 딸이 학교에서 잘하는지 걱정하던 어머니 Laura(A)에게 Nelson 선생님(B)이 아주 잘하고 있다고 칭찬했을 때 놀라면서도 기분 좋은 어머니가 할 말로는 ③ '그 애가 학교에서 잘 행동하고 있다고 들으니 마음이 놓이는군요.'가 적절하다.

① 제가 그 문제를 이해할 수 있는지 볼게요.
② 당신이 당신의 자녀를 격려해야 한다고 생각해요.
④ 선생님 수업에서 공손하라고 그 애에게 충고해야 할 것 같아요.
⑤ 당신이 아이였을 때부터 죽 항상 당신을 자랑스러워했어요.

W: Laura is the mother of 11-year-old Christine. Today is Parent-Teacher Conferences at Christine's school. She goes to her daughter's school and sees her teacher, Mr. Nelson. Laura asks him **how Christine is doing** in school. Actually, she is worried about Christine because she is quiet and shy but sometimes **gets irritated at home**. But to her surprise, Mr. Nelson says Christine is a very good student. When Laura tells him she is worried about her daughter, Mr. Nelson says Christine **is really good at figuring things out** and learning. He says she tries to actively participate in the class activities. Laura is very surprised but feels good. In this situation, what would Laura most likely say to Mr. Nelson?

Laura: I feel relieved to hear she behaves well in school.

여: Laura는 11살짜리 Christine의 어머니이다. 오늘은 Christine의 학교에서 학부모 회의가 있다. 그녀는 딸의 학교로 가서 아이의 선생님인 Nelson 선생님을 만난다. Laura는 그에게 Christine이 학교에서 어떻게 하고 있는지 묻는다. 사실 그녀는 Christine이 조용하고 수줍어하지만, 가끔 집에서 짜증을 부리기 때문에 딸이 걱정된다. 그러나 놀랍게도 Nelson 선생님은 Christine이 아주 훌륭한 학생이라고 말한다. Laura가 Nelson 선생님에게 딸이 걱정된다고 말하자 그는 Christine이 문제를 이해하고 배우는 것을 정말 잘한다고 말한다. 그는 그 애가 수업 활동에 적극적으로 참여하려고 한다고 한다. Laura는 매우 놀라지만 기분이 좋다. 이 상황에서 Laura가 Nelson 선생님에게 뭐라고 말하겠는가?

Laura: 그 애가 학교에서 잘 행동하고 있다고 들으니 마음이 놓이는군요.

어휘 conference 회의; 협의 get irritated 짜증을 부리다 to one's surprise 놀랍게도 figure A out A를 이해하다[알아내다]; 계산[산출]하다 actively 적극적으로, 활발히 participate in ~에 참여[참가]하다 | 선택지 어휘 | encourage 격려[고무]하다 relieved 안도하는 behave 행동[처신]하다 advise 충고[권고]하다

16~17 세트 문항   16 ⑤ 17 ④

* **16** 외식이 소박한 음식의 즐거움을 잊게 할 수 있다고 했고, 자극적인 맛에 익숙해지면 다양한 건강 문제로 이어질 수 있다고 말하며 건강을 위해 소박한 식사의 즐거움을 다시 깨달으라고 조언하고 있다. 그러므로 담화의 주제는 ⑤ '건강을 위해 담백하고 소박한 음식을 먹는 것의 가치'이다.

① 가정 요리의 건강상 이점
② 즉석 식품을 먹는 것의 부정적 영향
③ 유기농 방식으로 채소를 재배하는 법
④ 폭넓게 다양한 식단을 먹는 것의 중요성

* **17** 해석 참조.
① 옥수수 ② 연어 ③ 멜론 ④ 양파 ⑤ 토마토

W: Are you a person who enjoys eating out? If so, I'd like to give you some advice. Much of today's cooking, particularly in restaurants, is designed to excite the senses more than to provide **what your body needs**. This comes with the risk of forgetting the pleasures of simple foods. Can you still **take pleasure in** an ear of sweet corn, just picked, lightly cooked, and eaten plain without butter or salt? Or a slice of really fresh salmon only with lemon? Or a section of perfectly ripe melon? If you cannot imagine salad and tomatoes without creamy dressing, then **you've lost touch**

with plain foods. I am not urging you to live on oatmeal and water. Once we become accustomed to eating spicy foods, we want even stronger flavors. My concern is that if strong flavors are the main appeal of food, **our health will suffer**. The ingredients that create these strong flavors can cause a variety of health problems as well as stomach pain. So, why not try to relearn **the joys of simple meals** for your health?

여: 여러분은 외식을 즐기는 사람인가요? 그렇다면 여러분에게 조언을 좀 드리겠습니다. 오늘날의 많은 요리들이 특히 식당에서는 여러분의 신체가 필요로 하는 것을 공급하는 것보다 더 많이 감각을 자극하도록 만들어집니다. 이것에는 소박한 음식의 즐거움을 잊게 하는 위험이 따라옵니다. 여러분은 막 따서 살짝 익히고 버터나 소금 없이 있는 그대로 먹는, 단 맛이 나는 ① 옥수수 하나를 여전히 즐기실 수 있습니까? 아니면 레몬만 곁들인 정말 신선한 ② 연어 한 조각은요? 아니면 완전히 익은 ③ 멜론 한쪽은요? 여러분이 크림이 많이 든 드레싱 없는 샐러드와 ⑤ 토마토를 먹는 것을 상상할 수 없다면, 그러면 여러분은 담백한 음식의 감촉을 잃어버린 겁니다. 저는 여러분에게 귀리죽과 물을 먹고 살라고 설득하고 있는 건 아닙니다. 일단 우리가 양념 맛이 강한 음식을 먹는 것에 익숙해지면, 우리는 훨씬 더 자극적인 맛을 원하게 됩니다. 제 걱정은 자극적인 맛이 음식의 주된 매력이라면 우리 건강은 고통받을 것이라는 겁니다. 그러한 자극적인 맛을 내는 재료들은 복통뿐만 아니라 다양한 건강 문제를 일으킬 수 있습니다. 그러므로 건강을 위해 소박한 식사의 즐거움을 다시 깨닫기 위해 노력해보는 것은 어떨까요?

어휘 eat out 외식하다 particularly 특히, 특별히 pleasure 즐거움, 기쁨 *cf.* take pleasure in ~을 즐기다[좋아하다] simple 소박한, 간소한 an ear of corn 옥수수 한 대 salmon 연어 ripe 익은; 숙성한 plain 담백한; 있는 그대로의 urge A to-v A에게 v하라고 설득하려 하다 accustomed to A A에 익숙한 spicy 양념 맛이 강한 flavor 맛, 풍미 concern 걱정, 우려 appeal 매력; 호소(하다) suffer 고통받다; 시달리다 ingredient 재료, 성분; 구성 요소 | 선택지 어휘 | instant 즉석의, 즉각적인; 순간 organic 유기농의

19회

01 화자가 하는 말의 목적 ②

* 담화의 일부 내용이 아니라 중심 내용을 파악해야 한다. 치과에 가지 않고 가정에서 제품을 사용하면 단 며칠 후에 치아가 더 하얗게 보일 것이라고 하면서 웹사이트를 방문해 주문하라고 하고 있다. 그러므로 담화의 목적은 ② '치아 미백 제품을 광고하려고'임을 알 수 있다.

M: Would you like to light up the room with your smile? It can be done. Most people aren't aware of how easy it is to get a bright smile. Our product can be used at home without visiting the dentist. Just apply the product to your teeth every night after your regular brushing. It's that simple. Maintain your usual cleaning habits, and after just a few days, your teeth will start to look whiter. Unlike similar products, ours is guaranteed not to hurt sensitive gums. Why wait? Visit our website at www.whiteteeth.com and order it today. You'll see why our company has the highest sales of all dental product companies in the nation.

남: 여러분의 미소로 방을 환하게 밝히고 싶으십니까? 그렇게 할 수 있습니다. 대부분의 사람들은 밝은 미소를 얻는 것이 얼마나 쉬운지 깨닫지 못하고 있습니다. 저희 제품은 치과를 방문하지 않고 가정에서 사용할 수 있습니다. 매일 저녁 규칙적인 칫솔질 후에 여러분의 치아에 제품을 바르기만 하십시오. 그렇게 간단합니다. 여러분의 평상시의 (치아를) 닦는 습관을 유지하십시오. 그러면 단 며칠 후에 여러분의 치아는 더 하얗게 보이기 시작할 것입니다. 유사한 제품과는 다르게 저희 제품은 예민한 잇몸을 상하게 하지 않는 것을 보증합니다. 왜 기다리십니까? 저희 웹사이트 www.whiteteeth.com을 방문하셔서 오늘 그것을 주문하십시오. 왜 저희 회사가 전국의 모든 치과 제품 회사 중에서 최고의 매출을 내는지 알게 되실 겁니다.

어휘 light up ~을 환하게 밝히다; 불을 붙이다   be aware of ~을 깨닫다[알아차리다]   apply 바르다; 적용하다; 지원하다   maintain 유지[지속]하다   guarantee 보증[보장]하다; 보증(서)   sensitive 예민한, 민감한   gum 잇몸

02 의견 ④

* 우선 지시문에서 명시한 화자의 성별을 보고 어느 화자의 말에 주목할지를 판단해야 한다. 특히 의견이나 주장을 표현하는 어구(I think ~, You should ~ 등)가 이끄는 내용을 잘 들어야 한다. 아들이 폐건전지를 다른 쓰레기와 함께 버리려고 하자 어머니는 폐건전지가 환경에 해로우므로 재활용되어야 한다고 말하고 있다. 그러므로 여자의 의견은 ④ '오염을 막기 위해 폐건전지는 재활용해야 한다.'이다.

W: Bruce, can you help me clean the basement?
M: Sure, Mom. Oh, there are some old batteries in this box here.
W: They're used batteries. I've kept them there.
M: Can I throw away these old batteries with the other garbage?
W: No, you shouldn't do that. They contain harmful metals and chemicals that can get into our air and water supply.
M: Really?
W: Yes, if you do that, it's harmful to our environment. American people throw away about 180,000 tons of batteries per year.
M: Wow, that's a lot of batteries.
W: Yes, they should be recycled.
M: Oh, I see. Then what should we do?
W: I'll send them to a battery recycling center tomorrow.
M: Okay. Then I'll just leave this box here.

여: Bruce, 지하실 청소를 도와줄 수 있니?
남: 그럼요, 엄마. 아, 여기 이 상자 안에 오래된 건전지가 좀 있어요.
여: 그것들은 다 쓴 건전지란다. 거기 보관해두었지.
남: 제가 이 오래된 건전지를 다른 쓰레기와 함께 버려도 될까요?
여: 아니, 그래서는 안 돼. 그것들은 대기나 상수도로 들어갈 수 있는 해로운 금속과 화학

물질을 포함하고 있어.
남: 정말이요?
여: 응. 네가 그렇게 하면 그건 우리 환경에 해롭단다. 미국 사람들은 일 년에 약 18만 톤의 건전지를 버려.
남: 와, 그거 많은 건전지네요.
여: 그래, 그것들은 재활용되어야 해.
남: 아, 알았어요. 그러면 우리가 뭘 해야 하죠?
여: 그것들을 내일 건전지 재활용 센터로 보낼 거야.
남: 알겠어요. 그러면 이 상자를 여기 그냥 둘게요.

어휘 basement 지하실[층]   garbage 쓰레기; 음식 찌꺼기   contain 포함하다; 억누르다   chemical 화학 물질; 화학의   water supply 상수도   recycle 재활용하다

03 관계 ②

* 직업을 나타내거나 추론할 수 있는 힌트가 대화 전반에 걸쳐 드러나므로, 대화를 전체적으로 이해하는 것이 필요하다. 박물관이나 미술관 내부 사진 촬영의 가능 여부 및 추후 여행 일정을 알려주고 있다. 그 외, 지도를 주는 것으로 미루어 보아 두 사람의 관계는 ② '관광 가이드 – 여행객'임을 알 수 있다.

M: If you have any questions while we're going along, please don't hesitate to ask.
W: I have a question actually.
M: Sure, what's that?
W: Are we allowed to take pictures once we get inside the museum?
M: Oh, I'm glad you asked that. I forgot to mention that taking photographs inside the art gallery and the museum is not allowed.
W: Okay. And what time do we have lunch?
M: After visiting the museum, we'll meet back at the bus at 12:15 exactly. Then we'll have lunch.
W: Okay. I have another question. I'd like to know if we're going to visit any castles today.
M: No, I'm afraid all of the castles are far from the city. We're going to visit them tomorrow.
W: Oh, thanks for the information.
M: My pleasure. I'll give you a map. It shows where all of the castles are.

남: 우리가 가는 동안 질문이 있으시면 망설이지 말고 질문하세요.
여: 사실 제가 질문이 하나 있어요.
남: 그래요, 뭐죠?
여: 우리가 일단 박물관 안으로 들어가면 사진 찍는 게 허용되나요?
남: 아, 그걸 물어봐 주시니 기쁘네요. 제가 미술관과 박물관 내부에서 사진 찍는 게 허용되지 않는다고 말하는 것을 잊었습니다.
여: 알았어요. 그리고 언제 우리가 점심을 먹죠?
남: 박물관 방문 후에 정확히 12시 15분에 버스에서 다시 만날 겁니다. 그리고 나서 점심 식사를 할 겁니다.
여: 좋아요. 또 다른 질문이 있는데요. 오늘 우리가 성을 방문할 건지 알고 싶어요.
남: 아뇨, 유감이지만 모든 성은 도시로부터 멀리 있어서요. 우리는 내일 그곳들을 방문할 겁니다.
여: 아, 알려줘서 고마워요.
남: 도움이 되어 저도 기쁩니다. 제가 지도를 드릴게요. 그게 모든 성들이 어디 있는지 보여줍니다.

어휘 hesitate 망설이다. 주저하다   mention 말하다. 언급(하다)

04 그림 불일치 ⑤

* 대화가 나오기 전에 각 사물의 위치 관계와 외형(형태나 무늬, 개수 등)의 특징을 미리

확인하는 것이 좋다. 신랑 신부 이미지 중 신랑이 실크 모자를 쓰고 있어서 우스워 보인다고 했으므로 그림 중 모자를 쓰지 않은 신랑의 이미지인 ⑤는 대화의 내용과 일치하지 않는다. 모자를 벗겨달라고 하는 것은 청첩장 그림에 모자가 이미 있음을 나타내는 것이다.

W: Brian, our wedding planner just e-mailed us our wedding-invitation card design.
M: Let me see. Oh, it's pretty.
W: Yeah, they put a banner saying "WEDDING DAY" at the top left.
M: Right. There are **two birds facing each other** under the banner.
W: I like this heart between them. And they placed our names, Brian and Emily, under the birds.
M: That's great. There's also the wedding date and time at the bottom left. June 16th, Saturday, 3 o'clock in the afternoon. Perfect!
W: What do you think of this bride-and-groom image on the right?
M: The bride looks great. She is wearing a wedding gown and a long veil.
W: I agree. But **the groom is wearing a silk hat**. It looks funny.
M: I think so. Why don't you call them and **ask to take off the hat**? That's the only thing we want to change.
W: Okay. I'll do that.

여: Brian, 우리 웨딩 플래너가 방금 우리 청첩장 디자인을 이메일로 보냈어요.
남: 어디 봐요. 아, 예쁘군요.
여: 네, 'WEDDING DAY'라고 쓰인 현수막을 왼쪽 상단에 두었네요.
남: 그렇군요. 현수막 아래에 새 두 마리가 서로 마주 보고 있네요.
여: 나는 새들 사이의 이 하트가 마음에 들어요. 그리고 우리 이름 Brian과 Emily를 새들 아래에 배치했어요.
남: 그거 좋군요. 왼쪽 하단에 결혼식 날짜와 시간도 있어요. 6월 16일 토요일 오후 3시. 완벽해요!
여: 오른쪽의 이 신랑 신부 이미지는 어떻게 생각해요?
남: 신부는 아주 좋아 보여요. 웨딩드레스를 입고 긴 면사포를 쓰고 있군요.
여: 동의해요. 하지만 신랑은 실크 모자를 쓰고 있네요. 우스워 보여요.
남: 나도 그렇게 생각해요. 그들에게 전화해서 모자를 벗겨달라고 요청하는 건 어때요? 그게 우리가 바꾸기를 원하는 유일한 것이네요.
여: 좋아요. 내가 그걸 할게요.

어휘 bride 신부 (bride) groom 신랑 veil 면사포; 베일 take off (옷, 모자 등을) 벗(기)다; 이륙하다; 휴가를 보내다

05 추후 행동   ④

✻ 대개 대화는 어떤 일을 하게 되는 상황이 먼저 제시된 뒤에 남자와 여자가 각각 할 일들과 이에 대한 수락/거절의 응답이 나열되는 식으로 전개된다. 여자는 파티 인원이 변경된 것을 식당에 전화해 알리겠다고 했으므로 여자의 할 일은 ④ '식당 예약인원 변경 알리기'이다.

W: Honey, did you order a cake for your mother's birthday party?
M: No, I didn't yet. **I am about to do it**. Oh, did you make a reservation for the birthday dinner already?
W: Of course. Seven Hills is a fancy and popular restaurant, so **we should make reservations**.
M: How many people did you reserve for?
W: I reserved a table for twelve people.
M: Then we need to **change the number of people** to ten.
W: Why?
M: I just got a call from Aunt Sophia this afternoon. Her husband, Uncle Jerry, hurt his back.
W: I'm sorry to hear that.
M: She said she has to take care of him, so those two can't come to the party.
W: Okay. I'll call the restaurant and **let them know about the change** while you order the cake.
M: Thanks, honey.

여: 여보, 당신 어머니 생신 파티를 위해 케이크를 주문했어요?
남: 아뇨, 아직 하지 않았어요. 막 하려고요. 아, 당신은 생신 저녁 식사 예약을 벌써 했어요?

여: 물론이죠. Seven Hills는 고급스럽고 인기 있는 식당이라서 예약을 해야 해요.
남: 몇 사람을 예약했어요?
여: 12명이 앉을 테이블을 예약했어요.
남: 그러면 인원수를 10명으로 바꿔야 해요.
여: 왜요?
남: 오늘 오후 Sophia 고모님의 전화를 막 받았어요. 고모님의 남편 Jerry 고모부님이 허리를 다치셨어요.
여: 참 안됐군요.
남: 고모님도 고모부님을 돌봐야 한다고 하셨으니까 그 두 분은 파티에 오지 못하세요.
여: 알겠어요. 당신이 케이크를 주문하는 동안 나는 식당에 전화해서 변경에 대해 알릴게요.
남: 고마워요, 여보.

어휘 be about to-v 막 v하려 하다   make a reservation 예약하다 cf. reserve 예약하다   fancy 고급의; 화려한   back 허리; 뒤쪽의

06 금액   ③

✻ 여러 개의 수치 정보가 등장하므로 필요한 정보를 메모하면서 듣는 것이 좋다. 40달러짜리 에티오피아 커피 한 팩과 30달러짜리 콜롬비아 커피 한 팩 그리고 10달러짜리 커피 필터 한 팩을 구매하므로 남자가 지불할 금액은 ③ '$80'이다.

W: Good afternoon. How can I help you?
M: I'd like to buy some coffee beans.
W: We have various types of coffee beans. **Which type do you want**?
M: I like coffee from Kenya. Can I know its roasting date?
W: Its roasting date was a week ago. **Newly roasted beans** are from Ethiopia and Columbia.
M: How much are they?
W: The Ethiopian coffee and Kenyan coffee are **$40** a pack, and the Columbian coffee is **$30** a pack.
M: Hmm... I'll take one pack of Ethiopian coffee and one pack of Columbian coffee. The fresh coffee **has more flavor**.
W: Right. Is there anything else?
M: I also want one pack of paper filters, the big size. **That's all**.
W: They are **$10** a pack. Okay. One Ethiopian coffee, one Columbian coffee, and a pack of coffee filters.
M: Right.

여: 안녕하세요. 어떻게 도와드릴까요?
남: 커피 원두를 사고 싶습니다.
여: 다양한 종류의 커피 원두가 있습니다. 어떤 종류를 원하시나요?
남: 케냐산 커피가 좋아요. 그 커피 원두의 볶은 날짜를 알 수 있나요?
여: 그것의 볶은 날짜는 일주일 전입니다. 최근에 볶은 원두는 에티오피아와 콜롬비아산입니다.
남: 그것들은 얼마죠?
여: 에티오피아 커피와 케냐 커피는 한 팩에 40달러이고 콜롬비아 커피는 한 팩에 30달러입니다.
남: 음... 에티오피아 커피 한 팩하고 콜롬비아 커피 한 팩을 사겠어요. 신선한 커피가 더 풍미가 좋으니까요.
여: 그렇죠. 다른 건 없으신가요?
남: 종이 필터 한 팩도 큰 사이즈로 원합니다. 그게 다예요.
여: 그것들은 한 팩에 10달러입니다. 알겠습니다. 에티오피아 커피 하나, 콜롬비아 커피 하나와 커피 필터 한 팩이요.
남: 맞습니다.

어휘 various 다양한   roast (콩, 커피 원두 등을) 볶다; (특히 고기를) 굽다   flavor 풍미, 맛

07 이유   ③

✻ 지시문을 통해 여자가 룸메이트를 바꾸고 싶어 하는 상황이며 여자의 말에 단서가 있을 확률이 높음을 파악한다. 여자의 룸메이트는 친구가 많지 않고 여자의 물건에 손을 대지도 않지만 방을 전혀 청소하지 않고 금방 더럽힌다고 했다. 그러므로 여자가 룸메이트를 바꾸고 싶은 적절한 이유는 ③ '방을 너무 더럽게 사용해서'이다.

M: Hi! What are you doing here at the library? Are you studying?

W: No, I watched a movie in the media room. What about you?

M: I'm **just hanging around**. You look upset. What's wrong?

W: It's because of my roommate. I don't want to go into our room.

M: Oh, does she always have guests over?

W: No, she doesn't have many friends.

M: Then does she **touch your stuff without asking**?

W: No, she doesn't. But **she never cleans our room**. Her hair covers the floor, and she throws away her trash on the floor.

M: Oh, that's terrible.

W: Yeah! I have cleaned the room, but it gets dirty again two hours later.

M: Did you talk to her about it?

W: Yes, I did, but nothing's changed. I'll ask the dormitory manager **to switch roommates**.

남: 안녕! 너 여기 도서관에서 뭐 하고 있니? 공부하는 거야?

여: 아니야, 미디어 실에서 영화를 봤어. 넌?

남: 그냥 어슬렁거리는 중이야. 너 화가 난 것 같아. 무슨 일이야?

여: 내 룸메이트 때문이야. 우리 방에 들어가고 싶지가 않아.

남: 아, 그 애가 항상 손님을 초대하니?

여: 아니, 그 애는 친구가 많지는 않아.

남: 그러면 물어보지도 않고 네 물건에 손을 대니?

여: 아니, 그렇지 않아. 하지만 그 애는 방을 전혀 청소하지 않아. 그 애의 머리카락이 바닥에 덮여 있고 자기 쓰레기를 바닥에 버려.

남: 아, 그거 끔찍하다.

여: 그래! 내가 방을 치우지만, 두 시간이 지나면 다시 더러워져.

남: 그 애에게 그것에 관해 이야기해봤니?

여: 응, 해봤지만 아무것도 바뀌지 않았어. 난 룸메이트를 바꿔 달라고 기숙사 관리인에게 요청할 거야.

어휘 hang around 어슬렁거리다, 배회하다   floor 바닥; 층   dormitory 기숙사

08 언급하지 않은 것 ③

※ 대화의 진행은 대개 선택지와 같은 순서이므로, 선택지를 보면서 언급된 내용을 소거하는 식으로 푸는 것이 좋다. 모임 인원 여섯 명이 모임 장소인 지역 카페에서 만나고 책의 종류는 보통 소설을 읽지만 전기 등도 읽는다고 했다. 또한, 자기가 읽고 싶은 책을 제안하고 함께 선정한다고 책 선정 방법에 대해서도 말했지만 모임 횟수에 대해서는 전혀 언급하지 않았으므로 답은 ③이다.

M: Oh, hi, Rachel. You're reading a book.

W: I've got my book club this evening, but I haven't had time to finish the book.

M: You're in a book club? What do you do? I mean what is the club?

W: Well, we're a group of friends. **There's six of us**. We meet in a local cafe and talk about the book we've read.

M: You like reading. So **what sort of books do you read**?

W: It's usually a novel, but sometimes we read a biography or something like that.

M: And who chooses it?

W: We all do. We suggest books that **we'd like to read** and then decide together.

M: That's cool.

W: If you are interested, just tell me.

M: Okay. I'll think about it!

남: 아, 안녕, Rachel. 책을 읽고 있구나.

여: 오늘 저녁에 독서 클럽이 있어, 하지만 책을 다 읽을 시간이 없었어.

남: 네가 독서 클럽에 있는 거야? 뭐 하는데? 내 말은 무슨 클럽이야?

여: 음, 우리는 친구 모임이야. 여섯 명이 있어(① 모임 인원). 지역 카페에서 만나고(② 모임 장소) 우리가 읽은 책에 대해 이야기를 나눠.

남: 너 독서를 좋아하는구나. 그러면 어떤 종류의 책을 읽는 거니?

여: 보통 소설이지만 때로는 전기나 그런 것도 읽어(④ 책의 종류).

남: 그럼 누가 그걸 선택하는 거야?

여: 우리 모두가 해. 우리가 읽고 싶은 책을 제안하고 나서 함께 결정해(⑤ 책 선정 방법).

남: 그거 멋지다.

여: 네가 관심이 있으면 내게 말만 해.

남: 알았어. 생각해 볼게!

어휘 sort 종류, 유형   novel (장편) 소설; 새로운   biography (인물의) 전기

09 내용 불일치 ③

※ 담화의 진행은 대개 선택지와 같은 순서이므로, 선택지를 보면서 일치하는 내용을 소거하는 식으로 푸는 것이 좋다. 오디션은 필요 없다고 했으므로 ③ '오디션은 1월과 7월에 실시한다.'는 내용과 일치하지 않는다. 일 년에 두 번 1월과 7월에는 회비를 내는 것임에 유의한다.

M: I'd like to invite anyone **who has ever been in** a high school band to join the Four Corners Community Band. We meet **every Monday night** from 7 p.m. to 9 p.m in the Cortez Community Hall. The band plays all styles of music, including classical and jazz. The band is open to **adults over the age of 18**. Membership fees are $20 twice a year. Members must pay in January and again in July. Membership fees are used for the rental of our practice room. **No auditions necessary**. If you want to join us, please e-mail us! We'd love for you to come join us!

남: 고등학교 밴드에 계셨던 적이 있는 분은 누구나 Four Corners Community Band에 가입하시라고 요청하고 싶습니다. 우리는 ① 매주 월요일 밤 오후 7시부터 9시까지 Cortez Community Hall에서 만납니다. 밴드는 클래식 음악과 재즈를 포함하여 모든 유형의 음악을 연주합니다. ② 밴드에는 18세가 넘는 성인들이 참가할 수 있습니다. 회비는 일 년에 두 번 20달러입니다. ③ 회원들은 (회비를) 반드시 1월에 지불하고 다시 7월에 지불해야 합니다. ④ 회비는 우리 연습실을 대여하는 데 사용됩니다. ⑤ 오디션은 필요 없습니다. ⑤ 가입하고 싶으시면 저희에게 이메일을 보내주십시오! 여러분이 오셔서 저희와 함께하신다면 좋겠습니다!

어휘 including ~을 포함하여   membership fee 회비   rental 대여, 임대   necessary 필요한, 필수의

10 도표 이해 ②

※ 대화의 진행은 대개 도표 항목의 나열 순서대로 진행된다. 대화를 들으면서 도표의 각 항목 중 선택되지 않은 것을 소거하는 식으로 푸는 것이 좋다. 두 사람은 부피가 350에서 500밀리리터 사이의 텀블러를 원했고(⑤ 소거) 소재는 스테인리스 강철을 선호한다(① 소거). 또한, 손잡이는 없는 것을 선택했고(④ 소거), 남은 둘 중에서 가격이 30달러 이하인 것을 골랐으므로 두 사람이 구매할 텀블러는 ②이다.

W: We need to get tumblers for Christmas gifts for our staff.

M: Of course. Let's buy them online.

W: Okay. Let's check a price comparison website.

M: There's one here. It has **a variety of styles** to choose from. First, which size of tumblers do you want?

W: Between 350 to 500 ml. Something bigger than 500 ml is **hard to carry in bags**.

M: Okay. I think plastic would be better since it's much lighter.

W: No, stainless steel is better because it's the safest material for hot drinks and easy to clean. **I prefer stainless steel**.

M: All right. I didn't know that. And how about **tumblers without handles**? Sometimes the handles are inconvenient with a car's cup holders.

W: I agree. Then let's order this one because our maximum price is $30 per tumbler.

M: All right. I'll order 15 tumblers.

여: 우리는 직원을 위한 크리스마스 선물로 텀블러를 사야 해요.

남: 물론이죠. 그것들을 온라인으로 삽시다.

여: 좋아요, 가격 비교 웹사이트를 확인합시다.

남: 여기 하나 있군요. 선택할 다양한 스타일이 있어요. 우선 어떤 크기의 텀블러를 원하나요?

여: 350에서 500밀리리터 사이요. 500밀리리터보다 더 큰 건 가방에 넣어 다니기 힘들어요.

남: 알았어요. 내 생각에는 플라스틱이 훨씬 더 가벼우니까 더 좋을 것 같아요.

여: 아니요, 스테인리스 강철이 뜨거운 음료에 가장 안전한 소재이고 세척하기도 쉽기 때문에 더 좋아요. 난 스테인리스 강철을 선호해요.

남: 알았어요. 그걸 몰랐네요. 그리고 손잡이가 없는 텀블러는 어때요? 가끔 손잡이가 자동차 컵홀더에는 불편하더라고요.

여: 동의해요. 그러면 우리 최고 가격이 텀블러당 30달러이니까 이걸로 주문합시다.

남: 좋아요. 내가 15개의 텀블러를 주문할게요.

어휘 comparison 비교, 대조; 비유 a variety of 다양한 material 소재, 재료; 물질적인 inconvenient 불편한

11 짧은 대화에 이어질 응답 ②

✲ 책을 빌려줄 수 있냐는 여자의 질문에 대한 남자의 응답으로는 ② '왜 안 되겠어? 내가 다 읽으면 너에게 알려줄게.'가 가장 적절하다.

① 물론이지. 난 그걸 몇 번 읽었어.
③ 이해해줘서 고마워. 내일 그걸 돌려줄게.
④ 좋아. 네가 나한테 책을 빌려줄 수 있는지 궁금했어.
⑤ 그게 내가 생각하는 바야. 넌 다음에 더 좋은 성적을 받을 거야.

W: Hunter, **did you buy the book** which Dr. Levi recommended to us?
M: Yes, I did. It's almost $60, quite expensive. I've almost finished the book.
W: Well, when you're finished with the book, **can I borrow it from you**?
M: Why not? I'll let you know when I'm done.

여: Hunter, 너 Levi 박사님이 우리에게 추천해 주신 책 샀니?
남: 응, 샀어. 거의 60달러라서 꽤 비싸더라. 그 책을 거의 다 읽었어.
여: 음, 네가 그 책을 다 읽으면 너한테서 그걸 빌릴 수 있을까?
남: 왜 안 되겠어? 내가 다 읽으면 너에게 알려줄게.

어휘 recommend 추천하다; 권고[권장]하다

12 짧은 대화에 이어질 응답 ③

✲ 비행기가 취소되어 여자가 고객과의 회의에 갈 수 없을 것 같다는 남자의 말에 대한 여자의 응답으로는 ③ '그렇다면 회의를 취소할 수밖에 없군요.'가 가장 적절하다.

① 당신은 지금 그를 만나기 위한 준비가 아직 안 되었군요.
② 만일 그렇다면, 우리는 이 지역을 즉시 떠나야 해요.
④ 지금은 기상 정보를 이용할 수 없어요.
⑤ 그에게 전화해서 취소하는 이유를 알아봐요.

M: Camila! All flights to Florida have been canceled due to the hurricane.
W: Really? My flight is scheduled for 2:35 p.m. I have a meeting with a client there.
M: That's too bad! **I don't think you can make it.**
W: I have no choice but to cancel the meeting then.

남: Camila! 허리케인 때문에 플로리다로 가는 모든 비행기가 취소되었어요.
여: 정말이에요? 내 비행기는 오후 2시 35분에 예정되어 있어요. 난 거기서 고객과 회의가 있는데요.
남: 너무 곤란하게 되었는데요! 당신은 갈 수 없을 것 같아요.
여: 그렇다면 회의를 취소할 수밖에 없군요.

어휘 client 고객, 의뢰인 make it (시간에 맞춰) 가다[참석하다]
| 선택지 어휘 | area 지역; 구역 immediately 즉시; 직접적으로 have no choice but to-v v할 수밖에 없다, v하지 않을 수 없다 available 이용할 수 있는; 시간이 있는

13 긴 대화에 이어질 응답 ④

✲ 대화의 전체 맥락 하에 마지막 말의 의미나 의도를 정확히 파악하는 것이 좋다. 보고서에 집중해야 해서 전화를 받고 싶지 않다는 남자의 말에 대한 여자의 응답으로는 ④ '알겠습니다. 아무도 방해하지 않도록 하겠습니다.'가 가장 적절하다.

① 죄송합니다. 그런 전화에 주의를 기울이겠습니다.

② 네, 제게 Carter 씨의 전화번호를 주세요.
③ 이해합니다. 우리는 나중에 그것에 관해 이야기를 나눌 수 있어요.
⑤ 걱정 마세요. 점심으로 샌드위치를 주문하겠습니다.

M: Good afternoon, Sydney. Did anyone call me while I was out?
W: Yes, Mr. Carter called an hour ago. He'd like you **to call him back** at this number as soon as possible.
M: I see.
W: Mr. Carter said **it's urgent**.
M: Okay. I'll call him right away. By the way, **did you reschedule** my appointment with the dentist?
W: Yes, it's next Tuesday afternoon at 3 p.m.
M: Good. I'm quite busy today. I have to finish up this report by 2.
W: I see. If you don't have time for lunch, I'll prepare some sandwiches.
M: Thanks, Sydney. I want to fully focus on my report. Whoever calls me, **I don't want to answer the phone.**
W: Okay. I'll try not to let anyone disturb you.

남: 안녕, Sidney. 내가 외출한 사이에 누가 전화했나요?
여: 네, Carter 씨가 한 시간 전에 전화했어요. 그는 당신이 가능한 한 빨리 이 번호로 다시 자신에게 전화해주기를 원해요.
남: 알았어요.
여: Carter 씨가 급하다고 했어요.
남: 알겠어요. 바로 그에게 전화할게요. 그런데 내 치과 예약 일정을 변경했나요?
여: 네, 다음 화요일 오후 3시입니다.
남: 좋아요. 오늘 내가 상당히 바빠요. 이 보고서를 2시까지 끝내야 해요.
여: 알겠습니다. 점심 드실 시간이 없으면 샌드위치를 좀 준비할게요.
남: 고마워요, Sydney. 내 보고서에 완전히 집중하고 싶어요. 누가 전화해도 받고 싶지 않아요.
여: 알겠습니다. 아무도 방해하지 않도록 하겠습니다.

어휘 urgent 긴급한; 절박한 appointment 예약; 약속; 임명 fully 완전히, 충분히
| 선택지 어휘 | pay attention 주의를 기울이다 disturb 방해하다

14 긴 대화에 이어질 응답 ②

✲ 대화의 전체 맥락 하에 마지막 말의 의미나 의도를 정확히 파악하는 것이 좋다. 남자가 여자에게 집중해서 공부할 때 기억력에 도움이 되도록 걷기를 하라고 조언하자 그렇게 해보겠다고 여자가 답한다. 이에 대한 남자의 응답으로는 ② '좋아. 그게 너에게 생기를 되찾아 줄 거라고 확신해.'가 적절하다.

① 그렇구나. 조언 고마워.
③ 도움이 되어 기뻐. 전혀 문제가 되지 않아.
④ 그래. 네 성적이 걱정돼.
⑤ 괜찮아. 난 널 귀찮게 하고 싶지 않아.

M: Miranda, you look depressed. Is there anything wrong?
W: I made many mistakes in the mid-term exam.
M: Come on. **Don't be depressed.** I'm sure you'll do better next time.
W: Lately I can't seem to remember what I've studied.
M: Maybe you should **try walking regularly**. That might help your memory.
W: Are you sure?
M: Yes! A lot of research has shown that after exercise, people **perform better on tests** of memory and attention.
W: **That makes sense**.
M: If your brain has to concentrate for hours at a time, it loses the ability to remember things.
W: Okay. I'll walk when I feel tired while studying.
M: Great. I'm sure it'll refresh you.

남: Miranda, 우울해 보인다. 문제가 있니?
여: 중간고사에서 실수를 많이 했어.
남: 이봐. 우울해하지 마. 분명히 넌 다음번에 더 잘할 거야.
여: 최근에 나는 공부한 것을 기억하지 못하는 것 같아.
남: 아마 넌 규칙적으로 걷는 걸 시도해야 할 것 같아. 그게 네 기억력에 도움이 될 수도 있어.

여: 확실한 거니?

남: 그래! 많은 연구에서 운동한 후에 사람들이 기억력과 주의력 테스트에서 더 좋은 성적을 낸다는 걸 보여주고 있어.

여: 그거 이해가 돼.

남: 뇌가 한 번에 여러 시간 동안 집중해야 하면 그건 기억하는 능력을 잃어버려.

여: 알았어. 공부하다 피곤할 때 걸을게.

남: 좋아. 그게 너에게 생기를 되찾아 줄 거라고 확신해.

어휘 depressed 우울한 mid-term exam 중간고사 lately 최근에 regularly 규칙적으로, 정기적으로 attention 주의(력); 관심; 보살핌 concentrate 집중하다
| 선택지 어휘 | bother 귀찮게 하다; 신경 쓰다

15 상황에 적절한 말 ②

* 지시문을 통해 누가(A) 누구에게(B) 할 말인지를 우선 정확히 파악한다. 담화는 대개 A와 B에 대한 배경 설명과 B가 처한 문제 상황, 그리고 이에 대해 A가 어떤 말을 하려고 하는지에 대한 설명의 순서로 전개된다. 바쁜 프로젝트 중에 부하직원인 Deborah(B)가 아파서 조퇴하면서 사과를 한다. 이때 건강이 중요하다고 생각하는 Deborah의 상사(A)가 Deborah(B)에게 할 말로는 ② '걱정 말아요. 우리는 당신이 건강했으면 해요.'가 가장 적절하다.

① 그럼요. 병원은 길 건너에 있어요.
③ 이번에는 그를 믿을 수 있어요. 그에겐 하루가 더 있어요.
④ 이해해요. 당신이 Ronald의 일을 해야 할 거예요.
⑤ 프로젝트는 내일까지예요. 우리는 서둘러야 해요.

M: Deborah recently took on a big project at her company and she is working very hard. Today she doesn't feel very well and has **a headache and fever**. Seeing that Deborah is really sick, her co-worker, Ronald, tells her to go home and take a rest. Since Deborah is finding it difficult to work, she asks her boss if she can take the rest of the day off. Her boss says **she can leave early** because he clearly sees that she is ill. Deborah apologizes because she has so much left to do for the project. But her boss thinks that **her health is important** to perform well for the project. In this situation, what would Deborah's boss most likely say to Deborah?

Deborah's boss: Don't worry. We need you to be healthy.

남: Deborah는 최근에 회사에서 큰 프로젝트를 맡았고 매우 열심히 일하고 있다. 오늘 그녀는 몸 상태가 별로 좋지 않고 두통과 열이 있다. Deborah가 정말 아픈 것을 보고 그녀의 동료 Ronald가 그녀에게 집에 가서 쉬라고 말한다. Deborah는 일하기가 어렵다는 것을 알았기에 상사에게 조퇴해도 되는지 묻는다. 그녀의 상사는 그녀가 아픈 걸 분명히 보고 있기에 그녀가 일찍 퇴근해도 된다고 말한다. Deborah는 프로젝트에 할 일이 너무 많이 남아 있기 때문에 사과한다. 그러나 그녀의 상사는 프로젝트를 잘 수행하려면 그녀의 건강이 중요하다고 생각한다. 이 상황에서 Deborah의 상사가 Deborah에게 뭐라고 말하겠는가?

Deborah의 상사: 걱정 말아요. 우리는 당신이 건강했으면 해요.

어휘 take on (일 등을) 맡다, (책임을) 지다, (의미, 중요성을) 가지다 co-worker 동료
perform 수행하다; 공연하다 | 선택지 어휘 | due ~하기로 되어 있는, 예정된

16~17 세트 문항 16 ⑤ 17 ③

* 16 신체 이미지에 대한 부정적인 생각은 큰 문제가 될 수 있고, 어릴 때 발달시키는 신체 개념은 성인기까지 영향을 미칠 수 있다고 했으므로 담화의 주제는 ⑤ '아이들에게 있어서 긍정적 신체 이미지를 발달시키는 것의 중요성'이다.

① 아이들의 신체를 형성하는 영양소
② 아이들의 신체를 튼튼하게 하는 효과적인 방법
③ 아이들이 이상적인 몸매를 갖도록 돕는 방법
④ 아이들을 변화에 대비시키는 것의 필요성

* 17 해석 참조.
① 우울 ② 불안 ③ 과도한 갈증 ④ 미네랄 결핍 ⑤ 성장 지연

W: We want our kids to feel great about themselves and their appearance. But most teens say they don't feel thin enough or attractive enough. Although 80% of youth have a normal body weight, over 60% are unhappy **with their body image** and want to change their weight. In a society where thinness is important, young people's weight and appearance naturally affect **how they see themselves**. This can quickly become a huge problem with symptoms of depression, stress, and anxiety. Body image worries can lead to unhealthy dieting and food obsessions. These behaviors can result in a lack of vitamins and minerals, and growth delays. We can help our children lay the foundation for **a positive body image** early on. We can give our kids the sense that they are beautiful regardless of how they look. We can support them by **not sharing negative ideas** about the body. Remember, the body concept our sons and daughters develop in their early years **will stay with them** into adulthood.

여: 우리는 우리 아이들이 스스로와 자신의 외모에 대해 근사하다고 느끼기를 바랍니다. 하지만 대부분의 십 대들은 자기들이 충분히 마르거나 충분히 매력적이라고 생각하지 않는다고 말합니다. 80%의 청년들이 정상 체중임에도 불구하고 60%가 넘는 청년들은 자기 신체 이미지에 불만이 있고 체중을 변화시키고 싶어 합니다. 마른 것이 중요한 사회에서 젊은이들의 체중과 외모는 그들이 자신을 보는 방식에 자연스럽게 영향을 줍니다. 이것은 빠르게 ① 우울, 스트레스와 ② 불안의 증세가 있는 큰 문제가 될 수 있습니다. 신체 이미지 걱정은 건강에 좋지 않은 다이어트와 음식 강박으로 이어질 수 있습니다. 이런 행동은 비타민과 ④ 미네랄의 결핍과 ⑤ 성장 지연을 유발할 수 있습니다. 우리는 우리 자녀가 어릴 때 긍정적인 신체 이미지를 위한 토대를 마련하도록 도울 수 있습니다. 우리 아이들에게 자신이 외모에 상관없이 아름답다는 것을 느끼게 해줄 수 있습니다. 신체에 대한 부정적 생각을 공유하지 않으로 그들을 지지할 수 있습니다. 우리 아들딸이 어릴 때 발달시키는 신체 개념은 성인기까지 그들과 함께할 것임을 기억하십시오.

어휘 appearance 외모; 출현 attractive 매력적인 affect 영향을 주다 symptom 증세, 증상; 조짐 depression 우울(증) anxiety 불안, 걱정; 열망 lead to ~로 이어지다
obsession 강박 관념, 집착 behavior 행동; 태도 result in (결과적으로) ~을 야기하다
lay the foundation 토대를 마련하다, 기반을 다지다 concept 개념, 관념
| 선택지 어휘 | nutrient 영양소, 영양분 strengthen 튼튼하게 하다, 강화하다
necessity 필요성; 필수품 ideal 이상적인

20회

01 ③　02 ③　03 ④　04 ⑤　05 ③　06 ④　07 ③　08 ③　09 ⑤　10 ③
11 ②　12 ④　13 ③　14 ⑤　15 ③　16 ①　17 ④

01 화자가 하는 말의 목적　③

★ 담화의 일부 내용이 아니라 중심 내용을 파악해야 한다. 호텔 직원으로서 많은 기회가 여러분을 기다리고 있고, 처음엔 하우스키퍼로 시작하지만 매니저로 승진할 수 있다고 했으므로 신입 사원을 상대로 말하고 있음을 알 수 있다. 이제 호텔 투어를 시작한다는 것으로 보아 담화의 목적은 ③ '호텔 신입 사원들에게 호텔을 안내하려고'이다.

W: Welcome to the Fairmont Hotel chain. As a hotel employee, many opportunities await you. You may be starting out as housekeepers, but any one of you **could advance to manager** as you gain experience. Our goal at the Fairmont Hotels is to provide the highest level of service possible. Our customers pay high rates to stay at our hotels, and they expect **the very best service** in return. In order to meet this expectation, a positive and professional attitude is required on the part of our employees. We expect the highest quality service from all of you. Now, we **are ready to start our tour** of the hotel before you begin work. We'll begin right next door in the dining room, and then move on to the kitchen. This way, please.

여: Fairmont 호텔 체인에 오신 것을 환영합니다. 호텔 직원으로서 많은 기회가 여러분을 기다리고 있습니다. 여러분은 하우스키퍼로 시작할지 모르지만 경험을 쌓아가면서 여러분 중 누구라도 매니저로 승진할 수 있습니다. Fairmont 호텔에서 우리의 목표는 가능한 최고 수준의 서비스를 제공하는 것입니다. 우리 고객은 우리 호텔에 묵기 위해 높은 요금을 지불하고 그들은 보답으로 단연코 최고의 서비스를 기대합니다. 이 기대를 충족시키기 위해서 우리 직원 측에서는 긍정적이고 전문적인 태도가 요구됩니다. 우리는 여러분 모두에게 최고 품질의 서비스를 기대합니다. 이제 우리는 여러분이 일을 시작하기 전에 호텔 투어를 시작할 준비가 되었습니다. 식당 바로 옆방에서 시작해서 그 다음에 주방으로 이동할 것입니다. 이쪽으로 오십시오.

어휘 employee 직원, 고용인　opportunity 기회　await 기다리고 있다, 기다리다　advance 승진(하다); 진보(하다)　rate 요금; 비율　in return 보답으로, 답례로　meet 충족시키다; 마중 가다　professional 전문적인; 프로의　attitude 태도, 자세

02 의견　③

★ 우선 지시문에서 명시한 화자의 성별을 보고 어느 화자의 말에 주목할지를 판단해야 한다. 특히 의견이나 주장을 표현하는 어구(I think ~, You should ~ 등)가 이끄는 내용을 잘 들어야 한다. 엄마는 아이가 듣는 노래 가사에 나쁜 말이 있고 주제가 폭력적이어서 아이에게 해로운 영향을 줄 수 있다며 그런 음악 듣는 것을 허용하지 않으므로 여자의 의견은 ③ '폭력적인 가사는 아이들에게 나쁜 영향을 준다.'가 적절하다.

W: Brandon, what are you listening to?
M: Oh, Mom. I'm sorry if it's too loud. It's the most popular song nowadays.
W: Are you sure? I was very shocked by the words. **It has such bad language.**
M: Mom, it's a rap song. Please don't **take it too seriously.** It's just for fun.
W: Brandon, you're only 11 years old, and I won't allow you to listen to any music like this.
M: It's not that bad.
W: This song is for adults not children.
M: But everybody listens to hip hop and rap music in our school.
W: Think about what it's saying. **The themes are violent**, and the language is extremely unpleasant to me.
M: Oh, I see.
W: In addition, the violent lyrics could have **a harmful effect on** you. It could change your behavior.
M: Okay. I won't listen to it.

여: Brandon, 너 뭐 듣고 있니?
남: 아, 엄마. 너무 시끄럽다면 죄송해요. 요즘 제일 인기 있는 노래예요.

여: 정말이니? 난 그 가사에 무척 충격을 받았단다. 너무나 나쁜 말이 있더구나.
남: 엄마, 이건 랩이에요. 너무 진지하게 받아들이지 마세요. 그냥 재미를 위한 거예요.
여: Brandon, 넌 겨우 11살이고 난 네가 이와 같은 어떤 음악도 듣게 허용하지 않을 거야.
남: 이건 그렇게 나쁘지는 않아요.
여: 이 노래는 어른을 위한 것이지 아이들을 위한 건 아니야.
남: 하지만 우리 학교에서는 모두가 힙합과 랩 음악을 들어요.
여: 그것이 말하는 바를 생각해보렴. 주제가 폭력적이고, 그 표현은 내게 아주 불쾌하단다.
남: 아, 알겠어요.
여: 게다가, 폭력적인 가사는 너에게 해로운 영향을 줄 수 있어. 그게 네 행동을 바꿀 수 있단다.
남: 알겠어요. 그걸 듣지 않을게요.

어휘 nowadays 요즘, 현재는　take A seriously A를 진지[심각]하게 받아들이다　allow A to-v A가 v하도록 허용[허락]하다　theme 주제, 테마　lyric 노래 가사; 서정시(의)　behavior 행동; 태도

03 관계　④

★ 직업을 나타내거나 추론할 수 있는 힌트가 대화 전반에 걸쳐 드러나므로, 대화를 전체적으로 이해하는 것이 필요하다. 남자가 여자의 집을 살펴보면서 여자에게 요구하는 가격을 약간 낮춰야 한다고 하고 집을 구매할 고객에게 보여주기 위해 집 사진을 찍는 것으로 보아 여자는 집을 팔려고 하고 남자는 그 일을 맡아 해주는 ④ '집주인 – 부동산 중개인'임을 알 수 있다.

W: Do you want some coffee? I have a fresh pot.
M: Yes, please. Thanks. You have a beautiful garden with flowers, trees, and a fountain.
W: Thanks. My husband is a gardener, so we've taken very good care of the garden.
M: Great. Actually, a well-maintained garden can **add value to your house**. There are four bedrooms, right?
W: Yes. It also has a great view of the beach from upstairs.
M: Yes, it's a lovely house. The only problem is that **your asking price is too high**.
W: I think I can get that much.
M: The prices have been falling in this area recently. I think you need to lower your price a bit.
W: Oh, I'll talk it over with my husband.
M: Okay. I need to take some pictures of your house to **show to our clients**. Is it okay with you?
W: Sure. Go ahead.

여: 커피를 좀 드시겠어요? 방금 내린 커피가 있는데요.
남: 네, 주십시오. 고맙습니다. 꽃과 나무와 분수가 있는 아름다운 정원을 갖고 계시는군요.
여: 고마워요. 제 남편이 정원사라서 우리는 정원에 무척 정성을 기울였어요.
남: 굉장합니다. 사실 잘 가꾸어진 정원은 이 집에 가치를 더할 수 있죠. 침실이 4개죠, 맞나요?
여: 네. 또 위층에는 해변의 훌륭한 전망이 있답니다.
남: 네, 멋진 집이군요. 유일한 문제는 요구하는 가격이 너무 높다는 것인데요.
여: 그만큼은 받을 수 있다고 생각해요.
남: 최근에 이 지역의 가격이 떨어지고 있어서요. 가격을 약간 낮추셔야 한다고 생각해요.
여: 아, 남편과 그것을 한번 얘기해 볼게요.
남: 좋습니다. 저희 고객에게 보여주기 위해 고객님 댁의 사진을 좀 찍어야 하는데요. 괜찮으신지요?
여: 그럼요. 찍으세요.

어휘 fountain 분수　well-maintained 잘 가꾸어진, 손질이 잘 된　area 지역; 구역　client 고객, 의뢰인

04 그림 불일치 ⑤

✽ 대화가 나오기 전에 각 사물의 위치 관계와 외형(형태나 무늬, 개수 등)의 특징을 미리 확인하는 것이 좋다. 대화에서는 크리스마스트리 꼭대기에 별을 올려두었다고 했는데 그림에서는 산타 모자가 있으므로 ⑤가 대화의 내용과 일치하지 않는다. 산타 모자는 남자가 제안한 것으로 여자가 바꾸겠다고 한 것임에 유의한다.

W: Our department store is planning to hold a Santa Claus event. This is my design plan for the event.
M: Let me see. Wow, **I see a fireplace** on the left. Good idea!
W: I think a fireplace is the best place for Christmas gifts.
M: Exactly. So you put three big gift boxes in front of the fireplace.
W: I also put **this big armchair** in the center. It's for Santa Claus to sit on.
M: That's good. I like this arch behind the chair. You put up **a banner** saying "SANTA" **on the arch**.
W: Yes. And I placed a Christmas tree on the right.
M: Well, **you put a star on top of the tree**. How about putting a Santa hat there instead of a star?
W: Oh, it's a good idea. I'll change it.
M: Thanks. You did a good job.

여: 우리 백화점이 산타클로스 행사를 열 계획이에요. 이게 그 행사를 위한 디자인 설계도예요.
남: 어디 봅시다. 와, 왼쪽에 벽난로가 보이네요. 좋은 아이디어예요!
여: 벽난로가 크리스마스 선물을 두기 위한 최고의 장소라고 생각해서요.
남: 바로 그렇죠. 그래서 벽난로 앞에 세 개의 커다란 선물 상자를 두었군요.
여: 난 중앙에 또 이 큰 안락의자를 두었어요. 산타클로스가 앉을 장소죠.
남: 그거 좋군요. 의자 뒤의 아치가 마음에 들어요. 아치에 'SANTA'라고 쓰인 현수막을 달아놓았군요.
여: 네. 그리고 난 오른쪽에 크리스마스트리를 두었어요.
남: 음, 트리 꼭대기에 별을 올려두었네요. 별 대신 산타 모자를 올려두는 건 어때요?
여: 아, 그거 좋은 생각이에요. 그걸 바꿀게요.
남: 고마워요. 잘 했어요.

어휘 hold 열다; 잡다 plan 설계도; 계획 fireplace 벽난로 armchair 안락의자

05 추후 행동 ③

✽ 대개 대화는 어떤 일을 하게 되는 상황이 먼저 제시된 뒤에 남자와 여자가 각각 할 일들과 이에 대한 수락/거절의 응답이 나열되는 식으로 전개된다. 스포츠 물병을 주문하는 상황에서 여자가 자기네 회사의 상호와 로고를 물병에 프린트하기를 원했고 남자가 가능하다고 하면서 그것을 이메일로 보내라고 하고 있다. 이에 대해 여자가 바로 보내겠다고 했으므로 여자의 할 일은 ③ '회사 상호와 로고 보내주기'이다.

[Telephone rings.]
M: This is Promotions Now. How can I help you?
W: This is Sarah Palmer from Silvertech Company. We're interested in your sports bottles on your website.
M: Great. We have several different sports bottles. **Which one do you want**?
W: I like your aluminum sports bottle. Its model number is 204PB.
M: That's the top seller. How many do you need?
W: Four hundred bottles. Can you offer a quantity discount?
M: Yes, we can give you a five-percent discount.
W: Thank you. Can you put **our company's name and logo on** the bottles?
M: Sure. Why don't you e-mail us your company's name and logo? We can print it on the bottles.
W: Great. **I'll send you an e-mail** right away. By the way, do I have to pay an extra charge for the logo print?
M: No, it's free **since you are ordering** more than 300 bottles.

[전화벨이 울린다.]
남: Promotions Now입니다. 무엇을 도와드릴까요?
여: 저는 Silvertech 사의 Sarah Palmer입니다. 그쪽 웹사이트의 스포츠 물병에 관심이 있어요.
남: 좋습니다. 저희는 몇 가지 다양한 스포츠 물병이 있는데요. 어떤 걸 원하십니까?

여: 알루미늄 스포츠 물병이 마음에 듭니다. 모델 번호는 204PB입니다.
남: 그건 가장 잘 나가는 물병입니다. 얼마나 필요하신지요?
여: 400개요. 대량 구입 할인을 해주실 수 있나요?
남: 네, 5퍼센트 할인을 해드릴 수 있습니다.
여: 고맙습니다. 우리 회사 상호와 로고를 물병에 넣을 수 있나요?
남: 그럼요. 회사 상호와 로고를 저희에게 이메일로 보내주시겠어요? 물병에 그걸 프린트할 수 있습니다.
여: 좋아요. 제가 당장 이메일을 보낼게요. 그런데 로고 프린트에 대한 추가 요금을 지불해야 하나요?
남: 아뇨. 물병을 300개 넘게 주문하시기 때문에 무료입니다.

어휘 quantity discount 대량 구입 할인, 수량 할인 extra charge 추가 요금

06 금액 ④

✽ 여러 개의 수치 정보가 등장하므로 필요한 정보를 메모하면서 듣는 것이 좋다. 원래 대여 총액인 320달러에 일정 변경으로 더 큰 차로 변경하게 되어 추가로 70달러를 더 내야 하므로 여자가 지불할 금액은 ④ '$390'이다.

[Telephone rings.]
M: Speedy Car Rental. How may I help you?
W: Uh, this is Angela Ford speaking. We've rented a car from you for two weeks from next Friday. But **we need to change the date** to a week later.
M: Hold on, please. Yes, Ms. Ford. You wanted a compact car for two weeks.
W: Yes, that's right. Our total was **$320**.
M: Sorry, but if you change the reservation, we'll have to give you a bigger car. Is that all right?
W: Is that more expensive?
M: Yes, you need to pay 35 dollars more per week.
W: Oh, dear. So **we have to pay 70 dollars extra** for the two weeks?
M: I'm afraid so.
W: Okay. **We have no choice**. I'll reserve that car. Thanks.
M: I'll send you the updated information. Goodbye.

[전화벨이 울린다.]
남: Speedy 자동차 렌탈 회사입니다. 뭘 도와드릴까요?
여: 어, 저는 Angela Ford입니다. 다음 주 금요일부터 2주 동안 그쪽 회사에서 자동차를 대여했는데요. 하지만 날짜를 일주일 뒤로 변경해야 해서요.
남: 잠깐만요. 네, Ford 씨. 소형 승용차를 2주 동안 원하셨군요.
여: 네, 그게 맞아요. 저희의 총액은 320달러였어요.
남: 죄송합니다만, 예약을 변경하시면 더 큰 차를 드릴 수밖에 없습니다. 괜찮으세요?
여: 그게 더 비싼가요?
남: 네, 일주일에 35달러를 더 지불하셔야 합니다.
여: 아, 이런. 그러면 2주 동안 추가로 70달러를 지불해야 하는 거군요.
남: 유감스럽지만 그러셔야 하겠는데요.
여: 알겠어요. 선택의 여지가 없네요. 그 차를 예약하겠어요. 고마워요.
남: 새로운 정보를 보내드리겠습니다. 안녕히 계세요.

어휘 compact car 소형 승용차 reservation 예약 *cf.* reserve 예약하다; 보유하다

07 이유 ③

✽ 지시문을 통해 여자가 보고서 성적을 나쁘게 받은 상황임을 파악한다. 선생님께서 보고서에 이름을 쓰지 않은 것이 성적을 나쁘게 받은 것과 아무 관련이 없다고 했고 여자는 보고서의 분량도 채웠다. 주제 역시 창의적이라고 했지만 자료의 출처를 밝히지 않고 자기 것처럼 썼기에 나쁜 성적을 받은 것이라 했으므로, 답은 ③ '자료의 출처를 밝히지 않아서'이다.

W: Excuse me, Mr. Goldstein.
M: Come on in. What's up?
W: Uh, I didn't get my paper back yet.
M: I have a paper with no name on it. Is this yours?
W: That's it! Oh, I got a D minus. Is it because I didn't write my name on it?
M: No, that **has nothing to do with** the grade.
W: You said the paper should be two pages long, so I wrote two and a half

pages.

M: Yes. And your ideas for the theme were creative. But you **copied parts of a book** into your paper.

W: No! I never copied anyone's paper.

M: Some of the ideas came from books. But you made it seem like they were yours.

W: Oh, I didn't know that would be such a big problem.

M: It's a huge problem. **Not leaving the names of your sources** is dishonest and wrong.

여: 실례합니다. Goldstein 선생님.

남: 들어오렴. 무슨 일이니?

여: 어, 아직 제 보고서를 돌려받지 못했어요.

남: 이름을 안 쓴 보고서가 있는데, 이게 네 것이니?

여: 바로 그거예요! 아, 제가 D 마이너스를 받았네요. 제가 보고서에 이름을 쓰지 않기 때문인가요?

남: 아니, 그건 성적하고 아무런 관련이 없단다.

여: 선생님께서 보고서가 2페이지 길이여야 한다고 말씀하셔서 저는 2페이지 반을 썼는데요.

남: 그래. 그리고 주제에 대한 네 아이디어도 창의적이었어. 하지만 넌 네 보고서에 책의 일부를 베껴 넣었더구나.

여: 아뇨! 저는 결코 누구의 보고서도 베끼지 않았어요.

남: 아이디어의 일부가 책에서 나온 거야. 하지만 넌 그것들이 네 것인 것처럼 보이게 만들었어.

여: 아, 그게 그렇게 큰 문제가 될 줄은 몰랐어요.

남: 그건 큰 문제야. 네 자료 출처의 이름을 남기지 않는 건 부정직하고 잘못된 거야.

어휘 have nothing to do with ~와 아무 관련이 없다 source (자료의) 출처, 자료; 원천 dishonest 부정직한, 불성실한

08 언급하지 않은 것 ③

✻ 대화의 진행은 대개 선택지와 같은 순서이므로, 선택지를 보면서 언급된 내용을 소거하는 식으로 푸는 것이 좋다. 금요일과 토요일에 투어를 제공하고, 투어가 약 한 시간 걸리며 점심 식사는 예약하면 가능하고 진주를 이용한 특별 체험이 있다고 말했지만 이용 요금은 언급하지 않았다. 그러므로 답은 ③이다.

[Telephone rings.]

W: Hello, this is Paua Pearl Farm.

M: Hello. We're planning to visit your pearl farm. I'd like to know **when your farm opens**.

W: Our farm is open from Monday to Saturday, and we offer guided tours for visitors on Friday and Saturday.

M: How long does the tour take?

W: It takes about one hour. You can discover how the pearls come to be and see **what we do with them**.

M: Good. Do all tours include lunches?

W: No, all tours include tea and snacks, but you need to **book lunch in advance**.

M: Are there any special experiences offered?

W: Sure. You can make a unique souvenir from pearls by yourself.

M: Okay. Thanks for the information.

[전화벨이 울린다.]

여: 여보세요, 여기는 Paua 진주 양식장입니다.

남: 여보세요, 저희가 그곳 진주 양식장을 방문할 계획을 세우고 있는데요, 언제 문을 여는지 알고 싶습니다.

여: 저희 양식장은 월요일부터 토요일까지 개장하고 금요일과 토요일에는 방문객을 위해서 가이드가 있는 투어를 제공합니다(① 운영 요일).

남: 투어 시간이 얼마나 걸리나요?

여: 약 한 시간 걸립니다(② 소요 시간). 진주가 어떻게 나오게 되는지 알게 되고 저희가 그걸로 무엇을 하는지 보실 수 있습니다.

남: 좋네요. 모든 투어가 점심을 포함하나요?

여: 아니요, 모든 투어가 차와 간식을 포함합니다만, 점심은 사전에 예약하셔야 합니다(④ 점심 제공 여부).

남: 제공되는 특별 체험이 있나요?

여: 그럼요. 손님이 직접 진주로 독특한 기념품을 만들 수 있습니다(⑤ 특별 체험).

남: 알겠습니다. 알려주셔서 감사합니다.

어휘 pearl 진주; 귀중한 물건 book 예약하다 in advance 사전에, 미리 souvenir 기념품

09 내용 불일치 ⑤

✻ 담화의 진행은 대개 선택지와 같은 순서이므로, 선택지를 보면서 일치하는 내용을 소거하는 식으로 푸는 것이 좋다. 자전거 주차 공간을 직원이 주시할 것이긴 하지만 자전거에 어떤 귀중품도 남겨 두지 말라고 했으므로 ⑤ '직원이 없으므로 귀중품을 남겨 두면 안 된다.'는 내용과 일치하지 않는다.

M: Do you want to ride your bike to the game at the main stadium? Madison City provides free bicycle parking. The bicycle parking space **is sponsored by** Saria Bike Company. The space will be available for bicycle parking from two hours before the game until one hour after the Madison City football game ends. There is **no charge for** the bicycle parking space. Staff there will greet you and provide instructions for parking your bike. **You should bring a lock** for your bike. The space will also **be watched by staff members**, but don't leave any valuables with your bicycle.

남: 주 경기장의 경기에 자전거를 타고 오길 원하십니까? Madison 시가 무료 자전거 주차를 제공합니다. 자전거 주차 공간은 ① Saria 자전거 회사가 후원합니다. 이 공간은 ② 경기 시작 두 시간 전부터 Madison 시 축구 경기가 끝난 한 시간 후까지 자전거 주차가 가능할 것입니다. ③ 자전거 주차 공간에 대한 요금은 없습니다. 그곳에서 직원이 여러분을 맞이하고 여러분의 자전거를 주차하기 위한 지침을 제공할 것입니다. 여러분은 ④ 여러분의 자전거를 위한 자물쇠를 가져와야 합니다. ⑤ 직원이 또한 이 공간을 주시할 것이긴 하지만 여러분의 자전거에 어떤 귀중품도 남겨 두지 마십시오.

어휘 sponsor 후원하다; 주관하다 charge 요금, 비용 instruction 지침; 설명(서); 교육 valuables 귀중품

10 도표 이해 ③

✻ 대화의 진행은 대개 도표 항목의 나열 순서대로 진행된다. 대화를 들으면서 도표의 각 항목 중 선택되지 않은 것을 소거하는 식으로 푸는 것이 좋다. 제일 먼저 사계절 텐트를 사지 않겠다고 했으므로 ②와 ⑤가 제외되고 2-3인용 텐트를 원했으므로 선택할 것이 ①과 ③ 중 하나가 된다. 여자는 가격이 싼 것을 원했지만 결국에는 더 가벼운 것으로 선택하기로 했으므로 두 사람이 구매할 텐트는 ③이다.

M: Honey, we really need to buy a tent since we go camping every weekend. So I brought a brochure of tents.

W: That's a good idea.

M: Do you think we need a four-season tent?

W: I don't think so. We're not going camping in the winter. Let's **go for a three-season tent**.

M: Okay. Then think about the size. How about a tent for four people? It has more space inside.

W: I prefer a tent for **two or three people**. A bigger tent is heavy to carry. And it's difficult to find a big enough space to set up the tent.

M: Okay. We'll choose a 2 or 3 person tent. Now there are two options left.

W: Of course, **the cheaper**, **the better**.

M: But the cheaper one is heavier. And there is only a 20-dollar difference in prices.

W: That's true. **Let's choose the lighter one**.

남: 여보, 우리는 매주 주말 캠핑을 가기 때문에 텐트를 정말 사야 해요. 그래서 텐트 책자를 가져왔어요.

여: 그거 좋은 생각이에요.

남: 우리가 사계절 텐트가 필요하다고 생각해요?

여: 그렇게 생각하지 않아요. 우리는 겨울에는 캠핑을 가지 않잖아요. 세 계절 텐트로 합시다.

남: 좋아요. 그러면 크기에 대해 생각해봐요. 4인용 텐트는 어때요? 안에 공간이 더 넓잖아요.

여: 난 2 또는 3인용 텐트가 더 좋아요. 더 큰 텐트는 들고 다니기 무거워요. 그리고 텐트를 세우기 위한 충분히 큰 공간을 찾기도 어렵고요.

남: 알았어요. 2-3인용 텐트를 고릅시다. 이제 선택할 게 두 개 남았어요.

여: 물론 가격이 더 싼 게 더 좋죠.

남: 하지만 가격이 더 싼 건 더 무거워요. 그리고 가격도 겨우 20달러 차이예요.

여: 그건 맞아요. 더 가벼운 걸 선택합시다.

어휘 brochure (안내·광고용) 책자 set up 세우다; 설치하다

11 짧은 대화에 이어질 응답 ②

＊ 세탁기 수리를 신청을 하는 상황에서 여자가 수리에 돈이 드는지 질문했을 때 응답으로는 ② '보증 기간 중이라서 무료로 수리될 것입니다.'가 가장 적절하다.

① 늦지 않게 그걸 수리할 수 있는 방법이 없습니다.
③ 우선, 우리는 필요한 부품을 주문해야 합니다.
④ 가능한 한 빨리 사람을 보내겠습니다.
⑤ 그걸 저기 놓아주시면 제가 살펴보겠습니다.

W: I need someone to fix my washing machine. It isn't working.
M: Okay. Can you tell me its model number and when you purchased it?
W: The number is MA17, and I bought it seven months ago. **Should I pay for the repair?**
M: It'll be fixed for free under the warranty.

여: 제 세탁기를 고쳐줄 사람이 필요해요. 그게 작동하지 않거든요.
남: 알겠습니다. 그 모델 번호와 언제 그걸 구매했는지 알려주시겠어요?
여: 번호는 MA17이고 7개월 전에 샀어요. 수리하는 데 돈을 지불해야 하나요?
남: 보증 기간 중이라서 무료로 수리될 것입니다.

어휘 purchase 구매(하다), 사다 | 선택지 어휘 | under warranty 보증 기간 중인

12 짧은 대화에 이어질 응답 ④

＊ 연필깎이를 찾지 못해 여자가 전기 연필깎이를 사자고 하자 남자가 동의하면서 바닥에 끈끈한 고무가 있는 것으로 사자고 한다. 이에 대한 응답으로는 ④ '좋아. 그런 식으로 그건 내가 놓아둔 곳에 있을 거야.'가 적절하다.

① 하지 마. 그건 그렇게 나쁘지 않아.
② 응. 상자 안에 연필이 좀 있어.
③ 기다려. 내가 거기 있는 오래된 잡동사니를 모두 치울게.
⑤ 맞아. 그건 네 것보다 훨씬 더 비싸.

M: Do you know where a pencil sharpener is? We have two, but I can't find either.
W: **They often disappear.** How about buying an electric pencil sharpener?
M: Good idea. **Let's get one with sticky rubber** on the bottom.
W: Okay. That way it will stay where I put it.

남: 연필깎이가 어디 있는지 아니? 우리는 두 개가 있지만 난 어느 것도 찾을 수가 없어.
여: 그것들은 종종 사라져. 전기 연필깎이를 사는 건 어때?
남: 좋은 생각이야. 바닥에 끈끈한 고무가 있는 걸 사자.
여: 좋아. 그런 식으로 그건 내가 놓아둔 곳에 있을 거야.

어휘 sticky 끈끈한, 들러붙는 rubber 고무; 지우개 bottom 바닥, 맨 아래 (부분)
| 선택지 어휘 | junk 잡동사니, 폐물

13 긴 대화에 이어질 응답 ③

＊ 대화의 전체 맥락 하에 마지막 말의 의미나 의도를 정확히 파악하는 것이 좋다. 아내와 출장에서 한 달 후 돌아오기로 한 남편이 나누는 대화이다. 가족 모두가 그리워하는 상황에서 남자가 일이 잘되어 다음 주에 돌아온다고 했을 때 여자의 응답으로는 ③ '그거 굉장한 소식이네요! 아이들이 아주 기뻐할 거예요.'가 가장 적절하다.

① 아이들에게 사랑한다고 전해줘요. 곧 다시 전화할게요.
② 당신이 도착을 연기해야 한다 해도 이해해요.

④ 이번 출장 덕분에 당신 사업이 성공하기를 바라요.
⑤ 가끔은 중국 음식이 나와 맞지 않아요.

[Telephone rings.]
W: Hello?
M: Honey, it's me!
W: Oh, Anthony, I was hoping I'd hear from you soon! How is your business trip to China going?
M: It's going well. **How's it going** over there?
W: Well, you know, same as usual. Life's good, except that I miss you so much!
M: I miss you too. How are the kids?
W: They miss you **even more than I do.** They ask about you every day.
M: I think about you guys all the time, too.
W: Well, I've told them that you'll be coming back in a month, so they can't wait for that.
M: Well, honey, things are going so well over here that I think **I might be able to come home** next week.
W: That's wonderful news! The kids will be so happy.

[전화벨이 울린다.]
여: 여보세요?
남: 여보, 나예요!
여: 아, Anthony, 당신한테서 곧 소식 듣기를 바라고 있었어요! 중국 출장에서 어떻게 지내고 있어요?
남: 잘 되고 있어요. 거기는 어떻게 지내요?
여: 음, 알다시피 평상시와 똑같아요. 당신을 너무 많이 그리워한다는 걸 제외하고는 생활은 즐겁죠!
남: 나도 당신이 보고 싶어요. 애들은 어떤가요?
여: 애들은 나보다 훨씬 더 당신을 그리워해요. 매일 당신에 대해 물어요.
남: 나도 내내 당신하고 애들을 생각해요.
여: 음, 당신이 한 달 후에 돌아올 거라고 말해서 애들은 그걸 몹시 기대하고 있어요.
남: 음, 여보, 여기 일들이 아주 잘 되어서 내가 다음 주에 집에 갈 수 있을 것 같아요.
여: 그거 굉장한 소식이네요! 아이들이 아주 기뻐할 거예요.

어휘 business trip 출장 except ~을 제외하고, ~외에는
| 선택지 어휘 | delay 연기하다, 미루다 arrival 도착; 등장 thanks to A A 덕분에

14 긴 대화에 이어질 응답 ⑤

＊ 대화의 전체 맥락 하에 마지막 말의 의미나 의도를 정확히 파악하는 것이 좋다. 영화가 이번 토요일에 상영이 끝나는데 서로 시간이 맞지 않아 못 보는 상황이다. 이때 어쩔 수 없다는 여자의 말에 대한 남자의 응답으로는 ⑤ '아쉬워요. 그러면 우리는 그 영화를 DVD로 봐야겠네요.'가 적절하다.

① 괜찮아요. 사실 난 액션 영화를 좋아하지 않아요.
② 그거 좋겠네요. 대신에 록 콘서트를 갑시다.
③ 우린 선택의 여지가 없어요. 일요일에 영화를 봅시다.
④ 서둘러요. 다음 상영 관객이 기다리고 있어요.

M: Lauren, how about seeing the movie, *Bumblebee*, this Saturday?
W: Great idea. I'd like to see it.
M: Let's have lunch at a nice restaurant and see the movie.
W: Oh, hold on. Aren't we going somewhere this Saturday?
M: Oh, right. I completely forgot. We **are supposed to visit** my grandmother.
W: Well, how about watching the movie Friday evening?
M: I have a dinner appointment Friday evening. What about Thursday evening?
W: No, I have a dentist appointment on Thursday. I probably **won't feel like watching** a movie then.
M: Let's check when they stop running the movie. *[pause]* Oh, they **stop playing it** this Saturday.
W: I guess **there's nothing we can do.**
M: Too bad. We'll have to watch the movie on DVD then.

남: Lauren, 이번 토요일에 영화 'Bumblebee'를 보는 게 어때요?

여: 멋진 생각이에요. 그걸 보고 싶어요.
남: 근사한 식당에서 점심을 먹고 영화를 봅시다.
여: 아, 잠깐만요. 우리 이번 토요일에 어디 가지 않아요?
남: 아, 맞아요. 까맣게 잊었네요. 내 할머니를 방문하기로 되어 있죠.
여: 음, 영화를 금요일 저녁에 보는 건 어때요?
남: 금요일 저녁에는 저녁 식사 약속이 있어요. 목요일 저녁은 어때요?
여: 안 돼요. 목요일에 치과 예약이 있어요. 그때 아마 난 영화를 볼 기분이 아닐 거예요.
남: 언제 영화 상영을 끝내는지 확인해봅시다. *[잠시 후]* 아, 이번 토요일에 상영을 끝내네요.
여: 어쩔 수 없는 것 같아요.
남: *아쉬워요. 그러면 우리는 그 영화를 DVD로 봐야겠네요.*

어휘 completely 완전히 be supposed to-v v하기로 되어 있다 appointment 약속;
예약: 임명 feel like v-ing v하고 싶다 | 선택지 어휘 | audience 관객; 청중

---

15 상황에 적절한 말 ③

❋ 지시문을 통해 누가(A) 누구에게(B) 할 말인지를 우선 정확히 파악한다. 담화는 대개 A와 B에 대한 배경 설명과 B가 처한 문제 상황, 그리고 이에 대해 A가 어떤 말을 하려고 하는지에 대한 설명의 순서로 전개된다. Carol(A)의 차가 긁히고 가해자가 사라진 상황에서 그 건물에서 일하는 친구 Jeff(B)를 만나 그가 주차장에 보안 카메라가 있음을 알려준 상황이다. 우선 감사를 표하고 같이 보안 카메라를 보러 가자고 청하는 말로는 ③ '고마워! 그것을 확인하러 나와 함께 갈 수 있니?'가 가장 적절하다.

① 정말 안심이다. 네 보안 카메라가 어디 있니?
② 끔찍하구나! 네 자동차는 언제 사고가 났니?
④ 그거 좋아 보인다. 네 자동차 얼마 주고 샀어?
⑤ 네 차를 건물 앞에 주차하지 그러니?

M: Jeff and Carol are friends. Today Jeff runs into Carol in the parking lot of his office building. Jeff notices Carol is very upset and asks her why. Carol says she's visited this building **to meet her client**. She parked her car there and she's just found a scratch on her parked car. Someone hit her car and ran away **without leaving a note**. Her car is almost brand-new, so she is very upset. Jeff knows that there are some security cameras in the parking lot. So, he advises Carol to go to the parking lot office and check the cameras. Carol **wants him to go with her** because he works in the building. In this situation, what would Carol most likely say to Jeff?

Carol: Thanks! Can you come with me to check them out?

남: Jeff와 Carol은 친구이다. 오늘 Jeff는 자신의 사무실 건물 주차장에서 Carol을 우연히 만난다. Jeff는 Carol이 매우 화가 난 것을 알아채고 그녀에게 이유를 묻는다. Carol은 자신의 고객을 만나기 위해 이 건물을 방문했다고 말한다. 그녀가 차를 거기에 주차했고 자신의 주차한 차에서 긁힌 자국을 방금 발견했다. 누군가가 그녀의 차를 치고 메모도 남기지 않고 도망가 버렸다. 그녀의 차는 거의 완전히 새것이라서 그녀는 매우 화가 난다. Jeff는 주차장에 보안 카메라가 몇 대 있는 걸 안다. 그래서 그는 Carol에게 주차장 사무소로 가서 카메라를 확인하라고 조언한다. Carol은 그가 그 건물에서 일하기 때문에 자신과 함께 가주기를 원한다. 이 상황에서 Carol은 Jeff에게 뭐라고 말하겠는가?

Carol: *고마워! 그것을 확인하러 나와 함께 갈 수 있니?*

어휘 run into 우연히 만나다 notice 알아차리다; 주목(하다); 통지(서) brand-new 완전히 새것인 security 보안, 안전; 안심
| 선택지 어휘 | relief 안심, 안도; 경감 awful 끔찍한, 지독한 accident 사고; 우연

16~17 세트 문항 16 ① 17 ④

❋ **16** 저녁 식사 초대를 받아서 갈 때 따라야 할 규칙이 있다고 하면서 식사 초대를 받았을 때 갖추어야 할 예의에 대해 이야기하고 있다. 그러므로 담화의 주제는 ① '훌륭한 저녁 식사 손님이 되는 법'이 가장 적절하다.

② 더 건강하게 먹기 위한 통상적인 방법
③ 저녁 식사 파티를 계획하는 방법
④ 주인을 위한 선물을 선택하는 데 도움이 되는 조언
⑤ 세계 곳곳의 식사 예절

❋ **17** 해석 참조.
① 꽃 ② 와인 ③ 양초 ④ 접시 ⑤ 화분

M: If a friend or family member invites you over **for dinner**, there are certain rules that **need to be followed**. Remember, this person took the time to invite you, plan a meal, clean their house, pay for food, and get everything set up. So call the host and ask if there's anything you can do to help. You can bring dessert or **arrive early to help set up**. If the host insists they don't need any help, bring over a small gift such as flowers, a bottle of wine, or a candle. A houseplant or a picture frame is terrific too. Always **make sure you arrive on time**. During your meal, make sure you don't speak with your mouth full or **make noises while eating**. This is considered rude and distasteful. Finally, it's common for people to send a thank-you card after the meal. A simple thank-you card with a few words will be enough. **Keep these points in mind** the next time you're invited to a dinner party.

남: 친구나 가족 구성원이 여러분을 저녁 식사에 초대한다면 여러분이 따라야 할 어떤 규칙들이 있습니다. 이 사람이 여러분을 초대하고, 식사를 계획하고, 자신들의 집을 치우고, 음식에 돈을 지불하고, 모든 것을 마련하는 데 시간을 냈다는 것을 기억하십시오. 그러므로 주인에게 전화해서 여러분이 도와줄 수 있는 게 있는지 물어보십시오. 여러분은 후식을 가져가거나 상차림을 돕기 위해 일찍 도착할 수 있습니다. 주인이 어떤 도움도 필요하지 않다고 단언한다면 ① 꽃이나, ② 와인 한 병, 혹은 ③ 양초 같은 작은 선물을 가져가십시오. ⑤ 화분이나 액자도 아주 좋습니다. 언제나 꼭 제시간에 도착하십시오. 식사하는 동안 음식을 입에 가득 넣고 말하거나 먹으면서 소리를 내지 않도록 하십시오. 이것은 무례하고 불쾌하게 여겨집니다. 마지막으로 식사를 하고 나서 감사의 카드를 보내는 것은 흔한 일입니다. 몇 마디 적은 간단한 감사 카드면 충분할 것입니다. 다음에 여러분이 저녁 식사 파티에 초대받을 때 이 점들을 명심하십시오.

어휘 certain 어떤, 어느; 확실한 host 주인 insist 단언하다, 주장하다; 강요하다
terrific 아주 좋은, 훌륭한 consider 여기다; 고려[숙고]하다 distasteful 불쾌한, 혐오스러운; 맛없는 keep A in mind A를 명심하다

ANSWER

01회
01 ⑤ 02 ③ 03 ④ 04 ⑤ 05 ③　06 ③ 07 ④ 08 ⑤ 09 ③ 10 ⑤
11 ② 12 ③ 13 ② 14 ③ 15 ④　16 ① 17 ③

02회
01 ④ 02 ② 03 ③ 04 ④ 05 ④　06 ④ 07 ② 08 ⑤ 09 ⑤ 10 ⑤
11 ③ 12 ④ 13 ① 14 ① 15 ⑤　16 ④ 17 ④

03회
01 ② 02 ③ 03 ④ 04 ⑤ 05 ②　06 ③ 07 ④ 08 ⑤ 09 ④ 10 ③
11 ③ 12 ② 13 ① 14 ① 15 ④　16 ③ 17 ④

04회
01 ② 02 ④ 03 ③ 04 ⑤ 05 ④　06 ③ 07 ③ 08 ⑤ 09 ⑤ 10 ①
11 ③ 12 ⑤ 13 ⑤ 14 ④ 15 ④　16 ④ 17 ②

05회
01 ① 02 ⑤ 03 ② 04 ⑤ 05 ④　06 ② 07 ③ 08 ④ 09 ⑤ 10 ⑤
11 ② 12 ⑤ 13 ③ 14 ④ 15 ③　16 ④ 17 ⑤

06회
01 ④ 02 ② 03 ③ 04 ⑤ 05 ③　06 ④ 07 ⑤ 08 ④ 09 ④ 10 ⑤
11 ② 12 ② 13 ② 14 ③ 15 ③　16 ③ 17 ④

07회
01 ⑤ 02 ④ 03 ② 04 ⑤ 05 ④　06 ④ 07 ③ 08 ④ 09 ③ 10 ④
11 ② 12 ③ 13 ⑤ 14 ① 15 ④　16 ② 17 ⑤

08회
01 ④ 02 ③ 03 ③ 04 ④ 05 ⑤　06 ④ 07 ③ 08 ⑤ 09 ④ 10 ⑤
11 ③ 12 ③ 13 ③ 14 ② 15 ②　16 ③ 17 ④

09회
01 ② 02 ③ 03 ④ 04 ④ 05 ④　06 ② 07 ④ 08 ④ 09 ③ 10 ④
11 ③ 12 ④ 13 ④ 14 ③ 15 ④　16 ② 17 ④

10회
01 ② 02 ① 03 ④ 04 ④ 05 ③　06 ④ 07 ④ 08 ④ 09 ③ 10 ⑤
11 ⑤ 12 ⑤ 13 ② 14 ③ 15 ⑤　16 ② 17 ②

11회
01 ④ 02 ② 03 ④ 04 ④ 05 ②　06 ② 07 ④ 08 ④ 09 ③ 10 ④
11 ⑤ 12 ⑤ 13 ③ 14 ② 15 ⑤　16 ⑤ 17 ⑤

12회
01 ② 02 ④ 03 ③ 04 ⑤ 05 ⑤　06 ④ 07 ④ 08 ② 09 ⑤ 10 ④
11 ③ 12 ④ 13 ② 14 ① 15 ③　16 ① 17 ④

13회
01 ④ 02 ④ 03 ③ 04 ④ 05 ③　06 ④ 07 ⑤ 08 ③ 09 ④ 10 ⑤
11 ② 12 ③ 13 ① 14 ④ 15 ④　16 ④ 17 ③

14회
01 ④ 02 ③ 03 ② 04 ④ 05 ②　06 ③ 07 ② 08 ⑤ 09 ⑤ 10 ①
11 ② 12 ④ 13 ② 14 ④ 15 ③　16 ④ 17 ④

15회
01 ② 02 ④ 03 ② 04 ③ 05 ④　06 ③ 07 ④ 08 ④ 09 ⑤ 10 ⑤
11 ① 12 ③ 13 ② 14 ③ 15 ③　16 ① 17 ②

16회
01 ④ 02 ④ 03 ⑤ 04 ⑤ 05 ⑤　06 ③ 07 ④ 08 ④ 09 ⑤ 10 ⑤
11 ④ 12 ② 13 ② 14 ⑤ 15 ②　16 ⑤ 17 ④

17회
01 ③ 02 ② 03 ④ 04 ④ 05 ⑤　06 ⑤ 07 ④ 08 ④ 09 ④ 10 ①
11 ⑤ 12 ⑤ 13 ② 14 ② 15 ③　16 ② 17 ④

18회
01 ⑤ 02 ② 03 ② 04 ③ 05 ③　06 ③ 07 ③ 08 ② 09 ⑤ 10 ③
11 ① 12 ② 13 ① 14 ② 15 ③　16 ⑤ 17 ④

19회
01 ② 02 ④ 03 ② 04 ⑤ 05 ④　06 ③ 07 ③ 08 ③ 09 ③ 10 ②
11 ② 12 ③ 13 ④ 14 ② 15 ②　16 ⑤ 17 ③

20회
01 ③ 02 ③ 03 ④ 04 ⑤ 05 ③　06 ④ 07 ③ 08 ④ 09 ⑤ 10 ③
11 ② 12 ④ 13 ③ 14 ⑤ 15 ③　16 ① 17 ④

MEMO

첫단추 BUTTON UP